# WASHINGTON, D.C.

## A map of the center of the city

W9-ASO-939

1 THE CAPITOL
2 SENATE OFFICE BLDGS.
3 SUPREME COURT
4 LIBRARY OF CONGRESS
5 ANNEX TO LIBRARY
6 U.S. COURT HOUSE
7 HOUSE OFFICE BLDG.
8 NEW HOUSE OFFICE BLDG.
9 DEPT. OF AGRICULTURE
10 SMITHSONIAN INST.
11 FREER GALLERY OF ART

12 AIRCRAFT BLDG.
13 ARTS & INDUSTRIES BLDG.
14 EAST ADMINISTRATION BLDG.
15 FEDERAL TRADE COMM.
16 ARCHIVES BLDG.
17 DEPT. OF JUSTICE (F.B.I.)
18 BUR. OF INT. REVENUE
19 POST OFFICE DEPT. DEPT. OF LABOR
20 DEPT. OF HEALTH, EDUCATION & WELFARE
21 DEPT. OF COMMERCE

22 TREASURY DEPT.
23 WHITE HOUSE
24 EXECUTIVE OFFICE BLDG.
25 GENERAL SERVICES BLDG.
26 DEPT. OF STATE
27 DEPT. OF INTERIOR
28 FEDERAL RES. SYSTEM
29 NAT. SCIENCE FOUND.
30 JEFFERSON MEMORIAL
31 WASHINGTON MON.
32 BUR. OF ENG. & PRINTING

33 PENTAGON    34 LINCOLN MEMORIAL
35 NATIONAL GALLERY OF ART

J. MacDonald

DAVID FELLMAN
*Professor of Political Science, University of Wisconsin*
ADVISORY EDITOR TO DODD, MEAD & COMPANY

# GOVERNING AMERICA

*The Politics of a Free People*

SECOND EDITION

*National Government*

# GOVERNING AMERICA

*The Politics of a Free People*

### SECOND EDITION

*National Government*

## THOMAS H. ELIOT

*Chancellor, Washington University*

DODD, MEAD & COMPANY

NEW YORK    TORONTO    1965

TO LOIS JAMESON ELIOT

# Editor's Introduction to Second Edition

As advisory editor to Dodd, Mead & Company in the political science field, it is a great pleasure to have had a hand in the publication of the second edition of Thomas H. Eliot's fine textbook on American government. As in the case of the first edition, which appeared in 1960, this book is designed for the basic college or university course in American government. The basic structure of the book has not been altered, and the over-all point of view is retained. The factual material has been brought up to date throughout, and new factual materials have been added. Perhaps the principal new feature of the second edition is the addition of a substantial number of charts and tables which set out, in convenient and orderly form, and often dramatically, large amounts of otherwise scattered information.

One of the central responsibilities of professors of political science in this country is to give students an adequate survey course on American government and politics. This responsibility has several dimensions. First of all, the course is generally the entry course for most students; that is, it is their introduction to the discipline. At this point, therefore, a taste for political science is either encouraged or dulled. First impressions are obviously important merely because they come first. The student who has to plod his weary way through a dull and ponderous textbook is not likely to continue his studies in the political science field. Secondly, the general American government course is important because what it contains ought to be part of the culture of every American citizen, whatever his profession or business or occupation or station in life may be. Our world has always been engaged in an endless struggle with ignorance, and nowhere is ignorance more dangerous than in the governmental field. An understanding of the main elements of American government and politics is essential for creative citizenship and even for good neighborliness. All studies show, for example, that there is a direct correlation between education and tolerance. That is to say, educated people consistently display greater tolerance than the uneducated for differences, even for eccentricities, among their fellow men. The educated are less prejudiced, more likely to judge men and institutions on their true merits, and more willing to stand by general principles in concrete situations.

In a broader sense, however, the study of American government is essential to the success of our democratic form of government, since it is not only government *for* the people, but also necessarily *by* the people. Democratic government requires, by definition, the active participation of very large numbers of people, and one can hardly dispute the fact that informed participation is vastly preferable to the uninformed variety. The American ethos has always put a high value on education, and the serious study of government and politics is a classic part of even the most minimal program of preparation for the good life.

Finally, the quality of the basic textbook for the general survey course in American government and politics is especially important because so many students take the course. In most institutions the enrollments are apt to be very large indeed, and where the students gather in unusually large classes, the textbook must do double duty: it must not only inform, but also inspire; it must explore ideas as well as describe facts; it must talk to the student simply because he will normally have small opportunity, on account of the sheer numbers involved, to talk to his professor. In a very real sense the dialectic is between the student and his textbook.

I think Professor Eliot's textbook measures up to these exacting requirements of a basic text in the general American government course. It is, for one thing, a well-written book. It has a lively style and moves along at a brisk pace. The author has a good sense of narrative and drama and a sure touch in selecting just the right event or person or document to illustrate a general rule. In a very real sense the author is talking directly to the student, and as in the case of all good talk, the book constantly shifts from one gear to another, from exposition to evaluation to argument, even to an occasional exhortation. For the author's commitment to the moral foundations of democracy is very genuine. Above all, from the literary point of view, this book was written for a specific student audience and in the light of its specific needs.

Furthermore, Professor Eliot is no closet philosopher, and therefore his book does not smell of the lamp. He has always been directly concerned with politics in one way or another. He once served as a member of the federal House of Representatives, and while he has in recent years been a professor, he has never lost touch with practical politics. For example, during the past few years he has been closely identified with the movement to reorganize the jungle of local governments in the St. Louis area, and no political experience could possibly be more demanding than such an enterprise.

To be sure, Professor Eliot gives adequate attention to our institutions and the basic pattern of American constitutional law upon which they rest. Indeed, as a professor of constitutional law he has a sure grasp of the great constitutional principles which undergird our governmental institutions. But this book recognizes the dynamic quality of American political processes, and thus goes beyond the customary institutional descriptions and analyses to examine functions in a workaday world. In short, this is a book about American government *and* politics, and thus deals with the real world of public affairs as well as its structural and legal framework.

The student will find in Professor Eliot's book a well-written, lively and interesting account of the fundamentals of both American governmental institutions and American politics. It is learned without being dull or stuffy, and gives serious attention to the actual political behavior of men, public as well as private. It should whet the student's appetite for further study in political science. It should also make him a better citizen.

DAVID FELLMAN

# Preface to Second Edition

Revision of the book, for this new edition, has included selection of some new relevant facts and figures (the process is called "updating") and presentation of much more of the information in graphic, tabular form. The march of events has required especially a considerable expansion of the chapter on the equal protection of the laws. With respect to concepts and theories, a more thorough treatment of the products of voting behavior research has been made appropriate by the advance of that branch of social science. Comments and criticisms by many teachers and students who used the first edition have helped to make this, hopefully, a more useful text.

My original selection has a multiple foundation. It is based, first, on classroom experience: it offers concepts which undergraduates, new to the subject, can understand and apply to new situations. Second, while many of the factual examples are drawn from American political history, for numerous others I have turned to relevant fragments of my own experience in government and politics. The whole book, finally, has been written in the conviction that before a person can be effectively committed to the fundamental principles of American democracy he must subject those principles and the strengths and weaknesses of our political system to dispassionate analysis. Selection and emphasis in this book are pointed toward that end.

After examinations are over, students soon forget dozens of facts for every one that they remember. A central task of the teacher is to give them the memorable facts and a great deal of other information which, though easily forgotten, serves as the basis of theories and concepts that they may grasp firmly and retain. It is essentially a process of selection. Lectures must be highly selective; textbooks can be less so. Yet the textbook cannot include everything. It must strike a balance between its minor function of serving as a reference work, and its major role of presenting ideas backed up by solid and illustrative information. Which ideas and which information are matters for the author to decide.

When I went to college back in the 1920's the typical textbook merely described governmental institutions. Many modern political scientists, in contrast, focus primarily on what they believe to be the measurable political behavior of groups of human beings. Both approaches, the institutional and the behavioral, are necessary for the understanding of politics. Neither, by itself, is enough. And I wonder whether both together are quite enough: for if institutions seem to lack flesh and blood, so do human groups after they have been reduced to statistics. Individual conduct—a person's unforeseeable folly or unexpected greatness—plays a central part in politics too. This book is about what people do, not only in organized private groups or as members of governing bodies, but also as unpredictable individuals with the personal faults and virtues common to mankind.

How can the author of a book that could be written only because of his good fortune—in having been reared in a politically-aware family, in education as both student and teacher, and in public life—adequately acknowledge his debts to all who have helped to shape his thinking and his written words? With reluctance he must again select and omit. I would like, though, to thank first the teachers who long ago introduced me to political science, two youthful tutors named W. Y. Elliott and C. J. Friedrich. Nor should I overlook that great teacher of constitutional law, the late T. R. Powell. For opening the gates of public service to me I owe lifelong gratitude to Frances Perkins and Charles E. Wyzanski, Jr. And my brief fling in active politics—like the other things which have been most rewarding—would have been impossible without the active help and cheerful confidence of the lady to whom this book is dedicated.

I have learned much from both my students and my colleagues at Washington University. For the former I wrote out new lectures a few years ago, which somehow turned into the first chapters of this book; for reading those and encouraging me to proceed I thank William Oman, Edward F. Webster, and Victor Rosenblum. Later the whole manuscript * was read by Julius Paul and the proofs by Merle Fainsod, Martin Landau, Richard E. Neustadt, and Maurice Waters. I absolve them and all others, of course, of responsibility for any errors which it may contain, but I am grateful for their discerning criticism. With respect to illustrations, I owe a special debt to Daniel R. Fitzpatrick and Genia Graves. In the work of revising the original text and preparing an up-to-date second edition, Eugene P. Angrist has provided valuable help. Throughout the whole period of the book's preparation I have profited immeasurably from the meticulous pencil and wise advice of David Fellman.

---

* Except for the state and local chapters.

THOMAS H. ELIOT
*Washington University*
*St. Louis, Missouri*
*January, 1964*

# Contents

# Illustrations

## ILLUSTRATION CREDITS

# Charts and Tables

PART *One*

PART One

# CHAPTER 1

# Government and Politics

M en have been walking on two legs, on this planet, for at least a million years. How they lived, during most of those long ages, we do not know; but in the centuries known to history, the most extensive recorded experiment in human self-government has been that of the United States of America. Other nations, today and in earlier ages, have experimented with the idea of individual freedom under law. Americans have learned much from them, especially from the principles of government applied in ancient Athens and not-so-ancient England. But the American adventure, infused with similar ideals, is clearly the greatest in terms of the number of people affected, the duration of the system, the size of the country, and the development of its wealth and power.

It is indeed an experiment, an adventure. It always has been. We gained our independence less than two hundred years ago. We stayed together, as a nation, only at the cost of 618,000 lives lost in a fierce civil war. We grew to become a world power; and now that we have achieved that status, the success of our experiment may be, eventually, the lever which will swing the balance in the rest of the world away from tyranny and toward freedom. We are still being judged not on our might alone, but on how

3

fully we succeed in bringing "the blessings of liberty" to every person in the country, and how well we build, on the foundation of freedom, a social system wherein each individual can experience the durable satisfactions of life.

Quoting our Constitution, Americans sometimes say that our government exists to "provide for the common defense and promote the general welfare." The same thing could be said, however, about nearly every government that has ever existed. Why have men instituted governments anywhere, if not for these purposes? For that matter, if we value individual freedom as highly as we say we do, why have any government at all? The very existence of government means that we are not completely free to do exactly as we like. Someone has authority over us. Ordinarily, we obey that authority. Why?

There are many different notions as to why governments were created in the first place. One theory is that early men, living fairly close together in, say, a fertile valley, soon found that they had to protect their crops and themselves against marauders from the rocky hills nearby. For the "common defense" they organized, appointed leaders, decided on some rules of conduct, and agreed to obey those leaders and those rules. Have you ever wondered why the names of some cities end with "polis"—Indianapolis, for instance, or Minneapolis? Might there be a connection between such names and names ending in "burgh," or "borough"—Pittsburgh, say, or Edinborough—or in "ton," or "don"—Boston, London? There might be, for in different ancient languages "polis," "burgh," and "ton" meant essentially the same thing—a fortress, or a *fortified city*. Here, then, is a shred of evidence to support a conjecture that at least some governments of small city-states were established in self-defense against foreign aggression.

Perhaps, however, there did not have to be any danger of *foreign* attack. Perhaps the peril lay in human avarice closer to home. One great English philosopher, Thomas Hobbes, found the source of government in human depravity. It is normal, he suggested, for every man to want what every other man has, and hence for each person's hand to be raised against his neighbor. From this, Hobbes reasoned logically that men instituted governments to establish *order*—"domestic tranquillity," as our

Constitution's preamble puts it. Not community defense, but self-protection, was the aim. Only the strongest, fiercest individuals were able to protect themselves by their individual efforts; all the others, therefore, were ready to give up some of their independence in order to save their property or their lives. Hence they established governments, without which, according to Hobbes, man's life would be "solitary, poor, nasty, brutish, and short."

Another English philosopher, John Locke, who had great influence on the leaders of revolutionary America, was less pessimistic about human nature than was Hobbes. He taught that even without government there was a just unwritten "law of nature" applicable equally to all people. Nevertheless, this "law of nature," establishing rights and wrongs, was not clearly understood or fairly interpreted by every individual, nor could a weak person unlawfully injured by a stronger one gain redress for his injury by his own efforts. So, again, people agreed on some kind of organized society, to the end that natural justice should prevail; and the whole society then transferred or delegated its power to institutions of government. In the theories of both Hobbes and Locke, there was assumed to be an agreement among the people of a community—a "social contract" or compact, under which some authority was taken from each person and given to the "state."

Modern psychology has suggested other reasons for the establishment of government. The desire for power, like the sexual urge, is a dominant factor in many individuals. A strong man might organize a primitive community and set up a government (with himself as the ruler) simply to satisfy his own ambition. Conversely, many or most people, even those who say that they love liberty, may be afraid to be free. Some psychologists believe that each of us, at times, longs for the complete prenatal security of existence in our mother's womb; there, we had no freedom at all but neither did we worry about anything. So, naturally, the fearful many would gladly enough submit to the domination of the more adventurous, power-hungry few.

Now all these are theories about why government ever came to exist. The fact remains that the Europeans who settled in America had, long since, been accustomed to the existence of government and took its existence for granted. The real question before them was, what kind of a government? Their eventual answer, after the United States had gained its independence through war, gives meaning to our phrase about "a great experiment." For the government which they established was founded, more explicitly than any in history since 400 B.C., on the principle that the individual person is the most important thing in the world and that the state and its government exist to serve him and safeguard his "unalienable rights" to life, liberty, and the pursuit of happiness.

Think for a moment how different this was from the conception of the role of government shared by most nations in the eighteenth century, and you will see the justification for calling the American effort an "adventure." Our national republic was established when republics were philosophers' dreams or historians' memories. Most of the civilized world was ruled by kings or autocrats. The individual's chief significance lay in his role of member of the state, servant, if you will, of the government, rather than the other way around. For most of the world, "government by the people" was a phrase with no practical meaning whatever. And certainly no nation had ever sought to establish popular government over a territory as great as that covered by our original thirteen states. A self-governing republic, stretching from the Bay of Fundy to the Sea Islands of Georgia—this was something new on the face of the earth, and to make it succeed was one of the most challenging adventures ever undertaken by man.

Reflect, too, on the situation in the world today. There are many republics, or "constitutional monarchies," which are almost the same thing. These are free countries, where the people are not ruled by despots. One of them, Great Britain, is still a powerful state; another, India, is a new and potentially great state. But the majority of human beings do not live in these free societies. In population, the largest country is China; in might, the only present rival of the United States is the Soviet Union. Both China and Russia are essentially tyrannies. In both the prevailing ideology is that the good of the state (however that may be determined) is the *summum bonum,* the highest value in life, and that the individual is of secondary importance, his worth being assessed only in terms of the state's advancement. No matter how profoundly we may disagree with this ideology, we have to recognize that China and the Soviet Union possess not only material power, but influence over the minds of millions of men. To counteract that might and that influence the free world, in which the United States is much the strongest country, has got to show not only physical strength, but success in the workings of its individual-centered, democratic institutions. In the eyes of much of the world, our ideas of government are still on trial, their ultimate validity unproved. Our system is still an experiment—and we are proud to call it that. For, unlike the Communists, we do not exalt the state and punish criticism of the rulers. We believe that the state exists for us, not we for it, and that all government, being a human institution, is necessarily imperfect. Always it can and must be criticized, adapted, and improved. The adventure of a free society is new not just when the government is established, but every day thereafter; as long as it endures, it will always be an experiment.

## WHAT IS "GOVERNMENT"?

If governments can vary so greatly from country to country, what, then, do we mean by "government"? Briefly, "government" is the set of *rules* (for instance, constitutions, statutes, decrees) which are enforceable in a given territory, plus *institutions* (for example, regular elections, or Congress, or Praesidium, or police force) through which those rules are made or by which they can be enforced. The rules may and do vary widely both in their extent and in the way they are made. The institutions differ, too. But all governments have both.

All governments, too, if they are to endure for any length of time, must have the *power* to compel obedience to the rules. Ultimately, this power may be simply naked force. If the rulers have all the arms, they may think that they need nothing more. But men are men, even when they are armed. They can make the power of the rulers complete; but so can they use their arms against the rulers. Reliance on armed force alone is a two-edged sword. In the French Revolution, for instance, whole companies of soldiers, well aware of the misery of their own parents and brothers and sisters, promptly sided with the revolutionists. Over any extended period of time, government needs more than force.

Much of its power rests, instead, on the *willingness* of the great majority of the people to obey its commands—not because they like those commands, but because they think it proper to obey them. This willingness does not imply fear of the state, but rather, at one extreme, vehement pride in the state, and at the other, recognition of the fact that although government may be an unfortunate necessity, it *is* a necessity. Loyalty to the state, vociferous or grudging, is a vital part of the power without which government cannot exist. The habit of loyalty takes a firmer hold over a period of time as generations come to venerate the *symbols* of government. In the British Commonwealth of Nations, the crown is such a symbol. Respect is shown to the Queen not because of her personal qualities (highly respectable though they may be), but because in her royal capacity she represents an idea of a state, of a kind of government, of a social community, which generations of men of British stock have held dear. In America, perhaps the nearest equivalent to the symbol of the crown is the stars and stripes: "I pledge allegiance to the flag . . ." Familiar words, repeated by rote. Yet sometime, after months in a foreign desert, you may come to a seaport, still far from home. There in the harbor, unexpectedly, you will see a ship flying the American flag—and to your surprise a thrill will run down your spine.

Such a symbol connotes something more than government. It is a reminder of your homeland, and this, too, stirs your emotions. There is considerable evidence that the Russians fought so bravely and successfully in World War II not because of devotion to the totalitarian state or to Stalin, but out of devotion to "Mother Russia," their beleaguered homeland. The "national hymn" of many a country is devoted chiefly to its physical aspects and its natural beauty. The British and American anthems, of course, center on symbols—"God Save the Queen" and "The Star-Spangled Banner"; yet remember that of America we also sing "Oh beautiful for spacious skies, for amber waves of grain" and "I love thy rocks and rills, thy woods and templed hills."

Governmental power in the United States has always more obviously rested on popular willingness to accept it and emotional attachment to the symbols of the state than on bare force. For any government to be stable and lasting, such voluntary acceptance must be truly widespread. If the rules or rulers arouse the violent opposition of even a sizeable minority of the people, the whole governmental structure may topple. This is true in a society based on economic or social classes—witness, again, the French Revolution. It can be true, too, in a large country like the United States, where the economy, customs, and traditions of one section have differed sharply from those of another section. Ordinarily, rulers feel that it is their job to keep the country whole.[1] They are committed to prevent the dismemberment of the state. If, as happened in 1861, such dismemberment is seriously attempted, they will fight to prevent it. But where the tradition is one of limited government, with a refusal to glorify the state, the rulers will constantly try to avoid taking steps that would lead to disruption and dismemberment. The maintenance of national unity, of a broad base of popular approval or acceptance, is a constant concern of every responsible ruler.

This does not imply that for a nation to stay united, all of the people have to agree about everything. Far from it. But there does have to be a general, substantial acceptance of the fundamentals of government and social organization. This acceptance may be brought about by inertia, timidity, indoctrination, self-interest, or logical analysis—whatever the means used, the important thing is the existence of a *consensus* on basic ideas and institutions. In Communist lands, the consensus may be a general acceptance of Communist doctrine and the exaltation of the state. In the United States, the needed consensus is found in the acceptance of the Constitution and the readiness to debate issues and abide by the majority's decision. This might be stated in another way: the American political consensus is the generally shared belief in operating through a republican form of government.

---

[1] A possible exception to this may be President Buchanan, who was unwilling to use force even when the southern states seceded from the Union. For an example of how most rulers feel, however, recall the eloquent statement of former British Prime Minister Winston Churchill: "I did not become His Majesty's first minister in order to preside over the liquidation of the British Empire."

## A DEMOCRATIC REPUBLIC

*Democracy* has come to have many meanings, but for our purposes the best one is found in the origin of the word itself. The word came into our language as a derivative of an ancient Greek phrase *Demos Krateo*—which means, simply, "let the people rule." Democracy can exist without a republic; old-time city-states in Greece, and small New England towns, are often cited as examples of real democracy, because there the citizens "ruled" directly through decisions at meetings where every citizen could vote. In a large country, however, it would be difficult for democracy to exist—for the people to rule—except through a *representative* system. This is the essence of a republic: *a republican form of government* is one in which the ultimate power is said to be held by all the citizens of the republic, but they can exercise it only through a few people whom they choose, periodically, as their rulers.

In a democracy, people make decisions by voting. At a town meeting, for instance, they vote whether to raise the tax rate or build a new town hall or have the town collect the garbage. When they have a republican form of government, they vote for someone else—an alderman, a senator, a governor, a president—to make these and other governmental decisions for them. They elect these officials for a definite term, a period of time fixed in advance by law. After an official's term ends, the voters can, if they wish, elect someone else. Thus even in a republic, where they do not rule directly, the people have a continuing influence on the decision-making process, for the men who actually make the decisions are answerable to them on the next election day.

The people could participate in elections every month and still not have democracy unless those elections provided them with the opportunity of a *free choice* between alternatives. Totalitarian states have held "elections," but they have not achieved democracy, because in elections in Mussolini's Italy, Hitler's Germany, or the Soviet Union the voters were not free and had no real choice. They were not free to discuss the issues, to criticize their rulers, or to urge policies frowned on by the tyrants. Often they were not even free to hear both sides: the punishment for listening to "underground" or foreign broadcasts critical of the regime could be as savage as the punishment for speaking out. So when they started for the polling booths on election day, few of these people were equipped to make an intelligent choice. And when they got there, there was no choice which they could make, intelligently or stupidly, for the only names on the ballot were those approved by their rulers.[2]

Essential to democracy, then, are the right freely to criticize and listen to criticism, and the right, through election contests, to try to replace the rulers. This implies, in democracy, a definite value in discussion, dissent, and controversy, in peaceful struggle culminating periodically in victory or defeat at the polls. Democracy, indeed, cannot exist without *politics*—and it is to the politics of democracy that we now turn.

## WHAT IS "POLITICS"?

If you look up the word in an abridged dictionary, you may learn that "politics" is "the art of government," and be none the wiser. If you ask a sophisticated friend, he may answer that politics is what ambitious, unprincipled men do to gain office, a game in which the stakes are power and prestige and the weapons are the bribe, the false promise, and the shabby compromise. This tells you something, at least, but is it adequate? You might just as well define boxing as legalized mayhem in which one man tries to disable his opponent by kidney punches and blows below the belt. Boxing can be a dirty business and so can politics, but to define either of them solely in terms of their occasional rottenness is thoroughly misleading. It might be equally misleading to define boxing as "a character-building sport" or politics as "the noblest of the professions, public service." In speaking of politics, now, let us try to avoid these preconceived "value judgments," good

---

[2] To try to fool the world into thinking that they have great popular support, dictators sometimes give the people a "choice," permitting them to vote "No" as an indication of their dislike of the rulers or their policies. Then it is announced that hardly anyone voted "No." This is meaningless: most voters would be afraid to vote "No," for fear that they would be identified and punished. If many are brave enough to vote "No," the dictators' minions count the votes and can announce totally false results without anyone's being able to protest. And in any event, the ballot presents no real alternatives to the voter, for there is no opposition candidate.

and bad. Instead of using such words as "unprincipled," "shabby," or "noblest," let us try to develop a working definition that will describe politics as a process and that will apply whether politicians are good, bad, or indifferent.

Politics is an individual's or a group's effort to gain and exert influence, or to obtain and exercise power in the administration of government and the making of public policy, for their material advantage or for ends which they deem ideal. Note the references to government and public policy. People often speak of "politics" in the affairs of a fraternity, a college faculty, or a corporation, and indeed in all of those there are sometimes struggles for place or prestige or particular programs; but we are defining politics in terms of *governmental* power. Note, too, that the definition implies conflict and controversy. In any government effective enough to be worth studying there is bound to be a struggle to control its offices or direct its policies.

Now, having defined *politics,* how should we study it? What, if anything, is the central factor of politics, upon which we should focus our attention? Perhaps it is the *individual,* the politician or the voter. A typical history book, half a century ago, described American politics almost entirely in terms of a comparatively few political leaders. Elections were between Clay and Jackson, or Hayes and Tilden, or Bryan and McKinley, and the winner got his picture in the book. Like the contests for office, major policies were often described as individual creations, and controversies over them as duels between particular statesmen. Recently there has been a reaction against this kind of political history, this notion that political decisions are the products of personalities. Yet it is not irrelevant to consider the impact of an individual person's character, leadership, foibles, and ideas. The student of politics who emphasizes the individual's role can cite many examples of its importance. Here are a few illustrative explanations of political behavior at various levels:

A President of the United States says to his secretary: "I want that banking bill to pass, and I know that my addressing Congress in person is more effective than just sending up a written message about it; but I've had the flu and I just can't go up there and make a speech this week."

A legislator tells his assistant: "I don't like the banking bill and I don't believe many people back home like it, but I'm going to vote for it because Congressman Joe Black asked me to as a favor to him. Joe Black is my best friend in the House."

A humble male voter remarks apologetically to a candidate for office: "Oh, Mr. Edwards, you're a fine man. Wish I could vote for you. But I can't. Mr. Hurley, he got my old man a job, twenty years ago, so I gotta vote for Mr. Hurley."

A sophisticated female voter speaks heatedly of a candidate for office: "I'll certainly never vote for *that* man! I can't bear him! I saw him on television and he was kissing a baby!" (We might pause here to sympathize with the unfortunate politician. When someone thrusts a baby into his arms, what is he supposed to do—drop it?)

All these examples shed some light on the meaning of a typically pithy comment once made by Calvin Coolidge: "Politics is people. It is personal, it is individual, and nothing more." Except for the last three words, this is a statement worth remembering—especially if, like Mr. Coolidge, you embark on a political career.

Another starting point in the study of politics is the assumption that politics is essentially a conflict of *interests,* and that "interests" are usually ideas or goals held in common by *groups* of people. Farmers, let us assume, want higher prices for their products; with this goal held in common on the farms, there is a farming "interest." Worthy people disgusted by a corrupt city government might constitute a "reform" or "clean government" interest. Always people want to get, keep, or discard something; when they can achieve their desire through governmental action, they have a political "interest."

The concept of "conflict of interests" is illustrated most clearly when the struggle is between or among *organizations.* The "farming interest," for instance, may be relatively unimportant in politics save as it is represented by formally organized groups—the American Farm Bureau Federation, for example, or the National Grange, or the National Farmers Union. The kinds of organizations upon which the student of politics should concentrate are two: the "pressure group," which in the United States primarily seeks to influence public policy, and the "political party," which primarily seeks to win elections. Of course, these two primary objectives are not wholly separate and distinct. The pressure group can influence policy more effectively if its friends are elected to office. The party's success in elections may depend on the policies which its spokesmen advocate or adopt.

Again, we can illustrate the "interest" approach to politics by quoting a few actual or typical statements concerning political decisions.

A national party leader muses: "We can't nominate Joe for Vice-President; in the Senate, he has shown no sympathy at all for the interests of the farmers."

A senator explains: "I know a lot of radical outfits are for this bill, and some more conservative people are too, but the State Medical Association is against it so I guess I'd better vote against it."

A party's ward chairman says: "For the nomination to Congress, we'll back any decent man who'll promise to give jobs to members of our organization."

A labor leader warns the President: "If you appoint that labor-hating old buzzard to the Labor Board, Mr. President, our union people will figure that they'll never get a fair shake from the board, and there will be strikes all over the place."

In each of these statements, it is the conflict of interests—a broad interest like agriculture, or a narrower one such as a pressure group or a local party organization—which is seen as the factor leading to a political decision which will presumably be acceptable to one interest or another.

Whether politics is essentially an individual enterprise or a group conflict, its nature is profoundly influenced by the *institutions* of the country in which it takes place. In the United States, these institutions consist of the constitutional framework of our government, the continuing and developing organizations—the "going concerns"—pertaining to government, and the customs of the people in public affairs. The Constitution, for instance, sets up a system in which there are now fifty states, and each has its own elected governor and its own powers of government. Accordingly, much of the politics in each state is focused on winning office and influencing policy within the state rather than solely at the national level. This fact has a shaping influence on political behavior. The individual has a local outlet for his ambition. The pressure group has a stake in decisions made at the state capital. Three years out of four, the local party organization tends to be so concerned with state and local contests that our so-called national political parties seem to be mere loose alliances of state and local parties.

Some of the establishments created by the Constitution appear to have acquired a character of their own, which could not have been confidently predicted when they were formed. As a "going concern," the presidency has developed into one of the truly great offices of the world. Formerly this was not so. In the Constitution, the President's duties are chiefly those of an administrator, and people are not likely to become tremendously excited about who should be a "chief administrator." But, as we shall see, a preponderant measure of policy-making power, as well as administrative responsibility, has become attached to the institution of the presidency. Therefore it is upon control of that office that much of our politics is centered. Another example of institutional influence on politics is the development by each house of Congress of its own rules and customs. Long service in the Senate is an advantage to a senator seeking reelection or trying to promote a particular policy, not because he is old and wise (he may be feeble and stupid), but because the custom of the Senate is to favor those who have served longest by placing them in key positions which offer the greatest opportunities for prestige and influence.

Popular custom, too, often molds the contours of political behavior. In many states, for instance, there is no law forbidding a man to run for Congress in a district different from the one in which he lives. But if he dares to do so, he will usually have two strikes against him, for the customary assumption is that a representative should be a resident of the district which he represents. Consider, also, the custom of nominating presidential candidates at national conventions. No statute requires that such conventions be held. Yet they have come to be a part of our system of "political institutions"—and if you ever get seriously interested in becoming President, your first objective will be to win, not the general election, but a majority of the votes in your party's convention.

The student of politics, then, must consider how individual people act and react, must become fully aware of the perpetual clash of interests and organized group conflict, and must realize that political behavior is considerably limited or shaped by institutions.

The student of politics is, of course, a student of government also, for politics and government are inextricably intertwined. As we proceed to examine the way in which the United States is governed, we will continually be asking the political questions: *why* is it governed this way or that, *what* causes Congress to behave the way it does, *how far* can the President go in committing the country to a particular course in world affairs? We will take up, for instance, the framing of the Constitution, the ideas of federalism and the separation of powers, the functioning of the three branches of government, and the making of domestic and foreign policy—and in each case, we will not merely recount the decisions which were made and the action which followed, but we will also investigate the politics inherent in such public decision-making and governmental action. For government, especially in a democracy, is a vibrant thing, a dynamic process, and in that process all of us play a continuing part.

PART *Two*

# THE CONSTITUTION OF
# THE UNITED STATES

CHAPTER **2**

# The Fundamental Charter

The Constitution of the United States is the foundation stone of the Republic. It *establishes the instruments* of government; it *grants power* and authority to the national government; and it also *limits the power* and authority of both the national and state governments. When it was first written, in 1787, it did not do all these things, for it was then merely words written on paper, just a suggestion to be considered by the people of the original thirteen states. But the people did consider it. Through special state conventions they formally "ratified" or accepted it. Even though some of the framers of the Constitution did not feel confident that it would endure, the people continued to accept it as the years went by, and so the authority of the government which it established constantly increased.

Read the Constitution. Examine it carefully. You will see that as originally proposed and ratified, it consisted of seven major divisions or "articles." It establishes the instruments of national government—the Congress, the presidency, and the Supreme Court—in the first three articles. It grants power in several places, but especially in Article I, section 8, wherein many powers of Congress are specifically set forth. And it expressly limits governmental power, both in that section and elsewhere in the document. A whole set of further limitations were promptly added by the adoption of the so-called "Bill of Rights," the first ten amendments. Since 1791, it has been formally altered, by amendment, only thirteen times. The framers had built better than they knew. Who among them seriously expected that their work would stand so little changed nearly two centuries later?

## THE NEED FOR A CONSTITUTION

### A National Government

In a free society, no constitution is likely to work, or to endure, unless its basic provisions are compatible with the fundamental beliefs of the people about government and unless the major interests of the country have a chance to gain their ends within the constitutional framework. The people of the United States accepted our Constitution because it met the demand for a true national government without sacrificing the principles of popular rule and individual freedom. The Constitution has lasted because it continues to meet that central demand, safeguard those basic principles, and provide opportunity for the major interests within the country. The one occasion when its survival was imperilled was the Civil War, which broke out when southern leaders became convinced that because they had lost control of the national government, there was no opportunity or security for the slaveholding interest under the Constitution.

The first belief basic to the Constitution in 1787 and today is the need for a national government. We did not have one until 1788, when the Constitution was ratified: yet we celebrate July 4, 1776, as the birthday of our country, and Lincoln referred to 1776 as the year in which "our forefathers brought forth upon this continent a new nation. . . ." It is true that our American Revolution, our war for independence, was a prerequisite to our becoming a nation. It is also true, however, that the Declaration of Independence itself spoke not in terms of national independence but of the separate independence of the thirteen former colonies of Great Britain: these, it said, "are, and of Right ought to be Free and Independent States."

For the running of the war, the revolutionary colonies generally accepted the authority and sought the leadership of a "Continental Congress," which later was entitled the Congress of the United States. To win on the battlefield, the people of the thirteen new states realized that they had to work together; and in 1777, the Congress sought to make its own authority legitimate and to perpetuate the wartime cooperation among the states. It proposed a national charter called the Articles of Confederation, which finally became operative in 1781.

The Articles of Confederation, as we shall see, did not establish an effective national government; but their adoption reflected a basic awareness of the need for some form of union. Individual states had won independence, true enough, yet the men who had won it for them had been fighting in the armies of the "United States." They had made *national* existence possible; and in a world peopled by predatory foreign powers, national existence was desirable, for no state by itself could long feel secure. When the Articles failed to meet the need, nationally minded men gathered together to consider how to strengthen the bonds of union and make safe the independence which had been so hardly won. They met privately at Mt. Vernon, George Washington's home, in 1785, and in a convention at Annapolis, Maryland, in 1786; and finally heeding their demands, the feeble Congress called for a convention to be held at Philadelphia in 1787, "for the sole and express purpose of revising the Articles of Confederation." At Philadelphia the delegates, instead of revising the Articles, cast them aside and drew up a wholly new charter, the Constitution of the United States. They shaped a true national government, and the approval of the people gave it life.

## A People's Government

Although the trumpet call of the Declaration of Independence had not announced the birth of a recognizable nation, at least it had heralded its coming. And it did more than that. It expressed fundamental ideas about government—ideas which profoundly influenced the eventual shaping of our national institutions. Thomas Jefferson, its chief author, was a young man of unusual versatility and wide learning; and his colleagues, though perhaps less brilliant, generally shared the philosophy which he expressed.

That philosophy held that "all men are created equal, that they are endowed by their Creator with certain unalienable Rights, that among these are Life, Liberty, and the pursuit of Happiness. —*That to secure these rights, Governments are instituted among Men, deriving their just powers from the consent of the governed.*" This, as we saw in Chapter 1, is an echo of the teaching of John Locke. It places the source of government in the *people*, each of whom has certain "rights" which are inherent in his very existence: he cannot give them away even if he wants to. The Declaration of Independence goes on to say that when a government fails "to secure these rights"—that is, to protect them and make them safe—the *people* can properly abolish it and form a new government. Essentially, then, the Declaration of Independence is a democratic document. It assumes that government is created by the people and must be responsible to the people, who can change it when it fails to accomplish the purpose for which it was established. Thus the spokesmen for the revolutionary colonies, the potential leaders of the future nation, became committed to the fundamental principle of popular rule—government of and for and by the people. Any new Constitution would have to be founded on that principle.

## A True Union of States

Although none of the great nations of the world possessed written constitutions when our Constitution was drafted, the idea of formalizing the structure of government, the grant of power, and the limitations on its exercise in a written charter was not strange to the new Americans. Each of the thirteen states had its own charter. People in all the states were familiar with the three basic characteristics of such charters—establish, grant, limit. What was completely unfamiliar, however, was the idea of such a constitution for a union of states, for in 1787 there was not, and never had been, any true government of the whole country. The words "the United States of America" had expressed the unity of the thirteen separate states in the common effort to win independence from Great Britain. After the Revolution was won, what did the phrase mean? It referred to states; it included a governmental "instrument," a national Congress, which, however, had no real power or authority; it contained a reminder of past triumph and a hope for future unity. Today the phrase "United Nations" has a somewhat similar impact, although it refers to more than 110 "member states" instead of 13. But just as there is no true "United Nations Government" today, so there was no true "United States Government" in 1787.

Who was the first President of the United States? George Washington? Well, although there is some lingering historical dispute about this, it appears that the first person properly and officially to sign himself as "President of the United States" was a gentleman named John Hansen, in the year 1781. He was the presiding officer of the United States Congress, the feeble "instrument of national government" which existed in the years immediately prior to the Constitution. Because that Congress was not a government in the true sense—because, in those years, there was no real government of the United States—Mr. Hansen's position was of no great significance and his name is generally forgotten.

From 1776, when independence was declared, until 1788, when the Constitution came into effect, government in the United States was state and local government, operating differently in each state. The Articles of Confederation of 1781 did formally establish a Congress and purported to give it some powers, chiefly the power to conduct foreign affairs. But as a charter of national government the Articles of Confederation had fatal weaknesses. Each state, regardless of its population, had one vote in the Congress. Major legislation could be adopted only by more than mere majorities, and the Articles of Confederation themselves could not be changed except by a unanimous vote. In these respects, the Articles of Confederation sounded more like a charter for a league than a national constitution. Most important of all, the Congress did not have the power to compel individual people to obey its laws. For instance, it could, and did, make a treaty with England. During the Revolution a number of pro-British American "Tories" had fled from their homes, taking ship to Halifax or England. Frequently their houses had been taken over and occupied, free of charge, by Americans. After the war, the treaty with England declared that these American "squatters" should either turn the houses back to their rightful owners or pay a reasonable price for them. This the United States of America, through its Congress, solemnly agreed to. But the United States of America had no way to make the squatters either vacate or pay up. The national Congress which agreed to the treaty had neither force nor authority at its command. It could only *ask* the individual states—which did have force and authority—to see that the provisions of the treaty were carried out. When the states refused, the squatters stayed.

Just as it could not enforce a treaty, so the so-called national government had no actual power to raise an army or navy and obtain the money needed to maintain them. No young American of the 1780's awaited a letter from the nation's capital, beginning with the word "Greetings." No older American struggled with the intricacies of filling out a federal income tax form. The government under the Articles of Confederation neither drafted anybody nor taxed anybody. Although authorized to maintain an army and navy, it could do so only if it had money—and for this it had to depend on the highly uncertain generosity of the states.

There were many Americans who were not disturbed by this lack of a real national government, and some who were opposed to creating one. Deeply imbedded in our political traditions is a belief in "grass roots" government—rule of, for, and by the people of a particular locality. In the Revolution, men had fought against being ruled by faraway foreigners. Now would they wish to be ruled from some faraway spot, by largely unknown people? To be sure, one of their neighbors might have a voice in the distant government. Certainly, the nation's capital would be on the western shore of the Atlantic instead of the eastern. But even so, strangers would control the government, and they would make their decisions at a place almost as inaccessible as London. For Philadelphia (the capital under the Articles of Confederation) was a good two weeks' journey from Georgia, by horse and by stagecoach; and there were no telegraphs or telephones with which to close the gap.

Nevertheless, by 1787 many of the most respected citizens in the several states had concluded that there must be a real national government. Otherwise, they believed, the people of the the thirteen states were doomed to poverty and armed strife. All government, they feared, would fall into disrepute, and either tyrants would seize the reins or the individual states, one by one, would be gobbled up by England, France, or Spain. These dark forebodings were not the nightmares of the faint-hearted; there was considerable basis for them. In the 1780's, interstate strife actually grew into small wars. Connecticut settlers in the Wyoming Valley in Pennsylvania fought bloody battles with Pennsylvania troops. Maryland fishermen shot it out with Virginia fishermen over their rival "rights" to the fauna off the mouth of Chesapeake Bay. (They still do, occasionally!) States conducted "trade wars" against each other, forbidding the importation of eggs or saddles or tinware from one state into another; these were peaceable, but the irritations which they caused could easily lead to shooting.

The restrictions on trade had a serious economic consequence. The state borders were becoming barriers against commerce, and the man with goods to sell was thereby cut off from a potential market. This had the effect of stifling enterprise, because it made business success increasingly difficult. And business enterprise was desperately needed, for the long years of war had left the country depleted. The middle 1780's, indeed, were a period of serious economic depression. Individual states dealt with this depression in different ways, none of them satisfactory. In Rhode Island and North Carolina the impoverished debtors elected a majority of the legislature, which promptly tried to help the debtors at the expense of their creditors. The government of Rhode Island issued a vast amount of "paper money" and insisted that this paper, though actually worthless, be accepted by the creditors in payment of debts. Meanwhile, Massachusetts took the opposite course, sticking to "hard money" and refusing to inflate the currency. So while the substantial financiers suffered in Rhode Island, the poor farmers became desperate in Massachusetts. Unable to meet their mortgage payments, a number of them in the Connecticut Valley took up arms, apparently to keep their farms from being seized by their creditors. They surrounded the courthouse in Northampton, where many of the mortgages were filed, and, growing more desperate when opposed, tried to storm the arsenal at Springfield. They kept up a dwindling guerilla warfare with the state militia for several months in 1786-1787. This was "Shays'

Rebellion," named for its leader. Daniel Shays is pictured by some historians as a brave though unwise man who expressed the American idea of "do it yourself" by taking up arms to protect his home and family. Indeed, there is today a fine highway in Massachusetts named for him. But in 1787, the lawless violence of "Shays' Rebellion" sent a chill down the spines of many Americans of substance. To them it seemed a warning of what was to come— civil war, anarchy, and the seizure of property from those who possessed it by those who had none.

While internal strife mounted and more threatened, the foreign affairs of the country deteriorated. Men who had fought and suffered for independence could not take a cheerful view of the growing weakness of the United States. Georgia asked in vain for more military protection against the Indians harassing her western settlers. Ignoring the so-called "national government," Spain closed the mouth of the Mississippi, and the British refused to send a minister to the United States because, as they explained, they did not know whether to send one minister or thirteen. American shipping, unprotected by any adequate national navy, was an easy prey to seizure by the British and French and the depredations of the Barbary pirates. The breakdown of international trade added to the economic woes of the country. In some quarters, indeed, there was talk that particular states would fare better if they severed themselves from the United States and formed commercial and political attachments elsewhere. Although such talk was exaggerated, it was symptomatic. The disease of disunity was making disastrous progress.

## THE FRAMING OF THE CONSTITUTION

It was under these conditions, and with these fears, that the framers of the Constitution convened in Philadelphia in May, 1787. Ostensibly, their function was to propose some amendments to the Articles of Confederation. Actually, many of them had been in communication with each other during the preceding months and were determined not to revise but to replace the Articles of Confederation by a completely new charter of government. They intended to create, for the first time, a real national government in America. Many of them were familiar with the task of drafting a constitution for a single state, but the great challenge before them now was to write a constitution for a new kind of government—one which would govern a nation composed of many states. Just as disunity caused them to assemble, so unity was their goal. Yet they realized that they could achieve nothing if they recommended one single, unified, all-powerful national government, abolishing the states or making them subsidiary provinces. The people of the states would have spurned any such proposal. Somehow the men at Philadelphia would have to devise the framework of a national government capable of uniting the country while maintaining the separate and distinct governments of every state.

The fifty-five delegates to the convention (the average number attending on any given day was thirty) were agreed on creating a real national government while retaining the states as self-governing units within the nation. They agreed that the new national government should be so devised as to minimize the chance of any man or group seizing despotic power. Most of them also shared a distrust of direct democracy, but all of them knew that the nation was committed to the essentially democratic principles enunciated in the Declaration of Independence.

There was agreement, too, that the new Constitution must provide some cure for the economic ills of the country. It would have to establish a uniform currency and eliminate the state tariff barriers which kept each state an isolated and increasingly impoverished economic unit.

There were many other matters, however, which divided them. On several occasions, these divisions were so sharp that it seemed that the convention must disband. The major ones were settled not by an appeal to abstract principles, but by compromises.

## The Main Compromises

The so-called "Great Compromise" at Philadelphia concerned the demands of the delegates from the small states for equal representation in the national Congress. This, you will remember, they already had in the Congress existing pursuant to the Articles of Confederation. Delegates from the more populous states preferred to have the number of congressmen in each state determined by the state's population. The solution, reached after the Delaware delegation had threatened to go home, was to have a Congress of two "chambers," in one of which, the House, the states would be represented by population, whereas in the other, the Senate, each state would have two members. The idea of having a two-chambered or "bicameral" legislature was not novel. The significance of the decision lay in the different methods of representation. Both sides were reasonably satisfied. The large states' delegates believed that the House would be the more important legislative body because it would possess the "money power"—the sole authority to initiate measures for raising revenue. The small states' delegates foresaw an influential Senate, composed of elder statesmen wisely reviewing the ill-considered actions of a headstrong House. In one sense, too, this was a compromise between two attitudes toward government—the aristocratic and the democratic. To be sure, the "democratic" cause had few if any enthusiastic adherents in the convention except for Benjamin Franklin. The delegates, therefore, in making one house "democratical," were not resolving a conflict among themselves. They were, rather, yielding some of their preferences because they recognized that their handiwork would be subject to popular approval and that such approval would not be given a totally undemocratic document. The convention's proposals for the differing methods of election of senators and representatives, then, represented a compromise of not only the conflict of interests between large and small states, but also of the differing ideas, in the country as a whole, of the proper political role of the ordinary humble citizen. Yet the difference was not fundamental. The Senate might be more "aristocratical" than the House, but still be a fit instrument of popular government. Unlike its British equivalent, the largely hereditary House of Lords, the Senate was to be chosen by state legislatures—and the latter, after all, were elected by the people. While, then, the framers saw real or fancied dangers in popular rule, they nevertheless preferred "government by the people" to any other form of government.

A later yet equally vital compromise prevented a breakup on issues which divided many northern delegates from those of the deep South. The northerners wished to give to Congress (in Article I, section 8) the power to impose export taxes and tariffs on imports in the same manner—majority vote—that Congress could enact other measures. Southerners objected to this; if this power was to be given to Congress at all, they said, it should be exercised only when at least two-thirds of the Congress agreed. Meanwhile, some of these same northerners were bent on abolishing the infamous African slave trade by having the Constitution itself prohibit the importation of Negro slaves. Again, some southerners objected. The double stalemate was resolved by each side giving ground. The North abandoned the export tax but won on the tariff: the power of Congress to tax imports was not hamstrung by a two-thirds rule. The South won on the Negro issue in two ways. First, the slave trade was permitted for twenty-one years. Second, the slave states were awarded extra representation in the House of Representatives. This was done by counting a slave (though he was not a citizen and had no vote) as "three-fifths of a person" when computing the state's population, the basis of representation in the House.

This compromise boosted the convention over its last high hurdle. It cost the signature of one of the most respected delegates, George Mason, as we shall see below; and two other delegates, Edmund Randolph of Virginia and Elbridge Gerry of Massachusetts, also refused to sign the completed document. But thirty-nine citizens, at least one from every state represented, signed it on September 16, 1787. The first signature was that of the convention's chairman, George Washington. Anxious for the future of the country he had done so much to create, he expressed no optimism about the fate of the convention's proposal. He was, however, satisfied that the delegates had done their work well. "We have raised a standard," he said, "to which the wise and honest can repair. The event is in the hands of God."

## Ratification

Actually, the outcome depended on whether the proposed Constitution would gain approval in at least nine of the thirteen states. It would never come into effect at all unless at least nine states ratified it. The method of ratification was prescribed in the Constitution itself—special conventions were to be held in each state for the sole purpose of considering and voting on the new document. The delegates to these state conventions were chosen by the voters. Feelings ran high, for and against the proposed Constitution; and in some states there were hot campaigns for the position of convention delegate between men favoring it and others who denounced it. Newspapers printed long series of articles on both sides of the question. The most famous of these series, arguing for ratification of the Constitution, became known as *The Federalist* papers. They were all signed by a fictitious name, "Publius," but actually they were written by James Madison, Alexander Hamilton, and John Jay.

Although, technically, ratification by any nine states would put the Constitution into effect, it was obvious that if a real union was to be established, the most important states would have to be in it. In size, wealth, and influence, these were New York and Virginia. Accordingly, the campaign for ratification was most earnestly pressed in these two states. By very narrow margins in both of them, the proponents of the Constitution triumphed. The Constitution was ratified and the country proceeded to transform the new government from paper into flesh and blood by electing its officers in the fall of 1788. On April 30, 1789, in the city of New York, the newly chosen Congress assembled; and George Washington, a balcony roof shielding him from the driving rain, took the oath of office as President of the United States.

## BASIC ELEMENTS OF THE CONSTITUTION

Agreement at Philadelphia and approval in the states were gained by a document which met the needs of the time. It provided Americans with a national government, yet left the states in existence. It organized the national government in a fashion intended to prevent autocracy. The states' approval was in effect conditioned on the Constitution's being immediately enlarged by amendments protecting individual liberties. And this was possible because the original document itself provided for its own peaceful alteration.

### The Federal Principle

The framers agreed upon a document which promoted both unity and diversity. In essence, they *divided* the subjects of governmental control between the new national government, on the one hand, and the governments of the states on the other. They endowed the national government, for the first time, with the right to make rules affecting individual citizens and to enforce those rules. Thus they made it a true government. And they specifically sought to eliminate the causes of economic distress, in two ways: the Constitution endowed the national government with the powers to coin money and to regulate "commerce among the states," and it forbade the states to coin money and to impose tariffs or other barriers impeding trade. At the same time, they left to the several states a wide range of authority. In fact, in those days, the powers left to the states seemed to the average citizen much broader and more significant than those "delegated" to the national government, except in matters of monetary and foreign policy. Out of necessity, the framers came up with something new—something which we now call "the federal principle," or "federalism," a system in which each of us is ruled by two governments, national and state. This invention of federalism, and what has happened to it, will be the subject of the next chapter of this book.

## The Separation of Powers

Just as the framers knew that their proposals would be rejected if they included abolition of the states, so they realized that the people would disapprove any charter which failed to erect barriers against tyranny. They believed that a sure road to tyranny was the accumulation of all governmental powers, legislative, executive, and judicial, in the hands of a single man or group of men. To prevent this, they proposed that in the new national government these major functions should be *separated* by assignment to three distinct units or "branches." These were the legislative branch, consisting of Congress; the executive branch, headed by the President; and the judicial branch, composed of the Supreme Court and such inferior courts as Congress might establish. None of the three branches would be fully dependent on any of the others, and the personnel of each would be selected in a different manner. As a practical matter, however, their mutual independence could not be complete, for if each branch totally disregarded the others, the government might easily degenerate into chaos. Accordingly, the framers provided that in some instances action could not be taken unless at least two branches were agreed on it. Thus, a bill passed by Congress could be nullified by a presidential veto, and some executive appointments proposed by the President would not be effective unless the Senate approved them. To make the government work, there would have to be some interbranch cooperation—and the very fact that such cooperation was required meant that any branch, by refusing to cooperate in actions which it deemed unwise, could check the abuse of power by the other branches. This system of separating functions among branches composed of different people, with different constituencies, and of giving each branch some power to restrain the others, seemed admirably designed to minimize any danger of despotism. It has not worked exactly as the framers expected it to, but it remains a basic element of the Constitution. Its details, development, and present-day significance will be explained and discussed in Chapters 4 and 5.

## The Protection of Individual Rights

The third basic constitutional principle stems from the reason for the second. The people of America wanted liberty, and they viewed governmental power as the natural enemy of liberty. Separation of powers was one safeguard against tyranny, but the voters wanted more. At Philadelphia, to be sure, the framers did not sense the strength of this popular desire. They assumed, or professed to assume, that the new national government which they proposed, with its structural safeguards, would in no way threaten individual freedom. Nevertheless, they did write into the original document a few specific protections against injustice. It required a jury trial in criminal cases in federal courts and prohibited bills of attainder,[1] ex post facto laws,[2] the imposition of any religious test for office under the national government, and (save in cases of invasion or rebellion) suspension of the writ of habeas corpus.[3]

---

[1] A bill of attainder is, essentially, a legislative act (in contrast to a judicial decision) condemning or "attainting" someone.

[2] An ex post facto law is a statute which makes punishable a previous act which was lawful at the time when it was performed.

[3] The writ of habeas corpus is a court order directing the official who holds a person in custody to produce that person for a hearing in court, not to decide whether he is guilty or innocent but simply whether he is being held lawfully in custody.

These protections, however, were not enough. After the convention adjourned, its members soon learned that their handiwork had what many people considered a fatal flaw—the lack of a full, specific "bill of rights." To save the Constitution's chances for ratification, its proponents promptly agreed to sponsor amendments to it, filling the gap. This promise allayed the opposition. The promise was kept. One of the key figures at Philadelphia and in the fight for ratification, James Madison, became the chief draftsman of the amendments and formally introduced them at the first meeting of the first Congress. Ten were adopted, the first ten amendments,[4] often described as the "Bill of Rights." The first clause provided for freedom of expression and worship and the separation of church and state. Others of the amendments were designed to protect the individual from arbitrary or oppressive actions by the national government and to preserve his right to a fair trial in the federal courts.

## The Opportunity for Constitutional Change

The belief that government stems from the people includes the assumption that the people have the right to change it. As the Declaration of Independence put the matter: ". . . it is the Right of the people to alter or abolish it . . . Prudence, indeed, will dictate that Governments long established should not be changed for light and transient causes. . . ." Here Jefferson was justifying revolution. The Constitution, however, made no provision for revolution: the people might have an inherent right to overthrow the government, but the officials of the government had an implied duty to put down any revolt. Yet the framers did recognize the need for *peaceful* alteration of the rules. They specifically provided, in Article V, that the Constitution could be *amended*. They also agreed that it should not be amended "for light and transient causes," and so made the process of formal amendment complicated and cumbersome.

---

4 Actually the Tenth Amendment is quite unlike the others in this series. The first, and others, protect the citizen against the national government. The tenth, in contrast, is a specific reminder that the national government's powers are *only* those delegated to it by the Constitution. For the student's purposes, the Tenth Amendment's significance is in the fact that it confirmed the principle of federalism rather than in its impact on civil liberties or individual rights.

The usual process is for an amendment to be proposed in Congress, pass both the House and the Senate with the approval of at least two-thirds of those voting in each chamber, and then (without presidential signature) be submitted to the state legislatures. The proposed amendment must be approved by the legislatures in three-quarters of the states before it becomes an effective part of the Constitution.[5] It is permissible, under Article V, for Congress to submit the proposal to special state conventions instead of to the legislatures. This, of course, is what was done with the original Constitution, but the method has been used only once since, in the case of the Twenty-first Amendment. The framers provided for another way of initiating an amendment, Article V directing that upon the demand of two-thirds of the states, Congress must call a convention which may then propose amendments for ratification in the usual manner. This method has never been used. However, in late 1962 a meeting of the "General Assembly of the States," a group of state legislators affiliated with the Council of State Governments, proposed three new amendments and launched a campaign to have the requisite number of states demand a constitutional convention to consider them. The three amendments would (1) change the amending process of the Constitution so that two thirds of the states could propose constitutional amendments directly without the approval of Congress or a convention, (2) prohibit any federal court from ruling on cases concerning the apportionment of state legislators, and (3) establish a "Court of the Union" made up of the fifty state supreme court chief justices, to review United States Supreme Court decisions on federal-state questions.

These proposed amendments avoid some of the difficulties experienced in earlier attempts to use the convention procedure, for they are identical in form from state to state. By July of 1963, the apportionment entry was doing best, having been approved in thirteen states and by one house of the legislature in three others. Still, its chances of gaining approval in two thirds of the states seemed very slim. Even if it did so, the problem of whether the

---

[5] State ratification, to be effective, must be completed within a reasonable time of the submission of the proposed amendment to the states. Some recent amendments and proposed amendments have included a specific provision that ratification must be completed within seven years or not at all.

ensuing convention could change the amendment or adopt a wholly different one would remain unsolved. No one knows what kind of a convention would be held—what the basis of representation would be, or what the convention's mandate would amount to. If a convention were held, would it be confined to approving or disapproving the amendment proposed by the states—in which case, why require that a convention be held? Would it be merely a technical drafting body, putting the states' proposal into proper form? Or could it initiate other amendments, on its own? Article V does not answer these questions.

The framers assumed that their handiwork would be altered; indeed, they agreed to its prompt amendment by the addition of the Bill of Rights. They could not have foreseen, however, how much the meaning of the document would change through the process of *judicial interpretation*. Some of the language in the Constitution is broad and ambiguous; if its exact meaning was uncertain in 1787, it is even more obscure under the utterly different conditions of life today. To interpret the Constitution and to adapt its ancient phrases to modern needs has been a major function of the Supreme Court, as will be fully explained in Chapter 5.

These, then, are the four great ideas in the Constitution: federalism, separation of powers, protection of individual liberty, and opportunity for change. You might rephrase the first three to read: "states' rights, minority rights, individual rights," but that would be an oversimplification. Federalism's novelty lay not in preserving states' rights, but in setting up a national authority whose laws, in given spheres of action, would be "supreme." The separation of powers was to protect not only minorities against majority tyranny, but also everyone against any possible despotism; and it was part of a system designed to enable government to function. The protection of individual rights, as the framers tacitly foresaw, turned out to be unimportant for many years, but became significant when by further amendment (the Fourteenth Amendment) it was extended to protect citizens against their state governments. Its importance increased still more in the present century, when wars and tensions led to intolerance of political heresy and to governmental efforts to suppress dissent.

## THE POLITICS OF CONSTITUTION-MAKING

None of the thirty-nine men who signed the Constitution on September 17, 1787, assumed that it was "ideal" or "perfect." Each of them was dissatisfied with one part of it or another. But all the signers were agreed that their handiwork was practical. It was designed, imperfectly, perhaps, but effectively, to cure the ills of disunion which the people were suffering under the Articles of Confederation; and it was also calculated to obtain sufficient popular acceptance, though not without a struggle.

The Constitution was essentially a practical political proposal. It may well be worthy of veneration, today, but surely anything worth venerating is worth understanding. Our understanding of the Constitution would be incomplete if we examined it simply as a formal instrument, establishing the government and granting and limiting power. We must analyze it, too, as a political achievement; and that analysis should begin with the politics of its framing and its ratification.

We have seen that politics is essentially the struggle for power and influence, in or through government. Obviously the opportunities for power and influence will be greatly affected by the structure of the government. Necessarily, then, the decision as to what that structure shall be is a fundamental political decision. Both during the framing at Philadelphia, when delegates differed and debated and compromised, and later in the several states, when the question was the ratification of the completed document, politics was present all the time.

### The Institutional Framework

In studying politics, it may be well to start by considering the institutional framework within which it is carried on. There were certain institutions which obviously constricted the discretion of the men at the Philadelphia Convention and limited the scope of their political conflict. Some of these institutions were customs and widely held convictions. For instance, the framers were not, as a practical matter, at liberty to recommend that a king should be appointed or summoned from abroad to rule over America. The institution of popular government, the general belief in the rightness of republican principles, put any such notion beyond the pale. Other institutions were more formal—for example, the existence of the states with their constitutions and their governments in operation. What people thought constitutions should be was made plain to the framers by those which had been adopted by eleven states from 1776 to 1780. All of them proclaimed that sovereignty resided in the people and expressly preserved the individual right to liberty of conscience. All put paramount governmental power in a representative legislature, and in most this legislature was divided into two bodies, one of which—the "upper house"—was in some states chosen by voters possessing substantial property while men with less property were qualified to join in electing the members of the other. Every state had a governor, but his powers were small. In more than half the states the governor, being elected for a one year term by the legislature, was obviously subservient to it. Furthermore he had no right to veto legislation; and his authority to appoint state officials was made subject to approval by either a legislative body or a specially constituted "council." [6] While under these early state constitutions the judicial branch could presumably declare laws unconstitutional, the judges were in most instances elected for short terms by the legislature, and a displeased legislature could quickly vote them out of office. In building on the state constitutions, then, the framers had to pick and choose, according to their own purposes. Much they could use. As we shall see, however, the framers' conception of what interests most needed protection in a national constitution led them to one major departure from the pattern of the state constitutions. Where the clauses of the latter added up to virtual legislative supremacy, the men in Philadelphia, fearing that popularly elected legislatures would disregard established property rights, preferred to restrain the legislature by a system of checks and balances.

As we have seen, no one at Philadelphia, except Hamilton, felt free to suggest that the state governments should simply be wiped

---

6 There were eleven new constitutions instead of thirteen, because two states merely revised their colonial charters. The constitutional provisions diluting the governor's appointing power persist in many states. In Massachusetts and New Hampshire there are still, today, separately elected "governor's councils" which ratify (or reject) the governor's appointments and issuance of pardons.

out. They knew that any charter of government in a country devoted to the idea of self-rule must not destroy but instead reflect the popular institutions of that country. The recognition of these institutions not only kept the political debate from straying into profitless channels but actually helped the framers in writing the Constitution itself. Except for new restraints on the legislature —the President's veto power, for instance—the structure of the proposed new national government paralleled the structure of government in most of the states. Furthermore, many clauses in the Constitution were taken word for word, or very nearly so, from various state constitutions. Thus the clause saying that "Each house shall be the judge of the elections, returns and qualifications of its own members" is an echo of the Massachusetts constitution's provision that the state "Senate shall be the final judge of the elections, returns, and qualifications of its own members," and the provision that "no religious test shall ever be required as a qualification to any office" is taken directly from the Maryland constitution. The final solution of the problem of how to choose a President was based on the Maryland system of having specially chosen county "electors" select the members of the state senate.

Thus, in political terms, institutions narrowed the possible issues which the framers had to grapple with, and also made it easier for them to resolve these issues. Their proposals, drawing heavily on the existing state constitutions, gathered popular support in part because they left these institutions intact. The men at Philadelphia were fully aware of the significance of institutions in the political struggle.

## The Role of Individuals

They were aware, too, of the important roles played by individuals in the political process. The selection of George Washington as chairman of the Philadelphia Convention is evidence of this awareness. General Washington was not a political philosopher. He had no intellectual brilliance, nor was he an eloquent orator. But in his individual person, he was an overpoweringly commanding figure. His character and self-control, his achievements, and his presence struck awe and inspired respect. Not only did the men at Philadelphia feel this respectful awe; they also knew that if this one man, George Washington, were to sign and support the new Constitution, the prospects of its ratification would be immeasurably brightened.

In contrast to Washington's mere presence, other delegates affected the decision-making at Philadelphia and in the state conventions by their intellectual force and insight. Foremost among these were two young men, Madison and Hamilton. Without their individual capacities and their personal efforts, there might never have been a Constitution. They had very different ideals and ambitions, and they were later to become political enemies. In 1787, however, they both favored "a more perfect union," and their different abilities were invaluable to the success of the whole endeavor.

There were other great and famous men at Philadelphia: [7] Benjamin Franklin, for example, and James Wilson of Pennsylvania. Franklin's humor and mellow wisdom helped to dull the knife-edge sharpness of disagreement among the delegates. Wilson's learning and great legal ability made him a persuasive advocate. Another Pennsylvania delegate, Gouverneur Morris, had special facility with his pen and is often given credit for the dignity and grace with which the Constitution is written—although, as we have just seen, a considerable portion of his task was an editorial "cut-and-paste" job, lifting and adapting many appropriate clauses from existing state constitutions.

The individual's significance in politics often stems from his personal, selfish ambition. There is little or no evidence that at Philadelphia the delegates were so motivated. They were seeking neither office nor glory. To be sure, some of them were active in state politics and undoubtedly were not wholly indifferent to public opinion as it might affect their personal political fortunes. Probably Elbridge Gerry of Massachusetts, eager for political preferment in that state, refused to sign the Constitution partly because he thought that his refusal would enhance his chances.

---

[7] Not all the outstanding leaders of early America were at Philadelphia. Thomas Jefferson, chief draftsman of the Declaration of Independence, was in Paris; he was our ambassador to France. John Adams, revolutionary leader and chief architect of the constitutions of his own and other states, John Hancock, Thomas Paine, and Patrick Henry were likewise absent.

Probably, in the battle for ratification, John Hancock was persuaded to support the Constitution by an appeal to his vanity and ambition: it was suggested to him that if the Constitution were ratified, he might be the first vice-president of the United States. But certainly the framers, by and large, were not primarily motivated by personal selfishness. As James Madison wrote: ". . . there never was an assembly of men, charged with a great and obvious trust, who were more pure in their motives, or more exclusively and anxiously devoted to the object committed to them than were the members of the Federal Convention of 1787."

Granting the purity of their motives, however, the framers shared a general concern which incidentally included a concern for themselves. Virtually all of them were men of substance, well-to-do property owners.[8] Inevitably, they spoke with the voice of their class, and thus they spoke for their class and so, in the last analysis, for themselves. But in so doing, they were not expressing individual ambition, but were defending and promoting the interests with which they were identified.

### The Impact of Interests

Most Americans in 1787 owned some property. The special "property interest" which tended to unite the framers was more than ownership of large estates or bank accounts. It included an assumption of superiority—social and political superiority, as well as economic. Most of the men at Philadelphia were distrustful of democracy. They knew that the democratic theory that the ultimate source of governmental authority is the people themselves was already one of the accepted political institutions of America. In prudence, they could not publicly denounce popular rule or flout the demand for it by creating an openly undemocratic structure of government. Yet some of them wished that they could. Only three, it appears, privately favored establishing a "constitutional monarchy," but many shared the forebodings of Gouverneur Morris: "The mob begin to think and reason. Poor reptiles! They bask in the sun, and ere noon they will bite, depend upon

---

8 The one exception, well named, was William Few of Georgia, a small farmer.

it." Their feelings were well put, some years later, by a prominent clergyman, Rev. Jeremy Belknap: "Let it stand as a principle that government originates from the people; but let the people be taught that they are not able to govern themselves!"

Naturally, the Constitution which men with such convictions and such fears drew up was something less than an enthusiastically democratic document. It restricted the active role of the people in ways that seemed inconsistent with the principles of the Declaration of Independence and actual provisions of the state constitutions. And yet, with hardly any change, it later became the basic charter of a democratic people. Democracy could grow in the United States, under the Constitution, because regardless of their social prejudice and fears for their property, the framers upheld what they called "the republican principle" and based the nation's government on popular rule.[9]

They were anxious, however, to dilute that popular rule. Accordingly, they agreed that one branch of the government, the judiciary, should be essentially *undemocratic,* the judges to be appointed for life terms rather than elected for short terms. The head of the executive branch, the President, was to be elected, not by the people, but by electors specially chosen in each state, in such manner as each state's legislature might prescribe. (In the beginning, this meant that the state legislatures themselves chose the electors who picked the President; popular elections of electors came later.) This, at best, was democracy doubly diluted. As for the legislative branch, one part of it, the House of Representatives, was to be popularly elected, but it could be checked by the other legislative body, the Senate, whose members were to be chosen by the state legislatures. So, of the three great branches, only one-half of one of them was originally intended to be a fully democratic institution.

It sometimes seems hard to realize, today, how many safeguards against popular rule the framers wrote into the Constitution. For

---

9 Not all of the great and well-to-do were anti-democratic. At Philadelphia, old Benjamin Franklin frankly expressed his cheerful faith in the humble people, from whom he had sprung. Over in Paris was Thomas Jefferson, a large landowner, who had confidence in popular rule so long as the people were predominantly agricultural and not huddled in industrial cities.

over a century and a half, presidential electors have been chosen by the people, not the legislatures; and the same has been true of the Senate since 1913. Only the Supreme Court remains insulated from the winds of popular democracy, and it remains that way because the people wish it. The framers should not be described as prophets of democracy. They can be praised or blamed, however, for their forbearance; they did not slam the door against the growth of democracy. Their safeguards reflected their distrust of the people, but they still made it possible for the people to increase the scope and directness of popular rule without revolution and civil strife.

If the defenders of substantial property interests were mostly reluctant to oppose the theory of democracy openly, they were frank in expressing their fear of democracy in practice. For democracy in practice is, in effect, the rule of the momentary majority. The framers, by using the principle of the separation of powers, made it very difficult for any majority party or group to gain control of the whole government. Furthermore, the very size of the new republic would make it difficult for any selfish majority to form or to remain united. And if any majority "faction," as Madison called it, should manage to dominate the Congress, the presidency, and the courts simultaneously, there was still the fact that the national government was not all-powerful, for under the Constitution much authority remained in the various states. Thus both the separation of powers and the federal system imposed obstacles to real majority rule of the whole country. In *The Federalist* papers, arguing for the ratification of the Constitution, Madison and Hamilton described these brakes on majority rule as valuable safeguards against the oppression of minorities—as, in essence, guaranties of freedom. They drew an unhappy picture of tyranny, not merely an individual despotism but "majority tyranny," and then happily predicted that under the Constitution such tyranny would be impossible and individual liberty would be assured. They persuaded many voters that the Constitution provided for both majority rule by the people and the protection of minorities. This picture of the Constitution persists today. It was never a completely accurate picture, for even now many governmental decisions are not made by the majority of the people, even indirectly; yet it is closer to the truth today than it was in 1788.

Although the framers' arguments were usually couched in general terms, there was a particular minority interest which concerned them most—naturally, their own. Paper money in Rhode Island, Shays' Rebellion in Massachusetts, were typical causes of their fear of majorities: for most people were poor. They themselves, being comparatively rich, were members of a minority. They were alarmed by the possibility of a majority revolt, and even more by majority control of legislative bodies. The Rhode Island legislature, though it had gone to the greatest extremes, was not the only one in which poor farmers, deep in debt, had gained a strong or controlling voice. And if debtors got the votes and held control of legislatures, what was to stop them from enacting laws wiping out their debts and making rich men poor?

The framers met this threat in two ways. First, they consciously departed from one principle common to most or all of the states: namely, the supremacy of the legislature. It was in the legislative branch, even in at least one house of the new Congress, that the majority interest, the poor-debtor interest, might become dominant. But the Constitution would check the poor debtors and restrain them from ruining their creditors because under the Constitution, Congress would not be supreme. Anything a "majority faction" might achieve in Congress could be thwarted by the President or, perhaps, by the Supreme Court. Second, they wrote into the Constitution specific clauses prohibiting the *states* from helping the poor by "robbing the rich." The new Constitution forbade any state law "impairing the obligation of contracts," and it prohibited the coinage or issue of money by any state.

These clauses, like the separation of powers, reflect an economic interest shared by most or all the framers. This does not mean that the men who wrote the Constitution were greedy men or that what they proposed was solely for the benefit of themselves and others of the wealthy class. On the contrary, the record shows that most of those at Philadelphia were public-spirited citizens and devoted patriots. The document they drafted could not have lasted if it had been an unjust instrument, cruelly oppressing the poor. Nevertheless, the way they saw things and what they did were conditioned by the kind of life they lived, the friends they had, and the values which they and their friends most prized. Inevitably, they wished the new Constitution to protect property. Thus they wrote it—and it worked.

*Conflict in the Convention.* So far, we have considered the impact of an interest which virtually all the framers shared. But there are different kinds of property and different ways of acquiring it. The delegates could be unanimous in favoring the protection of property rights in general, but the impact of the Constitution on specific money-making occupations divided them sharply. The major conflict of economic interests at Philadelphia was between the agricultural or planting interests, whose spokesmen were mainly southerners, and the commercial and industrial interests, mostly represented by northern delegates. The southerners, exporting much of their crop, favored free trade with foreign nations. The northerners, in contrast, hoped for a protective tariff against foreign goods which might undersell their products in America. Northerners feared that free trade would ruin their industrial prospects. Southerners feared that taxes on imports and especially exports would ruin the economy of the agricultural South.

As we have already seen, this conflict became interwoven with another group struggle which formed along roughly similar geographical lines: the disagreement about permitting any more Negro slaves to be imported from Africa. Here the pro-slavery interest was fiercely upheld by the delegates from the deep South— Georgia and especially South Carolina. As we have seen, these two conflicts were resolved simultaneously, the northerners winning on the tariff and the southerners on slavery.

This compromise, or rather "deal," saved the Constitution, but it also cost it the support of one of the most distinguished delegates at Philadelphia, George Mason of Virginia. Mason, though a slave-holder, was a strong critic of slavery, and demanded immediate abolition of the slave trade. At the same time, he spoke the language of the southern planters when he warned that a congressional majority from northern states could bring the South to ruin and subjection by taxing exports. Mason said that the convention's decisions on these subjects opened the door to eventual war between the South and the North, for the former would become more and more dependent on its slave-holding, exporting economy, while the latter would become increasingly populous, gain control of the national government, and destroy southern agriculture. His critics claimed that he was an interest spokesman pure and simple—his anti-slavery attitude, it was charged, stemmed from the fact that Virginia was already prosperous and needed no more slaves, but feared competition from the deeper South if more slaves should be imported there. But whatever the reasons for them, Mason's objections were prophetic. He named correctly the two issues which for three-quarters of a century threatened the existence of the Union—the tariff and slavery.

To sum up: the framing and adoption of the Constitution were basic political decisions. They were shaped, in part, by the institutions of early American government and the generally shared beliefs concerning the nature and role of government. They were made or influenced by men of wealth and learning and ability. They reflected the values or interests common to those men, including their conviction that men like themselves were fit to govern and their distrust of the masses of people. They included, too, compromises between material and ideal interests which divided the framers. Those compromises left imperfectly resolved some fundamental conflicts which were eventually settled only on the battlefield; yet without those compromises, there might never have been a Constitution.

# CHAPTER 3

# *The Federal Union*

As we have seen, "federalism" was the one remarkable invention of the framers. We must, then, define that term as
exactly as possible, for unless we define it we are unlikely to understand it. Then we must explore its implications—and this will
lead us into some of the reasons why America's history includes
the dark and bloody pages of civil war. For the nature of the
union was a matter not made explicit by the Constitution. Then
and thereafter, men understood it differently, and for their differences, eventually, they fought and died. Since the Civil War,
while the federal principle has remained intact, its significance
has been altered. The question of the nature of the union, supposedly settled at Appomattox Court House, periodically gives
rise to new debate and dissension. Meanwhile the actual, observa-
ble nature of the union, regardless of theories and legal principles,
has altered astonishingly in less than a century, for although state
governments have grown and state functions expanded, the national government, in contrast to the states, has assimilated an overwhelming preponderance of significant governmental power. We
have remained a federal union while becoming a unified and
mighty nation.

46

## THE NATURE OF FEDERALISM

A good way to find what "federalism" is, is to describe what it is *not*. In 1787, it was an invention because there were no federal governments in existence. In the countries of the civilized world, the ultimate power of government was vested in a single national authority. That was true then, and it is true in much of the world today. In Great Britain, for instance, the final power to make public decisions, binding all over the kingdom, is possessed by Parliament—the central organ of the national government. True, there are counties and cities in England, each with its local government; but those local governments exist by permission of Parliament, and whatever they do can be undone by Parliament. They are the creatures of the national government, for the national government is ultimately supreme.

This British system—and you can observe it, too, in France and Ireland, Norway and Sweden, Venezuela and Chile, and many other nations—is known as a *unitary* form of government, one in which a single unit of government is supreme. If it is familiar to us today, it was the only system which the framers knew in 1787. Our own original thirteen states had such a system; each of them, in itself, was unitary, with all the power heading up in a single government of the state. Each of them, like Great Britain, included local governments, but these, again, existed at the sufference of the state government. The cities and counties and villages of Connecticut or Pennsylvania or Maryland were the "creatures" of the state, with no independent governing power of their own. That was so in 1787; in legal contemplation, it is still true today.

This, then, was the familiar unitary system which the framers knew. If they had wanted to finish their job quickly at Philadelphia, and cared not at all about the public acceptance of their handiwork, they might have agreed on such a system for the whole nation. Certainly this would have simplified their task. The possibility was, indeed, brought to their attention. Early in the convention, Alexander Hamilton urged that a single national government be established to possess all of the governing power in the United States. The states, Hamilton said, might retain their names and boundaries, but they should be merely administrative districts for exercising the national government's authority. As we have seen, this suggestion ran so completely counter to prevailing opinion and was so subversive of existing institutions that the delegates gave Hamilton a very cool reception, so cool, indeed, that he left Philadelphia, returning only at the end of the convention in order to sign the proposed Constitution.

A simple unitary approach was undesirable or politically impractical. What about an even easier way to shorten the Convention—namely, to tinker a little with the existing Articles of Confederation and then recommend that they remain in effect? That, of course, would have been an endorsement of a system neither "unitary" nor "federal." As we have seen, under the Articles of Confederation there was a mere shadow of a national government. The United States, in 1787, was a *confederation,* or a league of independent states. It was *not a union,* any more than the United Nations today is a union. In a league or confederation, the purported instruments of the central government (the Congress under the Articles of Confederation, the Council and Assembly in the United Nations) actually have *no power to compel individuals* to do anything or to refrain from doing anything. In a confederation, the central agency cannot tax anyone or conscript anyone; all it can do is to request the support of the states which are members of the league—to beg the states for money, or for men.

The framers rejected a continuation of confederation. They spurned that "easy way out." After all, their real intention was, through governmental change, to cure the country's ills as they perceived them—ills both political and economic. They were privately committed to a change from confederation to something else, but they could not endorse a unitary system. Hence, in replacing the league which they knew, they had to devise something which nobody knew anything about. As a matter of strict practical necessity, they did just this. So practical was their approach that neither they nor the Constitution's supporters pointed to their handiwork as a remarkable invention. The federal system which they proposed in 1787 was not based on philosophical ideas or political theory, or even practical experience. Instead, it was hammered out of the political realities of the moment.

Unrecognized, at home, as a great innovation, the American federal system was observed, admired, and in its essentials copied elsewhere. Many countries, today, claim to be "federal unions." Actually the number whose constitutions and practices conform to the basic principles of federalism are comparatively few, but they include, at the very least, Australia, Canada, India, and Switzerland.

## The Federal Principle

What, then, are these "basic principles" of federalism? A federal system is one in which the powers of government are divided up, some being allotted to a national or central government and some to each of the smaller political units which we call states. In the case of those powers which are assigned to the central government, the central government is supreme; it has the final say. For instance, under our Constitution, the central government has the power to run a postal system. Therefore it can direct that an ordinary letter will be delivered through the mail only if a five-cent stamp is affixed to the envelope. The people of Maine or California might not like this, but they could not do anything about it. In matters which, like this, are entrusted to the national government, that government has the last word.

In the same way, the states are supreme with respect to those subjects of governmental action which the Constitution allots to *them*. In the United States, for instance, each state has the power to decide, for itself, whether or not to permit or recognize divorce. If the state of South Carolina refuses to grant divorces to any of its unhappily married citizens, or if the state of Nevada decides to grant divorces to any of its citizens who asks for one, the United States Congress has no power to change the situation. It cannot make the divorce laws of South Carolina more lenient or those of Nevada more stringent. With respect to divorces for their own residents, the states have the last word.

It is sometimes said that in a federal system, there are "concurrent" powers allotted simultaneously to the national and state governments. These, however, are exceptional, and the chief one is concerned primarily with the very existence of government itself. This is the power to tax. Both the central and the state governments have the power to tax—but to say this is hardly more than to say that they have the right to exist. Revenue is essential to any government, and in a civilized democracy it is raised by taxes of general application rather than by waylaying camel caravans or robbing Spanish galleons "in the name of Her Majesty, the Queen!" So the fact that both governments can levy taxes does not significantly alter the basic federal principle of a *division* of governmental powers and their *allocation,* some to the central government, some to the states.

Basic also is the fact that each government, in exercising the powers allotted to it, can directly compel the individual citizen to obey its rules and can punish him if he disobeys. Suppose a man is caught promoting some fraudulent scheme through the mails. As we have seen, the postal system is operated by the national government, pursuant to a grant of power to it. So the national government has made laws to protect the postal system from being used to defraud people. Accordingly, the culprit is tried in a United States court and when convicted is sentenced by a United States judge to a term in a United States prison. (Often we use slightly less exact terminology when referring to these organs of the national government: we speak of "federal courts," "federal judges," "federal prisons." It means the same thing. A "federal court" is a "United States court," which signifies that it is an organ of the national government.)

Suppose, instead, that a thief is caught inside a private home in St. Louis, Missouri, packing the family silver into a violin case which he has thoughtfully brought along. The maintenance of public order and safety, within any state, is the job of that state; accordingly, it makes and enforces laws against crime. So our burglar, when arrested, is charged with violating a Missouri law, is tried in a Missouri court, and is sent away to a state prison administered by the state of Missouri.

Here, then, are the fundamentals of federalism: the division and allotment of powers; the rule that the government to which a particular power has been allotted has the final say as to how it should be exercised; and the right of both the central and the state governments to enforce, against individuals, the rules which they make in exercising their allotted powers.

## FEDERALISM IN
## THE UNITED STATES CONSTITUTION

### The Allotment of Powers

A federal system, as defined, could exist if specific powers were allotted expressly to both governments or if some specific powers were granted to the states and all the rest, unnamed, were allotted to the national government. In the United States Constitution, however, the powers which are expressly mentioned are allotted to the *national* government. The unnamed powers are assigned or "reserved" to the states, which, of course, possessed them prior to 1787.

Most of the allotment of power to the national government is expressed as a grant of authority to Congress in Article I, section 8. There you will find, for instance, the national government's right to establish a postal system, to coin money, to tax, to raise an army, to regulate interstate commerce. And in Article VI there is a vitally important statement which makes the national power enforceable against individuals—a clause which says that not only the Constitution itself, but the laws made (by the national government) pursuant to it, as well as treaties made "under the authority of the United States," shall be "the supreme law of the land." As for the states' powers, these are "reserved" (allotted) to the states, such reservation being expressly confirmed by the Tenth Amendment. The Constitution not only grants or allots power, but also prohibits both the nation and the states from doing particular things. So when we say that each government has the "final say" in matters assigned to it, we mean that it has the "final say" so long as what it does is not forbidden by the Constitution. For instance, public education is a subject of state control. A state could decree that all public schools within the state should open on September 8; and any act of Congress ordering that the opening date should be October 1 would be unconstitutional and ineffective. The states have the last word. Now you may ask why, if the states have the last word about the public schools, they nevertheless cannot maintain separate schools for white children and Negro children. The answer is that the Constitution, as interpreted by the Supreme Court, prohibits such segregation by the states. Both the national government and the states must obey the Constitution. Neither can make laws which the Constitution forbids.

In explaining the basic nature of federalism, we have emphasized the finality and exclusiveness of the exercise of particular powers by one government or another. A federal union could hardly endure, however, if in practice all of its constituent parts dealt with each other at arms' length. The basic idea of federalism is the division of powers; but the very existence of a union of states depends on a high degree of cooperation. From the earliest days the national government counted heavily on the states' assistance in the enforcement of national laws. Until World War I, there was no real national police force, no effective FBI, indeed not enough federal revenue and customs officers to collect taxes and tariffs. Law enforcement was largely the task of the local authorities, and in the days when there were few federal judges, cases involving federal offenses were even tried in state courts. Today, some of the congressional statutes regulating business activity specifically provide that people claiming compensation under such statutes may bring suit in the state courts; conversely, in many civil law suits in the federal courts, the federal judges apply the law of the state where the case arose. Aside from enforcement are matters of policy formation and execution; in these, as we shall see briefly in this chapter and again when we consider particular government programs in Part V of this book, there is a broad and increasing area of intergovernmental cooperation. In the actual operation of much of the public business today, hostility and jurisdictional strife between state and national governments is far less common, and usually much less significant, than the habits of accommodation and coordinated action toward common goals. The fact remains that we still have a federal Constitution, in which certain subjects are allotted to one government for handling, and other subjects to the other. It is also, fortunately, a flexible Constitution, under which voluntary coordination is possible.

## Expansion of National Power

The expressed powers of the national government have been expanded in three ways.

*Amendments.* First, the scope of congressional authority has been increased by amendment of the original Constitution. Of the specific powers which Congress formerly lacked but has today, the most significant is the power to levy an income tax without having to apportion the tax among the states in accordance with their population. Ever since 1913, when this authority was vested in Congress by the Sixteenth Amendment, the national government has been richer than the state governments, for the right to tax everybody's income gave it vast financial resources. The importance of the central government in comparison to that of the states has increased tremendously since 1913. It is reasonable to doubt whether this would have happened if the Sixteenth Amendment had never been adopted.

Congressional power was also broadened by the additions to the Constitution which were made right after the Civil War— the Thirteenth, Fourteenth, and Fifteenth Amendments. These amendments, in brief, were designed to prohibit slavery, protect individuals against unjust state action, and ensure former Negro slaves of the right to vote. Each of them ends with a clause giving Congress "the power to enforce this article by appropriate legislation." In Reconstruction days, this new power seemed an important one, justifying the enactment of "civil rights" laws between 1866 and 1875. Later, however, as the nation acquiesced in the reassertion of "white supremacy" in the South, this congressional authority was left largely unexercised and much of what Congress did do was held invalid by the Supreme Court. After World War II, however, as the drive for equal rights quickened, the fact that enforcement powers had been entrusted to the national government regained importance, and the desegregation controversies of the 1950's and 1960's heightened its significance.

The Eighteenth and Nineteenth Amendments, adopted in 1919 and 1920, also added to the national government's power by authorizing congressional "enforcement." However, the Eighteenth Amendment, prohibiting the sale of liquor, was later repealed; and the effectiveness of the Nineteenth Amendment, providing for nation-wide woman's suffrage, has not depended on continuing congressional supervision. Women, as a sex, are in no danger of being deprived of the right to vote.

*Implied Powers.* Second, the extent of Congress's power has been increased by the interpretation of the clause in Article I, section 8, which says that Congress, in exercising the powers expressly granted to it, may do whatever is "necessary and proper" to put them into effect. That phrase might reasonably be read as confining Congress to making laws which are absolutely essential to the exercise of its power; or it might just as reasonably be read as authorizing Congress to do some things, not mentioned in the Constitution, which enable it better to perform the duties expressly imposed on it. This second interpretation—the one which assumes that Congress has "implied powers" in addition to, and in aid of, the powers specifically granted to it—was announced by the Supreme Court in 1819, and has prevailed ever since.

The Supreme Court's decision itself illustrates what is meant by "implied powers." The dispute before it was between the state of Maryland and an officer of the Second Bank of the United States, and the case is known as *McCulloch v. Maryland.*[1] Congress had chartered the bank, and it had opened a branch office in Baltimore, Maryland. Previously, the financial system of the country had been largely controlled by state-chartered banks, and these, together with some state governments, were hostile to the new nationally chartered bank and hoped to cripple or destroy it. Accordingly, Maryland enacted a law taxing the new bank's banknotes. This tax was really designed to drive it out of the banking business in Maryland. The cashier of the Baltimore branch bank

---

[1] 4 Wheaton 316. This is the way in which judicial decisions are "cited." Here, it means that the decision in *McCulloch versus Maryland* can be found in the fourth volume of the reports compiled by Wheaton, the court reporter, and published under his name. The report of this case begins on page 316 of that volume. In those early days, reports of Supreme Court decisions were published under the name of the reporter at the time—Wheaton, Cranch, Wallace, Peters, etc.—but since 1874 they have been published by the government as "Supreme Court Reports," indicated by the initials "U.S." The U.S. Reports now run into hundreds of volumes. The first case reported in the 1963 term of the Court would be cited as "372 U.S. 1."

issued banknotes without paying the tax, and the state brought suit against him.

The Supreme Court's decision, written by Chief Justice John Marshall, dealt first with the argument that Congress had no power to establish or charter a bank. If you reexamine Article I, section 8, you will not find any authority to do this given to Congress—at least, not *expressly* given, in so many words. However, Chief Justice Marshall said, in effect, that the United States government had a right to exist; that any government must have money, if it is going to operate at all; and that the Constitution specifically recognizes this, by giving Congress the power to tax. So, said he (speaking for a unanimous Supreme Court), Congress can legitimately decide that, to carry out its financial responsibilities, the establishment of a national bank is "necessary and proper," because the *express* power to raise money *implies* the power to hold that money safely and invest it wisely. "Let the end be legitimate, let it be within the scope of the Constitution, and all means which are appropriate, which are plainly adapted to that end, which are not prohibited, but consist with the letter and spirit of the Constitution, are constitutional." Thus wrote John Marshall, and thus was established the doctrine of implied powers, strengthening and broadening the scope of national authority.

The decision in *McCulloch v. Maryland* is significant, too, for its bearing on another matter which is not expressly stated in the Constitution. After declaring that the Bank of the United States had been constitutionally established, Marshall went on to hold that Maryland's tax upon its banknotes was unconstitutional. In essence, the Court decided that a *federal* system, established by the Constitution, necessarily implied that the states could not cripple the national government in the exercise of its powers. The state of Maryland, admittedly, had the power to tax, but it could not use that power to prevent the national government from exercising *its* power to run a banking business. As Marshall wrote: "The States have no power, by taxation or otherwise, to retard, impede, burden, or in any manner control the operations of the constitutional laws enacted by Congress to carry into execution the powers vested in the general government." Thus, by implication, the national government not only has more affirmative powers than are specifically enumerated in the Constitution, but it also has the right to exercise all of its powers without interference by the states.

*Interpretation.* The third way in which national power has grown is through interpretation of the express powers themselves. In Article I, section 8, are certain brief clauses whose meaning is not altogether certain. For instance, Congress can tax (and therefore, presumably, spend money), "to promote the . . . general welfare." And it can "regulate commerce . . . among the several states. . . ." Does its right to spend for the "general welfare" mean that Congress can appropriate money to be paid to particular farmers who agree to refrain from growing crops that are in oversupply? Does its right to regulate interstate commerce mean that it can fix a minimum wage for the employees of manufacturing corporations whose products are sold all over the country? Ultimately these questions depend on whether the Supreme Court construes the appropriate clauses narrowly or broadly. And although the Court's decisions have not been consistent, we can say that, by and large, the trend has been in favor of a broad construction.

Chief Justice Marshall again pointed the way when, in the famous case of *Gibbons v. Ogden,*[2] he declared that "commerce among the states" included not only buying and selling, but all forms of commercial "intercourse"—in that case, steamboat navigation. After Marshall's death, however, the Supreme Court gradually inclined toward a narrower view of Congress's powers, and eventually, in the early part of the twentieth century, it began to call certain national laws unconstitutional even though Congress had enacted them in the belief that they were regulations of interstate commerce. Foremost among these cases in which the Constitution was construed as narrowing Congress's power was *Hammer v. Dagenhart,*[3] decided in 1918. Hoping to eliminate the evil of child labor, Congress had passed a law prohibiting the shipment, across state boundaries, of any goods upon which children less than twelve years old had worked. The Supreme Court, however, ruled that Congress had no power to enact such a statute.

---

2 9 Wheaton 1 (1824).
3 247 U.S. 251 (1918).

The Court said that *employment*—of children or anybody else—in a factory, mill, or mine was a matter for each state to deal with and that Congress's statute really intended to regulate such employment rather than commerce. Not all the nine judges who composed the Supreme Court agreed with this decision. Four of them, speaking through Justice Oliver Wendell Holmes, Jr., argued that whatever Congress's intention might have been, the statute it passed dealt with the shipment of particular goods across state lines and hence was a valid regulation of interstate commerce.

The four dissenters were a minority, yet their views eventually prevailed. *Hammer v. Dagenhart* was an extreme example of the restrictive, narrow interpretation of Congress's power to regulate interstate commerce. Less than twenty years later, Congress enacted new laws regulating the employment relationship, and one of these new laws was essentially similar to the original child labor law. Now on the Supreme Court were only three of the judges who had decided *Hammer v. Dagenhart;* the rest had died or retired. In 1937, the "broad constructionists," the judges who followed the views of Marshall and Holmes, prevailed. In that year and thereafter, Congress's powers to regulate and control the industrial life of the country was vastly expanded, through the greatly broadened scope which the Court gave to the meaning of the words "interstate commerce." Congress now can, and does, not only prohibit the interstate shipment of child-made goods,[4] but impose minimum wages, occasionally fix prices, and require that employers bargain with unions, all under its broadly construed power to "regulate commerce . . . among the several states."

Thus in different ways the central government has become dominant. Yet the states still exist. Not only do they exist, but as individual governments they have grown. While in comparison to the national government they have become less important, they actually are more active, employ more people, and spend more money than they did in earlier times.

---

[4] This was decided in 1941, in the case of *U.S. v. Darby*, 312 U.S. 100. In deciding this case, the Court specifically "overruled" *Hammer v. Dagenhart*: that is, it announced that the earlier decision had interpreted the Constitution incorrectly.

## State Powers

The powers allotted to the states are not spelled out in the Constitution. On the contrary, that document forbids the states to do certain things: coin money, for instance, or pass laws impairing the obligation of contracts. But the framers assumed that all other governmental powers not delegated to the central government remained in the states. The framers assumed this, but agreed to have it made explicit—and the Tenth Amendment expressly "reserves" these undelegated, unforbidden powers to the states.

Undelegated, unforbidden—and undefined. What, then, are these "reserved" powers? No short definition of the state's powers could be complete. Often, however, each state is said to possess the "police power,"—the power to ensure and promote the health, welfare, safety, and morals of the people of the state. And, as we have seen, it is taken for granted that each state has the power to tax its citizens.

The states, then, have the primary responsibility for making and enforcing the rules concerning such matters as education, sanitation, mental health, marriage and divorce, the sale of real estate, and the prevention of crime. (Much of this is accomplished, of course, by local units of government established by the state or pursuant to state laws—school districts, counties, cities, and villages.) They can also regulate industry, so long as their regulations are reasonable and do not obstruct interstate commerce or conflict with a valid federal regulation of commerce. Thus states have established "safety codes" for factories and mines, and unemployment insurance systems, and "fair trade" rules against price-cutting. On some subjects, many state legislatures have voluntarily adopted "uniform laws," such as the statutes governing negotiable instruments; and, more often, one legislature, in considering a new measure, draws heavily on the wording of some other state's statute concerning the same subject. Yet each state can do its job differently from every other state. One may be a pioneer in prison reform, another in clinical treatment of mental disease. One may establish a public, inexpensive life insurance system, while another experiments with a youth service program to combat juvenile delinquency. So it is not surprising that the states have sometimes been called "laboratories," where novel governmental experiments can be tried. If they fail, no one outside the particular state is harmed, and if they succeed, they may set a useful pattern for other states to follow.

There are grave difficulties, however, facing any state which embarks on an expensive new program. Where will it get the needed money? It can tax its citizens, including the corporations in the state; but if it increases taxes, will not people and especially large business enterprises move away to some other state where taxes are much lower? As transportation has become rapid and easy, and communication instantaneous, the old separateness of the states has lost much of its former reality. In economic and social terms, the boundary line that divides one state from another has come to have less and less meaning. In the old days, a man managing a factory in Indiana was likely to own the factory, to live in Indiana, and to sell most or all of his product in Indiana. Now, in contrast, his Indiana factory is likely to be owned by a large corporation which in turn is owned by stockholders. The corporation's headquarters may be not in Indiana, but in Delaware or New Jersey; and the stockholders live all over the country. Now, if Indiana's taxes should become unusually heavy, the corporation might close down the Indiana factory and do its manufacturing in other states. Hence, even the wealthy states are often reluctant to undertake public programs which are costly, for if they increase the state taxes they may be killing the goose which lays the golden eggs.

If wealthy states sometimes feel that they must refrain from making needed improvements—in school buildings, for instance, or hospitals or highways—the poorer states, which have little industry and hence fewer tax resources, have even less real freedom of action.

These financial impediments to state action might be unimportant to the nation as a whole, if the people and business of each state were wholly separate and apart from those of every other state. But they are not. We have become an interdependent nation; what happens in one state affects all the rest of us. Highways provide a familiar example of this. For business or pleasure we drive through many states, and you know what a difference it makes when you cross a state line and, leaving a fine divided turn-pike, suddenly find yourself jolting on a narrow two-lane road. Infectious disease is another illustration; germs take no notice of state boundaries. And the national interest in how good a job each state does has been made especially apparent in wartime, when too many young men were disqualified by physical defects or handicapped by inadequate schooling. Bad teeth and bad education both impaired the strength of the United States.

## FEDERALISM UNDER CHANGED CIRCUMSTANCES

### The Grant-in-Aid

While, then, individual states find it hard to build super-highways or schools or hospitals, there is often a real national interest in their doing just these things. That national interest is usually made concrete in the form of a device known as the "grant-in-aid." Very simply, this is a conditional gift of money by the national government to the states, the money to be used for a specific purpose. The states are legally free to refuse the grant, but almost invariably they accept it.

The "grant-in-aid" device was first used over a century ago, and the first real long-range federal "program" employing it was initiated in 1862, when Congress passed the Morrill Act. That law conveyed to the states certain land owned by the national govern-ment, on condition that it be used as a site for a college specializ-ing in agricultural training. Later laws broadened the permitted purpose, to include mining and technology. The "A & M" colleges, in many western states, are still called "land-grant col-leges" because a federal grant-in-aid brought them into existence.

In 1913, as we have seen, the financial balance of power shifted from the states to Washington with the adoption of the Sixteenth Amendment, authorizing Congress to levy an income tax. The federal government had, before that time, been a relatively small establishment. Now it had new financial resources. There would seem to be a reasonable cause-and-effect relationship between the adoption of the Sixteenth Amendment and the fact that, very soon thereafter, the national government embarked on a new and expensive grant-in-aid program.

Congress enacted the first major monetary "grant-in-aid" law in 1916, offering money to the states for highway construction. Since then, grants-in-aid have multiplied. The national government has provided the states with funds for fighting venereal disease, encouraging vocational education, paying old-age pensions, building hospitals, and many other purposes. This method of so-called "cooperative federalism" became firmly established in the 1930's.

Grants-in-aid are conditional in three ways. First, the money must be spent for a particular, specified program. Second, though the state administers the program, it must comply with certain standards laid down in Washington: for instance, to get federal money for old-age pensions, a state must employ civil-service or merit-system personnel throughout its public welfare agencies. Third, in most cases the state must contribute some funds of its own to the program.

The grant-in-aid device has some disadvantages. Although it is based on the idea that each state should run its own program, federal "standards" impose a certain degree of uniformity across the nation and limit the states' freedom to experiment, for better or worse, with new administrative devices or unusual programs. And the usual overwhelming temptation to accept the proffered grant sometimes leads to a distortion of a state's budget. For example, the expenditures for vocational education in some state departments of education are very high because of the availability of "federal money"; to qualify for the grant, the states spend more of their own funds for that purpose than they would if they were left alone, and so spend less on something which may be more important. In other words, state policies are shaped, somewhat, by the existence of the federal grant-in-aid, and to that extent policymaking on local matters is shifted from the state capitals to Washington.

Nevertheless, the grant-in-aid seems to represent a workable compromise between a wholly national, unitary system and one in which the separate states, though theoretically retaining important powers, find it impracticable to exercise them. Kept within bounds, the plan represents a sane development of the federal system. Of course, if the device were abused, it could harmfully change the federal pattern. If Congress offered huge grants, too big to be rejected, but surrounded them with extremely detailed conditions, this could lead to a virtual abdication by the state governments. Conversely, if Congress simply made large grants with no strings attached, we would have the odd situation of the nation's taxpayers supporting the state governments, with no voice in how their money should be spent. Both of these extreme positions have occasionally had defenders but neither is typical of the actual grant-in-aid laws on the statute books.

Grants-in-aid are no minor matter in terms of the amounts of money involved. Recently about 10 per cent of the tax revenue collected by the federal government has been redistributed to the states in this manner. The amounts allocated to each state and the major ways in which the money is spent are shown in the accompanying tables. Notice that the impact of grants-in-aid differs tremendously from state to state. In 1961, for example, Alaska received a share of the grant money over four times greater than its people's and corporations' share of the federal tax burden, while Delaware got back relatively less than half of what its people and corporations contributed. Thus the grant-in-aid programs are a means by which the richer states assume some of the burdens of development of poorer states.

### STATE ALLOCATIONS OF U.S. GRANTS-IN-AID, 1961

| State | Allocation (in thousands) | Per Capita | Share of Allocations | Share of Federal Tax Burden |
|---|---|---|---|---|
| Alabama | $221,154 | $67 | 2.25% | .97% |
| Alaska | 48,441 | 207 | .49 | .11 |
| Arizona | 91,701 | 66 | .93 | .62 |
| Arkansas | 129,735 | 72 | 1.32 | .45 |
| California | 829,170 | 51 | 8.43 | 11.16 |
| Colorado | 138,834 | 78 | 1.41 | .97 |
| Connecticut | 114,730 | 44 | 1.16 | 2.22 |
| Delaware | 21,948 | 48 | .22 | .52 |
| Dist. of Col. | 93,416 | 123 | .95 | .69 |
| Florida | 217,351 | 42 | 2.21 | 2.52 |
| Georgia | 243,724 | 61 | 2.48 | 1.33 |
| Hawaii | 51,144 | 78 | .52 | .34 |
| Idaho | 60,785 | 89 | .61 | .26 |
| Illinois | 457,511 | 45 | 4.65 | 6.93 |

| State | Allocation (in thousands) | Per Capita | Share of Allocations | Share of Federal Tax Burden |
|---|---|---|---|---|
| Indiana | $ 188,759 | $ 40 | 1.92% | 2.29% |
| Iowa | 139,719 | 50 | 1.42 | 1.15 |
| Kansas | 137,494 | 63 | 1.39 | .96 |
| Kentucky | 172,841 | 56 | 1.75 | 1.03 |
| Louisiana | 245,904 | 74 | 2.50 | 1.23 |
| Maine | 53,893 | 54 | .54 | .44 |
| Maryland | 130,189 | 41 | 1.32 | 1.94 |
| Massachusetts | 262,630 | 50 | 2.67 | 3.53 |
| Michigan | 356,158 | 45 | 3.62 | 4.47 |
| Minnesota | 211,785 | 61 | 2.15 | 1.64 |
| Mississippi | 154,098 | 70 | 1.56 | .46 |
| Missouri | 258,409 | 59 | 2.62 | 2.28 |
| Montana | 73,538 | 108 | .74 | .30 |
| Nebraska | 100,937 | 71 | 1.02 | .65 |
| Nevada | 28,015 | 94 | .28 | .21 |
| New Hampshire | 38,043 | 61 | .38 | .33 |
| New Jersey | 193,745 | 31 | 1.97 | 4.29 |
| New Mexico | 96,301 | 98 | .98 | .37 |
| New York | 660,045 | 39 | 6.71 | 13.54 |
| North Carolina | 194,843 | 42 | 1.98 | 1.45 |
| North Dakota | 85,230 | 133 | .86 | .21 |
| Ohio | 429,586 | 43 | 4.37 | 5.74 |
| Oklahoma | 215,277 | 91 | 2.19 | .94 |
| Oregon | 136,430 | 76 | 1.38 | .95 |
| Pennsylvania | 450,156 | 39 | 4.58 | 6.92 |
| Rhode Island | 47,139 | 54 | .47 | .52 |
| South Carolina | 121,705 | 51 | 1.23 | .65 |
| South Dakota | 82,559 | 120 | .84 | .22 |
| Tennessee | 223,916 | 62 | 2.27 | 1.19 |
| Texas | 485,855 | 50 | 4.94 | 4.26 |
| Utah | 74,181 | 81 | .75 | .37 |
| Vermont | 36,338 | 92 | .36 | .17 |
| Virginia | 163,301 | 40 | 1.66 | 1.70 |
| Washington | 170,827 | 59 | 1.73 | 1.58 |
| West Virginia | 112,416 | 61 | 1.14 | .68 |
| Wisconsin | 163,183 | 41 | 1.66 | 2.07 |
| Wyoming | 57,403 | 170 | .58 | .18 |
| Territories | 137,349 | — | — | — |
| Undistributed | 216,439 | — | — | — |
| Total | $9,826,279 | $54 | 100.00% | 100.00% |

SOURCE: *Congressional Quarterly*, Vol. 20, June 29, 1962, p. 1,111.

## THE NINE LARGEST GRANTS-IN-AID PROGRAMS, 1961

| Program | Total Allocation |
| --- | --- |
| 1. Highways | $2,590,788,486 |
| 2. Old-Age Assistance | 1,215,164,973 |
| 3. Aid to Dependent Children | 701,302,286 |
| 4. Temporary Extended Unemployment Compensation | 481,151,560 |
| 5. Army National Guard | 415,461,084 |
| 6. Unemployment Compensation Administration | 358,552,447 |
| 7. Conservation Reserve Program | 350,547,651 |
| 8. Readjustment Benefit | 253,489,629 |
| 9. Air Force National Guard | 234,540,158 |
| Total—Nine Programs | $6,600,998,274 |

SOURCE: *Congressional Quarterly*, Vol. 20, June 29, 1962, p. 1,112.

## The Interstate Compact

Far less important than the grant-in-aid is a device permitted by the Constitution, which can be used to foster cooperation not between the national government and the states, but among states themselves. All that the Constitution says about it (in Article I, section 10) is that "No State shall, without the consent of Congress, . . . enter into any Agreement or Compact with another State." This implies that, if Congress approves, individual states can make compacts with each other, and occasionally they have done so. Usually these compacts have concerned the joint management of resources which affect more than one state. For example, the water in the Colorado River, which flows through several states, was needed by communities in different states for irrigation and other purposes. Six states, therefore, entered into the "Colorado River Compact," in an effort to divide up the water on an equitable basis. Likewise, the operation of the port of New York is not the concern of a single state. It includes the docks and airports in New Jersey as well as those in New York. Accordingly, by compact the two states established the Port of New York Authority, which regulates seagoing and airborne and even automobile traffic on both sides of the line which separates the states. In St. Louis, with a metropolitan area lying on both sides of the Mississippi River, an Illinois-Missouri compact created a Bi-State

Development Agency which has done little "developing" but does run the bus lines in the area.

## National Leadership

The adaptation of the federal system to the conditions and requirements of the modern world has been accomplished by various means. It has followed the changes in circumstances rather than causing them. We began with a federal system because the principle of federalism was, necessarily, the basis of the original union. We still have it because it is traditional and familiar, because it conforms to a still fairly general faith in the efficacy of local government, and because it has been adaptable, able to meet the people's new demands on government.

Some of these new demands are the product of the industrial age. With the coming of the railroads and the invention of the corporation, nation-wide industry began to displace the typical small local business of the eighteenth century. But big business, while accomplishing productive marvels, also created new problems of social and economic justice. Workers, consumers, and small producers demanded that government impose some controls on big business. By definition, however, big business and, in recent years, "big labor" transcended the limits of any one state. No single state could regulate them effectively. Only the national government could.

Other new demands for governmental action have arisen from the workings of the "economic cycle," in which prosperous periods have usually been followed by hard times. The country's worst economic depression occurred in the early 1930's. Millions of Americans were unemployed. They could not find work, and they were close to starvation. Again, no single state was able to save the situation; no single state could reform the nation's economic system, nor did it have the financial resources needed to feed desperate people. Again, the people turned to the national government.

The third new demand on government was not wished for by the people, but was created by the tragedy of modern war. Both world wars showed that the nation's security depended on strong national action in the economic sphere as well as the military. In World War I the federal government took over the railroads. In World War II it controlled prices and wages and virtually assumed the direction of all large private industry through production requirements and the allocation of materials. Few people would have wanted the government to do these things in prosperous times of peace; few could argue against its doing them in time of war. In the dangerous world in which we now live, the need for the national government to possess these powers, and to be ready to use them when necessary, cannot be sanely questioned.

All of these demands were, of course, totally unforeseen by the men of 1787. To meet them might well have required drastic amendment of the Constitution. Instead, they have been met because our federal system had the flexibility to meet them. Both the broader interpretation of the Constitution and the wider use of the grant-in-aid were responses to the hard realities and necessities of the 1930's. The important point is that these responses could be made without internal strife or constitutional change, and without abandoning the federal principle.

Today the national government is in full control of many areas of economic life. In power and prestige, it overshadows the states. Where it does not exercise full control, it often steers state action, through grants-in-aid or simply through the offering of expert advice in technical matters. The fact remains that the states still have much important work to do, and many significant policy decisions are made at the state and local levels—decisions which affect the daily lives of American citizens. For Americans are not only citizens of the United States, they are also citizens of particular states. We are still a Federal Union.

## THE POLITICS OF FEDERALISM

### The Institutional Issue

From the beginning of our national life, the federal principle has been an issue in the struggle for governmental power which is politics. Not everyone, originally, accepted the definition of federalism given in this chapter. And even agreement with that definition did not settle every question about what kind of a

Union the Constitution had established. It could still be asked, how closely are the member states bound to each other and to the Union, and what recourse have the states if, in their view, the national government abuses the power delegated to it? We have suggested that one way of studying politics is by analyzing institutions; here, a basic question was for many years the institutional one—the nature of the Union.

The party battles of early days were fought largely on this issue —the very names of the first parties show this. On one side were the believers in a closely knit Union with a strong central government, the "Federalists" of Hamilton and Adams. Against them were the "Anti-Federalists" headed by Jefferson and Madison, arguing that the Constitution allowed broad discretion to the states and established only loose and flexible bonds among them. As the nineteenth century advanced, the basic questions became still more acute: did we have a Union of people, or of states? Did a state have the right to judge, for itself, when the conditions upon which it entered the Union had been broken? Could it then withdraw from the Union?

Arguments over these questions punctuated the long and tragic march toward civil war. Statesmen orated about the meaning of the Constitution and the "sovereignty" of the states. Great men helped to sharpen the issues by describing what they thought the institutional framework was or should be. Many of the historic words of the struggle that echo down the halls of history concern institutions: witness Andrew Jackson's ringing toast, "Our Federal Union, it must be preserved!" and Daniel Webster's "Liberty and union, now and forever, one and inseparable!" Yet underlying the debates about the nature of the Union were deep and bitter conflicts of interests, conflicts foreshadowed at Philadelphia in 1787 and reaching a climax at Gettysburg in 1863. The tragedy of these conflicts—perhaps the factor which made them insoluble in legislative chambers and forced them to be decided on the battlefield—was that the contending interests were to a large degree divided along *geographic* lines. It was not just a matter of manufacturers contending for advantage against farmers doing the same. In the last analysis, it was North against South.

*The Interests.* The interests involved were not entirely economic. Philosophies, like institutions, gain adherents. It is too easy to say that arguments about the proper role of government, or sovereignty, or other abstract ideas are always cloaks disguising a selfish drive for material advantage. There can be an "ideal interest"—a group of people firmly wedded to an idea which, at least as far as they can see, is not connected with any practical gain for themselves. Thus large bodies of people are quite impractically loyal to particular institutions: all through recorded history, men have died for their country or for their ideals.

In the early politics of federalism, the problem of loyalties was obvious. Each American was subject to two governments, national and state. Each had to decide for himself which had the prior claim on his patriotic devotion. If this seems odd to us, today, remember that the states existed before the Union did. Loyalty is, in part, a tradition handed down from one generation to another, based on love of one's homeland. For most Americans in 1787, the homeland was Virginia, or Pennsylvania, or New York, and *not* the United States of America. And so, for many years and for large numbers of people, the states more than the Union were the chief objects of patriotism. In the South, this tradition was pervasive for many decades. It was still alive in 1861, when a distinguished officer of the United States Army resigned his commission because, though he considered himself a loyal American, he was a loyal Virginian first. In war between state and nation, he cast his lot with his state. His name was Robert E. Lee.

Although state loyalties endured, new emotions of patriotism centered on the nation as a whole. The thirteen original states might maintain their hold on the people's affections, but the nation was growing. New states, with no traditions, were being hewed out of the wilderness. The pioneers, moving west, could feel no deep inherited attachment to these new states. They looked to the national government for help, and they eagerly pressed their claims to be admitted to the Union. Their patriotism was likely to be national patriotism. Add their growing numbers to the minority in the seaboard states who had fought for the United States or otherwise been fired by the vision of Union, and you have a sizeable "interest," with its spokesmen and its symbols. Every threat from abroad, every battle with a foreign foe, sharpened this national devotion. And so in 1805 an American naval commander could carve a niche in history by crying "My *country,* right or wrong!" and in 1814 a Maryland poet, referring not to his state but to his country, could sing of "the land of the free and the home of the brave."

Less emotional and hence much narrower in scope was the "interest" in a political idea: the belief that local government is best for men who love freedom. Decisions made close at hand, it is assumed, are better than those made far away. First, they are made by people who know local needs and customs; second, more people can participate effectively in making them. This theory is as old as Aristotle. For most people, probably, it is not a matter of intense conviction or grave personal concern. But it has always been sincerely believed by a substantial number of Americans, and its adherents have always, therefore, been participants in the politics of federalism.

All of these abstract interests are real, even though they are abstract. They have motivated political action. The fact remains that they can also serve as a "cover" for far more concrete interests. They lend themselves to stirring slogans and patriotic hymns, and so they are useful to practical men whose materialistic objectives have no popular appeal. In very recent times, the success with which symbols can be used to disguise real political aims has become well understood by American politicians. In the early days of the Republic, however, there were no "public relations" firms specializing in symbols and slogans. Nor, probably, was there any such consciousness as there is today of the difference between the professed abstract interest and the underlying material interest. Men whose *economic* advantage lay in having the national government remain weak and loosely united could sincerely present the *ideal* advantages of strong local government and state sovereignty. Who can say which, the ideal or the practical, was the chief factor motivating them and their supporters in the political struggle?

The conflict in economic terms was, in general, between the agrarian interest and the commercial interest. It grew obvious and intense almost as soon as the new government was established. In George Washington's first cabinet were the two antagonists, Jefferson and Hamilton. Jefferson spoke for the farmers, for democracy, for individual liberty, for states' rights, and against having a strong and active national government. Hamilton spoke for industry and finance, for national unity, for leadership by the national government—and, when pressed, he burst out against democracy: "Your 'People', sir," he cried to Jefferson, "are a great beast!" The Hamiltonian viewpoint gained adherents, and its supporters, mainly from the North and calling themselves Federalists, gained control of Congress and elected John Adams to the presidency in 1796.

Now came the first open clash over the nature of the Union. The Federalists, the party of Hamilton and Adams, wished to maintain power because they liked it, because they believed that business would thrive if they kept it, and because they distrusted Jefferson and feared that he would hurt business if he became President. They sought to hold on to the reins of government and eliminate Jefferson as a threat to their domination and their pocketbooks by suppressing all criticism of the Adams administration. The Alien and Sedition Acts, passed in 1798, in effect made it a crime to criticize the government or any official thereof. Both Jefferson and James Madison, who had become his chief political lieutenant, counterattacked. The front upon which they mounted their offensive was a surprising one. They did not merely say that the Alien and Sedition laws were harsh and tyrannical. They went much further than that. They induced the Kentucky and Virginia legislatures to pass resolutions, drafted by themselves, setting forth a theory of the nature of the Union. These resolutions were intended to serve as a rallying call for political opposition to the Federalists, and they served their purpose.

The Kentucky and Virginia Resolutions did not appeal primarily to the ordinary man's occasional desire to denounce the Congress or the President. Instead, they appealed directly to the tradition of state loyalty and the belief in local government. They declared, in essence, that the states, as parties to the Constitution, had the right to decide whether an Act of Congress was unconstitutional. Then, on behalf of Kentucky and Virginia, they indicated that the Alien and Sedition laws were indeed unconstitutional—mere usurpations of power by the national government—and called upon all of the states to refuse to enforce those laws.

Madison, in the Virginia Resolutions, went even further, suggesting that individual states "interpose" statutes of their own, to prevent the enforcement of the national laws within the states.

In one way, the Virginia and Kentucky Resolutions were a political maneuver. Jefferson and Madison were carefully developing an issue which would have wide appeal and on which their "Anti-Federalist" party could campaign for office in 1800. But the doctrine which they expressed, concerning the nature of the Union, was of significance far beyond the next election. It was a doctrine of essential state sovereignty, state freedom to decide what its relationship to the Union should be.

Because the national government, under Hamilton's influence, had fostered policies to encourage industry rather than agriculture, the agricultural interests naturally aligned themselves on the states' rights, anti-centralist side. In appealing to traditional loyalties, Jefferson and Madison were simultaneously arousing farmers to political action, making them the basis of the first broad-scale American political party.

These interwoven interests—the "ideal" (states' rights) and the "practical" (agriculture)—were dominant in national politics for a good part of the period from 1800 until the Civil War. Whenever they lost their dominance even temporarily, the very fabric of the Union was in danger of being torn asunder.[5] In 1830, the northern commercial interests having succeeded in persuading Congress to increase the tariff on foreign goods, southern planters feared that their fortunes were imperilled. They sold their cotton in England, and they reasoned that if the United States put a tariff on British goods, the British might retaliate by putting a tariff on American goods. This would ruin the South. So the legislature of South Carolina, using the example of the Virginia and Kentucky Resolutions, resolved to "nullify" the tariff, even though the tariff was a properly enacted national statute and supposedly the "supreme law of the land." It was this crisis which brought forth

---

[5] Conversely, northern commercial interests, chiefly shipping, were behind an abortive movement to cause the New England states to secede from the Union in 1815. These interests had been damaged by the War of 1812, which put a stop to most American shipping.

President Jackson's toast (and, too, his threat to use force against South Carolina) and Senator Webster's peroration, the final words of his reply to Senator Hayne of South Carolina, who had set forth the state-sovereignty view of the nature of the Union.

Even in 1830, another interest conflict was gathering force. This was a battle between, on the one hand, a "moral" interest, and on the other an interest both economic and "moral." The anachronism of human slavery in "the land of the free" was producing a growing belief that in the name of justice and decency, slavery must be abolished. This anti-slavery interest was based in the North. In the South, the pro-slavery interest was overwhelmingly dominant. It was an economic interest, for financial success of the whole cotton-planting system depended on slavery. It was also a "moral" interest. The abolitionists might claim that slavery was immoral, but slave-owners answered that the Negroes were better off as slaves than they would otherwise be and that to give them freedom and equality would go against the laws of nature and would do endless harm to the Negroes, their white masters, and the whole future of both races.

Crusading individuals played a great part in sharpening the new conflict. The pamphleteer, William Lloyd Garrison; the editor, Elijah P. Lovejoy; the orator, Wendell Phillips; the novelist, Harriet Beecher Stowe: all these and others aroused moral fervor against slavery, and if they had never existed, who knows whether the course of history would have been the same? The great philosopher on the southern side, weaving together the ideas about the Union, the economic interests, and the alleged beneficence of slavery into a comprehensive political theory, was Senator John C. Calhoun of South Carolina. But it was neither individual leaders nor political theory that brought about the final crisis. The economic interest of the planters led them to press for the expansion of slavery westward; and against such expansion the majority of northerners stood united. In 1860 the northerners triumphed in the presidential election. Now the southern states technically violated even their own theory of the nature of the Union. They had said that each state could decide if the compact—the Constitution—had been broken. After Lincoln's election, however, they did not wait for him to become President the following March.

# The Pennfylvania Packet, *and Daily Advertifer.*

[Price Four-Pence.]    WEDNESDAY, September 19, 1787.    [No. 2690.]

WE, the People of the United States, in order to form a more perfect Union, eftablifh Juftice, infure domeftic Tranquility, provide for the common Defence, promote the General Welfare, and fecure the Bleffings of Liberty to Ourfelves and our Pofterity, do ordain and eftablifh this Conftitution for the United States of America.

### ARTICLE I.

*Sect.* 1. ALL legiflative powers herein granted fhall be vefted in a Congrefs of the United States, which fhall confift of a Senate and Houfe of Reprefentatives.

*Sect.* 2. The Houfe of Reprefentatives fhall be compofed of members chofen every fecond year by the people of the feveral ftates, and the electors in each ftate fhall have the qualifications requifite for electors of the moft numerous branch of the ftate legiflature.

No perfon fhall be a reprefentative who fhall not have attained to the age of twenty-five years, and been feven years a citizen of the United States, and who fhall not, when elected, be an inhabitant of that ftate in which he fhall be chofen.

Reprefentatives and direct taxes fhall be apportioned among the feveral ftates which may be included within this Union, according to their refpective numbers, which fhall be determined by adding to the whole number of free perfons, including thofe bound to fervice for a term of years, and excluding Indians not taxed, three-fifths of all other perfons. The actual enumeration fhall be made within three years after the firft meeting of the Congrefs of the United States, and within every fubfequent term of ten years, in fuch manner as they fhall by law direct. The number of reprefentatives fhall not exceed one for every thirty thoufand, but each ftate fhall have at leaft one reprefentative; and until fuch enumeration fhall be made, the ftate of New-Hampfhire fhall be entitled to chufe three, Maffachufetts eight, Rhode-Ifland and Providence Plantations one, Connecticut five, New-York fix, New-Jerfey four, Pennfylvania eight, Delaware one, Maryland fix, Virginia ten, North-Carolina five, South-Carolina five, and Georgia three.

When vacancies happen in the reprefentation from any ftate, the Executive authority thereof fhall iffue writs of election to fill fuch vacancies.

The Houfe of Reprefentatives fhall chufe their Speaker and other officers; and fhall have the fole power of impeachment.

*Sect.* 3. The Senate of the United States fhall be compofed of two fenators from each ftate, chofen by the legiflature thereof, for fix years; and each fenator fhall have one vote.

Immediately after they fhall be affembled in confequence of the firft election, they fhall be divided as equally as may be into three claffes. The feats of the fenators of the firft clafs fhall be vacated at the expiration of the fecond year, of the fecond clafs at the expiration of the fourth year, and of the third clafs at the expiration of the fixth year, fo that one-third may be chofen every fecond year; and if vacancies happen by refignation, or otherwife, during the recefs of the Legiflature of any ftate, the Executive thereof may make temporary appointments until the next meeting of the Legiflature, which fhall then fill fuch vacancies.

No perfon fhall be a fenator who fhall not have attained to the age of thirty years, and been nine years a citizen of the United States, and who fhall not, when elected, be an inhabitant of that ftate for which he fhall be chofen.

The Vice-Prefident of the United States fhall be Prefident of the fenate, but fhall have no vote, unlefs they be equally divided.

The Senate fhall chufe their other officers, and alfo a Prefident pro tempore, in the abfence of the Vice-Prefident, or when he fhall exercife the office of Prefident of the United States.

The Senate fhall have the fole power to try all impeachments. When fitting for that purpofe, they fhall be on oath or affirmation. When the Prefident of the United States is tried, the Chief Juftice fhall prefide: And no perfon fhall be convicted without the concurrence of two-thirds of the members prefent.

Judgment in cafes of impeachment fhall not extend further than to removal from office, and difqualification to hold and enjoy any office of honor, truft or profit under the United States; but the party convicted fhall neverthelefs be liable and fubject to indictment, trial, judgment and punifhment, according to law.

*Sect.* 4. The times, places and manner of holding elections for fenators and reprefentatives, fhall be prefcribed in each ftate by the legiflature thereof; but the Congrefs may at any time by law make or alter fuch regulations, except as to the places of chufing Senators.

The Congrefs fhall affemble at leaft once in every year, and fuch meeting fhall be on the firft Monday in December, unlefs they fhall by law appoint a different day.

*Sect.* 5. Each houfe fhall be the judge of the elections, returns and qualifications of its own members, and a majority of each fhall conftitute a quorum to do bufinefs; but a fmaller number may adjourn from day to day, and may be authorifed to compel the attendance of abfent members, in fuch manner, and under fuch penalties as each houfe may provide.

Each houfe may determine the rules of its proceedings, punifh its members for diforderly behaviour, and, with the concurrence of two-thirds, expel a member.

Each houfe fhall keep a journal of its proceedings, and from time to time publifh the fame, excepting fuch parts as may in their judgment require fecrecy; and the yeas and nays of the members of either houfe on any queftion fhall, at the defire of one-fifth of thofe prefent, be entered on the journal.

Neither houfe, during the feffion of Congrefs, fhall, without the confent of the other, adjourn for more than three days, nor to any other place than that in which the two houfes fhall be fitting.

*Sect.* 6. The fenators and reprefentatives fhall receive a compenfation for their fervices, to be afcertained by law, and paid out of the treafury of the United States. They fhall in all cafes, except treafon, felony and breach of the peace, be privileged from arreft during their attendance at the feffion of their refpective houfes, and in going to and returning from the fame; and for any fpeech or debate in either houfe, they fhall not be queftioned in any other place.

No fenator or reprefentative fhall, during the time for which he was elected, be appointed to any civil office under the authority of the United States, which fhall have been created, or the emoluments whereof fhall have been encreafed during fuch time; and no perfon holding any office under the United States, fhall be a member of either houfe during his continuance in office.

*Sect.* 7. All bills for raifing revenue fhall originate in the houfe of reprefentatives; but the fenate may propofe or concur with amendments as on other bills.

Every bill which fhall have paffed the houfe of reprefentatives and the fenate, fhall, before it become a law, be prefented to the prefident of the United States; if he approve he fhall fign it, but if not he fhall return it, with his objections to that houfe in which it fhall have originated, who fhall enter the objections at large on their journal, and proceed to reconfider it. If after fuch reconfideration two-thirds of that houfe fhall agree to pafs the bill, it fhall be fent, together with the objections, to the other houfe, by which it fhall likewife be reconfidered, and if approved by two-thirds of that houfe, it fhall become a law. But in all fuch cafes the votes of both houfes fhall

**The fundamental charter.** This is the first published edition of the original Constitution as it appeared in a Philadelphia newspaper the day after it was signed.

**The Federal Union, "one and inseparable."** At top, Senator Webster (at the right) debating with Senator Hayne of South Carolina, a defender of "nullification"; below, Abraham Lincoln, guarded by sharpshooters stationed around the unfinished Capitol dome, delivers his first inaugural address in 1861, in which he explains that the South's secession cannot be lawful but is, instead, rebellion.

They did not wait until a northern-dominated national administration took office and did something of which they disapproved. They assumed that the Lincoln administration would soon prohibit the expansion of slavery, a prohibition which they deemed unconstitutional, and so, led by South Carolina, they promptly left the Union.

Lincoln's first inaugural address, on March 4, 1861, dealt powerfully with the question of the nature of the Union. He adopted Webster's contention that it was a union in its nature indivisible; "no government proper," Lincoln said, "provides for its own dissolution." If, therefore, the people of a state felt that their interests were damaged by any action of the national government, they had but two choices. "They can exercise their constitutional right of amending it, or their revolutionary right to dismember or overthrow it." These are their only alternatives. Either the states remain in the Union and try to persuade Congress to change the laws, or to get the Constitution amended; or they *revolt*. They cannot peaceably leave the Union. They cannot just secede. If they try to do so, they are in fact conducting a revolution against the United States; and the President, being sworn to defend the Constitution against all enemies foreign and domestic, will have to use force to put down the revolution. Thus Lincoln laid the groundwork of legitimacy for his later call to arms in the defense of the Union.

Now most of this is ancient history. We have dealt with it at some length for several reasons. It illustrates the difficulties of keeping any people united under a national government, especially in a federal system. It reminds us that interests can be of different kinds. It shows how various kinds of interests, emotional, economic, and moral, can work together to create great opposing forces in the struggle to control the government. And, finally, it is not irrelevant history. The North-South economic conflict is no longer significant. But the states' rights slogans, though far less stirring than they were in days of yore, still are used to arouse opposition to increases in the national government's power.

"States' rights" was the banner raised by Franklin D. Roosevelt, of all people, when, as governor of New York in the prohibition era, he was objecting to the vigorous enforcement of the Volstead Act by federal policemen. New York's police, he said, could keep New York dry. It was the slogan of a later New York governor, Thomas E. Dewey, in his insistence that the state of New York should control the business of disposing of the electric power generated by federally financed dams on the St. Lawrence River. It provides a continuing undertone to much of our political discussion today, whether the argument concerns contracts wherein an employer agrees to hire only union members or proposals for meeting the financial needs of public schools. More often than not, its relationship to some economic issue, its use for the advantage of some economic interest, is fairly obvious—and as the wheel turns, the states' righters of yesteryear become the nationalists of today or tomorrow, or vice versa.

Finally, what we have called the "moral" issue, pertaining to the status of Negroes in America, has risen to the fore once again, though in a new guise. Once again, now in the 1960's, we hear talk of "interposition" and "nullification." Disputes over the nature of the Union will not, surely, by themselves lead to armed strife. But the issue of segregation (rather than slavery) will for a time be a source of political conflict and will keep alive the need for understanding what our federal system is.

# CHAPTER 4

# The Separation of Powers

$F$ ederalism, as we have just seen, is a *division* of powers between a central, national government and constituent, state governments. Now we turn to the second fundamental of our Constitution, the *separation* of powers within the national government itself. Some confusion may arise from the use of the word "powers" in both instances. Actually, the "powers" that are divided in a federal system are not the same as the "powers" which are separated within the national government. In a federal system, *authority to deal with specific subjects* is given to one government or the other: thus, authority to regulate commerce, coin money, or declare war is allotted to the national government, whereas authority to control sanitation, education, or local crime is reserved to the states. Within the national government, it is really the *functions* that are separated: the law-making function is given to Congress, for instance, and the function of deciding judicial controversies is given to the Supreme Court and such inferior courts as Congress may establish.

When we speak of powers being divided in a federal system, then, we are referring to the subjects with which government deals. When we speak of the separation of powers, we mean a splitting up of functions among different branches of a single government. It is important to understand this distinction. Here in the United States, we happen to have both a federal system and a separation of powers, but it is perfectly possible to have one without the other. Australia has a federal system, but no separation of powers: there the law-making and executive functions are both assigned to the same governing body. The same is true of Canada. Conversely, a "unitary" state could have a separation of powers, even though it is not a federal union. The two concepts are different, and neither is dependent on the other.

What, then, do we mean by a separation of powers? We mean that the Constitution assigns three major functions to three distinguishable branches of the national government. First, the effective part of the Constitution begins by saying: "All legislative power shall be vested in a Congress of the United States." This means that the function of law-making is Congress's business, and Congress is, therefore, the law-making or "legislative" branch of the government. The function of law-making is the task of making general rules, applicable all over the country, which must be obeyed. Congress makes a law when it enacts a statute. It decides, for instance, that all employees shall be paid old-age benefits after they retire at a certain age, or that it shall be a crime to transport a woman across a state line for immoral purposes, or that ordinary postage stamps shall cost four cents. These are all matters of national policy, requiring legislation, and the framers assigned to Congress the task of legislating on these and the other subjects specified in Article I, section 8 of the Constitution.

Second, the executive power, or function, is vested in the President of the United States. By this is meant the task of carrying out and enforcing the laws made by Congress. The President, for instance, is responsible for seeing to it that the retired old people do, in fact, receive their old-age benefits; that the "white-slaver" is caught and prosecuted; that the postmen deliver the letters which bear four-cent stamps but not those which do not. The executive function also includes primary responsibility for the peaceful relationships between the United States and foreign nations. The conduct of diplomacy is the job of the President, his ambassadors, and the Department of State. To accomplish the thousands of administrative and diplomatic tasks, of course, the President has to have the help of literally millions of government employees. These employees are appointed by him or his subordinates and are assigned to particular departments and divisions and bureaus; taken all together, they constitute the "executive branch," of which the President is the head.

Technically, as we shall see in Chapter 16, some of the administrative organs of the government occupy a special and ill-defined place in the total structure. These are the regulatory commissions, to which Congress has entrusted some functions much like those normally performed by courts. These commissions are composed of officials who are appointed for definite terms by the President with the consent of the Senate. The President can remove them, without senatorial consent, only for reasons specifically stated by Congress. They are not, therefore, exclusively under the President's control. In that respect they are different from the rest of the executive branch. Sometimes they are called "legislative commissions," but they are not a part of the legislative branch; and despite their "quasi-judicial" duties they are not courts, and so do not belong to the judicial branch. For present purposes, we can realistically classify them with the executive departments, especially as Congress has in most instances granted the President the authority to designate and to remove the commission chairman, thus giving the chief executive great influence in their operations.

The judicial function is allotted to the Supreme Court of the United States and such "inferior" courts as Congress may establish. Basically, the judicial function is the peaceable decision of controversies in which one or both parties claim that their rights have been violated and seek redress. The controversy may be between two corporations, one claiming that the other has damaged it by breaking a contract which the two had made. It might be a lawsuit for damages, brought by an injured person against the owner of the automobile which ran him down. Or it might be a "criminal case," in which the government, defending the right of the community to be orderly and secure, seeks to punish that man who transported a woman across state lines for immoral purposes. These are just a few examples of the kinds of controversies which must be decided by the judicial process. The Supreme Court, established by the Constitution, and the other federal courts created by Congress constitute the "judicial branch."

## REASONS FOR THE SEPARATION OF POWERS

Most governments, even in free and democratic countries, do not split up these three functions in this fashion. The British "parliamentary" form of government, for instance, assigns both legislative and executive responsibilities, and even some judicial functions, to a single Parliament. The British prime minister is an elected member of the legislative body, and thus votes on proposed laws, but he is also the chief executive. Around the world, this is a much more familiar pattern than our own.

Nevertheless, when the framers designed our national institutions of government in 1787, they were not inventing something new, as they were, perhaps unconsciously, when they proposed a federal system. The device of separating functions between distinct branches of government was familiar to them. In some of the colonies, there had been some degree of such separation. Most of the new state constitutions provided for it. And virtually all of the framers were aware of the logical reasons for it—reasons suggested by the English philosopher, John Locke, and later set forth by the French baron, Charles de Montesquieu. The framers seem to have been especially impressed by Montesquieu's logic. It boiled down to this, as restated later by James Madison: "The accumulation of all powers, legislative, executive, and judiciary, in the same hands, is the very definition of tyranny." Therefore, each of these powers should be placed in separate hands.

This belief that a scheme of separated powers was an excellent protection against tyranny was shared by many of the early American leaders. It had been formally expressed in 1780 in the constitution of Massachusetts. That document, written largely by the revolutionary leader John Adams, explicitly split up functions among three branches and then emphasized the purpose of doing so in the following language: "The legislative department shall never exercise the executive and judicial powers, or either of them: the executive shall never exercise the legislative and judicial powers, or either of them: the judicial shall never exercise the legislative and executive powers, or either of them: to the end it may be a government of laws and not of men."

That is a historic phrase, "a government of laws and not of men," but what does it mean? We all know that government is a human institution and that men do the governing. John Adams knew this, too. What he meant was this: our human rulers, with power at their command, can either use their power exactly as they see fit to use it or they can use it in accordance with law or, as Adams put it, "laws." The law or laws which constrain the rulers are both written—constitutions, statutes, ordinances—and unwritten—solidly established customs and widely shared beliefs as to how governmental power may be used. Adams, like Montesquieu and the framers, felt that if a ruler was entrusted with *all* the functions and powers of government, he might yield to the temptation of ruling by his own whim rather than in accordance with law—for with so much power in his own hands, he would feel that there was nothing to stop him from doing whatever he pleased. And this —the power of the ruler to do whatever he pleases—is the central quality of tyranny. In history there have been wicked dictators and benevolent despots, but they all have had this in common. Until and unless they were overthrown by force, they could all rule just as they liked.

The framers wrote the separation of powers into our Constitution because they feared that if one man or one group obtained too much authority, arbitrary, tyrannical rule might soon ensue. But they feared more than this. As Madison made clear in *The Federalist* papers, they feared the "force and violence of faction": more explicitly, the attempt of a majority of the people to gain control of the government. Today, we assume that majority rule is a normal attribute of democracy. The framers, however, were not exactly enthusiastic about democracy, and their coolness toward it was made evident by their fear of majority rule. The specific majority which they distrusted was the great mass of the people, comparatively unlettered, uncouth, and in the framers' eyes unfit to rule. And so in deciding on a separation of powers, they were building walls against the seizure of unbridled power not only by a single tyrant or a small despotic group, but by the majority of the voters as well.

## THE DIFFERENT CONSTITUENCIES

The separation of powers assumes that separate institutions will exist, to which different functions can be assigned. The Constitution establishes these separate institutions clearly enough: Congress in Article I, the office of the President in Article II, the Supreme Court in Article III. Merely mentioning them in different parts of the Constitution, however, is no guarantee of their separateness. The factor in the original Constitution which set each branch apart from the other branches was the difference in the way in which people would be chosen to fill the offices in each branch. Each had a different constituency.

In this respect, indeed, one branch, the legislative, had two different constituencies. Congress was divided within itself into two distinct bodies. The representatives were responsible to the voters in their districts. These voters elected them and could throw them out of office at the next election. The other half of the legislative branch, however, did not answer directly to the voters. Senators were elected, not by the people, but by the state legislatures.

The President was not chosen by either the people or the legislatures. Instead, each state selected a group of "electors," who were given the task of deciding who should be President of the United States. The Supreme Court's members were not elected at all. They were appointed by the President, with the consent of the Senate, and once in office they did not have to answer to anybody, for they had life terms.

The fact that each branch's constituency was different contributed to the independence of each branch. Thus, congressmen did not depend on the President for their jobs. The President was not dependent on Congress for his position. To be sure, there were two exceptions to this interbranch independence, but not very significant ones. First, the judges were dependent on the President and Senate for their initial appointments, but this dependence ended the moment they took their places on the bench, for they did not have to worry about being reappointed. Second, both the judges and the President, on charges of wrongdoing, could be impeached and removed from office by Congress. In all our history, however, no President and very few judges—none on the Supreme Court—have actually been removed.

## SHARED RESPONSIBILITIES AND MUTUAL RESTRAINTS: "CHECKS AND BALANCES"

Thus far, we have been analyzing factors which were designed to make each branch separate and independent. Inevitably, however, a serious question arises. Such a separation may be a good obstruction to tyrannical government, but is it not also a major obstacle to any government at all? In such a system, how can government function? Congress might make a law, only to have the President refuse to enforce it. The courts, applying their own idea of justice, might condemn a man for doing something which Congress had authorized him to do—and then the officers of the executive branch could either put the man in prison, carrying out the sentence of the court but flouting the will of Congress, or could set him free, agreeing with Congress but defying the court. What a mess! No wonder that in 1787 early critics of the proposed Constitution, noting the emphasis which its supporters placed on the separation of powers as a preserver of liberty, replied that it was also the creator of chaos. But they were wrong. The framers had foreseen this difficulty. They were not doctrinaire. They were practical. They had fashioned a Constitution which would work: "a government of separated institutions *sharing* powers." [1]

As we have seen, each of the first three articles of the Constitution begins by vesting a particular function—"all legislative power," for instance—in a particular branch of the government. Actually, however, the language is too sweeping. Reading the Constitution closely, you will see scattered through it various statements, expressed or implied, which modify those opening sentences of the first three articles. For instance, Congress is not really allotted "all" the legislative or lawmaking power, for the President can try to prevent a bill, which a majority of the Congress wants, from becoming law. He can "disapprove" it, as the Consti-

---

[1] Richard E. Neustadt, *Presidential Power* (New York: Science Editions, 1962), p. 33.

tution puts it; today, we ordinarily say that he can "veto" it. The executive power includes the vitally important executive task of appointing high officials. but the President cannot do this alone: he must share this power with the Senate, which has the right to reject the men whom he wishes to appoint. Likewise, the President's command of diplomacy is less than complete, for treaties which he makes with foreign nations will not become effective unless the Senate, by a two-thirds vote, approves of them. As for the judicial branch, the Supreme Court is established in the Constitution, but Congress (subject to the President's veto) can decide how many judges it shall consist of, and whether there shall be inferior courts and, if so, how many, and even whether the courts shall be allowed to decide certain types of disputes. Finally, Congress holds the purse strings for both of the other branches. Only by its action can they get the money with which to operate. Congress even fixes the salaries of the President and (with some restrictions) the Supreme Court justices.

Thus the "separation" of the powers of government turns out to be incomplete and indistinct. There are three definitely recognizable branches. Each branch is to a large degree independent of the others, yet each is partially dependent on the others. Each, accordingly, is forced into cooperation with the other branches where it is necessary that they pull together in order for the government to operate. The partial interweaving of their functions prevents the chaotic confusion which would follow from a complete, doctrinaire separation of powers.

Cooperation, where necessary, is one side of the coin. On the other side are the *restraints* which these same clauses of the Constitution allow one branch to impose on the others. Thus the presidential veto is assumed to have a restraining influence on Congress. The fact that it must ask Congress for its money presumably restrains the executive branch from indulging any tendency to extravagance in performing its executive duties. From this kind of restraint arises the familiar phrase *"checks and balances."* That phrase has a negative implication. One branch "checks" another; its power "balances" the other's; they all restrain each other. That is one legitimate way to describe the system, but, as we have seen in the previous paragraph, it is not the only legitimate way. If you say: "We have a system of separation of powers except for some necessary cooperation," you will be speaking just as accurately as when you use the more customary phrase, "separation of powers, with checks and balances."

One reason for the historic emphasis on the negative "checking" aspect is that this viewpoint was advanced by Madison and Hamilton in *The Federalist* papers as an argument in favor of the Constitution. The argument centered around the old fear of tyranny. Even if the branches were separate, what was to prevent one of them from becoming dominant and eventually ending the separation by capturing the whole governmental establishment? In answer to this, Madison pointed to the system of checks and restraints, by which each branch could defend itself from encroachment by the others. Men love power, he reasoned, and if they have some they are ambitious for more; but in the Constitution we have a system where "ambition is made to counteract ambition."

The separation of powers between three branches, each selected in a different way by different people; the limited but necessary cooperation between branches, and the mutual restraints which the provisions for cooperation entailed—this was the system designed to forestall autocratic tyrants and hold democratic majorities in check. How has it worked?

## THE SYSTEM IN OPERATION

In all the years since 1787, the United States has never been ruled by a despot, nor has any temporary majority ever gained full control of all the branches of government and used its power arbitrarily and tyrannically. Yet times and ideas change. Americans are as anti-dictator as they ever were, but they have much less fear of "tyrannical majorities." Many people feel that majorities are not necessarily despotic and that the democratic principle requires majority rule. For the protection of minorities, these people would rely not on the separation between President and Congress, but rather on the constitutional safeguards of everyone's right to dissent and criticize. They would count on the Supreme

Court to enforce these safeguards, for even the "majoritarians" have largely accepted the independence and restraining role of the Supreme Court of the United States. The Court, as an institution, has grown to a stature which far exceeds the expectations of the framers. It has done so through exercising its function of interpreting the Constitution in cases brought before it for decision. A judicial decision which restrains the executive, or strikes down an act of Congress, is a check on the other two branches of government. The "restraining" influence of the Court could, therefore, appropriately be discussed in connection with "checks and balances," but actually when the Court checks the other branches it is simultaneously performing a more significant task. It is saying what the Constitution means. That interpretative function is of such vital importance in our whole governmental system that it deserves special treatment and is accordingly discussed in full in the next chapter.

## The Causes of Change

We turn now, therefore, to the separation of powers between the legislative and executive branches. Time and necessity have wrought great changes in the system. We have noted that the difference in constituencies among the House, the Senate, and the presidency was important to the framers in two ways. First, the fact that the representatives were answerable to voters in small districts, the senators to state legislatures, and the President to some future group of carefully selected electors, made it easier for each branch to assert its independence of the others. Second, in their mistrust of democratic majorities, the framers were glad that only the House was democratically chosen.

Now this has changed. The constituencies still differ, but they are all *popular* constituencies; representatives, senators, and Presidents are all answerable directly to the voters. This has come about partly because of the Seventeenth Amendment (1913), which put the election of senators in the hands of the people instead of in the legislatures. It has resulted, partly, from the decision of the states to have presidential electors chosen by direct popular vote, and from the custom of having the presidential electors morally bound to vote for particular candidates for President rather than choosing anyone they like. But primarily it reflects two broader developments: the increased faith in democracy and the growth of the party system.

The careful dilution of democracy, so painstakingly written into the Constitution, was probably doomed from the outset. How could it have been otherwise in a country based on the principle of popular rule? The wonder is that the Senate remained an indirectly elected body for so long. The principle of direct democracy gained ground more quickly in the case of presidential elections. The framers had pictured the electors as wise and trusted statesmen who would confer together and choose whomever they thought was the best man for President. Within a dozen years, however, the role of the electors was becoming automatic: electors were chosen not because they were good and great, but because they had pledged themselves to vote for Jefferson or Adams or King or Clay for President. Today, when we go to the polls in a presidential election we are actually voting for electors, yet in many states the names of the would-be electors do not even appear on the ballot. We assume that we are choosing between actual candidates for the presidency, whose names do appear on the ballot. In substance and effect, that is just what we are doing, even though technically we are merely selecting electors who are expected to vote for our favorite.

This democratization of elections has been made possible by the rise of the party system, a development which began before 1800. If each of the presidential electors had promised to vote for a different man from all the rest, no President could have been picked by the electors or indirectly by the people. But the party system enables the voters to make an effective choice, especially when it is a two-party system. Each party agrees in advance on its one nominee for President. The candidates for the position of presidential elector are themselves party candidates, pledged to vote for the party's nominee.

The party system has had a profound effect on the separation of powers. The President, usually elected democratically in fact if not in form, is the one man for whom the party's adherents all over the country vote. Inevitably, therefore, the voters look on him as a party leader and a party spokesman. Inevitably, too, he and his party, in their appeal for votes, take positions on matters of policy, and often promise new legislation or the repeal of unpopular laws. Legislative policy, of course, is primarily the business of the legislative branch. The Constitution expressly authorizes the President to inject himself into it affirmatively only by "making recommendations from time to time," and, negatively, only by interposing a veto. But if a party has a legislative program, and the President is a party leader, can the President sit idly by while the Congress, for one reason or another, stalls or eviscerates his party's program? In the last thirty years, his problem has become still more acute, for the voters have come to speak not so much of "the party's program" as of "the President's program." If the President is expected, as he seems to be, to put through a program of new laws, and the law-making power is essentially entrusted to a separate, independent branch, how can the President live up to the peoples' expectations? More significant, how can any coherent, constructive legislative program be adopted?

*The Inherent Problem.* Ever since the national government became engaged in great and historically crucial undertakings at home and abroad, these questions have been acute. Under a party system, in a democratic society, can the separation of powers actually be made to work? That it has worked, at least fairly well, may be due to the readiness of both the Congress and the President to use in new ways the built-in devices of cooperation which are part of the constitutional framework. Nowadays, for instance, the President may exercise his constitutional right to "make recommendations" in a fashion that is more effective than a mere written communication to the Congress, the method used throughout the nineteenth century. He may decide to address the Congress in person; he may confer with congressional leaders and make direct, personal pleas to individual congressmen; he may seek to arouse public opinion and to cause the public to bring pressure on Congress by making a speech from the White House over a national TV hookup.

In all of this, oddly enough, he may be helped by the fact that he is a party leader. The party system created the problem because it put unofficial legislative responsibilities on the shoulders of the President. The party system can also help to solve the problem which it created, for the President is a party leader and so his recommendations may carry great weight with members of his own party in the Congress. However, the less disciplined and unified the party, the less the impact of the President's party leadership—a fact that leads to a host of other problems to be discussed later in this book. In 1963, some observers felt that even with an apparently comfortable Democratic majority in the House, Mr. Kennedy, a Democratic President, was up against the same kind of obstacle that his predecessor had faced; his legislative program ran afoul of a "conservative coalition" of Republicans and southern Democrats.

The difficulty of developing any coherent long-range program is increased when the party conflict results in one party controlling one or both houses of Congress while the President is of the opposite party. This tends to create a legislative stalemate. The President's recommendations are rejected by Congress, and Congress's bills are vetoed by the President. Compromise, which may be unsatisfactory to everyone, is often the only way to get anything accomplished. The dangers of inaction, resulting from such a stalemate, were exemplified in the national government in the early years of the great depression: most of what President Hoover planned to do ran into congressional disapproval, and the Democratic House knew that its own program was sure to be blocked by the President. More recently, in 1959, we again had a Republican President and a Democratic Congress, with the result that some legislation was enacted only after being modified to escape a veto, and some important measures, such as a public housing bill, were never passed at all. So we see not only that the party system affects the working of the separation of powers, but also that the separation of powers diminishes the possibility of party responsibility to the electorate.

While the rise of parties has altered the system as originally envisaged by the framers, the growth of America into a world power and the development of its economic life at home have changed it as much or more. They have, in effect, given new legislative responsibilities to the executive branch.

The Constitution, as we have seen, entrusted the conduct of foreign affairs primarily to the President. But foreign policy was relatively unimportant through most of the nineteenth century. Since 1914, in contrast, it has been of vital concern to all of us. As foreign policies have developed, some programs, though initiated by the President, have required legislative action. Congress thus plays a constantly greater formal part in the shaping of foreign policy. But—and this is a significant factor—in dealing with foreign affairs the President has special strength. When America speaks to the world, it does so through the President; he is the spokesman for the nation. The President, too, has the benefit of all of the secret intelligence which is gathered all over the world. Congress does not have the same access to vitally important information. And so in foreign affairs, the President's recommendations to Congress carry special weight, Congress and the people are prone to follow him, and he has a greater opportunity for legislative leadership than the framers ever thought he would possess.

The executive branch's intrusion into the legislative field has also increased as America's economic life has become more and more complex and the national government has sought to regulate it. The theory of the Constitution was that Congress would make the laws and the President, through his subordinates, would carry them out. However, Congress now finds many subjects too complicated to handle in detail, too quickly changing to be made subject to hard-and-fast laws. So, often guided by the experts in the executive branch and even accepting drafts of bills prepared in the executive agencies, it establishes general policies—that wages shall be kept from increasing in wartime, for instance, or that the government should buy surplus farm products at a fair price—and then delegates to the executive branch the job of filling in all the gaps in the statute. The President, or someone under him, is empowered to decide how quickly or slowly wages should rise, and in accordance with what formula; the President, or his appointee, is directed to decide, within stated limits, what a fair price for farm products is at any given time. These decisions which the President has to make are legislative decisions. In making them, the executive branch is making new laws, though always within a general framework prescribed by Congress.

This delegation of legislative authority does not seem consistent with the theory of the separation of powers. It does not appear to square with the plain words of Article I, *"All* legislative power . . . shall be vested in a Congress."* Yet it is necessary. The Supreme Court has ruled that it is constitutional, so long as Congress's general policy is enunciated clearly enough to guide the executive, and so long as the executive branch's procedures in making such legislative decisions provide safeguards against mere whimsical, arbitrary action.

## THE POLITICS OF THE SEPARATION OF POWERS

### "Ambition Against Ambition"

Institutional strife is virtually implicit in a system which relies on "checks and balances," even when that system also necessitates interbranch cooperation. "Cooperation" means "working together." But people can work together without cordiality, and when they cooperate only because they have to, there is a real likelihood of strained relations between them. All through our history there has been conflict between the President and Congress, a conflict caused by their separation and the devices of restraint included in the Constitution. Even when the majority of both the House and the Senate are of the same party as the President, the struggle between the branches runs like a half-unseen fire along the ground, to break into a blaze when it reaches the trees. When Madison spoke of pitting "ambition against ambition," he was prophetic. For it is ambition—not so much for power as for the trappings of power, prestige, admiration, and fame— that underlies this institutional strife.

Actually this kind of conflict is visible, though unimportant, within the legislative branch itself. There is some jealousy between the Senate and the House. Each of them has its own rules, traditions, and self-respect; each is in some ways a social unit as well as an official one, with a "club spirit" carefully cultivated by the older members. Therefore, a spirit of latent rivalry is always present, to the point where some care is taken to prevent this rivalry from becoming offensively overt. An amusing example of this is the House rule which forbids any representative, on the floor of the House, to mention the Senate or any senator by name.

Instead, the representative who wishes to mention action taken by the Senate refers mysteriously to "a bill which was passed by *another body.*"

Senators and representatives are very much alike, however, in their reactions to the executive branch. Even as distinguished a figure as President George Washington quickly learned that separation inculcated jealousy and that "checks" implied hostility. He went personally to call upon the Senate, seeking its "advice and consent" pursuant to the Constitution. The senators gave him a frigid greeting; were it not for the rather terrifying dignity of Washington, one would say that they gave him the brush-off. They declined to "advise" him, and they made clear that they could decide whether or not to "consent" without his presence.

Few, if any, senators have ever had the personal dignity of Washington, and the public does not always view the conduct of Congress as dignified. But the members are acutely conscious of the dignity of the *institution* in which they serve. They are jealous of its prestige because, for many of them, their own prestige depends upon it. The average member of Congress works very hard to get the job and undergoes considerable abuse while he holds it. Unless he is a person of unusual independence, his *amour propre,* his self-esteem, depends in part on the respect accorded to the position which he holds.

Legislators realize, of course, that more prestige is attached to the presidency than to any other office in the land. They are usually ready, accordingly, to treat that office with respect and even deference, even though they may chafe at a President's assertion of leadership and grumble when, by appealing "over their heads" to the people, he puts them on the spot. But they do not feel a similar ready respect for the other officers of the executive branch. These they are inclined to view with suspicion and occasional hostility. If a talented cabinet member lucidly explains a complicated subject to a congressional committee, they are likely to call him too smart, too smooth, too prone to "talk down" to them. If another cabinet member exhibits ignorance of just one subject within his field, they may treat him ever after with a mere scoffing politeness. In dealing with Congress, almost any high executive official has one strike against him, simply because he is in the executive branch and Congress is the legislative branch. As for the lesser executive officials, especially the publicly unknown "experts," they have two strikes against them. Being experts, they often think they know what should be done, and sometimes they say so. The congressman's reaction is likely to be: "Who does that guy think he is, to be telling us what to do? When did he ever get elected to anything? He couldn't get twenty votes in any city in my district." (Getting elected, the knowledge that they have won the approval of "the folks back home," is the common denominator of self-esteem for virtually all senators and representatives. Whatever else they do or fail to do, of that they feel they can be proud.)

Note the baseball simile, of "one strike" and "two strikes." It was deliberately selected. A batter with one or two strikes on him is not out. He still can hit safely. And so with executive officials: they start under a handicap but they still may score with Congress. Their attitude, their effort, and their personal qualities may win congressional liking and approval. But it takes a lot of doing.

If the legislative branch tends to be jealous and touchy, the executive branch inclines to suspicion and disrespect. It is perfectly true that many of the experts never won an election, or even tried to win one. Furthermore, they may understand very little about practical politics. They may assume that it is a dirty game and that those who win it are shrewd, self-interested men who may know how to make a demagogic speech but can have no useful opinion on matters of high policy.

This atmosphere of mutual stand-offishness (mutual hostility would probably be too strong a phrase) is largely the result of the separation of powers. Compare it with a government in which no such separation exists—Great Britain's, for example. There all the top executive posts are filled by members of the legislative branch, the Parliament. The interbranch suspicion and jealousy that is typical of the Washington scene is insignificant in London. But with us, such suspicion and jealousy are part and parcel of our whole constitutional scheme. If they opposed insuperable barriers to interbranch cooperation, they could very nearly bring the machinery of government to a halt. Fortunately, though they are barriers, they are by no means insuperable. Still they do exist, and in the politics of national policy formation they are real factors.

*The Individual Viewpoint.* Also important, in such politics, is the individual factor—the personality, say, of a President, and the way in which he interprets the presidential function under the Constitution. To illustrate this, let us look at the impact, on both the separation of powers principle and the formation of policy, of two twentieth century Presidents. William Howard Taft, a "strict constructionist," believed, in accordance with the letter of the law, that the President was and should be primarily a chief *executive*. This was his conviction. It suited his tastes; he had never held or sought a legislative office, and much of his public experience had been in the administrative field. Accordingly, during Taft's term the formation of policy requiring legislation was left almost wholly to the legislative branch—with results that were displeasing to many people who had voted for Taft and, in at least one instance, to Taft himself.

Woodrow Wilson, who succeeded Taft, had likewise never held legislative office, but he had hankered for it ever since his college days, when he had practiced writing his signature in a copybook: "Thomas Woodrow Wilson, Senator from Virginia." As a university professor, he had highly praised the British system, wherein the chief executive is also the chief legislative leader. As President, he acted according to his beliefs. He did so happily, for he enjoyed leadership and was a skilled persuader. Great domestic issues faced the country in Wilson's first term. The national policies formed to deal with those issues would have been different if Wilson had taken a more literal and respectful view of the separation of powers.

*Interests in Conflict.* Underlying much of the argument about the proper role of the two branches, however, is the ever present conflict of interests. When this conflict is reflected by the President advocating one policy and the Congress rejecting it, we have a typical instance of legislative politics, to be considered at length later in this book. When, however, the interests' concern is expressed in terms of constitutional theory—when one group praises the separation of powers and another deplores it—we may say that those interests which wish to maintain the status quo in domestic matters tend to favor sharp separation and strong checks, while those desiring major change are likely to favor presidential leadership and interbranch cooperation. This is because without very

To the House of Representatives:

I return herewith, without my approval, H. R. bill 9870, entitled "An Act to provide for the immediate payment of World War adjusted service certificates, for the cancellation of unpaid interest accrued on loans secured by such certificates, and for other purposes."

On May 22, 1935, in disapproving a bill to pay the bonus in full immediately instead of in 1945, I gave in person to a joint session of the Congress complete and explicit reasons for my action.

The bill I now return differs from last year's bill in only two important respects: first, it eliminates the issuance of unsecured paper currency to make the payments required and substitutes interest bearing bonds, which, however, may be converted into cash for face value at any time; second, it adds $2,000,000,000 to the total payments by forgiving interest after October 1, 1931, on amounts borrowed.

In all other respects, the circumstances, arguments and facts remain essentially the same as those fully covered and explained by me only eight months ago.

I respectfully refer the members of the Senate and of the House of Representatives to every word of what I said then.

My convictions are as impelling today as they were then. Therefore I cannot change them.

Franklin D. Roosevelt

The White House
January 24, 1936

**The separation of powers.** Above, the President "checks" Congress in unusual fashion, Franklin D. Roosevelt dramatizing his disapproval of a veterans' bonus bill by writing the veto message in his own hand. Below: The separation of powers system is one of not only mutual restraints, but shared responsibilities. Especially in times of international crisis, Presidents and Congressional leaders of both parties realize the need to consult together. Here at the White House in September, 1963, President Kennedy meets with Senate leaders of both parties to discuss prospects of getting strong bipartisan backing of the nuclear test ban treaty. Left to right: Secretary of Defense Robert S. McNamara; Senate Democratic leader Mike Mansfield; President Kennedy; and Republican leader Everett M. Dirksen.

**The United States Supreme Court building.** For many decades the Court met in the old Senate Chamber where Webster had uttered his defense of the principle of Union (see page 72). In 1935 the Justices moved into their new palatial building, which no one can enter without being reminded of any court's basic function —that of providing "equal justice under law."

strong leadership, which it seldom finds within its own ranks, Congress is less likely to construct major new policies or change old ones. Conversely, the President who charges into the legislative arena does so only because he wants change, through the enactment of new laws. It is not surprising that the so-called "strong" Presidents, those who have assumed that the job of the President includes legislative leadership, have almost uniformly aroused bitter hostility in the conservative camp.

The position which an interest group takes on the question, however, may change from time to time. It depends on what will benefit the group most at any given moment. If a "strong" President leads Congress toward goals which the group shares, it will, for the moment, hail his broad reading of his constitutional powers. If, later, his leadership takes Congress along roads which the group fears, it will denounce him for usurping legislative authority. An example of this was the shift in attitude of large numbers of businessmen and financiers, and their editorial spokesmen, toward President Franklin D. Roosevelt in his first term. Many cheered when, at the depth of a great economic depression, he assumed the role of leader and told Congress what to do, driving a great mass of "recovery" legislation to swift enactment in the spring of 1933. They praised him for doing this; they praised the Constitution for being so remarkably flexible that it permitted him to do it. In 1934, however, and even more in 1935, Roosevelt, still leading Congress, pushed for "reform" legislation (stock market regulation, abolition of large holding companies, rights for labor unions) and for welfare laws that would increase taxes. Now the same interests which had praised the President's legislative leadership and the flexibility of the Constitution sang a different song: they suggested that the President was smashing the salutary safeguards of the Constitution on his way to becoming a dictator.

In the same way, many leaders of organized labor denounced President Truman's broad interpretation of his executive power when he sought to break the railroad strike of 1946 by seizing the railroads. At that time the statutes previously passed by Congress, dealing with industrial disputes, were satisfactory to the labor leaders. But in 1947 Congress enacted a new law, the Taft-Hartley Act, which displeased them. And so in 1952, when Mr. Truman again intervened in a strike, this time seizing the steel mills, labor's spokesmen hailed his action as a proper exercise of executive power. They felt, by then, that he was more sympathetic to their interest than was Congress.

Once again, then, when the argument waxes hot and heavy over "constitutional principles," a certain amount of cautious skepticism may be appropriate. The principles don't change, but those who defend them today may decry them tomorrow. Nevertheless, a completely dispassionate observer might correctly feel that there is a real connection between the preservation of the separation of powers and the preservation of individual freedom in the United States. He would have to admit that many nations have long remained free without any separation of powers, but still, what works in England, or Norway, or Australia might not necessarily work as well in the United States. Our impartial analyst, then, might view with some alarm the increased merging of functions and the enlargement of the powers of the President. On the other hand, he might be disturbed by the delays, divisions, and incoherence in the formulation of national policy which are caused by the separation of powers and which show that the old principle still has vitality. Here is a real conflict of interests in the highest sense: the possible good done by the separation of powers as a deterrent to dictatorship, *versus* the possible harm it does by obstructing necessary governmental action in a push-button age. The question, of course, is not the formal abolition of the system. The issues are whether and how much it *can* be modified in practice without endangering individual freedom, and whether and how much it *must* be modified in practice if the nation itself is to remain prosperous and secure.

CHAPTER 5

# Judicial Review

The judicial branch of the national government consists of the Supreme Court, established by the Constitution and now consisting of a chief justice and eight associate justices, and such "inferior" federal courts as may be created by Congress. Since Congress first acted in 1789, there have always been such "inferior" courts, where trials are held and verdicts are rendered. The loser in the trial can appeal to a higher court, and eventually, in some instances, he can appeal to the Supreme Court. Appellate courts, including the Supreme Court, do not try each case all over again; their function is to decide whether the trial in the lower court was fair, and whether the rulings of the trial judge on questions of law were correct.

The functions of the Supreme Court of the United States could be discussed, appropriately enough, in connection with an analysis of the system of a separation of powers. Most of the signers at Philadelphia assumed that the Court might very occasionally serve as a "check," restraining Congress or the President from unlawful acts. They did not foresee, however, that this third branch, which they considered the weakest of the three, would not only acquire the unquestioned authority to tell the other branches what they could and could not do, but would assume a still more powerful

95

and much more affirmative role. The Court has become the supreme interpreter of the Constitution. When it says that the Constitution means a particular thing, that is what the Constitution means. Through the exercise of this great interpretative function, the Supreme Court has had a profound effect on our whole national life.

The Court decides controversies because that is what a court is for. It restrains the other branches, for that is its role in the separation of powers system. But in the course of doing both these things, it does much more. It is the arbiter of the federal system, when questions arise concerning the division of power between the national government and the states. It is the hoped-for shield of the oppressed, who believe that they have been deprived of rights which the Constitution gives them and depend on the Court to redress their wrongs. It interprets the Constitution, applying the words which were written in the horse-and-buggy days of 1787 to the complex issues of the nuclear age. "We live under a Constitution," Charles Evans Hughes said in 1907, "but the Constitution is what the judges say it is."

If language could always be crystal clear, and if statesmen could imagine every public problem two centuries in advance and write succinct solutions to each one into a constitution, there would be no need for interpretation. But the meaning of words is often ambiguous, even at the time when the words are written, and it changes as the years go by. What, precisely, was the meaning of "commerce among the states," when the framers wrote that phrase into the Constitution in 1787 and provided that Congress should have authority to regulate such "commerce"? Did they intend to refer to all the buying and selling that went on in the country? Did they mean merely the shipment of goods, for sale, across state lines? Did the phrase include navigation? If it did, did it embrace all navigation, or only ships carrying freight? These are all legitimate questions about the intention of the framers when they agreed on that wording. The questions multiply prodigiously when we try to apply the phrase to conditions of which the framers never dreamed. The sending of messages by telegraph, for pay; nation-wide telecasting; professional baseball, with teams playing in a league stretching from coast to coast; airplanes "seeding" fast-drifting clouds to produce rain—are all of these things, or any of them, "commerce among the states"?

And what is meant by the power of Congress to "regulate" such commerce? Does this clause authorize Congress to prohibit certain kinds of commerce which it deems harmful, or is prohibition something different from regulation? Can Congress "regulate" interstate commerce by promoting it, as when it authorizes the building of a highway bridge across a river which divides two states? Or is that not a "regulation" of commerce, and therefore not within the power of Congress? If all these problems—and there are hundreds more—can arise with respect to the meaning of just one clause in the Constitution, it is easy to see that the task of interpretation is essential and significant.

## THE SUPREME COURT AS INTERPRETER OF THE CONSTITUTION

The Supreme Court assumed this task because it had to in order to decide particular cases that came before it. For instance, when a man is arrested for violating a law of the United States, he may plead that Congress had no power to make the law, that the law is accordingly null and void, and that therefore he has done nothing illegal. How can judges decide whether or not to set him free unless they first decide whether the law which he violated was one which Congress, under its constitutional authority, could properly make?

The interpretation of written documents—wills, contracts, leases, ordinances, statutes, constitutions—is part and parcel of the work of virtually all courts, both federal and state. It is not something which courts do voluntarily, "on their own"; they do it only when they have to, in order to decide for and against the contending parties in a particular case. When the Supreme Court interprets the Constitution of the United States, it is performing a function which has come to be known as "judicial review." In cases where there is a need to do so, the Court "reviews" an act of Congress to see whether it is a law which Congress had the power to enact or whether, on the contrary, the Constitution withheld such power from Congress or prohibited its exercise in the particular fashion which Congress has prescribed.

Judicial review extends beyond acts of Congress. The Supreme Court occasionally reviews the validity (constitutionality) of actions taken or orders issued by the President, and it frequently reviews statutes passed by state legislatures. It does this when the contending parties in a case present a real question, which must be answered before their rights can be adjudicated, concerning the meaning and applicability of the Constitution of the United States.

## The Beginning of Judicial Review

Although a majority of the framers assumed that the Supreme Court would have the power of judicial review, and although the Court in 1794 exercised that power in a forgotten, unreported case which came before it, not until 1803 did it formally announce that it had that power and give its reasons. The statute which it held invalid was an insignificant one, but the 1803 case itself, *Marbury v. Madison*,[1] was one which grew out of a bitter political dispute and so excited much public interest.

In the background of that controversy was the first clear-cut party battle in American history. Thomas Jefferson, in 1800, defeated John Adams for the presidency. However, Jefferson and the new Congress did not take office until March 4, 1801. In February, 1801, the members of the "old" Congress, composed largely of members of Adams' Federalist party who had already been defeated at the polls but were still in office, decided to reward some of their political henchmen. They enacted a statute which established additional judgeships and new positions of justice of the peace in the District of Columbia. For one of these positions President Adams nominated a good party man, William Marbury. The Senate gave its approval, and Adams then signed Marbury's "commission" or order of appointment as justice of the peace. The Secretary of State duly affixed to it the seal of the United States. In those days, it was the job of the Secretary of State to see to it that such a signed and sealed commission was delivered to

---

[1] 1 Cranch 137.

the appointee. But the term of President Adams and the tenure of his Secretary of State were coming to an end. In the last-minute rush on the morning of March 4, 1801, before Jefferson took office at noon, the commissions of Marbury and some other appointees were left, undelivered, in the Secretary's office.

Jefferson was inaugurated and named James Madison as his Secretary of State. The Jeffersonians had previously denounced the last-minute creation of judgeships by the Adams administration as an attempt by the repudiated Federalists to capture permanent control of the judiciary after losing the presidency and Congress. Now they refused to further this "Federalist plot," as they deemed it. Secretary Madison declined to deliver the signed commissions to Marbury and the others who had been left empty-handed on March 4.

Marbury took legal action to compel Madison to deliver the commission to him. He petitioned the Supreme Court to issue a writ of mandamus—that is, an order directing Madison to deliver. The real question before the Court was whether, under these circumstances, it had authority to consider Marbury's application for the writ.

Marbury claimed that it did. He pointed to a statute—section 13 of the Judiciary Act of 1789—which provided that "the Supreme Court . . . shall have power to issue . . . writs of mandamus . . . to any . . . persons holding office under the authority of the United States." This, Marbury urged, gave the Court authority to do exactly what he was asking it to do: namely, to issue a writ of mandamus to James Madison, who was, certainly, a person "holding office under the authority of the United States."

The Supreme Court decided that it had no authority to issue the writ in this case. It agreed that the statute purported to authorize it to do so. But the statute, said Chief Justice John Marshall in the first of his many famous opinions, was in conflict with the Constitution. Remember that Marbury had come directly to the Supreme Court. He had not petitioned some lesser court, and later appealed to the Supreme Court; he had, instead, invoked the "original jurisdiction" of the Supreme Court. The statute appeared to give him the right to do this. Article III of the Constitution, however, expressly confines the Supreme Court's "original jurisdiction" to "Cases affecting Ambassadors, other public Ministers and Consuls,[2] and those in which a State shall be Party." William Marbury was not an ambassador or a public minister or a consul or, certainly, a state. Under the Constitution, therefore, the Supreme Court had no right to take original jurisdiction of his case. Congress had tried to give it that right, by enacting section 13 of the Judiciary Act, but it could not do so. The Constitution having specifically limited the Supreme Court's original jurisdiction, Congress had no power to enlarge it. Because section 13 did purport to enlarge it, section 13 was in conflict with the Constitution. And, said Marshall, when such a conflict occurs, there is only one thing which the judges can do. They must uphold the Constitution, as a "superior paramount law, . . . superior to any ordinary act of the legislature. . . . A law repugnant to the Constitution is void." So the Supreme Court held section 13 unconstitutional, null and void, and sent Marbury away, still empty-handed, because the Constitution had not authorized the Supreme Court to act on his petition for a writ of mandamus.

The notoriety of this case and the force of Marshall's opinion made *Marbury v. Madison* a landmark in constitutional history. The Chief Justice did more than just decide the case; he asserted that the Court had inherent power, in cases properly brought before it, to order the executive to perform administrative acts, and he set forth convincingly the reasons why the court had to review the validity of congressional legislation. Nevertheless, fifty-four years passed before another act of Congress was held invalid.

During that period, however, the Court fairly frequently passed on the validity of the acts of state legislatures and found them to be in conflict with the United States Constitution. The first of these cases was *Fletcher v. Peck*,[3] a dispute over title to property in Georgia. One of the claimants asserted that his right to the property was based on a grant made to him by the state legislature; the other answered that the grant had been later revoked, also by the state legislature. The Supreme Court held that the second statute, revoking the grant, was unconstitutional because

2 This refers to *foreign* diplomats only.
3 6 Cranch 87 (1810).

it violated the provision of Article I, section 10 of the Constitution that "No State shall . . . pass any . . . Law impairing the obligation of Contracts." The original grant, according to Marshall, created a contractual obligation on the state, which was "impaired" by the subsequent revocation.

Shortly after *Fletcher v. Peck*, Marshall led the way in solidifying the Supreme Court's position as the *final* interpreter of the Constitution. The states, after all, had courts too, and on those courts sat some judges as imperious and, in those days, as famous as Marshall. These state court judges did not object to judicial review, but they claimed that the highest court of a state had a right to interpret the Constitution just as finally and authoritatively as the highest court of the national government. Marshall, however, did not share the view that the Supreme Court was merely the "highest court of the national government" on a par with the highest court of each state. To him, it was the highest court of the *country*, and he and his colleagues acted accordingly. In two early cases, the Supreme Court insisted on accepting appeals from state courts in cases involving the meaning of the Constitution, even though the highest state courts had already passed upon them. At first there was resistance. Once, when the United States Supreme Court's decision differed with that of the Virginia supreme court, the indignant Virginia judges refused to issue the necessary orders to enforce the decision. But Marshall stuck to his guns, and the growth of the nationalistic spirit helped him. The people of the United States accepted the Court's authority to review state legislation. They accepted its assertion of power to be the final judge of constitutional questions, even when such questions had been dealt with in state courts. And eventually, at least, they accepted its right to invalidate acts of Congress, propounded so eloquently in *Marbury v. Madison*.

## Early Objections to Judicial Review

The Constitution itself does not expressly give the Supreme Court the power of judicial review. It does not say a word about the subject. Most of the framers assumed that the Court would have the power because of the nature of the judicial process: how could cases be decided otherwise? However, for a period lasting more than seventy years, not all of the country's leaders agreed that the Supreme Court possessed this implied right of judicial review, and even today the legitimacy of its power to hold statutes unconstitutional is sometimes questioned.

Two major objections have been made to the idea that under the Constitution itself the Supreme Court has the right, through judicial review of federal or state statutes, to make binding interpretations of the Constitution. First, consider a case wherein the Court strikes down an act of Congress. Why should the *Court* have the last word as to the meaning of the Constitution? The members of Congress, who passed that law, and the President, who signed it, are presumably intelligent and upright men, and they are all sworn to uphold and defend the Constitution. If they say that the statute is constitutional, why should the Court say that it is not? And if the Court does say this, with binding authority, is it not thereby becoming supreme in a government in which it is supposed to be only one of three *co-equal* branches?

Today, the Court's authority to declare acts of Congress unconstitutional is so generally accepted that it seems startling to question it. Yet as good a lawyer and as great an American as Abraham Lincoln questioned the conclusiveness of the Court's interpretation. In his first inaugural address in 1861, Lincoln agreed that to settle a dispute between individuals in a lawsuit, the Court might have to rule on the validity of a statute. But he suggested that only those individuals, and people in situations identical to theirs, should be considered bound by its decision. The Court, he implied, was not necessarily the final interpreter of the Constitution. If it said, as it had in the *Dred Scott* case [4] four years before, that Congress had no constitutional power to prohibit slavery in any territories of the United States, this settled the fate of Dred Scott, but did not determine the constitutionality of what Congress had done or might do. As an interpretation of the Constitution, Lincoln said, the Court's decision was "entitled to great respect"; but it was not the last word. In Lincoln's view, the question of whether Congress could prohibit slavery in the territories was still unsettled.

---

[4] *Dred Scott v. Sandford,* 19 Howard 393 (1857).

A different kind of challenge to the role of the Court as interpreter of the Constitution arose in connection with the dispute over the true nature of the federal system. If Congress made a law and the Court *upheld* that law, but the people of one or more states thought that the law was unconstitutional, why, once again, should the Court have the final say? The Constitution allots certain powers to the national government and reserves other powers to the states. When an act of the national government is challenged on the ground that it is not based on any power specifically granted to that government, why should the Supreme Court be the umpire? The Court is, itself, a part of the national government. To have members of the national government decide whether certain powers have been allotted to the national government or reserved to the states would be like having a World Series game umpired by the substitute pitchers of one of the contending teams. This criticism, though not illogical, never was persuasive enough to cause the Court much fear of reprisal, and it was assumed to have been laid to rest by the Civil War. As we shall see, however, it was revived, in slightly altered form, in the 1950's.

Despite these recurrent controversies, the Court has long since become established as the chief arbiter of federalism and the ultimate interpreter of the Constitution. But we must always remember that in performing these functions, the Court ordinarily does not take the initiative. Its central job is to decide the cases which other people bring before it. Only when that duty requires it to do so will it interpret the Constitution. Many constitutional questions, therefore, have never been decided by the Court. It does not render advisory opinions; and it refuses to decide a case when either of the contending parties lacks a direct, substantial interest in the outcome of the controversy. The Court is the final interpreter only of those provisions of the Constitution which it has to interpret.

## INTERPRETATION OF THE CONSTITUTION

### The Instruments of the National Government

The Constitution, as we have seen, established institutions or instruments of government; granted powers to the national government and left other powers in the states; and limited the scope and exercise of power by both national and state governments. In all of these respects it has needed interpretation, and judicial controversies have required the Supreme Court to interpret it.

The first instrument set up by the Constitution is the legislative branch, the Congress of the United States. In it is vested "all legislative power." Does that mean that Congress is prohibited from authorizing the President, or the executive branch, to make rules and regulations that have the force and effect of law? Can it, in this way, *share* the law-making authority entrusted to it? The Supreme Court has said that it can, but only if the executive's discretion, in such "law-making," is clearly defined and limited, and only if Congress insists on procedural safeguards to prevent the executive's action from being purely arbitrary. The Court held unconstitutional a statute which very broadly empowered the President to prescribe "codes of fair competition" for any or all industries when he saw fit, without adequately indicating what the codes should contain and without requiring that an industry should be given a hearing before becoming bound by any such code.

The meaning of "legislative powers" has been crucial, too, in decisions involving people who have been charged with "contempt of Congress." These have been people who, having been summoned before a congressional committee, are ordered to answer questions and flatly refuse to do so. Can Congress compel them to answer? When a congressional committee thus investigates, is it exercising a legislative, law-making power? In one such case, the Court suggested that Congress was usurping the judicial function. In other more recent cases, a minority of the justices expressed their opinion that Congress had no right to hold investigations for the purpose of harassing or "exposing" people. The leading case on the subject, however, includes congressional investigations within the meaning of "legislative powers" if the purpose is to find facts which may help Congress do its law-making job.

The constitutional powers of the President, and the relationships between the executive and legislative branches, have also required interpretation. If an official has been appointed by the

President with the consent of the Senate, can he be fired by the President without the Senate's consent? The Constitution does not expressly say; but when the ousted official brings suit for his salary, the Court must decide what it implies. Again, what are the limits of the President's "executive power"? Suppose Congress passed a law authorizing the President to take certain steps if a strike threatened the production of defensive weapons. Then a steel strike did occur in wartime and the President, deciding that these statutory steps would take too long, issued an order for the United States government to take over the steel mills. Did he have a right to do this, as "chief executive" or as "commander-in-chief"? If, in the absence of any statute, he could properly have done it, did the existence of the statute prescribing other procedures qualify or destroy his constitutional power to do it? These questions, and many more, about the powers of the President have come before the Supreme Court for decision. Here, as in the case of ambiguities with respect to Congress's powers, the Court interprets those clauses of the Constitution which established the instruments of government. It has permitted considerable blurring of the original sharpness of the lines separating the legislative and executive branches by approving a large amount of what is really executive "law-making." And it has inclined to construe broadly the President's powers to conduct foreign policy without congressional intrusion. At the same time, it has occasionally checked the exercise of presidential power, as when it nullified Mr. Truman's order seizing the steel mills on the ground that the order conflicted with an act of Congress.[5]

## The Grant of Powers and the Federal System

In the federal system established by the Constitution, certain specific "enumerated" powers were granted to Congress. As we have seen with respect to the power to regulate commerce among the states, the meaning of the clauses which grant these powers is often unclear. And except for the broad statement that all the powers not delegated are "reserved to the States," the Constitution is virtually silent with respect to the rights of the states in

---

[5] *Youngstown Sheet and Tube Company v. Sawyer,* 343 U.S. 579 (1952).

the federal Union. It is not surprising that, beginning in the early 1800's, cases arose in which the actions of the national government conflicted with those of a state, or vice versa. For instance, Congress passed a law under which ships were licensed for trade along the Atlantic coast. The state of Delaware, trying to improve the health of its citizens by getting rid of mosquito-breeding salt-water marshes, authorized the building of a dam across a creek in Chesapeake Bay. The dam was intended to shut off the upper end of the creek from the tide; unfortunately, it also blocked the channel for vessels sailing up to the head of the creek. A commercial sloop, licensed under the federal law, sailed up the creek and smashed into the dam. The owner of the sloop was sued for damages. His defense was that Delaware had no constitutional right to authorize the dam across that creek, for it obstructed interstate commerce. Here was a conflict between the national power over interstate commerce and the state's power to promote the health of its citizens. It was a minor dispute, to be sure, but it was typical of the kind of constitutional question which the Court has frequently had to answer. In deciding cases like this, the Court is, in a sense, acting as the umpire of the federal system.

The clause in Article I, section 8 authorizing Congress to regulate "commerce among the States" has been the chief source of dispute about the conflicting powers of the states and the federal government. It presents two major questions. First, what is the "commerce" which Congress is authorized to regulate? Second, can the states exercise their historic powers to regulate local affairs, when such state regulation incidentally prohibits some forms of interstate business or makes them less profitable? (The case of the dam across the creek raised this second question.)

As to the meaning of "commerce among the States," Chief Justice Marshall, in the early days, construed the words broadly. Then, as we saw in Chapter 3, for a hundred years the Supreme Court tended to interpret the commerce clause more and more narrowly. Congress, it said, could regulate the transportation of tangible goods, for sale, across state lines—but even such regulation was disallowed in *Hammer v. Dagenhart*. It could control the instruments of transportation—sailing vessels, steamboats, and railroads. But it could not prohibit a monopoly of sugar refining, even though the sugar was to be sold all over the country. It could not regulate labor conditions in coal mines or make marketing rules for poultry markets, despite the fact that the coal was to be shipped across state lines and the chickens had been brought to market from other states. Manufacturing, mining, and marketing, the Court said, were all local matters; they were not subjects which Congress could regulate. This was a far cry from Marshall's declaration that Congress had the power to govern "that commerce which concerns more States than one."

For years a strong minority of the Supreme Court—often four justices out of nine—disagreed with the narrow construction favored by the majority. Eventually, in 1937, the commerce clause was given a new, broad interpretation. In a series of major decisions from 1937 through 1941, the court said that Congress did, after all, have power to regulate manufacturing, if the goods being manufactured were destined for sale across state lines. As the years went by, "commerce among the States" was construed to include most private enterprise in the country. Old decisions, including the one in *Hammer v. Dagenhart* which had said Congress lacked authority to prohibit the shipment of goods made by child labor, were denounced and "overruled." Under its power to regulate "commerce among the States," Congress could now validly require employers to bargain collectively with their employees. (Collective bargaining, it was suggested, would promote industrial peace and prevent strikes, strikes prevent production, production is necessary if there is going to be any commerce; therefore, to impose a requirement of collective bargaining is an appropriate way to promote or "regulate" commerce.) Soon the Court was saying, clearly, that all employment in connection with the production of goods destined for interstate commerce was within the regulatory power of Congress. "The commerce power," wrote Justice Clark in 1951, "is commensurate with the economic life of the nation itself."

In handling the second question raised by the commerce clause —the scope of state power—the Supreme Court seems to have reached agreement on a few basic principles which guide its decisions. If a state law is intentionally "discriminatory"—that is, if it is intended to give businessmen inside the state an advantage over their out-of-state competitors—it improperly "burdens" inter-state commerce and is therefore unconstitutional. For instance, a state might wish to require that people who go from door-to-door trying to obtain subscriptions to magazines published in other states should pay a license fee before starting on their rounds. But such a law, directed at magazines published *outside* of the state but not at those published *within* the state, would be discriminatory. It would impede interstate commerce—the sale of magazines across state lines—and so would be void.

More difficult questions arise when the state law is not discriminatory, but applies to all alike. As a health measure, a state might say that all milk, before being sold inside the state, should be pasteurized within the state under the watchful eye of state inspectors. As a provision for safety, it might require that any large vessel entering its harbors should be steered up the channel by an experienced pilot licensed by the state. To raise revenue, it might levy a tax on all sales, including the sale of goods brought in from other states. If any such laws directly conflict with an act of Congress they are, of course, void, for acts of Congress are "the supreme law of the land." Often, however, Congress has not acted at all on the particular matter dealt with by the state law. Under such circumstances, is the state law valid?

In deciding this question, the Court attempts to "balance the interests" involved. It tries to measure the importance of having the particular subject—milk pasteurization, for instance, or port pilotage—dealt with uniformly on a national basis; it considers whether the subject is an appropriate one for varied local regulation; how much the state law benefits the state, and how seriously it obstructs interstate trade. The decision in each case (and there are several of them every year) depends on the application of these standards to the particular facts. In dealing with these problems, the Court quite consciously continues to play its part as "umpire of the federal system."

In cases involving the commerce clause and in other cases, too, the justices have frequently found occasion to express their ideas about the nature of the Union. "The government of the Union," wrote John Marshall in *McCulloch v. Maryland,* "is, emphatically and truly, a government of the people. In form and substance, it emanates from them." More than a century later another great judge, Benjamin N. Cardozo, declared that "The Constitution . . . was framed upon the theory that the people of the several States must sink or swim together, and that in the long run prosperity and salvation are in union and not division." These were mere *dicta*, not decisions of the Court. They were not even historical statements of proven accuracy. But the first was an expression of opinion which influenced history, and the second was an echo of an historic court decision—for in 1869 in *Texas v. White* [6] the Supreme Court held squarely that once a state joined the union, it could never leave it. The Union was "one and inseparable," Daniel Webster had cried in 1830, "now and forever." The Supreme Court, eventually, declared that he was right.

## Limitations on Governmental Powers Affecting Property

The Constitution establishes instruments of government and grants power to them; it also restrains them. Aside from the implied restrictions which keep the states from usurping federal power and vice versa, the restraints have two general purposes: the protection of property rights and the preservation of what have come to be known as "individual rights." In each case, it is the violation of these rights by *government* (state or national, as the case may be) which the Constitution seeks to prevent.

A major protection of property rights, at least as the framers saw it, was the clause in Article I, section 10 forbidding the states to make laws "impairing the obligation of contracts." This clause was understood differently by different people, and the Court was forced to interpret it in some famous cases. The most significant question about it arose from the fact that after issuing a charter to a corporation, without any limitation of time or express right to revoke it, a state sometimes sought to revoke the charter and bestow it on somebody else. The originally chartered corporation protested that this revocation was an impairment of the state's obligation of contract. The Supreme Court in the *Dartmouth College Case* [7] construed the clause strictly against the state. It thus upheld property rights; it also caused the states to change

---

6 7 Wallace 700 (1869).

7 4 Wheaton 518 (1819). Arguing as attorney for Dartmouth College, Daniel Webster spoke movingly: "She is a small college, but there are those who love her!"

their ways, so that today the organizers of a corporation receive their charter only with the specific understanding that the state can alter it or take it away from them.

*The "Due Process" Clause.* The other main protection of property rights is the provision, in two different places, that government shall not "deprive any person of life, liberty, or property without due process of law." This language in the Fifth Amendment restrains the national government, and in the Fourteenth Amendment it restrains the state governments. The "due process" clause, essentially, is a requirement that governmental action must be justly intended, well considered, and reasonable. Deliberately unjust, unconsidered, or unreasonable action would, on the other hand, lack "due process of law." This seems like a pretty clear definition, but when you put it to the test of some specific event, you will see that even so defined, the "due process" clause is still ambiguous. What action *is* "unjust" or "unreasonable"? Wise men have argued for centuries about the nature of justice, and intelligent people can and do differ as to what is reasonable and what is not.

The "due process" clause, therefore, from the first was ripe for judicial interpretation. As a protection of property rights, it became important after the adoption of the Fourteenth Amendment in 1868. (At that time, if any government threatened to interfere with property rights, it was likely to be a state; the national government regulated very little of the nation's business before 1887, and not a great deal of it until 1933.) Shortly after the Civil War, individual states began to enact laws imposing various regulations on industry. Objecting to these regulations, the corporations affected claimed that the state laws deprived them of property (their full control of their business, or their right to profits) or liberty (their freedom to make whatever contracts they liked) without "due process of law." To be sure, the Fourteenth Amendment protected only "persons," and the complaints against the state laws usually came from corporations, but this presented no difficulty: for, without explaining its reason for doing so, the Supreme Court declared that a corporation was a "person" within the meaning of the Fourteenth Amendment.[8]

---

8 *Santa Clara County v. Southern Pacific R.R. Co.*, 118 U.S. 394 (1886).

The essence of the corporations' complaint was that the state regulatory legislation was "unreasonable." A state law limiting the hours of labor in a bakery might have been proposed and enacted as a sensible health measure, but it was attacked as an unreasonable deprivation of property and liberty. The legislators, in fixing a minimum wage for female workers, might believe that they were doing the proper governmental job of promoting health and welfare and discouraging immorality. The employers answered that the law was arbitrary, unjust, and unreasonable; and they also persuaded employees to complain about such laws. Thus, a woman elevator operator in Washington, D. C., claimed that a statute, authorizing a board to fix a minimum wage sufficient for the maintenance of health and protection of morals, arbitrarily deprived her of her "freedom" to agree to work for thirty-five dollars a month.

As can be seen, the basic question in cases of this sort was not whether the state was simply depriving anyone of liberty or property. All regulatory laws do this, to some extent. The real issue was, was the state law *reasonable?* If it was, it was valid; if it was not, it lacked "due process of law" and so was unconstitutional.

In 1908, a Boston attorney, Louis D. Brandeis, not only perceived that this was the real issue, but invented a way of meeting it. Retained to defend the validity of a state labor law, Brandeis employed sociologists and statisticians to gather facts and figures. When the lawyers' briefs, their written arguments on points of law, were presented to the Supreme Court, Brandeis's was unlike any brief ever filed before. It included not only the usual kind of legal argument, with citations of precedents, but also over 100 printed pages of social and economic data, showing the real facts which had justified the enactment of the state law. This new technique was persuasive, while it was still new. It made it hard for any justice with a normal amount of humility to call the state laws "arbitrary" or "unreasonable." Two Oregon statutes regulating hours of labor were upheld by the Court after the Supreme Court justices had perused the "Brandeis briefs." But as the novelty wore off, a majority of the Court became less impressed by the facts and figures. Instead, they inclined more and more to follow their own reactions, regardless of the evidence. Their reactions were conditioned by their deeply held beliefs about the sanctity of property rights and the importance of limiting the role of government, particularly in economic affairs. And so in the 1920's and early 1930's, a whole series of state statutes were struck down as "unreasonable" and hence as violative of the "due process" clause: laws for minimum wages, for arbitration of labor disputes, for prevention of ticket "scalping," for requiring that only licensed pharmacists should operate drugstores, for control of the practices of private employment agencies, and many more.

In all of these cases a minority of the justices—including Brandeis, who by now was himself a member of the Court—vigorously dissented. Essentially, they disagreed with the majority's habit of substituting *its* opinion for that of the legislature, as to what was reasonable. "Courts," said Justice Stone caustically, "are not the only agency of government that must be assumed to have capacity to govern." The dissenters also suggested that in disregarding the legislature's judgment and deciding that a statute lacked "due process," the majority was really condemning the law not because it was arbitrary or unreasonable, but because the judges just didn't like it. As Justice Holmes put it: "I cannot believe that the (Fourteenth) Amendment was intended to give us (the justices) *carte blanche* to embody our economic or moral beliefs in its prohibitions."

These reminders of the fact that judicial discretion might have some proper limits never swayed four members of the majority. But the views of two other justices (these cases were decided, usually, by votes of five to four or six to three) began to change as the great business depression of 1929 grew worse and worse. The need for laws to regulate the sick economy now seemed apparent; it was harder than ever to call such laws "unreasonable." And so in the mid-1930's, the Court stopped striking down state laws as a matter of course. By the end of that decade, a very different conception prevailed as to the application of the "due process" clause to statutes governing business affairs.

Today, the "due process" clause is no longer a sturdy shield against government regulation of business. It still protects business against purely arbitrary oppression. For instance, today, if a state passed a law penalizing employers who employed any person over thirty years of age, it would seem easy to show that the law was arbitrary, whimsical, and not reasonably connected with any proper purpose of state government. Presumably, therefore, the Court would find a lack of "due process" and strike the statute down. But most statutes are not manifestly absurd or irrational. Most of them are designed to promote some recognized objective of government—health, for instance, or welfare or safety. In terms of such objectives, a legislature may be far-seeing or shortsighted, and its statutes wise or unwise. Mere shortsightedness and lack of wisdom, however, are faults common to mankind. They do not make a regulatory statute unconstitutional.

Thus far, in discussing judicial interpretation of constitutional limitations, we have been considering the restraints on governmental action affecting property rights. However, one normal, common-sense way of interpreting the due process clause is to view it as primarily a protection of an individual right of a very particular kind—namely, the right to a fair trial. "No person shall be deprived of life, liberty, or property without due process of law." Among other things, this may mean that "no person shall be fined (or ordered to pay damages), or imprisoned, or executed, except as the result of a decision reached after a fair trial."

The due process clause, moreover, protects more than the right to a fair trial. The "liberty" which it is designed to uphold against arbitrary action is not only freedom from unreasonable business regulation or freedom from unjust imprisonment. It also includes the *affirmative* liberties of the First Amendment—freedom of religion, speech, press, and assembly. And by the Fourteenth Amendment, no person can be denied the "equal protection of the laws" by a state.

These matters of every person's "constitutional liberties," every American's fundamental "civil rights," deserve separate, detailed treatment, which they receive in the next three chapters. They give rise to great continuing, largely unsettled questions of constitutional interpretation. In contrast, the questions of interpretation discussed more fully in the present chapter have been largely settled. Unforeseeable events may raise anew the issues of Congress's power to regulate interstate commerce, and the states' power to regulate local business. For the moment, however, what the Constitution means on these points seems reasonably clear; and the economic system has so thoroughly adapted itself to the existence and exercise of these governmental powers that there is little likelihood of a judicial reversion to the doctrines of the 1920's.

## THE POLITICS OF JUDICIAL REVIEW

If politics is a struggle for power in or through government, the Supreme Court is deep in politics, shocking as that idea may seem. For when it interprets the Constitution, the Court is constantly defining governmental powers. The real contestants in politics want those powers used, or withheld, for their own ends—ends which may be either ideal or material, as we have seen. Most national policy is made by Congress or the President, and political campaigns are waged to gain control of those branches of the government. But major national policies are also profoundly influenced, even shaped, by the decisions of the Supreme Court interpreting the Constitution. Those interpretations often strengthen the hand of one large interest group, and, conversely, step on the toes of another. It would seem natural, therefore, that the control of the Supreme Court's decision-making process would be a major political objective of such groups.

The actual making of decisions is the culmination of the judicial process, not the political process. But the question of *who* shall sit on the bench and make the decisions is decidedly a political question. Why, then, isn't control of the selection of the Court's personnel a legitimate and constant political objective?

The first answer to that question, of course, is that the justices are not elected. They are appointed by the President, with the consent of the Senate, and they serve for life. To control the Court, then, you would first have to capture the presidency and the Senate: and even if you succeeded in doing so, you might still not affect the Court's personnel. Judges seem to be congenitally long-lived; life on the Supreme Court, especially, appears to be healthy and sustaining. It is not quite true that "few die and none resign," yet in a particular four-year presidential term it may happen that no justices at all either resign or die. And so no President can count upon being able to appoint to the Court new justices whose ideas about the meaning of the Constitution are similar to his own.

Nevertheless, the possibility that a President will have just this opportunity is sometimes a behind-the-scenes factor in political campaigns for the presidency. There are times when justices are so very old or feeble that one can predict their early departure from the Court. Thus, in the 1920 campaign, William Howard Taft discreetly urged the election of Warren G. Harding as President on the ground that vacancies were likely to occur in the near future, and Harding could be trusted to fill those vacancies with "safe" judicial appointments: that is, Harding would appoint men whose views coincided with those of Taft and his friends. Mr. Taft, of course, was well aware of the tendency of a President to select justices on the basis of his approval of their approach to constitutional issues. Mr. Taft had been President, himself.

The possible impact of the presidential election on the future occupancy of the supreme bench is not, however, a customary topic of campaign oratory. It may be discussed by lawyers at lunch, but it should not be mentioned by any prudent candidate on the hustings. For since 1890, at least, a sacrosanct atmosphere has come to surround the Supreme Court. The Court is not immunized against criticism, but most Americans assume that it is beyond the reach of party politics and should be kept there. Accordingly, to make a partisan issue of control of judicial appointments would be to violate one of the basic "value" assumptions of our political life. Franklin D. Roosevelt might well have learned this in 1932 when he was first a candidate for the presidency. In the final week of the campaign, Mr. Roosevelt, a Democrat, said that the Republicans bore the responsibility for the country's bad economic plight because in 1929 they had controlled "the Executive, the Senate, the House of Representatives and, I may add for good measure, the Supreme Court as well." This suggestion that the Court was a partisan body offended many voters. It did not cost Roosevelt the election, but it was a tactical mistake which was sharply criticized even by newspapers supporting Roosevelt's candidacy. So we see that although control of the Court may sometimes be at stake in a national election, the adverse popular reaction to admitting that it is an issue effectively prevents its being made one.

The political concern with who shall sit on the Court can, however, occasion a struggle in the Senate over confirmation of the President's nominee for a judicial post. In 1929, for instance, President Hoover selected a reputable lower-court judge, John J. Parker, to fill a vacancy on the Supreme Court. Apparently believing that Judge Parker was "anti-labor" and "anti-Negro," a majority of senators opposed his confirmation and so prevented his appointment. This, however, is the only occasion in the last half-century when a nominee for a position on the Supreme Court has been rejected. Most senators are aware of their constituents' distaste for injecting even the appearance of "party politics" into matters pertaining to the Court.

If political combatants cannot overtly fight for control over judicial appointments, they can endeavor to limit or to maintain the power of the Supreme Court. Those who are displeased by the Court's interpretations can take political action by attacking the assumptions that underlie judicial review or by seeking to remodel the Court or restrict its power. These efforts give rise to political conflicts—the politics of judicial review.

Most of this political struggle is waged in institutional terms. Sometimes the Supreme Court justices have sparked the conflict by indulging in unnecessary, unwise *dicta* or by calling "unreasonable" laws which most people considered both reasonable and necessary. Usually, however, as we shall see, the members of the Court have tried to keep the Court clear of politics, and thus to safeguard its future and the future of judicial review.

In considering the politics of judicial review, we will find that the role of the individual is usually less prominent than it is in other political contests. This is chiefly because the Court is not composed of a single judge, but of nine; at least five men are responsible for its decisions, and they reach agreement in private. Nevertheless, great judges and famous statesmen have occasionally played historic parts in determining the scope of the Court's power and the extent of its authoritative independence.

Interest groups are inevitably concerned with who sits on the Court and how they decide cases. Although they cannot influence the actual decisions by lobbying or otherwise applying "pressure," [9] they can try to influence judicial appointments, and, more

9 Insofar as judicial interpretation is affected by the "climate of public opinion," interest groups may occasionally have an effect on the Court's decisions, for skillful publicity, propaganda, or education can help to alter that "climate." This matter will be explored further in Chapter 17.

particularly, they can participate in any battle over proposals to modify the Court's structure or limit its power of judicial review. To a consideration of the political factors in such battles we now turn.

## Institutional Factors

The justices themselves have never been ignorant of politics. From the first, they have understood that the Supreme Court is a governmental institution, existing in a political world. Within the national government, and in the nation as a whole, the Court did not acquire its great prestige and dominance just by happenstance. Its growth, as an institution, was nurtured by the justices and by those who agreed with the Court's decisions; and the institution of judicial review has prospered likewise.

From an institutional standpoint, Marshall's decision in *Marbury v. Madison* was a political masterpiece. Not only did the chief justice convincingly state the case for judicial review; he also asserted the judicial branch's right to give orders, under certain circumstances, to the executive branch. Yet in doing each of these things, he avoided a clash with anyone who might have defied him. True, the decision held an act of Congress, section 13 of the Judiciary Act of 1789, unconstitutional, but it is hardly likely that any member of Congress in 1803 felt affronted thereby; in fact, it seems improbable that many members had even been aware of the existence of section 13 before the case arose. It was an insignificant, noncontroversial statute. Furthermore, the majority in Congress, in 1803, were Anti-Federalists; they would not be prone to object to a court decision that deprived a Federalist appointee, Marbury, of a political plum. So the holding of the Court, dismissing Marbury's suit, was unlikely to displease Congress, and Marshall's unnecessary assertion that the Court could have ordered the commission delivered if the case had been properly before it could not incur defiance from the executive branch. There was no order to defy. What would have happened to the Supreme Court if in Marbury's case it had decided that it did have jurisdiction and ordered Madison to deliver? Almost certainly Madison, with the backing of President Jefferson, would have ignored the order, saying that the Court had no right to issue it. The

Court's prestige would have been damaged, perhaps fatally. Much of American history might have been different.

The avoidance of a damaging head-on collision, skillfully contrived in *Marbury v. Madison*, has become a standard judicial maneuver when the facts of a particular case make it possible. The court has to make plenty of decisions which displease many people. When somebody wins a case, somebody else loses. The justices, however, justifiably feel that they have no duty to interpret the Constitution in a particular case if they can reach a just decision without doing so. They ruefully recall one famous occasion when the Supreme Court quite needlessly undertook to construe the Constitution in regard to the most controversial issue in American history. That unnecessary venture was the opinion of the Court, written by Chief Justice Roger B. Taney, in the case of *Dred Scott v. Sandford* in 1857. It nearly finished judicial review.

**The Dred Scott Case.** Dred Scott was a Negro slave living in Missouri where slavery then was lawful. Many years before, back in 1820, Congress had passed an act called the Missouri Compromise, which prohibited slavery in what were then the northwestern territories of the United States. One of these "free" territories later became the state of Minnesota. Scott's owner took the slave with him to Minnesota, but later they both came back to Missouri. After returning, Scott claimed that by residing in free Minnesota he had become a free man, and he asked a United States court to declare his freedom. Eventually an appeal was taken to the Supreme Court.

The Supreme Court could have decided this case against Scott without any "judicial review" at all. It could have said that inasmuch as Scott had returned with his master to Missouri and was now residing there, his trips to other states were irrelevant. Whether he was a slave or not was a question of property rights to be decided in accordance with the law of Missouri. Thus the Court could have dismissed the case—without giving Scott his freedom, to be sure, but also without saying whether Congress had the constitutional power to outlaw slavery in the territories of the United States.

Instead, the Court went out of its way to try to settle the great political question of the time. Only three years before, the new Republican party had been organized largely to try to stop the expansion of slavery westward. The dominant southern wing of the Democratic party favored unlimited expansion. The issue was bitter: blood had already been spilled over it in Kansas. And now into the midst of this conflict moved the Supreme Court, quite unnecessarily reviewing the Missouri Compromise (already repealed) and finding that it had been unconstitutional. Congress, Taney's opinion said, had no power to outlaw slavery in the territories. (Therefore, a slave would not acquire freedom by going to Minnesota—logical reasoning, perhaps, but needless as far as reaching a decision in Dred Scott's case was concerned, for Scott had gone back into Missouri and resumed his status as a slave.) Even more gratuitously, the Court said that no Negro could ever attain full citizenship in the United States.

The *Dred Scott* opinion did not displease President Buchanan or the Democratic majority in Congress, but it cut northern sentiment to the quick. As we have seen, it led Lincoln publicly to assert that a Supreme Court interpretation of the Constitution was not authoritative or final. He argued this point forcefully in his debates with Senator Douglas in 1858. But his first inaugural, in 1861, was the speech which really illustrated the peril in which the Court had so needlessly placed judicial review. For judicial review rests, finally, on public acceptance, and here was the President of the United States saying that the public need not accept the Court's interpretations.

The Court survived its mistake. During the Civil War, Lincoln was able to appoint several new justices to it, and after the war the Court prudently avoided becoming embroiled in the political conflict over Reconstruction. But the lesson of *Dred Scott* was not forgotten. Often, since then, cases have come before the Court in which, though one party claims that a statute is unconstitutional, the Court declines to pass upon that question. Instead, the justices find that they can decide the case without interpreting the Constitution, because the statute is irrelevant; or they find that there is no real controversy between the parties, or that the controversy is not ripe for decision, or that it does not present a judicial question appropriate for a court to settle. A list of these reasons for not interpreting the Constitution is sometimes described as the Court's "self-denying ordinance," and indeed in such cases the Court is restraining itself and holding its own power in check. It may be doing so, however, not merely out of a sense of modesty or fitness, but also because of an instinct for self-preservation.

*Attacks on the Court.* The Supreme Court has survived political attacks of several kinds. Some were aimed at the justices who happened to be on the bench at the time. Some were aimed at the practice of judicial review. None succeeded in changing the nature of the Court or of its functions.

Congress, under the Constitution, is given several weapons with which to harass the Court if it deeply disapproves of what the Court is doing. First and least important is the power to impeach and remove federal judges. This is not significant, for no member of the Supreme Court has ever been removed—although, to be sure, hot-headed congressmen sometimes are so offended by a justice's opinions that they threaten to bring impeachment proceedings. Second, Congress is responsible for establishing, by statute, all federal courts except the Supreme Court. The power to establish such inferior courts includes the power to staff them, and it has been used once in a thoroughly political context. You will recall that in 1798 and 1799 Thomas Jefferson and his followers were highly critical of the federal courts for their occasionally ferocious enforcement of the Alien and Sedition laws. When Jefferson's Anti-Federalist party came to power, they promptly eliminated many of the judgeships of these inferior federal courts. This got rid of a lot of Federalist judges; it also made life harder for the justices of the Supreme Court, who had to resume the earlier custom of "riding circuit," each justice spending part of his time presiding over an "inferior" trial court.

Third, Congress can decide what jurisdiction the Supreme Court shall have, so long as its decision is consistent with the Constitution. Congress could not validly require the Court to perform nonjudicial duties, but it can forbid the Court to consider certain kinds of judicial controversies. On one occasion, Congress did just this, in order to make sure that one of its statutes should not be struck down. In 1868, while the Court was actually considering a case in which the validity of the Reconstruction Acts was chal-

lenged, Congress hastily passed a law depriving the Court of jurisdiction over the case. (The justices, it appears, were not unhappy
about this for it took them off a very hot spot.) This method was

Fitzpatrick in the *St. Louis Post-Dispatch*

### "Three-horse team" of the future?

The separation of powers created a system that could be portrayed as a team of three equally strong horses, pulling together,
side by side. Franklin D. Roosevelt, coming to the Presidency in
a time of economic emergency, had great influence on Congress
during his first term. At the start of his second term he proposed
to enlarge the Supreme Court. (This cartoon was drawn in March,
1937). Opponents of Roosevelt's plan assumed that the President
wished to dominate the judiciary, and believed that if he succeeded in doing so, the constitutional framework would be drastically altered in the direction of one-man rule.

more vengefully urged in Congress in 1958. The Court had just upheld individual rights in cases concerning congressional investigations, government employment, and the use of FBI files in criminal trials. There was some vehement criticism of all of these decisions, and some congressmen proposed that in the future such cases should be excluded from the jurisdiction of the Supreme Court.

Fourth, the Constitution allows Congress to fix the number of justices who shall compose the Supreme Court. Only once has a serious attempt been made to persuade Congress to use this power for the purpose of influencing actual Court decisions. This happened in 1937. The Court, by votes of five to four or six to three, had struck down half a dozen major statutes enacted during the first term of President Franklin D. Roosevelt. Now the constitutionality of two more statutes, the National Labor Relations Act and the Social Security Act, was being challenged. The majority of the justices had been adhering so firmly to a narrow construction of the interstate commerce clause that it appeared certain that they would find the Labor Relations Act, at least, invalid; and the Social Security Act, too, seemed to be in danger of feeling the judicial axe. Shortly before these cases were decided, however, President Roosevelt urged Congress to allow him to appoint as many as six new members to the Court. This "Court-packing" plan aroused a great political tempest and was eventually defeated. One of the objections to it was that it was "like changing the rules in the middle of the game." Certainly the plan was intended to change the membership of the Court so that the "New Deal" statutes would be upheld. As it happened, while the plan was being debated, the Court decided that the National Labor Relations Act and the Social Security Act were constitutional. These surprising decisions took the steam out of the fight for the President's bill; and the basic reason for the bill's existence disappeared completely soon afterwards, when one of the "old guard" justices retired and Roosevelt was thus able to name his successor.

Clearly, Congress has potential weapons to influence the trend of Court decisions, but is extremely reluctant to use them. Those who object to the Court's behavior sometimes feel, therefore, that their only recourse lies in the process of constitutional amendment. If the Court says that the Constitution prohibits a particular statute, the friends of the statute can always try to amend the Constitution. It is a difficult, long business, but it can be done, and it has been done. The federal income tax was struck down by the Court in 1895; eighteen years later, the Sixteenth Amendment was adopted giving Congress the right to levy such a tax.

One of the criticisms occasionally leveled at the Court and at the practice of judicial review is that the Court is undemocratic and irresponsible. These charges come most strongly when judicial review ends in nullifying statutes which have wide popular support. The critics say that the justices, never having to face reelection, possess too much unrestrained power and, being human, are prone to abuse it. One way to make them responsible to the voters would be to make judicial positions elective, for given terms. This would require a constitutional amendment, for Article III makes federal judgeships appointive for life. Such an amendment was urged in 1924 by the Progressive party, led by Robert M. LaFollette of Wisconsin; but LaFollette was defeated and the movement faded out.[10] The Progressives also unsuccessfully sought constitutional change in the system of judicial review itself. They proposed that Congress should be given the final power to reenact a law which the Court had held to be invalid. This proposal for the "recall of judicial decisions" had been urged earlier, in 1912, by the Progressive party of Theodore Roosevelt and was revived by LaFollette in 1924, again to no avail.

In the political conflicts over the Supreme Court's role, the institutional factor is perhaps the most significant. Many Americans believe that judicial review by an independent court is necessary and so will defend the system even though they disagree with particular judicial decisions. They think that it is necessary because, in their view, both the federal system and the protection of individual rights depend upon it. If the Supreme Court were not the umpire of the federal system, then there would be a struggle for

---

10 Many Americans seem to feel that in order to be impartial, judges *must* have the independence that comes from being appointed for life. They forget that the great majority of judges in the United States—the judges of most state and local courts—are elected for terms of a few years.

power between Congress and the states, and the national government, being the stronger, would usurp all the states' powers. If the justices were facing reelection, they would bend before public opinion and acquiesce when a "tyrannical majority" trampled on minority rights. So the arguments run; and whenever the Court has been under attack, these arguments have been persuasive. But defenders of the Court don't always stop with a logical argument. Emotions are involved as well. The Court has become a symbol of the rule of law as opposed to arbitrary despotism. "The first condition of political freedom," cried an eloquent opponent of Roosevelt's Court-packing bill, "is that we should stick to a regime of law, and not move off the path toward a regime of men. . . . Precisely because we live in a revolutionary period, it is no time to break down confidence in the basic institutions."

So it is that Article III remains unchanged and that challenges to the Court's authority have consistently failed. The fact remains that that authority rests on public acceptance. The justices themselves are aware of this and habitually avoid needless controversy. Frequently, however, they must make decisions that go to the heart of the political conflict. Then they make enemies; but, thus far at least, those enemies have not overcome the public's loyalty to the institutions of the Supreme Court and judicial review.

**The Individual Factor**

The Court-packing fight of 1937, the Progressive demands a quarter-century earlier, and the uproar over the *Dred Scott* decision eighty years before all provide case studies in the politics of judicial review. Once again, like so much of the conflict over federalism, these battles were waged largely in institutional terms. As we have seen, the Court avoided other attacks, but these three it endured instead. It sailed needlessly into the *Dred Scott* tempest and floundered, really, for years thereafter; weathered the Progressive storm with ease; and came triumphantly through the hurricane of 1937, though whether by accident or design no one will ever be quite sure.

Individuals played dramatic roles in all of these incidents. The *Dred Scott* tragedy seems to have got its start in the presidential ambitions of one of the members of the Court, Justice McLean, who was an Ohio abolitionist. The majority were ready to decide the case against Scott on narrow jurisdictional grounds. McLean, however, insisted on writing a separate dissenting opinion, in which he went out of his way to *uphold* the Missouri Compromise and the rights of Negroes as citizens. There was little reason for him, as a judge, to mention these matters, for the majority had not intended to discuss them. There was every reason for him, as an ambitious politician, to seize the opportunity to publish a political pronouncement on the burning issue of his time.

Unfortunately, McLean's dissent inspired Chief Justice Taney to reply in kind. Nearly forty years had passed since Taney had argued for the state in *McCulloch v. Maryland;* through all that period he had been a southerner, a strict constructionist, a believer in states' rights. Now, in his old age, angered at McLean and made unduly confident by the southerners' control of the national government, he decided to settle the slavery question once and for all. This was not the decision of a wise judge, nor, probably, would Taney have made it if he had been younger or had he been spared the irritation caused by McLean. (The significance of McLean's role is doubted by some historians—but the doubters' explanation of the Court's behavior is itself cast in terms of Taney's overweening confidence that his opinion would clinch the southerners' claims.)

The great names of the "recall" movement of the Progressive Era were Theodore Roosevelt and Robert M. LaFollette. The very fact that such famous national leaders supported it gave the movement impetus. Franklin Roosevelt, of course, was decidedly the personal leader of the Court-packing fight of 1937. He would have gone down to quick defeat had not the Court-packing bill been ardently supported by an influential senator, Joseph T. Robinson of Arkansas—and it was widely assumed that Senator Robinson's advocacy was based on the highly personal consideration that the President had promised to appoint him to the Court. When Robinson suddenly died, the bill died too. But, as we have seen, the real reason for Court-packing had already practically disappeared, for the Court had unexpectedly broadened its interpretation of the Constitution and upheld two major acts of Congress. This reversal was accomplished by a change in the opinions of two individuals, Chief Justice Hughes and Justice Owen J. Roberts. Did these men see a broader meaning in the commerce clause as a matter of intellectual conviction? Or did they, especially Roberts, shift their positions in order to thwart the Court-packing plan? Cynics, at the time, explained the change by saying "A switch in time saves nine." Motives are always hard to analyze, and most evidence indicates that self-preservation was not a substantial factor in the "switch" of Hughes and Roberts. But by that switch, those men, whatever their motives, made judicial and political history.

### The Interest Factor

What, then, of the role of interests and interest groups in these political clashes? Did not the line-up, in each contest, really turn not on the nature of the Court, the rightness of judicial review, or the ambitions of individuals, but rather on who liked the Court's decisions and who disliked them?

The answer to that question is a very qualified "yes-and-no." Presumably if there had been no *Dred Scott* case to anger the Republicans, Lincoln would never have suggested that the Court's constitutional interpretations were inconclusive. If Theodore Roosevelt and LaFollette had been content with what the Court did, they would have been less anxious to provide the machinery for undoing it. Franklin Roosevelt and his New Deal cohorts were plainly angered by particular decisions.

The interest line-up, then, depended partially on who stood to gain by change. The northern forces bent on restricting slavery might conceivably have crippled the Court when they took office in 1861 had not secession intervened and focused their attention elsewhere. The Progressives of 1912 were the believers in, or beneficiaries of, those early labor and welfare laws—the ten-hour day, for instance—which seem so picayune today but were so radical then. If those laws were to be struck down by the judiciary, so the Progressives argued, the legislators should have the power to revive them: good laws should stay in force. In the array of forces in 1937, one could expect to find standing with Franklin Roosevelt these same Progressives and their spiritual descendants, increased in strength, now, by the growing labor unions, whose successful fight for existence had been made possible by the New Deal.

To some extent this was, indeed, the line-up. The language of debate might concern the sanctity of the Court or its irresponsibility, the stability afforded by judicial review or its undemocratic nature; but one real issue was, "is the Court for us or against us?" Yet this is far from the whole truth. In 1937, particularly, it became clear that many Americans had a concern for the Court's prestige and were attached to the system of judicial review, even though they disliked the Court's decisions. On this issue Roosevelt, who had swept the country the previous autumn, could not keep his usual followers in line a few months later. The uproar against the Court-packing plan was partly caused, or inspired, by the big business organizations which were satisfied with the Court's decisions and hated the New Deal. They beat the drums for the cause of judicial review, for keeping the Supreme Court, in all its majesty, beyond the reach of politics. They used effective, emotional symbols and slogans. But if the Chamber of Commerce, the National Association of Manufacturers, and the American Liberty League had said nothing at all, there would still have been countless Americans whose objections to the Court-packing plan were based on devotion to the system.

To sum up: the warring factions have a material interest in the particular decisions of the Supreme Court, while a great mass of people, unconcerned with those decisions, have an ideal interest in the independence of the judiciary and the maintenance of judicial review. Numerically this last interest, though quite immeasurable, may well be greater than all the others put together.

# CHAPTER 6

# Freedom of Belief and Expression

The framers of the Constitution met two of the three requirements of constitution-making. They *established* an instrument
of government and they *granted powers* to it. But the third requirement, the one most basic of all to any idea of "constitutionalism" as opposed to tyranny, they did not meet so well. The draft
of the new Constitution which they signed on September 18, 1787,
failed adequately to *limit the power* of the government which
they sought to create. Or, at least, so many of their fellow Americans thought.

Most of the men at Philadelphia assumed that they had prepared a sufficiently limited government. The structure which they
had devised was supposed to prevent despotism. The new national
government was being given new duties, to be sure, but even
so it would perform only those duties expressly delegated to it;
all other governing would still be done by the states, which in
their own constitutions safeguarded the individual liberties of
their citizens. The separation of powers would prevent dictatorship and, as we have seen, the Constitution specifically prohibited
certain forms of injustice. Surely, the framers argued, these were
limitations enough; no one need fear that the national government would become tyrannical.

People did fear it, however, and among those who feared it were people otherwise friendly to the new Constitution. They argued from two major premises. First, they inclined to believe that individual freedom was best secured when government was close at hand; liberty, they thought, was safer when power was centered in the states rather than in some distant national capital. Any transfer of power to the new national government was, therefore, a threat to freedom. Second, they thought that any constitution was incomplete if it lacked a specific "bill of rights," a statement of those liberties which no government should take away and those guarantees of procedural fairness which would protect individuals from arbitrary injustice. State constitutions adopted during the American Revolution included such statements. Surely, if a bill of rights was appropriate in a state constitution, it was more than appropriate—it was necessary—in a charter for a strong national government.

Even before the campaign for the ratification of the new Constitution was fully under way, the friends of the document had recognized the force of these arguments. The framers may not have agreed with their critics, but they realized that without a firm promise to add a bill of rights to the Constitution, there was little or no chance of ratification by the state conventions. Accordingly, they made that firm promise. They agreed that if the Constitution was ratified, they would, in the first Congress, propose appropriate amendments. This promise was kept. James Madison, a key figure at the Philadelphia convention and a leader in the fight for ratification, helped to draft amendments and in 1789, as a representative, introduced them in Congress. Twelve were approved by Congress, and thereafter ten of them were ratified by the requisite number of states. These first ten amendments, generally called the "Bill of Rights," became an operative part of the Constitution on December 15, 1791.

## THE BILL OF RIGHTS

In understanding the significance of the Bill of Rights, the first thing is to know why it is there. This we have learned. It is there as a safeguard against tyranny by the national government. The First Amendment begins: "Congress shall make no law . . ." *Con-*

*gress*—the new *national* legislature. The next seven amendments do not specifically refer to Congress or any other branch of the national government, but they are to be read as if they did. Like the First Amendment, they were intended to limit the national government, not the states. Any possible question about this was settled in 1833, in the case of *Barron v. Baltimore*.[1] In that case, Chief Justice Marshall, speaking for the Supreme Court, declared that the Fifth Amendment afforded people protection only against arbitrary action by the national government and did not protect anyone against any abuse of state or local governmental power. For protection against such abuse by a state or local government, the citizen would have to look to his state constitution.

Second, the Bill of Rights includes two different kinds of provisions. The First Amendment is, in effect, a great affirmative declaration of individual liberty—freedom to worship, speak, publish, and assemble as one likes. The next seven amendments include a fairly long list of somewhat narrower "rights"—primarily, the right to be free from certain annoying types of governmental intrusion and from arbitrary governmental persecution or punishment. These cannot sensibly be considered apart from the First Amendment freedoms, for they provide much of the substance which gives reality to the promise of liberty. A person would not possess any freedom worth having if, despite a constitutional pronouncement that he had the right of free speech, he could be thrown into a dungeon and kept there without a trial the moment he used his right of free speech to criticize the officials of the government. "Procedural safeguards"—the assurance of fairness in the enforcement of the criminal law—are thus more than technical matters of judicial detail; their observance is vital to the *preservation* of liberty.

Third, we must look in passing at the Tenth Amendment, for on its face it is quite different from the others. It does not directly protect individuals against arbitrary governmental action. Rather, it says that of whatever legitimate powers governments may have, the national government can exercise only those which are granted to it by the Constitution; all others remain with the states. Thus

---

1 7 Peters 243 (1833).

it speaks not of liberties and rights, but of federalism: and, indeed, as a statement of the federal principle it has had its historic significance. Yet we may appropriately enough include the Tenth Amendment within the term "Bill of Rights," for it reminds us of the main reason why there was any Bill of Rights in the first place. That reason was fear of the national government. Out of that fear came the Tenth Amendment, just as did the First Amendment and the rest. The framers thought the Tenth Amendment unnecessary because without it the Constitution gave only certain powers to the national government and by implication left the rest with the states. The Tenth Amendment changed that *implied* "reservation of power" into an *express* reservation of power.

Finally, in searching for the present-day meaning of the Bill of Rights we must look behind the first ten amendments and beyond them, too. Behind them was the original Constitution, with those few specific safeguards against despotism and injustice which the framers thought were sufficient. Beyond them, to come into the Constitution seventy-seven years later, was the Fourteenth Amendment. We cannot usefully discuss American freedom and justice today without giving close attention to the Fourteenth Amendment. It was one of the constitutional changes which immediately followed the Civil War, and doubtless its central purpose was to protect the freed Negroes, the former slaves, in the southern states. One clause of the Fourteenth Amendment still seems chiefly to concern the descendants of those freed Negroes and their white neighbors: this, of course, is the clause forbidding any state to deny "equal protection of the laws" to any person within its borders. The "equal protection" clause we will take up in Chapter 8, which will be devoted to the theme of "equality." Here and in Chapter 7, in contrast, we are emphasizing not the equality of rights but the existence and nature of any individual rights which any person in the United States may assert against governmental oppression. The part of the Fourteenth Amendment which concerns us now, therefore, is the clause which protects individuals against deprivation of their liberty by the arbitrary action of state governments—the clause declaring that no state shall "deprive any person of life, liberty, or property without due process of law."

This "due process" clause has a familiar ring. Almost the same language appears in the Fifth Amendment. But, as we have seen, the Fifth Amendment protected the individual only against oppression by the national government. Since 1868, when the Fourteenth Amendment was ratified, the Constitution has afforded the same protection against oppression by any state. And judicial decisions have made it clear that the "liberty" protected by the Fourteenth Amendment includes freedom of worship, speech, press, and assembly.

## THE FIRST AMENDMENT FREEDOMS

### Religious Liberty

Separation of church and state and freedom of worship are the first great principles embodied in the First Amendment. The Pilgrims, so the poet sang, had crossed the perilous Atlantic seeking "freedom to worship God," but that was in 1620. In the intervening years, few of the earliest British colonies in North America had been havens of religious freedom. Quite the contrary. In several colonies, especially in New England, a dominant and intolerant clergy insisted on strict conformity to their own ideas of proper creed and worship. Dissenters were harassed; in the early days, some simply went away, striking into the wilderness and founding new colonies of their own. Thus the Reverend Thomas Hooker, disagreeing on matters of doctrine with his colleagues in Massachusetts, departed thence and settled the first colony in Connecticut. And again the dispiriting cycle was repeated: by the time the colonies became the United States, the ministers of Connecticut were as fearsomely intolerant of religious differences as had been the fire-and-brimstone preachers of Massachusetts.

Not only were they intolerant, they were also powerful. In Massachusetts, Connecticut, and other states, too, the clergy as a class had a dominant voice in political affairs. The link between "the state"—the government—and "the church," of whatever denomination happened to be supreme in a particular state, was often firmly forged. Thomas Jefferson, familiar with colonial history, believed that an "established church" (or "state church"), a religious sect with the power of government behind it, was in itself an enemy of intellectual liberty, freedom of mind and conscience. Accordingly, he took great pride in his authorship of Virginia's "Statute for Religious Freedom," which decreed that in his native commonwealth there should be no established church. It is not surprising that in drafting the First Amendment James Madison began with the same theme, for Madison was Jefferson's disciple.

*Separation of Church and State.* If there ever had been a serious idea of establishing a governmentally backed "national church" in the United States, it was laid to rest by the adoption of the First Amendment. Questions have arisen in recent times, however, concerning the financial relationships between churches and local governments. Can a state, or one of its subdivisions, excuse churches from paying property taxes? The answer is yes. So long as all religions and denominations are treated alike, this does not amount to an "establishment" of religion. More controversial is the furnishing, at public expense, of bus transportation to children attending parochial schools. In many places this has been a hot political issue; in some it has given rise to legal disputes over constitutional questions. In deciding such cases, not only has the Supreme Court been sharply divided, but individual justices seem to be of two minds. For instance, in a parochial school bus case, where taxpayers objected to such a use of public funds as violative of the First and Fourteenth Amendments, Justice Black wrote: "The 'establishment of religion' clause . . . means at least this: Neither a state nor the Federal government can set up a church. Neither can pass laws which aid one religion, aid all religions, or prefer one religion over another. Neither can force nor influence a person to go to or remain away from church against his will or force him to profess a belief or disbelief in any religion. . . . The First Amendment has erected a wall between church and state. That wall must be kept high and impregnable." Then, having stated these general principles, he and the majority of his colleagues decided that the furnishing of bus transportation was essentially a grant of assistance to school children rather than to any school. They therefore rejected the taxpayers' complaint and upheld the expenditure of public funds to pay the children's bus fares, even though this expenditure, as a practical matter, aided the children attending church schools of only one denomination.[2]

When state intervention takes other forms, the judicial answer is hard to predict. For example, some years ago the "released time" program in an Illinois school district was challenged, a public school parent claiming that it breached the constitutional wall between church and state. Under this program, a class period was set aside for religious instruction, which was given in the public school building by various church representatives. (Those children who did not want such instruction simply had a "free period.") The Supreme Court decided, eight justices to one, that such a released time program violated the Constitution.[3] Yet a few years later, by a six to three vote, the Supreme Court declared that a released time program was valid where the children who wanted religious instruction during a regular school day left the school building and received it elsewhere.[4] The difference between these two cases was that in the first the regular classrooms of the public schools were used for religious instruction and in the second they weren't. In view of the judicial language about the vast importance of the "high and impregnable wall" between church and state, critics found such a distinction oddly technical.

Public reaction to these decisions was mild compared to the stir caused by the Supreme Court's holdings in the "school prayer" cases in 1962 and 1963. In the first of these the Court declared that the reciting of a prayer, composed by the New York Board of Regents, during the morning exercises at public schools was unconstitutional because "it is no business of government to compose an official prayer for any group of the American people to recite as a part of a religious program carried on by government." [5] The later decisions [6] forbade public schools to include the reading of the Bible and the Lord's Prayer as part of the exercises, on the

2 *Everson v. Board of Education*, 330 U.S. 1 (1947).

3 *McCollum v. Board of Education*, 333 U.S. 203 (1948).

4 *Zorach v. Clauson*, 343 U.S. 306 (1952).

5 *Engel v. Vitale*, 370 U.S. 421 (1962).

6 *Abington Township v. Schempp*, 83 Sup. Ct. 1560 (1963); *Murray v. Baltimore School Board*, 83 Sup. Ct. 1560 (1963).

ground that while the government should not be hostile to religion it should be neutral, and these readings implied un-neutral support or "establishment" of the Christian faith.

*Freedom of Worship.* The clause which prohibits Congress from interfering with the "free exercise" of religion means that each person has a right to worship as he likes, or not at all. It also means, as we have seen, that such freedom of worship must be permitted not only by Congress, but by the states as well—or at least that the states cannot "unreasonably" interfere with it. Nowadays, only those small sects whose beliefs are shocking to the majority or whose practices are peculiarly offensive are likely to be the objects of repressive legislation. When such legislation is attacked as unconstitutional, the real question seems to be: how seriously offensive or dangerous are the practices of these people? The Supreme Court reads the Constitution as permitting complete freedom of religious *belief;* the difficulties arise when beliefs lead to *actions* which most people deem harmful. Because of the importance of freedom of belief, the Court is obviously reluctant to restrict freedom of action based on such belief except where the harm is great.

Sometimes, to be sure, the harmfulness of the action has seemed great enough to justify suppression of it. Thus many years ago laws prohibiting polygamy were upheld, even though, at that time, plural marriage was a custom consistent with the religious beliefs of a substantial sect, the Church of the Latter Day Saints. Such laws were justified as being proper measures in defense of public morals, although in the eyes of the Mormons of the 1890's they interfered with the "free exercise" of religion. Presumably, today, a local ordinance against public nudity could be enforced against members of a sect who honestly claimed that their religious convictions compelled them to disrobe on the city streets. But where the action is not so shocking or offensive, the Supreme Court is likely to strike down any state statute or local ordinance which forbids it.

One religious group, the "Jehovah's Witnesses," was the subject of considerable repressive legislation in the 1930's and 1940's. Again, this was not because of their private beliefs but because of what they did. In some quarters they made themselves unpopular by publishing violent attacks on another, much larger denomination. Other people were annoyed by their persistent, devoted door-to-door "missionary work." And still others, in a period of world crisis, professed to be alarmed because the "Witnesses" felt compelled by religious belief to refuse to salute the flag of the United States, which they considered an idol or "graven image" which God forbade them to recognize. Therefore, local ordinances were passed, not expressly aimed at the "Witnesses" but obviously intended to restrict their campaigning and their propaganda dissemination; and at about the same time, "Witnesses'" children refused to comply with state statutes requiring all school children to join in the daily pledge of allegiance to the flag.

The Supreme Court upheld the "Witnesses'" claim that they did not have to obey these laws. The local ordinances were held to interfere with the free exercise of religion, primarily because the Court wished to protect actions stemming from religious beliefs just as much as it reasonably could. Ringing doorbells and arguing, even arguing offensively, on sidewalks might be annoying to householders and casual pedestrians, but they were not harmful or dangerous acts, like polygamy. Therefore they could not constitutionally be prohibited. The Court had more trouble with the "flag salute" laws. Here again, however, it ended up on the side of the "Witnesses," holding that the children could not be compelled to join in the pledge of allegiance. This decision was difficult because with war spreading over the world (the cases were decided in 1940 and 1943) a strong argument could be made that a refusal to salute the flag was unpatriotic and harmful to the national interest. The majority of the justices finally decided, however, that such a "lack of patriotism," impelled by religious conviction, was not so harmful and dangerous as to justify punishment.[7]

---

[7] *West Virginia State Board of Education v. Barnette,* 319 U.S. 624 (1943). In contrast, young men who flatly refused to register under the Selective Service Act went to prison, even when they asserted that their refusal was based on religious convictions. There were two factors which made their situation different from the "flag salute" case. First, such refusal, if permitted, could do serious damage to the nation's war effort. Second, the Selective Service Act itself included special provisions for "conscientious (usually religious) objectors" who registered as such; they were compelled to render noncombatant service, but not to fight.

## Freedom of Expression

The right to say what we think is the First Amendment liberty which has been most often under attack, primarily because many people, even a majority, occasionally feel that the expression of particular ideas is dangerous to the security of the country. Before we examine this seeming conflict between individual liberty and national security, however, we should first see what "freedom of expression" does *not* include and then consider why any promise of such freedom is included in the Constitution.

Although we have a right of "free speech" (and "free press" and "free assembly") we do not have any right to utter or publish slander or libels or obscenities without being responsible for the consequences. If we say something slanderous about someone, he can sue us for damages. The same is true if we write something libelous about him. (The basic difference between slander and libel is that the former is spoken, the latter written or published.) And if we go about shouting obscenely, we can be fined or even jailed. These kinds of utterances are not "free speech" as that term is used in the Constitution. Sometimes there are bitter arguments—usually about books or plays—concerning what actually is "obscene" and what is not; but even though courts may hold that a particular book (e.g. *Ulysses*) is not obscene, the general principle remains intact—the principle that libel, slander, and obscenity are not protected by the First Amendment.

What "free expression" *does* mean, above all else, is that we have a right to express our opinions in all areas, including the field of public affairs. We have a right to criticize the existing political, economic, or social system and propose changes in any or all of them. We have a right to dissent from the majority's view and to say things which some people may think wrong and even dangerous. This right to criticize and dissent is not unlimited, as we shall see later in this chapter. Nevertheless, it is the heart of the First Amendment, the great affirmative promise of the Bill of Rights. Why so? What makes it so important?

***The Reasons for Free Speech.*** Some people think of "free speech" as a *natural right,* part of the "unalienable rights (to) . . . liberty" of which Thomas Jefferson wrote in the Declaration of

Independence. If, in your philosophy of life, you give first place to the individual human being, then you may believe that the freedom to think and to express what you think is very important indeed, for without it a person's development, both mental and spiritual, might be cramped and stunted. Almost equally as important as self-expression, you would believe, is the exploration of other people's thoughts—the right to grow intellectually by exchanging ideas and reading what other men have written. These rights, then, to speak and to listen are necessary for a person's self-fulfillment, his full realization of his human potentialities. It was from this kind of reasoning, reflecting a basic faith in the ability of individual human beings to grow in wisdom and virtue, that Jefferson wrote the famous lines which are carved today on the wall of his memorial temple in Washington: "I have sworn on the altar of God, eternal hostility against every form of tyranny over the mind of man."

Other people believe in "free speech" even though they are religious or philosophic skeptics with no high opinion of humanity or optimism about its future. They believe in it because they think it is *the best practical way to approach truth.* This is the usual defense made, today, of "academic freedom," the liberty of teachers and scholars to think and speak as they will—for, it is said, through such free expression and free interchange of ideas have come the great intellectual advances and scientific discoveries of human history. Yet the argument goes far beyond the college walls. Just as free intellectual exchange is good for scholarship and science, so it is good for deciding matters of public policy. The wisest policies can be arrived at—so the argument runs— only after full and unhampered discussion has shown the strength and weakness of every proposal. Probably the most famous statement of this position was that of Justice Holmes, in 1919: "Persecution for the expression of opinions seems to me perfectly logical. If you have no doubt of your premises or your power and want a certain result with all your heart you naturally express your wishes in law and sweep away all opposition. . . . But when men have realized that time has upset many fighting faiths, they may come to believe even more than they believe the very foundations of their own conduct that the ultimate good desired is better reached by free trade in ideas—that the best test of truth is the power of the thought to get itself accepted in the competition of the market, and that truth is the only ground upon which their wishes safely can be carried out. That at any rate is the theory of our Constitution." [8]

There is a third justification for "free speech," much like the second but reached from a different starting point. If you are committed to the *principle of democracy,* of "government by the people," then you must be committed to the principle of free discussion, for, as we saw in Chapter 1, democracy depends on people being able to make informed choices between policies, parties, or candidates. This means that for democracy to exist, there must be a broad opportunity to argue publicly about the issues—to argue and to listen to argument. If bad laws are passed, all is not lost so long as there is a chance to repeal them, and the existence of such a chance depends on people having a right to criticize them. This is the thinking behind the position taken by the late Chief Justice Stone and some other members of the Supreme Court that the First Amendment freedoms occupy a "preferred position"—the topmost position—in the hierarchy of constitutional rights and should be most firmly defended against all governmental attack.

Now you may say that without being a philosophic pragmatist or a democratic judge you believe in "free speech" for a fourth reason, much simpler than the other three. You believe in it because you like to be able to say what you think—it's a free country, isn't it? True enough: but does your satisfaction in being allowed to speak your mind amount to a belief in "free speech"? No, by itself it does not, for the real test is not whether you like to feel free to express *your* ideas, but whether you are willing to have other people express *their* ideas, even when you utterly disagree with them. Most people dislike hearing views expressed which differ sharply from their own. Most people incline to fear new ideas and unfamiliar doctrines. "Free speech" is part of American liberty, but at times in our history the power of government has been used to curtail it, and many people, perhaps most people, have agreed that it should be curtailed. These occasions have usu-

---

8 Holmes, J., dissenting in *Abrams v. United States,* 250 U.S. 616 (1919).

ally coincided with times of internal or international tension, and the intolerance of dissent which typifies them has been based chiefly on fear. In days of real or fancied peril, the faith in civil liberties is put to its severest test, and the limits of the First Amendment freedoms are pricked out by Supreme Court decisions. To these instances of tension and constitutional interpretation we now turn.

Fitzpatrick in the *St. Louis Post-Dispatch*

### As America goes so goes the world

If one views the world struggle as one of competing principles—democracy against totalitarian tyranny—the preservation of civil liberties in the United States is essential to the argument favoring democracy. This cartoon was drawn in 1953, at a time when free speech and free association were under heavy attack by Americans who believed that such freedom endangered the nation's security.

*The Standards for Judgment.* It is the expression and interchange of ideas on public policy, especially in the form of argument, advocacy, or exhortation, that give rise to the central question in many First Amendment cases. When the action of government—the enforcement of a repressive statute—is challenged on the ground that it abridges free expression, someone has got to decide whether such freedom is absolute or may be limited in the interest of the public safety or welfare—and, if so, when it may be limited and how much. The Constitution's language seems absolute: "Congress shall make no law." Yet no American court has ever held that we have complete, unbridled liberty to say whatever we want under any and all circumstances. For at least some statements that would cause harm we can be punished by public authority. The classic example of this was offered long ago by Justice Holmes: "No one has a right falsely to shout 'fire' in a crowded theatre." That seems like obvious common sense. But what if a majority of elected legislators feel that it is "obvious common sense" to punish people for criticizing public officials, for urging disobedience of authority, or for advocating drastic changes in foreign policy, the economic system, or the Constitution? Can they then enact a law making such criticism or advocacy illegal, or does the First Amendment forbid them to do so?

Since 1918, the Supreme Court has had to decide numerous cases involving questions like these. The justices have agreed that freedom of expression is limited and occasionally have held that it is quite strictly limited. Thus they have narrowed the meaning of the broad, flat, prohibitory language of the First Amendment. In another sense, however, they have broadened its meaning. Under the First Amendment, only Congress is expressly forbidden to abridge free expression. Yet since the Supreme Court's decision in *Gitlow v. New York* [9] in 1925, the same prohibition or one very much like it restricts the state legislatures,[10] for in the *Gitlow* case

---

9 268 U.S. 652.

10 All state constitutions also include clauses designed to protect freedom of expression. These, of course, restrict the state legislatures. However, as we saw in Chapter 4, a state law might be upheld by the state court as complying with both the state constitution and the United States Constitution, yet ultimately be struck down by the United States Supreme Court on the ground that it violated the Fourteenth Amendment.

the court said that "free speech" was part of the "liberty" which, under the Fourteenth Amendement, no state can take away without due process of law.[11] Furthermore, judicial interpretation has led to the unquestioned rule that where legislative bodies are forbidden to trespass so, likewise, all governmental authority is forbidden to trespass; whatever free speech cannot be validly curtailed by the legislature cannot be validly curtailed by the executive branch either.

The question, then, is when and how far government can restrict free speech—or, conversely, when we can say what we like and how extreme our expressed views can be. To decide that question different judges, at different times, have sought earnestly for some general rule or formula to guide them. In each case individual freedom has collided with some governmental conception of what is needed for public order or national security. Something has to give—but which, and how much? The judges are the referees in this contest, and they need a rule book. The Constitution's language being too sweeping or vague for their purposes, they have had to make up their own rules. Over the years, at least three judicially created rules or standards have been used by the courts in deciding "free speech" or "free press" cases.

*"Clear and Present Danger."* First to be expressed was the so-called *clear and present danger* rule or test. The question, wrote Justice Holmes for the Supreme Court in 1919, is whether the speech or publication which is made punishable by law in fact "created a clear and present danger of some substantive evil" which the government has a right to prevent.[12] Notice that under this doctrine, words by themselves are not evil; the man who speaks them can be punished only if his saying them makes plainly probable the immediate occurrence of an evil act. There must be

---

11 One school of judicial thought, whose most articulate spokesman was the late Chief Justice Stone, has interpreted the First Amendment as if it began: "Neither Congress nor any State legislature shall make a law abridging freedom of speech. . . ." Other justices believe that the restriction on state action is less direct; they hold that under the Fourteenth Amendment, a state can prohibit free speech if such prohibition is not "arbitrary and unreasonable." The difference is one of emphasis, the justices who follow Stone's lead being readier then the other group to question the legislature's "reasonableness" when the legislature has made a law abridging liberty of expression.

12 *Schenck v. U.S.*, 249 U.S. 47 (1919).

an *obvious* probability that such an act will result from the utterance of the words. It must be clearly likely that such an act will happen *immediately*. And, finally, the utterance of the words must make plainly probable the immediate commission of an *evil act*, the kind of action which government has a right to prohibit. These are the three elements of the clear and present danger rule. Where any one of the three is absent, a person cannot properly be punished for his criticism of authority or even his advocacy of revolution.

Four imaginary examples may illustrate how the clear and present danger rule works. First, suppose Congress makes a law saying that it is a crime to advocate changing the Constitution. John Jones writes an article eloquently urging that there be added to the Constitution a new amendment specifically allowing racial segregation in public schools. The article is published in a national magazine and is highly praised in southern newspaper editorials. Can John Jones be punished? He has broken the law, but is the law valid? Maybe Jones' article will so arouse people that the Constitution will indeed be amended—but does his urging the adoption of such an amendment amount to advocacy which may cause a "substantive evil which Congress has the right to prevent"? Is amendment of the Constitution such a "substantive evil"? Of course it's not. The Constitution itself provides that it can be amended by a specified democratic process. Mr. Jones is not preaching revolution; he is just urging that the amendment be properly introduced and adopted in the usual fashion. It does not matter what kind of amendment he wants; the point is that the Constitution itself permits the proposal of amendments and so, whether the amendments are wise or foolish, their proposal is not an "evil" which Congress can prevent. The law is unconstitutional and John Jones goes free.

Second, suppose a federal statute makes punishable any speech or publication which is designed to weaken or does in fact weaken the armed defenses of the United States. Lee Smith, a world-famous physicist, makes a televised speech advocating that the United States destroy all of its nuclear weapons immediately and stop making any more. He also urges that all nuclear physicists immediately refrain from working for the government. The speech is printed as a pamphlet and is sent to thousands of physicists. Here there is not much question about the "substantive evil" involved: the weakening of the country's defenses is surely something which Congress can rightfully forbid. But is it clearly probable that scientist Smith's speech will result *immediately* in a weakening of the country's defenses? If it is—if, for instance, upon receiving Smith's pamphlet many physicists promptly resign their Atomic Energy Commission and Defense Department jobs—then Smith is guilty. What he said created a clear and present danger of a substantive evil.

Third, suppose that Smith's speech is a little different. Instead of urging physicists promptly to resign their jobs, Smith calls for nuclear disarmament and says that if, within the next six months, Congress and the President fail to provide for such disarmament, then all the physicists should resign. A week later another great physicist, Edward Spiller, hotly answers Smith over a nation-wide television hookup. Did Smith's speech create an obvious likelihood of the *immediate* happening of an evil? Clearly not: Smith may be an influential man, but he has not urged that anything be done at the present moment. He has allowed plenty of time for those who disagree with him to answer him. Hence his speech, advocating action in the future, does not make probable any "present" occurrence. So to punish Smith under the statute would be unconsitutional, for he had a right to say what he did because his speech did not create a "present" (immediate) danger. In this example, you can see the connection between the "clear and present danger" test, which was first stated by Holmes, and the passage from Holmes' dissent in the *Abrams* case, quoted above. This connecting link is the conviction that "the best test of truth is in the competition of the market"—that advocacy even of a substantive evil should be permitted so long as there is time to refute it and to persuade people to pursue a sounder course.

Fourth, suppose that the immediate resignation of all nuclear physicists is advocated not by the great scientist, Smith, but by Bert Robinson, a twenty-one-year-old who has just flunked out of college. Robinson has little money and makes no speech; he prints his ungrammatical, misspelled message on a hand-printing press and sends the handbills to a few government physicists whose names he has read in scientific journals. Can Robinson be punished? The "evil" is substantial; there is also a demand for immediate or "present" action. But is it *clear* that Robinson's advocacy is likely to result in any action at all? There does not seem to be any reasonable likelihood that anything bad will happen, so Robinson, however wrong his views and his intentions, goes free.

Remember these four examples, and be ready to refer back to them as we proceed to analyze other judicial "standards" for deciding free speech cases. The results here have come from applying the clear and present danger rule; but the application of different rules or standards might lead to different outcomes. And the Supreme Court has not, by any means, always based its decisions on the clear and present danger rule.

*"Bad Tendency."* On the contrary, for a decade or more the majority of the justices applied what has come to be known as the *"bad tendency" test,* first articulated in 1925 in the aforementioned case of *Gitlow v. New York* and made more explicit two years later in *Whitney v. California.*[13] Under this standard, a person could be punished if what he said or published made the occurrence of an evil more likely than it otherwise would have been. The prosecution did not need to show that the speech or pamphlet made evil action clearly probable or that such evil action would take place immediately. A man could be convicted if his remarks *tended toward* the commission of a wrongful act. Under this bad tendency standard, freedom of discussion is limited much more strictly than under the clear and present danger rule.

To grasp the difference between the results of applying one standard or the other, look back to our four examples. In the first one, where the alleged "evil" was peaceable amendment of the Constitution, the accused man went free when the clear and present danger rule was applied. So would he go free under the bad tendency rule, and for the same reason: the alleged "evil" was not a wrong which Congress had any right to prevent.

The second example was that of physicist Smith, violating a statute by demanding that all physicists promptly leave the gov-

13 274 U.S. 374 (1927).

ernment service. We found that under the clear and present danger rule he might well have gone beyond his First Amendment rights. The question would depend on the circumstances: the extent of Smith's influence, the impact of his speech, and how likely it was that the speech would promptly disrupt the defense program. But under the "bad tendency" test, such considerations would be irrelevant. Under that standard, the statute could be enforced against Smith because Smith's speech pointed toward the weakening of the national defense.

The third example makes the contrast sharper. There, Smith urged physicists to quit after six months unless nuclear disarmament was undertaken in the meantime. The danger not being "present" or immediate, Smith would not be convicted under the clear and present danger test. But under the bad tendency standard, he would have had no right to say what he did. The fact that the action which he urged was not to take place for half a year would not excuse him.

Again, in the fourth example, one standard would lead to the acquittal of Robinson, the young "square," and the other would lead to his conviction. Robinson, a person of no influence, could not by his advocacy make "clearly probable" that what he advocated would happen; but his handbill, giving even a tiny push in the direction of the proscribed "evil," would run afoul of the bad tendency rule.

*"Balancing the Interests."* The bad tendency test, as we shall see, came to seem too restrictive of free expression. Conversely, at least to some justices, the clear and present danger rule seemed too broad; and others thought it just a catchy phrase without definite meaning. Beginning in 1951, the Court tended increasingly to develop a *balance of interest* approach. There is a national interest in the maintenance of order or the security of the state. There is an individual interest in freedom of expression. So suppression of free expression is bad, unless permitting it would be worse. Until the early 1960's, a majority of the justices usually gave the state's interest the edge, for two reasons: (1) The legislature had decided that suppression was desirable or necessary, and judges should give great weight to the legislature's judgment. (2) Most of these cases involved prohibition of Communist state-

ments or activity, and the danger of Communism made the state's security a paramount interest. On these points the dissenters (usually Chief Justice Warren and Justices Black, Brennan, and Douglas) answered in substance that (1) the legislators had less discretion in this field than in others, for they were forbidden by the Constitution to make any law abridging freedom of expression; and (2) while the Communist danger in the form of foreign hostility was real, in the form of domestic revolution it was either insignificant or conjectural.

*The Use of the Standards.* The First Amendment was 128 years old before the Supreme Court had to decide whether it had been violated by either a law of Congress or the enforcement of a law against particular defendants. A series of prosecutions occurred during World War I, under extremely repressive statutes prohibiting speech or publication interfering with recruiting or impairing the war effort. With the first three of these cases to come before them, most of the justices had little difficulty. They began by assuming that the interest of national security was paramount, especially in wartime. This assumption led naturally to a holding that the statutes were valid and the defendants (who had spoken against our participation in the war) properly convicted. Oddly, it was in one of these cases, *Schenck v. U.S.,* that Holmes first gave expression to the standard most favorable to civil liberties—the clear and present danger test. At that time, clearly, Holmes did not think that he was devising a standard of judgment. He was merely coining a felicitous phrase. He was writing a majority opinion, upholding the conviction of a Socialist whose statements had not, in fact, had any significant adverse effect on the war effort. Actually, if we analyze *Schenck* and the other World War I cases in the light of the three standards which we have considered, they seem to have been decided on the basis of the bad tendency test, or something very much like it.

This bad tendency test, as we have seen, was suggested in the *Gitlow* decision in 1925 and was made even more explicit in *Whitney v. California* in 1927. For at least a decade and a half after 1919, a Supreme Court majority, putting order and safety (even in peacetime) first, used the bad tendency rule and narrowed the scope of the First Amendment freedoms.

Meanwhile, however, the clear and present danger notion was being kept alive by its creator and his colleague, Justice Louis D. Brandeis. Six months after upholding the conviction of Schenck, Holmes voted against upholding the conviction of another insignificant "agitator," Abrams, and wrote the first of his famous dissenting opinions on the subject of civil liberties. "Clear and present danger," the casual phrase used to help justify Schenck's conviction, was quickly transformed by Holmes and Brandeis into a significant test—a test which eventually was to sway the balance in favor of First Amendment freedoms. So through the 1920's, these two justices disagreed with their colleagues, seizing every opportunity to expound the clear and present danger rule and to urge its adoption as a standard of judicial decision.

Holmes had died before "clear and present danger" came into its own, but Brandeis was still alive. The change came in the middle or late 1930's. New faces on the Court since the *Gitlow* days, especially Chief Justice Hughes and Justices Stone and Cardozo, contributed to the change; later there came to the bench other men devoted to civil liberties, Justices Black, Douglas, Murphy, and Rutledge. Through the late 1930's and most of the 1940's, the First Amendment received a broad interpretation, and freedom of expression was given the greatest judicial protection in our history.

The heyday of the clear and present danger test and the broad interpretation of the First Amendment ended with the decision in *Dennis v. U.S.*[14] in 1951. There had been changes in Court personnel; changes, too, in the climate of public opinion. New justices gave first place to the national security interest; some of the older justices, influenced by the threats inherent in the "cold war" with the Soviet Union, gave added weight to that interest. Dennis and his ten co-defendants, the top national leaders of the Communist party of the United States, were convicted of "conspiring to advocate" the violent overthrow of the government, in violation of a law which Congress had passed in 1940, a law commonly known as the Smith Act. The defendants appealed, contending that the Smith Act was unconstitutional or that, at the very least, its application to them deprived them of their First

14 341 U.S. 494 (1951).

Amendment rights. Their appeal was first heard by the U.S. Court of Appeals, presided over by Judge Learned Hand. Judge Hand upheld the Smith Act on the ground that the "gravity of the evil" (attempted revolution) which it sought to prevent justified the action of Congress, even when that "gravity" was "discounted by the improbability" that the attempted revolution would occur. In the Supreme Court, Chief Justice Vinson expressly adopted the same rationale for reaching the same conclusion, pointing out that the "improbability" of an effort forcibly to overthrow the government should not be taken for granted, in view of the known subservience of American Communists to the rulers of the Soviet Union. Dissenting were Justices Black and Douglas, who insisted that the clear and present danger test should be applied. They agreed that a "substantive evil" was involved, but they argued that the danger of such an evil's occurring was not "clear"— for the Communist party was very small and very unpopular—and was even less immediate or "present," as there was no evidence that the defendants were planning prompt revolution.

The *Dennis* case seemed to be a landmark, establishing the dominance of the national security interest over the individual liberty interest at least in cases involving communism or Communists. Yet, six years later, its significance was drastically and unexpectedly diminished by the Supreme Court itself. A group of leaders of the Communist party of California were indicted on charges generally similar to those in the *Dennis* case. The Supreme Court set aside most of their convictions, in *Yates v. U.S.*[15] In the course of its opinion, the Court drew a distinction between punishable advocacy "in a context of action," and advocacy which was essentially an expression of views and an attempt to persuade people to agree with such views, without any action immediately in prospect. The Court held that the trial judge had erred in failing to make this distinction clear to the jury. Critics, studying the *Yates* decision, concluded that in 1957 the Court wished to narrow the impact of the *Dennis* precedent. They noted that in *Yates*, no mention was made of the gravity of the evil doctrine. Furthermore, the Supreme Court seemed to be heading back toward the clear and present danger rule, for its opinion emphasized the lack

15 354 U.S. 298 (1957).

of immediacy of whatever violence might have been contemplated by Mrs. Yates and her co-defendants.

In two cases decided on the same day in 1961, the Court continued to be split on the question of what the government can do to control or suppress Communism. In *Communist Party v. Subversive Activities Control Board*,[16] the Court held that the registration requirements of the Subversive Activities Control Act of 1950 were not repugnant to the First Amendment and that an order of the Subversive Activities Control Board declaring the Communist party to be a Communist-action organization and requiring it to register with the Attorney General was properly made and constitutional. Chief Justice Warren and Justices Black, Douglas, and Brennan dissented. In *Scales v. U.S.*,[17] a prosecution for violation of the membership clause of the Smith Act, the Court, with the same dissenters, held that knowing and active membership in an organization engaged in illegal advocacy of the violent overthrow of the government could be punished, because such membership constituted a sufficiently close relationship to the criminal activity of actual advocacy as to render a member responsible for the acts of the organization.

To sum up: we are free to express our opinions and even to urge that unpopular or unwise action be taken, unless the action is something which the government has a right to prevent and unless what we say (1) creates an obvious danger that this evil action will promptly happen or (2) makes the happening of the evil action more probable.

Whether (1) or (2) is applied depends upon whether, at a given time, a majority of the Supreme Court prefers the clear and present danger test or the bad tendency test. It is possible that, instead of invoking either test, the Court might adopt the method used in the *Dennis* case, allowing speech to be restricted and punished when the action sought is very evil indeed and not wholly unlikely, but upholding freedom of speech when the action sought is not so very evil or seems wholly improbable. In any event, to be punishable the speech must be designed to lead to action; the government has no right to curtail mere speculative discussion.

---

16 367 U.S. 1 (1961).
17 367 U.S. 203 (1961).

WE SHOULD BE ETERNALLY VIGILANT...

SUPREME COURT DECISIONS

CALIFORNIA COMMUNISTS

JOHN STEWART SERVICE

JOHN T. WATKINS

PAUL M. SWEEZY

Fitzpatrick in the *St. Louis Post-Dispatch*

### In the tradition of Justice Holmes

The case of the "California Communists" was the *Yates* case, apparently limiting the restrictive impact of *Dennis v. U.S.* At the same time, the Court ordered the reinstatement of J. S. Service, a State Department official who, although cleared six times by various investigating boards, had been fired as a possible "security risk." It also put some limits on the power of legislative investigators to question people about their political beliefs and associations, in the *Sweezy* and *Watkins* decisions; the latter is discussed in Chapter 13.

## Freedom of Press and Assembly

The First Amendment's affirmation of the rights to publish freely and "peaceably to assemble" is subject to the same qualifications as its promise of the right of free speech. Publication is obviously one way of disseminating one's ideas, different from delivering an oration but entitled to similar protection. The recurring publication of newspapers or journals, however, does give rise to a question of a kind rarely involved in free speech cases. If a weekly newspaper regularly prints material so slanderous or treasonable as to forfeit its claim to the protection of the First Amendment, can a government suppress that newspaper? Can it forbid the publication of future numbers, or must it wait for the newspaper to appear and only then prosecute the publisher? This question came before the Supreme Court in 1931. Under a state law, the further publication of a scurrilous and defamatory weekly was forbidden. The Supreme Court held, however, that such suppression, in advance of publication, was an arbitrary denial of "liberty." [18] This judicial disapproval of "prior restraints" was extended to the free speech field, too, in *Thomas v. Collins*,[19] where a law requiring a union organizer to obtain a permit before making a speech was held invalid.

The case of the union organizer also served as a reminder of the intimate relationship between the freedoms of expression and the right "peaceably to assemble"—in other words, the freedom to join organizations. In 1958, an opinion by Justice Harlan pointed out how these liberties are, in practical meaning, indivisible. The case arose from the refusal of the National Association for the Advancement of Colored People to obey an order of a state court requiring it to divulge its membership lists. For the Supreme Court, Justice Harlan wrote: "Effective advocacy of both public and private points of view, particularly controversial ones, is undeniably enhanced by group association, as this Court has more than once recognized by remarking upon the close nexus between the freedoms of speech and assembly. *De Jonge v. Oregon*, 299 U.S. 353, 364; *Thomas v. Collins*, 323 U.S. 516, 530. It is beyond debate that freedom to engage in association for the advancement of beliefs and ideas is an inseparable part of the 'liberty' assured by the due process clause of the Fourteenth Amendment, which embraces freedom of speech. . . . In the domain of these indispensable liberties, whether of speech, press, or association, the decisions of this Court recognize that abridgement of such rights, even though unintended, may inevitably follow from varied forms of governmental action. . . . Compelled disclosure of affiliation with

---

18 *Near v. Minnesota*, 283 U.S. 697.
19 323 U.S. 516 (1945).

groups engaged in advocacy may constitute [an] effective restraint on freedom. . . ." [20] As this language suggests, the Supreme Court decided in favor of the NAACP and the "free enjoyment of the right to associate."

This chapter on the "First Amendment freedoms" does not pretend to cover all the issues and all the judicial decisions concerning individual liberty of conscience and expression. Such issues arise in many guises and in great numbers. This is inevitable, for at the heart of them is the age-old conflict between man and the state. As long as democracy endures, that conflict will continue; men will find that their freedom is never wholly secure against the harsh authority of government and at the same time will acknowledge that the state itself may not be secure against those who, unhindered, preach treason. Insofar as the United States, as a democracy and a "land of liberty," is committed to preserving free expression, that commitment itself can have real meaning only if Americans generally are aware of it. Nor can their awareness stop with the First Amendment. A constitutional right to criticize the government would be a hollow pretense if the government could nevertheless punish or destroy its critics. Protection against arbitrary punishment must be coupled with any affirmation of individual freedom. The two go together. Remember this as you read the next chapter on the procedural safeguards provided by the Constitution; keep in mind that it is dealing not with a separate topic, but with another phase of the general subject of constitutional liberties. You may be reminded of this when you note that our discussion of "the politics of freedom" does not appear here at the end of this chapter, but instead forms the concluding part of the next one. For the practice of freedom is confirmed by the Constitution not only in the First Amendment but also in subsequent sections of the Bill of Rights.

---

[20] *NAACP v. Alabama,* 356 U.S. 449 (1958). Apparently, however, disclosure can be compelled if the purpose of the inquiry is to expose subversion, particularly Communist subversion.

CHAPTER 7

# The Procedural Safeguards

## THE SIGNIFICANCE OF FAIR PROCEDURE

When you buy a house, you are quite likely to borrow some of the money you need to pay for it. Probably you will borrow from a bank. You will give to the bank your "promissory note," your promise to repay the loan at a stated time. But unless your name is Rockefeller, that note of yours by itself is not worth much to the bank. The bankers don't know whether you'll ever pay up or not. You might go broke, or run off to Brazil. So the bank insists on something as "security" for the payment of its loan to you. You therefore give them a mortgage on your house. This means that if you don't pay up, the bank can take your house and sell it, keeping enough of the proceeds of the sale to repay your loan and giving the rest, if any, to you.

As indicated above, one way of looking at the First Amendment is to view it as a great "promissory note"—our promise to ourselves and our posterity that Americans shall be free to worship, speak, and publish as they wish. The "security" which makes that promise reasonably effective is found in other parts of the Constitution—those provisions which protect accused persons, defendants, from arbitrary injustice. Look well, especially, at the Fourth, Fifth, Sixth, and Seventh Amendments. Mostly they have to do with procedure in criminal cases and so can be called "procedural

154

safeguards." Think twice before you fall into the tempting habit of calling them "*mere* procedural safeguards," for as Justice Frankfurter has truly said, they are "rights which the courts must enforce because they are basic to our free society," and, in Justice Black's words, "the people of no nation can lose their liberty so long as a Bill of Rights like ours survives and its basic purposes are conscientiously interpreted, enforced, and respected."

## THE NATURE OF "DUE PROCESS"

The "due process" clause appears in both the Fifth Amendment and the Fourteenth, and provides the over-all, general assurance that in any jurisdiction in the land, nobody who falls into the "toils of the law" will be punished without a fair trial. The clause comes down to us from centuries of English history: its progenitor was the Latin phrase *per legem terrae,* or "by the law of the land." It is the assertion of the *supremacy of law.* Where law is supreme, no tyrant can punish his enemies arbitrarily, merely because he dislikes them. They can be punished only if they have broken an existing law and are found guilty in proceedings which conform with law. This was a radical, revolutionary notion even in England three and a half centuries ago. King James the First thought it preposterous. He was the ruler: why shouldn't he rule as he saw fit? All his subjects, he told his chief justice Edward, Lord Coke, were "under the King." Yes, said Lord Coke; but he added defiantly that the King himself was "under God and the Law."

What, then, is "due process of law"? Elsewhere we examine the question of whether a legislature, in enacting a statute regulating business practices, violates "due process." Here, we are considering the procedural rights of individuals before tribunals, usually courts. In both instances, "due process" has one common denominator. It connotes basic *reasonableness, fairness, the absence of arbitrary, whimsical action by officials of government.*

In cases of criminal prosecution, this has been refined a bit by the judges, but the idea remains essentially the same. Someone is found guilty of a crime. Sent to prison, he complains that he is being deprived of his liberty without due process of law. What must he prove, to support this claim? He must show that in some essential respect, the conduct of the prosecution was arbitrary or his trial was unfair and his conviction unjust. The Supreme Court has often tried to make the meaning of "due process" plain. For instance, "by due process of law is meant one which, following the forms of law, is appropriate to the case, and just to the parties to be affected. It must be pursued in the ordinary mode prescribed by law; . . . whenever it is necessary to the protection of the parties, it must give them an opportunity to be heard respecting the justice of the judgment sought." [1] Pointed more directly to due process for defendants in criminal cases are the words of Justice Black: "From the popular abhorrence of illegal confinement, torture and extortion of confessions . . . evolved the fundamental idea that no man's life, liberty or property be forfeited as criminal punishment . . . until there had been a charge fairly made and fairly tried in a public tribunal free of prejudice, passion, excitement and tyrannical power. Thus, as assurance against ancient evils, our country, in order to preserve 'the blessings of liberty,' wrote into its basic law the requirement, among others, that the forfeitures of lives, liberties or property of people accused of crime can follow only if procedural safeguards of due process have been obeyed. . . . Under our constitutional system, courts stand against any winds that blow as havens of refuge for those who might otherwise suffer because they are helpless, weak, outnumbered, or because they are nonconforming victims of prejudice and public excitement." [2] The most quoted single phrase summing up the concept of "due process" appeared in the opinion in *Palko v. Connecticut*,[3] where Justice Benjamin N. Cardozo spoke of it as protecting those rights which are "of the very essence of a scheme of ordered liberty."

Now all this language has some meaning, but it can mean different things to different people. For instance, assume that a man goes on trial after the local newspaper has been filled with interviews with people who claim to have seen him commit a crime.

---

1 Field, J., in *Hagar v. Reclamation District*, 111 U.S. 701 (1884).
2 *Chambers v. Florida*, 309 U.S. 227 (1940).
3 302 U.S. 319 (1935).

Only one of the people interviewed appears as a witness in court. The members of the jury have read the local paper. If they find the defendant guilty, has he had a fair trial? Or was the jury so hopelessly prejudiced, before any evidence was presented, that the proceedings lacked "due process of law"? Again, a poor man is arrested and put on trial. He cannot afford to hire a lawyer, and the court does not offer him an attorney free of charge. So he acts as his own lawyer, defends himself incompetently, and is convicted. Was the trial so "unfair" as to be unconstitutional, or wasn't it? In other words, *just what is* essential to "a scheme of ordered liberty"?

This question has troubled judges for many years. Like all of us, they want the law to be certain and equal; more than the rest of us, they feel an obligation to make it so. Yet, obviously, in due process cases, what one judge will consider harmlessly irregular another may deem essentially unjust. So courts differ with each other and within themselves, and their decisions inevitably depend in part on the personal philosophy and outlook of individual judges. To violate the due process clause, Justice Frankfurter has implied, the conduct of the prosecution or the trial court must be such as to "shock the conscience." [4] For good or evil, consciences differ. Some are tender and some are tough. What "shocks the conscience" of one man—and a judge, after all, is a man—will leave his brother unshocked and undisturbed. Fortunately, judges are trained to use precedents in deciding cases, so what was considered shockingly unfair in one case will probably be held to be shockingly unfair in a later one with similar facts. Nevertheless, no two cases are exactly alike; and it must be recognized that the nature of "due process" often depends on the subjective judgment of the men who happen to form a majority of the Supreme Court at a given time. This subjective, personal element is inevitable even though the justices make a conscious effort to subordinate their own feelings. They try, as Justice Frankfurter has said, to apply "the impersonal standards (of fairness and justice) of society which alone judges, as the organs of Law, are empowered to en-

---

[4] *Rochin v. California,* 342 U.S. 165 (1952).

force." [5] But what even those "impersonal standards of society" really are is a subject upon which individuals can and do differ.

Most procedural "due process" questions arise under the Fourteenth Amendment, out of trials in the state courts. There are two reasons for this. First, numerically the state courts try many more criminal cases than do the federal courts. Second, defendants in federal courts can invoke other more specific procedural safeguards provided by the Bill of Rights rather than the somewhat vague "due process" clause. We will examine these specific safeguards in a moment. They include the right to counsel, the right not to testify against one's self, the right to jury trial; but under the United States Constitution, these rights are protections only against the federal government. In contrast to the specific guarantees in the Fourth, Fifth, Sixth, Seventh, and Eighth Amendments, the Fourteenth Amendment, which restrains the state governments, uses only the broad language of "due process of law." And so although in federal cases the aggrieved defendant can point to a host of more definite, concrete safeguards, in state cases the only way in which he can invoke the United States Constitution is by claiming a lack of due process. (He can also, of course, invoke the constitution of the state where he is tried.)

Questions have often arisen as to the relationship between the specific safeguards of the Bill of Rights and the "due process" clause of the Fourteenth Amendment. In 1947, Justice Hugo L. Black made a strong argument to the effect that the Fourteenth Amendment was designed to give to defendants in state courts *all* of the procedural guarantees afforded to defendants in federal courts. Three of his colleagues agreed with Justice Black, but five disagreed—and the five, of course, won the day. They believed that the Fourteenth Amendment did not automatically provide a state defendant with the right to counsel, jury trial, etc., but rather guaranteed him only what might be "essential justice" in his particular case. This was the decision of the Supreme Court in *Adamson v. California*,[6] and it seems to have settled the matter.

---

5 Frankfurter, J., concurring in *Louisiana ex rel. Francis v. Resweber*, 329 U.S. 459 (1947).
6 332 U.S. 46 (1947).

## THE DEFENDANT'S RIGHTS UNDER THE FEDERAL CONSTITUTION

So, then, let us take up what the Constitution does say about a defendant's rights in the federal courts, and see which of these, and to what extent, are so "essential" as to be Fourteenth Amendment safeguards against injustice in state courts as well. In making this analysis, we must bear in mind that despite our concentration on the federal Bill of Rights and the Fourteenth Amendment, in practice the ordinary defendant gets his effective protection from the constitution and statutes of the state in whose court he is tried. In the great majority of cases, these fix the procedure in his trial. Only in the comparatively rare instance does he claim that that procedure violates the United States Constitution. The states make substantial provision for fundamental fairness in criminal trials: for example, they provide for trial by jury, prescribe the steps to be taken in informing the defendant of the charges against him, and preserve the defendant's right to confront and cross-examine the witnesses against him. So when we speak of "the defendant's rights," we should remember that most criminal defendants, being charged with violation of state law and tried in a state court, have their rights preserved by state constitution or statute.

Nevertheless, occasionally a convicted man, claiming that the actual procedure in his trial was unfair and deviated from due process of law, appeals to the highest state court, loses there, and then appeals to the United States Supreme Court. Likewise in rare but significant instances, a procedural rule formally prescribed by a state constitution or statute is challenged as being in conflict with the Fourteenth Amendment. In both these situations, the United States Supreme Court must decide whether the United States Constitution has been violated. As the United States Constitution is the subject of our present study, let us examine the nature and extent of the protection offered by that national charter to the man accused of crime. Let us look at the various questions in the order that they arise as a criminal case unfolds, from the original arrest to the imposition of sentence. We know that human beings are fallible and that a basic purpose of government is to provide security and safety for the citizens. Therefore, criminals must be firmly prosecuted and punished. But we have also seen that if a people is to remain free, the prosecution of persons charged with crime must be fair and just.

## Arrest and Confinement

A person can be arrested only when there is some good reason to suspect that he has broken a law—a law that exists at the time he allegedly broke it. As we have seen, *"ex post facto* laws," both state and federal, are outlawed by the Constitution. You cannot properly be arrested for doing something which was lawful when you did it, even though since that time a statute has made it illegal.

Now suppose that you are arrested properly enough (you are innocent, but it looks as though you had committed a crime), and you are put in a cell in the local jail and simply left there. What can you do about it? If you can ever get an attorney to help you, or even a piece of paper to write on, you can prepare an application for a *writ of habeas corpus.* This is the historic common-law corrective for arbitrary imprisonment. As we have seen, it is a court order directing whatever official holds you in custody to produce you in court and to justify, if he can, your continued confinement. When a writ of habeas corpus is issued, the question is not whether you are guilty. The question is whether you are properly confined or have been jailed for no good reason. The judge may find that your arrest and confinement were wholly arbitrary and set you free. Or he may find the other way and return you to the custody of your jailer.

Habeas corpus is a powerful element in the rule of law and the maintenance of freedom. One of the most horrifying things in a totalitarian tyranny, as anyone who has read or seen *The Diary of Anne Frank* will realize, is the midnight rap on the door, the entry of the secret police and the speedy disappearance of their victims into concentration camps or death houses. In a free society, the rights that have persisted for centuries—those of the arrested man to seek the writ and of the judge to issue it—are bulwarks against such horrors. For the existence of such rights has created habits and expectations and assumptions—including a general reliance on the fairness of the courts—which restrain the police and are often fully shared by the police themselves. The use of habeas corpus can be suspended only in times of rebellion or invasion, the latter term being deemed to include war whether or not enemy troops are on our soil.

But, you may ask, what good is habeas corpus if an arrested man is simply held incommunicado, without any opportunity to consult a lawyer or petition the court? This does happen: suspects are "picked up" and sometimes questioned for hours, even for days. But the *implication* of the right to habeas corpus is that extended confinement and questioning, without any formal charges being made, is unjust and wrong—in other words, it is inconsistent with due process of law. And the Supreme Court in recent years has grown increasingly insistent that the period for which the suspect is held helpless by the police must be short. Perhaps the sharp awareness of how totalitarian police methods are an essential element of tyranny has made the court readier to restrict the leeway of the police in free America.

## The Charges

People accused of violating a federal criminal statute have the right, under the Sixth Amendment, "to be informed of the nature and cause of the accusation" before they go on trial. This protection, obviously necessary if the trial is to be fair, likewise covers persons accused of a crime by a state, not because of the Sixth Amendment but because of the due process clause of the Fourteenth and also, of course, because of a state constitutional provision or law. If you don't know exactly what offense you are charged with, how can you possibly defend yourself? And so either the Sixth or the Fourteenth Amendment is violated if a person is forced to defend himself against vague and uncertain accusations. The vagueness may crop up in the charges as framed by the prosecution or may be inherent in the law which the defendant is accused of breaking. For instance, one Lanzetta was accused of violating a state statute making it a crime to be a "known . . . member of any gang of two or more persons." The Supreme Court ordered Lanzetta's conviction under this statute to be set aside because the statute was "so vague, indefinite, and uncertain that it must be condemned as repugnant to the due process clause" of the Fourteenth Amendment.[7] If the statute had been not a state law but an Act of Congress, the Court would presumably have held that it violated the specific requirements of the Sixth Amendment.

Criminal prosecutions formally begin with the filing, in an appropriate court, of the charges against an accused man. These are included either in an "indictment" or an "information." An *indictment* ordinarily is made by a *grand jury*. The latter is a body of from twelve to twenty-three persons to whom the government's prosecuting attorney ordinarily presents a draft of a "bill of indictment" against someone suspected of crime. Meeting behind closed doors, the grand jury hears such evidence as the prosecutor presents or as it requests him to present. The suspect may himself be brought in to testify or may request to be heard, although often he is unaware of the fact that the grand jury is hearing evidence against him. The grand jury may find that there is sound reason for putting the suspected person on trial. It does so by a vote of at least twelve grand jurors that the "bill of indictment" is a "true bill." After such a vote, the indictment is presented to the court and the suspect becomes a defendant. In contrast to this historic precedure is the commencement of a criminal case by an *information,* a statement of the charges drawn up by the prosecutor and supported by sworn statements tending to show that there are reasonable grounds for putting the accused on trial. In some states an information is issued only after examination of the witnesses by a magistrate or a judge in court; if you have ever perused the "Perry Mason" stories of Erle Stanley Gardner, you will have noticed that Perry Mason, as defense attorney, often wins his most spectacular victories not at a trial before a jury, but in these preliminary hearings where the question is whether his client shall be committed for trial.

The Fifth Amendment specifically provides that, with certain exceptions for the military, no one shall be tried for a "capital or otherwise infamous crime" unless a grand jury has first issued an indictment. Today, essentially, this means that you cannot be tried for murder (a "capital crime" because the guilty man could

---

[7] *Lanzetta v. New Jersey,* 306 U.S. 451 (1939).

be executed—in ancient days, beheaded or "decapitated") in a federal court without first being indicted. However, there are very few trials for murder in federal courts. Murderers on the high seas are tried there, but most murders are committed on dry land, within some particular state, and so almost all murder trials are held in state courts. As we have seen, the Fifth Amendment restrains only federal action. Does the due process clause of the Fourteenth Amendment prevent states from trying persons for murder without an indictment? The Supreme Court has held that it does not.[8] The Court felt that there was nothing "essentially unjust" in California's starting the proceedings by the filing of an information rather than summoning a grand jury to indict the accused.

## The Trial

*The Tribunal.* Under the Sixth Amendment, an accused person has the right to a "speedy" and "public" trial. "Speedy," of course, does not mean "instantaneous"; months usually elapse between arrest and trial, the delay often being requested by the accused's lawyer in order to give him time to prepare his defense. But unnecessary and protracted postponement by the government is forbidden. It is forbidden in federal prosecutions by the Sixth Amendment, and in state prosecutions not only by state constitutional provisions but by the due process clause of the Fourteenth Amendment—for lengthy imprisonment without trial is open to the same kind of criticism as prolonged imprisonment for questioning before arraignment.

The requirement that the trial be "public" is made binding on the federal courts by the Sixth Amendment and ordinarily on the state courts by the Fourteenth (as well as, again, by state constitutions and laws). However, there have been peculiarly unpleasant state trials, usually involving sex crimes, when the judge has cleared the courtroom of all merely curious spectators. Under such circumstances this action by the judge did not deprive the defendants of due process.

The due process clauses of the Fifth and Fourteenth Amend-

---

8 *Hurtado v. California,* 110 U.S. 516 (1884).

ments give to every accused person, whether in a federal or a state court, the right to a fair trial. This, as we have seen, is the central meaning of "due process." The real question is, what are the elements of fairness and unfairness? It is sometimes pretty easy to find that a trial is unfair because it is held in a place, or before a particular judge or jury, under conditions which make fairness just about impossible. In prohibition days, for example, there were so many violations of both federal and local "dry" laws that some states established special tribunals for the sole purpose of trying bootleggers. One of these state laws provided that such cases should be tried by a special judge who would be allowed to pocket a percentage of the court costs, assessed to the defendant whenever the latter was found guilty. The temptation to which this exposed the special judge was so obvious and made the chance of an impartial trial so slim that the Supreme Court invalidated the statute as a denial of due process of law.[9] And in a case tried before a southern jury, a shouting mob in the courtroom, threatening harm to the jury if they did not quickly convict the defendant (which they did in a hurry), made "due process" plainly impossible.[10]

But what are the affirmative elements of "fairness"? Impartiality of the tribunal, yes: the Sixth Amendment requires an "impartial" jury, and the Fourteenth requires impartiality on the part of whomever decides the case. But does the due process clause compel the states to grant jury trials to all persons who want them? The idea of a jury trial as important in achieving justice goes way back to Magna Carta in the year 1215, and its significance to our forefathers is obvious, for they wrote the right to it into the original Constitution before the Sixth Amendment enlarged upon it. Yet the Supreme Court does not insist, today, that a jury trial is always essential to "due process" and so must be granted by the states. The problem is not an acute one, for the states do grant jury trials; but "some states have taken measures to restrict . . . (their) . . . use; others diminish the required number of jurors. Some states no longer require the unanimous

---

9 *Tumey v. Ohio*, 273 U.S. 510 (1927).
10 *Moore v. Dempsey*, 261 U.S. 86 (1923).

verdict. . . ." [11] Such state modifications of the jury system do not violate the Fourteenth Amendment.

*The Witnesses and Their Evidence.* The idea of a criminal trial is that the truth, the whole truth, and nothing but the truth, all the relevant facts bearing upon the question whether the defendant is innocent or guilty, shall be brought out before the jury. The jury must then decide whether all these facts convince them, beyond any reasonable doubt, that the defendant is guilty as charged. If they are not so convinced, they must acquit him—find him "not guilty." To achieve a fair verdict on the basis of the evidence, at least five things seem to be necessary.

*First,* all the witnesses who can possibly be found must be brought to court to testify. The prosecution—the government—through its investigative and police services is in a good position to find witnesses and order them to appear, but the defendant, lacking such resources, is not. There is no official duty to help him find the people who can testify that he didn't commit the crime in New York because at the time it was committed he was playing poker with them in Buffalo. But if he can find them, he is given official assistance in getting them to come to the trial. In federal cases, the Sixth Amendment gives him the right to "compulsory process for obtaining witnesses in his favor. . . ." That means that upon his request, the court will issue a subpoena (order) directing such witnesses to appear. This right of "compulsory process" is so necessary, if a trial is going to serve its purpose, that a denial of it by a state court would appear to be a violation of due process of law.

*Second,* the defendant or his attorney must have the right to confront and cross-examine the witnesses against him. This is vital if it is the truth which is sought. Not that most witnesses are perjurers. Most do their best to tell the truth. But their job is simply to answer questions, and the prosecutor may not ask the questions which permit them to tell the whole story. Moreover, witnesses often state what they sincerely believe to be facts, which simply cannot be facts at all. For example, a young war veteran

---

11 *Fay v. New York,* 332 U.S. 261 (1947). Actually, in criminal cases, all states require that the jury, to render a verdict, must be unanimous; nonunanimous majority verdicts are permitted in some states, but only in civil lawsuits.

was prosecuted for being a hit-and-run driver. The prosecution's star witness was the driver of another car. Both cars were going east on a divided highway. The witness was in the right lane. He testified that he had seen the defendant's vehicle whiz past him, swerve up onto the strip which divided the highway, and there strike a small boy with its left front fender. Sitting in court, the defendant, who had no recollection of any accident, looked very sad when he heard this testimony. Then, however, his attorney rose to cross-examine the witness. Where was defendant's car when it struck the boy? A few feet ahead of witness's car, and to the left of it. It struck the boy with its left front fender? Yes. Then to see this happen, witness looked diagonally *through* defendant's car, from its right rear to its left front? At this question, the witness looked puzzled, but stood his ground. The attorney proceeded: What time did the alleged accident occur? Seven o'clock on a December evening. What was the weather? It was snowing hard.

That ended the cross-examination. The witness had been honest. What had happened was that the defendant's car had indeed passed him, close to the strip; a boy playing on the strip had cried out; the witness, going slowly, had heard the cry, stopped, and walked over to where the boy was rolling in the snow, seemingly injured. The witness genuinely thought he had seen the boy hit because "that must have been what happened." Actually, as the cross-examination brought out, he could not possibly have *seen* the defendant's left front fender hit the boy.[12]

That is an example of the importance of cross-examination of an honest witness in arriving at the real facts. As for dishonest witnesses, we can go back to what is perhaps the earliest recorded cross-examination. Do you remember the Old Testament story of Susannah? She was accused by the Elders and sentenced to death; but up rose young Daniel and cross-examined the Elders, and they contradicted each other—and they were executed instead of Susannah, because they had borne false witness against her.

The constitutional right of cross-examination is found in the

---

[12] The fact that the boy himself was in court, alive and well, only three weeks after allegedly being struck by the front of a car going forty-five miles an hour, also helped get the defendant acquitted.

Sixth Amendment (implied from the right of the defendant to be confronted with the witnesses against him) and the due process clause of the Fourteenth, and so is possessed by all defendants, whether in federal or state courts.

*Third*, to get the evidence properly before the jury a defendant needs the help of counsel. The examples given above remind us of the importance of the attorney's role. If you ever get arrested for something more serious than speeding, get a lawyer! A lawyer has many more functions than just examining and cross-examining witnesses; he may, for instance, move to dismiss the complaint against you because the law you have violated is unconstitutional, and if you are convicted he knows how to "preserve your rights" while he prepares an appeal. But his role in the trial itself, and particularly in connection with eliciting testimony, is so central that it can properly be considered here under the general heading of "The Evidence." He is trained in the art of getting friendly witnesses to tell their stories and cross-examining unfriendly ones. If defendant has no counsel, the evidence which the jury has before it when it finally considers its verdict is likely to be very different from what it would be if he had an attorney.

This being so, it would seem that assistance of counsel is essential to a fair trial. And so it is, although up until 1963 the Supreme Court didn't quite see it that way. The Sixth Amendment specifically gives the right of counsel to federal defendants; if a defendant in federal court cannot afford to have a lawyer, the court will appoint a lawyer to defend him free of charge. In the case of *Gideon v. Wainwright* [13] the Supreme Court held that this Sixth Amendment guarantee was fundamental to a fair trial and therefore was binding on the states under the Fourteenth Amendment.[14]

---

[13] 83 Sup. Ct. 792 (1963).

[14] Prior to *Gideon v. Wainwright* the Court had held that there could not be fairness in a trial where the death penalty was possible unless the defendant had an opportunity to be represented by counsel; but in all other criminal cases, the justices examined the circumstances and often held that the lack of the right to counsel did not make the trial so unfair that it "shocked the conscience." Thus the Court let numerous lawyerless defendants be imprisoned. The rationale for this was spelled out in *Betts v. Brady*, 316 U.S. 455 (1942), which was specifically overruled by *Gideon v. Wainwright*.

*Fourth,* turning now to the evidence itself, we find that by implication the Fourth Amendment makes certain evidence inadmissible in federal trials. This is whatever evidence the prosecution has obtained by "unreasonable search and seizure." The Fourth Amendment, to be sure, says nothing at all about evidence. It was put into the Constitution by people who remembered the hated "writs of assistance" of colonial days—military orders which directed British soldiers to enter any colonist's home at any time, paw over his belongings, and take away—at least temporarily—anything which seemed to them suspicious. It has long been said that "a man's home is his castle." He has some right to privacy there, if nowhere else in this crowded world. And today, certainly, most police searches of any private premises are based on search warrants issued by courts, naming the premises to be searched and the general object of the search. But what if there should be an unwarranted and unreasonable search, by some overenthusiastic officer of the FBI? The Fourth Amendment forbids it, but what remedy has the householder? He can sue the officer for trespass, but as a practical matter that is no real remedy at all.

The Supreme Court has protected this householder by making unreasonable searches by federal police officers largely useless. It has achieved this by holding that evidence obtained by such means cannot be used in court. If the evidence can't be offered, there is no purpose in searching for it and seizing it. Until 1961, always with strong minority dissent, the Supreme Court confined this rule to federal cases. It held that if a state wanted to admit evidence improperly seized by state or local policemen it could do so, and implied that the admission of such evidence did not deprive a trial of essential fairness.

In the case of *Mapp v. Ohio,*[15] however, the Court decided that the state courts, too, must exclude evidence obtained by "unreasonable search and seizure." In the *Mapp* case allegedly pornographic books and pictures were taken from Mrs. Mapp's house by Cleveland police acting without benefit of a search warrant. The Court reversed her conviction on a charge of knowingly possessing obscene literature.

---

15 367 U.S. 643 (1961).

Although the Court frowns on evidence obtained by the unwarranted search of a private home or office, it does not bar evidence obtained by eavesdropping on a person's telephone conversation or by fixing an amplifying instrument on the wall adjoining his office and thus overhearing his conversation. When wire-tapping was in its infancy, a strong claim was made that it violated the Fourth Amendment, and three justices joined Justice Holmes in arguing that it did just that. Holmes described wire-tapping as "dirty business" and said that: "We have to choose, and for my part I think it is a lesser evil that some criminals should escape than that the government should play an ignoble part." [16] But this was a dissenting opinion, for only a minority of the court. Today the use in federal courts of evidence obtained by wire-tapping is prohibited, not by the Constitution, but by an act of Congress passed in 1934, the Federal Communications Act. Few states, however, have adopted any similar prohibition.

*Fifth,* in our consideration of the evidence in a criminal case, is the so-called *privilege against self-incrimination.* This privilege to remain silent—to refuse to answer proper questions in court or other official proceedings—stems from the Fifth Amendment's statement that nobody shall "be compelled in any criminal case to be a witness against himself." By interpretation, this "right to silence" has been extended beyond federal criminal cases, to include all federal proceedings wherein, but for this privilege, a witness can be compelled to testify. (As we shall see much later, the privilege has often been claimed by witnesses before congressional investigating committees.)

The privilege is an ancient one in Anglo-American law. It means, in effect, that nobody can be compelled to talk himself into jail. However, it is a decidedly limited privilege. It cannot properly be claimed unless the witness reasonably believes that his answer will tend to subject him to prosecution or to increase the likelihood of his conviction. Not only that: the prosecution which he fears must ordinarily be by the federal government, not any state government. And the witness loses the privilege altogether —"waives" it—if he answers a series of related questions and then

---

[16] *Olmstead v. U.S.*, 277 U.S. 438 (1928).

wants to remain silent when faced with further interrogation on the same subject.

Specifically, of course, the Fifth Amendment makes it unnecessary for a defendant to testify in his own defense if he does not wish to do so. This implies that neither the judge nor the prosecutor may criticize or otherwise comment on his failure to take the witness stand. And such is the rule in federal trials. The Constitution, however, does not make it the rule in state trials. If a state wishes to permit a judge to tell the jury that the defendant's failure to testify is tantamount to a confession of guilt, it can do so. Most states forbid comment on the defendant's silence; but those that allow it are within constitutional bounds, for the Supreme Court has held that the privilege against self-incrimination is not essential to due process of law.[17]

One form of "compelling" testimony, however, does without question violate the due process clause. That is the extraction of a confession by torture, physical or mental. Shocking to say, torture by police is not unknown in modern America. In the last few decades, there have periodically reached the Supreme Court cases where a prisoner's own signed confession was introduced in evidence against him, even though the confession had been wrung from him by protracted beatings and near-starvation. Thus in *Brown v. Mississippi,* 297 U.S. 278 (1936), two defendants "were laid over chairs and their backs were cut to pieces with a leather strap with buckles on it" until "they changed or adjusted their confessions in all particulars of detail so as to conform to the demands of their torturers." In another case five days of relentless questioning of a group of ignorant and terrified defendants, culminating in an all-night interrogation, ended with their "confession." They were convicted and sentenced to death. Their convictions were set aside by the Supreme Court, which said: "To permit human lives to be forfeited upon confessions thus obtained would make of the constitutional requirement of due process of law a meaningless symbol. . . . Today, as in ages past, we are not without tragic proof that the exalted power of some govern-

---

[17] *Twining v. New Jersey,* 211 U.S. 78 (1908).

ments to punish manufactured crime dictatorially is the hand-maid of tyranny." [18]

## The Sentence

The Eighth Amendment prohibits "cruel and unusual" punishments; and it seems natural to assume that such punishments would be inconsistent with due process of law and so are forbidden by the Fourteenth Amendment also. Of course, there will be disagreements as to just what the words "cruel and unusual" mean. Presumably they would include the kind of sentences carried out in England in Elizabethan times, such as hanging a man, cutting him down alive, and then deliberately carving his body into four quarters. But is flogging, still occasionally used in some states, a "cruel and unusual punishment"? This, again, is the kind of question that might well be answered differently by different judges. A strange case which divided the Supreme Court involved the execution of a murderer who had been sent to the electric chair and had actually been strapped into it only to have the power fail. He was taken back to his cell and held for execution after the machinery was repaired. Would sending him back to the chair, after his earlier experience in it, be "cruel and unusual"? Yes, said four justices; but the other five disagreed with them, and the prisoner was executed.[19] In the late 1950's public attention was drawn to another death sentence in a southern state, where the prisoner had been found guilty not of murder, but of armed robbery in the nighttime. Actually he had stolen less than two dollars. Was the sentence so harsh as to be "cruel and unusual" and hence to violate due process?

## Federal Limitations on State Procedure

Now that we have some acquaintance with the meaning, significance, and application of the "procedural safeguards" of the Bill of Rights and the phrase "due process of law," it is time to look again at the Constitution. Which of those safeguards that limit federal power under the Bill of Rights also limit state power

18 *Chambers v. Florida,* 309 U.S. 227 (1940).
19 *Louisiana ex rel. Francis v. Resweber,* 329 U.S. 459 (1947).

under the Fourteenth Amendment? For simplicity's sake, let us take up the Bill of Rights amendments in order and present the matter in a kind of tabular form.

Fourth Amendment:
Prohibition of unreasonable search and seizure, made effective by exclusion of evidence obtained thereby. *Prohibited* by Fourteenth Amendment.

Fifth Amendment:
(a) Requirement of indictment in capital cases. *Not required* by Fourteenth Amendment.
(b) Prohibition of double jeopardy. *Not prohibited* by Fourteenth Amendment.
(c) Privilege against self-incrimination. *Not granted* by Fourteenth Amendment.
(d) Due process of law (rarely invoked in federal cases, where more specific safeguards are available). *Required* by Fourteenth Amendment.

Sixth Amendment:
(a) Speedy trial. *Effectively required* by Fourteenth Amendment.
(b) Public trial. *Required in at least most cases* by Fourteenth Amendment, though under certain circumstances some exclusion of spectators might be reasonable and so not violate the due process clause.
(c) Requirement that accused be informed of charges. *Required* by the Fourteenth Amendment.
(d) Confrontation (cross-examination) of hostile witnesses. *Required* by the Fourteenth Amendment.
(e) Compulsory process for obtaining favorable witnesses. *Required* by the Fourteenth Amendment.
(f) Right to counsel. *Required in every case* by the Fourteenth Amendment.

Seventh Amendment:
Right to jury trial. *Not provided* by the Fourteenth Amendment.

Eighth Amendment:
(a) Prohibition of excessive bail. *Not prohibited* by the Fourteenth Amendment.
(b) Prohibition of cruel and unusual punishments. *Prohibited* by the Fourteenth Amendment.

In reviewing this table, remember again that just because the Fourteenth Amendment fails to provide certain safeguards, it does not follow that state defendants are necessarily unprotected. State constitutions or statutes provide in one form or another for jury trials and the privilege against self-incrimination. Remember, too, that the potential scope of the due process clause is so broad that in a particular case the conduct of the prosecution may be held to violate it, even though such conduct might seem to fall within a category here labeled "not prohibited by the Fourteenth Amendment." Thus to use a stomach pump on a man to extract narcotics which, on being arrested, he had hastily swallowed, and to use the pills thus obtained as evidence against him, was held to violate the due process clause—even though it seems to bear a resemblance to "unreasonable search and seizure." Remember, finally, that the constitutional safeguards are not provided out of soft, sentimental sympathy for the accused. Many of them reflect society's concern in a fair trial for the purpose of protecting society itself, by adhering to those procedures which are most likely to elicit the truth, punish the guilty, and set the innocent free. All of them together are guarantees against the arbitrary suppression of the people's liberties.

## THE POLITICS OF FREEDOM

The struggle for freedom is the fight against suppression. As we have seen, the instinct to suppress your opposition is a strong one. The preservation of individual liberty, therefore, is a difficult and never-ending task. It is most difficult and most crucial in those periods when fear stalks the land—fear of the unknown, fear of change, fear of revolution or of a foreign foe. At such times people think first of their own or their country's security and are readier than usual to see individual liberty sacrificed.

### Times of Tension

The first of such periods in the United States was at the end of the eighteenth century. The French Revolution of 1789, hopefully viewed at first as a great democratic uprising, had degenerated into terror and a new autocracy. There were rumors of impending war with France. More important, there was a widespread belief that French agents in America were secretly fomenting a revolution here. Men of large property, knowing that many French aristocrats had gone to the guillotine, began to have nightmares about what they called the "Jacobins" in America—a word which in some circles had as alarming a connotation as "Communists" had a century and a half later. These propertied men composed a majority in Congress. In 1798 they enacted the Alien and Sedition Acts, designed to silence the "Jacobins"—to protect the country from the teachings of those who allegedly sympathized with the French Revolution and who dared to criticize the administration of government in the United States. These acts were enforced, here and there, with something bordering on ferocity, and free discussion became a dangerous thing to undertake. Listen to the words of a despairing congressman from New York, Edward Livingston, uttered in 1798: "The hours of the most unsuspected confidence, the intimacies of friendship, or the recesses of domestic retirement, afford no security. The companion whom you must trust, the friend in whom you must confide, are tempted to betray your imprudent or unguarded follies; to misrepresent your words; to convey them, distorted by calumny, to the secret tribunal where jealousy presides—where fear officiates as accuser, and suspicion is the only evidence that is heard."

This assault on free speech was the only one in our history to become a major issue in a presidential campaign. As we shall see, the forces of freedom triumphed, the suppressive statutes lapsed, and offenders were pardoned. One wonders, however, if this would have happened if the fear of war with France had not abated first.

Yet it does not seem to be war or fear of war with a foreign foe that is always the chief cause of suppressive legislation. Perhaps more terrifying is the real or fancied danger of social revolution and the secret machinations of unknown revolutionaries. The United States fought three foreign wars in the nineteenth century, and one great civil war, yet in those periods nothing like the Alien and Sedition laws was placed on the statute books. Not until we entered World War I in 1917 were any statutes enacted that approached them in severity. And while these new espionage and sedition laws were enacted in wartime, we should not forget that our entry into the war was not the only historic event of 1917. That was the year of the Russian Revolution. Beginning in 1917, the fear of communism became a commonplace part of the American atmosphere. There was no alarm, in those days, over Soviet power. There was fear of secret, subversive plotting within the United States. Before the war was over, the statutes presumably intended to protect the war effort against Germany were being used to prosecute "Bolsheviks"—a term which connoted Communists, anarchists, and other widely assorted "radicals." For some years after the war, suppression of radical ideas was widely respectable, and the underlying fear of social revolution persisted.

Thus it was that in late 1917 and for several years thereafter, pacifists and political radicals were lumped together under the general charge of "sedition," and hundreds were imprisoned for expressing their opinions. In August, 1918, for example, the police in St. Louis were ordered "to arrest any person who publicly criticizes the United States for entering the war, or who questions the constitutionality of the selective draft." Nor was private criticism protected; a man in Lansing, Michigan, was sentenced to twenty years imprisonment for telling a relative that this was "a rich man's war." On the political front the most conspicuous victims were the socialists, including the Socialist party's leader, Eugene Debs, who was jailed for making an anti-war speech in 1918. In the years immediately after the war, the socialists were subjected to further political penalties: Congress refused to seat Victor Berger, a duly elected representative from Milwaukee, though his constituents twice reelected him, and the New York legislature declared vacant the seats of five elected socialists. In 1919 and early 1920, when it was obvious that among the "radical" activists were numerous aliens, Attorney-General A. Mitchell Palmer instituted a series of sweeping "raids." Ostensibly designed to round up aliens unlawfully in the country, these police raids resulted not only in mass deportations but also in the arrest of thousands of peaceable citizens. The great "Red scare" began to abate in the early 1920's, though not until December, 1924, were the last of the wartime "political prisoners" pardoned by President Coolidge.

The next new federal statute designed to check revolution was the Alien Registration Act of 1940, commonly known as the Smith Act. This, to be sure, was passed when war with Germany again impended, but it is noteworthy that 1940 was a year of the brief pact between Germany and the Soviet Union. The Smith Act was used during and after World War II not against Nazis but against Communists—anti-Stalin Trotskyites while Russia was our fighting ally and orthodox Stalinists when Russia was our cold war enemy. During the cold war period from 1947 to 1954, and especially while our forces were engaged in a "hot" war in Korea (1950-1953), the atmosphere surrounding American discussion became remarkably like that which Representative Livingston had described a century and a half earlier.

Yet despite the latent instinct to suppress, the ease with which we become prey to fancied terrors, and the real and endless perils of national life in an atomic age, our constitutional liberties endure. This is somewhat surprising for at least two reasons. First, a great number of people don't know what their liberties consist of and are especially unaware of the connection between freedom to criticize and the procedural guarantees of the Bill of Rights.[20] Second, the real defender of civil liberties is a believer in tolerance; on principle, he upholds the rights of those with whom he profoundly disagrees. In contrast, the person who cares nothing for civil liberties is likely to be intolerant of dissent, ruthless in attacking the dissenters, and ready to lump together everyone who opposes him, as enemies dangerous to the country's welfare.[21]

**Institutional Factors**

The factors which keep the Bill of Rights alive are, of course, largely *institutional*. The promise of freedom and its guarantees are in the Constitution itself. To be sure, this did not prevent the passage of the extreme laws of 1798. Sometimes it is asked why the Alien and Sedition laws, which seem so obviously unconstitutional, were not held so by the Supreme Court. The answer is that

20 See S. A. Stouffer, *Communism, Conformity, and Civil Liberties* (New York: Doubleday & Co., 1955).

21 Thus in the 1952 presidential campaign, Senator Joseph R. McCarthy told an audience that if he could board the Democratic campaign train "with a slippery elm club" he could make "a good American" out of the Democratic nominee—thus simultaneously using the language of force and implying that the nominee was not a good American.

at that time, Congress had not yet conferred on the Supreme Court "appellate jurisdiction"—the right to hear and decide appeals—in criminal cases. Furthermore, of course, the court had not yet formally asserted the right of judicial review: *Marbury v. Madison* was not decided until 1803. Instead, as we have seen, Jefferson and Madison raised the issue not so much in terms of civil liberties as in terms of the Constitution as a charter of confederation—the "states' rights" argument, which was particularly appealing in those days when so many people assumed that freedom could be preserved only by keeping the decision-making power in local hands. This Jeffersonian invocation of the Constitution to protect civil liberties could not be used today, for it was based on a doctrine long since repudiated. Today, we do not argue that the way to protect freedom is to turn the federal Union into a loose league of states. Instead we look to the Bill of Rights and the Supreme Court.

Often the Supreme Court is called "the defender of our liberties." Actually, it has not always provided a stalwart defense of freedom. As shown above, it has often sustained statutes which severely restrict free speech and punish its exercise: in fact, no such act of Congress has ever been invalidated. At other times, however, the Court has struck down state statutes, even those which imposed only minor restrictions on free speech. In all of its work, the Court is not unaffected by the "climate of public opinion," for the justices themselves live in that climate and breathe its atmosphere. One wonders whether the *Yates* case, upholding the right of revolutionary talk so long as it is not "in a context of action," would have been decided the same way if it had come before the same justices in 1952, when public alarm over "subversion" was at a high pitch and being constantly whipped up by Senator Joseph R. McCarthy of Wisconsin.

On the other hand, the Court has, on the whole, been insistent on upholding the procedural safeguards embodied in the Bill of Rights and the Fourteenth Amendment. And these, as we have seen, are vital to the preservation of freedom. Court and Constitution, together, have helped keep alive a traditional belief—an often-expressed faith in fundamental principles. This faith may not always run deep, or even be consciously shared, but the ideas of justice and individual freedom persist. What may be lip-service eventually becomes habit; what becomes habit is hard to change. Our human impulse to shut the other fellow's mouth and to cast him into a dungeon is counteracted by our habit of allowing him to speak and assuring him of justice.

## The Clash of Interests

The assumption that freedom and justice are here to stay has largely removed issues concerning civil liberties and justice from the arena of national politics since 1800. (Aside, of course, from the question of human slavery, to be considered in the next chapter.) Occasionally, parties or candidates have sought victory on the ground they can best protect the country's security, and to some this implies that they care little for individual constitutional rights. In 1920, for instance, Attorney-General A. Mitchell Palmer sought the Democratic nomination for President on his record of fighting the "Bolsheviks" in America: he had ruthlessly arrested thousands of persons as subversive aliens, though many of them turned out to be innocent citizens. In the years preceding 1952 and in the campaign of that year, one element of the Republican party, with Senator McCarthy as its chief spokesman, sought to convince the voters that concern for civil liberties was equivalent to being "soft on communism" and that the Democrats had been guilty of such softness. The Republicans won that election, though probably not for that reason. But people got tired of the issue, millions of Democrats resented being called "soft on communism," and the Supreme Court soon made major decisions putting some brakes on oppressive law-making and prosecution. In the elections of 1956 and 1960, the issue played no consequential part.

If the partisan concern for individual freedom is sporadic, this does not mean that interests are not affected or interest groups unconcerned with civil liberties issues. Both material and ideal interests are involved. For many years, when employers often viewed labor unions as sinister conspiracies, they sought governmental protection against such plotters. From this came local and state laws so framed and so enforced as to prevent union leaders from trying to persuade people to join a union: witness the Texas statute struck down by the Supreme Court as late as 1941, in

*Thomas v. Collins.*[22] More recently, some men of wealth have contributed substantially to the right-wing "fringe" groups which attempt to suppress the expression of ideas with which they disagree by bracketing the economic views which they find distasteful with other ideas (support for the United Nations, for instance, or for integration) and then calling the whole lot radical, communistic, subversive, and dangerous. This is not surprising. Men at the top of the economic heap want to stay there; men with great power have been known to abuse their power, and they may have much to gain, or to preserve, by the silencing of critical opinion.

There is also, however, an ideal interest, or a clash of such interests. Fortunately for civil liberties, the great and powerful and the influential and well-educated as a group are more fully aware of the nature of our constitutional freedoms than are other groups in the society.[23] Therefore, there are many men of large property and influence who place the ideal interest first or who are convinced that freedom for all is really the best long-run safeguard for their material interest. Such people are often effective in combatting restrictive local laws, such as those prohibiting the presence of United Nations documents in the schools, denying tax exemption to churches whose officials refuse to take loyalty oaths, and the like. Sometimes they win; sometimes they don't.

Not many organizations devote themselves to the ideal interest in favor of individual liberties. The chief one is the American Civil Liberties Union. It has about 60,000 members and an annual budget of about $500,000. Mostly the ACLU operates in the legal field, offering the help of counsel to defendants who appear to have been deprived of their constitutional rights. The organization also maintains an office in Washington, has branches which seek to influence legislative action in state capitals, and issues a newsletter and an annual report. The latter, which usually contains a "balance sheet" of civil liberties' gains and losses during the year, is widely quoted in the nation's press.

A number of organizations show occasional concern for civil liberties issues. Usually on the side of a broad protection of

---

22 See page 152.
23 See Stouffer, *op. cit.*

individual rights can be found such groups as Americans for Democratic Action and the American Veterans Committee. Often insisting that national security requires the stricter limitation of individual freedom have been, among others, the Daughters of the American Revolution and the American Legion, especially some local legion posts. On both sides there have been numerous "fringe" groups—extremists whose interest may be "ideal," but whose motives are obscure. On one side, some of these have been "fronts" for the communist movement; on the other, "fronts" for particular corporations or well-heeled violent anti-libertarians.

## The Influence of Individuals

We know that governmental decisions are influenced not only by institutions and discernible interests, but by individuals too. The most famous name in the history of our civil liberties is Thomas Jefferson. Being a shrewd politician, Jefferson did indeed subordinate the "free speech" issue as he organized his party for victory in 1800, preferring to emphasize state's rights rather than the First Amendment as the bulwark of freedom. Yet it was Jefferson who penned the great assertion of human rights, the Declaration of Independence; it was he who wrote the Virginia Statute for Religious Freedom and who swore himself to defend freedom for the human mind. In our own century, as a natural result of the transfer of the issue from the partisan to the judicial arena, the greatest names on the side of individual liberty are those of judges. One of these, to be sure, achieved enduring fame for his defense of civil liberty not when he was a judge, but in a period when, between two separate terms of service on the Supreme Court, he was a practicing lawyer. This was Charles Evans Hughes, who denounced the exclusion of the socialists by the New York legislature in 1920. Hughes' stand, at the height of the hysteria, took courage; it also had a profound effect. Of other Supreme Court justices, mention must certainly be made of the eloquent Justice Holmes, his colleague Brandeis, and in mid-century Justices Black and William O. Douglas. The first two, dissenting, paved the way for the libertarian decisions of the 1930's and 1940's. The latter two, in opinions and, in the case of Douglas, books, spoke forcefully for civil liberties when they were under heavy attack, making more real the possibility that the tide would turn—as it did, to some degree, soon after Earl H. Warren became chief justice in 1953, and more noticeably since Arthur Goldberg's appointment to the Court in 1962. In addition to these judicial figures, two other men should be mentioned: a legal scholar, Zechariah Chafee, and an organizer, Roger N. Baldwin, founder of the American Civil Liberties Union. These men, unprotected by judicial office, typify a larger number who spoke up for the right to utter "dangerous thoughts" when such an unpopular stand took courage.

The outstanding names on the other side are fewer simply because in times of fear and tension it is the popular side, and countless editors, politicians, and publicists speak for it. Hence, particular individuals do not loom as large. Even the framing of the Alien and Sedition laws is ascribed to a party or faction rather than to the leadership of one or two people. In the present century, however, two names stand out, those of Attorney-General A. Mitchell Palmer and Senator Joseph R. McCarthy. Hoping for a presidential nomination in 1920, and sensing the political potentialities of "anti-Boleshevik" hysteria, Palmer used the powers of his office ruthlessly to hunt down scapegoats, lumping the innocent with the guilty in his effort to "purge" the country of subversive aliens. More recently, for the brief period spanning the Korean War, McCarthy emerged as the most effective spokesman for those who feared for the security of the country's institutions and felt no qualms about suppressing civil liberties for the sake of such security. McCarthy proclaimed himself as the enemy of communism in America, and millions agreed with him that the importance of checking such subversion justified any harm done to non-Communists who by accident, folly, or their concern for civil liberties happened to get caught in the wide anti-Communist net. The senator's admirers were not disturbed by the fact that "McCarthyism" made many people afraid to speak their minds or even to discuss "controversial" subjects in public, thus effectively limiting free speech.

The effect of particular individual efforts, on either side, is primarily to preserve or modify the "climate of public opinion"— thus affecting legislative and executive decisions and probably, to some extent, judicial decisions as well. Many view the issue at its simplest as one of individual liberty versus security—security against both national subversion and local lawlessness. However, the libertarians argue that this is not a proper statement of the issue. They say that in the long run, the national security is best ensured by free discussion, and that both free discussion and security of person and property against crime are best ensured by strict adherence to the ancient procedural safeguards against arbitrary punishment. The dominance of either view depends in large part upon the assumptions, preferences, ideals, or indifference of ordinary people. Hence in determining the meaning and limitations of the Bill of Rights, every citizen plays an inescapable role.

**Civil rights march.** Demonstrators in Washington mass at the Lincoln Memorial.

CHAPTER **8**

# The Protection of Equal Rights

I n most of the world today, the great principles of liberty and justice which we have been considering have little or no influence on how governments behave or on how people think. In many countries, even some of the large "uncommitted" nations which have not been engulfed by communism, there has been no tradition of individual freedom. National liberty, yes: for this black men and brown have struggled in this century, as white men did in the young America of 1776. But each person's freedom to worship, speak, and publish as he likes is not recognized as of first importance even in some countries whose basic charters give lip service to these principles. The reason is plain. Most people in the world go to bed hungry every night. If you are half-starved, your central concerns are survival and the betterment of your material condition; you are not likely to have either the inclination or the energy to demand the right to dissent. Furthermore, if your forefathers never had such a right, you may be unaware that any human beings claim it, and even if you are aware of that, still you will not understand the significance they attach to it.

Yet men everywhere can understand one part of the American dream. That is the vision of equality. In the most backward countries of the world, even the poorest uneducated people yearn for

183

recognition of their worth as human beings. Conversely, they resent the scorn of those who view them as inferior animals—who deny them even the humble human *status* to which, by their very existence, they feel entitled. This yearning and resentment lie beneath the great revolutionary movement of the present century, the rising of the nonwhite peoples to independent nationhood. A spirit of nationalism, by itself, might not have sparked that revolution. But when to the desire for national independence was added a vast bitterness against those who had at best patronized them, at worst treated them like beasts of burden, the nationalist cause struck fire in millions of hearts. It made the issue not just one of independent statehood but one of individual status, not political freedom but human equality.

So it is not surprising that in today's world-wide ferment, there ever echo the words of our own Declaration of Independence in 1776: "We hold these truths to be self-evident: that all men are created equal. . . ." It is natural, too, that our opponents in the struggle to win the hearts of men are forever stressing and exaggerating our own apparent failure to abide by that "self-evident" truth. They know that having enough to eat and being accorded respect as human beings are two of the most universal desires in the world. The implications of being "created equal" are the goals of men's yearning everywhere.

## THE MEANING OF EQUALITY

Insofar as the Declaration of Independence expressed fundamental American aspirations, a belief in equality became a national axiom even though our original Constitution made no explicit mention of it. Yet always, people have differed as to its meaning and significance. Some deny both. They say that it is obvious that people are not created equal: one person is born healthy and intelligent, another not, one inherits wealth and another is consigned to poverty. Certainly they would be right, if "equal" meant "in all respects the same." We are all different, and some of us from the start are either more or less fortunate than others.

To escape from this criticism of Jefferson's doctrine, many

Americans say that the Declaration of Independence means that all men are equal "in the sight of God." This may be true, but it is not a particularly useful answer. Ideally, it should result in our treating each other with utmost respect. Instead, it seems often to serve as an excuse for treading on the toes of the weak, for it lifts from our own shoulders the responsibility for according equal treatment to everyone. Not God, but men, make the operative everyday laws of the land. The millions who by those laws are relegated forever to an inferior status may gain some comfort from the assurance of divine impartiality, but the yearning for equal recognition by living men persists.

In the United States, the question of equal status, or equality of opportunity, has risen to the forefront of men's minds in various guises. We will have occasion later to consider two campaigns in which "equality" was the watchword—the drive for women's suffrage and the long struggle of organized labor to obtain power balancing that of management in collective bargaining. Here let us examine two other questions of broad scope in the hope that they may shed light on the meaning of "equality" in the United States. The first is the relationship of equality to democracy; the second, the relationship of both of these to the status of American Negroes.

## Equality and Democracy

The basic idea that freedom was better than tyranny had its counterpart in the conviction that, as opposed to government by tyrants, there should be government by the people. Holding this conviction, the framers of the Constitution had to accept democracy, much as they distrusted it. What they distrusted most was that element of the democratic faith which assumed the rightness of social equality among the citizens. Soon the French Revolution, even before it descended into the barbarism of the Terror, frightened the American gentry with its slogan of, "Liberty, Equality, Fraternity." They wouldn't quarrel with "liberty" as a proper objective, but "equality" was something else again. They saw, as we see today, that "equality" may be virtually inseparable from democracy. If today you ask someone to define "democracy," there is a good chance that he will answer that it means everybody having an equal vote, or being treated equally, or having equal opportunity. In the same way, a Rockefeller cheerfully eating pizzas and warmly shaking humble hands is praised as being "so democratic." In this sense, democracy is the opposite of aristocracy; and as an aristocrat is assumed to be—or assumes himself to be—better than other people, so in contrast a democrat is automatically "no better than anyone else."

Even so, a strong claim can be made that democratic principles are not violated by the process of selection which brings to posts of great responsibility men most suited for such positions. In government, especially, it was once assumed that background, training, and experience fitted some men for high office, while those who lacked these assets were unqualified. To early American democrats, this did not seem to be a departure from the democratic faith, nor did it deny the validity of the notion of basic equality. It was merely a recognition of the fact that particular tasks demand particular qualities. A baseball club would not sign a one-legged man to play center field, nor would a sick person ask a carpenter to operate on him. Likewise the people of a democracy, in selecting their rulers, should naturally choose those best qualified to rule.

The trouble with this idea was, and is, that there is no clear and recognized training ground for elective office. You have to go to medical school to become a good doctor, but must you be a political science major to become a good senator? A century and a half ago, a good many Americans would have answered that you should have at least had a good education and sufficient affluence to permit you to devote yourself unselfishly to public affairs. This answer, however, contained the seeds of its own demolition. For in young America, by and large, only the sons of the rich went to college; and the rich were few in number and all too often scornful of the poor. Though the early democrats—in terms of Presidents, the "Virginia dynasty" of Jefferson, Madison, and Monroe and Massachusetts' John Quincy Adams—were themselves men of aristocratic background, the very preachments of democracy fanned anti-aristocratic, egalitarian sentiment. On such sentiment, in large part, Jefferson built his party, and eventually it was bound to overcome the assumption that though the people should choose their rulers, only the wise and great were fit to rule.[1]

The opposite assumption, that virtually anyone can govern, became generally pervasive in the middle 1820's, the period which marked the first ascendancy of Jacksonian or what Walter Lippmann has deplored as "Jacobin" democracy in the United States. For "Jacobin," a word carried over from the French Revolution, we can substitute "egalitarian"—a form of democracy in which all are deemed *equally* fit to rule. This spirit of equality in political affairs persists. It underlay the later drive for women's suffrage and the extension of "direct democracy" typified by the direct primary and the initiative, referendum, and recall. Born of the frontier, where everybody, to get along, had to be fairly competent at just about every task that came to hand, it helped, too, to justify the "spoils system"—the bestowal of government jobs on faithful party workers. For if everyone could do everything equally well, what harm could there be in dismissing experienced officials and replacing them with untrained but politically "deserving" people?

After more than a century, some of the ideas basic to Jacobin or egalitarian or Jacksonian democracy remained effective. Some, indeed, are embodied in such institutions as the direct primary. But the Jacksonian principle of equality of fitness for public service has been modified. Appointments to office, in most of the federal government and to some extent in the states, are now based on the opposite principle: namely, that the person appointed must prove that he possesses at least minimum qualifications for the job. What of elective office? The belief in equality made a Lincoln acceptable, despite his log-cabin birth and lack of education. Indeed, these evidences of humble status were assets to him and many others in political life. Yet, today, a combination of factors may be taking us back toward the pre-Jackson days, at least in the matter of the selection of a President. The leading

---

[1] It has sometimes been suggested that the broadening of the franchise—the elimination of property qualifications for voting—caused the change from aristocratic rulers to "common men" in high office. The evidence does not support this. The extension of the franchise was virtually complete well before the election of 1828. A popular belief in equality, enhanced by the social conditions of the expanding frontier, became dominant in response to the logical demands of the democratic faith.

A campaign poster in 1840—when the anti-Jackson Whigs cannily stole the Jacksonian thunder by portraying their candidate as a humble frontier farmer.

pre-convention Presidential candidates in 1964 were all men of substantial wealth; one, indeed, was fabulously rich. Nobody considered this a handicap. This suggests that we have become a far more egalitarian society *in fact* than in days of yore. The gulf between rich and poor seems less significant, and the hatred of the rich by the poor is no longer a cauldron to be stirred by demagogues. And so today the ownership of a mountain-top mansion or a Venezuela ranch no more destroys a politician's popularity than did birth in a Kentucky cabin a century ago. We do not feel that we are betraying the spirit of equality when, like the early Jeffersonians, we vote for a man we believe specially qualified regardless of his wealth.

There is one great flaw in this picture of a society sufficiently well off to cast aside the old class bitterness. It does not take adequately into account the particular situation of most of some 21,000,000 Americans. Not all of these are poor, but all of them, to a greater or less degree, have a Negro heritage. They comprise the great minority, still denied the full benefits of equality. The question of their status has been a political, legal, and moral issue all through our history, and is today.

## The Great Minority

Almost all of the Negroes in the United States are the descendants of slaves. Their forefathers were enslaved before they ever came to these shores. They were captured and held in bondage in Africa by enemy tribes, which then sold them to the white "slave-traders" of the eighteenth and early nineteenth centuries. Chained together like wild beasts, they were jammed into the slavers' ships, and those who survived were put to work for white masters, mostly in the cotton fields of the South. This began long before we were an independent nation.

What, then, did the Declaration of Independence mean when it spoke of all men being "created equal"? And what status, if any, did the framers of the Constitution accord to the Negro—the freed Negro as well as the slave? The Constitution provided no answer. All it said of slavery was that Congress could not forbid the importation of slaves before 1808 and that fugitive slaves should be returned; its only other reference to slaves was in the curious provision that in computing a state's population for the purposes of determining the number of its representatives in Congress and apportioning taxes, each slave should be counted as "three-fifths of a person." It said nothing about Negroes as such. Yet in 1857, in his *Dred Scott* opinion, Chief Justice Taney declared that the Constitution itself implicitly prohibited *all* Negroes, slave or free, from being citizens of the United States.

The questions of the meaning of the Declaration of Independence's "self-evident" truth, and of the validity of Taney's *Dred Scott* opinion, were debated eloquently in 1858 by the rival candidates for senator in Illinois, Stephen A. Douglas and Abraham Lincoln. Because his ultimate political triumph and the North's military victory effectively replaced Taney's views with those of Lincoln, we would do well to see what Lincoln said: "There is no reason in the world why the Negro is not entitled to all the natural rights enumerated in the Declaration of Independence, the right to life, liberty, and the pursuit of happiness. I hold that he is as much entitled to these as the white man. I agree with Judge Douglas that he is not my equal in many respects—certainly not in color, perhaps not in moral or intellectual endowment. But in the right to eat the bread, without leave of anybody else, which his own hand earns, he is my equal and the equal of Judge Douglas, and the equal of every living man."

These words were uttered when most Negroes were still slaves. Four years later came the Emancipation Proclamation, and after the Civil War the Constitution was amended to confirm not only their freedom, but their citizenship. Now, after a hundred years, millions of Negro citizens still long for what they assume to be the proper fruits of equal citizenship. Social prejudices or customs which keep them apart from other people and are designed to deny them equality are beyond the scope of this book. We must consider carefully, however, what governments in the United States have done or left undone, in impairing the Negro's status or giving him assurance of equality. The "Reconstruction Amendments" to the Constitution—the Thirteenth, Fourteenth, and Fifteenth Amendments—pointed the way toward equality. The first formally abolished slavery, the second established the native Negro's citizenship, the third presumed to assure him of the privilege of voting. Today there are no slaves, nor is there any serious inclination to go back to *Dred Scott* and deprive all Negroes of citizenship. Unfulfilled, however, is the Fifteenth Amendment's promise of the vote. And still unresolved are the questions which long ago arose from the same Fourteenth Amendment which conferred citizenship. That amendment includes a clause stating that no state shall deprive any person of the equal protection of the laws. The meaning of that "equal protection" clause, and its application to specific instances of discriminatory action, has become a burning issue and the Supreme Court's decision that the clause forbids racially segregated public schools has not by itself given equal status to the American Negro.

## THE EQUAL PROTECTION OF THE LAWS

Although the Fourteenth Amendment makes no mention of Negroes, the chief reason for its "equal protection" clause was the need for federal protection of the freed slaves against hostile action by the southern states. As Justice Miller wrote: "In the light of the history of these [Reconstruction] Amendments, and the pervading purpose of them, . . . it is not difficult to give a meaning to this. The existence of laws in the states where the newly emancipated Negroes resided, which discriminated with gross injustice and hardship against them as a class, was the evil to be remedied by this clause, and by it such laws are forbidden." [2] Yet while this indeed was the clause's central purpose, the sweep of the words used goes far beyond the freed slaves or their descendants. It implies a promise to "any person," that he shall be the subject of "equal laws." [3] Does this mean that every state law must apply in identical fashion to every person in the state? Before concentrating on the equal protection clause's application to the Negroes' struggle for equality, we must ascertain the answer to that question, for we need to gain an awareness of the scope of state action, even discriminatory action, still permissible despite the restraining words of the Fourteenth Amendment.

---

[2] *Slaughter-House Cases*, 16 Wallace 36 (1873).
[3] *Yick Wo v. Hopkins*, 118 U.S. 356 (1886).

## "Reasonable Classification"

By and large, when a state law is challenged as violating the equal protection clause, the Supreme Court uses the same approach that it has adopted in considering whether a state law violates the due process clause. Was the legislature *reasonable* or *arbitrary?* A state might levy a graduated income tax requiring rich people to pay a larger percentage of their income than poor people. It might prohibit long hours of work by women, but not by men. Or it might seek to destroy industrial monopolies but not agricultural monopolies. In each instance, the question is whether the *classification* (rich and poor, male and female, industrial and agricultural) is reasonably suited to promote the legitimate concerns of the state. The inequalities of treatment are obvious, yet they are permissible in each of the three examples given: for a legislature could reasonably decide that taxation in accordance with ability to pay was fair, that the physical endurance of women was less than that of men, and that monopolies in manufacturing damaged small business in the state whereas small farmers were faced with no similar threat. And certainly the revenue of the state, the health of its people, and a competitive economic system are all legitimate interests which a state can promote.

To violate the equal protection clause, therefore, a state would have to discriminate *arbitrarily and unreasonably* between different "classifications" of persons. For example, Oklahoma once passed a law authorizing the sterilization of "habitual criminals," but defined the term "habitual criminals" in such a way as to exclude embezzlers, tax evaders, and some other kinds of law-breakers. Under this law a thief could be sterilized, but an embezzler escaped such a penalty. The Supreme Court noted that in actual practice, the distinction between theft and embezzlement is often unclear. It condemned the statute for drawing a "conspicuously artificial" (or arbitrary) line between the two types of offenders.[4]

Such decisions are comparatively rare, for the present-day Court pays "a large deference" to the legislative judgment. One kind of discriminatory classification, however, it often views with suspi-

---

4 *Skinner v. Oklahoma,* 316 U.S. 535 (1942).

cion or hostility. The Court inclines to find that laws which are aimed at a particular minority group violate the equal protection clause when that minority group is identified by national origin or color. When we remember the origin of the Fourteenth Amendment, we can understand why the Court looks askance at state action designed to limit the activities of members of such a group—whether they are Orientals, or merely aliens, or Negroes.

In fact, the leading case wherein the equal protection clause was invoked involved the rights not of the freed slaves, but of Chinese immigrants in San Francisco. The Chinese having taken over most of the laundry business in that city, a city ordinance was passed requiring anyone running a laundry in a wooden building to get a permit from a city official. On its face, this ordinance looked like a reasonable fire-protection measure. As enforced, however, it was a means of driving the Chinese out of business, for while the few white launderers got their permits, most of the Chinese were denied theirs. The Supreme Court's opinion said that though the ordinance looked fair enough, "it [was] applied and administered by public authority with an evil eye and an unequal hand" and so violated the equal protection clause.[5] Many years later, California sought to restrict another "national origin" group, the Japanese, by denying to "aliens ineligible to citizenship" the right to fish in coastal waters. At that time, by federal law, Japanese immigrants could not become citizens. The state statute was aimed at excluding them from the fishing business. The Supreme Court held that no sound reason existed for putting California residents who happened to have been born in Japan into a special classification making them ineligible to fish for a living and struck down the state law.[6]

These were important decisions, but their significance pales beside the cases wherein the equal protection clause was invoked by those whom it was originally intended to protect. After the end of Reconstruction, near the close of the last century, the southern states sought to restore the old social, political, and economic conditions of the South through legislation aimed at the suppression of the Negroes. These laws took various forms. The central

[5] *Yick Wo v. Hopkins, supra.*
[6] *Takahashi v. Fish & Game Commission*, 334 U.S. 410 (1948).

idea of many of them was to require segregation on the basis of color. Others, particularly those concerning political activity, were designed to exclude Negroes from full participation in political life.

### The Constitution and Segregation

For more than sixty years, segregation—the enforced separation of white and colored people—was customary in the former confederate states and some of the border states as well. If a Negro boarded a bus in Washington, D. C., and took a front seat, as soon as the bus crossed the bridge into Virginia that Negro would have to move to the back of the bus. Southern railroad trains had "Jim Crow" cars for Negroes only. Terminals had separate rest rooms for white and colored. Negroes were excluded from public parks and playgrounds and swimming pools. And in seventeen states and the District of Columbia, all public schools and state colleges and universities were segregated.

Did these statutes and ordinances comply with the Fourteenth Amendment? Judging by Justice Matthews' language in the *Yick Wo* opinion, they didn't. Even more obviously, they departed from the concept of equal protection described by the Court in 1880 in a case deciding that the systematic exclusion of Negroes from jury service was unconstitutional. Speaking of the equal protection clause, the Court said: "The words of the amendment . . . contain a necessary implication of a positive immunity, or right, most valuable to the colored race,—the right to exemption from unfriendly legislation against them distinctively as colored,—exemption from legal discriminations, implying inferiority in civil society, lessening the security of their enjoyment of the rights which others enjoy, and discriminations which are steps toward reducing them to the condition of a subject race." [7] Yet in 1896, after the personnel of the Supreme Court had almost totally changed, a Jim Crow statute of Louisiana, segregating Negroes from white people in trains and streetcars, was upheld by the Court, eight justices to one. This was the famous case of *Plessy v. Ferguson*, 163 U.S. 537, which established the legal doctrine of "separate but equal." In *Plessy v. Ferguson*, the Court denied that

[7] *Strauder v. West Virginia*, 100 U.S. 303 (1880).

Jim Crow legislation was "unfriendly" to the Negro or implied his "inferiority in civil society." It declared that the equal protection clause was satisfied if, under a statute compelling segregation, the facilities accorded to Negroes were "equal" even though separate. The only justice remaining from the 1880 Court, John M. Harlan,[8] dissented bitterly, his dissent including the telling aphorism that "the Constitution is color-blind."

Through the "separate but equal" doctrine, the Supreme Court thus accommodated the Constitution to the customs and beliefs of the white people of the South, once the latter had regained their dominance there. And for nearly sixty years it appeared that segregation was valid, even though, to Negroes and many other observers, the separate facilities provided for colored people often appeared to be not equal, but inferior. Gradually, however, without openly repudiating *Plessy v. Ferguson,* the Court moved toward a more realistic position.

*Education.* Especially in the field of education, the justices began to examine the "equal" nature of the opportunities given to Negroes. A Negro sought to enroll in the University of Missouri's Law School. He was denied admission because of his color, but the state offered to pay his tuition at some law school in another state where no segregation was required. The Supreme Court said that this offer was not enough to satisfy the equal protection clause, whereupon Missouri opened a Negro law school at its separate state university for Negroes. Within a few years, even this hardly seemed sufficient. After denying a Negro, Herman Sweatt, admission to its state university law school, Texas purported to establish a separate Negro law school in which Sweatt was the only student. The Supreme Court held that this action failed to provide Sweatt with an opportunity for a legal education "equal" to that of white students, and compelled his admission to the regular University of Texas Law School.[9] Encouraged by decisions of this sort, the enemies of the "separate but equal" doctrine finally brought to the Court the larger and more basic issue, that of segregation in the public schools.

---

[8] Justice Harlan's grandson, also named John M. Harlan, was appointed to the Supreme Court by President Eisenhower in 1955.

[9] *Sweatt v. Painter,* 339 U.S. 629 (1950).

The public school segregation cases, directly challenging the validity of statutes in four states (out of the seventeen that then compelled such segregation) and the District of Columbia, were first argued before the Supreme Court in late 1952. No prophet could safely predict the result. The Court might reaffirm *Plessy v. Ferguson* and dismiss the challenge. It might abide by the "separate but equal" doctrine but say that the Negro schools were not "equal" to the white schools. Or it might repudiate "separate but equal," once and for all. The justices themselves, well aware of the significance of their ultimate decision, appeared to hesitate, even to stall. In the spring of 1953, instead of deciding the case, they asked for new attorneys' briefs, devoted to the intentions of those who drafted and adopted the Fourteenth Amendment. Did those men of 1868 intend to outlaw segregated public schools? The question was futile: in Civil War days and theretofore, there had been no state-wide public school systems in the South, and so the men who wrote and ratified the equal protection clause were not thinking specifically about public education one way or the other. Eventually, on May 17, 1954, the Supreme Court handed down its historic opinion in *Brown v. Board of Education of Topeka*, 347 U.S. 483. It chose the third alternative. It repudiated "separate but .equal," and it overruled *Plessy v. Ferguson*.

Chief Justice Warren wrote the opinion for a unanimous Court. He cited works of sociologists and psychologists to support his finding that segregation *in itself* created inequality, regardless of the kind of buildings in which Negroes went to school or the amount of money spent by the state on Negro education. In this respect, the effect of the *Brown* decision appeared to be confined to public schools. Yet it was soon obvious that the justices had agreed upon much more than the issue of segregation in education. In the years since 1954, they have consistently refused to review lower court decisions in which other Jim Crow laws were held unconstitutional. In effect, segregation by state law, on the basis of color, has been held to amount to a denial of equal protection to Negroes. If old Justice Harlan had lived long enough, he would thus have seen his lone dissent in *Plessy v. Ferguson* vindicated and would have rejoiced in the Court's return to that broad interpretation of the equal protection clause in which he had joined way back in 1880.

Fitzpatrick in the *St. Louis Post-Dispatch*

### Liberty Bell, 1954

Approving of the Supreme Court's decision of May 17, 1954, cartoonist Fitzpatrick combined the liberty bell with the school bell in this picture. The decision elicited a very different response in much of the South.

The Supreme Court's decision, however, far from closed the issue. The justices themselves, perhaps worried about possibly violent defiance and perhaps as a price of the judicial unanimity which they deemed important, kept the door open. Instead of ordering prompt integration in compliance with the Constitution, they first postponed the issuance of any order and then decreed that integration should proceed, school district by school district, "with all deliberate speed," under the general supervision of the United States district courts in the various states. In a few cities, without even waiting for this somewhat vague directive, school officials promptly ended segregation: the largest of these were Washington, St. Louis, and Louisville. But much of the South was defiant. Not only did school district officials fail to act, but in some states legislation was passed to prevent them from acting. When districts in Front Royal and Norfolk, Virginia, were ordered to "desegregate" by the district court, the governor of Virginia responded by closing the schools. In Little Rock, Arkansas, the school board promulgated and the district court approved a plan for gradual integration to begin in September, 1957, but Governor Orval E. Faubus ordered the Arkansas National Guard to patrol outside the Central High School and prevent any Negro child from entering it. Not until President Eisenhower ordered United States troops to Little Rock to "uphold the Constitution" did nine Negro children enter Central High School.

More serious violence erupted in the fall of 1962 when a federal court ordered that James Meredith, a Negro, be admitted to the University of Mississippi. Governor Ross Barnett of Mississippi refused to obey the court order; and he and his Lieutenant Governor, Paul Johnson, turned Meredith away three times during the last weeks of September. Meredith was finally placed on the campus at Oxford, Mississippi, on the night of September 30, under escort of over four hundred federal marshals, who were then besieged in the University's administration building through the night by a rock-throwing mob of several thousand. Two persons were killed and hundreds injured before federal troops and Mississippi National Guardsmen, federalized by order of President Kennedy, arrived and restored order early in the morning. On October 1, Meredith registered for classes while sixteen thousand troops patrolled the campus and town.

In January, 1963, Harvey Gantt, a Negro architectural student, was peacefully enrolled at Clemson College in South Carolina. And, when in June, 1963, three Negro students were admitted to the summer session of the University of Alabama—after Governor George Wallace abandoned his "stand in the schoolhouse door" on order of the federalized Alabama National Guard—at least one

Negro went to college at some level with whites in each of the fifty states.

At the elementary and secondary school level, however, no such claim could be made. Eight years after the *Brown* decision was handed down, out of 3,047 biracial school districts in states segregated in 1954, 912 were wholly or partially integrated. To many this appeared more like "deliberation" than speed, particularly when one looked behind the gross figures. As the accompanying chart shows, what integration had occurred had taken place overwhelmingly in the so-called border states. In the states of the deeper south, Arkansas, Florida, Georgia, Louisiana, North Carolina, and Virginia, and even in Tennessee, less than one per cent of enrolled Negro pupils actually went to school with whites, while in Alabama, Mississippi, and South Carolina no cracks at all showed in the wall of public school segregation.[9a]

State resistance by legislation, such as laws closing or abolishing public schools whenever a federal court ordered them integrated, seemed unlikely to succeed for two reasons. First, the outright abandonment of public education would strain southern loyalties to the utmost, forcing parents to decide between surrendering the doctrine of segregation and depriving their children of schooling. Second, any attempt to avoid this eventuality, by giving state support to white "private" schools, appeared sure to run afoul of the equal protection clause. The resisters, basically, were playing for time. As they saw it, the crisis had been caused by the Supreme Court. If they could hold out against the Court's decision long enough, perhaps new justices would modify or reverse it. After all, the Supreme Court in 1880 described the equal protection clause in words which obviously implied that segregation was unconstitutional, yet by 1896 it upheld segregation. White southerners could dream, at least, that a similar reversal would be achieved in the 1960's.

These dreams were dealt a considerable shock in May, 1963, when the Supreme Court reversed a decision of a district court which had upheld the "slow and gradual" desegregation of mu-

---

9a By the autumn of 1963, five small school districts in Alabama, and one in South Carolina, had been desegregated.

SEGREGATED-DESEGREGATED STATUS OF PUBLIC SCHOOLS IN FORMERLY
SEGREGATED STATES—May, 1962

| State | School Districts | | | Enrollment | | In Deseg. Districts | | Negroes in School with Whites | |
|---|---|---|---|---|---|---|---|---|---|
| | Total | with Negroes and Whites | Deseg. | White | Negro | White | Negro | Number | %‡ |
| Alabama | 114 | 114 | 0 | 523,303 | 276,029 | 0 | 0 | 0 | 0 |
| Arkansas | 418 | 228 | 10 | 320,204 | 108,841 | 54,737 | 13,237 | 151 | .139 |
| Delaware | 92 | 92 | 92 | 70,249 | 15,917 | 70,249 | 15,917 | 8,540 | 53.7 |
| Dist. of Col. | 1 | 1 | 1 | 23,462 | 103,806 | 23,462 | 103,806 | 88,881 | 85.6 |
| Florida | 67 | 67 | 5 | 927,331 | 242,097 | 348,209 | 61,883 | 648 | .268 |
| Georgia | 198 | 196 | 1 | 641,710 | 303,005 | 59,319 | 48,963 | 8 | .003 |
| Kentucky | 209 | 169 | 141 | 600,000* | 43,000* | 432,996* | 34,000* | 22,058 | 51.3 |
| Louisiana | 67 | 67 | 1 | 450,000* | 295,000* | 38,217 | 56,095 | 12 | .004 |
| Maryland | 24 | 23 | 23 | 481,276 | 143,879 | 476,473 | 143,879 | 59,729 | 41.5 |
| Mississippi | 150 | 150 | 0 | 293,600* | 286,800* | 0 | 0 | 0 | 0 |
| Missouri | 1,692 | 214* | 203* | 760,950* | 84,550* | — | 75,000* | 35,000* | 41.4 |
| North Carolina | 173 | 173 | 11 | 787,405 | 332,962 | 130,439 | 60,044 | 203 | .061 |
| Oklahoma | 1,292 | 240 | 195 | 508,750* | 41,250* | 295,525* | 33,817* | 10,555 | 25.6 |
| South Carolina | 108 | 108 | 0 | 363,768* | 265,076* | 0 | 0 | 0 | 0 |
| Tennessee | 154 | 143 | 17 | 663,065 | 155,500* | 225,096 | 74,524 | 1,167 | .750 |
| Texas | 1,483 | 890 | 149 | 1,892,044* | 300,867* | 805,000* | 95,700* | 4,000* | 1.33 |
| Virginia | 131 | 129 | 20 | 657,162 | 216,860 | 261,528 | 76,252 | 536 | .247 |
| West Virginia | 55 | 43 | 43 | 411,790* | 25,000* | 362,577* | 25,000* | 15,500* | 62.0 |
| Total | 6,398 | 3,047 | 912 | 10,376,069 | 3,240,439 | 3,583,827† | 918,117 | 246,988 | 7.6% |

* Estimated.
† Without Missouri.
‡ Proportion of Negroes in school with whites to total Negro enrollment.
SOURCE: *Southern Education Reporting Service*, May, 1962.

nicipal recreation facilities in Memphis.[10] The Court, speaking through one of the new justices, Arthur Goldberg, held that the "deliberate speed" formula of the *Brown* case did not apply to recreation facilities because the special problems involved in school desegregation were not present. The language of the opinion was broader than this, however, as Justice Goldberg went on to say that ". . . . [it was] never contemplated that the concept of 'deliberate speed' would countenance indefinite delay in elimination of racial barriers in schools, let alone other public facilities. . . . The basic guarantees of our Constitution are warrants for the here and now. . . . they are not merely hopes to some future enjoyment of some formalistic constitutional promise." The Supreme Court's patience seemed to have been stretched to the breaking point by the South's tactics of delay.

*Accommodations.* As we have just seen, the impact of *Brown v. Board of Education* extended beyond the field of public education. Statutes and ordinances barring Negroes from public parks and playgrounds were struck down; Jim Crow laws governing public transportation were set aside. *Plessy v. Ferguson* seemed to be dead. In practice, however, it remained alive. A local court, state or federal, might invalidate a local ordinance, ending segregation in a particular city's parks; but in thousands of other places, segregation persisted. Those who sought to end it by legal means had to proceed ordinance by ordinance, case by case—a long, expensive, and arduous process.

The equal protection clause, of course, was now on their side. Indeed, even before 1954 the Supreme Court had occasionally found in the Fourteenth Amendment the means to protect the rights of Negroes to go where they liked and live where they wished. It had held unconstitutional, for instance, a state court's enforcement of a "restrictive covenant," which is a contract among neighbors whereby each of them agrees not to sell his house to a person of a particular race or religion. In violation of such a covenant, a white man in St. Louis sold his house to a Negro. On the petition of the white neighbors, the Missouri court set the sale aside, on the ground that it violated the restrictive covenant. The Supreme Court then, however, in *Shelley v. Kraemer,* 334

10 *Watson v. City of Memphis,* 83 Sup. Ct. 1314 (1963).

U.S. 1 (1948), reversed the Missouri court, declaring that when the state court thus enforced a contract discriminating against Negroes, it was denying to Negroes the equal protection of the laws. (The case was unusual, in that the state's denial of equal protection was perpetrated by the state's judicial branch; most equal protection cases involve discriminatory legislative action or, as in the *Yick Wo* case, unfair administrative action.)

In transportation, too, Congress and the courts had whittled away at Jim Crowism for many years. Exercising its power to regulate interstate commerce, Congress outlawed segregation on interstate buses. This meant that no longer could bus drivers starting from Washington order Negroes to rear seats as soon as the bus crossed the Potomac into Virginia. Virginia claimed that within the state, its Jim Crow law was paramount; but the Supreme Court said "no." [11] The court likewise upheld a Negro's claim that under the Interstate Commerce Act's provision that all passengers on interstate trains should be treated equally, he could take any vacant seat he liked in the dining car.[12] And the same act has been found to be violated by the segregation of facilities in bus stations used by interstate travelers even though the stations are not owned by interstate carriers.[13]

The fact remains that purely local accommodations (or seats on intrastate buses, for instance) are still subject to local laws, that many such laws require segregation, and that they are still enforced despite their inconsistency with the equal protection clause as now interpreted. Furthermore, the Constitution does not forbid racial discrimination by private individuals or groups. It may make such discrimination unenforceable by the state courts, as in *Shelley v. Kraemer,* but it forces nobody to associate with anyone he dislikes in his home, his club, or his business office. The exclusion of Negroes from privately owned but publicly used accommodations—restaurants and hotels, for instance—is forbidden in numerous places outside the South; but the prohibition is found in local laws and ordinances, not in the Fourteenth

---

11 *Morgan v. Virginia,* 328 U.S. 373 (1946).
12 *Henderson v. United States,* 339 U.S. 816 (1950).
13 *Boynton v. Virginia,* 364 U.S. 454 (1960).

Amendment. However, as a part of civil rights legislation urged on Congress in the summer of 1963, President Kennedy advocated the enactment of a federal public accommodations law. This proposed law would use the interstate commerce clause as a constitutional basis for outlawing racial discrimination in a large number of private business enterprises, including many hotels, motels, and "hamburger stands."

*Employment.* The fact that the equal protection clause forbids certain forms of discrimination by state and local governments but does not directly affect the scope of private choice means that when private employers refuse to employ Negroes, they are not violating the Constitution. They may, however, be breaking a local law. In a few nonsouthern states, with New York leading the way in 1946, laws have been passed to outlaw racial and religious discrimination in private employment. Their starting point was an executive order issued by President Roosevelt in World War II, creating a federal Fair Employment Practices Committee (FEPC). This committee was charged with the "policing" of clauses in government defense contracts which forbade contractors to follow a discriminatory hiring policy. However, it lacked real enforcement powers. In contrast, the FEPC later established in Massachusetts and the State Commission Against Discrimination in New York can, after receiving complaints and holding hearings, issue an order requiring an employer to "cease and desist" from discriminatory practices, and such an order is enforceable by the courts. Even where such laws exist, of course, covert discrimination may persist, not only against Negroes but against other groups as well; [14] it is often difficult, if not impossible, to decide whether a company failed to hire a Negro because of his color or because of his lack of competence. When the Boston Red Sox in April, 1959 "farmed out" a Negro rookie, "Pumpsie" Green, was it because of his color? Objectors claimed that it was, pointing out that no Negroes played for the Red Sox. The club owners answered that "Pumpsie" was unsteady at shortstop

---

[14] For many years in Boston, well into the present century, many "help wanted" signs posted by employers concluded with the words: "No Irish need apply."

and obviously needed "seasoning." [15] The incident was a reminder of the difficulties confronting FEPC officials.

The map shown here gives some idea of the extent of state laws outlawing discrimination in the summer of 1963. These laws vary widely in coverage, enforcement, and effectiveness, however; the mere existence of such a law is no indication that the outlawed discrimination does not continue. In 1963 Governor Bert Combs of Kentucky took a somewhat different approach, issuing an executive order banning racial discrimination in any business licensed by the state.

### The Negro's Voting Privilege

The equal protection clause, by itself, would seem to make invalid any state action designed to keep Negroes (as distinguished from other people) from voting. And any doubt about the unconstitutionality of such discrimination was surely removed by the Fifteenth Amendment, which flatly forbids it. Yet in 1961 nearly a hundred years after the adoption of the Fourteenth and Fifteenth Amendments, only about 28 per cent of adult Negroes residing in the eleven former confederate states were registered voters—in Mississippi, only 6 per cent. To be sure, voting participation is generally less in the South than in the rest of the nation, but still about 56 per cent of southern whites are registered to vote. The especially low Negro registration reflects more than general voter apathy. It is partly the product of intimidation and partly the result of state laws designed to defeat the intentions of the equal protection clause and the Fifteenth Amendment.

One type of measure which discourages Negro voting is the poll tax, a small tax on each registered voter which must be paid before he can vote. This applies to everyone regardless of color, and so presumably does not violate the equal protection clause. It bears equally on poor people, regardless of color; white sharecroppers who live on what they raise or barter and handle only a couple of hundred dollars a year are as reluctant as their neighboring Negroes to pay even the small poll tax and as careless about keeping the receipt if they do pay it. The original and ex-

---

15 By July, Green was back with the Red Sox as a second baseman.

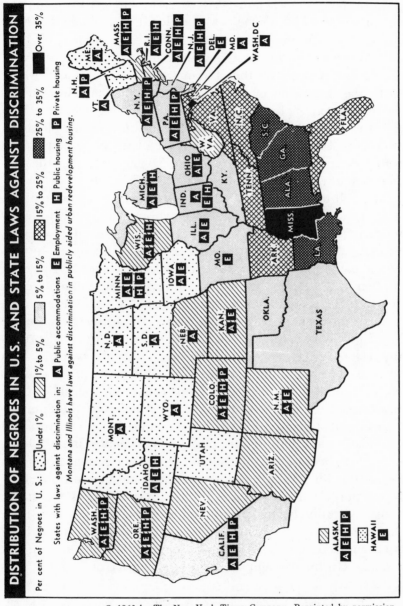

DISTRIBUTION OF NEGROES IN U.S. AND STATE LAWS AGAINST DISCRIMINATION

Per cent of Negroes in U. S.:  Under 1%   1% to 5%   5% to 15%   15% to 25%   25% to 35%   Over 35%

States with laws against discrimination in:  **A** Public accommodations  **E** Employment  **H** Public housing  **P** Private housing

Montana and Illinois have laws against discrimination in publicly aided urban redevelopment housing.

© 1963 by The New York Times Company. Reprinted by permission.

press purpose of such poll tax laws, however, was to discourage Negro voting. This purpose was achieved in a dozen southern states. Gradually the poll tax laws have been repealed; by 1963 only five remained in effect, and these five faced extinction with the recent passage of the Twenty-fourth Amendment which curbs the inhibiting effects of poll taxes by the states on national elections. The impediment to voting created by a poll tax was dramatically illustrated by the outpouring of voters after its repeal. Thus in Louisiana, in the last state-wide primary before the poll tax law was repealed, 379,000 voted; in the first one after its repeal, the number jumped to 540,000.[16]

The poll tax was never held unconstitutional, but more direct state action to keep Negroes from voting has been. In most southern states for many years and to a considerable degree today, winning a Democratic nomination has been tantamount to winning the election. The real contest, then, for senator or governor, is often in the Democratic party's "primary," the public election at which the party's nominees are chosen. A Texas statute made Negroes ineligible to vote in the Democratic primary. When the Supreme Court held that this statute violated the equal protection clause, the Democratic party's officials, acting as if they constituted a private club, adopted a resolution declaring that no Negroes could join the party. By this maneuver, the judicial axe was escaped for several years. Eventually, however, the Supreme Court decided that a primary for the nomination of congressional candidates was a part of the congressional election itself.[17] Logically, then, because the state administered the elections it was also responsible for administering the primary, and the "private club" which purported to hold the primary was acting as the state's agent. Accordingly, the party's action in barring Negroes from the primary was really state action, and thus it, too, violated the equal protection clause. *Smith v. Allwright,* 321 U.S. 649 (1944).

South Carolina sought to escape the impact of *Smith v. All-*

---

16 V. O. Key, *Southern Politics in State and Nation* (New York: Alfred A. Knopf, Inc., 1949).

17 *U.S. v. Classic,* 313 U.S. 299 (1941). This case did not involve Negroes' rights; Classic was a white election official, accused of stuffing a ballot box. But the decision had an inevitable logical effect on the Negroes' right to vote in primaries.

*wright* and to maintain the Democratic party as "lily white" by simply repealing all its primary laws. Whomever the party, acting in accordance with its own rules and procedures, certified as its nominee would have his name go on the ballot in the final election. The party's rules and procedures included a nominating primary but, of course, excluded Negroes from participation. This device was struck down as an obvious subterfuge: said Judge John J. Parker of the U. S. Court of Appeals: "No election machinery can be upheld if its purpose or effect is to deny to the Negro, on account of his race or color, any effective voice in the government of his country or the state or community wherein he lives." [18]

Yet such election machinery exists. No sooner was the "white primary," a direct exclusionary measure, struck down by the courts than southern state legislatures began to devise an indirect way of keeping Negroes from voting. This was the "literacy test." In most states this is just a requirement that a person should be able to read and write before he can qualify as a voter. In the South, however, further conditions have been added, and local election officials have been granted (or have assumed) very wide discretion. The law of Alabama, passed in 1951, is typical of the region-wide pattern. It provides that "the following persons shall be qualified to register: . . . those who can read and write any article of the Constitution of the United States in the English language which may be submitted to them by the Board of Registrars, provided, however, that no person shall be entitled to register . . . except those who embrace the duties and obligations of citizenship . . . and provided further, that . . . each applicant shall be furnished . . . a written questionnaire. . . . Such questionnaire shall be answered in writing by the applicant, in the presence of the Board without assistance. . . ." Such a statute gives local boards of registration (or their equivalent in other states) a virtually free hand; if they so desire, they can exclude most

---

[18] *Rice v. Elmore,* 165 F. 2nd 387 (1947). State officials sought review by the Supreme Court, but this was denied. The decision casts a long shadow over the plans in South Carolina and elsewhere, to escape the impact of *Brown v. Board of Education* by simply repealing all the state laws concerning public schools and then giving public financial support to segregated private schools.

Negro applicants under conditions which make it difficult to prove that they are discriminating arbitrarily. Mounting evidence that this was just what some of them were doing, however, caused Congress to establish a temporary Federal Civil Rights Commission in 1957 and to authorize the attorney-general of the United States to institute civil proceedings to prevent such discrimination. This congressional Act had little immediate effect, although by early 1963 the Justice Department had bought thirty-three such actions in various parts of the South, mainly in Mississippi, Louisiana, and Alabama. The statute's efficacy depended on the federal government's being able to discover the facts on which to base a case in court; and numerous state and local election authorities made such fact-finding difficult, if not impossible, by refusing to permit federal agents to inspect their records.

In another Civil Rights Act passed by Congress in 1960, courts were permitted to appoint referees to register qualified Negroes, if the court first found a pattern of voting discrimination in the area. In 1963 President Kennedy proposed new legislation to speed up the process of abolishing discrimination in voter registration. The proposed law had four main features. It would prohibit denial of the right to vote on the basis of errors or omissions on records or applications, where the error or omission was not material in determining whether the applicant was qualified to vote. It would prohibit the use of literacy tests not administered in writing. Where literacy tests were used it would require the presumption that anyone with a sixth-grade education is literate. In areas where less than 15 per cent of the Negroes are registered (in 1963 these included 261 counties in eleven states) and a voting suit has been started in the courts, it would allow the court to appoint referees to register qualified Negroes before a decision had been reached in the court. And it would provide for speeding up action on voting right suits in the federal courts. This proposed legislation spotlighted many of the problems which have existed in the fight for equal voting rights. Its constitutional basis appeared to be the operative sentence at the end of the Fifteenth Amendment, which gives Congress the power to enforce the prohibition of discriminatory voting practices.

## Citizens and Aliens

The equal protection clause is designed to protect all "persons" from discriminatory state action, just as the due process clauses of the Fifth and Fourteenth Amendments presumably protect all "persons" from arbitrary treatment by the federal and state governments, respectively. "Persons" is a word which includes aliens as well as citizens of the United States. Nevertheless, in several respects aliens have been subjected to discrimination or punishment which would not have been applied to them had they been citizens. Aside from the fact that no state permits them to vote, they are not on an "equal" footing with citizens.

The bases of citizenship, set forth briefly in the Fourteenth Amendment, were defined more fully by the Nationality Act of 1940. They are *birth* and *naturalization*. Ordinarily (the usual exception is the birth of a child to foreign diplomats) anyone born in the United States is a citizen, and so is a child born abroad to parents who are citizens.[19] Persons not born citizens can become so by being naturalized. To be eligible for naturalization, in the normal course of events, an alien must first have been admitted to the United States for the purpose of establishing a permanent residence here, must have resided here for five years, must have established a reputation as a law-abiding citizen capable of self-support, and must have passed an examination testing his knowledge of the English language and American institutions. The enforcement of these rules and the management of the prescribed procedures are the responsibility of the Immigration and Naturalization Service in the Department of Justice; the formal granting of citizenship is a function of the United States district courts.

The first step that an alien takes toward citizenship, then, is lawful entry into this country. For most of our history, the gates were wide open, equally to all. Emma Lazarus's famous verses, in-

---

19 If one parent is a citizen and the other an alien, the child born abroad can become and remain a citizen if both he and his citizen parent meet certain residence requirements specified by statute. If the parent is abroad on a governmental or other recognized mission, however, these requirements do not have to be met.

scribed on the wall near the base of the Statue of Liberty, were appropriate:

> Give me your tired, your poor,
> Your huddled masses yearning to be free . . .
> I lift my lamp beside the golden door.

Early in the present century, however, pressure to restrict immigration increased. In a single year, 1907, a total of 1,285,349 alien immigrants arrived on our shores. Organized labor had long seen in such great hordes a threat to decent wages and working conditions, for the newcomers often took jobs for whatever wages were offered them. At about the turn of the century, furthermore, the sources of immigration began to change perceptibly. Nineteenth century immigration had come largely from Anglo-Saxon or Celtic countries—chiefly Ireland, Germany, and Scandinavia. Now, more and more, the "huddled masses" were arriving instead from southern and eastern Europe. Suspicion of foreigners seems to come naturally to many people, and anti-foreign sentiment had been strong in some parts of the United States in the 1800's. It increased when the new immigrants were in background, religion, language, and customs even more "different" than their forerunners.

The restrictive immigration laws of 1921 and thereafter, therefore, not only drastically limited the number of aliens who could be admitted for permanent residence but also abandoned the old idea that all nationalities should be treated equally. A *quota system* was established under which the maximum number of immigrants from each country was fixed in such a way that many more aliens were admissible from certain countries than from others. The statute of 1924, for example, set each country's quota at 2 per cent of the number of people from that country living in the United States in 1890, before the great flood of immigration from southern and eastern Europe had reached its later heights. Accordingly, under that law 141,000 aliens from northern and western Europe were admissible each year, but only 20,000 from southern and eastern Europe and only 4,000 non-Europeans. Furthermore, the Act forbade naturalization to "Orientals"—a discriminatory prohibition which was lifted in the case of the Chinese during World War II and in the case of the Japanese and other nationalities a few years thereafter. (The quotas for such Asiatic countries, however, have remained extremely small.)

The accompanying table shows the present immigration quotas under the McCarran-Walter Act of 1952 which fixed the total permissible number of aliens to be admitted at 154,657 per year. The formula applied to determine these quotas was to allow ⅙ of 1 per cent of those of that national origin in the United States in 1920 to enter annually, but with a ceiling of 2,000 placed on the Asia-Pacific Triangle. No transfer of quotas from country to country and no carryover from year to year were to be permitted.

How then do we explain the discrepancies between the quotas and the annual average immigration for the decade of the 1950's revealed by the chart? First, Congress permits a large number of aliens to enter the United States every year under private bills which cover their specific cases. Furthermore, Congress has also passed more general laws almost every year to relax the existing restrictions to meet the needs of international events.

The quota or "national origins" system, which persists as a fundamental of our immigration policy,[20] seems a denial of the basic assumption of human equality. Essentially it is an expression of preference, a determination to welcome some people more readily than others. And not just different treatment for different nationalities, but distinctions based on past individual behavior and past or present political beliefs are also required by Congress. The record of an alien seeking citizenship must be free from moral taint or adherence to subversive doctrines. A nation composed entirely, aside from American Indians, of immigrants and the descendents of immigrants has, as it were, said to the world that we have just about enough people here now and that we should and will exercise our discretion in closing the door against those whom we don't like.

Furthermore, we feel free to treat aliens in this country differently from citizens. The equal protection clause does, it is true, inhibit state action designed specifically to discriminate against

---

[20] It does not apply to United States possessions; in recent years the migration from Puerto Rico has exceeded the immigration from all of the European countries combined.

## IMMIGRATION QUOTAS UNDER McCARRAN-WALTER ACT

| Country | Present Quota | Av. Annual Immigration 1951-60 | Pending Visa Application 1963 | Country | Present Quota | Av. Annual Immigration 1951-60 | Pending Visa Application 1963 |
|---|---|---|---|---|---|---|---|
| *Europe* | | | | *Asia* | | | |
| Austria | 1,405 | 2,968 | 4,590 | China | 205 | 3,274 | 24,860 |
| Belgium | 1,297 | 1,292 | — | India | 100 | 314 | 14,057 |
| Czechoslovakia | 2,859 | 2,880 | — | Indonesia | 100 | 1,012 | 8,576 |
| Denmark | 1,175 | 1,370 | 3,071 | Iran | 100 | 291 | 10,384 |
| Finland | 566 | 668 | 2,992 | Iraq | 100 | 190 | 7,320 |
| France | 3,069 | 3,802 | 7,765 | Israel | 100 | 935 | 15,196 |
| Germany | 25,814 | 34,545 | — | Japan | 185 | 4,467 | 8,882 |
| Greece | 308 | 4,844 | 105,659 | Jordan | 100 | 511 | 3,194 |
| Hungary | 865 | 6,455 | 17,470 | Korea | 100 | 702 | 1,192 |
| Ireland | 17,756 | 6,455 | — | Lebanon | 100 | 337 | 5,358 |
| Italy | 5,666 | 18,700 | 268,723 | Philippines | 100 | 1,809 | 8,124 |
| Latvia | 235 | 1,913 | 1,709 | | | | |
| Lithuania | 384 | 1,186 | 2,286 | *Africa* | | | |
| Netherlands | 3,136 | 4,719 | 8,666 | Morocco | 100 | 216 | 5,278 |
| Norway | 2,364 | 2,467 | — | Tunisia | 100 | 137 | 4,518 |
| Poland | 6,488 | 12,798 | 57,657 | Union of S.A. | 100 | 232 | 3,286 |
| Portugal | 438 | 2,043 | 50,559 | United Arab Rep. | 100 | 618 | 11,966 |
| Rumania | 289 | 1,743 | 13,892 | | | | |
| Spain | 250 | 1,072 | 16,396 | *Oceania* | | | |
| Sweden | 3,295 | 1,886 | — | Australia | 100 | 500 | 4,982 |
| Switzerland | 1,698 | 1,719 | 3,392 | New Zealand | 100 | 189 | 1,586 |
| Turkey | 225 | 684 | 18,123 | | | | |
| United Kingdom | 65,361 | 20,887 | 48,573 * | | | | |
| USSR | 2,697 | 4,650 | 8,613 | | | | |
| Yugoslavia | 942 | 5,866 | 79,732 | | | | |

* Mostly from West Indies which form separate subquota areas.

SOURCE: Congressional Quarterly, Vol. 21, March 22, 1963, p. 402

aliens as a classification. States have tried to take such action, but have occasionally been thwarted by Supreme Court decisions: thus an Arizona statute limiting the percentage of aliens whom any one employer could employ was struck down as a denial of equal protection,[21] and a California law designed to exclude aliens of Japanese extraction from commercial fishing was likewise held invalid.[22] But neither the alien nor, indeed, the naturalized citizen possesses safeguards against federal action equal to those possessed by native-born citizens. The Supreme Court takes the position that admission of foreign-born to citizenship is a subject peculiarly within congressional discretion: Congress should set the conditions and prescribe their enforcement, and what Congress can confer it can take away. So although an alien accused of a crime must be given a fair trial by a state court, he may have no redress against the federal immigration authorities who hold him for possible deportation from the country. Deportation—away from family and friends—may really be a far graver penalty than six months in jail for theft; yet it can be exacted after only an administrative hearing, without the benefits of judicial procedure. And not only an alien may be deported for violating in some manner the conditions of his entry into this country. A naturalized citizen, too, may be divested of his citizenship and deported if he is guilty of breaking some particular law—and it does not even matter that the law which he broke was enacted after the time that he performed the act which allegedly broke it. In other words, the Constitution's prohibition of *ex post facto* laws does not apply to the deportation of aliens or "denaturalized" citizens. In legal theory, deportation is part of an administrative process rather than a judicially imposed criminal punishment. Thus in 1952 it was possible, lawfully, to deport a law-abiding man who had lived in the United States for twenty-eight years because for a few weeks in 1934 he had belonged to the Communist party— although no law in 1934 forbade such membership and the Act of Congress (the McCarran Act) making past membership in the

---

21 *Truax v. Raich*, 239 U.S. 33 (1915).

22 *Takahashi v. Fish & Game Commission*, 334 U.S. 410 (1948). Remember, also, the *Yick Wo* case, where the Court protected Chinese laundrymen from discriminatory administrative action.

Communist party a ground for deportation was not passed until 1950.

The extension of the Fourteenth Amendment to all "persons," therefore, requires equal treatment of everyone by the states, but not by the federal government. To be sure, the federal government's unequal treatment of certain groups—e.g., Negro school children in Washington, D. C.—has been judicially condemned as a violation of the Fifth Amendment's due process clause. Nevertheless, at times the federal government has dealt harshly and, it would seem, unequally with particular minorities. The most glaring instance was the internment of thousands of Japanese during World War II. These people, who were accused of no crime and who obviously could not be deported back to Japan, were herded into what hostile critics called concentration camps, and many of them were kept there for more than three years. Many had lived nearly their whole lives in the United States, had prospered in business and agriculture, and doubtless would have been naturalized had the laws then permitted them to be. Many had sons fighting in the armed forces of the United States. No matter. They were incarcerated, and the Supreme Court upheld their confinement. They claimed a denial of equal protection: the Court replied that the federal government was not required to accord equal protection to everyone. They claimed a loss of liberty without due process of law, under the Fifth Amendment: the Court answered that in view of the exigencies of war and the danger to the country, the executive orders restraining the Japanese-born aliens were not arbitrary, but reasonable actions taken for the nation's safety. These were war time decisions. They were not surprising, for historically in war time the Court has upheld the use of governmental power. But in the cooler light of peace, the harsh treatment of this minority came to seem less and less defensible, and eventually, in 1959, the federal government, speaking through the President, issued a formal apology to the people who had suffered so many years before.

## THE POLITICS OF EQUALITY

In the early days, as we have seen, the demand of humble people for equal recognition played a significant part in the development of American politics. It underlay the clash over the ratification of the Constitution; it was a major stone in the foundation of the first enduring political party. Equality was the watchword of Jacksonian democracy; typically, workingmen marched the streets in Andrew Jackson's 1832 campaign, singing a song which denounced "the proud, the banking faction." (This was hardly an immortal verse, for "faction" was made to rhyme with "Jackson," but it did indicate the temper of the times.) Since Jackson's day the recognition of equal status—at least for white people—has been a working principle of politics which few prudent politicians would publicly question, any more than they would query the importance of the concept of "equal justice under law." [23]

"At least for white people"—yet even some white people have at times been the intended victims of political action based on the idea that they were not entitled to equal rights. Before the Civil War there arose, in some states, the American or "Know-Nothing" party, whose one objective seemed to be the suppression of the new immigrants, especially those of the Catholic religion. The "Know-Nothings" gained brief power in Massachusetts, where for many generations thereafter the bitterness arising from the intolerance of the earlier settlers toward the Irish immigrants largely shaped political life. [24] Anti-Catholicism and anti-Semitism, too, played an ugly role on the national scene as recently as 1924, when the old "Know-Nothing" doctrines were revived by an organization calling itself the Ku Klux Klan.

The original Ku Klux Klan, of course, was a body of white

---

23 As early as 1840, humble birth in a log cabin became a recognized political asset. Oddly, the party which capitalized on that asset, in that year, was the Whig party, the anti-Jackson "proud banking faction." They nominated an old frontier Indian fighter for President, adopted no platform, and outshouted the Jacksonians in a roisterous campaign devoted to praising the rugged virtues and alcoholic vices of the "common man."

24 The "Boston Irish" were welcomed by the Democratic party organization and became loyal Democrats—so much so that for many decades most Bay Staters assumed that nearly every Democrat was a Catholic and vice versa. Protestant Democrats, known as "Yankee Democrats," were rare birds indeed. Not since 1940 has any "Yankee Democrat" been elected to Congress from Massachusetts. The unwillingness to grant equal status to poor immigrants a century ago had an enduring influence on Massachusetts politics, although in 1962 a former Harvard All-American football player, Endicott Peabody, a Protestant "blue blood," won the Democratic nomination and the governorship.

southerners who organized way back in Reconstruction days for the purpose of restoring "white supremacy" in the defeated southern states. Whether or not their lawless tactics—including the systematic terrorizing of uneducated and superstitious Negroes —were effective, their main objective was won before the end of the nineteenth century. By that time, southern Negroes had been effectively excluded from public office and even, to a large degree, from the voting process. Segregation laws had been upheld by the Supreme Court. Northern Negroes, few in number, wielded little or no political influence. Because Lincoln, a Republican, had freed the slaves, they voted Republican; but most conservative Republican leaders showed no more concern for equal rights for Negroes in the South than did the Democrats. For roughly half a century, "the politics of equality" was a meaningless phrase to most Negroes in the United States. They were excluded from politics and they were denied equality.

Today, in contrast, the claim of equal rights for Negroes is a burning political issue all across the country. There are five chief reasons for this change. First is the change in the South itself, from agriculture to industry. The ignorant Negro cotton-picker could be kept ignorant, without the means for any effective protest, but Negroes in steel mills and factories required some competence and inevitably shared with their fellow workers a common interest in decent wages and working conditions. Many observant southerners came to feel that the future of the region depended on the gradual amelioration of the hardships of inequality. Second is the change in the North, arising from the great migration of Negroes into northern cities. This has given Negroes, in some states, a political voice much louder than ever before; politicians of both parties can ill afford to disregard the insistent demand for equality. Third, in both North and South, the Negroes constitute an economically depressed group in a time of widespread affluence; generally speaking, it is they who are the first to lose jobs when automation reduces the work force, and it is their children who cannot find employment when they leave school. The contrast between the relative prosperity of the white population and the relative poverty of the Negroes is a persistent source of unrest, even when Negro leaders give first place to the desire for desegregation of schools and public accommodations. Fourth, the involvement of the United States in an endless struggle for influence throughout the world has made vivid in men's minds the danger of discrimination against colored people here at home. "For Whites Only" is not a slogan likely to win America the friendship of the non-white peoples of Africa and Asia. Fifth—in part, at least, in response to all of the first four factors—the Supreme Court has determined that state-enforced segregation violates the Constitution. The Court's decisions did not create the political issue of equality, but they certainly assured it of a place in the forefront of the political battle for many years to come.

### The Institutional Framework

The struggle for equal rights for Negroes has always been profoundly affected by the Constitution itself, as interpreted by the Supreme Court. The original document recognized the existence of slavery and permitted its perpetuation. The Court in the *Dred Scott* opinion construed it as permanently denying the possibility of Negro citizenship. The Fourteenth Amendment, invented as a shield for the freed slaves, was shot full of holes by the decision in *Plessy v. Ferguson*. The overruling of *Plessy v. Ferguson* in 1954 gave new shape to the ancient issue. Indeed, it stimulated vehement criticism of a part of the institution itself—that is, the role of the Court as interpreter of the Constitution.

The institution of federalism, likewise expressed in the Constitution, has had a steady impact on the quest for Negro equality. It served as a safeguard for slavery and, later, a cover for discrimination. As we saw in Chapter 3, the old cry of "states' rights" has been raised anew in the current effort to preserve the system of racial segregation.

Not only the Constitution, but the institutional qualities of Congress—its long-standing rules and customs—have come to play a large part in the conflict. For decades, efforts have been made to promote equal rights by congressional action. Bills were introduced, for instance, to outlaw the poll tax as a prerequisite for voting in national elections and to create a National Fair Employment Practices Commission with enforcement powers. Such measures were thwarted by the congressional custom of seniority, which often brought southerners to the powerful post of committee chairman, and the Senate's custom of unlimited debate. The latter permits a determined group of southern senators to "filibuster"—that is, to talk so long against a pending measure that it is ultimately withdrawn without a vote. To be sure, since 1917 the Senate's rules have permitted a two-thirds majority to end a filibuster by voting to close debate—but, perhaps significantly, the southerners could count on enough northern Republican votes to defeat any such motion for "cloture." From the end of Reconstruction in 1877 until 1957, therefore, "civil rights" bills in Congress produced what were really sham battles. Such bills had no substantial chance of passage.

A final political institution affecting the issue has been our national electoral machinery—a combination of the electoral college system provided by the Constitution, the apportionment of congressional districts by the state legislatures, and the rise of national political parties. To win the presidency, a party's candidate must gain a majority not of the national popular vote but of the vote of the members of the electoral college. If he wins a popular majority or even only a popular plurality (the largest vote among several candidates, though less than 50 per cent of the vote cast) in a particular state, he receives all of the electoral votes of that state. Ever since the Civil War, the Democratic party has been confident of winning most or all of the southern states for its presidential candidate: conversely, it has generally been assumed that when the "solid South" is broken by some states voting Republican—as some did for Harding, Hoover, and especially Eisenhower—the Democratic candidate is doomed to defeat. These assumptions have given the South a preponderant voice in Democratic party councils far in excess of its proportion of the nation's population. Accordingly, even when northern "liberals" have been the acknowledged leaders of the party, the need to keep the southern voters in the party fold has usually prevented the Democratic party from taking a clear-cut stand in favor of equal rights for all. The great increase in the number of northern Negro voters, however, has recently pushed northern Democrats toward insisting on a firmer "liberal" position, just as it has awakened some Republicans who traditionally paid only lip-service to the Negroes' demands for equality.

The peculiar dual impact of the Negro on the Democratic party and on the House of Representatives is illustrated by the table showing the thirty-five congressional districts with the highest non-white populations. All these districts were represented by Democrats in 1960, except for one vacancy, and all the candidates were either not opposed or were elected easily. Eleven of these districts are in northern urban areas, twenty-one in southern rural areas, and three, two of which are in border states, are southern urban. The northern urban representatives are heavily dependent upon Negro votes for their support. The southern rural lawmakers are just as dependent on the continued existence of a system which keeps a large number of Negroes from voting. It is thus apparent that within the Congress and within the Democratic party there are Congressmen who are going to take a strong position, one way or the other, on the issue of civil rights.

The impact of the Negro on the Senate and the presidency is somewhat harder to detail. The table showing Negro population by states makes it clear that although the states with the largest percentages of Negroes are in the South and border areas, Negroes also form a significant part of the electorate in many of the large northern states. The percentage of Negroes registered to vote is much higher in most of the northern states. Since elections in many of these states tend to be rather closely contested, the interests of the Negro are of concern to senatorial and presidential candidates, especially in large states such as New York, Pennsylvania, Michigan, and Illinois.

## The Interests' Influence

A party, of course, is not only a political "institution," but a special form of interest group, and this group in turn speaks for and is subjected to pressures from various other interests. The political impact of the Negroes' northern migration would have been slight if Negroes voted without regard to the interests of Negroes as an identifiable group. It would have been unimportant, too, if Negroes put party loyalty ahead of all other political

## DISTRICTS WITH LARGEST NON-WHITE POPULATIONS

| Rank | State | Dist. | Type | 1960 Per Cent Non-White |
|------|-------|-------|------|-------------------------|
| 1. | Illinois | 1 | U | 92.1 |
| 2. | New York | 16 | U | 88.5 |
| 3. | Pennsylvania | 4 | U | 73.8 |
| 4. | Hawaii | AL | U | 68.0 |
| 5. | Mississippi | 3 | R | 65.5 |
| 6. | Illinois | 2 | U | 51.7 |
| 7. | North Carolina | 2 | R | 50.5 |
| 8. | Michigan | 13 | U | 50.3 |
| 9. | Mississippi | 2 | R | 49.6 |
| 10. | Virginia | 4 | R | 48.0 |
| 11. | Michigan | 15 | U | 46.6 |
| 12. | South Carolina | 6 | R | 46.6 |
| 13. | Mississippi | 4 | R | 46.4 |
| 14. | Ohio | 21 | U | 46.4 |
| 15. | Maryland | 4 | U | 45.5 |
| 16. | South Carolina | 1 | R | 44.0 |
| 17. | North Carolina | 1 | R | 43.8 |
| 18. | Michigan | 1 | U | 41.4 |
| 19. | Georgia | 6 | R | 41.3 |
| 20. | Mississippi | 5 | R | 41.2 |
| 21. | Louisiana | 5 | R | 40.5 |
| 22. | New York | 10 | U | 40.0 |
| 23. | Alabama | 3 | R | 39.3 |
| 24. | Georgia | 2 | R | 38.9 |
| 25. | Alabama | 1 | U | 38.8 |
| 26. | Alabama | 6 | R | 38.7 |
| 27. | Georgia | 1 | R | 37.6 |
| 28. | Louisiana | 4 | R | 37.4 |
| 29. | South Carolina | 2 | R | 37.3 |
| 30. | Georgia | 3 | R | 37.2 |
| 31. | Tennessee | 9 | U | 36.4 |
| 32. | Pennsylvania | 2 | U | 36.2 |
| 33. | Alabama | 2 | R | 36.0 |
| 34. | North Carolina | 7 | R | 35.6 |
| 35. | Louisiana | 6 | R | 35.4 |

x = not opposed.
NA = not available.
SOURCE: *Congressional Quarterly,* Vol. 20, March 30, 1962, pp. 507, 514, 515.

| 1960 Incumbent | Winner's Per Cent 1960 Vote | Registered—1961 | |
| --- | --- | --- | --- |
| | | Per Cent Whites | Per Cent Negroes |
| Dawson (D) | 77.8 | — | — |
| Powell (D) | 71.6 | — | — |
| Nix (D) | 78.4 | — | — |
| Inoyne (D) | 74.4 | — | — |
| Smith (D) | 92.7 | 76.4 | 30.7 |
| O'Hara (D) | 66.6 | — | — |
| Fountain (D) | 87.8 | 84.9 | 17.1 |
| Diggs (D) | 71.4 | — | — |
| Whitten (D) | x | 84.0 | 17.1 |
| Abbitt (D) | x | 54.8 | 18.6 |
| Dingell (D) | 79.4 | — | — |
| McMillan (D) | x | NA | NA |
| Williams (D) | x | 99.8 | 30.4 |
| Vanik (D) | 73.0 | — | — |
| Fallen (D) | 65.5 | 71.9 | 51.9 |
| Rivers (D) | x | NA | NA |
| Bonner (D) | 86.5 | 103.3 | 25.1 |
| Nedzi (D) | 85.5 | — | — |
| Vinson (D) | x | NA | NA |
| Winstead (D) | x | 84.4 | 50.6 |
| Passman (D) | x | 76.9 | 6.9 |
| Kelley (D) | 76.6 | — | — |
| Andrews (D) | x | 64.6 | 10.0 |
| Pilcher (D) | x | NA | NA |
| Boykin (D) | x | 57.5 | 13.4 |
| Seldin (D) | x | 66.7 | 16.2 |
| Hagan (D) | x | NA | NA |
| Waggonner (D) | 54.5 | 69.2 | 8.2 |
| Vacancy | x | NA | NA |
| Forrester (D) | x | NA | NA |
| Davis (D) | x | 71.8 | 64.3 |
| Gramahan (D) | 72.3 | — | — |
| Grant (D) | x | 67.7 | 11.2 |
| Lennon (D) | 76.5 | 76.6 | 42.8 |
| Morrison (D) | 85.6 | 81.1 | 31.5 |

U = urban.
AL = at large.
R = rural.

## NEGRO POPULATION BY STATE

| State | Negro Population 1950 | Negro Population 1960 | Per Cent 1960 Population Non-White |
|---|---|---|---|
| Alabama | 979,617 | 980,271 | 30.1 |
| Alaska | NA | 6,771 | 22.8 |
| Arizona | 25,974 | 43,403 | 10.2 |
| Arkansas | 426,639 | 388,787 | 21.9 |
| California | 462,172 | 883,861 | 8.0 |
| Colorado | 20,177 | 39,992 | 3.0 |
| Connecticut | 53,472 | 107,449 | 4.4 |
| Delaware | 43,598 | 60,688 | 13.9 |
| Florida | 603,101 | 880,186 | 17.9 |
| Georgia | 1,062,762 | 1,122,596 | 28.6 |
| Hawaii | NA | 4,943 | 68.0 * |
| Idaho | 1,050 | 1,502 | 1.5 |
| Illinois | 645,980 | 1,037,470 | 10.6 |
| Indiana | 174,168 | 269,275 | 5.9 |
| Iowa | 19,692 | 25,354 | 1.0 |
| Kansas | 73,158 | 91,445 | 4.6 |
| Kentucky | 201,921 | 215,949 | 7.2 |
| Louisiana | 882,428 | 1,039,207 | 32.1 |
| Maine | 1,221 | 3,318 | 0.6 |
| Maryland | 385,972 | 518,410 | 17.0 |
| Massachusetts | 73,171 | 111,842 | 2.4 |
| Michigan | 442,296 | 717,581 | 9.4 |
| Minnesota | 14,022 | 22,263 | 1.2 |
| Mississippi | 986,494 | 915,743 | 42.3 |
| Missouri | 297,088 | 390,853 | 9.2 |
| Montana | 1,232 | 1,467 | 3.6 |

* Includes Orientals and others, 425,599.
† Includes other races, 12,131.
SOURCE: *Congressional Quarterly*, Vol. 20, March 30, 1962, pp. 509-512.

goals and values. The assumption of most politicians, however, is that a "pro-Negro" interest is shared by most Negroes and strongly influences their vote, and the election statistics make plain the shift in party allegiance among Negro voters.

| State | Negro Population | | Per Cent 1960 Population Non-White |
| | 1950 | 1960 | |
| --- | --- | --- | --- |
| Nebraska | 19,234 | 29,262 | 2.6 |
| Nevada | 4,302 | 13,584 | 7.7 |
| New Hampshire | 731 | 1,903 | 0.4 |
| New Jersey | 318,565 | 514,875 | 8.7 |
| New Mexico | 8,408 | 17,063 | 7.9 |
| New York | 918,191 | 1,417,511 | 8.9 |
| North Carolina | 1,047,353 | 1,116,021 | 25.4 |
| North Dakota | 257 | 777 | 2.0 † |
| Ohio | 513,072 | 786,097 | 8.2 |
| Oklahoma | 145,503 | 153,084 | 9.5 |
| Oregon | 11,529 | 18,133 | 2.1 |
| Pennsylvania | 638,485 | 852,750 | 7.6 |
| Rhode Island | 13,903 | 18,332 | 2.4 |
| South Carolina | 822,077 | 829,291 | 34.9 |
| South Dakota | 727 | 1,114 | 4.0 ‡ |
| Tennessee | 530,603 | 586,876 | 16.5 |
| Texas | 977,458 | 1,187,125 | 12.6 |
| Utah | 2,729 | 4,148 | 1.9 |
| Vermont | 443 | 519 | 0.2 |
| Virginia | 734,211 | 816,258 | 20.8 |
| Washington | 30,691 | 48,738 | 3.6 § |
| West Virginia | 114,867 | 89,378 | 4.9 |
| Wisconsin | 28,182 | 74,546 | 2.4 |
| Wyoming | 2,557 | 2,183 | 2.2 # |
| Dist. of Col. | 280,803 | 411,737 | 53.9 |
| Total U.S. | 15,042,286 | 18,871,831 | 11.4 |

‡ Includes other races, 26,302.
§ Includes other races, 52,801.
# Includes other races, 4,961.

Actually, it is hard (or impossible) to state with absolute certainty that as between two white candidates, Negroes vote for the one most favorable to their particular racial interest. In local elections wherein a qualified colored man opposes a qualified white man, Negroes without doubt vote heavily for the Negro candidate.[25] But in an election between white candidates, is the "racial" interest paramount, or does the Negro, like the white voter, make his choice on the basis of other issues? Politicians in both parties tend to assume that the Negro voter decides on the basis of the candidate's record, or that of his party, on issues concerning equal rights. And certainly Negroes are unlikely to vote for anyone who defends discrimination—hence the usual reluctance to nominate a southerner for President lest he lose the northern Negro vote. Yet the evidence seems to indicate that where neither candidate is hostile, Negroes vote in terms of more interests than those of color and equality alone. Particularly they are affected, like so many others, by their own economic condition and aspirations.

Economic circumstances plainly underlay the noticeable shift of northern Negro voters from Republican to Democratic in 1932 and the ensuing New Deal period. The failure of President Roosevelt to fight for civil rights legislation did not turn them against him; if he was not battling for racial equality, still he was, in their view, helping the poor people. Although the persistent opposition of dominant southern Democrats in Congress did drive southern Negroes, in large numbers, into the Republican ranks during the Eisenhower years, northern Negroes continued to vote heavily Democratic, for to them the Democratic party remained the party of the "little guy." Any political prophet, then, must tread cautiously when he tries to predict the "Negro vote." To the Negro the civil rights issue may be of first importance, but not of sole importance.

The "equal rights" interest includes white people as well as colored. After all, the first apostles of Negro freedom in this country were such white zealots as editor William Lloyd Garrison, orator Wendell Phillips, and the martyred publisher, Elijah P. Lovejoy. Thousands of white men and women feel keenly about the issue of equal rights. Many of these support the "educational" and comparatively nonpolitical organization for the improve-

25 Even in such situations, however, it cannot be assumed that Negroes vote as a solid bloc for the Negro candidate. For example, in a city-wide election in Atlanta, Georgia, among numerous candidates were two Negroes of excellent reputation; one got a far bigger vote than the other in the Negro wards.

ment of opportunities for Negroes, the National Urban League. Others have joined the more militant National Association for the Advancement of Colored People (NAACP). The latter organization, founded in 1909, has in recent years emerged as a powerful and effective pressure group. With only about 400,000 members, it has made an impact primarily because of the timeliness of its appeal and the skill and resourcefulness of its leaders, especially its former chief attorney, Thurgood Marshall, who was appointed by President Kennedy to the United States Court of Appeals. Despairing, at least temporarily, of favorable action in Congress, the NAACP immediately after World War II sought to gain its objectives through judicial decisions. Courts do not weigh pressure groups and decide cases accordingly; but litigants do have a better chance in court if their cases raise issues in proper form and at the psychological moment, are carefully prepared, and are ably argued. In guiding civil rights litigation (culminating in *Brown v. Board of Education*) the NAACP thus had an influence on the course of history.

In the long struggle to implement the Supreme Court's decisions in the South, the NAACP has taken the lead and hence has been singled out as the special enemy of the believers in the maintenance of "white supremacy"—the White Citizens' Councils and their legislative allies. Some states have tried to outlaw it, others to harass it into ineffectiveness. Public employees have been forbidden to join or support it; state investigators have demanded that it produce its membership lists, as if it were some kind of treasonable conspiracy. (This effort to learn the names of all members and contributors was halted by the courts, at least temporarily; but it persisted, for it was the keystone of a campaign to weaken the NAACP. The idea was that if membership lists were publicized people would resign from the NAACP for fear of social or economic reprisals.)

In recent years the NAACP and its dominant policy of progress through litigation have been incapable of satisfying the accelerating pressure for Negro rights. Other groups have come into existence which attempt to accomplish more and accomplish it faster than the NAACP. The Congress of Racial Equality (CORE), founded in 1942 but not prominent until the late 1950's, claims to have invented two of the major new weapons in the Negro's arsenal: the sit-in and the Freedom Ride. CORE, under National Director James Farmer, has advocated and carried out direct, non-violent assault on discrimination. Using similar methods have been the Southern Christian Leadership Conference, the organizational vehicle of the Rev. Martin Luther King, Jr., and the Student Non-Violent Coordinating Committee, a militant organization of southern Negro students and young people. The aspirations of these groups, and their sense of urgency, promised both continued pressure in the field of civil rights and considerable conflict within the movement.

Another element of conflict is afforded by emergence of the Black Muslims. This group cannot be called a civil rights group in the same sense as the others, for it rejects integration and preaches a racism of black supremacy. It advocates a separate Negro nation within the territory of the United States. Started in 1930, but not well known until the late 1950's, the Black Muslim movement appeals chiefly to the Negro in the lowest economic bracket. Estimates of its strength vary, but the consensus seems to be that it has at least 100,000 members, and the fact that Adam Clayton Powell, a Negro Congressman from Harlem, has praised it is a suggestive indication of its political power. The sect imposes high moral standards and heavy financial obligations upon its members and identifies with Moslem nations abroad. This movement's course under its principal spokesman, Malcolm X, is hard to predict, but its potential importance in the politics of equality is considerable.

The "white supremacy" interest, enlisting now the sympathy of many southern "gradualists," has become (or remained) dominant in the southern states. Its impact is felt, too, in Washington. Thus in 1950 a distinguished senator, Frank P. Graham, was defeated for renomination in North Carolina by a "smear" campaign charging that he was sympathetic to the Negroes' cause, and in 1958 Representative Brooks Hays of Arkansas lost his seat because he was not sufficiently vehement in his opposition to equal rights. Hays lost even though he was the regular Democratic nominee, and despite the fact that in 1956 he had been one of a hundred and one southern representatives and senators who signed the so-called "Southern Manifesto," a "Declaration of Constitutional Rights," denouncing the Supreme Court's desegregation ruling and urging that it be resisted until reversed.

For obvious reasons, the "white supremacy" interest is centered in the South. Its adherents, however, hope for its extension in those northern cities where the Negro population is increasing. Convinced that segregation is right and necessary, they believe that white people outside the South will come to share this conviction once they find large numbers of Negroes living in their immediate neighborhood. They have received encouragement from one widely read national weekly, whose editor, David Lawrence, has persistently denounced the *Brown* decision. Mr. Lawrence appears to argue out of a deep personal belief that the Court was wrong—which reminds us that individual reactions, apart from discernible interest groups, have their own impact on political developments.

## The Individual Impact

There is a temptation to look back, here, and mention the men and women, colored and white, who have played leading parts in the progress of the American Negroes "up from slavery." However, we are dealing with politics—the struggle for power which may be used by government to further or to impede the quest for equal rights. In that political struggle, few Negroes have gained high office and participated in far-reaching decisions. As late as 1962, for example, no Negroes sat in the United States Senate, and only four served in the House of Representatives. The names of Negro leaders, from "gradualist" Booker T. Washington, a founder of the Urban League, and "militant" W. E. DuBois, a founder of the NAACP, down to the present have been associated more with education, science, and the arts than with politics and government. Mainly it has been white people in positions of power whose personal characters and viewpoints have affected the search for equality.

The first and greatest, of course, was Abraham Lincoln. He was not an abolitionist; as he said, if he could save the Union without freeing a single slave, he would do so. The fact remains that by executive order, he set the slaves free—and eventually the military might of his armies made the order fully effective. A different President, although fighting like Lincoln to save the Union, might well have pursued a different course. The Emancipation Proclamation was Lincoln's personal decision.

In more recent times two Presidents, both Democrats, furnish an interesting personal contrast in the way they approached the issue. The first, Franklin D. Roosevelt (whose distant cousin, Theodore Roosevelt, had long before caused an uproar by inviting Booker T. Washington to dine at the White House) had a natural sympathy for the Negro cause. His own political judgment, however, led him to refrain from advocating noteworthy steps toward equal rights; he did not wish to alienate the white southerners in Congress. Then came Harry Truman, who hailed from a one-time slave state (where schools were segregated, indeed, until 1954) and who rather prided himself on not being a "do-gooder." This practical politician from Missouri took, on his own motion, a step of great significance: on July 16, 1946, he ordered an end to segregation in the armed forces. Thereafter he urged congressional action on civil rights, thereby cementing southern congressional hostility toward his whole domestic program. What motivated Truman? Perhaps he figured that many southerners, for economic reasons, would oppose his program anyway and that his pro-equality stand would keep Negroes voting Democratic. Perhaps he acted out of personal conviction; after all, he was a modern "Jacksonian." The point is that he did what he did, whereas a different person in the White House would have acted differently.

The effectiveness of the desegregation decision was likewise affected by the personalities of two Presidents, Dwight D. Eisenhower and John F. Kennedy. Both met defiance with a show of force, to uphold the Constitution; but neither was by nature a fervent crusader for equal rights. A different kind of President, in 1954, might have used all his influence, either to further the public acceptance of integration or, through new appointments to the Supreme Court, to reverse the desegregation decision. Eisenhower did neither; he even managed to refrain from expressing approval or disapproval of the decision. Kennedy, with a more active conception of the presidency, took a more affirmative position on the issue; but not until the widespread Negro demonstrations in the spring of 1963 did he come forward with a broad proposal for speeding integration and speak forcefully in favor of it.

In the South, the two governors whose resistance was broken by federal troops—Orval E. Faubus of Arkansas in 1957 and Ross Barnett of Mississippi in 1962—were presumably motivated, as most politicians are, by a combination of factors: personal beliefs and political ambitions. The latter seemed significant especially in the case of Faubus, who himself had won the governorship by defeating a "white supremacist." Ironically, he chose in 1957 to make himself a hero of the "white supremacists," by ordering the state guard to prevent Negro children from entering Central High School in Little Rock, even though the Mayor of Little Rock said that if any objectors to their entrance made any trouble, the local police could easily keep the peace. If Faubus's primary purpose was to gain re-election, it was a shrewd choice, for the popular reaction against the eventual federal armed intervention was sure to win him votes in Arkansas.

Governor Barnett appeared to be a more authentic spokesman of the die-hard opposition to integration. From 1960 onward, however, another southern political figure was making his influence felt on the opposite side—influence that was increased simply because of his southern background. This was the Vice-President, Lyndon B. Johnson, who emerged as a quietly persuasive advocate of the civil rights program.

All of these men, of course, were acting within a political context. What they said and did affected the course of action in the states and in Congress, and within the two great political parties. The same was true of the efforts made by Governor Rockefeller of New York in 1963, to rally the Republican party to the integration cause, or at least to establish himself as the leader of the pro-integration wing of the party. By 1963, of course, men who did not hold public office were nevertheless shaping the politics of the 1960's; of these, the best-known, over an extended period of time, was a still youthful Negro, the Rev. Martin Luther King, Jr., whose persistent leadership of "non-violent" demonstrations led his admirers to compare him with Gandhi, the great figure who led India to freedom.

To sum up: the drive for equal rights regardless of color, after a vigorous start in the Reconstruction period, ground to a halt in the 1880's and 1890's. It was stopped by state legislation and the Supreme Court's decision in *Plessy v. Ferguson*, upholding the keystone of that legislative arch. It remained halted for half a century. Population shifts and increasing uneasiness about anti-Negro discrimination in a largely colored world started it forward again at about the time of World War II. Facing great obstacles imposed by the country's formal and informal political institutions, the proponents of equal rights concentrated their efforts on the courts, achieving success in the desegregation decision of 1954. That decision brought new militance to the opposing interest, that of the upholders of "white supremacy." And with the main judicial battle over, the struggle shifted to the legislative halls, where the increase of Negro voting strength and the temper of the times combined to make action realistically possible for the first time since the days of U. S. Grant. Both parties had to tread warily, the Republicans having to choose whether to try to win back the northern Negroes at the cost of losing their foothold in the South, the Democrats being faced (as they had been in 1860 and 1948) with a choice between upholding equal rights or temporizing for the sake of party unity. In both parties, these decisions were in part shaped by the political judgments and personal convictions of responsible party leaders. And over the sounds of all the political discussions and debates could be heard, by those with ears to hear, the command of the Fourteenth Amendment that no state shall "deny to any person within its jurisdiction the equal protection of the laws," and the ancient reminder of 1776 that "all men are created equal."

PART *Three*

# THE POLITICAL SYSTEM

CHAPTER **9**

# Interests and Pressure Groups

N ext Tuesday is election day. It does not matter how you vote—but *vote!*" The truck with the loudspeaker rumbles down the street, roaring its message to the idling drugstore cowboys, the busy housewives, the crowds in the stands watching a high school football game. ". . . It does not matter how you vote— but *vote!*" On the face of it, what a ridiculous slogan! Of course it matters how you vote: if it doesn't, then there's no sense in your bothering to vote at all.

Let's analyze that slogan. To be fair, let's admit that "it does not matter how you vote" probably means "regardless of whether you intend to vote for the Republican candidate or the Democratic candidate." Then the command to "vote!" implies that you have a civic duty to express your preference at the polls. Somehow, if you don't cast your ballot, you are letting democracy down.

Surely, however, this assumes that there is a real alternative before you—not just some unknown names and meaningless symbols on a ballot—and that you know enough to make an intelligent choice. Know enough, that is, about the candidates, the parties, and their programs to have definite preferences, conscientiously arrived at. The real "get-out-the-vote" message, then, should not be broadcast the Saturday before election day. It needs to be sounded every day of the year, and it should say something about *preparing yourselves to vote intelligently.* The final week-end's slogan might well end up: "And if you still don't know what you're voting about, stay home."

As we shall see, the task of "getting out the vote" has traditionally been the job of local party organizations. Only in recent years has it been undertaken also on a nonpartisan basis, through an appeal to everybody in the name of patriotism and civic duty. Apparently there is a feeling that among the democracies we make a poor showing: roughly 60 per cent of those potentially eligible actually vote in even hotly contested presidential elections, whereas in France nearly 90 per cent go to the polls in the average general election. The graph printed here shows approximately the proportion of Americans eligible to vote, who have voted in modern elections, while the table indicates how this varies from state to state. Remember that the national percentages are considerably lowered by the fact that many southern candidates are unopposed in the general election; the real battle is often over when the results of the primary are in.

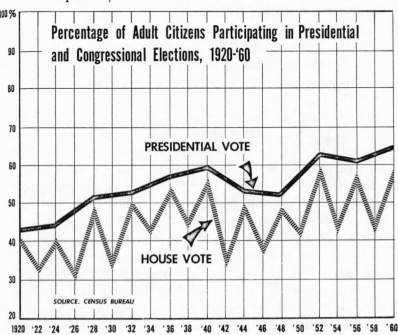

**Percentage of Adult Citizens Participating in Presidential and Congressional Elections, 1920-'60**

PRESIDENTIAL VOTE

HOUSE VOTE

SOURCE. CENSUS BUREAU

**PER CENT OF NUMBER OF CITIZENS OLD ENOUGH TO VOTE WHO VOTED**

| State | 1960 President | 1960 House | 1958 House | State | 1960 President | 1960 House | 1958 House |
|---|---|---|---|---|---|---|---|
| Alabama | 31.0 | 23.9 | 13.4 | Montana | 71.4 | 70.0 | 57.1 |
| Alaska | 45.3 | 44.1 | — | Nebraska | 71.5 | 67.7 | 46.5 |
| Arizona | 54.4 | 51.4 | 45.8 | Nevada | 61.3 | 59.2 | 53.2 |
| Arkansas | 41.0 | 6.7* | 5.9 | New Hampshire | 79.3 | 76.3 | 54.8 |
| California | 67.4 | 64.1 | 56.8 | New Jersey | 71.8 | 68.9 | 52.1 |
| Colorado | 71.4 | 69.4 | 53.6 | New Mexico | 62.0 | 60.2 | 46.4 |
| Connecticut | 76.9 | 76.6 | 66.1 | New York | 67.0 | 64.5 | 52.2 |
| Delaware | 73.4 | 72.9 | 56.4 | North Carolina | 53.5 | 50.9 | 24.2 |
| Florida | 50.0 | 40.4 | 18.1 | North Dakota | 78.4 | 72.3 | 49.3 |
| Georgia | 30.4 | 23.8 | 7.1 | Ohio | 71.3 | 65.9 | 54.6 |
| Hawaii | 51.3 | 50.7 | — | Oklahoma | 63.8 | 59.2 | 38.3 |
| Idaho | 80.8 | 78.0 | 63.6 | Oregon | 72.3 | 71.0 | 54.9 |
| Illinois | 75.7 | 73.8 | 51.8 | Pennsylvania | 70.5 | 69.8 | 56.4 |
| Indiana | 76.9 | 76.3 | 62.2 | Rhode Island | 75.0 | 72.6 | 62.7 |
| Iowa | 76.6 | 73.7 | 48.0 | South Carolina | 30.5 | 25.9 | 6.1 |
| Kansas | 70.3 | 65.9 | 56.8 | South Dakota | 78.2 | 76.8 | 64.3 |
| Kentucky | 59.2 | 48.1 | 25.3 | Tennessee | 50.3 | 30.7 | 18.2 |
| Louisiana | 44.8 | 28.8 | 10.7 | Texas | 41.8 | 36.9 | 14.5 |
| Maine | 72.6 | 70.3 | 48.5 | Utah | 80.0 | 78.9 | 62.4 |
| Maryland | 57.2 | 53.2 | 40.9 | Vermont | 72.4 | 71.9 | 55.6 |
| Massachusetts | 76.1 | 69.6 | 57.3 | Virginia | 33.4 | 27.7 | 19.8 |
| Michigan | 72.4 | 70.1 | 48.3 | Washington | 72.3 | 65.5 | 53.4 |
| Minnesota | 77.0 | 75.7 | 56.0 | West Virginia | 77.4 | 75.8 | 53.0 |
| Mississippi | 25.5 | 22.0 | 5.2 | Wisconsin | 73.5 | 70.6 | 49.5 |
| Missouri | 71.8 | 68.4 | 43.7 | Wyoming | 73.6 | 70.9 | 61.2 |
| | | | | Total | 63.8% | 59.4% | 43.6% |

* Arkansas does not tabulate votes for unopposed candidates.
SOURCE: *Congressional Quarterly*, Vol. 20, October 26, 1962, p. 2,033.

Surely the real standard of measurement, however, is not the number who vote but the number who want to vote—who feel concerned about the issues, the parties, and the parties' nominees. This concern, in turn, can be put to most effective use if it is enlightened by knowledge and some familiarity with analytical thinking. The informed man, the person of judgment, can first stimulate others to share his concern and then often influence them to share his preferences. Studies of individual voting habits show that many people make up their minds on the basis of what someone tells them—not a newspaper or a party boss, but a neighbor or friend whom they respect because he "knows his stuff."

The intelligent voter must have at least three skills in the general area of public affairs. He must understand the issues and know something about the candidates. This is current knowledge, deepened by what he has learned of history and by his judgment of human beings, but changing in content from day to day. A textbook can provide part of the background, but no more. Second, he must be familiar with the framework within which public policy is made. He needs some understanding of the American political system. In the larger sense, that is what this book is all about. You may feel, however, that "political system" is a term referring primarily to the active and endless struggle for public power, for the attainment of particular goals, waged by political parties and other groups and dramatized by candidates who enter crowded halls with bands playing or stroll down Main Street shaking hands. Who are the real rivals in this visible, familiar struggle, this striving for popular support? What factors sway the balance, and what is the meaning of victory or defeat for one contestant or the other? And by what rules, if any, is the "great game of politics" governed? In this sense, the "political system" is of primary concern to anyone who wants to vote wisely and to influence others: and it is the subject of this part of your text.

Heretofore we have ended several chapters with a discussion of politics—"the politics of federalism," "the politics of freedom," and so on. Now we deal centrally with politics itself. We deal with interests, institutions, and individuals in electoral contests and the making of public policy, always remembering that elections are only one way of settling political differences and that the governmental decisions which affect our lives are often many steps removed from the polling booths.

## THE MAJOR DISCERNIBLE INTERESTS

We have already made frequent references to very general "interests"—the "property interest" represented at the Philadelphia convention, for instance, or the less tangible interest in states' rights. It may be that politics is essentially a process of both reflecting and manipulating such interests or working out compromises between their different goals. Certainly political action does all three of these things. In the particular business of electoral politics, candidates or even whole parties may speak for an interest; campaigners regularly appeal to the voters' various real or supposed interests; party platforms and even presidential nominations often are the product of conscious compromise between interests.

In speaking of "interests" at this point, let us keep two things in mind. First, an interest is not necessarily organized. It can exist without any national association or public relations advisers. The framers at Philadelphia, for example, spoke for a "property interest" without benefit of the existence of any chamber of commerce. Second, whether organized or not, an interest is not necessarily evil. Madison, in *Federalist No. 10*, spoke of "factions" (by which he meant, conceivably, interests both unorganized and organized) as selfish and evil, and George Washington referred to the "pestilence of faction." In fact, however, interests are inevitable, natural, and human; and given our political process, organized interests— pressure groups—are virtually inevitable too. They may be selfish and harmful, they may even tend to national disunity and civil strife; but for better or worse they are the very soil at the base of our political landscape, and the plants which flourish in that soil do not necessarily bear bitter fruit. For a century our country has prospered in unity, despite sometimes fierce conflicts of interest such as those between "capital and labor" in former decades. Not even the deep emotions of the conflict between the "integration" and "segregation" interests will destroy it now.

In speaking of interests that have political significance, we must remember, of course, that numbers matter. If you love to play chess, make chess sets, or write books teaching the various ways to open a chess game, you have a "pro-chess" interest. You might want your state university to drop football and institute chess as a major sport, or perhaps have the legislature make chess a required school subject. But the likelihood is—and there hardly needs to be a scientific basis for this statement—that the "pro-chess" interest is very, very small. It represents no real voting strength. Covertly or accidentally this interest might get itself represented in the legislature for a short time; but it does not have enough votes, anywhere, for either candidates or legislators to pay it any serious attention. Perhaps if you could combine your concern with that of other enthusiasts, form a state chess association and operate as a pressure group, the "pro-chess" interest would be more important politically; as we shall see, even small pressure groups can sometimes get results. For the moment, though, you are unorganized and ineffective.

Even without organization, interests held in common by large numbers of people have great political effect. This broad community of interest has sometimes been termed an interest *grouping* as distinguished from an organized "group." The major groupings in our political history have been fairly easy to identify, even as they are today.

## Economic Interests

First, let us look at the groupings of what are essentially material or economic interests. Long ago Madison saw these as the ultimate cause of political conflict: ". . . the most common and durable source of factions has been the various and unequal distribution of property." [1] Various: the workman against the factory owner, the exporter against the importer. Unequal: the poor against the rich.

It is convenient, but perhaps a little too easy, to identify the economic interests which most affect politics as business, labor, and agriculture. These are very broad groupings indeed. True, a given issue might unite one or another of them to the point where

---

[1] *Federalist No. 10.*

you could correctly speak of the "business interest" or the "labor interest" or the "agricultural interest." Take the last of these. Suppose that a serious proposal were made, that hereafter it should be unlawful to sell any agricultural products above a particular price [2]—a price lower than those currently being charged. This would affect the earnings of all farmers, whatever they produced. Some would be hurt worse than others, but all would be hurt. Whoever made the proposal would be called an enemy of the "farmers"—in more sophisticated terms, he would be charged with hostility to the "agricultural interest."

On the other hand, a closer look at this particular "grouping" makes one realize that very few issues are likely to arise where it is safe to speak of the "agricultural interest" as a whole. Farmers make their living in different ways and under different circumstances. Some grow cotton, some raise hogs. Some live on a small acreage and struggle to meet their mortgage payments; others are wealthy ranchers. What some want from government is not at all the same as what others want and may even be drastically opposed to it—even though they are all "farmers."

A similar caution should be observed in speaking of "labor" and "business." For many decades, to be sure, the industrial wage earners were so emphatically at the bottom of the economic heap that they could all be classified together and a single appeal made to their interest—homesteads, minimum wages, maximum hours. The rise of unions changed the picture. In the larger industries unions gave promise of achieving not only better working conditions, but community status. Small artisans in the old tradition, however, did not feel the need for these and resisted unionization. Thus the labor interest began to split. As large-scale industry became dominant in the economy and depression threw millions out of work, it was possible once again to speak of a labor interest—a general wage earner's demand for employment, fair conditions,

---

[2] The first known law regulating farm prices in America was enacted in colonial Virginia in 1640, making it illegal to barter tobacco for a value less than sixpence a pound—a measure beneficial to the growers but adverse to the "smokers' interest" and to English traders who had been striking hard bargains. See J. K. Galbraith, *American Capitalism* (Boston: Houghton Mifflin Co., 1952) pp. 160-161.

and, now, the right to organize into unions; but this unity lasted only briefly. The union movement itself split, so that for twenty years you had to take care lest what you thought was the labor interest was only the voice of one league of unions, opposed to another league of unions. In the 1950's the bulk of the union movement once again coalesced, and some of its leaders spoke in terms of the labor interest on the assumption that it was one and the same as the combined unions' interest.

Even though most of them are under "one big tent," however, on some issues the unions' interest itself dissolves into separate pieces. The coal miners in the east central states, for instance, favored the building of the St. Lawrence Seaway; the New England longshoremen opposed it. So if you were a Massachusetts congressman courting labor's support, you opposed the seaway; and later, if you wanted to run for President, you found that you had made some enemies in West Virginia and Pennsylvania.

The clash between particular goals, such as those of cotton growers and stockbreeders, or coal miners and longshoremen, is of course repeated over and over again within the general grouping of the "business interest." The latter must be subdivided in various ways: big business and small (though on most issues this difference is unimportant), industries dependent on exports or on imports, companies unionized and nonunion, and, perhaps most significant, those whose commodities or services compete with other commodities or services. Thus to speak, for instance, of a "transportation interest" would be almost meaningless; railroads and trucking companies are both in the transportation business, but they have long opposed each other in legislative halls and before regulatory bodies as well as in the search for customers.

If it would be a mistake to think in the oversimplified terms of business, labor, and agricultural interests, it would be an even greater error to assume that all interests are altogether economic. We need not argue here whether the basis of every interest is economic motivation, in accordance with a materialistic interpretation of history and society. Suffice it to say that today in America we can identify numerous groupings which seem to lack a common economic background and whose professed concerns are not necessarily economic at all.

## National Origin Interests

The national background interests play a prominent part in American politics. These, surely, are as much emotional and environmental as anything else. In the American melting pot, old national customs, brought from afar, persist for generations; even the great-grandsons of immigrants, men successful in American life, are prone to feel some attachment to the country of their ancestors' origin. Why did the first Henry Cabot Lodge, long before World War I, make it his practice to "twist the British Lion's tail" in his senatorial campaigns in Massachusetts? A Boston Brahmin, Lodge was socially as close as any American could come to being an "English gentleman." Yet his speeches were often vehemently anti-British—and thus he won a substantial number of the normally Democratic Irish-American votes in his state, for those immigrants and sons of immigrants nursed an abiding hatred of Britain. The carefully planned campaign to keep the United States out of the League of Nations, a campaign in which Lodge was a leader, was based on special appeals to various national origin interests. The idea was to arouse opposition to the Treaty of Versailles (of which the League Covenant was an integral part) by turning Italo-Americans against it on the ground that it denied Italy its "right" to an Adriatic port, Irish-Americans against it because it failed to provide that Ireland should be united and free, and so on. If this example seems dated, look around you. Proclaim that Poland's freedom is no conceivable concern of ours, and then try to get elected mayor of Buffalo: you won't have a chance. Look at the election returns in a district populated by Americans of Italian heritage: other things being equal, Margiotti will beat Schmidt every time.

One interest which is likely to be of significance in our foreign policy for years to come is harder to classify, yet probably comes closer to the "national origin" tag than anything else. This is the Jewish grouping—which, again, must be subdivided into a Zionist interest and a non-Zionist or anti-Zionist interest. The Jewish vote, if identifiable, could be assumed to be strongly anti-Nazi twenty-five years ago. It is less homogeneous now, but a strong subgrouping (as well as a vigorous organized movement) is deeply and emotionally concerned for the security of another country—Israel. The recognition of this political interest was a factor in the original American commitments to Israel in 1947. It continues to be an unacknowledged factor in the development of American policy in the Middle East.

## Religious Interests

Some would say that any Jewish "grouping" should come under the heading of "religious" rather than "national origin." However that may be, it is certainly true that a religious interest has always been a real factor in American politics. Two principles—those of separation of church and state and respect for every person's religious beliefs—tend to submerge this factor in political campaigns. Occasionally, however, it rises above the surface. Back in the 1850's, a whole political party, the "Know-Nothings," spoke for the extremely intolerant wing of Protestantism against Catholicism. In our own century, in 1928, Alfred E. Smith, the Democratic candidate for President, lost much support in the usually Democratic South because he was a Catholic—and carried Massachusetts and Rhode Island for the same reason. John F. Kennedy, the first Catholic to become President, met the "religious issue" squarely in the 1960 campaign; his statement on the separation of church and state made to Protestant clergymen at Houston, Texas, and televised and retelevised nationally, probably allayed the fears of many Protestant Democrats.

Politicians are well aware of the religious interests among their constituents and are careful not to offend the voters' religious sensibilities. Thus it became a custom for candidates to invoke the deity, usually at the very end of their campaign speeches, lest their hearers accuse them of being irreligious. In state and local governments, the Christian clergy and lay denominational leaders have often played an active part in the shaping of public policy, openly forwarding their conception of the religious interest.

## Ethnic Interests

To speak of "ethnic" or "racial" political interests may involve a misuse of language, depending upon what you mean by "race." Realistically, however, we can say that whether color differentiates races or not, it creates an interest "grouping." Not only that: one particular interest, that of the Negroes, has a major impact on American politics today. Negroes have a common interest in policies which foster or impede equality of opportunity and status. They vote in large numbers in many big northern cities, and how they vote is influenced by their appraisal of the rival parties and candidates in terms of the issue of equal rights. Conversely, there exists in most of the South a discernible "white" interest in the perpetuation of segregation, reflected by the "Southern Manifesto" which the majority of southern congressmen signed in 1956.

Here, then, is the broad classification of the nation's major political interests, based on economic position, national origin, religion, and color. But there are other "ideal" interests, some of which we have mentioned earlier: a conscious concern for individual liberty, or peace through international cooperation or isolation, or patriotism in terms of retaining ancient customs or achieving world domination—or simply "anti-communism," which might include economic, national origin, religious, and patriotic factors. Of these the most widely shared are, surely, opposition to communism and desire for peace. These interests are not always easy to reconcile. In fact, the most difficult task of the American statesman today and for many tomorrows is the reconciliation of those interests—to find the way to stand firm against Communist power without blowing up civilization.

Most of us, within ourselves, represent a variety of interests and belong to more than one interest "grouping." Let us imagine a Colonel Thomas Jefferson Fairfax. Brought up to venerate his namesake, the Colonel has an emotional commitment to the principles of the Declaration of Independence. He is also a white Virginian, part of the anti-segregation interest; a war veteran and patriot, favoring larger expenditures for national defense; and a man of property, anxious for lower taxes. Here there is a clash between the last two interests, and perhaps between the first two as well. Truly the Colonel is a hard man to classify! So are we all. When forced to do so—when faced with a political choice—we have to sacrifice one thing that we value for another which we value more. But we would prefer to avoid having to make any such choice. To be at peace within ourselves, we try to compromise. And so in our political society, domestic tranquility requires frequently that a clash of interests be compromised.

That clash is given form and shape not by the broad interests which we have just been identifying, but by *organized groups* which often claim to speak for particular interests. Except for the political parties, whose somewhat different role we shall examine in the next chapter, these organizations are our active political combatants. Defending or furthering a special interest, they are called *interest groups*. Historically having sought their goals by applying "political pressure" to lawmakers, they are also called *pressure groups*. Neither is a term of reproach. Either will do.

## THE PRESSURE GROUPS

Since the enactment of the Federal Regulation of Lobbying Act in 1946, over six thousand individuals and organizations have complied with the law requiring the registration of all individuals and groups which seek to influence the legislative decisions of the United States Congress through direct communication to Congressmen. Many of these registrants represent the same organizations or pressure groups, but it is probably safe to say that the number of groups represented is in the thousands. Alphabetically, the list may run from Active-Retired Lighthouse Service Employees Association to Zantop Air Transport, Inc. To these we can safely add thousands more organizations which also qualify as pressure groups, even though they are not active in Washington. The Podunk Citizens Committee for More Off-street Parking is a pressure group just as is the National Association of Manufacturers, even though it seeks action not by Congress but by the Podunk city council. A pressure group is any organization, other than a political party, which aims to influence governmental decisions by legislatures or executives, national, state, or local.

Many pressure groups were originally formed for purposes other than political action. For instance, a quarter of a mile from the White House is the headquarters of a league of labor unions. Labor unions were formed to fight economic battles, not political ones. Their job was to strengthen the position of the worker as he bargained with his employer over what hours he should work and what wages he should receive. And today collective bargaining is still one of their central concerns. But the conditions under which collective bargaining is carried on, the legality of management-union contracts, and indeed the worker's right to belong to a union, have long depended on legislation. And so to its basic economic purposes, a union added specific political aims and thus inevitably became a political pressure group. In the same way, as the area of governmental activity has widened, many basically professional societies have assumed the pressure group's role. One of these we have mentioned—the National Education Association. It was originally an organization of and for educators, devoted to the exchange of ideas, the defense of academic freedom, and the improvement of the curriculum and the quality of teaching in the schools. But before long the NEA found that if unqualified persons were to be kept from teaching, there would have to be state laws setting minimum standards which every teacher must meet: and so the association, through its branches, put pressure on the state legislatures to enact such laws. In recent years the NEA has believed that adequate schooling depends on better financing and has continually pressed Congress to enact laws granting federal financial aid to local schools.

Even further removed from government and politics, at its inception, was the American Medical Association. This was and is a great professional society, whose meetings and journal bring to doctors all over the country news of the latest developments in all branches of medicine. Yet the AMA became a powerful national pressure group, too, when in the 1940's its leaders decided that professional progress was threatened by proposals that Congress should pass a compulsory health insurance law.

So we see that all manner of organizations, even though not organized for political purposes, can and do operate as pressure groups. They do so whenever they take action to influence governmental decisions. Long ago men found that alone they had little or no influence, but that when organized they could get the results they sought. And so they organized for political action; or if they first came together for quite different reasons, when political action became advisable they were well prepared to take it. They possessed the first prerequisite of effectiveness: organization.

It is easy enough to classify these organizations along lines somewhat similar to the interest groupings which we have just discussed. It is not so easy to realize that in each category, the largest or best-known groups by no means monopolize the field. Thus we can say truthfully enough that the American Federation of Labor-Congress of Industrial Organizations (AFL-CIO), whose constituent unions include some 13,000,000 workers (nearly five-sixths of all organized labor) is the most sizeable and prominent pressure group for the labor interest. But we must also keep in mind that other labor groups are effective too—the Railway Brotherhoods for many years had more legislative success than any other unions, the United Mine Workers virtually "wrote their own ticket" in 1935, and the Brotherhood of Teamsters played a vigorous part in the strife over labor legislation in 1959. In the same way, the "big two" of the business interest—the National Association of Manufacturers and the United States Chamber of Commerce—and the "big three" of agriculture—the American Farm Bureau Federation, the National Grange, and the National Farmers Union—are not the only spokesmen for businessmen and farmers. The registered lobbyists before Congress represent a multitude of individual unions, corporations, businesses, and farm organizations.

Economic interests include more than labor, business, and agriculture. In recent years, as we have just seen in the case of the AMA and the NEA, groups based on particular professions have become active politically. They have done so in part, at least, to preserve or improve the economic circumstances of their members. Their purposes, of course, go far beyond crass monetary goals. Good medicine and good schools are objectives which most of us share. It is for these that doctors and teachers contribute and work. A doctors' organization, however, is likely to assume that good medicine is threatened by proposals to alter the economic structure of the profession to the physicians' possible detriment. In the same way, a teachers' organization is naturally convinced that better pay for teachers will produce better education. Thus material and ideal ends become inextricably interwoven, in the efforts of these and many other groups. Perhaps materialism is dominant, perhaps idealism; conceivably, on occasion, they are identical.

Since Civil War days, the special interests of veterans have been pressed so successfully by national organizations as to justify placing "veterans' groups" in a category of their own. The Grand Army of the Republic, composed of former Union soldiers, was an early example, with pensions for its members the chief fruit of its labors. After World War I arose the American Legion, the largest and politically most potent of the veterans' organizations today. The Veterans of Foreign Wars, and, later, the American Veterans of World War II have also operated as effective pressure groups. All of these are primarily concerned with governmental action concerning people who have served in the armed forces: bonuses, disability payments, hospitalization, or educational benefits. All of them, however, also presume to speak for "Americanism." In this aspect, they fall into the classification of "patriotic" pressure groups, along with somewhat shriller but less influential bodies such as the Daughters of the American Revolution.

Further out on the "patriotism" front are a spate of ultra right-wing organizations which became visible in the early 1960's. These groups, such as the John Birch Society, the Christian Anti-Communist Crusade, or the intriguingly named National Indignation Conference, call for a variety of actions, usually including the repeal of the income tax, curtailment of federal government functions, and drastic action against Communism—though their definition of "Communism" and identification of "Communists" seem at times to be highly irresponsible.[3]

Among the galaxy of other groups we have already noted some which might be classified as "ethnic" (the NAACP) or "idealistic" (the ACLU); in our later discussion of the political struggles over particular public policies we will encounter more. Every one of these organizations, no matter how various their aims, seeks to influence the making of governmental decisions. Every one of them is numerically a small, often a tiny, minority of the voting population. Insofar as any one of them, then, shapes public policy,

---

3 For example, consider the written statement of the founder of the John Birch Society that President Eisenhower was a "dedicated, conscious agent of the Communist conspiracy."

does its success mark a departure from the democratic principle of government by the people through the expressed will of the majority of the people?

## The Reputation of Pressure Groups

James Madison was not the last to imply that "factions," a term which included interest groups, were both selfish and evil. In the late nineteenth century the word "lobby" gained a bad name for itself, because it was in the "lobbies" outside the legislative chambers that the pressure group representatives were assumed to be bribing the lawmakers. At the turn of the century the noun "interests" was in bad repute: it stood for powerful and wealthy monopolies who allegedly bought governmental favors. In more recent times "lobby" and "interests" have become more respectable words but books have been written about gentlemen obviously up to no good ends, called "the pressure boys." However, the notion that pressure groups are the "bad guys" in the picture is oversimplified and misleading. This must be obvious from the examples we have already considered. All of us have known doctors and teachers, and most or all of those whom we have known are worthy citizens; when they organize, and their organizations take political action, do they suddenly become evil?

The first thing to remember is that a great many people sincerely believe that what *they* want, what will benefit them, will also benefit the nation as a whole. "What's good for General Motors is good for the country," said Charles E. Wilson, president of General Motors, when he was nominated for secretary of defense in 1953. Mr. Wilson was forthrightly speaking his mind. So might labor leaders speak: laws ensuring the existence of a strong union would mean better wages for the members and this would be "good for the country." Often you may be apt to consider that your own economic well-being and the national welfare are one and the same thing. You could be wrong, but you could still be honestly patriotic. Second, the pressure group provides opportunities for participation by the ordinary citizen in the affairs of his government, beyond merely voting every two years. It insures that broad interests which might otherwise be neglected will at least receive some notice from the official decision-makers. In these respects, it seems to be a political instrument appropriate to a democracy. There are those who remind us, however, that the framers of the Constitution established a republic and distrusted democracy; that powerful pressure groups may exert economic coercion on their members and so themselves be undemocratic; and that the notion that pressure groups are desirous of the national welfare is frequently a delusion. Such reminders may temper undue enthusiasm over the democratic role of pressure groups and provide a useful warning against permitting them to dominate the political scene. But they cannot cause the clock to be turned back. Pressure groups are in politics to stay. And both the representation of interests and increased individual participation are consistent with the democratic philosophy which has been prevalent in the United States since the days of Andrew Jackson.

Third, as we shall see, most pressure groups, in operation, have become less sleazy and more respectable than in days of yore. There is still some outright monetary corruption of the lawmakers, and there are more subtle hints of rewards and reprisals. But the "group representatives"—the lobbyists—have achieved a reputable status in the capitals of many states and of the nation. "While the methods of the 'old' lobby have not been everywhere abandoned, the 'new' lobby is everywhere respected, accepted, and causes few editorial writers to thunder. It is not difficult to discover the reasons—active citizens are themselves caught up in the system while the passive citizen, if he pays any attention to it at all, sees nothing unusual in it." [4]

## Methods of Pressure Groups

An organization which wants a legislative body to reach a particular decision in its favor may adopt one or more of several methods to achieve its goal.

*Direct Persuasion.* First, it may seek *directly to persuade the legislators.* This can be attempted legitimately, or illegitimately, or by means that are perhaps legal but seem a bit shady. In Washington, these days, proper persuasion is the usual method employed, the registered lobbyist laying data and opinions before

[4] Donald C. Blaisdell, "Foreword," *Annals of the American Academy of Political and Social Science,* September, 1958, p. ix.

Fitzpatrick in the *St. Louis Post-Dispatch*

### New national anthem

This war-time cartoon (1943) reflects indignation with any and all claims of private interests in a time of national danger. The fact remains that the various "blocs," so unattractively portrayed, were not necessarily or wholly forgetful of the public interest; we all tend to identify our own demands with those of the public good.

committees and individual congressmen. This has become a part of the whole legislative picture, and will be discussed more fully when we deal with Congress in Chapter 14. Direct persuasion, however, has not always been just a matter of argument, of trying to convince the lawmaker of the justice of one's cause. Outright bribery is always possible and probably occurs on rare occasions in Washington, though it is a risky business as well as a dishonest one.

*Campaign Contributions.* Between lawful persuasion and criminal bribery lies a possible tactic which has helped some legislators but has brought about the downfall of at least one representative in recent times and has prevented the passage of some legislation. This is the device of "paying off" a legislator not in cash for himself, but in the form of a campaign contribution. Campaigns cost a lot of money. Many a congressman, planning to seek re-election, worries about how he is going to finance his next campaign. Along comes a lobbyist with a large check or a promise to make a payment—for campaign expenses only, of course. Who knows how this affects the vote of that congressman on a bill in which the lobbyist is interested? It is legal to make campaign contributions, and the "contributor" has exacted no pledge from the lawmaker. But the business smells bad. So bad does it smell, indeed, that when in 1956 Congress passed a bill favored by the oil industry after a senator publicly declared that, shortly before the Senate voted on the bill, an oil company representative had offered him a $2,500 campaign contribution, President Eisenhower killed the bill with a veto. The President did so even though he had recommended that the bill be passed. He said that he could not approve legislation adopted in an atmosphere of suspicion of bribery.

Direct persuasion, then, can be corrupt or at best dubious, but is usually straightforward and legitimate. It is not the only way to influence a legislator, however. Although the elected representatives of the people may be deaf to logical or emotional argument, they can hear very clearly the voices of their own constituents. Most of them want to be reelected. Most of them, too, feel that they have a duty, as representatives, to pay some heed to what the voters "back home" are saying. A pressure group, therefore, may adopt the method of *indirect persuasion,* arousing people in a particular representative's district to write him, telegraph him, telephone him, pound him with demands that he vote for the measure which the group wants passed.

*Intervention in Campaigns.* Another pressure group technique is *active participation in the electoral process.* Long ago, before the days of the Eighteenth Amendment and its prohibition of the sale of liquor, the "temperance" forces used this method with great effect. Where the cause of prohibition had numerous adherents, its leaders judged candidates for Congress on the basis of whether they were "wet" or "dry." The largest organized "dry" group, the Anti-Saloon League, then went into the political campaign urging the election of a "dry" or, at least, the defeat of a known "wet," regardless of party—regardless, too, of any other issue. As in those days temperance and prohibition were causes which stirred men and women to true crusading fervor, the temperance forces could swing elections by their unity and ardor. Gradually more and more men in Congress were, if not personally "dry," at least unwilling to risk the enmity of the Anti-Saloon League and its ally the Women's Christian Temperance Union. Thus the prohibition forces triumphed, not by persuasion in the capitol but by their power at the polls.

In more recent times, a dramatic use of this technique nationwide was in the congressional elections of 1950, when the American Medical Association went directly into various contests for representative and senator, aiming always to defeat candidates who favored any form of governmental health insurance. Some doctors who had never before been interested in politics dashed by airplane to political meetings, carrying the message to the voters—always, essentially, the same message: "Senator X is for socialized medicine; vote against Senator X." In countless homes which doctors visited, they left with their prescriptions a printed political message—vote against Senator X. Doctors' wives telephoned voters by the thousand—all with the same message. Here, with a vengeance, was political action by an interest group.

In actually intervening in campaigns, or in scaring a legislator by threatening to do so, a pressure group can be effective even though it is small. Where a legislator faces a close fight for renomination, or in a district in which party strength is almost evenly divided, a few votes make the difference between victory and defeat. A few energetic people, campaigning ardently for a cause they deem noble and against a candidate they imagine to be utterly evil, can sometimes swing the balance.

*Influencing Public Opinion.* A further technique, less direct, continues over long periods of time rather than being concentrated in a few autumn weeks: the method of seeking to *create a favorable atmosphere of public opinion.* Here again the AMA furnishes an example. During the several years when President Truman was urging the passage of a health insurance bill, you could hardly pass a drugstore window without seeing in it a reproduction of a famous and emotion-laden painting called, simply, "The Doctor"—a picture of a wise, kindly, bearded medico at the bedside of a child, with the parents, in the semi-darkness, placing all their trust and hope in him. The AMA used this picture as a symbol of the private practitioner, whose practice and, presumably, whose patients were threatened by Mr. Truman's dark and dangerous plans. The organization hired a successful public relations firm to "spread the gospel" as well as to plan and advise in both persuading congressmen and fighting electoral battles.

On a long-range basis have been many organizational efforts— regular radio and television programs, sponsorship of essay contests, magazine and billboard advertising, and the publication and wide distribution of innumerable books and pamphlets. Modern examples include the weekly television shows of large unions such as the automobile workers; the electric power industry's full-page advertisements in monthly magazines, designed to dramatize the alleged unfairness of government competition in developing and selling electric power; and the continuing efforts of the American Legion and the National Association of Manufacturers to foster certain attitudes among the school children of the land. The American Legion seeks to inculcate patriotism through essay contests and the like. The NAM promotes a feeling of satisfaction with the system of private economic enterprise. All of these various efforts have two objectives: to create good will for the organization and to bring people around to their point of view. In the last analysis, it is the votes which matter. And as the NAM pointed out in emphasizing its school program. "We rely on the schools to make citizens. Thirty millions of voters of [ten years hence] are in our schools today."

We have now considered several methods of persuasion in terms of legislative decisions. Aside from logical persuasion and crass bribery, all of them are based on what we have called "electoral politics." Campaign contributions, outpourings of letters from constituents, direct participation in campaigns, the cultivation of popular support even among future voters: all these methods are subject to the ultimate test of the ballot box. As long as we have free elections and people want to be elected, all are likely to remain in frequent use.

*Access to Decision-Makers.* Legislative action is only one form of governmental decision-making. Many significant decisions are made by the executive branch as well as by the Congress. The nature of the presidency and the respect in which that office is held insulate the White House from direct lobbying, unless the President wishes to listen to the interest group spokesmen. This "unless," however, is important. Early in Franklin D. Roosevelt's first term, a prominent banker was asked to explain his personal bitterness toward the administration. "Why," he replied, "until now we've always been invited to the White House and could talk to the President whenever we had something to say. But now this man won't even listen to us!" At the very least, interest groups want "access" to the centers of official power. Therefore, they are not unconcerned with presidential nominations and elections and often try indirectly to influence presidential appointments, especially to the agencies which regulate industry. More directly and continuously, they are involved in the day-to-day decisions made by such regulatory agencies and other executive departments. The efforts of group spokesmen do not stop with formal appearances and arguments before these rule-making bodies. The rule-makers themselves often come to lean heavily on pressure group representatives for expert information; and in the course of time personal friendships are likely to be established between people whose work brings them constantly together. The conscious cultivation of such friendships is one part of the job of many a successful lobbyist.

The third main area of governmental decision-making is, of course, the judicial branch. Here the ordinary lobbying tactics would boomerang, for any self-respecting judge is thoroughly aware of his duty to be impartial. Furthermore, courts are not like legislatures; they cannot provide remedies for social ills on their own initiative but must confine themselves to deciding disputes—"cases or controversies"—formally brought before them by contending litigants. Some groups, such as the American Civil Liberties Union and the National Association for the Advancement of Colored People, through their attorneys, often participate in litigation and even plan it; but this is normal legal representation, not to be confused with the other persuasive tactics of "pressure politics." The NAACP, to be sure, has been credited or charged with influencing judicial conduct by the indirect method of altering the climate of public opinion, in favor of equal rights, through a long campaign of civic education or public relations. Judges, however, although not impervious to public opinion, are not necessarily or quickly responsive to it. Aside from normal legal argument, therefore, pressure groups' influence on judicial decisions must be so gradual, slight, and uncertain that few organizations try to exert it.

## What Makes a Pressure Group Effective

The factors of success in pressure group activities are being studied, analyzed, and measured by many scholars. Oddly, political scientists were slow in realizing the significance of interests in politics; not until 1908 was the central role of interest groups widely recognized,[5] and not for many years after that were many serious studies made of their activities. As for measuring the elements which produce success, any such undertaking is fraught with great difficulties. There are too many "variables," as the social scientists put it. What works for one group under certain circumstances may fail tomorrow under only slightly varied conditions. We can, however, identify a number of factors which, alone or together, are likely to make one organization more effective than another. We cannot give any factor particular weight, but there is enough evidence to say that a group's success may well depend on its numerical size, cohesion, program, internal organization, leadership, and financial resources.

*Size.* An organization like the AFL-CIO, with about 13,000,000 members, starts off with the advantage of numerical strength. Obviously, the more people that belong to an organization, the greater its potential impact. In national affairs, a group of 1,300

---

[5] The ground-breaking work was that of A. F. Bentley, *The Process of Government* (Chicago: University of Chicago Press, 1908).

people would have two strikes against it—though as we have just
seen even a small group may be effective, if it is located in a politically crucial spot.

*Cohesion.* The weakness of a very large organization is that the
more people who belong to it, the less unified it becomes. Differences of opinion become substantial, and the very hugeness of the
group makes a person feel that his own membership in it is of
little significance. Unable effectively to influence the group's decisions, he may well lose interest and make no effort to further its
program. These difficulties are compounded when the organization is a league or combination of smaller groups and membership is therefore indirect. In the last analysis, group effectiveness
depends on all or the great majority of the group standing together. A small cohesive organization, whose members will all vote
as the group decides, can be more effective than one whose seeming numerical strength is dissipated by internal differences.

*Program.* Because cohesion is so important, a group's effectiveness may be predicted on the basis of whether its program is one
which enlists the united enthusiasm of all its members. Theoretically, at least, it would seem that the advantage lies with the organization which has a single, easily understood goal. One clear-cut
purpose, such as to prohibit the sale of liquor or to obtain bigger
old-age pensions, brings together the people who want these
things: and once organized, they are likely to stay together as long
as they all have one common objective. Conversely, an organization which adopts an eight-point program ranging from national
policy in the Far East to the internal reorganization of the U.S.
Children's Bureau is opening the door to internal dissension and
defection. The more single-minded the program, the more cohesive the organization is likely to be. Even a united group, of
course, will not achieve much quickly if its program is utterly
inconsistent with the general beliefs and customs of the people;
yet endless persistence has sometimes changed unpopular causes
into victorious ones. Nor will a group which exists essentially for
a limited purpose be as persuasive when it strays far afield, even
though all its members are agreed. For example, the AMA, being
composed of doctors, carries great weight on issues directly concerning health and medicine; its opinions on highway construc-

tion or Far Eastern policy would presumably be much less influential.

*Organization.* More than one group in our history failed for years to realize its political potential by neglecting its own organizational structure. Often it employed a part-time "executive secretary" whose office, as the saying goes, was in his hat. Its membership lists were kept in desultory fashion, dues went uncollected, and the members merely talked or listened to each other at "inspirational" annual meetings. The great move toward more formal organization got fully under way after World War I. More and more groups decided that to be effective, they must have a full-time paid staff and permanent headquarters. As a group's success came to depend increasingly on its ability to furnish full and accurate information, the headquarters staff was expanded to include a research department. To inform officials, their own members, and the public, publicity bureaus were established and periodicals published. The tremendous and relatively recent development of formal organization is reflected by many handsome edifices in Washington—which are still a-building.

*Leadership.* If one prerequisite for success is the institution of a full-time, well-paid position at the controls, another is the selection of the right man to fill it. The strength of many an organization can be assessed only in terms of the personal effectiveness of its executive director or salaried president. Individuals of ability, personal force (sometimes ruthlessness), and political acumen have built some pressure groups into dynamic forces. They have so dominated their organizations that in the public mind their names have become inseparable from the group they lead—witness John L. Lewis and the United Mine Workers, Walter Reuther and the United Automobile Workers, or the late Edward A. O'Neal and the American Farm Bureau Federation. After a weak organization has become powerful thanks to able leadership, it may run for a while on its own steam, with less colorful men at the top; but its continuing influence is likely to depend in part on the ability of the men who manage it.

*Finance.* A national pressure group cannot be really effective without money. Headquarters, salaries, research staffs, publications—all these cost plenty. More than twenty years ago, in the middle of a prolonged economic depression, the National Association of Manufacturers was said to have spent $36,000,000 on one phase of its public relations program alone—publishing pamphlets describing the virtues of free enterprise and distributing them to public schools all over the country. The 1948-1951 campaign of the American Medical Association, directed by a California public relations firm, cost at least $4,678,000. Congress requires that lobbyists submit official reports on their expenditures for actual lobbying activities in Washington. The table presented here summarizes these reports for 1961 and the first half of 1962. When it is borne in mind that these amounts represent only a part of the actual expenses of the pressure groups concerned, it is obvious that a great deal of money is involved in attempting to influence public policy.

Where does this kind of money come from? For mass organizations, membership dues can make up most or all of it; a union with hundreds of thousands of members, or a combination of unions with many millions, can fill sizeable treasuries while keeping individual membership dues reasonably small. A smaller but substantial organization like the NAM, almost all of whose 20,000-odd members are corporations large and small, can raise great sums through higher dues and special contributions when needed. The AMA financed its campaign of 1948-1951 by a special $25-a-year assessment on its members; as defiance of the AMA could cost a doctor his practice in some local hospitals and even cause virtual professional ostracism, most doctors paid up. Small organizations whose members are not rich and cannot be coerced must depend on dues and occasional contributions to meet their modest budgets. In view of the great financial power of their bigger or wealthier competitors, the wonder is that they are effective at all. But although "money talks," people can talk too—and sometimes the little fellow can be persuasive after all.

It is so easy to imagine pressure groups possessing all of the foregoing attributes of success that we may forget that even such groups are not all-powerful. They are limited by several factors. For one thing, they compete with each other. For another, they are composed of individuals who, like that old Virginian colonel,

**LOBBYING EXPENDITURES REPORTED**

| Type of Group | 1961 | | | | 1962 (First Six Months) | | | |
|---|---|---|---|---|---|---|---|---|
| | No. of Groups Reporting | Amount Reported Spent | Largest Spenders Reporting | Amount Reported Spent | No. of Groups Reporting | Amount Reported Spent | Largest Spenders Reporting | Amount Reported Spent |
| Business | 171 | $1,598,091 | U.S. Savings & Loan League<br>Nat'l Committee for Insurance Taxation<br>American Trucking Assn. | $101,802<br>90,058<br>84,986 | 149 | $820,757 | Nat'l Committee for Insurance Taxation<br>U.S. Savings & Loan League | $81,203<br>62,082 |
| Citizens | 52 | 437,695 | Nat'l Housing Conference<br>Nat'l Rivers & Harbors Congress | 88,141<br>46,706 | 44 | 262,202 | Nat'l Rivers & Harbors Congress<br>Citizens Committee on Natural Resources | 33,660<br>25,529 |
| Employee and Labor | 40 | 857,759 | AFL-CIO<br>Int'l Brotherhood of Teamsters | 139,919<br>81,918 | 36 | 475,542 | United Federation of Postal Clerks (AFL-CIO)<br>AFL-CIO | 84,006<br>70,703 |
| Farm | 22 | 365,888 | American Farm Bureau Federation<br>Nat'l Farmers Union | 111,364<br>88,273 | 21 | 211,036 | American Farm Bureau Federation<br>Nat'l Farmers Union | 59,567<br>48,552 |
| Military and Veterans | 10 | 133,734 | American Legion<br>Disabled Officers Assn. | 103,566<br>15,000 | 6 | 68,196 | American Legion<br>Disabled Officers Assn. | 53,859<br>7,500 |
| Professional | 17 | 376,912 | American Medical Assn.<br>American Hospital Assn.<br>Nat'l Education Assn. | 163,405<br>67,688<br>51,910 | 17 | 170,133 | American Medical Assn.<br>American Hospital Assn. | 67,386<br>30,526 |

have within themselves a conflict of interests and loyalties. Comparatively few people put heart and soul wholly into one organization for a lifetime. They belong to several, and their attachment to any one, over a period of time, is more likely to be lukewarm than intense. Finally, pressure groups operate on a political stage where both law and custom have given the political parties the main spotlight.

## Pressure Groups and Political Parties

The crucial distinction between a pressure group and a political party lies in the fact that the latter seeks control of the government by electing its candidates to office and the former does not. A local party organization, or party leaders in Congress, at times act like a pressure group, threatening or cajoling or otherwise trying to persuade a particular legislator to vote the way they want him to. A pressure group occasionally throws itself into an electoral campaign and so, for a brief period, resembles a party. But the basic distinction remains. The party is the active contender for office—office which is gained by getting the most votes. Therefore, the party depends for success on winning popular support for its candidates; if possible, a popular majority. The pressure group, on the other hand, cannot by itself muster any popular majority. Its membership is small. Its objective is not full control of the government, but satisfactory governmental decisions on matters it deems most important. For success it depends chiefly on holding a critical balance of power in closely contested elections, on its direct influence on a few key lawmakers, and on the personal persuasiveness of its spokesmen with others. Only secondarily does it try to sway public opinion as a whole, and any such effort is necessarily limited to the richest organizations. The pressure group, in representing interests and providing for political participation, may be, as we have noted, a democratic instrument, but insofar as it gains influence by short-cutting the normal process of majority elections, it seems anachronistic in a democratic system. The recognizable instrument of a democratic polity is the political party.

As we have seen, however, pressure groups are concerned about who gets elected to office even though elections are run on a party basis, the candidates of one party opposing the candidates of another. Not only that: pressure groups seek favorable action from a Congress organized along party lines, where the congressional leaders are party leaders. The President, also, is among other things a party leader. Now, no one can ever be absolutely sure which party will win an election, and the loser this time may be the winner next. Most pressure groups, therefore, want friends in both parties. They also want to keep their own membership united. Many people consider themselves to be Democrats or Republicans for reasons quite unconnected with the goals of the interest groups to which they may belong; if one such group formally became a constituent part of the Republican party, many of its Democratic members would resign in a huff—and vice versa. So most groups active in campaigns have tacitly adopted the nonpartisan policy announced long ago by Samuel Gompers, first president of the American Federation of Labor: "Reward your friends and punish your enemies."

These friends and enemies may be candidates for office, bearing either party's label, or they may be aspirants for nomination by either party. As the final election is between party nominees, a pressure group may find that its first political task is to get its friends nominated. It may, therefore, inject itself into party primaries, those "nominating elections" in which the party standard-bearers are chosen; it may even try to influence the nomination of presidential candidates by national conventions. There, the pressure groups are interested not only in the nominations but in the platforms or programs adopted by both parties. Seventy were represented, for instance, before the Republican platform committee in 1952, arguing for or against the inclusion of particular "planks" or items in the program; and these formal appearances were probably only a small part of some groups' efforts to influence the committee members. Many of the same representatives, after presenting their case to the Republicans, obtained a similar hearing when the Democratic platform committee met a fortnight later.

Pressure groups, then, concern themselves with party activities, because what the parties do—the platforms they adopt, the candidates they nominate, the leaders they select—profoundly affect the decisions made by government. The parties, in turn, depend for success on their appeal, if not openly to pressure groups, at least to the broad interest "groupings" within which the pressure groups have originated. Seldom can either afford to make an enduring alliance with the other: the pressure group because outright permanent partisanship would divide its membership, the party because it must appeal to so many interests that official federation with one group would alienate many voters. So although pressure groups and parties need each other, they keep their formal distance, remaining both rivals and collaborators. Surely it is not surprising that "pressure politics" is a familiar catchword to describe our political system—but the older phrase: "party politics," is at least as descriptive. Aware of the existence of interests as fundamental in politics and of the effectiveness of pressure groups in promoting those interests, we advance now to consider the strange phenomenon around which our whole electoral structure is built—the political party.

CHAPTER **10**

# The Political Parties

A body of men united for promoting by their joint endeavors
the national interest, upon some particular principle in
which they are all agreed." That is the famous definition of a
political party propounded by Edmund Burke, a British statesman, over a century and a half ago. Read it over—think it over.
Does it seem to define something *other* than a party—something
about which we have just been reading? Assume that, as so often
happens, the people who form an organization for one special
purpose are convinced that their goal is in "the national interest"
and that their ends are to be attained through governmental
action. What have they formed—a party? Or a pressure group?

Burke's definition does, indeed, seem to fit a modern pressure
group. When it was first expressed, it may have described political
parties in Great Britain—for in those days, there was no mass
electorate. Comparatively few people were qualified to vote. A
party, then, was not a great agglomeration of citizens scattered all
over the country. It was a *parliamentary group*—a body of members of Parliament united to push or obstruct particular policies.
In contrast, in both Great Britain and the United States today
the great parties are *popular* parties which arose in the last century along with the spread of popular democracy. The parties

include not just legislators, but millions and millions of voters spread across the length and breadth of the land.

Can any such huge entity be called "a body of men united"? We have just seen that all manner of various and competing interests divide people; does a party unite them again? Current American history seems to cast grave doubts on that proposition. In the first place, a party that seeks control of the government must concern itself not with just "some particular principle," but with many pressing issues of foreign and domestic policy. And as we have just seen, the more numerous the issues upon which an organization must take a stand, the more certain the difficulty of keeping people united in that organization. In the second place, a *national* party must try to include people who obviously start off with different viewpoints because of the wide geographical differences among them. If it does include them, can it do so and still claim to speak for a group united on some particular principle? The price of being a mass party in the United States is almost always lack of unity and coherence. Parties exist, but hardly fit into Burke's picture of "a body of men united." Senator Eastland of Mississippi is pro-segregation and anti-labor; Senator Humphrey of Minnesota is anti-segregation and pro-labor; yet they both are—or were, anyway, as late as 1964—elected leaders in the Democratic party. Jacob Javits, a believer in expanded federal government action, was a Republican senator; so was Barry Goldwater. Such drastic internal divisions of opinion are quite typical of both our major parties.

In sharp contrast to Burke's definition is one formulated some years ago by a scholar who observed its flaws and despaired of finding any "unifying principle" in either party. He was the late E. M. Sait, who said that a party is "an organized group that seeks to control the personnel and policy of the government." The trouble with that definition is that it is too narrow, in two aspects. First, is an American party really an "organized group"? It *includes* organized groups, which we will discuss later in this chapter. But it also includes millions of men and women who are not "organized" and who do not form a group in any normal sense of that word, yet who consider themselves Democrats or Republicans as the case may be. Second, if the only thing that makes a party tick is a desire for power, why should those millions feel any loyalty to either party? They won't obtain office or influence policy; they are busy making a living, and their only political activity is voting on election day. Yet they consider themselves partisans—and they prefer one party to the other. They must think, then, that there is some difference between the parties— that one stands for something better, in their eyes, than the other.

They tend to believe, in other words, that there is at least a lingering grain of truth in the old Burkean definition. But many also realize that Sait's less idealistic phrase may include much truth. Many Americans, therefore, priding themselves on their realism and independence, claim that they are nonpartisan. Alleging that there is no real difference between the policies of the parties, they say that they "vote for the best man, not for the party." The astonishing thing is how consistently one person finds that the "best man" just happens to be a Democrat while for another the "best man" is almost always a Republican. Studies of election returns show that while many people "split their tickets," and many others switch easily from one party to the other, most voters vote either Republican or Democratic pretty consistently over the years. Furthermore, both private polls and official registration figures indicate that most voters consider them- selves to be either Republicans or Democrats. Rightly or wrongly, these voters think that there are reasons for their preference— reasons presumably to be found in the promises and the records of the parties. In our effort to discover what a party is, let us turn briefly to those records and consider why it is that for a century there have been in this country just two major parties, with which millions of voters have felt at least some sense of affiliation. Then we will examine the other picture of a party as essentially an organized group hungry for office and power.

## "UPON SOME PARTICULAR PRINCIPLE"

### The Development of Party Attitudes

*The Beginnings.* Thomas Jefferson is hailed by Democratic politicians as the founder of their party—even though Jefferson's original party was called "Republican" ("democratic" then having a dangerous sound to respectable ears) and was organized before the days of mass participation in the political process. The Constitution made no provision for parties and George Washington, at least, abhorred the idea that they would arise. Yet they were inevitable. In a free legislature, some men are bound to unite on "some particular principle," and others to unite against them. Likewise in free elections, someone is bound to realize, as Samuel Adams did in colonial Boston, that those who organize and vote together can often elect whom they like to office.

Actually the first political party in the United States was a legislative party in the Burkean sense—the so-called Federalist party of the 1790's, whose intellectual leader was Alexander Hamilton. A majority in the Congress agreed on the policies of the Washington and Adams administrations (1789-1801)—centralized financial leadership, encouragement of manufacturing, a tariff on imports, peaceful settlement with England, hostility to revolutionary France, and, finally, the condemnation and suppression of strong criticism of the government. This congressional majority exuded an air of respectability. Like the Philadelphia convention, it spoke for major property interests. Its philosophy was simply stated by John Jay: "The people who own the country ought to govern it." Controlling Congress, the Federalists, largely through Hamilton's persuasive skill in dealing with President Washington, soon captured the executive branch—and after that, the judiciary, as the President nominated "sound men," i.e., Federalists, to judgeships. Jay himself became Chief Justice of the United States.

Against the Federalists' policies stood the congressional minority, at first informally called "Anti-Feds." They spoke for the agrarian interests, the exporters, the people who feared a strong central government as a threat to freedom. The cleavage was both economic and ideological, and it was deep. It became fierce and bitter when, in 1798, the Federalists sought to perpetuate their monopoly of power through the Alien and Sedition Acts.

Jefferson's original contribution to party-building lay in the fact that he went outside of the nation's capital and took his case to the people. He did this partly by writing thousands of letters—a prodigious task in those days when there were no typewriters and carbon paper and mimeographs—and persuading "Anti-Feds" to organize in their own states for the next election. His persuasion was the more effective because the time was ripe. The nature of the issues aroused men's passions. The Jeffersonian party— called first, Republican, then Democratic-Republican, and eventually Democratic—arose out of the deeply felt need to oppose the policies of those who controlled the government.

The same kind of need gave rise to the Republican party which we know today. It was organized in 1854. By that time, of course, the issues had changed. So had the Democratic party. From an amalgam of "little men" in the north, southern planters, and frontiersmen exemplified by Andrew Jackson, the Democratic party had become increasingly the political instrument of the southern planters. By 1844, party control had come firmly into the hands of the cotton-growing, slave-owning group, and by the mid-1850's that group, bent on the expansion of slavery westward into the newly developed territories beyond the Mississippi, had gained virtual control of all branches of the national government as well.

Now it is true that by this time, "Jacksonian democracy" with its overtones of social equality and its increased exercise of the suffrage (for men only, however!) had brought mass parties into existence, and the Democrats had recognizable partisan opposition. Their opponent was the Whig party. The Whigs, however, based their strength on distinguished leaders such as Senators Clay and Webster, and on the financial interests which hated Andrew Jackson and favored the old Hamiltonian policies of a national bank and a protective tariff. As the southern Democrats pressed for slavery's expansion, the old Whig leaders died and the old anti-Jackson issues became insignificant. A great issue—slavery's expansion, containment, or abolition—stirred men's hearts and minds: but the opposition party, the Whigs, first sought compromise and then found it impossible to unite on any side of the issue. So once again there was a deep and bitter cleavage, and a vacuum where opposition pressure should have been exerted. Politics abhors a vacuum: into this one quickly came the new Republican party, formed of old Whigs and many northern Democrats who wanted the spread of slavery stopped. The Republicans had no

Jefferson to guide their organization, but they had a burning cause.

This brief account of the beginnings of the Democratic and Republican parties is not included here simply as a matter of historical interest. It may be significant as an indicator of the conditions which must exist if, in the future, any effective new national party is to arise. In both instances, one party or faction was dominant in all three branches of the government. Each time, the dominant group's policies, vigorously pushed, excited the vehement emotional opposition of great numbers of citizens. When the old Federalists were in control, the need to make this opposition effective was met by the creation of a new rival party. When the southern Democrats were riding high, the rival party could not even agree that they should be unhorsed and offered no alternative program of its own; accordingly, another opposition party was established. We can at least guess, therefore, that our present two parties will remain the major parties in the country at least until and unless (1) one of them has full control in Washington; (2) the party in control pursues strong policies which arouse searing resentment in millions of hearts; and (3) the minority party fails to fight for opposite policies or evades the burning issues altogether.

*After the Civil War.* The War Between the States gave to the nation a new hero and to the Republican party a new issue— the preservation of the Union. It was followed by a great expansion westward, typified by the completion of the transcontinental railways. The three post-bellum decades were the era of unbridled "venture capitalism," with mammoth corporate enterprise changing the face of American business. Private fortunes and monopolies grew to enormous size, and so much economic power was wielded by investment bankers that New York's Wall Street, where their offices were located, became a symbol of concentrated wealth.

During this period the Democratic party, stigmatized continually as "the party of rebellion," had above all else to be respectable. Furthermore, it responded to the dominant interests of the time as readily as did the Republicans. For thirty years they were both "business" parties. Because the exporting South was still a major factor in the Democratic party, the Democrats were moderately opposed to the Republicans' desire for a high tariff, but otherwise the party conflict was largely a sham battle, at least in terms of issues. Even in personalities, there was little difference between them. The Democratic leader of the 1870's, Samuel J. Tilden, was a wealthy corporation lawyer. The only Democrat elected President in this thirty-year span, Grover Cleveland, was a solid conservative; except for the tariff, he was squarely on the side of the financial giants and industrial magnates.

As we shall see in more detail in Chapter 18, however, this was also a period when gaping fissures appeared in the economic system. The fortunes of the mighty contrasted ever more sharply with the poverty of the farmers and the factory workers. The latter sought to organize for economic action, but the forces of government—including Cleveland's administration—were against them. The farmers put their hope of economic salvation not into organization, but into political action to obtain an inflationary monetary policy. They demanded that prices be raised through increasing the supply of money by the free coinage of silver.

*Since 1896.* The period when it was reasonably accurate to say that the parties were "just alike except for the tariff" ended abruptly on July 10, 1896, in Chicago. There, on that day, the embattled farmers of the west gained control of the Democratic party and nominated a young orator, William Jennings Bryan, for President. Bryan was for "free silver": later he was to speak for the nationalization of railroads and the protection of labor's right to organize. He put a lasting imprint on his party. He infused it with a readiness to experiment, a willingness to use the powers of government affirmatively to cure the real or fancied ills affecting the body politic. In one sense, this meant turning away from Jefferson and Jackson, with their dislike of strong centralized direction of affairs from Washington. In another sense, Bryan brought the Democrats back to the Jefferson-Jackson path, making it once more a party whose chief appeal was to the humble folk who felt that they were at a disadvantage economically, in the factory or on the farm.

Many traditional Democrats disagreed with Bryan, and the party did not always follow his leadership. Nevertheless, in the twentieth century, the Democrats have won the presidency only with candidates who made his kind of affirmative, pragmatic appeal—their critics might say demagogic appeal—to masses of people, who called for vigorous action and proclaimed their readiness to "take arms against a sea of troubles."

The nomination of Bryan did not change the character of Republican policies, but did serve to make the Republicans more than ever the party of the so-called sound business interests; for Bryan's initial campaign was waged on the issue of drastic monetary inflation, an idea which scared the daylights out of the leaders of industry and investment banking and also many moderate men of all the trades and professions. So in 1896, with sound currency at stake, big business moved openly to the center of the Republican stage. Marcus Hanna of Ohio, a steel "tycoon" as we would call him today, virtually took command. For the first time, millions of dollars were raised and spent—to elect the Republican candidate, McKinley, and save the integrity of the dollar. From that day to this, in every presidential campaign the Republican party has always been able to obtain much larger campaign funds than its opponent.

Now, however, let us heed one solemn warning. We must not assume that the Republican party is "a body of men united" to promote the purposes of business and uphold conservative principles [1] or that the Democratic party is the political arm of labor and utters liberal or radical doctrine with a clear and single voice. On domestic issues, both parties are divided within themselves. Among the Democrats in Congress, for instance, the pro-labor programs of Presidents F. D. Roosevelt and Truman were opposed by many southerners and a few northerners, too. The Republican party after the 1930's was likewise plagued by internal disagreement: some Republican leaders were ready to assume that the measures of Roosevelt's New Deal were here to stay, whereas others wanted to fight the battles of the 1930's all over again and denounced even the moderately conservative administration of President Eisenhower as "socialistic." Journalists, adopting the

---

[1] In January, 1959, the chairman of the Republican National Committee told his fellow Republicans that "we must change the false image of the Republican party as the party of big business, the party of the vested interests."

language of European politics, thus found it easy to speak of left (liberal or radical) and right (conservative or reactionary) wings in both parties. The fact remains that in general, for the last sixty years and more, Democratic policy at the national level has been more in favor of change than has Republican policy, although in the 1960's the most "pro-change" faction was the extreme right wing of both parties, the so-called "radical right" that sought to alter the Constitution and sharply limit the authority of the national government.

In this very brief bit of party history we have left to the last two great areas of policy formation which today, as in the past, tend to destroy party unity. One of these is the whole field of foreign policy. On such questions as collective security to stop Nazi aggression in the 1930's and aiding Britain in the early 1940's, both parties split, vigorous opposition to Roosevelt's "internationalist" course coming from his fellow Democrats such as Senators Wheeler of Montana and Walsh of Massachusetts, as well as from many, but not all, Republicans. More recently, President Eisenhower on several occasions received less congressional support, on foreign policy issues, from his fellow-Republicans than from Democrats. The other great divisive force, disturbing the Democratic party's solidarity, is the difference of opinion concerning the status of the American Negro. This broke the party asunder a century ago; it has continually threatened to repeat the process ever since World War II.

## The Foundations of Partisanship

In a great nation of over 190,000,000 people, voters are so numerous and their interests so diverse that a national party can hardly expect to develop a clear-cut program upon which a majority can wholeheartedly unite. Both major parties, to win office, must therefore appeal simultaneously to many groups or groupings whose goals conflict with each other. For instance, in a largely industrial society, a victorious party must get many votes from both businessmen and labor union members. Its program must be couched largely in general terms, so framed as not to drive any major segment of the population wholly over to the opposition.

Not only are most party programs vague, but they are not necessarily carried out even when the party wins a national election. For our parties are not disciplined organizations. A senator may defy his party's leaders, including the President: he may vote against the measures urged in his party's platform; and still he remains a party member in good standing. As we shall see, two major reasons for this lack of party discipline and hence of party unity are the separation of powers, which inhibits the President from being a fully effective party leader, and the federal system, which tends to scatter the organized strength of the parties among state and local bodies rather than center it in a national party executive. So even if a President is elected with a clear and affirmative program, and his fellow partisans gain a majority in both houses of Congress, there is no assurance that the program will be enacted. Conversely, it becomes very difficult justly to place the responsibility for action or inaction on one party or the other.

If, then, party programs are usually vague and party responsibility is largely an illusion, why are so many people partisans?

One reason has already been suggested: namely, that in a general way the parties' stands have differed, and one is more commonly identified with the "little man" and experimentation than the other. But there are other causes of continuing partisanship that may be much more important.

The first is *family tradition*. Great-grandfather, grandfather, and father and mother were Democrats; therefore, without thinking much about it, son and daughter vote the Democratic ticket. A little girl in 1876 saw a Republican torchlight parade in which an effigy of the Democratic candidate, Tilden, was carried by, decorated with satanic horns and a tail. She got the impression then that Democrats were devils, and her father, whose brother had died fighting for the Union, encouraged that impression. Eighty years later that little girl's descendants were still voting the Republican ticket. We need not labor this point: most of us know people who, if asked their party affiliation, reply with surprise: "Oh, we've always been Republicans" (or "we've always been Democrats"). The significant words are "we've always been" —referring to a family unit for several generations.

INTERGENERATIONAL RESEMBLANCE IN PARTISAN
ORIENTATION, POLITICALLY ACTIVE AND
INACTIVE HOMES, 1958

| Party Identification of Offspring | One or Both Parents Were Politically Active | | | Neither Parent Was Politically Active | | |
|---|---|---|---|---|---|---|
| | Parents Democratic | Parents Republican | Parents Had No Consistent Partisanship | Parents Democratic | Parents Republicans | No Consistent Partisanship |
| Strong Democrat | 50% | 5% | 21% | 40% | 6% | 20% |
| Weak Democrat | 29 | 9 | 26 | 36 | 11 | 15 |
| Independent | 12 | 13 | 26 | 19 | 16 | 26 |
| Weak Republican | 6 | 34 | 16 | 3 | 42 | 20 |
| Strong Republican | 2 | 37 | 10 | 1 | 24 | 12 |
| Apolitical | 1 | 2 | 1 | 1 | 1 | 7 |
| Number of cases | 333 | 194 | 135 | 308 | 187 | 199 |

SOURCE: *The American Voter*, p. 147, Table 7-1.

The second is *social and economic environment*. If you come
from another country and settle in a community where everyone
else is a Democrat, the chances are strong that when you get your
citizenship you will register as a Democrat too. The pressure to
conform to community values is a strong one; the political opinions which you hear are pro-Democratic; and if as a newcomer
you are in need of help, a vigorous local party organization may
well make it advantageous for you to be a Democrat. Thus the
impoverished Irish immigrants of the nineteenth century settling
in the poorer quarters of New York and Boston found themselves
living among Democrats and succored by Democratic "machines."
Thus, too, the Scandinavian and German farmers who settled in
the west central states after the Civil War were likely to find all
around them the families of Union veterans and other pro-Union
homesteaders from the North; their neighbors being Republicans,
the newcomers became Republicans, too. Conversely, sometimes

a change of status or environment will mean a change of party affiliation. Most southern whites were brought up as Democrats. If one of them, a rising businessman, moves to a wealthy northern town, family tradition and his own emotional commitments may keep him in the Democratic fold. He may, however, find that both his intellectual sympathies and his dislike of being thought odd by his neighbors are strong enough to break the old ties and make him vote Republican. At the present time political analysts are trying to ascertain whether the "flight to the suburbs," of urban wage earners moving into more affluent communities, is likewise causing a substantial shift from the Democratic party to the Republican. If environment were the only factor, such a shift would be overwhelming in the metropolitan areas of the North where residential suburbs have been traditionally Republican. But there have been few evidences of any such overwhelming shift —which indicates that environment is only one factor among several in determining a voter's partisanship.

Other causes of continuing partisanship include admiration for a party leader, one's own political ambitions and, finally, the connection which a person makes between his own policy preferences and the two parties. Dynamic leadership can enlist a man under a party banner and very likely keep him and his children in that party's ranks. A person who earnestly desires a political career may coolly decide that his chances of success depend on his affiliating with the party which is dominant in his community—and once affiliated, it is not likely that he will change. (Politicians have, to be sure, occasionally "swapped horses" in mid-career, but it is a risky business, for the party they have deserted will not eagerly welcome them back, nor will their new fellow partisans fully trust them.) As for the connection between the parties, the issues, and one's personal experience, this is often a basis for partisanship even though it may not always be logical to fix the responsibility for success or disaster on either party. For seventy years after the Civil War northern Negroes voted heavily Republican largely because Lincoln, a Republican, freed the slaves. Since 1930, many voters have cast Democratic ballots because they or their parents suffered in the "Hoover depression." Undoubtedly personal grief arising from the Korean War drove some voters into the Republican ranks to stay—because they heard that war called "Mr. Truman's War," and Truman was a Democrat.

We have been speaking here, of course, of the continuing partisans—the "rock-ribbed Republicans" and "unterrified Democrats." Millions of voters do not fall into either category. Many express only a temporary preference; many others profess to have no partisan preference at all. If a great number of people have no feeling of loyalty to either party but, on the contrary, are dissatisfied with both, why is it that only the two major parties dominate the political scene? Why not a third national party, or a fourth, to give vent to the interests and enthusiasms of the switchers and the independents?

## The Two-Party System

For a century, at least, most national elections have been contests between the candidates of the Republican and Democratic parties—candidates for the presidency and for seats in Congress. In most parts of the country, today, the only significant local party organizations are, again, Republican and Democratic. Yet, as we have seen, neither of these parties is "a body of men united . . . on some particular principle." If they are not united, one might think that people who believed strongly in "some particular principle" would form a new united party and seek control of the government. Yet this seldom happens, and when it has happened, in the last hundred years, it has been unsuccessful.

*Belief in Party Responsibility.* Without being dogmatic, we can suggest several reasons for the continued existence of a two-party system in the United States, as distinguished from a multi-party system. First, there is the idea (whatever the reality may be) of party responsibility, where the people can hold the majority party responsible for its acts when it is in power and, if dissatisfied, replace it with the opposition party. Obviously nobody can fix responsibility on the majority party unless it is in fact a single, identifiable party. If the government is run by a coalition of several parties, as was the case in France for many years, it is bound to be both irresponsible and unstable. This was the argument strongly expressed by President Eisenhower in emphasizing the value of a two-party system and urging Republican solidarity in elections, however much individual Republicans might differ with each other between times. Insofar as people accept this argument, it offers one reason why there *is* a two-party system as well as why there should be.

*Only One Can Win.* Another reason, based less on what should be and more on what is, is that our elections are held in "single-member districts." At a given time, normally, a congressional district elects *one* representative, a state *one* senator, and the nation, of course, *one* President. Now if you don't like your representative or senator or President and want to defeat him in the next election, do you put up several candidates against him? Of course not. If the opposition vote is split among several contenders, the incumbent will probably get re-elected. The best chance of defeating him lies in uniting behind a single opponent. As the presidency is the biggest prize, and a unified effort either to retain or to oust the President must be nation-wide, each national party sticks together.

*State Laws.* A third reason, nowadays, for two parties to be dominant is that party structure itself is prescribed by law in most states, with many states making things very difficult for a new party to get itself established. A typical state law permits a new party to be designated on the ballot only if it submits petitions signed by a specified number of voters or a certain percentage of the number in the state who voted at the last state-wide election for governor. In large states, this means gathering tens of thousands of signatures, a formidable task—in both California and Ohio, for example, over 300,000 signatures. Furthermore, a small new party that manages to get on the ballot can stay there, in some states, only if its candidate for governor receives at least 5 per cent of the total vote.

*Seniority in Congress.* Still another reason for having just two parties is the custom of giving senior members of Congress the various committee chairmanships. As we shall see in Chapter 13, Congress organizes itself on a partisan basis. The majority party in either house is entitled to the chairmanships of the committees. These positions are powerful, and customarily they go to the party members who have had the longest continuous service on the committee. So if the Democrats, say, have a majority in the Senate, the senior Democratic senators will not want to make a formal break with the Democratic party even though they profoundly disapprove of its platform and its presidential candidate. By severing their connection with the party, they would be depriving themselves of power and perquisites in the Senate.

The foregoing are all possible reasons for the maintenance of a two-party system, but perhaps more important than any of them are *inertia* and *consensus*. "Inertia" does not mean laziness. Here it means simply that the two parties are going concerns, recognized by law and custom. Anyone trying to form a new party not only must spend great quantities of energy and probably money, but must fight an uphill battle against the entrenched political habits of most Americans. "Consensus" refers to the general agreement of the great majority of the people on the fundamentals of our social, economic, and political life. Widely shared are the broad beliefs in a society where the individual is reasonably free to speak, worship, and rise to the top by his own efforts, an economy where the profit motive and private enterprise play dominant roles, and a political system designed to provide democratic government in a united republic. Under this capacious roof of shared beliefs or consensus, two parties can usefully differ on details, but people find little need for more than two. It is only when the consensus is broken, when a truly basic disagreement leads to profound conflict of ideas and ideals and the parties fail to reflect this breach, that a third party is likely to gain a foothold despite the handicaps it faces.

## "Third Parties"

The lack of a consensus on social matters—specifically, the deep emotional differences concerning the social status of the Negro in American life—has threatened the two-party system for more than a century. This cleavage, coupled with the failure of the Whig party to reflect it, motivated the establishment of the Republican party, which was a "third party" when it was formed in 1854. The same cleavage split the Democratic party wide open in 1860, so that in the presidential election of that year Lincoln was opposed by two separate "Democratic" candidates and a "Constitutional Liberty" candidate. Many years later, in 1948, the Democratic party was again split, the "Dixiecrats" or States' Rights Party, composed of southern Democrats, nominating a presidential ticket which won majorities in four states. That new party was impermanent, being organized for one election only; but it was formed because of resentment against the social views—the "equal rights" position—which a majority of delegates to the Democratic national convention wrote into the party platform. On this social question, the major parties officially see very nearly eye to eye, each ostensibly favoring equal rights. Yet among the people, consensus has crumbled since World War II just as it did a century earlier, once again making it difficult indeed to contain all sizeable groups of voters within the two familiar parties.

Consensus concerning our political and governmental system has been comfortably apparent for most of the time since the vexed question of the nature of the Union was seemingly settled on the battlefield. As we have seen, however, there have been occasional disruptions concerning one branch of government, the Supreme Court. Vehement disapproval of the Supreme Court's role contributed to the rise of the Progressive party of 1912; still more vehement disapproval threatens the unity of the Democratic party today. And any southern third-party movement now would also build on a possible lack of consensus on the old question of the rights of the states, assuming that that question was not closed, after all, at Appomattox Courthouse. In recent years, since foreign policy has become so obviously a matter of life or death for all of us, consensus in that area becomes increasingly important to the two-party system. If there is a general agreement as to aims, two parties can represent differences as to methods. But if the people are divided in purpose, or if the major parties agree on methods which many Americans feel fraught with death, again a new party might arise. This was the disagreement underlying the establishment of Henry A. Wallace's ill-starred Progressive party of 1948—ill-starred because Communists got control of its machinery, but still able to attract about 1,500,000 votes.

The Republican party was the last significant "third party" to endure, though the Populists put candidates into the field for some twenty years. The others rise suddenly and fade away as the urgency of the issues lessens or the old parties take over the new one's program, as the Democrats stole the Populists' thunder in

1896. A few minor parties have, to be sure, lasted for a long time. The Prohibition party, the Socialist Workers, the Socialists, the Communists: all have had their names on many ballots in many election years. None ever carried a state for its presidential candidate; none ever changed the result of a national election. In the worst days of depression, in the presidential election of 1932, an attractive Socialist candidate got only 2.2 per cent of the popular vote; the Communist nominee got less than a third of one per cent. These doctrinaire groups were outside of the consensus altogether and had no general appeal.

In the states "third parties," operating locally rather than nationally, have had occasional influence. The American Labor Party, despite its name, was indigenous to New York. Arising out of the dissatisfaction of labor leaders with the policies of the older parties, it elected two men to Congress and seemed likely to play an increasingly important role in state politics. This new party split, however, on the issue of cooperating with Communists. The ALP was soon dominated by Communists and quickly faded from the scene, unable to get enough votes to retain its place on the ballot. The anti-Communist dissidents formed the Liberal party. The latter's numerical strength in New York is not great, and usually it merely endorses Democratic candidates rather than nominating its own; but in close state elections between Democrats and Republicans, the Liberal endorsement may be a deciding factor. In contrast are the minor parties which pop up now and then in states whose laws do not severely restrict or handicap such movements. Often these are not really parties at all, but just names chosen by independent candidates. Thus in New Jersey in 1958, the ballot carried the names of alleged candidates of the Conservation of Life Advocates Party, the Keep People Working Party, the Light a Candle Party, and—the title selected by a pig farmer perennially running for office—the Politicians Are Jokers Party.

## "A BODY OF MEN UNITED"

However disparate may be the views of Democrats south and north, or Republicans east and west, or even fellow partisans in the same village or apartment house, one thing brings some of them together. For all kinds of different reasons, these people want their party to win elections—and they are willing to work to bring that result about. These willing workers cannot be effective alone. Victory is the product of "joint endeavors," and in politics as in other affairs a joint venture in which many men and women participate requires leadership and coherence. In short, it needs *organization*.

Partisans can be separated into several categories. Far removed from the center of party activity are the casual Democrats or Republicans, who may give their party designation to a pollster but refrain from political activities and vote a "split ticket" when they feel like it. Closer in are those who can be pretty well counted on to vote for the party's candidates; it is this group which the party strives to "get to the polls" on election day. Still nearer the center are the party regulars, who may dislike the candidates whom the party nominates but will support them faithfully nonetheless. At the core are those regulars who make politics either a full-time business or their major avocation—the members of the organization.

## The National Party Organization

We have just been imagining a party as a large sphere composed of concentric circles. When we concentrate on the hard core, the party organization without which the whole sphere might fly apart or disintegrate, we must change the picture. To put the party organization into a diagram, we should use a pyramid. Thousands of local clubs and committees form the base of the pyramid; halfway up come the state organizations; and at the top is the national committee.

The trouble with this picture is that it reminds one of a hierarchy, and in a hierarchy the ultimate power is at the top. You reach the summit, and you are supreme. But the national committee is anything but supreme. In a realistic sense, it is not alone at the top. The party leaders in Congress may have actual supremacy, particularly in the formulation of party policy when their party does not control the White House but does have a majority in Congress. Thus in the late 1950's the Democratic leader of the Senate, Lyndon Johnson, was more influential than the national committee's chairman in developing a Democratic program.

Each party's national committee includes two members, a man and a woman, from each state; the Republicans, in addition, have one extra member, the state party chairman, for each state that votes Republican. These national committeemen and women are elected every four years by the state's delegates to the national presidential convention. They choose their own chairman, and he tries to act, to some degree, as the spokesman for the party.

Yet he has very little control. For instance in the winter of 1954 the chairman of the Democratic National Committee, Stephen Mitchell, made a public appeal to Democrats in two congressional districts in California. In each case, he told them very emphatically that they should not nominate a particular man for Congress, and he gave reasons which seemed to him compelling. His command, or at least urgent advice, was completely ignored. The two men were promptly nominated by their own local Democrats.

Nevertheless, the national chairmanship is a potential center of party leadership. Every four years the chairman, though formally elected by the committee, is actually the choice of the party's presidential candidate; and if the candidate wins, the chairman can speak to the rank and file as the President's viceroy for the party's organization affairs. In recent times, moreover, he has become increasingly a propounder of party policy. The chairmen are often invited to appear, even to debate, on television programs, and are billed as the parties' "official spokesmen." Neither of them has official authority to speak for the party, nor has anyone else; but if millions of listeners think that they do, their potential influence on policy is thereby increased. This is particularly true of the chairman whose party is "out of power." As we shall see, the President is, or can be, the chief spokesman of his own party. The opposition, in contrast, speaks with many voices. Among these the voice of an effective chairman can be among the loudest.

The office of the national committee in Washington is largely a propaganda center. Its potentialities were first realized in 1930, when the Democratic chairman hired a newspaperman, Charles

Michelson, to work for the committee. Michelson, a man with an eloquent typewriter lubricated by vitriol, wrote hundreds of speeches and statements for Democratic senators and other party leaders, attacking the Republican administration of President Hoover. Today, both party headquarters roll out reams of public relations material every year, stepping up the output in campaign time. Each publishes a regular periodical, the Republican *Battle Line* and the *Democrat*.

Organizationally, the national office is occasionally effective in promoting local organization and maintaining the morale of party workers, both by propaganda and by personal visits. When the party has won the presidency, the national committee may also be a center for the disposal of patronage. But in the patronage business—the matter of appointing people to government positions—it has to compete with the President, his agency chiefs, and the party's members of Congress, all of whom may have their own ideas as to who should be appointed.

### Party Organization in the States

Statutes in each state establish the form of party organization, differing only in detail from state to state. By and large—there are exceptions—state chairmen are mainly figureheads, or scapegoats when the party loses. The typical state committee is chiefly a representative body of local organization leaders; even where its members are popularly elected, it has few significant functions and little influence, with one exception—in a good many states, the state committee is given by law a major role in the selection of delegates to the party's national convention. Occasionally, therefore, a real contest occurs for control of the state committee between supporters of different contenders for the presidential nomination.

Far more important are the local party organizations—thousands of them, in villages and townships and wards and cities and counties. Here, by law, there are official party chieftains—party committeemen and women, for instance, chosen by the voters, and local chairmen selected by the committees. Here you can find that monster, the political machine, or that fitting instrument of democracy, the party organization: your terminology is likely to depend on which side you favor, the *other* party having the "machine." And here is the real source of power in the party structure. Organizationally, a "national" party is in the main a conglomeration of ill-coordinated local units, each with its own concerns though all fly the same party banner.

In effectiveness and motivation, local organizations vary greatly. Though statutes establish the formal pattern of local partisan machinery, it's up to individual people to give life to the law. In a good many places the machine is made of paper. There just isn't enough daily, hourly interest to make people undertake the unpaid burden of political work. In many other places personal ambition or idealism drives a handful of men and women into political organization—but so few of them that you could hardly call them a party machine.

There are still many cities, though, where a real machine exists and functions. Let's look for a moment at the still-existing city or county machine—and it can be either Democratic or Republican, it doesn't matter which.

The machine is a little pyramid with the precincts at the bottom and the city or county chairman at the top—only in *this* pyramid, the real power is usually at the top. Typically, the chairman is the boss—after working his way up from the precinct to the ward leadership and thence to the summit. He rules the organization because the workers in it respect him and count on him for party success, or depend on him for favors, or fear his disapproval. We live in a democracy, and he can be overthrown; but while he's the boss, he runs the show.

*Purposes of Local Organizations.* If people did not care who won elections, there would be no party machines. But many people do care, for ideal or selfish reasons. A local organization can help win elections in several ways. By the unity and persuasive leg work of its members, it can often decide whom the party shall nominate for local office. Between elections, by constant enthusiasm, publicity, and the drudgery of getting people to register to vote, it can maintain or increase the party's strength. At campaign time, it "gets out the vote" and in many states, takes the responsibility of providing poll-watchers to see that the vote is fairly conducted and properly counted.[2]

*Fuel for the Machine.* What keeps an organization running? It depends on devoted volunteers; less than one-fifth of the active workers for fairly representative city machines which have been carefully studied hold government jobs. In the main, the "ward heelers," the precinct leaders, the official committeemen are privately employed and turn to politics in their spare time. It's hard work; why do they do it?

Historically the machine has run chiefly on *patronage*. People work for it, or for "the boss," in gratitude for past favors and more particularly in the hope of favors to come. The most direct form of patronage is appointment to public office—jobs ranging all the way from judge to janitor, from deputy sheriff to dog catcher. (Despite the familiar phrase about not having enough friends to be elected dog catcher, most dog catchers are appointed, not elected.) Work hard for the party, and if it wins and you need a job, you'll get one: that was the tacit assumption underlying much local political effort in former days, and it still is an important factor. Patronage has been bitterly criticized, with good reason. Tragic accidents have happened because men whose only qualification was doorbell ringing in Ward Four have been appointed to such responsible posts as elevator inspector. Furthermore, when party service is the sole test, dishonorable men may easily be named to positions of public trust. Against this patronage system, too, is the argument that it not only leads to bad government but departs from basic democratic principles: it makes vote-getting a matter of bribing people with promises of jobs rather than persuading them on public issues. However, the patronage system has its defenders. Surely, it is argued, policy-making positions should be filled by people who agree with what the party in power wants to do. The small jobs, assuming that minimum standards of character and competence are satisfied, might go just as well to party

---

2 Some old-time machines perverted this last function by hiring "repeaters" who voted under various names in different precincts, and by deliberately miscounting the ballots. These abuses used to be fairly prevalent; today they occur less frequently. The increasing use of voting machines makes falsification of the results more difficult.

workers as to anyone else. And for the public good they should go to the party faithful—for otherwise the organization would lose its members, and without organization the whole party system would crumble. So the arguments run.

*Favors* other than public patronage also bind people to a party machine. These include employment in private business; the fixing of parking tickets, the furnishing of bail; on a different economic level, the granting of loans and licenses for doing business. The organization may act as a service agency for humble people, too. Some of the great city machines got their real start when there was mass immigration into this country. Party workers went to the pier to meet the boat, to give their personal help to the poor, frightened foreigners who emerged from the steerage into a strange world—and those same immigrants were forever grateful. Sometimes the favor has been a ton of coal for a shivering tenement; in the 1920's, one local boss sent hundreds of turkeys to poor families on Thanksgiving Day. For a long time, in great cities especially, the local party headquarters was the center of the neighborhood's social life. Older people today, who grew up on New York's lower East Side, remember the glamor of the local assembly district boss, the occasional dances at the party's clubhouse in the ward, and the annual trip on the day boat up the Hudson—a great occasion, with the portly Tammany chieftains handing out cigars to the men, the beer flowing, and the women in their summer best posing on the deck for snapshots as the steamer sailed beneath the Palisades.

Some of the organization's most active workers, however, are not anxious for either appointments or picnics. Some are eager for elective office. Some are eager for the party's victory simply because they believe in what they think it stands for. In both these categories—the ambitious and the dedicated—are as devoted followers as any organization can hope for.

To last, an organization must have *voting power* and at least the reasonable hope of getting control of public office. Its leaders must be able to say to the elected officials: "Listen, we can reelect you or we can make it hard for you next time—we have *votes*. All our people will go to the polls, and all of their fathers and mothers and brothers and sisters and nephews and nieces will go to the polls, too. So you'd better listen to us." The greater its influence, the more it can hold its membership by threats—usually unspoken —as well as by favors. The ambitious politician fears being thwarted. The insecure worker fears unemployment. The humble family fears social disapproval. When the machine is both powerful and ruthless, of course, others fear it too: the businessman who affronts the boss, for instance, may be harassed. In Memphis there was an undertaker who defied the political machine, and they nearly ran him out of business by stopping his funeral processions on trumped-up charges of faulty brakes or reckless driving. They could do this, of course, only because they controlled the city government.

Yet even a powerful machine depends, in the last analysis, on popular approval. Its leaders have to face the ambitions of would-be rivals for the leadership, the fury of the disappointed party workers, and, in the case of machines that are either corrupt or tyrannical, the revolt of the voters. A change in leaders, to be sure, does not dissolve the organization. But misuse of power, or continued failure to deliver the goods, can do so. The Crump organization in Memphis, for instance, though reputedly "clean," was arbitrary and dictatorial—and eventually it was overthrown. A series of disastrous defeats can so discourage the partisans that they work halfheartedly or not at all. And inability or refusal to satisfy the demands of the party workers can cause the organization's practical dissolution. The vengeance of a disappointed party worker—his bitterness toward the boss who failed to reward him, and more especially toward the official whom the machine elected and who then ignored his campaign workers when appointments were made—can be vehement. An illustration of this appeared in anonymous verses printed some years ago in a local Boston weekly:

Y're looking well, Mulcahy, and mighty prosp'rous too.
Things came your way, election day, it's purty soft for you—
But wait a minute, till I'm through; there's one thing I can't see:
Just where do I come in at—where's the job you promised me?
I polled the ward, got out the vote, just git that in y'r dome,
I scraped the precincts t'rough and t'rough, just like a fine tooth
                                comb,

I hardly saw me home at all, and that's no idle whine:—
You got yours, Mulcahy, whin do I git mine?
Now I'm not insinuatin', but be that as it may,
I'll warn y' now, to watch y'r step, that's all I've got to say.
It's up to you to come across, make good y'r word, that's all,
Or something's going to happen whin the vote comes out next
                                    fall.
There'll be an upset in the ward, that'll dislocate y'r spine:—
You got yours, Mulcahy, whin do I git mine?

## The Changing Picture

We have been discussing the party machines of the past. The discussion is relevant because today in many places local organizations have the same characteristics and operate in the same way. Yet the nature of the machine is clearly changing. There are still city bosses and "county rings." Great cities still include "delivery wards," where a solid vote is "delivered" for the candidates endorsed by the local party leaders. Nevertheless, the local party organizations—which even in their heyday were really effective in only a portion of the electoral districts of the country—are taking on a different aspect, and probably, over-all, are declining in strength. At least their ability to present a *disciplined* united front is being steadily reduced.

An entertaining novel published in 1956, *The Last Hurrah* by Edwin O'Connor, suggested the reasons for the decline of the typical boss and the familiar machine. It presented a graphic picture of the old-style boss losing his grip, even though he was as eloquent, vigorous, cynical, and ruthless as ever. Why? What had happened to his machine? What is happening to local party machines in many cities?

First, civil service examinations slowly supplant patronage in the filling of more and more public positions.

Second, the needy can look to the government, not to the boss, for most of the help they want. The "welfare state" has taken over a vital portion of the machine's old stock in trade.

Third, television—the climax of a long development, beginning with Henry Ford's first cheap automobile, which has changed our social patterns. No longer do humble city folk depend on the local party headquarters to furnish entertainment, outings, clambakes, a natural meeting place. Now, with television, fewer and fewer will even go to political rallies: they can see the whole show right at home. The machine as a social center is fading away.

There are other reasons, too, not so clearly implied in O'Connor's novel. Unrestricted immigration ended about forty years ago; no longer do the city organizations enlist vast crowds of newcomers, help them to find work and to become citizens, and receive their votes on election day. The beneficiaries of such welcomes are passing from the scene. It appears, too, that party bonds are being progressively loosened. The "cult of personality" is fostered by television, which gives every citizen the chance to see and hear all major candidates; regardless of party labels, people decide that they like one contender better than the other, and it gets harder and harder for the organization to "deliver" a straight party vote. "Split ticket" voting becomes more common. Thus in 1956, we heard the unprecedented news of a Republican President being elected while a majority of the voters simultaneously voted for Democratic congressmen. In the off-year election of 1958, the splitting of tickets was widespread. In Pennsylvania, for example, a Democratic governor and a Republican senator were elected. The converse was true in Rhode Island. In Massachusetts, in 1960, Kennedy won by over 700,000 but simultaneously a Republican was elected governor. In 1958, in one upstate New York county, the voters gave Nelson A. Rockefeller, the Republican standard-bearer, a majority of 16,000; at the same time they were favoring the Democratic nominee for Congress by a 10,000 majority. This kind of thing has happened before, but it seems to happen more frequently now—partly, at least, because the candidates can project their personalities into every living room.

The fact remains that party organizations will continue to exist, to carry on the fight for victory at the polls. It may be that, increasingly, they will depend on dedicated people who want the party to win not because they want favors but because they believe that their party can best serve the community and the country. Perhaps, too, there will be a trend toward the replacement of "party" machines by strictly "personal" machines, composed of people devoted, for one reason or another, to a particular political leader.[3]

How, now, shall we define an American political party—or is it beyond brief definition? Some years ago, a charming children's book was entitled *A Hole is to Dig*. It was filled with brief definitions given by very small children: "A cow is to moo; a cow is to give milk." The little tots defined things in terms of functions. Perhaps we should follow their example. If we do, we won't be stating the whole truth about parties, but we may be getting close to the heart of the matter. "A party is to elect." That's what makes it different from a pressure group. That's why party organizations exist. So let us turn to this basic function: the selection of our rulers.

---

3 Such personal machines, separate from the legal party structure, have long been dominant in some areas. In the one-party regions of the South, where the real contest is for the Democratic nomination, it is natural that organizations should center around the ambitions of particular candidates. The Democrats in Massachusetts, too, have been oddly impervious to the official party mechanism. Many of them are faithful organization people, yet when a visiting governor at a party banquet in the 1940's asked some of them what county organizations they were affiliated with, he received stares of blank incomprehension. Then came the answers: "I'm a Curley man." "Me, I'm a Tobin man." They named politicians, not counties.

# CHAPTER 11

# The Nominating Process

B ack in 1941, the hardy voters of Cambridge, Massachusetts, were faced with a problem: how to choose nine from among *eighty-three* candidates for the city council. The city had just adopted a new charter, requiring that the councilors should be elected "at large" from the city as a whole, not, as formerly, by wards, and that no party designation should appear on the ballot. To become a candidate, all one had to do was file a petition with a few signatures on it. So it was every man for himself—and the befuddled electorate, struggling with yard-long ballots, marked down their "X's" here and there opposite familiar names, ruined the ballot by trying to erase an "X" when they saw a name they liked better further down the list, and went away wondering who in the world at least sixty of the eighty-three candidates might be.

For our purposes, that local experience has two lessons. The first we have already learned—that politics abhors a vacuum, and when one occurs, parties quickly fill it. Sure enough, before the next election one strong local organization in Cambridge was putting a "slate" of nine candidates into the field. The opponents of the organization promptly agreed to keep down the number of anti-organization candidates. Quite a few extraneous individuals got their names on the ballot, and in 1943 there were thirty-nine candidates; but although no parties were mentioned on the ballot itself, the voters were on the receiving end of a barrage of campaign literature telling them which candidates were "endorsed" by the Civic Association (essentially a local party) and which were opposed by it.

The second lesson follows from the first. The incident reminds us of the electoral shambles that can occur if there is no regular, accepted way of *narrowing the choice* which the voters must make on election day. Parties play a vital role in narrowing the choice. They do it by nominating candidates for elective office. In a democracy any qualified person can reasonably aspire to office— after all, every American baby has a proud parent, or at least a doting aunt, who predicts that he'll be President of the United States. It would be a bit confusing, though, if millions of these babies, having grown up, should all run for President at the same time. The list of "hopefuls" has got to be pared down somehow, lest the voters give up in despair and the winners gain office with the support of only a small minority of the electorate. To pare down the list to manageable size, to allow us to make an understandable decision between two main contenders and thus assure that the victor will be the choice of the majority or near-majority, is the purpose of the nominating process. In national politics, this job is done by the political parties.

Historically, they have used three methods of doing it: the caucus, the convention, and the popular or direct primary. The caucus, a meeting of the party's elected officeholders, went out of fashion long ago. The convention, which replaced it, was a more democratic device, for it brought together delegates of the party's many local groups. It is still used for the nomination of presidential candidates, which we consider in some detail later in this chapter. The primary, however, is today the nearly universal way of nominating candidates for senator, representative, and state and many local offices. A party primary is really a "nominating election" in which the voters adhering to one party decide among several aspirants for the party's nomination for an office, choosing one of them to be the party's candidate.

In the course of a lifetime, many of us may run for some elective office or be interested in someone else who is doing so. We should realize that in many or most instances, the first hurdle to be cleared is the primary: you can't get elected unless you first get nominated. And if our only political activity is merely voting, we should know why the choice confronting us is between the particular people whose names are on the ballot on election day: why those names, and not the names of other people for whom we have more respect? If we know about the nominating process, we not only gain understanding, but also may realize that opportunities exist for us to affect that process. Let us proceed, then, to examine the primary. In doing so, we may find it helpful to use words carefully. People who seek a party's nomination are often called "candidates"; but so are the people whom the parties nominate. If a senatorial seat is at stake, a person who wants the Republican nomination may announce that he is a "candidate for the Senate." Actually he is hoping that the Republican party will make him its candidate for the Senate. To avoid confusion, therefore, let us call the contenders for nomination *aspirants*—they aspire to be their party's choice. Once nominations are made, the race is between the parties' *candidates*.

## NOMINATION BY PRIMARY

Many writers have traced the origins of the primary back to 1867 in Crawford County, Pennsylvania, but it began earlier than that. There is evidence that it was used by the Democrats of Crawford County as early as 1842,[1] and newspaper records in St. Louis show that the Democrats in that city were invited to vote on whom their party should nominate for various offices in 1850. It began to be the official nominating system, prescribed by state law, very early in the present century, Wisconsin leading the procession in 1901. Today all U.S. senators and representatives are nominated in primaries, except in Connecticut and, in the case of senators, New York, Delaware, and Indiana. The last three states select the nominees for all state-wide offices at party conventions. Connecticut has passed legislation preserving the convention system but permitting a primary when the loser in the

---

[1] "Origin of the Direct Primary," *National Municipal Review*, April, 1935, pp. 222-223.

convention receives one-fifth or more of the votes cast by the delegates. A few other states have experimented with holding a convention before the primary to endorse aspirants for nominations, but those endorsed can still be opposed in the primary, and some of them have been defeated.

The impetus behind the spread of the primary in the "progressive era" early in this century was the spirit of democratic reform, which prescribed "more democracy" as the cure for all manner of social and political ills. The particular ills which the primary was supposed to remedy were the corruption and machine domination of the nominating process. The primary supplanted the convention system, which had long been a prey to those evils. The votes of convention delegates, it was said, were "bought and sold like cattle," and the selection of nominees was actually accomplished by a boss or group of machine leaders, regardless of the wishes of the people.[2] All this would be exorcised, so the reformers thought, by the powerful medicine of direct democracy.

The fact is that in many primaries, far more money is spent than was ever spent in a convention—not in bribing delegates to be sure, but in campaign expenses which sometimes run into six figures. Such costly campaigns must be financed by somebody, and those who found it worth while to "buy delegates" may see in the primary an opportunity not to "buy voters" but to put a future officeholder under heavy obligation to them. As for the influence of the party machine, in many places—for good or ill—it controls the primary just as it controlled the convention, with one important exception—in a primary the anti-machine people can, if aroused, reject the organization's slate. Very often, however, the primary appears to interest few voters except the full-time politi-

---

[2] In the "convention" state of New York, much was made in the campaign of 1958 of the undenied allegation that the Democratic senatorial nominee was selected by Carmine De Sapio, the "boss" of Tammany Hall (the party organization in Manhattan) against the wishes of even as powerful a person as the governor of the state. However, there is no evidence that Mr. De Sapio's selection of Edward J. Hogan was against the wishes of the rank and file of Democratic voters. And for many years, the record of nominations made by conventions in both New York and Connecticut has been the best defense of the convention system. The conventions have produced a large number of splendidly qualified candidates, especially for governor: one thinks of Smith, Roosevelt, Lehman, Dewey, Harriman, and Rockefeller in New York, and Cross, Bowles, Lodge, and Ribicoff in Connecticut, and wonders whether primaries could have done any better or as well.

cians and their faithful followers, and "direct democracy" ends up, after all, with the boss on top. Predominant influence of the party organization on the party's nominations may be defended as justified, useful, and necessary, as we shall see; what seems impossible to defend is the lackadaisical inertia, ignorance, and apathy of many Americans who vote on election day in November, but fail to vote in the primary.

## The Mechanics of Making Nominations

*The Significance of Legal Requirements.* The first thing that an aspirant for his party's nomination must do, if his name is to appear on the ballot in the primary, is to comply with the state laws concerning nominations and elections. The formalities of indicating an intention to run differ from state to state, but in general are fairly simple. Petitions must be filed with the appropriate officer—the election commissioner, or the secretary of state—bearing a requisite number of valid signatures. Some state laws say that these signatures must be geographically distributed among the counties, wards, townships, or other political subdivisions of the electoral district. And in some states the aspirant must not only file petitions, but must pay a moderate filing fee.

If you ever run for office, be sure you know what the laws of your state provide. Otherwise your hopes may be dashed at the outset. Here are three examples based on actual occurrences, of ambitions being ruined through ignorance of the law.

(1) A woman seeking nomination to a city office filed petitions bearing 1026 signatures, the law requiring only 850. She began enthusiastically to campaign. But when the election commissioners checked her papers, they found that many people had signed their names differently from the way their names appeared on the official list of registered voters. On the printed list, for instance, Mr. Johnson's name appeared as "Frederick C. Johnson," on the nominating petition, as "Fred Johnson." This disparity made his signature invalid. Likewise invalid was the signature of "John Smith, 80 Pleasant St.," because Mr. Smith had just moved and his address on the latest official list of voters was "75 Redfern Ave." Thus the commissioners threw out over 200 of the signatures and ruled the petitions insufficient.

(2) A distinguished diplomat retired, went to live in the college town where he had spent his boyhood, and promptly decided to run for the state senate. His party's leaders, who disliked the sitting senator (though he was of the same party), were delighted. They announced that they would support the diplomat in the primary. The senator said nothing. They filed petitions with plenty of valid signatures. The senator did the same, but remained silent. Finally the last day for filing came and went: the diplomat alone had filed to oppose the senator for the nomination. Then, when it was too late for the party leaders to get anyone else to run against him, the senator blandly pointed out that the diplomat, long in foreign parts, had established his legal residence in the senatorial district only eleven months before the date of the next election, whereas the state law required at least one year's residence in the district as a qualification for the state senate. So the discomfited diplomat and his friends went off to lick their wounds, and the senator was renominated without opposition.

(3) Two men sought the nomination for Congress in a district at the western end of the state. One was the vice-chairman of the party's state committee. The other was an unknown small-town lawyer, who seemed to be running for his health. The primary was to be held in September. On July 20, as the state law prescribed, the vice-chairman filed more than enough signatures at the office of the election commissioners in his county. Then, confident of the nomination, he went fishing. A week later, frantic messages reached him from the state capital, 150 miles away. Where were his papers? Didn't he know that the state law required that the petitions, certified by the county election commissioners, had to be filed with the secretary of state before five o'clock on July 27? It was already three o'clock. Desperately he dashed to the county courthouse, grabbed the petitions, chartered an airplane to fly to the state capital—and ran into a blind fog that grounded him fifty miles from his goal. The small-town lawyer, who had been more careful, thus won the nomination by default, was elected to Congress, and served respectably there for twelve years, retiring in 1958.

So the first thing is to know the law. What are the legal qualifications—citizenship, age, residence—for the office sought? What are the dates and requirements for the filing of intentions? The state legislature fixes not only those dates, but the date of the primary itself. In some states it is held in the spring before the November election; in some in mid-summer; in a few—Massachusetts, New York,[3] Wisconsin—in September. The early primary gives the voters a chance to become well acquainted with the rival parties' nominees.[4] But it encourages an exhausting six-month campaign leading up to the November election. In the "September states" the post-primary campaign is a more manageable seven-week effort, imposing less of a strain on both the candidates and the voters. Mid-summer primaries seem well designed (consciously or unconsciously) to discourage voting; many people are away on vacation, and the stay-at-homes may find it too hot to go to the polls.

*Types of Primaries.* As primaries are designed to produce *party* nominations, it is logical to assume that only faithful partisans should vote, each in the primary of his own party. However, there are two difficulties about this. The first is the fact that the parties are not membership organizations like private clubs; beyond accepting a man's word for it, how can you tell that he is a Democrat or a Republican? The second is that historically, the primary was looked upon as an essentially democratic device: if "pure democracy" is the goal, shouldn't we all be allowed to vote on the nominations of both parties for every office?

Most states—forty of them—take the view that primaries are essentially party elections and that anyone voting in a party primary should give some evidence of affiliation with that party. Many of these states require that he register as a partisan prior to the primary; a few provide that if challenged he must make a declaration of intention to support the party's nominees. The voter goes to the polls. There he (or the printed voting list) indicates his party affiliation, and he is handed the ballot of that party.

---

3 Although New York nominates candidates for state-wide offices (U. S. senator, governor, etc.) at party conventions, the nominations for Congress and the state legislature are decided by primaries.

4 In Great Britain, the candidate to oppose a sitting member of Parliament is ordinarily selected years before the election. This gives him and the voters ample opportunity to know each other and permits the actual intensive campaign to be as short as three weeks.

He votes for various aspirants for that party's nomination for the different offices involved. In the final election, he is under no legal obligation to vote for the party's candidates; but in the primary, he is performing a party duty, and only people who identify themselves with the party are permitted to participate. This system, which emphasizes the party's responsibility for making nominations, is known as the *closed primary*.

In contrast, other states have an *open primary*, emphasizing the free choice of the voter rather than the role of the party. In an open primary the voter is given both party ballots. In the privacy of the booth, he crumples one of them and marks the other. (Likewise where voting machines are used, he votes only for aspirants for one party's nominations.) The essential thing is that he need not publicly declare his party preference. Under this system, a lifelong Democrat can take part in choosing Republican nominees—and vice versa.

One state, Washington, is more "open" still. It provides for a *"blanket" primary*, where the voter is given both ballots and can mark them both, though casting only one vote for the nomination for any one office. Thus he might put his cross beside (or pull the lever under) the name of an aspirant for the Republican nomination for governor, an aspirant for the Democratic nomination for senator, and so on.

**The Winners.** In most primaries, victory goes to the aspirant with the largest number of votes. If there are several rival contenders, the one who wins the nomination may well have less than a majority. More likely he will have a *plurality*, less than 50 per cent of the total vote but nevertheless more than any of his opponents. Apparently our preference for having elective office filled by someone who has won majority support does not extend to party nominations; we are—or should be—quite used to nominees who got less than half the vote in the primary. When, however, nomination is equivalent to election—when everyone assumes that one party's nominee is certain to win in November —there is greater reason for majority rule in the primary. Therefore the southern states, in the days when they were solidly Democratic and any Democratic nominee was sure to be elected, adopted a plan insuring that the winner of the real contest—the primary—would be the aspirant receiving a majority of the votes cast. They devised the *run off system,* which is used in nine states. Under this system, if no aspirant gets a majority in the first primary, a run off is held two or three weeks later between the two strongest contenders. Thus, Colfax, Culpeper, Lee, and Ravenel may all be in the original primary, with the following result: Colfax 40 per cent, Culpeper 32 per cent, Lee 18 per cent, Ravenel 10 per cent. The run off is between Colfax and Culpeper, one of whom, inevitably, must receive over 50 per cent of the vote cast in that second election.

## Parties and Primaries

*The Contest for the Nomination.* Most primary battles are popularity contests, with the party organization's endorsement often helping to make one contender more popular than the rest. Issues are usually subordinated. After all, the aspirants all "belong" to the same party, and in a particular district the party may be fairly united in outlook. Even if it isn't, most of its leaders prefer to maintain the appearance of unity and therefore frown on the ambitious contender who deliberately opens up intraparty cleavages. Any future nominee will want united party backing in his campaign for election—why offend people by taking a stand which may incur the disapproval of many of your fellow partisans? It is much safer and easier to assume, or pretend, that the party stands for principles so well known that they do not need to be spelled out and to spend your time in (1) denouncing the other party, (2) convincing your fellow partisans that you would make a strong candidate, and (3) making yourself well and favorably known among the voters. The second may be enough where a strong party organization largely controls the primary voting. The third is vital for success where local party groups within the district or state are inactive or back different aspirants, or where you are "bucking the machine." So if you ever want to run for office, the questions you might ask yourself before deciding to seek your party's nomination are these: would I be a good candidate against the opposition party? Can I convince the leaders of most or all of the local party organizations of this, and will they therefore support me for the nomination? By primary day, can I make myself known and liked by a large number of my fellow partisans?

There are special factors and situations, however, that may make these questions irrelevant or insufficient. Sometimes issues are important. The conflict of interests within the party framework occasionally makes the primary a real battleground where questions of policy are at stake. This can be especially true in "one-party" areas; where nomination is equivalent to election, the primary is the only contest in which conflicting interests can fight it out.

The general rule, however, is that primary campaigns are essentially contests where personality and organization count much more than issues. Always present is the temptation to try to win by making a personal attack on your rivals. The severity of any such attack, however, is likely to be tempered by the knowledge that if you win the primary, you will need the support of your opponents and their friends to win the election. When the nomination is equivalent to election, it hardly matters how much you split the party, and "dirty" campaigning is unrestrained by fear of eventual defeat. When the election is a real party contest, however, there is no sense in gaining a nomination by means which jeopardize your chance of victory in the election. And, of course, many aspirants and many voters dislike and resent the use of smear tactics and below-the-belt campaigning. In a popularity contest, the contender who sneers at the private life or personality quirks of his opponent is himself likely to lose.

*The Role of the Party Organization.* In some states party organizations, by law or their own rules, refrain from formally taking sides in the nominating process. In most, however, if party organizations are strong and active, they usually affect the outcome of a primary contest. If they unite, they can decide it. The wise aspirant normally seeks their endorsement; in fact, he may not run at all unless he has received promises of organization support. The endorsement is effective. Remember that in most primaries the vote is light; only the most politically conscious people go to the polls. In old-fashioned machine wards, this means the party regulars, who will vote as the leaders decide. Where the newer type of organization is growing up, based less on patronage and more on principle, the endorsement is important too. The active members of the local club vote on which aspirant to support, and most of their fellow partisans will ordinarily follow their recommendation.

Yet the organization endorsement is not necessarily conclusive. An aspirant who fails to receive it may yet win the primary if he is personally attractive, endlessly energetic, and skillful in exploiting the advantages of his "independence." A successful anti-machine primary campaign can lead to election, for the defeated organization usually is wise enough to follow the old advice: "If you can't lick 'em, join 'em." Unless he has personally offended the bosses, they will support the upstart in the election campaign. Furthermore, his status as an independent in the primary may well attract the votes of independents in the election. Thus in the 1958 congressional elections in New York, two districts were easily won by candidates who had first successfully defied their party organizations in the primary. The dramatic way in which they won the nomination helped them to get elected.

Where party organizations are active, then, a primary may be a walkover for the aspirant whom they all endorse, a contest between aspirants each of whom has the endorsement of some organizations within the state or district, or, rarely, a battle between the organizations' choice and a daring individual who defies them. The latter, if successful, may himself become a party leader; but he is not likely to be successful.

A primary in which the party organization is feeble or inactive may result in the nomination of a weak candidate. Not only may the nominee be the favorite of only a small group within his own party; more important, he may be offensive to a large number of his fellow partisans and to independent voters. Even loyal party men often cannot bring themselves to vote for party candidates whom they profoundly dislike and distrust. So a primary where the party leaders are neutral can result in the party's putting its worst foot forward on election day and losing the election. Of course the leaders may make a poor choice too, but at least they ordinarily want to win the election and so are likely to back an aspirant who, if nominated, will appeal to all the partisan voters and many independents as well. In contrast, unguided voters in a primary are less prone to give much thought to victory on election day; many of them vote for the fellow they "like best," ignorant or heedless of the fact that in the final election he will be the easiest candidate for the opposition party to defeat.

To sum up: a primary is a theoretically and potentially demo-cratic device for making nominations. Insofar as powerful party machines influence or control it, the purposes of those who first fostered the primary are thwarted. However, if the real goal is to have each party nominate its best qualified man, the organization's domination of the primary can be, and often is, more of a help than a hindrance. The goal is at least as likely to be achieved when party leaders are active as when they are not, for party leaders usually want to win elections. Where the organization is active but unwise—where it presses for the nomination of un-qualified or unattractive candidates—the primary provides an op-portunity for intraparty revolt.

## PRESIDENTIAL NOMINATIONS

The most important and dramatic survival of the convention system of making nominations is shown to us on television every four years. It is the national party convention. More than a thou-sand delegates meet in a huge hall, together with a host of alter-nate delegates and a great crowd of spectators. They listen to speeches long and short; they march and cheer and sing; in dull periods they go out to confer, eat, drink, and maybe sleep; in mo-ments of decision they sometimes stay tensely on the convention floor all night; and always hundreds of people seem to be milling up and down the aisles, pushing and shoving while the chairman pounds his gavel and shouts ceaselessly for order. Out of this mael-strom comes the nomination of a man who will contend for the highest office in the land.

The convention system is a fascinating blend of party control and democratic influence. Since 1832, when Andrew Jackson caused the first Democratic national convention to be summoned, it has become one of our crucially important political institutions. Here the parties appear, as it were, in the flesh. In each convention the clash of interests and the rivalries of leaders come into full view. Each party adopts a platform—a statement of principles or a program which it will offer to the voters. Each concludes by selecting its candidates for President and Vice-President. As voters, our choice in November is effectively confined to the individuals whom the conventions name.

Party organizations are usually dominant in deciding who shall be the delegates at the convention. However, in numerous states the rank and file of the party's voters have some say in this decision. Likewise, party leaders in many cases decide how the delegates shall vote; yet they cannot determine who shall be nominated unless they effectively agree among themselves—a difficult thing for leaders from fifty states and countless cities and counties to accomplish. Even when the leaders are united, the "voice of the people" may thwart their desires: for many delegates may be more responsive to the rank and file than to the leaders, and, furthermore, party chieftains will not lightly pass over the man who has the greatest popular support, despite their personal preference for someone else. Responsible party leadership includes responsiveness to public opinion.

## The Choice of Delegates

Each national convention, as we have seen, is composed of over 1300 delegates. For 1960, the Republicans fixed 1331 as their total number of delegates' votes, the Democrats, 1521. The delegates are selected in the states, each state having a number of delegates prescribed by the national committee. The allocation is based primarily on population, as reflected in the number of senators and representatives each state has; traditionally, the state delegation to the convention has been double that number. Thus Nevada, with two senators and one representative, would have six delegates; New York, with two senators and forty-three representatives, would have ninety. The Republicans, however, have made this the minimum number, adding a few "bonus" delegates to various states in accordance with formulae designed to reflect the state's devotion to the party.[5] And the Democrats, in 1960, changed

---

[5] This bonus system was originated by the Republicans primarily to keep the southern states (where the Republican vote was habitually very small) from having disproportionately large voting strength in the convention.

the basic formula, not doubling the number of congressmen but multiplying that number by two and a half. In addition, each party allots a handful of seats to Puerto Rico, the Virgin Islands, and the Canal Zone.

Presumably to make faithful party workers happy, the parties long permitted states to select two, three, or four times as many delegates as the number of votes to which it was entitled. Thus a state with 40 votes could send 120 delegates to the convention—each of them casting only one-third of a vote, but all of them supposedly having a grand and glorious time. Then if you doubled the number of these "one-third" delegates, providing an alternate for each one, you brought pleasure and prestige to 240 loyal partisans. However, you also jammed the convention hall to bursting. With the coming of television, the party leaders, concerned about making a bad impression on millions of voters, gave thought to lessening the confusion by reducing the number of delegates and alternates; and fractional voting, therefore, is gradually becoming a thing of the past.

In about two thirds of the states, the selection of delegates is basically an organization matter. Techniques vary from state to state. In some, the choice of most delegates rests with the party's state committee. In others, most are chosen by county committees or by district conventions—the latter being composed of delegates from the city or county or township organizations. Rank and file party adherents can participate at the very bottom of the ladder in choosing delegates to the district conventions, but seldom do many of them bother to do so.

Whom does the organization select? The only general answer is that almost always, the state delegation includes the recognized party leaders—the governor and senator, for instance, and the state chairman and the national committeeman and committeewoman. The rest of the delegates, in the main, are people who want to go and whom the local organization leaders believe to be both deserving and compliant.

*"Presidential Primaries."* In fifteen states, delegates to the convention are elected by the party voters. These elections are called "presidential primaries," but unlike the primaries discussed earlier in this chapter, they are not held for the purpose of nomi-

nating anybody. They are *delegate elections*. They have some bearing on the eventual nomination of a candidate for President, but their effect is indirect and often very small.

A "presidential primary" in a given state, taking place weeks or months before the convention,[6] may indeed pit presidential aspirants against each other. A "slate" of candidates—a list of people uniting their campaigns—may announce a desire to be elected to the post of delegate so that, at the convention, they can vote for Jones, a serious presidential contender. A rival slate may announce that it is pledged to work for the nomination of Robinson, another serious presidential contender. The voters then vote for the candidates on one slate or the other, and the winners go to the convention. If the Jones slate wins, Jones' chances of being nominated are enhanced.

If such "delegate elections" were held in every state, they might come close to settling the nomination by popular choice. The fact is, however, that less than half the delegates at the convention are chosen in this fashion. And there are at least three other obstacles to making the "presidential primaries" instruments of effective popular choice.

(1) One or more of the major presidential aspirants may refuse to allow his name to be used by any candidate for delegate in a particular state. He may prefer to concentrate on other states where he believes he is more popular. So in numerous states there may be no contest at all.

(2) Prominent party leaders, undecided as to whom to support for President, may form a slate and run for delegate either "unpledged"—under no obligation to support any particular aspirant —or pledged to a "favorite son," some worthy local figure who is not seeking the presidency. If all the best-known party leaders are on such a slate, they are unlikely to have any opposition, and so the real contest for the presidential nomination never comes before the voters.

(3) The "pledges" of delegates cannot be enforced and some-

---

6 The "presidential primary" in New Hampshire is held in mid-March, that in California in early June; other states hold theirs at various times during the spring.

times do not imply even a moral obligation to vote for the favored aspirant for more than one ballot at the convention. As the convention often must take several ballots before any aspirant gets a majority, this means that as the balloting proceeds, Jones' delegates feel free to switch their votes to Robinson or Green or Smith. (Not all of them, to be sure, will feel free and willing to do this until Jones, despairing of his chances, "releases" them from their moral obligation to support him.) Thus the voter's April choice —as he viewed it—of Jones for President seems totally ineffective in July, when the very delegates for whom he voted desert Jones and help to nominate his rival.

For all of these causes, and especially because less than half the delegates are selected in "presidential primaries," these delegate elections are not *necessarily* significant. For instance, in 1916 the Republican convention nominated Charles Evans Hughes for President, and in 1952 the Democratic convention named Adlai E. Stevenson: in neither case had the winner entered any "presidential primary." Conversely, an aspirant can campaign successfully for the election of delegates pledged to himself, yet find that his victories are hollow: so it was with Estes Kefauver as he sought the Democratic nomination in 1952.

Yet "presidential primaries" can and sometimes do significantly affect the eventual action of the convention. The number of "pledged" delegates elected is not as important as the psychological factor. The party is looking for a winner. The aspirant who wins a "presidential primary" in which there is a real contest begins to look like a good vote-getter; if he wins another, he looks like a *very* good vote-getter. This was strikingly illustrated in 1960, when John F. Kennedy's triumph in Wisconsin showed that he had strength in a partially agricultural state, and his victory in West Virginia, a strongly Protestant state, seemed to disprove the thesis that Protestants would refuse to vote for a Catholic candidate.

The contest for the 1952 presidential nomination between Republican aspirants Dwight D. Eisenhower and Robert A. Taft illustrated both the affirmative and negative possibilities of the "presidential primaries." In New Hampshire, Taft organized confidently. At the last minute General Eisenhower, then in Europe, consented to the use of his name. There was a contest squarely between the two rival slates. Eisenhower's smashing victory removed one of his greatest obstacles, the doubts of his supporters that the people would vote for a soldier. Taft's defeat aroused the "he can't win" chorus to full cry and caused many of his friends to lose heart.

Probably defeats are more often significant than victories. Wendell Willkie, running last in the Wisconsin Republican "presidential primary" in 1944, promptly dropped out of the presidential race; Estes Kefauver, after losing to Stevenson in California in 1956, not only dropped out but announced his support for his rival. In any event, while "presidential primaries" do not insure a democratic system of nomination, they are not unimportant. They do not bind the nominating convention, but they may profoundly influence it.

*"Preferential Primaries" and "Polls."* Ten states provide for voting before the convention in a manner even less effective than the usual "presidential primary." The ballot includes the names of those aspirants who wish to be voted on; in two states, a person's name may be put on the ballot without his permission. This is not an election of delegates, but strictly a show of "preference" for one aspirant or another, and most states' delegates to the convention are not bound by it in any way. Only once has this type of popularity contest had any significant influence. That was in 1952, in Minnesota. Harold Stassen, Minnesota's governor, was the choice of the state's delegates, and General Eisenhower's name was not even on the ballot. Stassen's was: yet even so, nearly 100,-000 Minnesota Republicans wrote in Eisenhower's name. This provided further impressive evidence of Eisenhower's great popularity.

A new problem for presidential aspirants was produced by the Oregon legislature prior to the 1960 conventions. The new Oregon law provides for a "preferential primary" where the selection of the names to appear on the ballot is made by a state official, the secretary of state. He is supposed to be guided by the extent of active campaigning, newspaper comment, and other evidence showing that a person is a genuine contender for the nomination, but in fact his discretion is very broad. He can omit whom he wishes; more important, he can put onto the Oregon ballot the names of men who have no desire to compete in a popularity contest in that state. Only by filing an affidavit proclaiming that he is not seeking the nomination can any person selected by the state secretary keep his name off the ballot. This "puts on the spot" any covert aspirant who hopes to remain in the background until a convention deadlock between the avowed contestants results in his being "drafted" as a compromise choice.

Even the Oregon free-for-all is confined to a single small state. Political leaders may be more impressed by the unofficial polls taken by private nation-wide polling organizations.

These show something, at least, of the relative popularity of the aspirants. They fail, however, to indicate the extent and depth of active hostility to an aspirant—and this, as we have seen, may make him a poor man to nominate. This omission is corrected, in part, by the custom of arranging imaginary "horse races" between possible candidates, one for each party. If a polling organization reports in June that A, an aspirant for the Democratic nomination, would get 60 per cent of the vote in a race against X, a possible Republican candidate, and that other Democratic aspirants B, C, and D would get only 52 per cent or even lose to X, this index of A's superior capacity to win the election may have real influence at the Democratic convention in July. The delegates want a winner. They may argue correctly that A's advantage is temporary, that he leads the field only because he is better known and that B, C, or D could do even better when thrust into the limelight as the party's nominee; but still the results of the polls may significantly increase A's chances.

## The National Convention

The party's quadrennial convention meets in a city selected in advance by its national committee—Chicago, more often than not, because of its central location. For 1964, however, neither party followed this traditional course. The Republicans chose San Francisco and the Democrats Atlantic City. The choice of a site is big business. Both cities offered the party war chests of over $600,000 apiece for the privilege of playing host to the delegates.

*Organization.* Before the grand climax, the nominating of a presidential candidate, and the usually drab anti-climax, the selection of his running mate, the convention adopts a platform—a statement of principles and a program. And before it can do that, it must organize. Usually the matter of organizing the convention is a cut-and-dried business, decided in advance by party leaders and representatives of the leading contenders for the nomination. They agree on who shall be temporary chairman, with the honor of making the "keynote speech," and on who shall be permanent chairman, a potentially important position if the battle is hot. They agree on the rules—usually the continuation of rules guiding former conventions. And in most instances any disagreements as to who are properly entitled to act as delegates are likewise settled in advance.

Occasionally, however, contests over organization, rules, and the seating of delegates have occurred on the convention floor and have had great significance. If the national committee leaders are opposed to one prominent contender and select an enemy of his to make the keynote speech, the contender may seek an early show of strength by proposing a rival candidate for the post of temporary chairman. Or some well-known delegate may seek to commit the party to a particular course by proposing a change in the rules—as William Jennings Bryan did in 1912, when he struck at the alleged alliance between big business and Tammany Hall by moving to adopt a rule barring from the Democratic convention "August Belmont, Thomas F. Ryan (both of them millionaires, and both of them delegates) and any other member of the privilege-hunting, favor-seeking class." An attempt to have the convention adopt a rule binding all delegates to support the party's candidate nearly split the Democratic convention in 1952, for southern delegates did not wish to be committed until they knew what the platform said, who the nominee was, and whether he was hostile to their sectional interests.

Twice, contests over rules regarding delegates' *credentials* have made history. In 1952, rival sets of Republican delegates came to Chicago from several southern states. These were states which had no "presidential primaries." The "regular" delegates, certified by their local organizations, were generally favorable to Senator Robert A. Taft for President. But it was claimed that they had been improperly selected by local conventions illegally conducted and that a majority of Republicans, excluded from these local conventions, favored Eisenhower and had held proper meetings which selected delegates pledged to him. The issue of which set of delegates to seat was determined by the convention after a vote was taken on a proposed rule to provide a method for settling it. The victory of the Eisenhower forces, in adopting a rule which in effect assured the seating of the Eisenhower delegates and the exclusion of the Taft delegates, made the nomination of Eisenhower virtually inevitable.

The Taft family had no luck at all in the matter of delegates' credentials. Senator Taft's father, President William Howard Taft, had won a similar battle over the seating of southern delegates in 1912, but it was a Pyrrhic victory. The loser in that contest was Theodore Roosevelt. When a rule was adopted making certain that his southern supporters would be excluded, Roosevelt "bolted" the convention. With ebullient confidence ("I'm fit as a bull moose") and crusading fervor ("We stand at Armageddon and we battle for the Lord") he hurriedly organized a new party, ran for President, split Taft's support and carried sixteen states whereas Taft could capture only Utah and Vermont.

*Platform.* Each party's platform committee (selected by the national committee) meets a few days before the convention and holds hearings at which interest group representatives urge the party to adopt particular policies. Then the members get down to the job of drafting a document which will mean something yet not offend sizeable groups of voters. The result is usually a wordy document, long on diatribes against the opposition and short on specific positive promises. This eventually is read aloud to all the delegates and approved by them.

Occasionally, however, a platform includes a "plank"—a section on some one subject—which is explicit and controversial; and sometimes the convention is treated to a meaningful debate about it. The debate concerning adoption or amendment of the platform can have historic effects. It was in that debate in 1896 that Bryan, arguing for a "free silver" plank, by his eloquence and magnetism made himself the leader of the Democratic party. In 1924, a proposal that the Democratic platform should denounce, by name, the Ku Klux Klan threw the delegates into bitter controversy and helped destroy the party's chance for victory that year. And in still another Democratic convention, that of 1948, the adoption of a civil rights plank proposed from the floor caused Mississippi's delegates to walk out and gave rise to the short-lived "States' Rights" or "Dixiecrat" party, which carried four states in the election.

Platforms are not wholly useless. They give the voters an idea, at least, of the general attitude of delegates at a party convention. To a President such as Woodrow Wilson, who believed strongly in party responsibility, the platform consisted of pledges which he felt bound to try to fulfill. Yet the separation of powers, the absence of party discipline, and the fact that parties are loose confederations of local groups all conspire to prevent the platform from being carried out, and so the public's interest in it is justifiably tempered by more than a grain of skepticism. Even a presidential candidate does not always feel bound to agree with the platform adopted by the very convention which nominated him.

*Nominating a Presidential Candidate.* The technical procedure for making the nomination can be quickly described. The clerk of the convention calls the roll of states in alphabetical order. The first state, Alabama, through the chairman of its delegation may answer "Alabama desires to place a name in nomination," or "Alabama yields to the great state of New York" (or Georgia or Pennsylvania or Texas or any other state). Then a delegate, selected in advance, goes to the platform and makes a speech, putting the name of an aspirant from his state before the convention. Later, delegates from other states may do the same for their favorites; and still other delegates arise to make "seconding" speeches for those whose names have already been proposed.

Logically, this time-consuming procedure seems to make very little sense. It gives numerous politicians a chance to sound off in front of television cameras, but it seldom if ever has any effect on how the delegates will vote.[7] The same is true of the tumultu-

---

[7] Once, to be sure, a nominating speech affected the nomination, though not in the manner intended. In the Republican convention of 1880, James A. Garfield proposed the name of Senator Sherman of Ohio. Apparently Garfield's speech impressed the delegates. They did not nominate Sherman, but eventually selected Garfield himself.

**Campaigning.** Grover Cleveland's home town, Buffalo, New York, was the scene of this campaign parade in 1884. Today, despite television, politicians feel that the voters like to see them in the flesh; sixty years after this parade President Roosevelt, with his Scottie "Fala," rode slowly in an open car, through cheering crowds in New York City, for four hours in a driving rain.

**The National Convention,** a durable institution which has changed little in aspect in the last eighty years. Above, James A. Garfield putting the name of John Sherman into nomination at the Republican Convention of 1880, a speech which so impressed the delegates that they nominated not Sherman but Garfield himself (see page 310). Below, the Democratic Convention of 1960.

ous "demonstration" at the conclusion of a nominating speech. In earlier times, these demonstrations were reasonably spontaneous, delegates parading and cheering for their favorites. Recently professionalized glamor has replaced spontaneity; at a prearranged signal, a corps of high-stepping majorettes may suddenly invade the hall, cheering sections jump into action, and a convention band swings full blast into the "state song" of the man whose name has been presented. It's all good fun, but it gets boring—and television time is expensive, too. Both national committees have been giving serious thought to putting time limits on both speeches and demonstrations and have had some success in shortening the former.

The balloting is conducted by calling the roll of the states. In Democratic conventions, some state delegations are bound by vote of state committees or conventions, or by their own choice, to abide by the "unit rule," by which is meant that all of the votes of a particular state will be cast for the man favored by a majority of the delegates from that state. The "unit rule," however, seems to be passing from the scene. Frequently, when the clerk calls the name of a state, the chairman of its delegation will respond "five votes for Robinson, four votes for Green, four votes for Smith, and one for Jones."

Both parties today provide that the aspirant who receives a majority of the votes cast by the delegates shall be the party's nominee. For a hundred years, the Democratic party required that to gain the nomination, an aspirant had to get two-thirds of the vote; but this "two-thirds rule," which gave an effective veto to a minority faction, was abrogated in 1936.

When there is a real contest for the nomination among three or more aspirants, it is unlikely that any one of them will win a majority on the first ballot. So the roll is called again. And, if necessary, again and again and again: in several conventions over forty ballots were taken, and in one, a hundred and three. But again television has an effect. Such prolonged deadlocks are unlikely to be played out before the cameras. Eventually—and probably sooner, today, than in years gone by—all but one or two of the leading contenders get discouraged. Their supporters clamor to be "released" and may even change their votes without waiting to be released. The uncommitted delegates, the "favorite son" groups, sniff the wind and try to guess which way to jump. *They want to be with the winner.* Finally one aspirant comes very close to a majority: and as the last state is called, the delegates from a "favorite son" state are on their feet, demanding the chairman's attention, shouting that they want to change their vote. They make a timely leap onto the bandwagon—and the race is over.

So much for the procedure. But why does X win the nomination instead of Y? One factor is X's *availability.* Ideally, the delegates want their nominee to be a man of impeccable reputation and dynamic personality, with a distinguished war record (e.g., Eisenhower and Kennedy), governmental experience, and as few political enemies as possible. Preferably, he should come from a large and closely-contested state. These considerations partially explain why so many presidential candidates have been citizens of populous states—New York, Ohio, California, for instance— whose electoral votes can swing the election in November, and also why so many have been governors. A state governor can often establish a national reputation without taking a clear stand on many national issues. Conversely, in nine consecutive presidential elections in this century no senator was nominated, for senators make their records by voting on issues, and their votes are bound to offend various interest groups.

Old-fashioned "availability," however, is less important than it used to be. John F. Kennedy won the nomination after fourteen years in Congress, during which he had to cast many votes and offend many interests. A leading aspirant for the Republican nomination in 1964, Barry Goldwater, not only was a Senator but hailed from Arizona, which casts only four electoral votes. The change that these instances illustrate may have two related causes. First, the impact of issues on the voters' minds is more uniform than it was before the days of jet planes and television—national issues are recognized as such by most people simultaneously. Second, as great national and international life-or-death questions sink into the people's minds, their choice for President is more likely to be the man of experience, whatever state he comes from, who has taken positions on the great issues regardless of their passing unpopularity. The uncommitted compromise candidate may seem less attractive than in the past.

All of these factors—issues of policy, personal popularity, old-fashioned "availability" in terms of geography and lack of enemies—go into the convention's choice. That choice is produced by the votes of the delegates; but the delegates themselves may be guided to it by the preferences of the party leaders—the dominant chieftains of local organizations and the powerful party men in Congress. When a deadlock occurs, there are sometimes only two ways of breaking it. One is a "deal"; thus in 1932, when Franklin D. Roosevelt was the leading Democratic contender but John N. Garner had the support of Texas and California, the Roosevelt forces won the Texas and California delegates, and the nomination, by promising the vice-presidential nomination to Garner. The other is a compromise, and obviously thirteen hundred tired and excited delegates can't work out a compromise. That has to be reached by a small group, in comparative quiet—as it was reached in 1920 by the Republican leaders (who made such an unfortunate choice that it gave a permanent bad name to the "smoke-filled room") and, more respectably, by the Republicans in 1916 and the Democrats in 1952.

Much of the foregoing assumes a convention where there is a contest for the nomination. Normally there is no such contest when an incumbent President seeks renomination. Since 1912, every such President has won unanimously by acclamation or on the first ballot with slight opposition. A party can ill afford to admit a mistake by denying renomination to the man it successfully offered to the electorate four years before, and furthermore, the President and those around him are likely to have a firm hold on most of the party's organizational machinery.

*Nominating a Vice-Presidential Candidate.* Usually, the man nominated for President either hand-picks his running mate, as both Kennedy and Nixon did in 1960, or approves the choice made by some of the party leaders whom he trusts. The delegates have just hoisted the nominee to the top and are looking to him to lead them to victory; naturally he can "call the turn." The process of nominating someone for Vice-President may include the familiar rigamarole of speeches, nominating and seconding, and the ballot by roll call of the states, but the matter is normally decided long before the balloting begins.

This is one reason why the nomination of a vice-presidential candidate is often a dispiriting affair, conducted in a morning-after atmosphere. Another is that quite frequently the man selected for Vice-President is a man lacking in national distinction, a man who has never been seriously considered for the presidency itself. Typically he is chosen chiefly because he "balances the ticket." Is the presidential nominee an easterner and head of a utilities corporation? Then for Vice-President put up a westerner who advocates federal water power projects. Is he a northern Democrat? Then his running mate should be a southern Democrat. Unify the party, heal any breaches opened at the convention —these seem often to be the objectives, without much heed being paid to the fact that eight Presidents have died in office.

The 1956 Democratic convention marked a departure from this pattern. The presidential nominee, Stevenson, angered some of the leaders and startled the delegates by announcing that he had no choice for Vice-President; the nomination was up to the convention. A sharp, short contest developed, and on the second ballot the majority voted for Estes Kefauver. Only at the Republican convention of 1920 was there a somewhat similar choice by the delegates: they revolted against the leaders who had just caused the nomination of Warren G. Harding for President and unexpectedly selected Calvin Coolidge for Vice-President.

Again, when a President has just been renominated he can name his own running mate and usually agrees to the renomination of the incumbent Vice-President. An exception to this occurred in 1940, when a deep split had developed between President Roosevelt and Vice-President Garner and the latter strongly disapproved of running for a third term. With considerable difficulty Roosevelt successfully insisted that the convention nominate Henry A. Wallace for Vice-President. Four years later party leaders persuaded Roosevelt that Wallace would be a liability in the 1944 campaign, and the President acquiesced in their selection of Harry S. Truman.

Now Coolidge and Truman, of course, became President and each was reelected to that office. The fact remains that since the days of Andrew Jackson vice-presidential nominees, at the time of their original nomination, have very seldom been men who were seriously considered for the presidency itself. Originally, of course, the Vice-President was expected to be the runner-up in the contest for the presidency—the country's "number two" statesman. Thus when Adams, a Federalist, was President, Jefferson, an Anti-Federalist, was Vice-President. The rise of the party system made this conception of the vice-presidency quickly obsolete. Its incompatibility with partisan elections was proved by the tie in 1800, when the Anti-Federalist electors, each casting two votes, cast party-slate ballots for Jefferson and Aaron Burr. They intended to vote for Jefferson for President and Burr for Vice-President, but the original Constitution made no provision for their indicating any such differentiation. As a result Jefferson and Burr got an equal number of electoral votes, and the House of Representatives had to elect the President. (It chose Jefferson.) To prevent a recurrence of this situation, the Twelfth Amendment was adopted in 1804, separating the formal election of President and Vice-President. This marked a drastic departure from the original conception of the vice-presidential office and was a tacit recognition of the arrival of national party politics. For a candidate for Vice-President is a person willing to settle for second place on a party ticket, and not necessarily a contender for the presidency at all. To be sure, Lyndon B. Johnson, Kennedy's choice for the nomination in 1960, had been a strong aspirant for the top spot on the ticket; yet even this very well-known candidate was chosen chiefly because Kennedy believed, correctly, that he would "balance the ticket" and keep most of the South in the Democratic column. The use of the nominations merely to promote internal party unity and the complete removal of the selection from the control of the voters make the naming of vice-presidential candidates the least satisfactory and most undemocratic part of the entire nominating process.

CHAPTER 12

# The Electoral Process

The heart of a democratic system is the electoral process. Periodic free elections make "government by the people" a reality. As we have seen, this presupposes freedom to debate the issues; it also assumes that the voters' choice is made manageable and significant by a system of party nominations. Elections would have little meaning if they were not preceded by campaigns between recognized contestants. Nor would they epitomize the democratic spirit if all but a handful of citizens were forbidden to vote. Fortunately, in the United States, the suffrage is broad, and real choices are offered to the voters—choices between men and between policies. What manner of men are these who seek public office? What part do policies play in their appeal for votes? What is the nature of a campaign, and what roles in it are open to you and me and most other Americans? Why do we vote as we do? For that matter, who can vote, and what is the impact of the votes they cast?

These are the questions to be considered in this chapter. We will begin with the last ones, which have to do with the institutional formalities of the electoral process—for we need to know the ground rules of the electoral game. Then we can give thought to the game itself—the players and what they do to win. It is a

316

matter of immediate personal concern, for in this great game of politics all of us can take part, and most of us do or some day will.

**THE GROUND RULES**

### The Mechanics of Voting

The least we can do, in politics, is to vote. Whatever else we may lack, so politicians sometimes tell us, we have that precious right, the right to vote. To be sure, the "right to vote" is not universal; it was decidedly not included among those self-evident unalienable rights mentioned in the Declaration of Independence. Voting is a privilege conferred by the government on those whom it deems worthy. Yet such is its importance that we quite naturally think of it as a "right," possessed at least by all literate, law-abiding, mature citizens.

*A State Privilege.* Under the Constitution there is no such thing as any *national* privilege of voting. Instead, each state determines the voting qualifications of its own citizens. The Constitution does, of course, in the Fifteenth and Nineteenth Amendments forbid the states to deny the franchise to anyone because of color or sex. The Fifteenth Amendment was a natural aftermath of the Civil War and the conferring of citizenship on the freed slaves. The Nineteenth Amendment, guaranteeing woman's suffrage, was a plant of much slower growth. Traditionally, well on into the present century, in some democracies across the sea and in much of the United States as well, voting had been an exclusively masculine business. The idea that only men should vote was consistent with the prevailing social outlook, which pictured a woman as an odd combination of hard-working homemaker and fragile flower who should not be sullied by politics—or trade or business either, for that matter. Not surprisingly, then, the first of our states to give women the privilege of voting were in the pioneer West, where women often worked on the farms with men and were obviously not lilies of the field. Naturally, too, the movement for nationwide women's suffrage, guaranteed by constitutional amendment, achieved success at the close of World War I, for it was in that brief period of war that women all over the country were suddenly "emancipated" from the old Victorian taboos. Ladies from

Fitzpatrick in the *St. Louis Post-Dispatch*

**A right men have died for**

gentle homes cut their hair, smoked, drove trucks and worked in factories—why in the world, then, shouldn't they vote? Even so, the Nineteenth Amendment might well have been delayed had it not been for the courageous and sometimes militant persistence of a comparatively small group of women who fought, not always wisely but always indomitably, for the single cause of "votes for women."

Nevertheless the states, between them, withhold the privilege from millions of persons. In forty-six states, everyone under twenty-one years old is excluded; in Hawaii, those under twenty; in Alaska, those under nineteen; and in Georgia and Kentucky, those not yet eighteen. Others are excluded, too. The property qualifications which disfranchised a small proportion of the people in the Republic's earliest days were, indeed, soon abandoned, yet something like them long existed in the "poll tax" states of the South: as we saw in Chapter 8, the poll tax was designed to disfranchise Negroes, but it also prevented many poor white people from voting. As we saw in that chapter, too, some state requirements that a person, to be worthy of the suffrage, must be literate have been administered in such a way as to deny Negroes the ballot. More even-handed are the provisions, in most states, that to be eligible to vote a person must have resided for a given length of time within the state and a particular electoral subdivision thereof and that he must be out of jail.

*Registration.* Except in Arkansas, North Dakota, and Texas, the first stop on the road to the ballot box for most would-be voters is the requirement of registration. Throughout most states and in the sizeable cities of the rest, you must get your name on the official list of voters well before election day.[1] Some states insist that if you want to vote, you must register periodically, every two or four years; others have adopted a system of permanent registration, so that if you once register, you remain on the list unless and until you move out of the particular electoral district, the city or township or county where you resided when you first registered, or, in some states, until you have failed to vote in several consecutive elections. If you do so move or fail to vote you have to register over again.

For the citizen, registration is a normal prerequisite of voting: he must show by his birth certificate (or his appearance) that he is not too young and that he meets whatever other qualifications are imposed by state law. For the party politicians, it is something more. Occasionally, a dominant party machine, so entrenched as to be unresponsive to the electorate, has deliberately tried to discourage the enrollment of additional voters by making it hard for

---

[1] This applies to the election of most local, state, and national officials. In many places, however, registration is not required for voting in local school board elections.

MODERN REPRESENTATIVE GOVERNMENT

*Question :*   If a man represents the women of his household how can
he represent himself?

**I**T is a common notion that men represent women at the
polls.

**D**ID you ever know a man who asked his wife how she wanted
him to vote?

**I**F a man votes as his wife wishes him to do, he doesn't represent himself.

**O**R, if a man votes to please himself, he doesn't represent
his wife.

**T**HE predicament of a man who attempts to represent a family
consisting of a wife, mother and daughters who hold different opinions, is conclusive that it cannot be done.

**I**F there are sons, the idea of a family vote isn't applied; they
vote for themselves.

**C**AN you see any sense in the argument that men represent
women at the polls? Of course not; there isn't any sense
to see.

**VOTE FOR THE SUFFRAGE AMENDMENT IN 1915.**

EMPIRE STATE CAMPAIGN COMMITTEE

**303 FIFTH AVENUE**        46       **NEW YORK**

The long fight for woman suffrage was basically a campaign for
equality for women. In this handbill, however, the suffragists gave
the argument a new twist—votes for women would be a boon to hen-
pecked husbands and fathers.

them to register. For example, in some counties in a southern state, a few years ago, new registration had to take place on a single day, and the party-controlled press gave no publicity to that fact. Similarly, it has been written of the congested East Harlem section of New York City that in that area, political "power rests upon the preservation of vested economic interests in jobs and in real estate and, it is said by some, in gambling and narcotics traffic and prostitution. In any event, where political power represents economic investment, whether lawful or criminal, the poor are apt to be excluded from politics. In East Harlem they are practically speaking disenfranchised. In some election districts here, far more people are unregistered for voting than those who are registered, and no effort is made to reach or register or enroll them, much less admit them to the councils of the local political club." [2]

Sometimes registration methods have been misused by corrupt election commissioners who disregard the law and enroll non-existent people; [3] sometimes the law itself is too loosely drawn to insure that all the voters in a precinct are actual residents of that precinct. But always, whenever an effective political organization, democratically controlled, is on the job, the registration system presents a year-round challenge. In states where periodic registration is required, the party regulars must be persuaded to spend a few minutes or hours going to the election commission's office or, often, the local schoolhouse where the registrars make themselves available for an evening. In all states, all newcomers must be canvassed, and those who probably will vote the "right" way must be urged to register. (The urging may take the form of an automobile at the door, though no potential registrant has actually been kidnapped.) Registration work pays off in votes. It can result in party triumphs in districts and even in states. For, as we shall see later in this chapter, an astonishingly large number of mature American citizens not only fail to vote, but do not even take the trouble to register.

---

2 William Stringfellow, "Christianity, Poverty, and the Practice of the Law," *Harvard Law School Bulletin,* June, 1959, p. 4.

3 Hence the cynical phrase sometimes used to describe the voting turnout in a machine-controlled city ward: "the graveyard vote."

## REQUIREMENTS FOR VOTING

| State | Minimum Age | U.S. Citizenship | Residence Requirements | | | Literacy Test | Loyalty Oath |
| | | | State | County | Precinct or Ward | | |
|---|---|---|---|---|---|---|---|
| Alabama | 21 | Yes | 2 yrs. | 1 yr. | 3 mos. | Yes | Yes |
| Alaska | 19 | Yes | 1 yr. | — | 30 days | Read or speak English | — |
| Arizona | 21 | Yes | 1 yr. | 30 days | 30 days | Yes | — |
| Arkansas | 21 | Yes | 12 mos. | 6 mos. | 1 mo. | — | — |
| California | 21 | 90 days | 1 yr. | 90 days | 54 days | Yes | — |
| Colorado | 21 | Yes | 1 yr. | 90 days | 15 days | — | — |
| Connecticut | 21 | Yes | 1 yr. | — | 6 mos.* | Yes | Yes |
| Delaware | 21 | Yes | 1 yr. | 3 mos. | 30 days | Yes | — |
| Florida | 21 | Yes | 1 yr. | 6 mos. | — | — | Yes |
| Georgia | 18 | Yes | 1 yr. | 6 mos. | — | Yes | — |
| Hawaii | 20 | Yes | 1 yr. | — | 3 mos. | Hawaiian or English | — |
| Idaho | 21 | Yes | 6 mos. | — | 30 days | — | Yes |
| Illinois | 21 | Yes | 1 yr. | 90 days | 30 days | — | — |
| Indiana | 21 | Yes | 6 mos. | — | 30 days | — | — |
| Iowa | 21 | Yes | 6 mos. | 60 days | 10 days | — | — |
| Kansas | 21 | Yes | 6 mos. | — | 30 days | — | — |
| Kentucky | 18 | Yes | 1 yr. | 6 mos. | 60 days | — | — |
| Louisiana | 21 | Yes | 1 yr. | 1 yr. | 3 mos. | Yes | — |
| Maine | 21 | Yes | 6 mos. | — | 3 mos.* | Yes | — |
| Maryland | 21 | Yes | 1 yr. | 6 mos. | 6 mos. | — | — |
| Massachusetts | 21 | Yes | 1 yr. | — | 6 mos. | Yes | — |
| Michigan | 21 | Yes | 6 mos. | — | 30 days | — | — |
| Minnesota | 21 | 3 mos. | 6 mos. | — | 30 days | — | — |
| Mississippi | 21 | Yes | 2 yrs. | — | 1 yr. | Yes | Yes |

***The Ballot.*** Those who do vote may find at the polling booth either a ballot or a voting machine by which they cast their secret votes.[4] On the former they make their choices by drawing a penciled "X" beside the names they favor. On the latter, they

---

4 In the old days, voting was not secret. The "Australian ballot" reform, near the turn of the century, aimed at a secret ballot to protect the dissident voter from the wrath of his neighbors, his employer, or the local party boss.

| State | Minimum Age | U.S. Citizenship | Residence Requirements | | | Literacy Test | Loyalty Oath |
|-------|:-----------:|:----------------:|:----------:|:----------:|:-----------------:|:-------------:|:------------:|
| | | | State | County | Precinct or Ward | | |
| Missouri | 21 | Yes | 1 yr. | 60 days | 60 days * | — | — |
| Montana | 21 | Yes | 1 yr. | 30 days | — | — | — |
| Nebraska | 21 | Yes | 6 mos. | 40 days | 10 days | — | — |
| Nevada | 21 | Yes | 6 mos. | 30 days | 10 days | — | — |
| New Hampshire | 21 | Yes | 6 mos. | — | 6 mos.* | — | — |
| New Jersey | 21 | Yes | 6 mos. | 60 days | — | — | — |
| New Mexico | 21 | Yes | 12 mos. | 90 days | 30 days | — | — |
| New York | 21 | 90 days | 1 yr. | 4 mos. | 30 days | — | — |
| North Carolina | 21 | Yes | 1 yr. | — | 30 days | Yes | — |
| North Dakota | 21 | Yes | 1 yr. | 90 days | 30 days | — | Yes |
| Ohio | 21 | Yes | 1 yr. | 40 days | 40 days | — | — |
| Oklahoma | 21 | Yes | 1 yr. | 6 mos. | 30 days | — | — |
| Oregon | 21 | Yes | 6 mos. | — | 30 days | Yes | — |
| Pennsylvania | 21 | 1 mo. | 1 yr. | — | 2 mos. | — | — |
| Rhode Island | 21 | Yes | 1 yr. | — | 6 mos.* | — | — |
| South Carolina | 21 | Yes | 2 yrs. | 1 yr. | 4 mos. | Yes, or own property | — |
| South Dakota | 21 | Yes | 1 yr. | 90 days | 30 days | — | — |
| Tennessee | 21 | Yes | 12 mos. | 3 mos. | — | — | — |
| Texas | 21 | Yes | 1 yr. | 6 mos. | 6 mos. | — | — |
| Utah | 21 | 90 days | 1 yr. | 4 mos. | 60 days | — | — |
| Vermont | 21 | Yes | 1 yr. | — | 3 mos.* | — | Yes |
| Virginia | 21 | Yes | 1 yr. | 6 mos. | 30 days | Yes | — |
| Washington | 21 | Yes | 1 yr. | 90 days | 30 days | Yes | — |
| West Virginia | 21 | Yes | 1 yr. | 60 days | — | — | - |
| Wisconsin | 21 | Yes | 1 yr. | — | 10 days | — | — |
| Wyoming | 21 | Yes | 1 yr. | 60 days | 10 days | Yes | — |

* In these states the requirement is for residence in city, town, or township.
SOURCE: Adapted from *The Book of the States, 1962-1963* (Chicago: The Council of State Governments, 1962), p. 20.

pull down levers over the names of their candidates. Voting machines are comparatively expensive, but they are so much harder to tamper with, and the tabulation of the vote is so much quicker and more accurate, that their use has been rapidly spreading. Whichever device is used, the form of the ballot—the order in which the names appear and the choices made available to the voter—can have a decisive effect in close elections.

In general, there are two kinds of ballots—the "office block" type and the "party column" type. In the former, a separate "box" appears for each office, with the name of the office at the top and the name and party designations of the candidates below it, viz:

> For Assemblyman:
> Adam Allen        (Dem.)        ☐
> Wallace Widener (Rep.)        ☐

You vote for one of the two, and then you turn to the next box, which may be that for state senator. As a method it seems simple and straightforward enough—how does it affect the results? It can affect them in two ways. First—though this factor is far more important in primaries where all the aspirants are of the same party than it is in interparty elections—the candidate whose name comes *first* has a demonstrable advantage. This advantage is insignificant in contests for the highest offices. It is unimportant in areas accustomed to faithful party loyalty. But where party loyalty is not a major factor and the office is a minor one, with the men contending for it unknown to most voters, Allen will pick up more casual, unthinking votes than will Widener. His gain, to be sure, may be so small as not to affect the outcome, unless the latter is a virtual tie. In the primaries, however, his advantage in having the topmost spot among several contenders is more marked: in fact, it may be the reason why Allen got the nomination we are considering rather than his rivals for it, Banks and Crowley and Dineen.

Much more important to the practical politician is the fact that in the final election the "office block" type of ballot readily tempts a voter to "split his ticket." It increases the chance of his voting for a Democrat for one office, a Republican for another, rather than going "straight down the line" for all of one party's candidates. Common sense made this apparent to the politicians long ago; modern scientific "surveys" confirm it. Voters tend to split their tickets more in "office block" states than in "party line" states.

In the "party line" type of ballot, you can vote for all the party's candidates by drawing a single "X" or pulling down a single lever. You can still split your ticket, if you like, by scratching out the name of the party's candidate for a particular office, or by pulling down the lever over the name of his opponent; but for many voters, the temptation to follow the short and simple course is a considerable one. Therefore, where party leaders feel that the party's candidate for President, say, is very popular, they are happy to have a "party line" type of ballot, for many supporters of the presidential nominee will vote in a single motion for the entire party slate and so improve the chances of its candidates for minor offices.

Ordinarily the election is decided when the ballots are counted on election night. In contests for senator or representative, for example, whoever receives the highest vote wins. It does not have to be a clear majority; a plurality will suffice. (In a two-party race, of course, the winner does have a majority.) Most states provide for absentee voting by its residents who are away from home on election day and make timely application for absentee ballots, and federal law makes special provision for absentee voting by people in the armed forces. Seldom do these absentee ballots, counted a few days later, affect the result. The winners can usually celebrate within a few hours of the closing of the polls. Occasionally, however, a race is so close that every vote is vital: in a congressional contest in New Hampshire a few years ago, for instance, the first official count indicated that the result was a tie. (Imagine the feelings of the friend of one candidate, who had simply forgotten to vote!) In such instances, the counting of the absentee ballots may or may not settle the matter. The result may still be so close that the ostensible loser demands a recount. This is usually a futile gesture, but occasionally a recount shows that arithmetical errors were made in the original count or that improperly marked ballots (such as those where the "X" was drawn so large that the ends of it were opposite the names of both rivals) have been counted, and so turns election-night defeat into belated triumph.

The ballot in a presidential election—its form and its effect— is another story. The names of the candidates appear on it yet we do not vote for them. Instead, we vote for a group of relatively unknown people whose names may not even be on the ballot. This paradoxical situation results from the Constitution's plan for the indirect election of the President—a "ground rule" of politics which has profoundly influenced the nature of national political campaigns.

## Presidential Elections

The framers of the Constitution, after arguing for weeks about how the President of the United States should be chosen, came up with an eleventh-hour solution which was adopted with little further debate. It was based on one assumption which became obsolete within a decade—namely, that there would be no national parties—and on another which was rejected within forty years—namely, that democracy in the new Republic should be limited and indirect. The plan was to have each state legislature choose a group of electors, men of distinction and acknowledged wisdom, who would meet together in each state and select the best man in the country for President. These electors, all together, would form the "electoral college."

Today, as for more than a century and a half, the electors are not the wise and great, chosen to use their judgment; they are party nominees, often persons of only local repute and sometimes not even that, selected to register automatically the verdict of the voters. They are not picked by the legislatures, nor even from legislative districts. In each state, each party puts up a state-wide slate of candidates for the position of presidential elector. For these, as a group, we vote. (Their names may be on the ballot, but in some states their names do not appear and our vote for them is cast by our voting, ostensibly, for the party's candidates for President and Vice-President, whose names *do* appear.) The winners, then, are all candidates of the same party, pledged to vote for its presidential nominee.

This means that presidential campaigns must be designed to capture separate majorities or pluralities in various states, rather than a majority or plurality of all the country's voters. The number of electors chosen by each state—its "electoral vote"—depends largely on its population: it is equal to the number of seats in Congress (both Senate and House) allotted to that state. Thus sparsely populated states like Alaska and Nevada have three electoral votes apiece (equal to two seats in the Senate plus one in the House); in contrast, New York will cast forty-three electoral votes in 1964 and 1968; California, forty; and Pennsylvania, twenty-nine.[5] Ordinarily, therefore, victory in the election depends on winning in most or all of the largest states. A party which wins them, each one by only a narrow margin, could lose heavily in other states and still gain a majority of the "electoral college." Twice, indeed, in 1876 (a confused election, with competing sets of returns appearing in several states) and more clearly in 1888, a President was elected even though, in the whole country, he received fewer popular votes than his opponent. And even when the winner has a comfortable popular majority, the electoral vote is highly misleading. Thus Franklin D. Roosevelt, in popular votes, defeated Alfred M. Landon in 1936 by a little less than two to one—a big margin, but nothing like the horrendous 523-to-8 "final score" in the electoral college.

The accompanying table, which shows the results of presidential elections from 1856 to 1960 in terms of both popular and electoral votes, makes other curious results apparent: compare the narrow percentage difference between the candidates in, for instance, 1880 and 1960 with the comfortable electoral vote margin in those years.

Though the system seems ill suited to modern political realities, it is itself a political reality and a very sturdy one. It enhances the importance of all state party organizations. It gives an advantage to the interests centered in some of the large states, where a small majority may swing the whole election. Perhaps most important, it has been for a very long time a salient feature of our political geography, something to which politicians are accustomed and around which they make their plans. Many attacks have been made on the electoral college. Many suggestions have been advanced for abolishing or changing it. Of these, the most seriously pressed in recent years is a plan to eliminate the electors and to divide up each state's electoral vote in roughly the same proportion

[5] The size of each state's electoral vote may change after each decennial census; a state whose population has increased sharply will be allotted more seats in the House, and hence have a larger electoral vote, and the state losing population may lose a seat in the House and have its electoral vote reduced. Prior to the adoption of the Twenty-third Amendment in 1961, the nation's electoral vote (or "electoral college") was equal, numerically, to the size of the whole Congress. Now the District of Columbia, though unrepresented in Congress, has three electoral votes, so that the total electoral vote will be 538 in the 1964 election.

## PRESIDENTIAL ELECTION RESULTS, 1856-1960

| Election | Candidate Popular | Electoral | Candidate Popular | Electoral | Candidate Popular | Electoral | Candidate Popular | Electoral |
|---|---|---|---|---|---|---|---|---|
| 1856 | Buchanan (Dem.) 1,839,237 (45.63%) | 174 | Fremont (Rep.) 1,341,028 (33.27%) | 114 | Fillmore (Whig) 849,872 (21.08%) | 8 | | |
| 1860 | Douglas (Dem.) 1,379,434 (29.40%) | 12 | Lincoln (Rep.) 1,867,198 (39.79%) | 180 | Breckinridge (Dem.) 854,248 (18.20%) | 72 | Bell (Const. Union) 591,658 (12.61%) | 39 |
| 1864 | McClellan (Dem.) 1,805,063 (44.85%) | 21 | Lincoln (Rep.) 2,219,362 (55.15%) | 212 | | | | |
| 1868 | Seymour (Dem.) 2,703,933 (47.29%) | 80 | Grant (Rep.) 3,013,313 (52.71%) | 214 | | | | |
| 1872 | Greeley (Dem.) 2,833,711 (43.82%) | 66* | Grant (Rep.) 3,597,375 (55.63%) | 286 | O'Conor (Dem.) 29, 464 (.46%) | 0 | | |
| 1876 | Tilden (Dem.) 4,287,670 (50.93%) | 184 | Hayes (Rep.) 4,035,924 (47.94%) | 185 | Cooper (Greenback) 82,797 (.98%) | 0 | | |
| 1880 | Hancock (Dem.) 4,444,976 (48.21%) | 155 | Garfield (Rep.) 4,454,433 (48.32%) | 214 | Weaver (Greenback) 308,649 | 0 | | |

|  |  |  | | | |
|------|----------|-----------|---|---|---|
| 1884 | Cleveland (Dem.) 4,875,971 219 (48.50%) | Blaine (Rep.) 4,852,234 182 (48.26%) | Butler (Green) 175,066 0 (1.74%) | St. John (Proh.) 150,957 0 (1.50%) | |
| 1888 | Cleveland (Dem.) 5,540,365 168 (48.64%) | B. Harrison (Rep.) 5,445,269 233 (47.81%) | Fish (Proh.) 250,122 0 (2.20%) | Streeter (Union Lab.) 147,606 0 (1.30%) | |
| 1892 | Cleveland (Dem.) 5,556,982 277 (46.04%) | B. Harrison (Rep.) 5,191,466 145 (43.01%) | Weaver (Populist) 1,029,960 22 (8.53%) | Bidwell (Proh.) 271,111 0 (2.25%) | |
| 1896 | Bryan (Dem.) 6,516,722 176 (46.72%) | McKinley (Rep.) 7,113,734 271 (51.00%) | Palmer (Nat. Dem.) 135,456 0 (.97%) | Levering (Proh.) 131,285 0 (.94%) | |
| 1900 | Bryan (Dem.) 6,358,160 155 (45.50%) | McKinley (Rep.) 7,219,828 292 (51.67%) | Woolley (Proh.) 210,200 0 (1.50%) | Debs (Soc.) 95,744 0 (.67%) | Barker (Pop.) 50,605 0 (.36%) |
| 1904 | Parker (Dem.) 5,084,533 140 (37.59%) | T. Roosevelt (Rep.) 7,628,831 336 (56.40%) | Debs (Soc.) 402,714 0 (2.98%) | Swallow (Proh.) 259,163 0 (1.92%) | Watson (Proh.) 114,790 0 (.85%) |
| 1908 | Bryan (Dem.) 6,410,665 162 (43.05%) | W. H. Taft (Rep.) 7,679,114 321 (51.57%) | Debs (Soc.) 420,858 0 (2.83%) | Chafin (Proh.) 252,704 0 (1.70%) | |
| 1912 | Wilson (Dem.) 6,301,254 435 (41.85%) | W. H. Taft (Rep.) 3,485,831 8 (23.15%) | T. Roosevelt (Prog.) 4,127,788 88 (27.42%) | Debs (Soc.) 901,255 0 (5.99%) | Chafin (Proh.) 209,644 0 (1.39%) |

| Election | Candidate Popular | Electoral | Candidate Popular | Electoral | Candidate Popular | Electoral | Candidate Popular | Electoral | Candidate Popular | Electoral |
|---|---|---|---|---|---|---|---|---|---|---|
| 1916 | Wilson (Dem.) 9,131,511 (49.26%) | 277 | Hughes (Rep.) 8,548,935 (46.12%) | 254 | Benson (Soc.) 585,974 (3.16%) | 0 | Hanley (Proh.) 220,505 (1.19%) | 0 | Watkins (Proh.) 189,467 (.71%) | 0 |
| 1920 | Cox (Dem.) 9,147,353 (34.15%) | 127 | Harding (Rep.) 16,153,785 (60.31%) | 404 | Debs (Soc.) 919,801 (3.43%) | 0 | Christensen (Farm-Lab.) 265,421 (.99%) | 0 | | |
| 1924 | Davis (Dem.) 8,386,624 (28.82%) | 136 | Coolidge (Rep.) 15,725,016 (54.04%) | 382 | LaFollette (Prog.) 4,831,470 (16.60%) | 13 | | | | |
| 1928 | Smith (Dem.) 15,016,443 (40.79%) | 87 | Hoover (Rep.) 21,430,743 (58.22%) | 444 | Thomas (Soc.) 267,420 (.73%) | 0 | | | | |
| 1932 | F. D. Roosevelt (Dem.) 22,821,857 (57.41%) | 472 | Hoover (Rep.) 15,761,841 (39.65%) | 59 | Thomas (Soc.) 884,781 (2.23%) | 0 | | | | |
| 1936 | F. D. Roosevelt (Dem.) 27,751,841 (60.80%) | 523 | Landon (Rep.) 16,679,491 (36.54%) | 8 | Lemke (Union) 892,390 (1.96%) | 0 | | | | |

| Year | Democratic | | | Republican | | | Other | | | Other | | |
|---|---|---|---|---|---|---|---|---|---|---|---|---|
| 1940 | F. D. Roosevelt (Dem.) | 27,243,466 (54.69%) | 449 | Willkie (Rep.) | 22,334,413 (44.83%) | 82 | Thomas (Soc.) | 116,514 (.23%) | 0 | | | |
| 1944 | F. D. Roosevelt (Dem.) | 25,612,474 (53.39%) | 432 | Dewey (Rep.) | 22,017,570 (45.89%) | 99 | Thomas (Soc.) | 79,010 (.16%) | 0 | | | |
| 1948 | Truman (Dem.) | 24,104,030 (49.51%) | 303 | Dewey (Rep.) | 21,971,004 (45.13%) | 189 | Thurmond (States' Rights) | 1,169,032 (2.40%) | 39 | Wallace (Prog.) | 1,157,063 (2.38%) | 0 |
| 1952 | Stevenson (Dem.) | 27,314,992 (44.38%) | 89 | Eisenhower (Rep.) | 33,937,252 (55.14%) | 442 | Hallinan (Prog.) | 140,178 (.23%) | 0 | | | |
| 1956 | Stevenson (Dem.) | 26,035,504 (41.97%) | 73 † | Eisenhower (Rep.) | 35,589,477 (57.37%) | 457 | Andrews (Constitution) | 176,887 (.29%) | 0 | | | |
| 1960 | Kennedy (Dem.) | 34,221,349 (49.71%) | 303 | Nixon (Rep.) | 34,108,647 (49.55%) | 219 | Byrd (Ind. Dem.) | 440,298 (.64%) | 15 | Byrd (States' Rights) | 134,132 (.21%) | 0 |

\* Greeley died after the popular election but before the meeting of the electoral college, and his electoral votes were scattered among four others.

† One electoral vote was cast for Walter B. Jones (Dem.).

as the popular vote is divided. Thus Texas, where Kennedy in 1960 got 50.5 per cent and hence all of the state's twenty-four electoral votes, would have been credited with thirteen electoral votes for Kennedy and eleven for Nixon, or even with twelve apiece. But neither this plan nor any other seems likely to be written into the Constitution until and unless the anachronistic but ancient and familiar system results once more in the defeat of a candidate for whom most Americans have voted.

The electoral system necessarily dictates the nature of presidential campaigns, forcing the candidates to concentrate on larger states which are closely divided. As such it is a significant "ground rule" of the political game. That game becomes most visible, something in which we can all take at least a tiny part and which millions of us watch with fascination, at campaign time, the three or four months preceding a national election. Let us take a look at the people who play it and examine the way in which the game proceeds—always remembering that while politics may quite reasonably seem like a great game, it is one where the ultimate stakes may be both our liberty and our survival.

## CAMPAIGNS AND CAMPAIGNERS

At the center of any campaign for office stands the candidate himself. Around him may be the campaign managers, the party wheelhorses, the volunteer workers. All of them, including the candidate, are impelled by a variety of motives. What they do, too, varies somewhat from person to person as well as from place to place. It is hardly easier to make general statements about a typical campaign than it is to portray any one politician as typical of all politicians. Nevertheless, most political participants do have some things in common and face similar problems; and there are some general truths about campaigning which, if they cannot qualify as hard-and-fast rules, can serve as guides for both candidates and impartial observers.

### The Participants

A candidate for high and responsible public office may be young or old, brainy or dumb, independent or compliant—but whatever else he is, he is virtually certain to be ambitious. Normally he is eager to win the post he seeks, for its own sake or as a stepping stone to still higher office. Why he seeks it is often a question which only a psychologist could wisely try to answer: the reasons may run all the way from a family tradition of public service to a desire to "make a fast buck" by corrupt means. More often than many people realize, men enter politics and stay in politics because they enjoy it. They are willing to take the risks of what is an essentially unstable kind of profession, one in which luck plays a very large part.[6]

For their own satisfaction and success, they· need to be suited to the political "way of life." Perhaps more than anything else, they require two attributes: physical energy and enjoyment of all sorts of social contacts. To be elected, they must work vigorously and hard. To win votes, they must be liked by people; and this is the more easily achieved if they themselves like people.

Some men, of course, get started in politics at or near the top. They run for very high office after making a reputation in some other profession. Thus Woodrow Wilson shifted in his fifties from education to politics, seeking the governorship of New Jersey without having previously run for any office. George Romney in 1962 stepped directly from the presidency of American Motors Corporation to the governorship of Michigan; and of course General Eisenhower had been a military man all his life until he ran for President. Such men may not require all the qualities which are needed by the career politician who works his way up the ladder

---

6 We sometimes forget that among the greatest Americans in history have been "career politicians." Consider what Horace White, secretary of the Republican State Committee in Illinois before the Civil War, wrote later about a local politician whom he had known: "The popular conception of Mr. Lincoln, as one not seeking public honors, but not avoiding public duties, is . . . wide of the mark. He was entirely human in this regard, but his desire for political preferment was hedged about by a sense of obligation to the truth which nothing could shake. . . . Within this high enclosure, he was as ambitious of earthly honors as any man of his time. Furthermore, he was an adept at logrolling or any other political game that did not involve falsity. . . . He was one of the shrewdest politicians in the State. Nobody knew better how to turn things to advantage politically, and nobody was readier to take such advantage. . . . Fortunate was it for all of us that he was no shrinking patriot, that he was moved as other men are moved, so that his fellows might take heed of him and know him as one of themselves, and as fit to be a leader in a crisis."

from the precinct organization to local office to a national post. (To be sure, Eisenhower had the great asset of mass "likeableness" which vastly increased his political chances.) But even at the level of presidential politics, such men are comparatively rare. Some presidential candidates, many senatorial candidates, and most contenders for seats in the House, like most aspirants for state office, come up "the hard way."

To get some idea of what that means, let us consider the somewhat parallel careers of two men who sought the governorship of an eastern state, a dozen years apart. Each was a Republican. Each started at the bottom and climbed from minor offices to lieutenant-governor and, finally, the nomination for governor.

The first was an extrovert—a jovial, friendly, often incautious man who enjoyed mixing with his fellows and loved the limelight. Once in politics, he worked at it day and night. Of him it was said that each election night, he went to bed early, saying to his wife: "If we win, let me sleep; if we lose, wake me at six-thirty—I've got to start campaigning!" [7] Sunday mornings he went to church early and then dashed from church to church, often arriving in time to shake hands with the parishioners as they emerged. He was a veteran of both the war with Spain and World War I; on one occasion, when he attended a luncheon of one veterans' group and a mid-afternoon meeting of the other, he changed uniforms en route in the back of his automobile. His independence earned him the distrust of many party leaders, but he built a personal following, until finally he was in line for the gubernatorial nomination. And by that time it was 1934, when the Democratic tide was sweeping the country. He ran, and he ran well—but he lost.

There are some lessons to be learned from this man's career. Enjoying combat, notoriety, and fellowship, he found much happiness in it. Defeat did not stop him: he was preparing strenuously for another campaign when he died. He was not an orator or a demagogue: instead he counted chiefly on his vigor and his friend-

---

[7] In 1957, William Proxmire, upon being elected U.S. senator from Wisconsin, went this one better. Although he had won, he didn't sleep; he was shaking hands at a factory gate at six the next morning.

liness. It was fun to do favors for people and, as a by-product, to gain their esteem and loyalty. Some of those people attached themselves devotedly to him—any rising politician is likely to have around him (driving his car, doing errands, answering telephones) a handful of year-round helpers who have hitched their wagons to his star.[8] Hence his use of the word "we" rather than "I"—he was an egotistical man, but as a politician he felt himself part of an undefined group, and so said "if we lose" or "if we win." Largely by his own efforts he did win, time after time; and when at last he lost, the cause was simply the turn of the wheel, the unpredictable luck that makes politics an insecure career.

The second man went into politics, at least in part, because of a family tradition of *noblesse oblige*. Well educated, thoughtful, and serious, he felt that he had an obligation to serve the public. Quite specifically, he thought that he should be governor. Otherwise he was modest as well as dignified and reserved. To walk up to perfect strangers, introduce himself, and shake their often reluctant hands did not come easily to him; he learned to do it, but at a physical and nervous cost. Nor was it agreeable to him to subordinate his own views to those of the party leaders whose support he courted; but, again, he did it. Eventually he was elected governor. Next day, when two of his friends met on their way to work, one said "Great news!" The other shook his head, and replied "Poor John!" "Why 'poor John'? He won easily." "Poor John," repeated the other, "He's been running for governor, day and night, for at least ten years. That's all he's lived for. Now he's got it—so he hasn't anything to live for any more!"

The gloomy friend was at least half right. Partly because of the concessions he had made, the hostages he had given, and partly because of exhaustion or failing health, "John" was unhappy in the governorship. Perhaps, though, the main source of his disappointment was that the chase was over. Politics can have the same pitfall as immature courtship: the struggle for victory can become

---

[8] Louis McHenry Howe, who decided that Franklin D. Roosevelt was going to be President and for many years devoted all his time to giving destiny a push, was a conspicuous example of such a wagon-hitcher, but there were, and are, countless others who make a politician's fortunes their own.

an end in itself, with disillusion and discontent the fruits of ultimate triumph. This governor's career reminds us, too, that for men like him, men of serious purpose and family affection, large-scale politics exacts a considerable sacrifice. If with determination you set forth on a long path to the presidency or the governorship or the Senate or, sometimes, even just the House of Representatives, you will no longer be able to live as most other men do. You are at the beck and call of every voter. There can be no eight-hour days and few if any regular vacations. Evenings with your family, quietly at home, get rarer and rarer. The life of the career politician can be amusing, educational, and exciting, and can furnish opportunities for noble service, but the sensitive person of contemplative inclinations will find it hard and exhausting.

Anyone getting up toward the top in politics must reckon with one other factor peculiar to the profession. Not only does he live in a glass house, but he tends to become what people see through the windows, with all their possible distortions. Did you ever read Ray Bradbury's stories about Mars? In one of them, American settlers on Mars find themselves, after a number of years, quietly changing: dark-skinned they become, and golden-eyed, and they begin to call each other by Martian names hitherto unknown to them. So with the prominent politician: as the Martian atmosphere changed the settlers, so the political atmosphere may change him. The public gets an increasingly clear and fixed idea of what he is like—or rather of what they *think* he is like. Their idea may be quite wrong, but he is under steady pressure to make it right. If people like him because they think he is the kind of fellow who loves children, then he will umpire at Little League games and dress up as a clown at a hospital fair. If they admire his eloquence, he will strive to be consistently eloquent. To use an overworked phrase, politics creates a "public image" of each major politician. Lucky is the candidate whose public image is the same as his private personality. Often the two are different, and the politician must either act as though outside of his own home "all the world's a stage," or actually merge his old private self with his new public self until the two are indistinguishable.

Of most campaign participants, however, there is no "public image" at all—for these include not only candidates, but the men and women who work with them. Some of these, as we saw in Chapter 10, may be regular party leaders and party workers. In campaign time, however, many a candidate counts on more than the party organization. Around him are his own chosen friends and advisers (some of whom stick to him like leeches) and beyond them are the campaign volunteers. These may be young people sampling a bit of political experience. They may be zealots, young and old, inspired by a person or a cause or, alas, driven merely by hatred of the candidate's opponent. They are unpaid and they don't punch time clocks, so some will be missing at the crucial moment; but many a local campaign has been won by the hard work of ardent volunteers. What kind of work do they do? How does it fit into the general scheme of a campaign?

## Campaign Activities and Methods

Local customs vary, and even in the same region there are differences between a presidential contest and a campaign for the state legislature. Nevertheless, almost any candidate and his advisers can operate on a few workable assumptions, regardless of locality or of the office being sought. The first and most important assumption for all but presidential contests is that *most people have never heard of the candidate.* This is significant because of its corollary —namely, that people usually prefer to vote for someone with whose name they are familiar.

*The Need to Be Known.* It is hard for a candidate, centering all his attention on his campaign and surrounded by admirers, to realize how amazingly unknown he really is. "Oh yes," said a confident novice, "I'm well known in Gardentown." But the cynical questioner went to Gardentown and found that only one person out of ninety he questioned had ever heard the young man's name. Even a successful politician remains unidentifiable to most of the voters. A few years ago, surveys were made in two congressional districts, from each of which the representative was then serving his third term. In each district (in widely separated states) the voters were predominantly "middle class" or even "upper middle," with an unusually large proportion of college graduates. And in each the result of the survey was the same—only 27 per cent of the adult population was able to name the congressman. In one of those districts the congressman's opponent took a similar poll, two months before election day. To his dismay he found that only 5 per cent had ever heard of *him*.

From this basic assumption, then, stem many of the candidate's activities. He must make his name known. He must make *himself* known. And so he seeks publicity, dreaming up ways to get into newspaper headlines. He hires radio and television "spots," wherein his name can be repeated over and over again during the day. And he goes out and shakes hands at every opportunity. A seasoned campaigner does not barge in where he is not wanted; only an ill-advised and crude beginner, for instance, would attend the wake of a complete stranger. But for the active candidate no reasonably good-humored group is too small. If he sees six people waiting for a streetcar, he will stop his automobile, jump out, and introduce himself. He will keep his automobile's gasoline tank nearly empty, as an excuse to pull in at many filling stations and say hello to the attendants and the customers. He will remember, all the time, that while some people will respond to such tactics with ridicule or scorn, many more will be vaguely pleased by his courtesy and friendliness. And they will remember his name and the fact that they have met him.

Surely, you may say, although these efforts may be appropriate in local campaigns between insignificant contestants, they are not suited to electioneering for national office. Yet "meeting people" certainly is a vital objective of most congressional candidates and of many senatorial contenders as well; and in recent years endless hand-shaking has even become fashionable for aspirants for the presidential nomination. Estes Kefauver of Tennessee made it so. In 1952, against the wishes of the national and state party leaders, he entered the "presidential primaries" in New Hampshire, seeking the election of a slate of delegates pledged to him. Through the snow he marched along miles of streets, his right hand out and a smile on his face. He shook thousands of hands. (He even got his arm stuck, reaching through a teller's window to shake hands with a clerk.) And he won the primary.

Presidential contenders, however, cannot shake seventy million hands; nor can a candidate for Congress hope to meet all of the voters in his district. Both, therefore, must count on other ways of making themselves known. One they have put in motion by their hand-shaking; word passes from the voter whose hand was shaken to several who did not have that pleasure. But more is needed—and here is where the campaign volunteers are most useful. Long before radio and television were invented, people had fingers with which to push doorbells and hold pens. They could canvass from house to house, telling each voter about their favorite. They could address and stuff and stamp thousands of envelopes, so that every voter could learn about the candidate through "campaign literature" sent through the mail. They could organize a telephone barrage. These time-honored campaign methods have not been displaced by television. They still constitute the heart of most campaigns. Their effectiveness depends in good part on the number, devotion, and tact of volunteer helpers. The face-to-face personal canvass is the most difficult of these methods of publicizing a candidate, but it is also often the most fun and nearly always the most useful.

The other main route to getting known is the fullest possible exploitation of the normal media of publicity. In the case of presidential aspirants this begins, often, years before the nominating conventions. Take a look at old copies of the major national weeklies for 1958 and 1959; all of the contenders were the subjects of illustrated articles, often "cover stories," and although these may have been inspired by the dictates of up-to-the-minute journalism, they would hardly have been printed if the men they portrayed had not been newsworthy. The most sensational success of the "publicity build-up" was that of Wendell Willkie, a political unknown until three months before he was nominated by the Republican convention of 1940. Newspaper stories, illustrated magazine articles, and full-page advertisements made his name and face familiar in record time.

Increasingly in recent years, candidates have placed reliance on professional advertising or public relations firms, retaining them not only to publicize the candidate, but if possible to glamorize him, and in any event to create a "favorable public image" of him. Commercially, these firms normally concentrate on selling particular products, using modern advertising methods and constantly testing the extent and nature of consumer demand and consumer reaction to brand names, slogans, and packaging. In politics, they perform essentially the same operation. They try to sell their candidate to the voters. In doing this, they seek to discover what the voters want at that particular moment: what issues they feel strongly about, what personal traits they like or dislike about the candidate and his opponent, what slogans they most readily respond to. Sample polling techniques have been developed to the point where many public relations experts and their clients feel that the results of interviewing are reliable enough to serve as the basis of campaign strategy.

*Pleasing the Voters.* A second common assumption, then, is that a campaign can be most successful if the candidate, in his personality and his program, *offers the voters what they want.* This may appear to be a natural result of the democratic process. To some, however, it seems cynical and wrong. Voting, these critics say, is not like buying soap. The nonsense of singing commercials is not a fit substitute for reasonable debate. Political democracy can work only if candidates are responsible leaders who take a stand for what they believe, regardless of what the sample polls may show, and try to persuade the voters to their way of thinking. So goes the argument of those who deplore the growing dominance of public relations techniques in politics.

The assumption that a wise candidate follows the voters' wishes, instead of leading and molding public opinion, does not rest on ground as firm as the first axiom about the importance of becoming well known. It is subject to several uncertainties. First, even the pollsters don't know everything and opinions can change in the course of a campaign. Second, many voters like a man of obvious courage: witness the rise of Harry Truman in popular esteem in the autumn of 1948, when every poll seemed to prove that he didn't have a chance of being elected. Almost alone, he bucked the tide. His methods were not those of modern public relations, but of old-fashioned politics: like Bryan way back in 1896, he traveled all over the country, speaking bluntly and forcefully not only to city crowds, but at crossroads and whistle stops. Whether or not they liked what he said, many people liked him for saying it—and he won. Third, it is at least reasonable to guess that in the long run, the use of commercial advertising techniques in politics may become less and less effective, Television commercials may sell particular brands of cigarettes and beer, yet a good many viewers grow skeptical of their often extravagant claims. This skepticism is easily transferred to the claims of rival candidates for office, especially as so many Americans are traditionally dubious of the sincerity of all politicians.

Most candidates for major office, though, do need a great amount of help, and the public relations experts are a natural place for them to turn, at least for advice and the technical assistance needed to place advertising and sew up television time. The question is one of who dominates—the candidate or the professional expert, the product or the advertiser. Some candidates may feel that as the objective of a campaign is to win office, the tactics employed don't seriously matter so long as they are successful. They think that they can "put on an act" during a campaign, but become their real selves again after victory is won. Hence they yield to the expediency of the moment, taking positions which they care nothing about, or avoiding issues, or irresponsibly making promises which they cannot keep (e.g., the promises to cut federal expenditures uttered by Franklin Roosevelt in 1932 and Dwight Eisenhower in 1952). This is risky business. Unfulfilled promises may come back to haunt them. More important, a politician tends, as we have seen, to become what the voters think he is. The campaign costume is easier to don than to doff.

*Speechmaking.* For all candidates, then, the first task is to become well known. The second is either to "sell" themselves or be "sold" to the voters. Facilitating both is the ability to make a speech. The invention of the amplifier made it easier for a person with normal lungs and vocal chords to campaign. The coming of radio and television required the candidate to learn new techniques. Nevertheless, the rising politician still finds, not huge roaring rallies to be sure, but a great number of smaller audiences habitually searching for a speaker. If he is articulate and has a reasonably interesting subject to talk about, he can introduce himself to large numbers via the lecture platform and the after-luncheon speech. Styles of oratory change, but the political value of being a good speaker remains.

Oratorical style, of course, has been greatly modified by radio and television. The rolling periods of yesteryear swayed outdoor multitudes, but they are out of place in the living room. Since F. D. Roosevelt first saw the potentialities of radio and began his "fireside chats"—homey, friendly talks in a personal, conversational vein—in 1933, politicians have had to try to add to their repertoire the special skill of talking, first on radio and now on television, directly to listeners in their own homes. They have even had to attempt the impossible, in presidential campaigns, when their speech to a cheering crowd is televised. To whom are they talking—the people massed in front of them or the individual "viewers" all across the country? The style best suited for one audience is less appropriate for the other.

This problem is important only when television is widely used in a campaign, as it is and must be in many state-wide races and certainly all presidential contests. And even for those who solve it—who manage to get their message and personality across to their live listeners and their televiewers simultaneously—the use of television has further pitfalls. These might, indeed, be pitfalls for democracy itself. Television is an *entertainment* medium. Inevitably, a politician's performance on television is judged, at least in part, simply as a performance. This means that the paramount question may be, not "Did he make sense?" but "Did he put on a good show?" In 1960, the "debates" between Kennedy and Nixon had an impact on the election not so much because of what the candidates said about the issues as because Kennedy, despite his youthful appearance, seemed calm, collected, and remarkably well-informed, while Nixon, at least in the first encounter, appeared tense and ill.

*The Vagaries of Campaigns.* There remain now the questions of campaign organization and strategy and the place of issues in the electoral contest. About these, few if any general statements can be safely made. Two or three things a candidate—even one for President—does well to keep in mind. One is that wholly unexpected crises will occur before election day. An example is the exposure, in mid-campaign of 1952, of the private fund provided for the Republican candidate for Vice-President, Richard M. Nixon, during his term as a senator. No one, including presidential candidate Eisenhower, knew what the impact of this would be. There was serious talk of Nixon's withdrawing from the ticket. Instead, he made a dramatic presentation of his own defense on television, turning what seemed to be political disaster into political gain. Second, especially in lesser contests, each candidate is rightly warned of the possibility of eleventh-hour "dirty work" by his opponent or the latter's supporters. For instance, in a congressional campaign a postcard was printed, urging votes for one candidate because he supported a move for a new city charter—an issue with which in fact he was not concerned. This was carefully mailed, the day before election, to all of the known enemies of the new charter, for the obvious purpose of arousing their resentment against the candidate. In a gubernatorial race, last-minute publicity was given to the charge that one contender had committed perjury many years before. He was prepared for this attack, and the attempt to "smear" him backfired. Such last-ditch efforts are familiar in democratic elections not only in the United States but in England, where they have turned the tide of more than one national election. Seldom if ever are they effective in presidential elections here. But surprising "breaks" in the final days have been. Cleveland won the presidency because shortly before election at a dinner for Blaine, Cleveland's rival, a preacher named Samuel Burchard called the Democratic party the party of "rum, Romanism, and rebellion." Roman Catholics were insulted, and enough of them reacted by voting for Cleveland to swing New York into his column. In 1956, Eisenhower's margin of victory was unquestionably increased by the war between Israel and Egypt, which broke out the weekend before election day and caused great fear of another world war. In those closing hours, when the holocaust seemed at hand, the old warning against changing horses while crossing a stream was heeded, and thousands of Stevenson volunteers lost their enthusiasm and ceased to campaign.

There have been all kinds of presidential campaigns. The Whigs in 1840 did not try to make any sense: they engaged in a hoop-la campaign full of songs and rhyming slogans. Twenty years later, Lincoln stayed in Springfield, Illinois, and said nothing. In 1920 Harding likewise traveled little and said less; his managers, like Lincoln's, rightly assumed that the Republican party was sure to win. In contrast, Bryan and Truman "barnstormed," speaking hundreds of times and, in the case of Truman, specifically directing his appeal to a variety of private interests. Truman was an exception among Presidents seeking re-election; most of them let the opponents carry the ball until the final weeks, when they emerge from the White House to make a few major speeches in defense of their own records. In 1960, of course, neither Kennedy nor Nixon was an incumbent seeking re-election, and they nearly knocked themselves out dashing by jet to meet countless speaking and television engagements.

Off-year elections, when representatives and one-third of the senators are chosen, have traditionally been local affairs. More and more, however, there has been a tendency to "nationalize" them—that is, to consider the 469 contests as one nation-wide party contest. Thus F. D. Roosevelt assumed a general campaign leadership in 1934, and in both 1954 and 1958 Vice-President Nixon was the acknowledged spokesman of the Republican party in most of the country.

A campaign, whether for President or a state assembly seat, is a sizeable enterprise and often a chaotic one. Some form of organization is necessary to bring at least a little order out of the chaos. Again, however, there can be no all-embracing rule of procedure. Some candidates run their own campaigns; others appoint campaign managers and follow their bidding. There may be one rented headquarters, several, or none at all. People are needed—whether volunteers or salaried assistants—to perform essentially executive tasks, directing the mailing operation, for instance, arranging the schedule of rallies, other meetings, and television appearances, and satisfying the strangers who wander into the headquarters wanting to help, or to advise, or to meet the candidate, or just to cadge the price of a drink. In a presidential contest, of course, these needs are multiplied many times over. An extensive campaign tour requires careful planning, occupying the time of transportation experts to arrange the scheduling and of politicians to act as "advance men." The latter precede the candidate to a given state or city, make sure that arrangements for the candidate's appearance are complete, drum up enthusiasm, and try to discover what local internecine party conflicts exist, so that the candidate can be warned to avoid them. Nowadays, too, the campaign seems to require the services of expert speech writers. Arrangements must be made to furnish transportation to the working members of the press and to give local candidates the chance to be photographed with the presidential nominee. The vice-presidential candidate's schedule must be planned to avoid duplication with that of his running mate. Obviously a campaign for the presidency requires executive leadership—in other words, a recognized campaign manager. Ordinarily this is the chairman of the party's national committee, operating out of the party office in Washington or special campaign headquarters in New York.

## Campaign Finance

All of the activities we have just been considering cost a vast amount of money. In a close congressional contest in 1958, over $150,000 was spent, legitimately, in behalf of a single candidate—the bulk of it going for brightly colored billboards and choice television spots. Even in a more frugal district, the basic expenses mount up: one lone mailing to all the registered voters, by families, can cost $6,000 in stamps alone. Fifteen minutes on a local television station may cost $780; to make it worth while, the program must be advertised in the newspapers—another $60 or $100. So the costs mount up; and if one contender has the money and is spending it, his rival feels a desperate need to match his spending. The more populous the district, or the larger the state, the greater the legitimate campaign expenses. In presidential campaigns they total many millions of dollars. Even in years in which no national elections are held, the parties spend substantial amounts of money. The reported spending for recent non-election years is given in the accompanying chart.

### REPORTED NON-ELECTION YEAR SPENDING

| Year | Democrats | | Republicans | |
|------|-----------|----------|-------------|----------|
| | Receipts | Spending | Receipts | Spending |
| 1955 | $1,108,682 | $1,013,983 | $1,992,436 | $1,733,191 |
| 1957 | 977,344 | 1,058,491 | 1,745,543 | 2,502,188 |
| 1959 | 1,412,667 | 1,339,537 | 2,405,653 | 2,312,135 |
| 1961 | 4,202,492 | 4,178,108 | 2,303,989 | 3,071,717 |

*Control of Expenditures.* Laws have been enacted by Congress and forty-two states, in the hope of placing some controls on both campaign expenditures and campaign contributions. They have little practical effect. Those that prohibit the candidate or any individual contributor from spending more than a few thousand dollars of his own money can be easily circumvented. State and national laws limiting expenditures and requiring full reports thereof usually leave the door wide open: they permit special "political committees" to raise and spend money, and if several of these are all supporting the same candidate, it is of little use to limit the amount which can be spent by any one committee. Thus the second "Hatch Act," a federal law passed in 1940, placed a $3,000,000 maximum on campaign spending by any one committee in a presidential campaign. This was much less than the amount spent by each party's national committee two years before. And it was promptly circumvented by the establishment of numerous "committees" for both parties' candidates—so that in 1940, the total reported amount (probably far less than the actual totals) spent for Willkie, Republican, was $14,941,000 and for Roosevelt, Democrat, $5,856,000. Congress in 1904 prohibited campaign contributions, in national elections, by corporations, and broadened this in 1947 to forbid contributions by unions. Nothing, however, prevents the well-paid officers of corporations from donating large sums, nor are union members forbidden to pool their resources and thus make substantial contributions through labor's political committees. It is a crime to make or accept a campaign contribution as payment for governmental favors, but the commission of such a crime is virtually impossible to prove, for contributor and candidate rarely come close to making any express agreement. A tacit hope or expectation can hardly be the basis of a criminal prosecution.

Periodically, there have been attempts to bring down the cost of campaigning. These normally get nowhere. "Corrupt practice" statutes which set unrealistically low maximum figures are made to be broken or evaded: by common consent, a candidate should be allowed to write to all the voters and to speak to them on television. A reporting requirement does result in information

**Voting, yesterday and today.** While George Caleb Bingham's century-old "county election" scene is certainly gayer and more sociable than today's voting booth with its machine and its concealing curtain, the idea of "government by the people" is still confirmed on each election day.

**Election news.** In simpler times the outdoor stereoptican lantern made election night a time of prolonged suspense, as indicated by the genial mob scene (left) in Columbus, Ohio in 1884. In earlier days the news had traveled on horseback; below is a facsimile of the first message carried over the plains from St. Joseph, Missouri, to Denver by the "Pony Express," announcing the news of Lincoln's election. In contrast are today's electronic marvels, which usually make it possible for telecasters (as in the Columbia Broadcasting System newsroom, below) to end all doubts about the result long before midnight.

as to where some of the campaign funds came from—some, but not all, for there is no way of checking up on the folding money that may come into the campaign fund and go unreported, nor can every well-meaning individual who independently prints placards or sends out letters supporting his favorite candidate be expected to file a report. Usually he has no idea that he is supposed to do so. There might conceivably come a day when the government itself would finance campaigns or at least pay for a limited amount of mailing and television time for each candidate for national office. Plans of this sort have been advanced in Congress from time to time since 1910. But they are halted by doubts about the wisdom of saddling the taxpayer with campaign costs and skepticism as to their practical effectiveness; the contenders could and would continue to spend additional funds. The only effective way to reduce campaign expenditures is for the voters themselves to resent heavy expenditures and express their resentment at the polls.

*An Expensive Business.* Of course, the complaint about large expenditures does not concern the objects of the spending nearly as much as it concerns the sources of the money spent. Outright buying of votes may occur here and there, but most campaign costs are legitimate enough. The danger lies in the power which expensive campaigning confers on those who are able to contribute. "He who pays the piper calls the tune." The large contributor often can reasonably hope that the candidate whom he supports will perform as he, the contributor, desires. In 1936, a labor leader, John L. Lewis, obviously expected that a $500,000 contribution by his unions to F. D. Roosevelt's campaign fund would give him influence at the White House; when it did not, he growled furiously about the ingratitude of those who had "supped at Labor's table," and four years later opposed Roosevelt's re-election. Roosevelt hardly had to worry about this, but consider the case of an impecunious first-term congressman. Could he cheerfully offend the people upon whose contributions he depended for his next campaign? The greater the candidate's expenses, the harder it becomes for him to maintain his independence. This is what gives significance to the statutes requiring the reporting of contributions, incomplete though these reports may be. By studying the list of contributors we get some notion of the extent to which particular interests or individuals are committed to the fortunes of one candidate or party, and hence an idea—not necessarily correct—of the probable viewpoint of that candidate or party, in office, directly affecting these interests and people.

One thing which is certain is that large contributions are very important in financing political campaigns, particularly for the presidency. In spite of increasing attempts by both parties to broaden the base of their financial support, the effect of the gift of $500 or more continues to be great. The following table shows the percentage of amounts contributed by individuals to national-level committees in sums of $500 or over.

| National Level Committees | 1948 | 1952 | 1956 | 1960 |
|---|---|---|---|---|
| Democratic | 69% | 63% | 44% | 59% |
| Republican | 74% | 68% | 74% | 58% |

SOURCE: Herbert E. Alexander, *Financing the 1960 Election* (Princeton, N.J.: Citizens' Research Foundation, 1962), p. 57.

Of the 5,300 contributors of $500 or more in 1960, ninety-five persons gave $10,000 or more, sixty to Republican causes, and thirty-five to Democratic. Twenty-five of these people had also made contributions of at least $10,000 in both 1952 and 1956.

Of the total of $8,500,000 contributed by the persons listed as having given $500 or more, about $650,000, or 7 per cent, represented the contributions of members of twelve prominent families with obvious stakes in politics. These gifts are presented in more detail in the next table. It is obvious that the Republicans receive heavier support from these families than do the Democrats. But it is also interesting to note the wide variation in this kind of political participation on the part of these families.

Alexander's list of 5,300 contributors of $500 or more also discloses a startling singlemindedness. Only thirty-five of these individuals gave $500 or more to candidates or committees of both parties, with about half of these splitting their contributions approximately evenly and the other half clearly preferring one party, while giving to both.

**CONTRIBUTIONS OF 12 PROMINENT FAMILIES, 1960**

| Family | Number of Individuals Contributing | Total Contributions | Republican | Democratic | Miscellaneous |
|---|---|---|---|---|---|
| du Pont | 56 | $136,585 | $125,085 | $4,500 | $7,000 |
| Field | 3 | 13,250 | 8,000 | 2,750 | 2,500 |
| Ford | 11 | 31,000 | 31,000 | — | — |
| Harriman | 3 | 31,750 | 22,750 | 9,000 | — |
| Lehman | 7 | 39,200 | 14,000 | 24,700 | 500 |
| Mellon | 12 | 87,650 | 64,250 | 12,400 | 11,000 |
| Olin | 4 | 37,000 | 37,000 | — | — |
| Pew | 6 | 74,000 | 74,000 | — | — |
| Reynolds | 6 | 13,000 | 2,000 | 11,000 | — |
| Rockefeller | 19 | 115,875 | 114,875 | 1,000 | — |
| Vanderbilt | 6 | 29,500 | 18,000 | 10,500 | 1,000 |
| Whitney | 5 | 40,550 | 37,550 | 3,000 | — |
| Total | 138 | $649,360 | $548,510 | $78,850 | $22,000 |

SOURCE: Alexander, *Financing the 1960 Election*, Table 10, p. 61.

Another interesting question is the size and nature of financial support of political campaigns on the part of organized interest groups. Although it is difficult to get any complete information on this, clues are offered by Alexander's tabulation of the contributions of officials of thirteen selected trade associations and special interest groups. The results are summarized in the accompanying table. As we would expect, the bulk of these contributions goes to the Republican party. But more impressive is the relatively low level of participation. Only about 14 per cent of these presumably politically active persons are recorded as giving $500 or more to a political party.

In congressional elections, some money is raised and dispensed nation-wide on a purely partisan basis, but mainly it is a matter of each candidate for himself. The 1958 reports showed that in the Democratic triumph of that year, financial contributions from la-

CONTRIBUTIONS OF OFFICIALS OF 13 SELECTED GROUPS, 1960

| | | Number of Contributions and Amount of Contributions | | | | |
|---|---|---|---|---|---|---|
| Association | No. of Members | No. | Dem. | No. | Rep. | Measured Group |
| American Bar Association | 267 | 1 | $ 500 | 5 | $ 4,750 | House of Delegates |
| American Medical Association | 19 | – | – | – | – | Officers & Trustees |
| American Petroleum Institute | 164 | 3 | 6,000 | 34 | 113,700 | Officers, Directors, & Honorar Directors |
| American Iron & Steel Institute | 46 | 1 | 1,000 | 9 | 25,000 | Officers & Directors |
| Association of American Railroads | 34 | 1 | 1,000 | 5 | 3,500 | Officers & Directors |
| Business Advisory Council | 124 | 7 | 35,140 | 73 | 241,060 | Active & Grad. Members |
| Chiefs of Foreign & Special Missions | 27 | 6 | 22,115 | 1 | 4,000 | Non-career Officers |
| Manufacturing Chemists Association | 33 | – | – | 5 | 7,000 | Officers & Directors |
| National Assn. of Electrical Co. | 29 | – | – | – | – | Officers & Directors |
| National Assn. of Manufacturers | 172 | 2 | 1,000 | 18 | 44,050 | Officers, Directors, & Vice Presidents |
| National Assn. of Real Estate Boards | 265 | – | – | 3 | 3,500 | Officers & Directors |
| National Coal Association | 42 | 1 | 1,000 | 3 | 3,200 | Directors |
| U. S. Chamber of Commerce | 60 | – | – | 5 | 3,200 | Officers & Directors |
| Totals * | 1,286 | 22 | $62,255 | 161 | $425,710 | |

*Totals do not necessarily check because of duplications in individual giving and amounts of gifts.
SOURCE: Alexander, *Financing the 1960 Election*, adapted from Table 11, pp. 64–5.

bor sources may have played a considerable part. These contributions, however, were made to individual candidates rather than to the party as a whole. They included the following reported sums: $25,625, $24,950, $20,900, and $19,400 contributed to senatorial candidates in Wisconsin, California, New Jersey, and Connecticut respectively; $10,710 and $7,050 to congressional contenders in Virginia and Missouri. Through political committees, the United Automobile Workers raised and spent $243,789, the United Steelworkers $192,136, and "COPE" (the AFL-CIO's committee on political education) $709,813. All in all, these reported labor expenditures slightly exceeded the total spent by official Democratic party organizations. Even so, the whole amount spent for all Democratic candidates in 1958 was less than that spent on behalf of their Republican opponents. The Republicans received hardly any contributions from labor sources, but raised plenty elsewhere —the total reported was $4,657,652, as against the total Democratic spending (by party committees and labor committees) of $3,531,382.

Historically, the Republicans, have been able to raise more money than their rivals. In 1960, however, a combination of Democratic willingness to incur large debts and increased spending by labor groups resulted in Democratic and labor groups' outspending the Republicans. Witness the following comparisons of reported presidential campaign expenditures:

**REPORTED EXPENDITURES,
PRESIDENTIAL CAMPAIGNS**

|      | Republicans | Democrats |  |
|------|-------------|-----------|---|
| 1928 | $ 9,434,000 | $ 7,152,000 | |
| 1944 | 13,196,000 | 7,441,000 | |
| 1952 | 13,800,000 | 6,200,000 | (plus most of $3,200,000 spent by labor and other groups) |
| 1956 | 20,685,000 | 10,977,000 | (plus most of $941,500 spent by labor and other groups) |
| 1960 | 11,300,000 | 10,587,000 | (of which $3,820,000 was debt and plus most of $2,227,000 spent by labor groups) |

Throughout this whole period, the Republicans have had not only much more money, but the voluntary support of a great majority of the nation's newspapers. Nevertheless, between 1932 and 1952, the Democrats won five presidential elections in a row. Perhaps the lesson is that while substantial funds are necessary for a victorious campaign, at some point they begin to produce diminishing returns. A candidate is not likely to win if his campaign chest is empty, but his triumph does not depend on its being full to overflowing.

## THE BEHAVIOR OF THE VOTERS

Campaigns are to gain votes, and votes decide elections. Why people vote as they do is, therefore, a question of immediate importance to the campaigners and of challenging fascination to the political analysts. Some of the latter have made a business of predicting *how* people will vote, and others are developing a political market for their explanation of *why*. The predictions have sometimes been wrong and the analyses of motives are not yet of proven validity. The scientific study of "voting behavior" still has a long way to go before it can produce many significant general propositions. Even at its best, it may not be able to produce conclusive answers. In its present form, it is based primarily on interviews with a small number of individual people. These people are, very likely, representative of a much larger population. They are, however, human beings—and as such, their opinions change, perhaps unpredictably from moment to moment. What they tell the interviewers on Monday may be different from what they would have told him the previous Wednesday.[9] Furthermore, they may not know what motivates them and even the most sophisticated questioning may not elicit their real motive. Consider, for instance, some sample polls that were taken after the 1952 election. Many of the people interviewed had formerly voted Democratic but had switched to Eisenhower in 1952. Why? The reasons given, probably quite honestly, were their personal admiration of Eisenhower, their disgust with the alleged corruption in Truman's administration, their dislike of the Korean War, and their belief that it was time for a change. Possible reasons which they did *not* offer were the charges that the Democrats were "soft on communism" and the fact that Stevenson had been divorced. Republican campaigners had assumed that these last two issues would be particularly influential among Catholic voters. Were they mistaken? The answers given to the interviewers made it seem so. Yet the fact

---

[9] A striking example of "changeability" is offered by the Gallup polls during campaigns. In September, 1940, 44 per cent of those interviewed said they would vote for Willkie; four weeks later, 48 per cent. Able social scientists strive to overcome this difficulty by going back and interviewing the same people periodically.

was that the "switchers" to Eisenhower, in the sample groups interviewed, included Catholics far in excess of their proportionate share of the local population. Perhaps, therefore, the unexpressed and possibly unrecognized influences upon which the common-sense Republican strategists had counted had had far more effect than the motives revealed by the scientific interviews.

This example suggests that it is wise to approach "voting behavior" analyses with some caution. At the same time, we should recognize that such studies have revealed a good deal about what people *think* causes them to vote as they do and have provided insights and formulations which may lead to far more certain knowledge of man's political responses. When well-devised sample survey techniques are combined with the actual election returns, the results may provide at least workable hypotheses upon which to base both political strategy and further scientific analysis.

## Who Votes

*Situational Factors.* The percentage of people voting varies considerably from election to election and from state to state within a single election. It also varies in many other ways which we will outline here. The relationship between these variables is not fixed, but what we mean when we say, for instance, that men vote more than women is that *all other things being equal* a higher percentage of men than of women will vote.

It is well established that, in recent years, men have voted more than women. Likewise, people over 35 years of age vote more than those between 21 and 35. Whites vote more than Negroes, and highly educated people vote more than those with less education. The higher a person's income, the more likely he is to vote. Businessmen, professional people, white-collar workers, and skilled laborers tend to vote more than farm workers and unskilled laborers.[10] These are what have been called the "social correlates" of voting, the situational factors which tend toward voting.

Some other situational factors also seem to lead to different voting patterns. Residents of rural areas tend to vote in the lowest proportion, those in small towns and cities more heavily, and those

10 Seymour M. Lipset, *Political Man* (Doubleday & Co., 1959).

in large metropolitan areas heaviest of all.[11] Also, the kind of election seems to make a difference. As we might expect, the heaviest voting is for President. Generally, people vote more in national elections than in state or local elections, more for President or governor than for congressmen or state legislators, and (except in the South) more in general elections than in primary elections.[12]

*Motivational Factors.* If the situational factors described above help us to predict who will vote and to explain who has voted in the past, they are important; but they still do not answer the question of why some people vote and some do not. Analysis of the actual impact of what we have called "motivational factors" may provide the key to the answer to that question.

The Survey Research Center at the University of Michigan has made intensive analyses of carefully chosen samples of the electorate on a continuing basis since the election of 1948, and some of their findings are published in *The American Voter*.[13] One of the subjects they examine is that of motivational factors in voter turnout. The results of some of their work are presented in the accompanying table.

These findings indicate that in presidential elections a great many people vote simply because they think it is their duty, as citizens, to do so—or because, on election day, it's the thing to do. Of those who apparently were uninterested in the campaign and unconcerned about the result, more than half nevertheless cast their ballots. Only in the comparatively small group that admitted to a lack of civic responsibility was there a heavy proportion of stay-at-homes. Perhaps those sound trucks that we mentioned at the beginning of this chapter have had a big effect after all. But civic duty is not discharged by voting; ignorant voting is civic irresponsibility.

---

11 Angus Campbell, Philip E. Converse, Warren E. Miller, and Donald E. Stokes, *The American Voter,* pp. 409-416.

12 V. O. Key, *American State Politics; An Indroduction,* pp. 135-140, and Robert E. Lane, *Political Life,* pp. 318-319.

13 Angus Campbell, Philip E. Converse, Warren E. Miller, and Donald E. Stokes, *The American Voter* (New York: John Wiley & Sons, 1960).

## RELATION OF AGE, EDUCATION, SEX, AND REGION TO PRESIDENTIAL VOTE TURNOUT *

| | 34 or Less | | | Age 35-54 | | | 55 or Over | | |
|---|---|---|---|---|---|---|---|---|---|
| | Grade School | High School | College | Grade School | High School | College | Grade School | High School | College |
| Non-South Male | 60% (52) | 78% (175) | 88% (81) | 80% (156) | 87% (222) | 96% (103) | 87% (179) | 93% (96) | 100% (31) |
| Female | 44% (55) | 73% (285) | 90% (70) | 71% (170) | 85% (312) | 91% (85) | 71% (173) | 91% (126) | 93% (30) |
| South Male | 19% (32) | 55% (69) | 81% (32) | 55% (87) | 80% (54) | 88% (33) | 63% (72) | 71% (21) | 82% (11) |
| Female | 13% (47) | 41% (111) | 74% (23) | 22% (97) | 56% (86) | 82% (38) | 31% (75) | 58% (33) | 86% (22) |

* Entries indicate the proportion voting for President within the category. The number of cases involved in each proportion is indicated in parentheses. The table is based on a combination of data from the 1952 and 1956 election samples.

SOURCE: *The American Voter*, p. 495, Table 17-11.

## RELATION OF DEGREE OF INTEREST IN CAMPAIGN TO VOTING TURNOUT, 1956

|  | Degree of Interest in Campaign | | |
|---|---|---|---|
|  | Not Much Interested | Somewhat Interested | Very Much Interested |
| Voted | 58% | 72% | 87% |
| Did not vote | 42% | 28% | 13% |
| Number of cases | 540 | 695 | 520 |

## RELATION OF DEGREE OF CONCERN ABOUT ELECTION OUTCOME TO VOTING TURNOUT, 1956

|  | Degree of Concern Over Election Outcome | | | |
|---|---|---|---|---|
|  | Don't Care At All | Don't Care Very Much | Care Somewhat | Care Very Much |
| Voted | 52% | 69% | 76% | 84% |
| Did not vote | 48% | 31% | 24% | 16% |
| Number of cases | 230 | 367 | 627 | 459 |

## RELATION OF PERCEIVED CLOSENESS OF ELECTION AND INTENSITY OF PARTISAN PREFERENCE TO VOTING TURNOUT, 1956

|  | Election Perceived To Be | | | | | |
|---|---|---|---|---|---|---|
|  | One-Sided | | | Close | | |
|  | Intensity of Preference | | | Intensity of Preference | | |
|  | Weak | Medium | Strong | Weak | Medium | Strong |
| Voted | 70% | 71% | 73% | 71% | 79% | 89% |
| Did not vote | 30% | 29% | 27% | 29% | 21% | 11% |
| Number of cases | 130 | 170 | 88 | 301 | 360 | 226 |

**RELATION OF SENSE OF CITIZEN DUTY TO
VOTING TURNOUT, 1956**

|  | Sense of Citizen Duty * | | | | |
|---|---|---|---|---|---|
|  | Low | — | — | — | High |
| Voted | 13% | 42% | 52% | 74% | 85% |
| Did not vote | 87% | 58% | 48% | 26% | 15% |
| Number of cases | 89 | 78 | 146 | 639 | 812 |

\* Respondents were classified according to the strength of their sense of citizen duty on the basis of a cumulative scale formed from responses to four questions.
SOURCE: *The American Voter*, Tables 5-3 through 5-7.

## The Intelligent Voter

The study of motivational factors in voting does at least suggest that the voter, more than the non-voter, holds attitudes which reflect an understanding of the American system of government. He not only feels that it is his duty to vote, but is concerned about the outcome, and follows the campaign with interest. (Remember that our data tells us nothing about the absolute number of people who hold these attitudes but only that they are held by more of those who vote than of those who do not.)

How much do people know about the issues which are involved in the campaign? In order to attempt to answer this question the authors of *The American Voter* investigated the familiarity of their 1956 sample with a list of six foreign policy and ten domestic policy issues. The results are presented in the accompanying table.

In one sense, this table may be encouraging. For you may notice that the average proportion of people who know little or nothing about the issues is roughly the same as the proportion of people who fail to vote in presidential elections—about one-third of the potential electorate. Unfortunately, however, we cannot be sure that the ignorant people and the people who stay home are the same individuals. As we have seen, more than half the people interviewed who said they "didn't care" who won nevertheless

## PUBLIC FAMILIARITY WITH SELECTED ISSUES, 1956

| Issue | No Opinion | B * | C ** | D *** |
|---|---|---|---|---|
| *Foreign Policy* | | | | |
| Give aid to neutral countries | 28% | 19% | 53% | 18% |
| Send soldiers abroad | 20 | 13 | 67 | 22 |
| Economic aid to foreign countries | 17 | 16 | 67 | 23 |
| Act tough toward Russia, China | 20 | 11 | 69 | 36 |
| Avoid foreign involvement | 14 | 15 | 71 | 32 |
| Friendliness toward other nations | 12 | 10 | 78 | 32 |
| *Domestic Policy* | | | | |
| Firing of suspected Communists | 16 | 39 | 45 | 23 |
| Leave electricity, housing to private industry | 30 | 19 | 51 | 22 |
| Segregation of schools | 12 | 34 | 54 | 31 |
| Influence of big business in government | 28 | 18 | 54 | 35 |
| Influence of unions in government | 25 | 20 | 55 | 31 |
| Insure medical care | 12 | 29 | 59 | 24 |
| Cutting taxes | 19 | 18 | 63 | 30 |
| Government guarantee of jobs | 10 | 23 | 67 | 31 |
| Racial equality in jobs and housing | 14 | 19 | 67 | 28 |
| Government aid to education | 10 | 23 | 67 | 27 |

B *    Hold opinion, but don't know what government is doing.
C **   Hold opinion, and know what government is doing.
D *** Hold opinion, know what government is doing, and also perceive party differences on issue; the "D" group includes part of the "C" group.
SOURCE: *The American Voter*, p. 174, Table 8-1; p. 182, Table 8-3.

went to the polls, and it seems reasonable to guess that many of the voting "don't cares" were also the "don't knows." So our first happy assumption that the "issues" table shows the ignorant and indifferent staying home while the concerned and knowledgeable vote is probably overoptimistic.

The authors of *The American Voter* tested their sample to attempt to discover the "level of conceptualization," the qualitative way in which the voter looks at the political world. They asked questions about the individual's political preference and then ranked the answers on a scale which ranged from (1) a clearly or roughly defined ideological framework, through (2) varying perceptions of benefits to a given group, to (3) responses relating vaguely to the "nature of the times," to (4) responses that referred only to party or candidate, without any sense of what the party or candidate stood for, to (5) responses that indicated nothing, where issues, parties, and candidates all drew a blank. The investigations were not rigorous in their standards, but rather exercised a necessary generosity toward our collective ego. The results are shown in the accompanying table.

**SUMMARY OF THE DISTRIBUTION OF THE TOTAL SAMPLE AND OF 1956 VOTERS IN LEVELS OF CONCEPTUALIZATION**

|  | Proportion of Total Sample | Proportion of Voters |
|---|---|---|
| A. Ideology | | |
| I. Ideology | $2\frac{1}{2}\%$ | $3\frac{1}{2}\%$ |
| II. Near-ideology | 9 | 12 |
| B. Group benefits | | |
| I. Perception of conflict | 14 | 16 |
| II. Single group interest | 17 | 18 |
| III. Shallow group benefit responses | 11 | 11 |
| C. Nature of the times | 24 | 23 |
| D. No issue content | | |
| I. Party orientation | 4 | $3\frac{1}{2}$ |
| II. Candidate orientation | 9 | 7 |
| III. No content | 5 | 3 |
| IV. Unclassified | $4\frac{1}{2}$ | 4 |

SOURCE: *The American Voter*, p. 249, Table 10-1.

Notice that those whose responses had no issue content were almost 20 per cent of the sample, while only a little over 11 per cent thought of politics in ideological terms. When we also consider the large number who made only vague references to the "nature of the times," we find that over 40 per cent of the sample failed even to reach the level of shallow recognition of group benefits in discussing their political preference. This is only a small sample, and even the ablest interviewers cannot always devise questions and obtain responses that accurately reflect a person's perception of his political environment; nevertheless, the results suggest that the proportion of "intelligent voters" is smaller than is good for a democratic system of government.

## The Voter's Choice

Just how the voter makes up his mind is the most important question in campaign strategy and the most baffling to voting behavior research. In Chapter 10 we discussed the foundations of partisanship. In this section we will see what some of the voting behavior research has shown about partisanship and its importance.

*Party Identification.* It seems clear that identification with a political party is a powerful element in the voter's choice. The relationship between party identification and how people voted in two presidential elections is shown in the table.

### RELATION OF PARTY IDENTIFICATION TO PRESIDENTIAL VOTE

|  | Strong Dem. | Weak Dem. | Inde- pendent | Weak Rep. | Strong Rep. |
|---|---|---|---|---|---|
| **1952** | | | | | |
| Republican | 16% | 38% | 67% | 94% | 99% |
| Democratic | 84% | 62% | 33% | 6% | 1% |
| Number of cases | 262 | 274 | 269 | 171 | 199 |
| **1956** | | | | | |
| Republican | 15% | 37% | 73% | 93% | 99% |
| Democratic | 85% | 63% | 27% | 7% | 1% |
| Number of cases | 286 | 270 | 305 | 194 | 211 |

SOURCE: *The American Voter,* p. 139, Table 6-5.

The distribution of party identification as found by a series of sample surveys is shown in the next table. We can see that, while there are fluctuations, the pattern was relatively stable over an eight-year period.

On page 271 we considered the "foundations of partisanship." Now, the social scientists produce evidence that however party identification is formed, it is stable. We have seen this already in the table of party identification for the period from 1952–1960, but it is made even clearer by the next table. Most people just don't change parties.

## THE DISTRIBUTION OF PARTY IDENTIFICATION

|  | October 1952 | October 1954 | October 1956 | October 1958 | October 1960 |
|---|---|---|---|---|---|
| Strong Republicans | 13% | 13% | 15% | 13% | 14% |
| Weak Republicans | 14 | 14 | 14 | 16 | 13 |
| Independent Republicans | 7 | 6 | 8 | 4 | 7 |
| Independents | 5 | 7 | 9 | 8 | 8 |
| Independent Democrats | 10 | 9 | 7 | 7 | 8 |
| Weak Democrats | 25 | 25 | 23 | 24 | 25 |
| Strong Democrats | 22 | 22 | 21 | 23 | 21 |
| Apolitical, don't know | 4 | 4 | 3 | 5 | 4 |
|  | 100% | 100% | 100% | 100% | 100% |
| Number of cases | 1,614 | 1,139 | 1,772 | 1,269 | ? |

SOURCE: *The American Voter*, p. 124, Table 6-1; Bone and Ranney, *Politics and Voters*, p. 10.

As people get older, their attachment to the party with which they identify themselves strengthens. As we see in the next table, only 24 per cent of the youngest voters identify strongly with their party while over 50 per cent of the oldest groups are strong "identifiers," and the proportion of independents decreases steadily. The significance of these findings lies not in the percentage of those who "identify" with the Republicans or the Democrats, but in the reminder that party identification is still widespread and tends to remain stable for long periods—although, as we have seen, there have been occasional major realignments in our political history.

Party identification, however, does not tell the whole story. Throughout the period since 1952, as we have seen, the surveys revealed that most people thought of themselves as Democrats, yet a Republican, Eisenhower, was elected President in 1952 and 1956 and a Democrat, Kennedy, won by only the thinnest of margins in 1960. Clearly a lot of things contribute to the voter's decision besides party identification.

Old-fashioned political observers, who still view scientific samplings with suspicion, used to say that a voter "voted his pocketbook." If he was out of work, he blamed the party in power. Surely, that was what happened in 1932. If he was a farmer and

## STABILITY AND CHANGE IN PARTY IDENTIFICATION, 1956

|  | Strong Dem. | Weak Dem. | Ind. Dem. | Ind. | Ind. Rep. | Weak Rep. | Strong Rep. |
|---|---|---|---|---|---|---|---|
| Have not changed from one party to other | 93% | 89% | 69% | 68% | 55% | 74% | 85% |
| Were Republican, changed to Democrat | 7 | 11 | — | — | — | — | — |
| Were Republican, changed to Independent | — | — | 13 | 10 | 8 | — | — |
| Were Democratic, changed to Independent | — | — | 18 | 22 | 37 | — | — |
| Were Democratic, changed to Republican | — | — | — | — | — | 26 | 15 |
|  | 100% | 100% | 100% | 100% | 100% | 100% | 100% |
| Number of cases | 364 | 397 | 108 | 145 | 144 | 250 | 261 |

SOURCE: *The American Voter*, p. 148, Table 7-2.

## RELATION OF AGE TO PARTY IDENTIFICATION,* 1952-1957

| Party identification | Age | | | | | | | | | | | |
|---|---|---|---|---|---|---|---|---|---|---|---|---|
|  | 21-24 | 25-29 | 30-34 | 35-39 | 40-44 | 45-49 | 50-54 | 55-59 | 60-64 | 65-69 | 70-75 | Over 75 |
| Strong Democrats | 16% | 20% | 21% | 21% | 24% | 22% | 25% | 23% | 23% | 26% | 28% | 25% |
| Weak Democrats | 32 | 29 | 29 | 31 | 29 | 24 | 23 | 22 | 21 | 18 | 17 | 17 |
| Independents | 31 | 26 | 24 | 23 | 22 | 23 | 19 | 20 | 19 | 15 | 14 | 16 |
| Weak Republicans | 13 | 18 | 16 | 15 | 15 | 16 | 17 | 16 | 18 | 19 | 16 | 16 |
| Strong Republicans | 8 | 7 | 10 | 10 | 10 | 15 | 16 | 19 | 19 | 22 | 25 | 26 |
| Proportion of strong identifiers | 24 | 27 | 31 | 31 | 34 | 37 | 41 | 42 | 42 | 48 | 53 | 51 |
| Number of cases | 552 | 1,088 | 1,201 | 1,221 | 1,081 | 977 | 915 | 741 | 677 | 473 | 354 | 297 |

* These data are combined from seven national samples interviewed by the Survey Research Center between 1952 and 1957.
SOURCE: *The American Voter*, p. 162, Table 7-5.

farm prices were unsatisfactory, he voted for a change: witness the falling-off of the vote, in 1956, for Eisenhower in his native Kansas. But since the coming of the nuclear age, one other factor —the question of peace or war—may well be of greater influence on the voters' choice than ever before, whether or not the investigators find it out or the voters themselves fully realize it. And since the coming of television, the factor of the candidate's personality, always important, may well be even more significant than in bygone days.

For one hundred years, never did the presidential candidate of one party win while the opposition party won a majority in both houses of Congress—never, that is, until 1956. Then it happened. This could hardly have been caused by a sudden attack of socio-economic schizophrenia or by quarrels in millions of families. Instead, the influence of "social characteristics" was modified by what people thought and how they felt. The threat of war, including the last-minute Suez crisis, made many think first of the national security. This influenced their vote for President—for the President is the nation's chief diplomat and the commander-in-chief of its armed forces. It did not affect their votes for senator or congressman: in casting those, they were, perhaps, still reflecting their environment. Probably even more important, however, was their personal feeling about the candidate. This, above all, was a positive liking for President Eisenhower.

In many congressional races, the "personality" factor was and is of first importance, too. If you examine the election returns, you may be surprised to find that numerous representatives win reelection even though the opposition party easily carries their districts for every other office. In such a district, the representative may have worked hard to build an effective organization: but his continuing majority, in the face of his party's defeat, depends largely on the fact that people like him. In his introduction to a brilliant little book on politics by a recent congressional candidate,[14] David Riesman has written: "The nice citizen who is lured

---

14 From: *To Be a Politician*, by Stimson Bullitt. Copyright © 1959 by Stimson Bullitt. Reprinted by permission of Doubleday & Company, Inc.

into voting either by a particular candidate's personality or because he regards voting as a kind of minimal civic decency is not likely to care about issues. Morris Janowitz's analysis of consent and manipulation in national elections, based on survey data, reveals that those voters who feel least involved rely most heavily on 'personality' as the basis of choice. My friend, Lewis Dexter, who has been a precinct worker and poller in many campaigns, tells me that a congressman's votes on even the most hotly debated legislation are seldom known in his home territory, let alone count as a factor in his re-election (save as such votes open the purses of wealthy backers or, more occasionally, as a particular stand wins the enthusiasm of hard-working people who can marshal a group of voters). Mr. Bullitt's own experience as a campaigner is identical: in accosting prospective voters at factory gates, taverns, street corners, and shopping centers, he found that he hardly ever was questioned about a stand he had taken."

## The Campaign's Impact

If most voters are faithful to one party, and the vote of the rest is predestined by their social or economic status, of what possible use is a campaign? One answer to that question we have just observed: namely, that the candidate's personality may break the supposedly preordained pattern. Another is that "socioeconomic status" is not a monolithic concept: the banker's friends may be Republicans, but his father was a Democrat and a friend of Woodrow Wilson, whereas the skilled electrician may be both a union man (hence, in theory, predisposed to the Democratic party) and a vestryman of the Presbyterian church, where most of the congregation is Republican. Thus even the mechanistic conception of the voter is that of a frequently confused and troubled person, subject to cross pressures competing for his vote. The more such cross pressures beat upon him, the slower he is to make up his mind. For this or other reasons, even in presidential elections 10 per cent or more of the voters remain uncertain until the last minute—or so the public opinion polls indicate. The authors of *The American Voter,* for example, report the following results in their sample surveys of the two Eisenhower victories:

**REPORTED TIME OF VOTE DECISION**

|  | 1952 | 1956 |
|---|---|---|
| 1. Knew all along how they would vote | 30% | 44% |
| 2. Decided when Eisenhower or Stevenson became a candidate, or at time of convention | 35 | 32 |
| 3. Decided after conventions, during campaign | 20 | 11 |
| 4. Decided within two weeks of election | 9 | 7 |
| 5. Decided on election day | 2 | 2 |
| 6. Do not remember | 1 | 1 |
| 7. Not ascertained | 3 | 3 |
|  | 100% | 100% |
| Number of cases | 1,195 | 1,291 |

SOURCE: *The American Voter*, p. 78, Table 4-4.

Campaigns, then, are primarily efforts to bring to the polls *all* of those who are favorably inclined and to persuade *most* of the uncommitted and uncertain. A close national election, as Thomas E. Dewey learned in 1948, can be lost by the overconfidence or lack of enthusiasm which produces stay-at-homes on election day and by the decision reached by a few hundred thousand people on election day itself. In congressional elections, campaigns have still more impact. As we have seen, a preponderant number of voters are ill informed about issues in congressional campaigns and even about the identity of the candidates. Therefore a well-run campaign, promoting an attractive candidate, can fairly often swing a district from its traditional partisan moorings and turn predicted defeat into an "upset" victory.

Such swings are most predictable, however, when discontent is obvious and is focused on the party in power. Economic disaster produces a shift in voting habits. When depression hit the country in 1929, after eight and a half years of Republican rule, even regular Republican voters began to lose their partisan faith. Seizing the opportunity, the Democrats bent every effort to convince the public that this was President Hoover's depression. By the time that Mr. Hoover came up for reelection, in 1932, a Democratic campaign was hardly necessary, so great was the Democrats' advantage. A more recent example of the impact of economic conditions on voting was furnished in 1958 by the congressional elections in West Virginia. There was much unemployment in that state and a Republican was in the White House—hence the Democrats made unprecedented gains.

The obvious relationship between conditions and how people vote makes some candidates stress economic issues in their campaigns regardless of the economic situation. "Talk about the 'gut' issues," Adlai Stevenson's advisers told him in 1956. It may or may not have been good advice: certainly a call to take arms against poverty and economic blight is not particularly persuasive with people who are enjoying prosperity, as most Americans were in that year. And except in areas for years scarred by disaster, the "gut issues" have been displaced in their position of prime significance by the issues of peace, war, and survival. In local contests, local issues—contracts for local corporations, more welfare aid for the needy, a new housing project, the high price of gas—may still be of first importance. In the great struggle for the presidency, however, the stakes are infinitely higher. War—the danger of it or the waging of it—dwarfs everything else. "He kept us out of war" was the slogan that won Wilson his reelection in 1916. "Your sons are not going to be sent into any foreign wars," was the carefully worded and misleading promise that helped Franklin Roosevelt win in 1940. "I will go to Korea," said Eisenhower in 1952, implying that he would bring peace with honor out of that frustrating war—and that one sentence was worth more votes to him than anything else in his campaign.

Perhaps our study of the "great game of politics," in the four chapters which compose this part of this book, has yielded what seem to be discouraging results in terms of democratic principles. The organized participants seem to be mainly selfish pressure groups or party machines, neither of them necessarily concerned with the public weal. The individual players must, if they are to play successfully, make efforts seldom required of other men and develop hides thicker than the elephant's. The voters, by and large, appear to lack both interest and information. Under these circumstances, can democracy work? Some of the social scientists whose analyses of voting behavior we have briefly considered believe that it can—that even though individual citizens fail to live up to the demands of democratic theory, "the system of democracy does meet certain requirements for a going political organization." They assert that the system can survive so long as the intensity of conflict is limited, a pluralistic social organization exists, and a "basic consensus" prevails.[12] We might add to this another note of optimism—namely, that whatever their political shortcomings, the American people have adhered to their faith in democratic principles for a very long time, and for nearly a century the nation has stayed united and grown in prosperity and power.

Yet we cannot smugly conclude that a democratic system will run forever under its own steam, regardless of the civic irresponsibility of individuals and groups. In the long run, its future must depend on the use which human beings make of it. If few vote, and still fewer vote intelligently and responsibly, it has a dim future. Its prospects are bleak, too, if the ablest citizens disdain politics and shun political life. Even if many vote and competent politicians abound, the path is uncertain so long as the mechanics of politics remain a mystery. For competent men may be selfish, dishonest, and ruthless, and uninformed voters can be deceived. That is why, in this part of this book, we have dwelt in some detail on the mechanics and realities of politics in the United States. The wider the understanding of the political system, the greater the chance that patriotic men and women can direct it for the national good and the freedom and safety of future generations.

---

[12] Bernard R. Berelson, Paul F. Lazarsfeld, and William N. McPhee, *Voting* (Chicago: University of Chicago Press, 1954), pp. 312, 313. Compare our discussion in Chapter 10 of the importance of "consensus" to the maintenance of the two-party system.

Tom Little in *The Nashville Tennessean*

**Another helmsman**

PART *Four*

# THE ORGANS OF GOVERNMENT

# CHAPTER 13

# Congress: Making the Laws

All of the political behavior discussed in the preceding chapters—Part III of this book—ultimately concerns the making of policy. Pressure groups are active because they want something officially decided in the manner they prefer. Elections are held to put men in office whom the majority of the people trust or who will do what most voters believe should be done. Now we turn to an examination of the agencies of government which in fact are entrusted with the task of "doing things"—of making policy, carrying it out, and confirming its validity or preventing its execution. Broadly speaking, these are the three great branches, legislative, executive and judicial. The first of these, established in the first article of the Constitution, is of course the Congress of the United States.

Modern students of politics tend to portray Congress as a political battleground for the organized interests of the country—a cockpit of factional strife where group conflicts are fought out and resolved. Earlier writers—and, interestingly, most professional politicians who have written on the subject—have described Congress in a different way. They give first importance to it as an institution designed to govern in the national interest, and they stress the improvements in its organization and procedure which they believe are needed if it is fully to achieve that purpose. Between these different emphases we need make no choice. Institutions are shaped by politics—Congress itself was given its form and its powers in a great political compromise—but, in turn, institutions mold political behavior. And whether the results of group conflict and compromise are adverse to the national interest or are themselves expressions of the national interest is one of the great unresolved and forever debatable questions of democratic governance.

Our approach, instead, will be to emphasize the functions of Congress. In the present chapter, we will consider the legislative or law-making function; in the next, the representative function, the task imposed on 535 men and women of giving reality to the ideal of "government by the people." Throughout our examination of these subjects, we will bear constantly in mind that Congress is indeed an arena of political struggle and that it has an institutional life of its own which profoundly affects the nature and outcome of that struggle.

## THE LEGISLATIVE TASK

Congress's essential job is to consider and adopt or reject proposed laws. As proposals, these are called *bills* or resolutions. If and when they are enacted—agreed upon by both House and Senate and approved by the President or repassed over his veto—they become *laws* or acts or statutes. In barest, briefest outline—we will fill it in later in this chapter—a successful bill runs the following steeplechase on its way to enactment: after being written or "drafted," it is introduced by a member of either house—for the purpose of this example, let us say the House of Representatives. It is referred to one of the standing committees of the House, not as a subject of "investigation" but for the committee's consideration. (The committee may hold hearings, at which the witnesses appear voluntarily because they want to air their opinions.) The committee may or may not make changes in the bill; it then "reports" the bill, favorably. The scheduling committee of the House, known as the Rules Committee, fixes a time for its consideration by the whole House. At that time it is debated and again may or may not be amended. It "passes" the House by majority vote and is sent to the Senate, where virtually the same process is repeated. If, before passing the bill, the Senate makes more changes in it, it is resubmitted to the House  Unless the House then accepts the Senate's amendments, a "conference committee" representing both chambers is appointed to iron out the differences between the House and Senate versions. The conference committee, usually compromising, agrees on recommending a single version of the bill. Both houses accept this recommendation and the bill, signed by the Speaker of the House and the Vice-President, is sent to the White House. The President approves of it and signs it and it becomes law.

## The Substance of Legislation

There would be little use in learning about how Congress legislates unless we have some understanding of the significance of what it does. We can get a pretty fair idea of the scope of its authority to make laws if we reexamine Article I, section 8 of the Constitution. As we know, however, that section is couched in very general terms. Moreover, it includes matters which take very little of Congress's time today. What we need to know, now, is what the substance of the legislative task consists of. What are the chief questions of policy facing Congress in the middle of the twentieth century? We cannot cover all the ground here, and we will leave the development of many major programs, foreign and domestic, for detailed examination in Part V of this book: but we can profitably identify a few of the most important categories of legislation.

*Taxing and Spending.* The Constitution empowers Congress to levy taxes "for the common defense and the general welfare." This implies that Congress can also direct that money shall be spent for these broad purposes. And broad, indeed, they are. Vast funds may be expended, and are, in exploring space, stockpiling bombs, and providing economic and military aid to foreign nations. Billions more may be spent, and are, in old-age benefits, grants to states for aid to the needy, drought and disaster relief, urban renewal, college scholarships. (Both lists, of course, could be expanded almost indefinitely.) All of these expenditures require congressional authorization. All of them raise issues which squarely confront the congressmen. Is this a proper activity for the federal government? How much should be spent for it? How will the expenditure of larger or smaller sums or none at all affect the nation's security, its economic system, the daily lives of its people? Involved in all of these questions, inevitably, are the competing demands of the interest groups concerned—and underlying them all is the never-ending conflict between the taxpayer's interest and the desire of every group which favors a particular expenditure.

Spending some $100,000,000,000 a year, as we do, we must raise most of that money in taxes if we want to stay out of bankruptcy. Every tax bill, so exposed is the voter's "pocketbook nerve," is the source of inevitable controversy in the House and Senate. Which taxes shall be raised or lowered—personal income tax, corporation tax, excise tax on cigarettes or theatre tickets? In addition to deciding whether and how to increase the total amount of the government's revenue, Congress also has to consider tax legislation designed for objectives other than revenue-raising—objectives which sometimes seem to be identical with the goals of particular pressure groups. A familiar example is the old tax on oleomargarine colored to look like butter. That tax was not intended to raise any substantial revenue; it was meant to protect dairy farmers by making yellow oleomargarine so expensive that it could not compete with butter. In the same way, the protective tariff, which is a tax on imports from foreign countries, is not primarily a money-raising device. Its chief purposes are to discourage foreign producers from importing their goods into this country and to raise the price of the goods that are imported; and so every tariff bill sets off a dispute between the American producer who wants to be free from competition and the consumer who would like to buy things, imported or not, at low prices.

The terrific local pressures for tariff "protection" (the organized producers' voices being far louder than the unorganized consumers') and the seemingly disastrous effects of the high tariff of the 1920's on the nation's economy led Congress, in the 1930's, to turn over most of the work of tariff-making to the executive branch. Nevertheless, the question of renewing this delegation of authority to the executive comes periodically before the Congress, and between times there is perpetual pressure for congressional tariff legislation. From the larger issues of how much and what to tax, how much to spend and what for, Congress can never escape. Nor can the congressmen ever forget that although foreign policy may be primarily the responsibility of the President, much of it today involves vast expenditures which only Congress can authorize. The fate of the nation, perhaps of mankind, rides with the decisions made not only in the White House but on Capitol Hill as well.

**The Regulation of Interstate Commerce.** The clause of Article I, section 8 authorizing Congress to "regulate commerce . . . among the several states" is the source of legislative controversy every year. Under that authority, Congress passed a law in 1887 to regulate railroads; today its laws direct that airlines and buses and trucks be regulated as well. There is a constant demand for changes in these laws; a major railroad statute was passed, for instance, in 1958. But the "interstate commerce" power, as we saw in Chapter 5, is not confined to transportation. If you became a congressman tomorrow, you could be pretty sure that during your first year in Washington you would have to make up your mind about many other bills authorized by the "interstate commerce" clause: measures to change the government guarantee of farm prices, for instance, or to prohibit "racketeering" in union-management relations, to raise minimum wages or to end federal regulation of the price of natural gas. The impact of such bills on the national economy is obvious; you would also find that individual people and pressure groups feel very strongly about them.

**Protection of Civil Rights.** The additions to the Constitution made right after the Civil War—the Thirteenth, Fourteenth, and Fifteenth Amendments—authorized Congress to implement, by statute, the civil rights promised by those amendments. After the Reconstruction days ended, however, half a century elapsed before much congressional attention was given to such matters as the protection of the Negro's rights to vote and to have a fair trial. Now, civil rights legislation, or the possibility of it, is constantly in the minds of the legislators. It is such an emotional issue that it threatens party disruption and involves the organization and procedural rules of Congress itself.

**Development and Management.** A century ago, a major question before the country and the Congress was what to do with millions of square miles of "public lands"—vast undeveloped tracts owned by the nation as a whole. Even today, the public domain (exclusive of Alaska, where close to 365,000,000 acres are government-owned) consists of some 376,000,000 acres, and it is Congress which determines how it shall be used—for grazing, lumbering, or mining under a system of licenses, for instance, or for national parks. The Constitution, furthermore, gives Congress power to legislate concerning the "navigable waters" of the United States. So it is up to Congress to decide whether and how to develop the great waterways of the nation—whether to dredge rivers and harbors to protect shipping, or dam the rivers for flood control; and if dams are built, whether to use the stored water for irrigation and the falling water for the generation of electric power. The Tennessee Valley Authority, for instance, with its huge dams controlling floods and furnishing cheap electricity to homes, factories, and farms was established by Congress pursuant to its power to make laws governing "navigable streams." The long-run national significance of much of this kind of legislation is matched by the immediate concern it arouses among particular interests such as private power companies, the transportation industry, rural cooperatives, and farmers on land where little rain falls during the year. It gives rise, too, to ideological debates about the proper role of government and to recurrent charges of "creeping socialism."

The earliest "socialistic scheme," of course, was the post office— a national business of delivering the mail. Congress is the ultimate policy-maker for the postal system: witness the inauguration of the parcel post service in 1911 (over the opposition of the express companies, who cried "socialism!") and the legislation raising the price of ordinary stamps. Under the heading of "development and management" we can place, too, the congressional tasks of fixing policy for the government of the territories and possessions of the United States and the governing of the District of Columbia, for which Congress has to act as a virtual city council.

*Appropriations.* Whatever else it does, one thing Congress must do every year if government is to function: it must supply the various agencies of government with money to pay salaries, rent or maintain buildings, buy supplies, and carry out the duties imposed on them by law. It does this by voting a series of "supply" or appropriation bills. Under the rules of House and Senate, an appropriation for a new agency or a new activity requires two distinct stages. First, a law is passed *authorizing* the making of future appropriations. Thus, a statute may begin by saying something like: "For the purpose of making grants to the states for slum clearance as defined in this Act, there is hereby authorized to be appropriated annually a sum not to exceed $1,000,000,000" or perhaps, "such sums as may be necessary." The enactment of this law does not provide any money for anything. In effect, however, it does commit the Congress to make money available, within the limits, if any, set by the authorizing statute. Exactly how much money to appropriate is decided later, when Congress considers a wholly separate appropriation bill.

The federal government's fiscal year runs from July 1 through June 30. Accordingly, each year Congress tries to pass all major appropriation bills before midnight on June 30. The arduous work of going over the President's budget (the document showing in great detail what funds the President is requesting for each agency) begins in the autumn before the budget is even formally prepared and submitted. Usually by early spring, appropriation bills are drafted and brought before the House. And usually, though not always, they pass both the House and the Senate and are signed by the President before the deadline.

Agreement is not always easy. Appropriation bills contain the seeds of major controversy over matters of policy. At their broadest, they concern the whole fiscal policy of the government—the question of a total balanced budget.[1] In detail, they can determine the effectiveness of various governmental programs. One

---

[1] In 1946 Congress sought to provide machinery to insure that this over-all fiscal consideration would be uppermost. It established a special joint committee on the annual budget, which was supposed to recommend a "ceiling" which should not be exceeded by the total of all appropriations. But public budget-making is a dynamic process affected by fast-moving events. A "ceiling" fixed in March could be made obsolete by unexpected drought, foreign crisis, or the launching of new "Sputniks." And major interests and pressure groups customarily feel that if the total budget must be cut to fit under a "ceiling," it must be the other fellow's appropriations, not their own, which must be reduced. For both these reasons, committee members felt that their task was futile and abandoned their efforts.

Congress may establish a program for protecting the consumer against false and deceitful advertising. A later Congress, unsympathetic to this program but reluctant to engage in a violent controversy over its repeal, can make it innocuous by drastically reducing the money available for its enforcement. Today every appropriation bill for foreign-aid programs is a potential source of this kind of conflict, which is essentially less about fiscal policy than about foreign policy.

## Supervision of Other Branches

Appropriation acts are, of course, essential parts of the process of interbranch cooperation or checks and balances discussed in Chapter 4. They exemplify both of these aspects of the separation of powers, especially when Congress is passing upon the budgetary requests for the operation of the departments and agencies of the executive branch. Often there is close cooperation between a department's budgetary officers and the members of the House subcommittee which is assigned the duty of preparing the bill appropriating money for that department. The members of that subcommittee take an active interest, and often a very sympathetic one, in the detailed affairs of that department; sometimes the subcommittee's salaried staff experts know as much about the department as the department head himself. Conversely, Congress's "power of the purse" is a perpetual check on executive extravagance. Some congressmen seem to feel that their most useful function is the prevention of waste, and some Appropriations Committee chairmen have gloried in the nickname "Watchdog of the Treasury."

Congressional legislation is necessary, too, for establishing and modifying the structure of the executive branch. No departments were created by the Constitution; they were created by acts of Congress, and they can be merged or abolished by Congress. Yet here a rather curious development has taken place. Many years ago, Presidents began complaining that although they were saddled with the responsibility of running the executive branch, they lacked the power to make it efficient and economical by merging agencies which duplicated each other's work. As the activities of the federal government increased, the problem of executive efficiency and the need for recurrent reorganization of the executive branch became more pressing. Everyone seemed to recognize this, but Congress found it difficult to do anything about it. Each department head was likely to agree on the need for reorganization on condition that his department should remain untouched. Virtually every department could muster a pressure group to support its claim of untouchability, whereas there was no pressure group effectively fighting for the cause of reorganization.[2] So agencies multiplied and duplication and overlapping of jurisdiction got worse. Eventually, during the presidency of Herbert Hoover, Congress in effect transferred to the President effective power to initiate reorganization, and similar power has been given to each President since. The system selected, which has never been tested in the courts, seems to turn the Constitution upside down. Under it, the President formally proposes a "reorganization plan," which might, for instance, shift functions from one agency to another or merge several bureaus into a single new department like the Department of Health, Education, and Welfare. If the President's plan is not formally rejected by either the House or the Senate within sixty days, it goes into effect—it becomes law. The ordinary constitutional assumption with respect to law-making, of course, is that Congress proposes and the President can only veto; here, in sharp contrast, the President proposes and the Congress can only veto. However, this upside-down system was, after all, established by Congress itself and can be eliminated by it at any time. Moreover, it is not exclusive; Congress still can initiate and pass legislation of its own in the ordinary manner, establishing executive agencies and reorganizing the executive branch.

Through appropriations and its constitutional power to establish inferior courts and prescribe the appellate jurisdiction of the Supreme Court, Congress also has a general supervisory power over the administration of the judicial branch. The traditional importance of "keeping the courts out of politics" tends to remove such legislation from the usual stream of clash and controversy. Occasionally, as we have seen, Congress's power to make laws re-

---

[2] The "National Citizens' Committee for the Hoover Report," 1948-1957, sough*t* to fill this void; its activities are discussed in Chapter 16.

specting the size and jurisdiction of the Supreme Court gives rise to sharp political conflict.

Congress's "supervisory" authority also includes the power of the Senate to confirm or reject the nominees proposed by the President for major public office, an executive function which also may give rise to questions of essentially legislative policy. The Senate's right to reject or approve the ratification of treaties with foreign governments is more clearly a policy-making one. Finally, as far as formal action is concerned, Congress can impeach and remove persons from executive and judicial office. An *impeachment*, voted by the House, is rather like a grand jury's indictment: it is not a finding of guilt, but rather a set of formal charges which forces an official to stand trial. The "trial" is held by the Senate, which by a two-thirds vote can find the defendant guilty and remove him from his position. This supervisory weapon is seldom used, and when it has been wielded against executive officers, as in the impeachment of President Johnson, its exercise has been caused by differences over policy—political conflict—rather than because of any personal wrongdoing. Nevertheless it remains a "club in the closet," a warning against malfeasance and corruption.

The weapon that by no means remains in the closet, however, is that of open criticism and denunciation. Plenty of executive officials quake in their boots at the thought, not that they might be impeached, but that they might be the victim of damaging personal attack in a speech by a single representative or senator. Such attacks are important because of Congress's legislative power. Executives cannot afford lightly to offend the people who hold the purse strings, and some congressmen are prone to read a personal insult into even the most unintentional slight. A glaring example of this was furnished some years ago by a gentleman of long experience and high repute, Senator Carter Glass of Virginia. The Social Security Board was in the process of enlarging its staff and establishing regional and local offices. Senator Glass wanted the board to give a good job to one of his constituents and to establish its southern Virginia office in his home town of Lynchburg. The board, however, offered a less desirable position to the constituent and selected Roanoke as the site of its office in southern Virginia.

Senator Glass was personally affronted, especially because the board's executive director was a fellow Virginian. He succeeded in writing into the board's next appropriation act a provision that the positions of the executive director and the board's bureau chiefs, all of whom were serving under appointments made by the board, must hereafter be filled by nomination by the President, subject to senatorial confirmation. The President promptly nominated all of the incumbents, but for weeks Senator Glass managed to prevent the Senate from acting on their confirmation, so that they had to serve without real authority and without pay. In that instance, the President and the board stood fast and Senator Glass eventually relented, but it is easy to see how such an impasse would tempt a President or department head simply to drop the individual who had offended the congressman. Thus in 1953 and 1954, fear of denunciation by Senator Joseph McCarthy unquestionably contributed to the firing or forced retirement of executive officials, especially in the State Department.

In Senator McCarthy's onslaught, however, questions of personal patronage were insignificant: the issues, at least in part, were those of policy. Congress's supervisory function includes seeing to it that executive personnel are carrying out the policies which it has formulated. This means that executive action is a proper subject for congressional debate. It means that executive officials can be asked for information as to what they are doing—information which, to be sure, is not always forthcoming, as the President has authority to direct that some, at least, of the executive branch's files be kept secret. And it means that Congress, just as it does in connection with the general run of legislative subjects, occasionally embarks on a formal investigation of one or more agencies of the executive establishment.

## Congressional Investigations

Seldom does any congressional activity hit the front pages as readily as its investigations. Law-making is a meticulous, complicated business; debates on policy are learned and long-winded; but investigations are political Westerns and whodunits, full of good guys and bad guys, sharp verbal clashes, chilling exposures, and threats of dire punishment. Drama comes ready-made when a "probe" is on. So publicized are the probers, their inquiries and their statements, that one might almost think that Congress's major function was that of investigating crime and subversion. Actually the Constitution does not expressly authorize Congress to investigate anything; Congress does so merely in aid of its legislative power, on the theory that it must obtain information before it can wisely make laws.

But what is this implied investigative power? Congressmen naturally need and seek information; when they ask you your opinion on a pending bill or invite you to appear before a committee and express your views, are they "investigating"? Such inquiries—the inquiries normally made by legislative committees, where views and data are requested and citizens voluntarily ask to be heard by the law-makers—are not "investigations" as we use the term here. What differentiates an investigation from the ordinary inquiry is that *an investigating committee has the power to compel testimony.* Anyone who refuses to obey a properly made order by such a committee, to answer questions or produce documents, is subject to being fined or imprisoned for contempt of Congress.

Investigations are carried on by committees of the House and Senate. In the past, these were almost always special committees, created for the purpose of examining one particular subject. Both houses, in 1946, tried to put an end to the proliferation of such special committees by giving investigative authority to their regular, permanent legislative committees: such general authority is now possessed by all such "standing" committees of the Senate and by three committees of the House. However, short-lived special committees are still established from time to time.

Most standing committees seldom embark on investigations. They don't need to do so; they can get all the information they need, for their law-making purposes, on a voluntary basis. Furthermore, investigations cost money: the House or Senate must be asked to appropriate funds with which to hire counsel, employ researchers and investigators, and pay travel expenses and witness fees. However, some committees regularly obtain such funds and are perpetually investigating: these include, in the House, the Committee on Government Operations and the Committee on Un-American Activities, and in the Senate the Permanent Investigating Subcommittee of the Committee on Government Operations and the Internal Security Subcommittee of the Committee on the Judiciary. Other committees usually obtain the authority or financial support required when they request it.

*Constitutional Justification.* The authority to make people answer questions, on pain of being put in jail if they refuse, is so obviously one that could be used to harass individuals and impair their freedom that it might seem to run counter to the idea of the Constitution as a restraint on governmental power. Courts have always had such authority, but its exercise by a political, legislative body needs justification in constitutional terms. Not until 1927 did the Supreme Court spell out that justification. In the case of *McGrain v. Daugherty*,[3] the court held that Congress could properly compel testimony in aid of its law-making function. This means that if you are summoned to appear before an investigating committee, you must obey the summons. If you are ordered to answer a question, you must answer it—unless you prefer to remain silent on the ground that your answer might tend to incriminate you. However, you can insist that the question be relevant to the inquiry being conducted: if in an investigation of racketeering you are asked whether as a boy you played on the high school football team, you would probably be safe in refusing to answer. Certainly you would have a right to withhold your reply until the committee had explained why such a question was pertinent and proper. Imprisonment for refusing to answer questions when the authority of the committee to ask them is not clear, or where the pertinence of the questions is doubtful and, upon being challenged, is left unexplained, amounts to arbitrary punishment and so violates due process of law. This the Supreme Court held in 1957, in *Watkins v. United States*.[4]

The "legislative purpose" justification is adequate for most investigations. Every such inquiry into the conduct of an executive agency can be said to be "in aid of legislation," for as we have seen Congress must legislate—must consider an appropriation bill—with respect to that agency every year. Likewise most "probes" of eco-

---

[3] 273 U.S. 135 (1927).
[4] 354 U.S. 178 (1957).

nomic or other activity—banking operations, labor unions, the stock market—can be tied easily to pending legislative proposals or the possibility of changing the existing laws on those subjects. Sometimes, to be sure, the connection seems far-fetched. A Senate committee once investigated the political activities of public school teachers in New York City, despite the fact that public school administration is a job for local government, not Congress. Nevertheless, if that committee had been challenged, it could presumably have replied that Congress might soon consider a bill for federal aid to states for education and that therefore its inquiry had a legislative basis.

Sometimes another justification for the investigative power is asserted: namely, that Congress has a duty to look into all matters of national concern, discover the facts, and expose wrongdoing. "It is the proper duty of a representative body to look diligently into every affair of government," wrote Woodrow Wilson long ago, "and to talk much about what it sees." The Supreme Court, however, has never indicated that the Constitution imposes any such implied duty or confers any such implied authority on the Congress. If Congress is the "grand inquest" of the nation, it is so only in connection with its legislative function.

*Purposes and Results.* Leaving aside, for the moment, the special questions that arise out of investigations of alleged subversion and "un-American activities," it is hard to prove that other famous investigations have actually helped Congress to *draft* wise or needed laws. Usually the need for legislation is already obvious, at least to some congressmen, before the inquiry starts. The information needed in preparing detailed bills is at hand or can be obtained without compulsion. The investigation, therefore, is less likely to aid Congress in *preparing* legislation than it is to help get legislation *enacted.* The publicity creates an atmosphere, often an atmosphere of public indignation, which makes it easy to vote for a bill curbing the alleged evils which have been exposed. And the facts that are gathered are themselves helpful in persuading reluctant or uninterested representatives and senators that "something must be done."

Certainly a number of investigations seem to have played a major part in getting legislation enacted. Twice committees have looked deeply into the country's banking system. Each time, their efforts heightened public awareness of that system's shortcomings and made easier the passage of important statutes—the Federal Reserve Act of 1914 and the National Banking Act of 1934. The facts adduced by a comparatively unpublicized committee in the 1930's, concerning the union-busting tactics of certain employers, were doubtless persuasive in winning congressional votes for bills protecting unions and, later, against bills designed to weaken them; and the "McClellan committee" hearings of the late 1950's created a public demand for a law to prevent union "racketeering."

These examples suggest that more is involved, in investigations, than technical assistance in bill-drafting. Partisan advantage, dominance of one interest over another, and the fortunes of individuals are often at stake. A Congress controlled by one party has often delighted in investigating executive conduct when the President is of the other party, hoping to discredit the opposition by exposing its misdeeds in office. Investigations of management-labor relations are of importance to interest groups whether any bills are passed or not; each group hopes that public disfavor will be turned against the other. As for individuals, two kinds of people are affected, in very different ways. Politicians generally thrive on publicity, and more than one has gained national prominence as an investigator. Estes Kefauver was a little-known senator when he commenced his televised inquiry into "interstate crime"; a few months later, his name was a household word and he was a contender for the presidency. Representative Richard M. Nixon made his reputation as acting chairman of the House Committee on Un-American Activities; he was soon promoted to the Senate and available for the vice-presidency. During World War II, a special Senate committee was set up to oversee the conduct of the temporary wartime agencies in the executive branch; hard-hitting but fair, the head of that committee emerged with lustre from obscurity. His name was Harry S. Truman.

But if investigations are stepping stones for politicians, they can also bring humiliation and disaster to private citizens. Sometimes they do so by bringing to light facts which lead to further investigation and successful prosecution by the Department of

Justice. This may be a fortunate by-product of a legislative inquiry. Less fortunate is the temptation to which committee chairmen and their counsel sometimes yield, to pursue individuals as if that were the Congress's chief object in life. For every criminal whose exposure begins at a committee hearing, there have been dozens or hundreds of people never prosecuted for any crime but portrayed before the public eye as if they were the most miserable miscreants. The widespread publicity which almost any investigating committee can command places in jeopardy the reputation of any witness summoned to appear before it.

*Inquiries into Political Opinion and Activity.* What has just been said about the politics of investigations is particularly true of inquiries into people's beliefs or their loyalty to the United States. Partisan and factional advantage can be gained by painting the opposition as subversive; prestige can be won by the investigator who exposes disloyalty, and ruin may be the lot of those accused before the committee. In the late 1930's and for ten years thereafter, the House Committee on Un-American Activities had a virtual monopoly in the field of investigating people's opinions. Later, Senate groups, especially the Permanent Investigating Subcommittee and the Internal Security Subcommittee, moved onto the same stage. The pattern became familiar: a "friendly witness," usually an ex-Communist, would testify, accusing various persons of having been or being active Communists, and the accused might then be summoned and subjected to inquisitorial questioning by a committee chairman or counsel who sounded far more like a storybook prosecutor than like either a judge or a legislator. Public alarm over the extent of domestic subversion was aroused. Confidence in the administration in power was undermined on the ground that it was harboring Communists in governmental positions. Some individuals were exposed as having been members of the Communist party; others denied the charge, but walked ever after under its shadow.

One difficulty about this kind of investigation was, and is, that unless they had violated the Smith Act, those being accused were not charged with any crime. There was no way for them, therefore, to get their "day in court." Another difficulty lies in the vagueness of such terms as "subversive" and "un-American."

Those words mean different things to different people. Actual participation in the Communist party may seem definite enough to come within them: but what about mere membership in a society—a league for better housing or to abolish poll taxes—which includes a Communist among its officers? Is that subversive? There is no definite answer. A third difficulty is a constitutional one. If the First Amendment's promise of freedom of speech has for its primary purpose the protection of dissenting views, can a person be compelled to state or explain his views? A few witnesses have refused to answer a committee's questions, basing their refusal on their alleged constitutional right to be free from questioning as to their political beliefs and activities. That such a right might exist was hinted in Chief Justice Warren's opinion in the *Watkins* case, but two years later the Supreme Court held that whether or not there is any "right to be silent," it does not justify a witness's refusal to answer questions about his membership in the Communist party.[5]

In two cases decided in 1961 the Court held that a witness could not refuse to answer questions asked by the House Committee on Un-American Activities about his membership in the Communist Party on the grounds that the sole reason for his being called was his opposition to the work of the Committee,[6] and that a witness before the same Committee was not immune from conviction for refusing to answer questions when relying on his (or his attorney's) understanding of previous decisions of the Supreme Court.[7]

**The Procedure of Investigating Committees.** "The rights you have are the rights given you by this committee," thundered the chairman of the House Committee on Un-American Activities to a witness in 1948. "*We* will determine what rights you have

---

[5] *U.S. v. Barenblatt* 360 U.S. 109 (1959). This was a five to four decision, with Chief Justice Warren and Justices Black, Brennan, and Douglas dissenting. For the majority, Justice Harlan's opinion implied that although a witness might properly refuse to answer questions as to whether he was a Republican or Democrat or Socialist or Prohibitionist or States' Righter, communism is not just a "political belief" but a movement endangering the national security, and so is a fit subject for inquiry.

[6] *Wilkinson v. U.S.*, 365 U.S. 399 (1961).

[7] *Braden v. U.S.*, 365 U.S. 431 (1961).

and what rights you have not got before the committee." That statement, autocratic though it may seem, brings into sharp focus the nature of investigating committee procedure. The committee's hearings are not judicial proceedings. Before the committee, a person summoned to appear has only two constitutional rights. One is to refuse to answer a question on the ground that his answer might tend to incriminate him. This invocation of the Fifth Amendment's "privilege against self-incrimination" has its drawbacks. People wonder what the witness is trying to hide: referring to witnesses who claimed the privilege, Senator Joseph McCarthy popularized the damning term "Fifth Amendment Communist." Furthermore, by statute the committee (with the approval of the Attorney General) may offer certain witnesses immunity from federal prosecution arising from their testimony, and if such an offer is made, the privilege is lost.

A second right is to refrain from answering irrelevant questions. But this puts onto the witness the risk of deciding whether the question is relevant or not. He may guess wrong—in which case he may be cited for contempt and go to jail. Since the *Watkins* decision of 1957, however, whenever there is reasonable doubt as to the relevance of a question, a witness has had a right to insist on an official explanation of its relevance.

What about other rights which a defendant has in a federal court and most state courts—the right to be represented by counsel, to testify by answering his lawyer's questions, to confront and cross-examine his accusers—indeed, the right to know the charges against him? A witness before an investigating committee has none of these. A committee may grant him one or more of them, but what the committee grants it can take away. Actually, most investigating committees have only allowed a witness to bring an attorney with him to the hearing—and this doesn't mean much, for the attorney is not allowed to put the witness on the stand and question him, nor can he cross-examine the people who have accused his client. All of the questioning, ordinarily, is done by the committee members and the committee's counsel, and often the witness is not allowed to make any statement of his own: he can only answer the questions put to him.

This points up the basic fact that *investigations are not trials*. The attorney for the Senate's "Rackets" investigation was frequently quoted as saying that "we have proved" or "we will prove" this or that, but if judicial procedure makes any sense, investigating committees do not "prove" anything at all. The judicial safeguards, remember, are not just for the protection of individuals; they are supposed to protect society by providing the soundest method of getting at the truth and determining a person's guilt or innocence. Although they do not always achieve this result, they seem likely to come closer to achieving it than the one-sided investigating procedure in which the committee often seems to have prejudged the case and acts as prosecutor, judge, and jury all rolled into one.

Many suggestions have been made for the improvement of investigating procedure. Yet they are seldom acted upon—and for this there is a sound reason. Congress is not a judicial or law-enforcement body: it is a law-making one. If, into its many investigations, it injected all of the "procedural safeguards" of judicial trials, investigations would proceed at a snail's pace and many members of Congress would have to spend all of their time, all year long, attending the hearings. If the procedure, then, seems unfair to individuals and a highly uncertain way of judging guilt or innocence, the remedy lies largely with the investigators themselves, and with the House or Senate as a whole. And it can only begin with the public realization of the fundamental premise, again, that investigations are not trials, but rather are held to aid Congress in its law-making function—that the committee's job is to find facts, not to condemn people. The fact-finding function, as we have seen, is by itself of great significance. Felix Frankfurter emphasized this in his professorial days: "The power of investigation should be left untrammeled. . . . The safeguards against abuse and folly by investigators are to be looked for in the forces of responsibility which are operating from within Congress, and are generated from without." [8]

---

[8] Felix Frankfurter, "Hands Off the Investigations," *The New Republic*, May 21, 1924.

## THE ORGANIZATION OF THE HOUSE
## AND SENATE

With this reminder that Congress's central job is to make the laws, we turn to the matter of how it organizes to perform that task. Obviously a House composed of 435 men and women—or a Senate composed of 100, for that matter—is too large to act coherently unless ways of dividing up the work and assigning responsibility are established. Even a small club needs a president, committees, and rules of order. And so with Congress, where great issues are at stake and bitter division is possible, there must be clear-cut lines of authority and a recognized code of procedure. The four central facts about the organization of the House and Senate are these: (1) the party system, loose though it may be in the country as a whole, is all-important in the allocation of responsible positions in the Congress; (2) each house, and each party in each house, has a recognized system of entrenched leadership; (3) much the largest portion of the actual law-making job is done by standing committees; and (4) members rise to posts of power and influence largely through the operation of the unwritten "seniority rule."

### The Partisan Basis of Organization

For many decades, almost every member of Congress has arrived in Washington wearing a party label, either Democratic or Republican. Regardless of how much they may differ in viewpoint among themselves, all the Democrats work together in deciding on matters of organization and the filling of responsible positions, and so do all the Republicans. The majority party can elect the Speaker, the presiding officer of the House, and the Senate's "president *pro tem*" who occasionally deputizes for the Vice-President as the Senate's presiding officer. In both chambers it can determine how large committees shall be, and how many Democrats and Republicans shall sit on each committee. It selects the top members of the paid staff of the House and Senate—the sergeant at arms, for instance, the doorkeeper, and their assistants.

Formally, all these choices are made by the House or Senate, but the effective decision is made by the party members. Here is what happens in the House, for instance: normally on the day before a new Congress convenes in early January, each party "caucuses." The representatives who carry the party label meet behind closed doors. By majority vote, they select their candidates for Speaker, the presiding officer of the House, and for various staff positions. They also decide the stand they will take on committee representation. All of these decisions are subject to ratification by the whole House the next day. Each party puts its candidate for Speaker, for instance, into nomination, but the result is normally a foregone conclusion: the majority party's candidate will be elected. For on matters of organization, if on little else, the party members stick together. This is true in both chambers, the Senate as well as the House, and for both parties, though the Republicans call their party gathering a "conference" rather than a caucus.

There is a highly practical reason for this custom of party unity. Congress can't get to work until it organizes, and if its members failed to follow party lines on organizational questions, prolonged and futile turmoil could easily follow. For instance, in a large eastern city some years ago, a nine-man city council was elected on a nonpartisan basis. It convened in early January, and its first task was to organize, beginning with the selection of a council president. But with no party lines to follow, not even a majority of merely five men could be mustered by any one councilor for president. On ballot after ballot, the score was three to three to three, or four to four to one. Over 1,100 ballots were taken before, in mid-March, a council president was chosen—and meanwhile, for more than two months, the city's business languished. Congressmen long ago recognized the potential harm in such a situation, and therefore they usually vote almost automatically for the party caucus's nominees.[9]

---

[9] Quite a stir was created in January, 1957, when a senator hinted that he might break party lines in organizing the Senate. The 1956 election had produced a Senate of 49 Democrats and 47 Republicans. One of the Democrats was a highly independent gentleman from Ohio, Frank J. Lausche. If Lausche had voted with the Republicans, it would have created a 48-48 tie, with the Republican Vice-President, Mr. Nixon, then casting the deciding vote. However, when the chips were down Senator Lausche stuck with his party.

The positions or party "leader" are not filled by vote of the whole House or Senate, but by each party's caucus. In each chamber there is a majority leader and a minority leader, and each party also elects a "whip"—a term borrowed from Parliament and indicating the task of "whipping" party members into line on controversial issues. Each party also selects its own "committee on committees," the group which assigns the members to the standing committees; [10] and each party in the Senate selects the members of its Policy Committee and Steering Committee.

The institutionalization of the party system in Congress is a real factor in legislative behavior. It is only one factor. Party-line voting on questions of organization and the accepted structure of agencies of party leadership do not mean that party members suddenly become a "body of men united" when they reach Washington. Factionalism and localism persist: these and the constant interplay of clashing interest demands tend to break down party unity when issues of policy are at stake. To some extent, however, these divisive forces are counteracted by the custom of partisanship that prevails in the earliest days of every Congress.

**The Power Structure**

Potentially, the most powerful single position in the Congress is that of Speaker of the House. The Speaker is not only the presiding officer; he is also the majority party's choice, and so automatically is a top party leader. In addition he is, by statute, the number three man on the presidential totem poll; if both President and Vice-President should die, he would become President.

The authority of anyone who presides over a responsible body of 435 people is inevitably great. It has to be, if business is to proceed in any orderly fashion. By itself, the Speaker's power to "recognize" members who wish to speak is so considerable that the prudent representative prefers to be on friendly terms with him; when several people are simultaneously clamoring for the

---

10 The House Democrats do this by selecting people to serve on the standing Committee on Ways and Means, for the Democrats on that committee make the committee assignments for their fellow Democrats.

floor, the presiding officer can be curiously deaf to the cries of "Mr. Speaker" emanating from those whom he does not wish to hear. Furthermore, there is no appeal from his decision as to who "has the floor." To maintain the respect of the membership any presiding officer must be generally fair and just. But the Speaker's dual position as chairman and as party leader is such that in any borderline case, such as a doubtful claim by a member that he has been unjustly treated, the House membership will "uphold the chair." The Speaker not only presides; he refers bills to committees, appoints special committees, and names the members of the "conference committees" which iron out differences in bills passed in varying form by both House and Senate.

The Speaker used to have more power than this. Before 1911, he named the members of all the standing committees and largely determined the order in which bills would be presented to the House. This great power caused one Speaker to be known as "Czar" Reed and eventually gave rise to a revolt and a drastic change in the rules of the House. Even though shorn of much of its earlier authority, however, the speakership remains an august and towering position.

The post of party leader carries less formal power. This is especially true in the House, where the "majority leader" actually plays second fiddle to the Speaker. In the Senate, where a tradition of individual self-importance (or of the dignity of representing a sovereign state) persists, party leaders have a harder time still, in ordinary human terms: you can't lead if nobody will follow. Nevertheless, in the late 1950's a majority leader in the Senate, Lyndon B. Johnson of Texas, brought new lustre to that position by his energy and skill in personally influencing his Democratic colleagues to pursue the legislative course which he prescribed. Party leaders in the Senate are aided by their accepted authority to schedule the bills for consideration. It may be noted here that as a presiding officer, the Vice-President has far less influence in the Senate than the Speaker has in the House. For one thing, his discretion is much more limited because at any given time, only a small body of senators—often fifteen or twenty—are on the Senate floor, and for another, he is not a senator chosen by the majority party in the Senate. Even so, the Vice-President has occasional importance in his role as presiding officer. He can vote to break a tie; subject to any senator's appeal to the whole Senate, he can interpret the rules; and on occasion his power to refer bills has affected the course of legislation.

In both chambers, leadership is far from wholly centralized. Rather it is largely dispersed among the chairmen of the various standing committees, which we will consider in a moment. The measure of the influence of a Speaker or party leader depends in good part on their relationships with these chairmen, and they know it: at least one House majority leader, therefore, made it his invariable practice to vote in favor of every bill supported by the chairman of the committee which had worked on that bill and to oppose all amendments to which the chairman objected. Conversely, a committee chairman's effectiveness is substantially affected by the respect which the Speaker or party leader has for him. The tendency, therefore, is for the whole leadership echelon to stick together—not on every issue, but on all matters concerning the leadership structure itself. Proposals for drastic change in the organization and procedure of the House or Senate are likely to run head on against a well-nigh united opposition from those who already have attained the most powerful positions.

### The Standing Committees

When a bill is formally proposed in either House or Senate, it is referred to one of the standing committees. Of these there are twenty-one in the House and seventeen in the Senate. Each is assigned to deal with matters pertaining to a particular subject or subjects, usually indicated by its name. The standing committees, with the numbers of Democrats and Republicans who composed them in 1963, are as follows:

|                  *House*                  |              *Senate*              |
| --- | --- |
| Agriculture (21 D., 14 R.) | Aeronautical and Space Sciences |
| Appropriations (30 D., 20 R.) |   (10 D., 5 R.) |
| Armed Services (21 D., 16 R.) | Agriculture and Forestry (11 D., |
| Banking and Currency (18 D., |   6 R.) |
|   12 R.) | Appropriations (17 D., 10 R.) |

| *House* | *Senate* |
|---|---|
| District of Columbia (15 D., 10 R.) | Armed Services (11 D., 6 R.) |
| | Banking and Currency (9 D., 6 R.) |
| Education and Labor (19 D., 12 R.) | |
| | Commerce (11 D., 6 R.) |
| Foreign Affairs (20 D., 13 R.) | District of Columbia (4 D., 3 R.) |
| Government Operations (19 D., 11 R.) | Finance (11 D., 6 R.) |
| | Foreign Relations (11 D., 6 R.) |
| House Administration (15 D., 10 R.) | Government Operations (6 D., 3 R.) |
| Interior and Insular Affairs (19 D., 14 R.) | Interior and Insular Affairs (11 D., 6 R.) |
| Interstate and Foreign Commerce (20 D., 13 R.) | Judiciary (9 D., 6 R.) |
| | Labor and Public Welfare (10 D., 5 R.) |
| Judiciary (21 D., 14 R.) | |
| Merchant Marine and Fisheries (19 D., 12 R.) | Post Office and Civil Service (6 D., 3 R.) |
| Post Office and Civil Service (14 D., 11 R.) | Public Works (11 D., 6 R.) |
| | Rules and Administration (6 D., 3 R.) |
| Public Works (20 D., 14 R.) | |
| Rules (10 D., 5 R.) | Select Small Business (11 D., 6 R.) |
| Science and Astronautics (17 D., 11 R.) | |
| Un-American Activities (5 D., 4 R.) | |
| Veteran's Affairs (15 D., 10 R.) | |
| Ways and Means (15 D., 10 R.) | |
| Select Small Business (7 D., 6 R.) | |

Most committees establish subcommittees, either on a continuing basis, or *ad hoc*—that is, to serve for a particular purpose such as the consideration of one proposed measure.

Each representative has at least one committee assignment (a few have two), and ordinarily each senator has two.[11] Assignments,

---

[11] In 1959 seven Senate committees were increased in size in an effort to assure every new senator of a major assignment and apparently to increase the Democrats' margin on several committees. This resulted in the appointment of senators to three committees instead of two.

as we have seen, are made by specially chosen party groups. Once a person is assigned to a committee he can stay there, if he wants to, unless his party's membership in the House (or Senate) is so greatly reduced that it loses a seat or seats on that committee. For instance, if there is a Democratic majority in the House as a whole, a 25-member House committee may include 16 Democrats and 9 Republicans. Then suppose that in the next election, the Republicans gain a majority in the House and divide up the committee seats in the same proportion, 16 to 9. Obviously 7 Democratic seats are lost. If the Democratic committee members were all reelected, that means that 7 of them must leave the committee, presumably to be assigned to other committees where several Democrats failed of reelection. In this situation, the Democrats "bumped" from the first committee are those with the least seniority—that is, with the shortest length of continuous service on the committee.

The assignment of members to committees involves partisan, interest group, personal, and seniority factors. The majority party in effect decides the partisan proportions on each committee. Often these are nearly even—in the House 14 to 11, say, or 13 to 12, and in the Senate 9 to 6; but if one party has a very large majority, it is likely to be nearer 16 to 9 in the House and 10 to 5 in the Senate. Congressmen usually have a preference as to which committees they wish to join, but their preferences cannot always be satisfied nor does the selecting group necessarily want to satisfy them. If the men making the assignments are, say, strongly in favor of the American Farm Bureau Federation's position on aid to agriculture, they may reject the request of a new representative for a place on the Committee on Agriculture because he is known to be hostile to the American Farm Bureau Federation. Often new members are assigned to comparatively minor committees in whose work they are not much interested. When one committee vacancy is sought by several applicants, custom decrees that the post will go to the member with the greatest seniority—in this case, the longest continuous service in House or Senate, as the case may be.

The committees are the graveyards of most proposed legislation. They are the high hurdles which any bill, if it is ever to become law, must surmount. In the committees the real legislative labor is performed, of considering, approving, rejecting, perfecting, or rewriting the measures offered by individual representatives and senators. They are at the very heart of the legislative maze: they cannot make a bill into a law, but they can kill it or they can speed it on its way toward enactment. That is why they are important—so important that Woodrow Wilson's description of them in 1885, in his *Congressional Government* (Boston: Houghton Mifflin Co., 1885, 2nd ed., 1900) is still reasonably accurate: "The rules are so framed as to put all business under their management. . . . [T]here is one principle which runs through every stage of procedure, and which is never disallowed or abrogated,—the principle that the Committees shall rule without let or hindrance. And this is a principle of extraordinary formative power. It is the mould of all legislation."

Committees being so significant, it is not surprising that committee chairmanships are positions of great power. The chairman is the member of the majority party who has served the longest period, without a break, on the committee. The nature of Congress's power structure is such that habitually deference is paid to him, and with good reason. For the chairman, ordinarily, can "call the shots" in many committees. He determines the order in which bills will be considered; he appoints subcommittees; he speaks for the committee; he sets the date when hearings shall be held and presides at the hearings; and when a measure favored by the committee is debated in the House, he decides which supporters of the bill shall speak and for how long. None of these things, except of course presiding, are *necessarily* his functions; no immutable law confers these powers on him. Revolt within a committee is possible—but it is very, very, rare. Only the unusual chairman who has lost all standing with his fellow leaders can safely be defied.

## The Seniority Rule

Not by formal regulation but by unwritten custom, seniority—the length of unbroken service—is a prime factor in the advancement of congressmen to positions of power. In the committee structure, members are ranked, by parties, in the order of their seniority. (If you look at the semiannual *Congressional Digest*, you will see, for each committee, two columns, one for each party;

you can assume that the names at the bottom of each list are the relative newcomers and those at the top the old-timers.) As members are defeated or retire or die, those remaining move up a notch and eventually may reach the top. The senior man in the majority party becomes chairman of the committee. The senior man in the minority party is known as the "ranking" minority member; should his party win a majority in the next election, he will automatically become chairman. By "senior man," of course, we do not mean oldest in years, but senior in terms of having the longest period of uninterrupted membership on the committee.

Seniority in a slightly broader sense—namely, in terms of uninterrupted service in the particular house of Congress—is also important, as we have seen, in the assignment of members to committees. The custom of making such assignments on the basis of seniority, giving first choice to the senior members, is not unbreakable. It was modified slightly in the Senate in 1957 and again in 1959, when in two or three instances strict seniority was ignored so that junior men could be placed on committees for which they seemed particularly suited. This was an unusual event, however, and was possible only because of the remarkable hold which the leader who decided on the change, Senator Johnson, had over his fellow Democrats.

The impact of seniority is felt all through the deliberations of Congress. If a "conference committee" has to be appointed, the senior members of the appropriate standing committees are named to it. If two members ask a House committee chairman for a chance to speak during a floor debate, he will ordinarily give the first opportunity to the one who has served the longest. Although the Speaker and the party leaders do not reach their positions by the workings of an automatic seniority rule, seniority has an effect on their election: startling indeed would be the choice of anyone who had not served in the House or Senate for many years. The emphasis given to seniority has a profound effect in both chambers, but particularly in the House, where it brings to the top only a very small proportion of the whole large membership. Most representatives remain for many years "back-benchers," with comparatively little influence.

The seniority rule brings to power, in committee chairmanships, many men who come from virtually one-party districts or states, because such men are more likely than others to be reelected year after year. In a Democratic Congress, therefore, you can expect to find more than half the chairmanships held by southerners.[12] When the Republicans were in a majority, in 1947-1949 and 1953-1955, many of these posts were filled by members from mid-west rural constituencies. In both instances, the chairmen held generally conservative views, not necessarily consistent with the opinions of the President, the party leaders, or the majority of the nation's voters. The seniority rule, therefore, tends to foster and perpetuate internal party disunity on policy questions, making it extremely difficult for any party leader to formulate a coherent legislative program and get it enacted.

This obvious divisive effect of the seniority rule, coupled with the fact that seniority occasionally brings to power men who are incompetent or corrupt, makes one wonder why Congress puts up with it. The basic answer is that its automatic quality diminishes strife among ambitious members of Congress. The whole power structure depends on mutual respect among the members of the leadership echelon. The influence of the men at the top is secure so long as they uphold each other's authority, no matter how much they may disagree with each other's views. If committee chairmanships were made the subject, every two years, of factional warfare and personal intrigue, authority would become fleeting and temporary, and the prestige of all the leadership positions would crumble. So, at least, the men of greatest congressional influence appear to reason. They have a stake in the present system, and will not lightly see it changed.

## THE PROCEDURE OF THE HOUSE AND SENATE

Early in this chapter we took a quick glance at the route which a bill must follow on its way to becoming a law of the land. We saw that it goes through many stages: drafting, introduction, com-

---

12 In April, 1963, out of the seventeen standing committees of the Senate, eleven were chaired by southerners, only one chairman came from a state east of the Mississippi and north of the Potomac, the most populous region of the country.

mittee consideration, scheduling, debate and amendment, and passage in one house; committee consideration, scheduling, debate and amendment, and passage in the other house; conference committee consideration to eliminate disparities; final passage in both houses; presidential signature. Now let us look a little more closely at what happens at each of these stages.

## The Origin of a Bill

All kinds of people propose legislation: "there ought to be a law" is an old American saying. Only members of Congress, however, can actually put it before the House or Senate for consideration. In theory, of course, senators and representatives draft bills themselves—and sometimes they actually do so, with the technical assistance of a highly skilled, nonpartisan corps of legislative draftsmen which each house employs.[13] Seldom, however, does the first draft of any significant measure spring full-panoplied from the brain of any individual legislator. It may, instead, be the work of a congressional committee; it may be the product of a pressure group's legal staff; it might even be a combination of the two. Or the initial version of a bill may be prepared by lawyers and experts in the executive branch of the government: this was where most major legislation began during the New Deal period, and many proposals emanate from this source today. Wherever it commences, the proposal cannot become a bill until some legislator introduces it. This he does by the simple process of depositing a typed draft in a box (called the "hopper") on the desk of the clerk of the House or, in the Senate, by gaining recognition to announce its introduction and handing it to the clerk who reads its title aloud. The clerk gives it a number ("H. R. 1" or "S. 1" for the first bill introduced in each house) and the Speaker or Vice-President promptly directs that it be printed and referred to the appropriate standing committee.

---

13 These anonymous technicians have greatly improved the quality of legislative drafting since they were first hired in 1917, and are so conscientiously impartial that they have won the full confidence of members of Congress. The pattern was fixed by the House's long-time Legislative Counsel, a selfless and able public servant named Middleton Beaman. Not all of the drafting staff remain forever anonymous: a former member of it, Gerald Morgan, eventually became Deputy Assistant to President Eisenhower.

### Consideration by Committee

Most committees, in both houses, have regular meeting days, and most bills referred to them are dealt with quickly in "executive session," behind closed doors. Quickly, because there appears to be no significant support for most measures and they can be simply put in a pigeonhole (more precisely, the chairman's desk drawer or filing cabinet) and left there. When, however, a bill seems important—because it is being advocated by the President, or a department head, or the party leaders, or substantial pressure groups, or influential congressmen, or a member of the committee itself—the committee spends plenty of time on it. (It is often referred to a subcommittee, as we have seen, in which case the subcommittee's procedure is the same.) The members agree—usually at the chairman's suggestion—that on such a measure public hearings will be appropriate, both to inform the committee and to give people a chance to state their views. The hearings may be held promptly or after long delay, and may be brief or prolonged, largely depending on the chairman's discretion. At a hearing members of Congress are given the first chance to "testify"; after them, customarily, representatives of the executive branch. Then citizens are heard for and against the measure. The spokesmen for pressure groups are likely to appear in full force, armed with arguments, statistical data, and sometimes legal briefs.

The atmosphere in these hearings is usually very different from that which often prevails in the hearings held by investigating committees. No one is being accused of anything. Congressmen attend not to badger witnesses but to learn from them, and discourtesy, though it sometimes occurs, is the exception. All of the testimony is transcribed and printed.[14] After the hearings end, the committee meets again in executive session—perhaps for many days—deciding what to do. It may still reject the bill. It may approve it. More likely, it will approve it with modifications, and if the changes are many it may decide to draft a new "clean" bill to be introduced by the chairman, under a new number. When

---

14 Ordinarily a proof is sent to the witness before publication, and the final printed version differs considerably from what was actually said. Try having your own conversation taken down sometime: you are likely to be startled or appalled by your oral departures from the rules of English grammar.

this happens, the new bill is referred right back to the committee, which, of course, promptly approves it.

A subcommittee's disapproval ordinarily kills a bill, but its approval does not necessarily mean that the bill will clear the hurdle of committee consideration. The full committee must still vote on it. Further hearings before the full committee, however, are extremely unlikely; after all, the testimony before the subcommittee is available in print.

Committee procedure is generally similar in both House and Senate, even to the point of duplicating the hearings. When a House committee has held full hearings on a bill which later passes the House, it seems hardly necessary for a Senate committee to hold more hearings. The fact that it usually does so is a reminder of the independent status of each house in the eyes of its own members and of the general procedural insistence on deliberation as a safeguard against hasty action.

### Getting a Bill to the Floor

To be assured of consideration by the House of Representatives as a whole, any important bill approved by the appropriate committee must also be given a favorable push by the House Committee on Rules. All major measures are placed on the House's "Union calendar" and referred to the Rules Committee.

*In the House: the Rules Committee.* In theory, the House Rules Committee is quite different from other standing committees. For one thing, it is much smaller, with only fifteen members. For another, it is customarily divided two to one—or, rather, ten to five—in favor of the majority party. Most important, it is not supposed to be a legislative committee, weighing the pro's and con's of proposed legislation. Instead it is a scheduling committee, deciding when a bill shall come before the whole House and recommending the rules to govern its consideration, such as the length of time to be allotted for general debate and the number of amendments which may be offered from the floor.

The Rules Committee, therefore, is often likened to a "traffic cop," but it is also described as a bottleneck. For its members are human. Like other congressmen they have strong personal opinions and sometimes speak for strong interest groups. Therefore

they are always tempted to go beyond merely directing the legislative traffic so that it will flow smoothly, and to put up a permanent stop signal against any bill of which they disapprove.
They can do this by simply failing to act—refusing to "give the bill
a rule" or a green light. Thus a small group, eight members of the
Rules Committee, can effectively halt the progress of a measure
which has been approved by the appropriate standing committee
and may have the support of a large number of congressmen.

From the 1930's to the present, a working bipartisan alliance
has often seemed to dominate the Rules Committee—an alliance
between Republicans and southern or other conservative Democrats. Such a combination has at times held up major legislation
including wage and hour legislation in the 1930's and civil rights
bills in the following two decades. In 1949, a liberal Democratic
majority in the House sought to reduce the Rules Committee's
power by adopting a "twenty-one-day rule," under which the
appropriate standing committee's chairman was authorized to
call up a bill for consideration by the whole House if the Rules
Committee had failed to act on it for twenty-one days after receiving it. The "twenty-one-day rule" was rescinded two years
later. In 1961, the enlargement of the Committee by three new
positions weakened the grasp of the "conservative coalition" only
slightly.

The only recourse, when the Rules Committee does bottle up
a bill, is for the bill's friends to get it to the floor by petition. If
a majority of the whole House—218 members—sign a formal petition on the Speaker's desk—called a "discharge petition" because
its effect is to "discharge the committee from further consideration
of the bill"—the measure will be assured of House consideration.
The petition device is naturally not popular with the Rules Committee or, usually, with the leaders of the House. Often the
Speaker appears to glare balefully or resignedly at a "back-
bencher" bold enough to approach the rostrum and affix his name
to a discharge petition. Nevertheless some important measures,
such as the Fair Labor Standards Act, are on the statute books today only because a majority of representatives did pry the bill
away from the Rules Committee through use of the petition.

*In the Senate.* The Senate has no true counterpart of the

House Rules Committee; the latter's seeming opposite number, the Senate Committee on Rules, has no scheduling function. As its name implies, it confines itself to the consideration of proposed changes in the standing rules of the Senate. Scheduling is handled primarily by the party leaders, the majority leader constantly trying to devise a rational program so that every senator may know in advance when a particular measure will be placed before the Senate for action. One difficulty facing him is the fact that he can seldom foresee how long the Senate will debate a certain bill; and another arises from the authority of any senator who wants to kick over the traces to "call up" any bill on the calendar —i.e., any bill reported by one of the standing committees. The senator who tries to get a bill considered in conflict with the leadership's schedule is most unlikely to succeed, but he and a few colleagues can stall the proceedings for many hours by discussing merely the motion to take up the bill. In the main, however, important measures come up in the order planned by the leadership —an order worked out by the majority leader in conference with the relevant committee chairmen and, significantly, with the minority leader. Seldom if ever is there a strictly partisan "hassle" over the scheduling of bills to come before the Senate.

### Consideration on the Floor

If you visit Washington when Congress is in session, get a card from your representative or one of your senators admitting you to the visitors' galleries of the two chambers. Don't be dismayed by the sight which greets your eyes. In the House, you may find less than a hundred representatives present on the floor of the handsomely remodeled room in the south wing of the Capitol, and some of these are almost sure to be chatting quietly together, or reading newspapers, or standing smoking in the rear "behind the rail." The long rows of seats, arranged in a semicircle, are sparsely occupied. In the front of the chamber, facing his few listeners, a gentleman is orating: he sounds as if he had leather lungs, but really it's only a powerful amplifier that makes him seem to shout. Somebody must be paying attention to him, for now and then a representative pops up from his seat and asks "Will the gentleman yield?" continuing by asking a question of the speaker.

Mostly, though, the members seem indifferent to what is being said. Throughout the speech they move to and fro, signaling constituents in the gallery to join them for lunch, shifting seats to whisper to one another, or disappearing through swinging doors into the lobby behind the Speaker's desk or the small canteen in the rear.

Is this, then, debate on matters of high policy, as carried on in the more representative body of the United States Congress? The question would be a very disturbing one if you did not know already that most of the hard work that goes into the making of legislative decisions is performed in the committee rooms. It would still be disturbing if it could be fairly asked about all of the discussion of important bills on the floor of the House. However, although the scene we have been witnessing is what most casual visitors see, it is not typical of two stages of the consideration given to major measures.

*In the House: The Committee of the Whole.* The view from the gallery is likely to be different when formal debate opens on a controversial matter. A bill, let us assume, has been reported by the appropriate standing committee and has "got a rule" from the Rules Committee, which recommends that it be debated in Committee of the Whole for, say, eight hours, four hours to be allotted or "controlled" by the chairman of the standing committee and the other four hours by its ranking minority member. The House accepts this recommendation, as it usually does, without discussion, goes into relatively informal "committee" session, and the debate begins. In the first hour or two, when the chairman or, if the chairman allots him time to speak, the originator of the bill is explaining the measure, a substantial number of representatives remain in their seats, listening. They want to know about the bill and about the arguments for it or against it; some of them want to ask questions about it or to prepare answers to these opening speeches. Eventually, of course, the arguments get stale and there are no new questions to ask, and in the closing hours of debate interest dwindles and so does the audience on the floor.

After the scheduled debate is over, however, comes the best "show" ordinarily put on by the House. It considers proposed amendments to the pending bill. It is acting as a "Committee of the Whole House on the State of the Union." The clerk reads the bill, paragraph by paragraph, and at the end of each paragraph any representative may offer an amendment to that paragraph. His proposed amendment is then debated, in staccato fashion: no speech can last more than five minutes, and most of these short speeches stick to the question. The issue is thus joined in rapid-fire debate, and, usually after a few arguments are presented pro and con, a vote is taken. Then the clerk reads the next paragraph, another amendment is offered, and the five-minute speeches begin again.

Thus if he is lucky enough to be present during one of these sessions of the "committee of the whole," the visitor is treated to a considerable amount of brief, pithy argument and the sight of legislative decisions being made in full public view. Not that all of these decisions are final or even made clear-cut matters of record. True enough, if the decision is to reject a proposed amendment, that is final; the amendment is dead. If, however, the amendment is accepted, that is merely a committee decision; the amendment will not be written into the bill unless, later, the House in formal session adopts it. And it may not do so; for though the sessions of the committee of the whole are often well attended, they seldom attract much more than half of the full House membership. As for the decisions being made in full public view, this is true as far as it goes. It omits, however, the important fact that in the committee of the whole, no representative has to answer "aye" or "no" and have his vote recorded. The voting is done by "voice vote" ("All in favor say 'aye' "), standing vote, or "passing through tellers," a process wherein all favoring an amendment walk up the middle aisle and are counted as they go by two counters or "tellers," and then all of the opponents do the same. It is virtually impossible for even the most experienced correspondents in the press gallery to be sure of all the names of those who, by shouting in unison, standing, or walking quickly up the aisle vote for or against the amendment. The significance of this procedure, this method of killing amendments by unrecorded voting, on the values of responsible representative government we will deal with in the next chapter.

After the bill's last paragraph has been read and all amendments have been voted up or down, the committee "rises." Its work is done. The House reconvenes in formal session. Before it is the report of its Committee of the Whole House—referring the bill back to the House itself with, let us say, a recommendation for two amendments which the committee has adopted by voice vote. Now a "roll call vote" can be demanded, in which every representative's name is called by the clerk and he answers "aye" or "no." So on amendments adopted in committee (as distinguished from those rejected in committee) there can be a record vote, showing the position of every representative; and what was done by the committee can be undone by the House.

After the House decides whether or not to agree to the amendments, one last chance remains to obtain a record vote on some controversial aspect of the measure. A motion can be made to "recommit" the bill—that is, to send it back to the appropriate standing committee, perhaps with instructions that it be changed. Thus when the House considered the bill which became the Social Security Act, in 1935, a motion was made to recommit and instruct the Ways and Means Committee to strike from the bill two of its eleven chapters, those creating the national old-age insurance system. When the roll was called on this motion to recommit, each representative had the opportunity to declare himself; more important, every voter could know whether his representative favored old-age insurance or not.

Assuming—as is usually the case—that the motion to recommit is defeated, the only thing left to do is to pass or defeat the bill. This may be done by voice vote or, on the demand of one-fifth of the representatives present, by role call vote. And so the bill is passed and goes to the Senate.

*In the Senate: Filibuster and Cloture.* Now let us follow the bill from the Senate gallery. Once again the scene is likely to be dispiriting. The chamber is dignified, with individual desks for every senator. Comparatively few, however, are occupied. These few senators, perhaps, are listening to a senator who is standing beside his desk, orating, and if the orator lacks an attentive audience on the floor, he may favor the gallery, appearing to address his remarks directly to the visitors. But worse is the frequent incoherence of the debate. Our bill, now passed by the House and reported by a Senate committee, has been called up. Let us say that it is a measure concerning the price of wheat. The committee's chairman has just made the opening statement for the bill's proponents. Then up rises another senator, and—what's this? Is he talking about wheat? No, he seems to be discussing iniquities on the San Francisco waterfront. A colleague asks him to yield; he says, "I yield the floor to my friend the senator from Nevada," and the Nevadan then pays a graceful tribute to the Vice-President on the occasion of the latter's birthday. Presiding, the Vice-President smiles somewhat sheepishly as three other senators add their congratulations. But now—ah! The majority leader is rising; perhaps he will get the Senate back on the track. Alas, all he says is that after the wheat price bill is disposed of, the senators can expect to take up the matter of Defense Department appropriations. Finally a Minnesota senator is recognized and resumes the discussion of wheat prices.

Unlike the situation in the House, there is ordinarily no time limit on debate in the Senate, nor is there any special procedure for the consideration of amendments. Any senator can offer an amendment at any time, and this can be discussed at virtually any length. Often, however, a definite hour is fixed for a vote on an amendment or on a bill by the unanimous consent of the senators present—most procedural decisions, and many legislative ones, are made in the Senate by unanimous consent. Controversial amendments are likely to be accepted or rejected by recorded roll call votes.

The outstanding feature of Senate consideration is the general custom of unlimited debate, which in turn sometimes gives rise to the *filibuster*. When a senator or group of senators talk for many hours *for the purpose of preventing a vote,* they are engaging in a filibuster. The same term (which originally meant "freebooter," but mysteriously changed its locale from the high seas to the Senate) is often loosely applied to any prolonged Senate debate, but such loose use deprives it of its real significance. A very strong case indeed can be made for prolonged debate. It assures full consideration of important bills; more important, it gives the people "back home" adequate time to let their senators know how they feel about the matter being discussed in Washington.

The long debate concerning our joining the old World Court was, from the standpoint of democratic theory, fully justified; during it senators were flooded with mail and telegrams which turned the tide against the resolution. When, in 1941, Senator Wheeler and other "isolationists" spoke for days against the lend-lease bill for aid to beleaguered Britain, they were not really filibustering. They were hoping, in vain, that there would again be an outpouring of adverse opinion from the country, and in this hope they were delaying the vote; but they were not trying to prevent the vote from ever being taken. It is the intention to keep the Senate from ever voting on a measure that is the essence of a filibuster.

When the life of a particular Congress is coming to an end, or, more realistically, when Congress has already agreed to adjourn, say, at midnight on August 31, any individual senator has an opportunity to stage a one-man filibuster. In the last-minute rush, numerous bills are awaiting final enactment. A single senator, obtaining recognition in mid-afternoon, can stop all these bills by simply talking till midnight—a feat of physical endurance which is within the capacities of many senators. (Individual speeches have run as long as twenty-two hours.) He may do this because he is opposed to one bill; and if, to save the rest, the Senate agrees to drop that bill, his mission is accomplished and he will sit down. He may do it, as Senator Huey Long did in 1935, not out of opposition to any bill but as a protest against the Senate's failure to pass his own pet measures—or, perhaps, just to make trouble.

More frequently effective than the one-man filibuster is the planned effort of a sizeable group of senators to "talk a bill to death." In recent years, the typical filibuster has been that arranged and carried out by a dozen or more southern senators against civil rights legislation. The filibusterers assume that if the bill is brought to a vote, the Senate will pass it. Therefore their objective is to prevent its coming to a vote. They know that much important legislation is on the Senate calendar awaiting consideration. Reasoning that many senators will not want to see all these other bills indefinitely delayed, they plan to hold the floor, one after the other, and make prolonged speeches. They can do this when the question is whether to consider the bill, and they can do it again, if necessary, when the bill itself is before the Senate. They figure that if they can show that they can keep talking for many weeks, the pressure to pass the many bills awaiting action will grow so great that the Senate will agree to drop the one measure which they oppose. In other words, their filibuster is a monkey wrench thrown into the Senate's legislative machinery. The easiest way to get the machinery running again is to persuade them to pull out the monkey wrench—to stop talking—which they will do only at a price. Their price is the withdrawal from Senate consideration of the bill which they deem objectionable.

There are several ways of stopping a filibuster or defeating its objectives if the majority is sufficiently determined. A one-man filibuster designed to last until the preordained hour of adjournment can be ruined by delaying the time of adjournment; but this is highly inconvenient for senators who already have made travel arrangements and engagements back in their own states. A group filibuster can be made extremely difficult by holding all-night sessions. These put an intolerable physical strain on the filibusterers. However, they also make such heavy physical demands on all the other senators that they are held only when the majority is vehemently determined to break the filibuster. Finally and most important, the Senate can end a filibuster by voting "cloture"— by deciding to limit the debate. The cloture procedure is complicated. It can be begun only if sixteen senators petition for it. It can be adopted only if two-thirds of the senators present vote for it. Even then, every senator can still speak for an hour before a vote is taken: but the adoption of cloture does, at least, assure that eventually the bill will be voted on.

However, many senators appear extremely reluctant to vote for cloture. They recognize that a successful filibuster means minority control, an idea inconsistent with normal democratic practice. Yet they know that sometime they may feel so strongly against some bill that they, too, will want to kill it by a filibuster. Usually these senators justify their unwillingness to vote for cloture by making vague references to the Senate's being "the greatest deliberative body in the world" and by describing "the right of unlimited debate" as a fundamental American principle. More sophisticated philosophers favor retaining the filibuster on the ground that it prevents Congress from making laws which would be bitterly resented by a sizeable minority of the population. Opponents of the filibuster—in late years these have been mainly advocates of civil rights legislation—answer that the majority's rights should be considered, too, but in the Senate they have not succeeded in their attempts to make significant changes in the rules.

## Ironing Out the Differences

Now our bill that passed the House some time ago, having avoided the vicissitudes of a filibuster, passes the Senate—but not until the Senate has made several changes in it. It now is returned to the House. The latter can agree to the Senate amendments and pass the amended bill; but if the changes made by the Senate are substantial, the House is likely, instead, to reject them and to request a conference. The Senate agrees to this request and a "conference committee" is appointed—usually composed, as we have seen, of the chairman and senior members of the standing committees of House and Senate to which the bill was earlier referred. The conferees (called "managers" for the House and Senate, respectively) are under heavy pressure to reach an agreement. After all, the bill has passed both houses, and normally the Senate amendments have not changed its basic purposes. They trade: the House's men accept the first Senate amendment if the Senate's men will drop the second. They compromise: if the bill as it passed the House authorized an appropriation of $10,000,000 and a Senate amendment cut that figure to $6,000,000, the conferees may agree on some figure between the two. But, behind closed doors, conference committees sometimes do more than trade and compromise. Occasionally they write wholly new clauses into the bill. For this they have been assailed as a "third house," unrepresentative and irresponsible. They can answer this criticism by pointing out that their final recommendations may still be rejected by the House or Senate. This is not a wholly realistic defense, however. Although the conference committees' reports are printed, they contain no explanations, and they are written in terms ("Section 4, subsection (c), strike out 'on and after January 1, 1961,' and insert in lieu thereof 'when a finding has been made in accordance with section 3, subsection (f)' ") which cannot be understood unless the reader possesses a copy of the bill and has the time and inclination to study it with great care. Again the pressure is heavy to get the bill passed. Representatives and senators naturally incline to "go along" with the conferees' decisions and usually do so by unanimous agreement.

## Presidential Approval or Disapproval

After the bill passed by both houses goes to the White House, the President has ten days (excluding Sundays and holidays) in which to decide what to do about it. If he signs it during that ten-day period, it becomes a law. He may let it become law without his signature, simply by doing nothing about it—if, during the ten-day period, Congress is still in session. Most bills are signed, sometimes with photographed ceremonies including the presentation of presidential pens to congressmen who led the fight for their passage. When the President dislikes a bill but sees no purpose in fighting against it, he makes an ineffectual gesture of distaste by allowing it to become law without his signature.

The President may, however, register his disapproval more strongly. He may veto the bill, returning it to the house in which it originated with a message stating his reasons for disapproving it. It can still become law, without his approval, but only if both houses re-pass it, each by a two-thirds vote—that is, only if in each house at least two-thirds of those present and voting cast their votes in favor of "overriding" the veto. When Congress adjourns during the ten-day period following the passage of a bill, the President can kill the bill by doing nothing about it; the combination of his failure to sign it and Congress's adjournment results, at the conclusion of the ten-day period, in what is called a "pocket veto" of the bill, which cannot be overridden.

To sum up: the great legislative duties imposed on the Congress are performed in an institutional setting where customs and rules militate against hasty affirmative action. Party labels play a decisive part in the formal organization of House and Senate. The power structure in both chambers is basically affected by seniority, and is held together in the face of wide ideological differences by the stake which the power holders and those who expect soon to succeed to powerful posts have in the continuation of the system. In the tortuous route which a bill must follow if it is to become a law, there are many "pressure points" where a particular interest group, working through sympathetic congressmen, can delay or wholly halt its progress. Small minorities—in both chambers the standing legislative committees, in the House the Rules Committee, in the Senate a dedicated body of filibusterers—can often prevent its enactment. Major decisions as to what the legislation should contain can be made, especially in the House, without any sure way of holding a congressman responsible or even of knowing how he voted.

Are these all flaws in the legislative process- or are they wise safeguards against ill-considered action? Are they, at least, inevitable parts of any legislative system—inevitable because of the natural complexities of the business of law-making? If so, are they consistent with the other reason for the existence of Congress? Congress is not just a law-making body; it is a representative body, designed to give real meaning to the ideal of "government by the people." Since 1913, the Senate has been likewise popularly elected and so directly representative of the people. The question, then, is whether and to what extent congressional government, as described in this chapter, is popular government—how much it does or can or should do to make policies in accordance with the people's will, and how effectively the people can hold it responsible for what it does. To these questions we now turn.

# CHAPTER 14

# Congress: Representing the People

In a republic, self-government is achieved through representation. Because of their numbers, a hundred and eighty million people cannot collectively decide questions of policy and make laws. These tasks they entrust to the men and women whom they elect to represent them. Congress, then, is a representative body, and each individual congressman represents constituents—the people who reside in his constituency, the district or state where he was chosen. Just what this representative function is, and how it is performed by individual members of Congress and by Congress as a whole, are the subjects for examination in this chapter.

First, we will look at the individual representative's function and see how he looks at it. Should he think for himself, try to mold the thinking of his constituents, or simply try to reflect their views? What, in fact, *does* he do? Then we must ask a series of questions about Congress as a representative body. Is it, in truth, fairly representative of the people of the country? Does it act in a fashion that is responsive to the wishes of a majority of the people? Can the voters justly hold their congressmen, or Congress as a whole, responsible for the passage of bad laws or the failure to pass good ones? To the extent that both responsiveness and responsibility are lacking, what, if anything, can or should be done to increase them and so bring our system more into line with the democratic principle of majority rule?

## THE LEGISLATOR'S REPRESENTATIVE ROLE

*Independent Judgment.* Our old friend Edmund Burke, who coined the classic definition of parliamentary political parties more than a century and a half ago, was also the author of a historic statement on the proper relationship between a representative and his constituents. He wrote it when he was a candidate for election to the House of Commons from the city of Bristol in southwestern England and called it "Address to the Electors of Bristol." Essentially, Burke's position was that a representative from (or "for") Bristol was, first and foremost, a member *of* the *national* legislature. Election, Burke suggested, meant that the voters trusted him to use his best judgment for the good of the country. The representative, therefore, while listening respectfully to the views of his constituents, should make up his own mind as he saw fit, putting the national welfare, as he saw it, ahead of the special interests of his constituency. If the voters then disapproved of his decisions or lost confidence in his judgment, they could defeat him in the next election.

This theory of the representative function is based, of course, on the assumption that most people want to be represented by men of courage and integrity, men who will do what they think is right. It assumes, too, that the people prefer legislators concerned more about the country's needs than the demands from a single small district. Is this too idealistic? Even if it is practicable in Britain, can this theory be applied in the United States, which has so deeply-rooted a tradition of localism in politics? Well, there are plenty of American examples of the validity of the first assumption underlying the theory—namely, that voters respect courage, integrity, and independence. The second assumption, however, is more troublesome. Will a majority of voters in a particular state or district be willing to sacrifice their local interests for the national good—especially where nobody can prove that the sacrifice will actually be beneficial to the nation? As a representative you may think that freer trade is vital for both world peace and the stability of the American economy. But if the chief industry in your district is a large watch factory, whose managers and workers fear being forced out of business by Swiss competition, can you expect these constituents to approve of your vote for reducing the tariff on Swiss watches? You can explain to them how lower tariffs will promote peace and American business in general. You may even persuade them that this is so. Yet even if they understand your reasons for favoring tariff reduction, will they favor it when it seems sure to hurt them personally? Aside from the demands it makes on human unselfishness, the second assumption also overlooks a point emphasized heretofore in this book: namely, the tendency of people sincerely to believe that the national interest and their own personal advantage are one and the same.

Nevertheless, American senators and representatives have acted occasionally on Burkean principles and been reelected again and again. Senator George W. Norris of Nebraska was one. His courage led him to vote against entry into World War I, knowing that he would be vilified as something close to a traitor. His independence took him out of all party alignments. And his historic monuments are national laws of no particular concern to his own state, especially the Tennessee Valley Authority. In the House, a representative who wrote a series of authoritative works on Congress, Robert Luce of Massachusetts, likewise frankly told the voters that he would do as he thought was right, whether they disagreed with him or not—and Mr. Luce, a conservative Republican, even won reelection in 1936 in the face of a Democratic landslide. Two years later he won again. In that campaign, his opponent was urged by a Democratic audience to denounce Mr. Luce for flouting the demands of his constituents. The candidate, yet another Burkean, refused to do so. He said that he agreed with Mr. Luce's theory of the representative function. The audience murmured discontentedly. Most of them disagreed with the notion that a representative in Congress should simply use his own judgment and let the chips fall where they may. They believed, instead, that he should try to reflect or "mirror" the opinions of his constituents.

*Mouthpiece of Constituents.* The "mirror" theory of representation appears to be far more prevalent in the United States than Burke's theory. It assumes that the man sent to Washington is the spokesman for the voters who elected him: he should say what they would say were they there in his place. In this view, the representative's task is to find out what public opinion in his constituency is, on any given issue, and to argue and vote in accordance with that opinion. And often congressmen try to do just that. They do it both because they believe it is their job to do it and also because they want to be re-elected. As realists they assume that voters, consciously or unconsciously, tend to vote selfishly.

This theory is consistent with much of American political history and practice. In a federal union, legislators come from separate states. The older states have their own significant history; every state has its own government around which party organizations grow. It is natural, therefore, for senators to feel that they must speak for their states and for representatives to assume the parallel task of speaking for their districts. Nevertheless the "mirror" theory, like its opposite, has flaws which make its complete application impossible. There are irreparable cracks in the mirror.

The first flaw is the assumption that any general "popular will" exists on most issues that come before Congress. It doesn't. Poll-takers can get answers if they ask questions: but in many instances the "opinion" of the person interviewed is wholly "off the cuff" concerning a matter in which he has little interest and no knowledge. Most voters, most of the time, have only a dim idea of what Congress is doing and of what they want Congress to do. However, there are occasions when broad public sentiment is aroused: nearly everyone knew and had some opinion about bills to repeal the Prohibition Amendment, for instance, just as today they would know of measures to eliminate selective service or to draft all young women. So on some issues, at least, congressmen can assume that the people do have opinions.

Even so, however, it is very nearly impossible to find out what the majority of the constituents want their representative to do: and this is the second flaw in the "mirror" theory of the representative function. Some congressmen give great weight to the letters and telegrams they receive from home. The volume of mail, however, is a poor indication of public opinion. Even on widely publicized, controversial issues a representative is hardly likely to hear from more than 1000 constituents out of, say, 150,000 voters in his district; and the 1000 do not represent a true cross section of opinion in the district.

One way to get a cross section is to hire a professional polling agency to select a scientific sample of the constituency and conduct private polls, but this costs more money than most congressmen can afford. The published public opinion polls, like those reported by Gallup and Elmo Roper, may give some clues as to what people are thinking, but their figures are seldom broken down by states and never by congressional districts. And even if they were, the senators or representatives whose primary desire was reelection could not put full reliance on them. The policies which most people favor in March they often dislike by November. The congressman whose vote for a bill in the winter faithfully reflected his constituents' attitude then may be bitterly blamed for it when he seeks reelection in the fall. People will say that he should have known better than to follow their opinions—he was in Washington, wasn't he, with access to information which they did not possess? Unreasonable, perhaps, but that's the way people often are.

There is another and quite different weakness in the "mirror" theory. It assumes that a representative must be willing to be a virtual automaton, simply registering the opinions of his constituents. Congressmen, however, are the law-makers of the land. They occupy important positions—and they are likely to feel important themselves. They are human beings, with opinions and consciences. It is not easy for a congressman of character wholly to subordinate his own opinions, compromise with his conscience and defer to his constituents when he is convinced that they are wrong. If he does so, can he maintain his self-respect? For that matter, will he retain the respect of his constituents? Comic-strip senators who always say what they think people want to hear are portrayed as objects of ridicule and scorn. Who wants to be that kind of a senator, and who wants such spineless men in the Senate?

So we see that neither of the foregoing theories of the representative function can successfully stand thorough analysis. There is some soundness in each of them. Congressmen act in accordance with both of them, sometimes defying the fates (and the voters) and sometimes mechanically registering what they think are their constituents' opinions. Most of them, certainly, feel that they should constantly consult influential and informed people in their districts. Many of them feel that it is their duty (and good publicity, too) to keep their constituents informed about what they are doing, through monthly newsletters or frequent radio broadcasts or telecasts. Some use these means to try to mold public opinion to their own way of thinking by analyzing the issues and explaining their personal views. None of them has much time to theorize: as they go about the business of law-making, they are up against hard, immediate, practical questions. How will this measure or that affect the country? Their party? Their own constituency? Will an affirmative vote on a bill impair their influence and usefulness in the Congress? Will it injure their chance of reelection? For most of them, how they answer these questions, day after day, will indicate toward which theoretical pole they lean. The record will prove their independence or their attempt faithfully to reflect the voters' wishes.

### The Pressures on the Legislator

Not only the cartoonists but serious political analysts have sometimes assumed that the one thing a congressman wants more than anything else in the world is reelection and that this single desire dictates how he votes on the bills before him. There is enough truth in this assumption to warrant our examining it closely. True enough, most congressmen—not all—are eager to be reelected. There is nothing wrong about that. It is a worthy ambition. Very human, too, is the wish to have one's record vindicated by the approval of the voters. And the wish for reelection is not always just a yearning for success, prestige, power, or vindication. Sometimes members of Congress want to get some big legislative job done, which takes years to accomplish—like Norris's ten-year fight for the development of electric power on the Tennessee River. They can't lead the battle for such legislation if they are not in Congress.

The real question relates to the extent that the desire for reelection affects the congressman's behavior. Clearly it makes him

more eager to comply with requests from constituents for personal favors—a matter which we will touch upon more fully in a
few moments. But what about the impact on his legislative decisions? In voting on most bills, he may try to please his constituents and will claim a reasonably respectable justification for
doing so. Or, if he does not try to please them, he will at least
endeavor not to offend a substantial segment of them. If a bill
comes before the House, say, which he personally favors, but
which has been vehemently condemned by the American Legion
posts or the strong labor unions in his district, how should he
vote? If he considers the bill to be relatively unimportant and it
is going to be defeated anyway, he may decide to vote against it.
Not a courageous choice, this, but a prudent and perhaps a defensible one: why risk one's seat in the House and one's chance to
make major legislative decisions for the sake of a lost cause, and
an unimportant cause at that? (This type of reasoning, of course,
can lead to serious temptation. It may inculcate the habit of betraying one's convictions, always with a plausible excuse.)

The desire for reelection leads a congressman, then, to refrain
from stepping needlessly on anybody's toes. It leads him, too, to
want to stay "in right" with the local party organization leaders
in his constituency (fortunately for him, these are only sporadi-
cally interested in legislative controversies), and, all too often, with
the potential financial contributors to his next campaign. Campaigning having become an extremely costly business in many
districts, the continued support of these contributors may be the
vital factor in his bid for reelection. Finally, he is aware that his
potential opponents will criticize him for not doing enough for
the district or the state. To prevent such criticism, he will not
only do favors for individuals but will try to obtain legislative
favors for his constituency—the authorization of a dam or several
new post offices, for instance. Even as free-wheeling a senator as
Wayne Morse of Oregon, whose independence led him to switch
parties, during his first term spent many hours on the Senate floor
pleading for legislation beneficial to the sheep raisers of eastern
Oregon.

If doubts about his reelection make a congressman tread carefully, the pressures that pound on him from organized groups and

individuals have their own effect on his legislative conduct. Some of these pressures, of course, are intimately tied up with his chances of being reelected. But aside from that, they have a steady impact. Many important bills arouse little or no excitement among his own constituents. How, then, will he vote? Here the pressure groups descend on him. They cannot threaten him, but they try to persuade. Conscientiously he listens to all sides—legislative controversies have a way of being at least heptagonal—and eventually may reach a completely rational decision. But factors of personal friendship, his respect for particular interest spokesmen, and his impatience with or dislike for others may make his choice a partly emotional one. And when two of his closest friends and advisers take sharply opposing sides and give him contradictory advice, he again must weigh the personal factors involved. If he votes "aye" will he lose a valued friend—and if so, should he risk losing the other friend by voting "no"? To base a vote in Congress on which friend you most want to keep may seem like a curious way to reach legislative decisions, but it can happen.

This matter of friendship is significant. Most politicians, as John F. Kennedy emphasized in the introduction to his book about courageous congressmen,[1] like to be liked. They want to make friends and to keep friends: friendships are among the stablest rewards of the politician's chancy, insecure life. More particularly, representatives and senators want to be liked within the House and Senate. Each, as an institution, has its own "club spirit"; senators are fond of describing the Senate as "the most exclusive club in the world." The surest way to get along in Congress is to "go along"—to observe the customs of the club, treat all members with respect,[2] and win the liking and confidence of the leaders, especially in your own party. Are you anxious to have Congress pass your bill establishing a new federal judgeship in your state? Nobody else cares particularly about your bill: it will pass if the committee chairman and party leaders help you, and

---

[1] John F. Kennedy, *Profiles in Courage* (New York: Harper & Brothers, 1956).

[2] A committee chairman, on being criticized by a "freshman" representative for his committee's procedure, once brought most of the House to its feet by his declaration that "The first thing a new member must learn to do is to love and respect every member of this House!"

conversely it will get nowhere if they don't. Therefore, as a legislator, you realize that your own effectiveness depends in part on the
congressional alliances you can make, especially with the men who
wield the greatest influence. This means that the price you pay
for independence—for voting against the leadership's wishes on
important bills—may be a high one. It might make you briefly
popular at home, but permanently ineffectual in Congress.

Finally, though the congressman must live most of the time
among his constituents and his colleagues and wants them to like
him, there is one person he has to live with all the time. That is
himself. The need for self-respect is one more continual pressure
influencing a legislator's major decisions. Truly the legislative
life is not an easy one. The man who leads it is yanked and pulled
and pounded—by his own convictions and desires for self-respect;
by his wish for friends and his need for friends; by his fear of
defeat for himself or the causes he is fighting for; by the arguments of insistent lobbyists; by the appeals for party loyalty; by
the demands of his organized and individual constituents. If we
say that our representative is in Washington to speak "for us," we
should at least realize the complexities of every choice he has to
make. It may be that when he votes as we would not have voted,
he is not betraying us but is, instead, making himself abler to
represent us more satisfactorily on other issues at other times.

### The Legislator as "Washington Representative"

The cracks in the mirror theory of the representative function
are most evident in those states or districts which reelect congressmen time after time, apparently regardless of how they vote on
legislative matters. They withstand opposition party landslides.
They win because they are personally popular—but what makes
them popular? Curly hair and a winning smile? Sometimes—
though not, usually, for long. Respect for their character, ability,
or length of service? Sometimes, especially the last: after years in
Congress they become "household words" in their constituencies,
and people take pride in the habit of voting for them. But personal attributes and modest fame are seldom enough. It is what
they do for the district or state, and for their individual constituents, that keeps them popular.

*Courtesy and Concern.* The first rule for a congressman to follow is to answer his mail promptly, courteously, and if possible warmly. Surprisingly often, a quick, full, thoughtful answer to a critical letter turns a hostile critic into at least a grudging admirer. Many people seem to get a "kick" out of saying "I got a long better from the Senator yesterday." Even more effective is a telegram or, best of all, a long distance telephone call. Almost all of us are flattered by such attentions being shown us by a busy statesman.

A second rule is to pay attention to the particular demands of his constituency for favored treatment in the form of special legislation (like the bill creating a new judgeship) or executive decisions, such as to locate an air base in the state or give financial support to an urban renewal project in the chief city of the district. A man can overcome the handicap of personal unattractiveness if he can point with pride to the visible evidence of the many things which he has done for the constituency as a whole.

*Finding Jobs for People.* Most important of all, however, is the constant granting of individual favors. These fall into two broad categories. The first is patronage. At its simplest, patronage is the business of getting jobs for people. It has long been the chief stock-in-trade of many local party organizations, as we saw in Chapter 10, and a representative from an urban district where the party machine is strong can sometimes turn most of his patronage problems over to the local party chieftains. Other congressmen, however, cannot thus pass the buck. Men and women who canvassed for them in the primary, or who drove voters to the polls on election day, ask them for regular public employment. In times of economic depression, these requests come flooding in—find us jobs, jobs, jobs. Even in prosperous days a surprisingly large number of people seem to prefer public employment to whatever they are doing. The famous story of a century ago, of "orfice-seekers" climbing through windows and down chimneys to ask President Lincoln to appoint them to government positions, does not seem particularly exaggerated—or very comical, either—to many a newly-elected representative today.

A congressman himself can employ, directly, only a handful of people, and most of these he must choose on the basis of ability.

He can hardly afford to select as his own executive assistants, secretaries, and stenographers people whose only qualification is the campaigning they have done in his behalf. Aside from them, however, he may have from one to half a dozen jobs to hand out, in the Capitol or the House or Senate Office Buildings: positions such as those of elevator operator or file clerk. To meet most of the humbler patronage demands, he must persuade officials in the executive branch to fill minor vacancies with the people he recommends. Fortunate is the congressman who, through his influential position or more simply through personal acquaintance, gets the inside track to a government agency which is growing fast and hiring employees outside of the Civil Service requirements. In a single two-year period one such congressman, allotted one lone elevator operator's position as his share of the Capitol patronage, managed to appoint twenty-two elevator operators. How? His secretary was a personal friend of the personnel director charged with staffing a new agency, which needed a large number of comparatively unskilled employees. The first elevator operator appointed, after a month during which he gave indications of being an intelligent and personable fellow, was sent up to see this personnel director. The latter hired him at once. Now the congressman could appoint another young man to the elevator vacancy —and a month later, the whole process was repeated, and so it went for the whole two years.

There is an old myth that congressmen dislike the patronage system. Finding a man a job, it is said, makes "nine enemies and one ingrate." As far as the employment demands of humble job seekers are concerned—people who don't request a particular position but just want work—this is largely nonsense. By and large, the people who get the jobs are grateful, and those who can't be placed immediately remain hopeful. Only when there is hot competition for appointment to a specific position does the congressman face real patronage trouble. The naming of candidates to West Point and Annapolis, for example, was long a congressional perquisite of somewhat doubtful benefit to the congressman as well as to the armed services: the selection of one youngster always brought bitter disappointment to several others. Some present congressmen, realizing this, have long tried to take them-

**A joint session of Congress.** The President delivers his annual "State of the Union" message each January to a joint session of Congress in the House chamber.

PRESS GALLERY

VICE PRESIDENT

SPEAKER

PRESIDENT

SUPREME COURT JUSTICES

SENATORS

REPUBLICAN REPRESENTATIVES

DEMOCRATIC REPRESENTATIVES

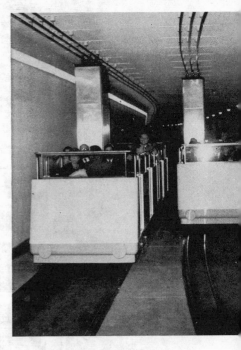

**Congress at work.** At top, committee member Senator Sam J. Ervin, Democrat, North Carolina (left) quizzes Attorney General Robert F. Kennedy (right) over legal technicalities of the administration's civil rights legislation during the latter's appearance before the Senate Judiciary Committee. Next to Kennedy is Burke Marshall, Assistant Attorney General in charge of the Civil Rights Division. Lower left, a Senator's mail: Senator Russell of Georgia and some of the letters he received about a civil rights bill. Lower right, Senators hastening from their offices to the Senate floor on the new subway running under the Plaza (Representatives, equally distant from the Capitol, have to walk).

selves "off the spot" by insisting on competitive examinations for all the applicants in their constituency. More recently the academies themselves have reduced the pressure further by stiffening their entrance requirements. Another example of competitive patronage, where there are no examinations, is the appointment of judges to the United States courts. The selection, of course, is made by the President, usually on the advice of his attorney-general. Nevertheless, when there is such a judicial vacancy in a state, that state's senators are likely to be pressured to recommend the naming of Jones or Smith or Robinson to the bench. If they back Jones and he is eventually appointed, they may incur the enmity of Smith and Robinson and their friends. And if none of the three is appointed, the supporters of all three may speak scornfully of the senators, describing them as men who would not fight hard for their friends or who obviously lacked influence in Washington.

Every senator understands the political dangers and difficulties inherent in this kind of "high-level" patronage. At the very least, each of them has a stake in preventing the appointment to high federal posts of men from their own states who are their personal or political enemies. Accordingly, there is in the Senate a custom known as *senatorial courtesy*, designed to stop just such appointments. When the President sends to the Senate a nomination—for a judgeship, say, or to fill such a post as that of Collector of Customs or United States Marshal—the Senate will usually refuse to confirm the nomination if the nominee is "personally objectionable" to the majority party's senator or senators from the state where the nominee resides. With the help of this system of mutual protection against positively hostile appointments, senators readily put up with the political risks of high-level patronage. Most of them figure that, on balance, the dispensing of patronage makes them more friends than enemies. The very proof that they have influence disarms the disappointed. Those who didn't get the job may feel sore about it, but are likely to nurse their wounds privately, for, after all, they may later want the senator's help when another appropriate vacancy is to be filled.

Patronage of all kinds, as we have seen, helps to hold a political organization together. It is often indispensable to many congressmen who rely on their own personal "machines." And for some—especially representatives from relatively low-income districts—it has the additional effect of freeing the law-maker from local pressures affecting his legislative decisions. If large numbers of his constituents need jobs and he finds jobs for them, as far as they are concerned he can vote as he pleases on any bill that comes before the House. He is their "patron," and they are for him.

*Access to the Executive Branch.* Congressmen do more for their constituents than find work for them. As government has become more complex, the demands for *intercession* with an executive agency, on behalf of some private citizen or corporation, have constantly increased. This intercession can, of course, go to improper lengths, as when a representative seeks to persuade the Federal Communications Commission to award a television channel to one out of several competing applicants. Usually, however, congressmen stay within defensible limits. They arrange an appointment for their constituent with an official of the agency concerned; they may telephone the official—in the constituent's presence—and ask him to give "all proper consideration" to the constituent's claim. Much of the business of "interceding" for the constituents is simply a matter of obtaining information. People feel, correctly, that a request for information from a congressman will get fuller and prompter attention than will a similar request from an unknown citizen.

Senators and representatives assume that this kind of intercession, like the business of running a specialized employment agency in their Washington office, is part of their job. As a practical matter, they are right. Errand-running, or, as most congressmen prefer to describe it, service to constituents, not only helps them to get reelected, but is something which most of their constituents expect. Purists shudder at the time and energy a congressman expends on doing favors—time and energy necessarily diverted from the essential task of law-making. But many a congressman enjoys doing favors for people, and even the purists have been known to ask for favors when they thought their congressman could help them. From the standpoint of both the representatives and the represented, it is part of the job.

Depression, war, and the increasing complexity of government have made this "service" function such a time-consuming one that in 1946 Congress tried to equip itself to handle it better. In the old days, of course, being a senator or representative was only a part-time job. It took only about eight months, on the average, out of a two-year span. Most congressmen meanwhile maintained their private businesses or professions without much difficulty. Now the situation has changed. Being a congressman is virtually a full-time job. Congress has raised the pay of its members accordingly ($22,500 per year), has established a contributory retirement system for those who serve six years or more, and has provided funds for nearly three times as much staff assistance as congressmen had only twenty years ago. A typical senator's staff may include an executive assistant at a $15,000 annual salary and eight secretaries, assistants, and clerks—all paid from public funds and all, like their chief, working hard from morning till night. Congress is often criticized for voting itself these and other minor perquisites, but congressmen feel that they are justified. Their job has grown to such proportions that they cannot perform it without help, and if they had to pay for that help out of their own pockets only men of independent wealth could afford to serve in Congress. A Congress of rich men would hardly seem to most of us to be "representative" of a democracy.

## CONGRESS AS A REPRESENTATIVE BODY

It is time now to reexamine Congress's performance of its lawmaking function in terms of its role as a representative body. Let us remember that whichever theory of representation we tend to favor, Burke's or the mirror of public opinion, both concern a relationship between the electors and the elected. In both, the essence of that relationship is *responsibility*. Even if we believe that a legislator is chosen to do what he thinks is wise, we are not saying that the people should simply abdicate: we assume that the voters will pass judgment on that legislator's conduct in frequent elections. They will authorize him to act as he sees fit, for a short period, but they will hold him responsible for what he does. If, on the other hand, we incline toward the mirror principle, we again assume that the people will hold their representatives responsible; and we add to the legislator's duties the obligation to be continuously *responsive* to the wishes of the voters.

The questions before us, then, are whether the House and Senate as national representative bodies are responsible to the people of the nation and responsive to national opinion, and whether individual congressmen can likewise fairly be held responsible by their constituents and are responsive to their wishes. These boil down to one central issue: to what extent do we really have democratic self-government in the United States? How well do we conform in practice to the fundamental concept of democracy outlined in the first chapter of this book?

### Factors Favoring Responsibility and Responsiveness

Operating in favor of responsible democratic government are the facts that we do have periodic elections in which almost all mature Americans can vote and that we do possess, on the whole, broad freedom to discuss, advocate, and criticize. The members of both houses of Congress are elected by the people. Certainly the nation's press has not felt under restraints in criticizing Congress or, at times, the other branches of the government. Furthermore, we have available a great amount of material to enhance our knowledge of public affairs and our representatives' conduct. Numerous newspapers and the press services maintain large staffs of Washington correspondents, television and radio provide frequent discussions of public issues, and for the serious student there are always the daily official *Congressional Record,* printing verbatim [3] the proceedings on the floor of House and Senate, and the privately compiled *Congressional Quarterly Weekly* which provides succinct analyses of voting behavior, pressure group activity, and party unity in Congress. It is still true, too, that our legislators make many of the policy decisions which affect our lives

---

[3] Actually, proof sheets of the recorded remarks of members are ordinarily given to them to correct, and their corrections often alter what was actually said. This may be a boon to the English language (few people can express themselves orally, for an extended period, in perfect English) and to the congressmen involved, but it robs the *Record* of historical exactness.

and that in making them they take heed of what we want them to do—if we bother to tell them. All of these are factors strengthening responsible and responsive law-making.

## Factors Decreasing Responsibility and Responsiveness

*Delegation and Complexity.* On the other hand, there are some elements of our political society which militate against the satisfactory operation of the democratic and representative principles. One of these is the fact that a considerable amount of law-making is not done by our elected legislators but by appointed administrators to whom Congress habitually delegates wide authority. Some of these administrators, being subordinate to the President, are indirectly responsible to the people; but those in the "independent" regulatory commissions have only the most tenuous connection with the electorate. And insofar as the Supreme Court, in interpreting not only the Constitution but also acts of Congress, plays a legislative role, the ideal of democratic representation fades still further into the background. Appointed for life, the justices are not held responsible to the people, nor do they pretend to be responsive to temporary popular demands.

More significant still is the complexity of public affairs. Nowadays, to legislate wisely requires a great amount of knowledge, understanding, and skill. Obviously most citizens simply don't have the time to acquire them. The more complicated the issues, the less able the people are to deal with them. This weakens the idea of responsibility, for uninformed voters cannot well hold a legislator responsible for decisions which they know so little about that they can neither praise nor denounce. It also casts doubt on the value of responsiveness: our representatives can hardly be responsive to our opinions if we have no opinions. These are general weaknesses in the application of the basic theory of self-government through representation, somewhat counterbalancing the factors which give it practical validity. But there are also special adverse factors arising out of the apportionment of congressional seats, the nature of Congress, and our party system which require our more detailed examination.

*Apportionment.* The goal of having Congress responsible and responsive can be reached only through the ballot box. At the minimum, each citizen has the effectiveness represented by his one vote on election day. If Congress is to answer to the majority of the people, and if we are to have a fully just political society, it would seem obvious that that minimum of effectiveness should be the same for everyone—that each citizen's vote should count just as much as the vote of every other citizen. However, it doesn't. *The arrangement of constituencies,* the "apportionment" of seats in both the Senate and House, gives people differing amounts of voting power, depending upon where they live. To a degree, it makes Congress more responsive to some people or groups than to others and can result in minorities being abler to hold Congress responsible than majorities are.

(1) *The Senate* was intended by the framers of the Constitution to be indirectly elected. Senators were supposed to represent not the *demos,* the people, but the sovereign states whose legislatures chose them. This being the Founding Fathers' intention, the equal representation of each state, large and small, in the Senate had a sound justification in principle. The Seventeenth Amendment, however, changed the picture. Since its adoption in 1913, senators have been elected by the people of their states. This was a move in the direction of democracy, but it did not go the whole way. It made senators popular representatives, but it did not make the Senate truly representative of the people of the nation. It did not do this because it did not eliminate the requirement that each state should have two senators regardless of its population.

So today, although each senator is answerable to his own constituents, the Senate as a whole is not necessarily going to reflect the opinions of a majority of all the voters in the country. Vermont with a population of 390,000 has two senators; so has Alaska with 226,000 people and Nevada with 285,000. But these small or sparsely settled states have just as much voice in the decisions of the United States Senate as have New York (16,782,000), California (15,717,000), and Pennsylvania (11,319,000).[4] Theoretically, indeed, a bill could pass the Senate with the support of 52 senators representing, in all, approximately 30,000,000 people, over the

---

[4] These are the 1960 census figures; since 1960, California has become the most populous state in the Union.

opposition of 48 senators representing about 150,000,000 people. That is what we mean when we say that the Senate, as a body, is not necessarily representative of the people of the nation, and when we suggest that an individual voter in Vermont has more influence at the ballot box than an individual voter in New York.

Nothing can be done about this. The one provision of the Constitution which cannot be amended—unless the states adversely affected agree, which is unthinkable—is the requirement of an equal number of senators from every state. If this seems anachronistic today—if the possibility that Alaska and Vermont together can carry more weight than New York seems inconsistent with the democratic principles of equal voting power for every citizen and of majority rule—we can solace ourselves by remembering that it was a price that had to be paid for the sake of our national existence.

The impact of such state-by-state inequality on what the Senate does has long been obvious. Today we are largely an urban country: two-thirds of the American people live in cities. They are underrepresented in the Senate. Generally, the rural areas are overrepresented, for many of the less populated states are largely rural. The tendency then is for agricultural interests to make themselves felt in the Senate more than their numerical size would lead one to expect, and labor interests less. Economic interests and issues are not the only ones affected; at times the people of small rural states have had a powerful voice in foreign policy questions, out of all proportion to their numbers.

(2) *In the House of Representatives,* the only constitutional obstacle to equality of popular representation is comparatively minor. It is the provision that every state shall have at least one representative. At the moment this means that Alaska, Delaware, Nevada, Wyoming, and Vermont each has a representative even though, in each of these states, the population is less than that of the average congressional district. But this disparity is inconsequential compared to others which unnecessarily distort the principle of representation in the House. These are the gerrymander and the failure to draw new district lines when the centers of population shift within a state.

In 1910, Congress by statute fixed the membership of the House at 435. Under the Constitution, the number of seats allotted to each state is to be in accordance with its population, except for the special provision for the smaller states mentioned above. Every ten years, then, after each national census, each state is informed of the number of seats it will have in the House during the next decade, with a few—such as Texas, California, and Michigan in recent years—gaining several new seats, reflecting their rapid growth, and a few others losing a seat or two because their population has declined or failed to increase at the national rate. Representatives are elected from districts within the state, the drawing of district boundaries being the job of the state legislature. When the number of seats is changed, the legislature must draw a whole new set of district lines.[5]

This redistricting is a political task performed by politicians for politicians' purposes. Almost invariably it gives rise to anguished cries of "gerrymander." That word (properly pronounced with a hard "g") is a combination of the name of Governor Elbridge Gerry of Massachusetts and the salamander-shaped district which he caused to be established in the northeastern part of his state in 1814. A gerrymander is the drawing of district lines in such a way as unduly to benefit the party which has a majority in the state legislature doing the redistricting. Assume that the census shows that 2,000,000 people live in a state, 500,000 of whom have come there since the last previous census. This state has grown rapidly enough to be entitled to one more seat in the House than it formally had; as the average population of a congressional district is almost exactly 400,000, the state is now allotted five seats. The four old districts must be replaced by five new ones. There is a Democratic majority in the state legislature. The voters in the state usually divide about 60 per cent Democratic to 40 per cent

---

5 If, in a state which has gained a seat, the legislature fails to redistrict the state, the additional representative is elected "at large"; his district is the whole state. If the state loses a seat and the legislature fails to redistrict, all the old districts are abolished and the whole "delegation"—all the representatives of the state—run "at large." When, as a result of the 1960 census, Alabama lost one seat in the House, each of the former nine districts chose a candidate in the 1962 primaries. These nine then participated in a runoff election to choose the eight representatives to which the state was entitled.

Republican:—so, it would seem, the state's delegation in the next
House should consist of three Democrats and two Republicans.
But the Democratic legislators have other ideas. They devise a
monstrous district, stretching in a long narrow corridor from one
end of the state to the other, weaving as it goes so as to avoid all
the large cities. This strangely shaped district, wholly rural, is almost solidly Republican. Hardly any Democrats live in it; as a
result, there are enough Democrats in each of the four remaining
districts to produce Democratic majorities in every one of them.
So the partisan lineup in the House will be four to one instead of
three to two—which, of course; was the purpose of this gerrymander.  If this imaginary example seems to you far-fetched, take
a look at the map of New York's 14th and 15th congressional districts. The 15th is designed to elect a Republican congressman

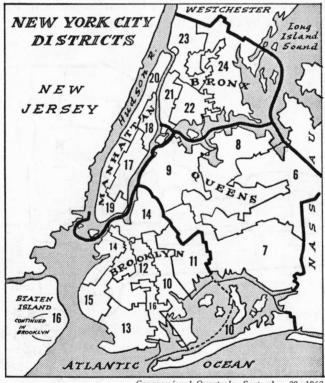

*Congressional Quarterly,* September 28, 1962

from Brooklyn. It wanders through various middle- and high-income residential areas which are considered safely Republicans. The Democratic voters who might have elected both congressmen from this area are funneled into the 14th Congressional district, two highly industrialized and low-income areas connected by a long narrow strip of curb along the waterfront. This arrangement is the product of the Republican-controlled legislature's 1961 redistricting plan.

In another gerrymander by the same legislature, there was a different purpose. Representative Samuel S. Stratton of Schenectady, a Democrat, was marked for political extinction by putting his home city together with Albany, which already had a Democratic congressman. Stratton thereupon ran in the new 35th district which stretched over a hundred miles westward across the state, an area deemed to be safely Republican. The Republican legislators' purpose was not achieved; Stratton performed a minor political miracle by carrying the new 35th district in 1962.

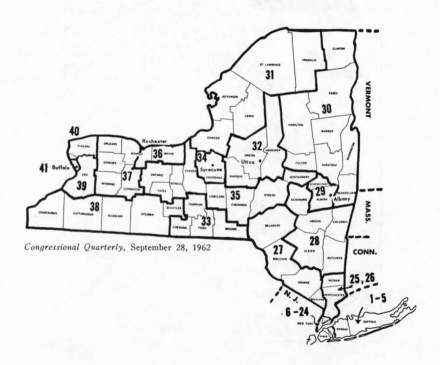

*Congressional Quarterly*, September 28, 1962

Partisan advantage is not the only goal of gerrymanders. Personalities enter in: every redistricting affects the sitting congressmen one way or another. A legislature may deliberately draw the new lines to make safer the majority of a veteran representative or to create a district "made to order" for a popular local politician. And often affecting the personal fortunes of representatives is an intraparty factional fight, a clash of interests struggling for advantage.

Comparatively few states have their allotment of seats changed after a decennial census. In most, the size of the House delegation remains the same for two or three or four decades. But even within these states, sharp population shifts occur. Thousands of people leave the farms and villages and move to the big cities. Yet if the number of seats is not changed, most state legislatures let the old district lines stand even though migration has depleted the population of one district and swollen that of another. Even when they do redistrict, legislatures often seem to pay little heed to the disproportionate size of the districts they create. In the early 1960's, for example, the twelfth congressional district of Michigan had 177,000 people; the population of the same state's second district was over 800,000. A more detailed idea of the disproportion in size of congressional districts can be gained from the table showing the twenty largest and smallest districts after the redistricting which followed the 1960 census.

Like the gerrymander, failure to redistrict is frequently a partisan political decision. More than that, it is often the choice of a predominantly rural and small-town legislature hostile to big-city urban interests, for the problem of creating equal representative constituencies goes back to the state legislatures and the state constitutions which established them. Many states, in fixing the constituencies for their own legislators, depart from the principle of numerical equality. They give a heavy advantage to rural counties and tiny villages. Thus in the lower house in the Connecticut legislature, every town has two representatives: Colebrook, with a population of 492, has representation equal to that of Hartford, with 177,397 people. Recently, with the massive movement of people from the city to the suburbs, the class of voter most hurt by malapportionment of congressional districts has been the sub-

# TWENTY LARGEST AND SMALLEST CONGRESSIONAL DISTRICTS

| | Largest Districts | | | | Smallest Districts | |
|---|---|---|---|---|---|---|
| District | Rep. 88th Congress | | 1960 Population | District | Rep. 88th Congress | | 1960 Population |
| 1. Texas 5th | Alger | (R) | 951,527 | Michigan 12th | Bennett | (R) | 177,431 |
| 2. Georgia 5th | Weltner | (D) | 823,680 | South Dakota 2nd | Berry | (R) | 182,845 |
| 3. Michigan 16th | Lesinski | (D) | 802,994 | Colorado 4th | Aspinall | (D) | 195,511 |
| 4. Ohio 3rd | Schenck | (R) | 726,156 | Arizona 3rd | Senner | (D) | 198,236 |
| 5. Maryland 5th | Lankford | (D) | 711,045 | Texas 4th | Roberts | (D) | 216,371 |
| 6. Indiana 11th | Bruce | (R) | 697,567 | Alaska AL | Rivers | (D) | 226,167 |
| 7. Michigan 18th | Broomfield | (R) | 690,259 | Alabama 7th | * | | 236,216 |
| 8. Connecticut 1st | Daddario | (D) | 689,555 | Tennessee 8th | Everett | (D) | 223,387 |
| 9. Texas 20th | Gonzalez | (D) | 687,151 | Oklahoma 3rd | Albert | (D) | 227,692 |
| 10. Ohio 12th | Devine | (R) | 682,962 | Tennessee 7th | Murray | (D) | 232,652 |
| 11. Texas 22nd | Casey | (D) | 674,965 | Ohio 15th | Secrest | (D) | 236,288 |
| 12. Michigan 7th | O'Hara | (D) | 664,556 | Wisconsin 10th | O'Konski | (R) | 236,870 |
| 13. Arizona 1st | Rhodes | (R) | 663,510 | Florida 9th | Fugua | (D) | 237,235 |
| 14. Florida 6th | Rogers | (D) | 660,345 | Michigan 11th | Knox | (R) | 240,793 |
| 15. Colorado 2nd | Brotzman | (R) | 653,945 | Florida 8th | Matthews | (D) | 241,250 |
| 16. Connecticut 4th | Sibal | (R) | 653,589 | Maryland 1st | Morton | (R) | 243,570 |
| 17. Alabama 9th | * | | 634,864 | Texas 1st | Patman | (D) | 245,942 |
| 18. Tennessee 9th | Davis | (D) | 627,019 | Texas 6th | Teague | (D) | 248,149 |
| 19. Michigan 6th | Chamberlain | (R) | 623,842 | Alabama 6th | * | | 251,765 |
| 20. Maryland 2nd | Long | (D) | 621,935 | Oklahoma 4th | Steed | (D) | 252,208 |

* Because of a deadlock over redistricting after the 1960 census reduced the delegation from 9 to 8, all Alabama Representatives to the 88th Congress were elected at large.

SOURCE: Congressional Quarterly, Vol. 20, September 28, 1962, p. 1,604, and November 9, 1962, pp. 2,146-2,147.

urbanite. The table on "regional comparisons" shows something of the impact of outmoded and discriminatory apportionment on the urban, suburban, and rural voter.

**REGIONAL COMPARISONS OF URBAN, SUBURBAN, RURAL REPRESENTATION IN HOUSE OF REPRESENTATIVES, 87TH CONGRESS, 1960 CENSUS**

| Predominant Characteristic of Population | Number of Districts in Group | Total Population of Districts in Group | Average District Population | Relative Values of Vote (100 = Average) |
|---|---|---|---|---|
| *The United States—Totals* | | | | |
| Urban | 126 | 54,427,014 | 431,960 | 95 |
| Suburban | 60 | 32,902,170 | 548,370 | 75 |
| Rural | 250 | 91,230,035 | 364,920 | 112 |
| National Total | 436 * | 178,559,219 | 408,602 | |
| *Eastern States* | | | | |
| Urban | 46 | 16,471,438 | 358,075 | 109 |
| Suburban | 33 | 15,885,354 | 481,374 | 81 |
| Rural | 49 | 17,728,429 | 361,805 | 108 |
| Regional Total | 128 | 50,085,221 | 391,291 | |
| *Southern States* | | | | |
| Urban | 24 | 13,367,384 | 556,974 | 73 |
| Suburban | 9 | 2,995,411 | 599,082 | 68 |
| Rural | 91 | 32,438,960 | 356,472 | 114 |
| Regional Total | 120 | 48,801,755 | 406,681 | |
| *Midwestern States* | | | | |
| Urban | 36 | 15,329,068 | 425,807 | 94 |
| Suburban | 12 | 7,285,536 | 607,128 | 66 |
| Rural | 81 | 29,004,535 | 358,081 | 112 |
| Regional Total | 129 | 51,619,139 | 400,148 | |
| *Western States* | | | | |
| Urban | 20 | 9,259,124 | 462,956 | 103 |
| Suburban | 10 | 6,735,869 | 673,587 | 71 |
| Rural | 29 | 12,058,111 | 415,797 | 114 |
| Regional Total | 59 | 28,053,104 | 475,476 | |

* The Connecticut-at-large seat is not included.
SOURCE: *Congressional Quarterly*, Vol. 20, February 2, 1962, p. 153.

The ideal picture of Congress as representing all the people is marred, then—in the Senate by constitutional fiat, in the House chiefly by state legislative action or inaction. In both the effect is the same. Rural areas and interests are overrepresented in comparison with their share of the total population. Within a single state or district, of course, the individual senator or representative considers himself to be the representative of his constituents. But as a national law-making body, Congress is made less responsive to the majority of the people, and they less able to hold it responsible, by the vagaries of the apportionment system.

*The Structure and Customs of Congress.* As we have seen, neither the House nor the Senate is a fully representative body equipped to speak for the entire population. The establishment of constituencies which are grossly unequal in numerical size gives disproportionately great influence to some individuals and interests, disproportionately little to others. Congress, therefore, tends to be more responsive to some groups in the society, less responsive to other groups. Its responsiveness to any general majority will—when such exists—is even more noticeably limited by its own customs, organization, and procedure. Again and again, as must be clear by now, the cards are stacked in favor of the minority. Vivid examples are the power of eight members of the House Rules Committee to stop legislation and the ability of perhaps a dozen or two senators to filibuster a bill into oblivion. In the House, procedures designed to safeguard the majority's rights— the petition device, for instance—do exist, but the customs of the House and the importance of conformity to those customs prevent their frequent use. In the Senate not a simple majority, but an extraordinary one (two-thirds) is needed to break a filibuster.

All of these built-in devices for the protection of the minority distort the responsiveness of Congress as a representative institution. They do not mean that individual congressmen fail to consider the wishes of their own constituents. However, although most individual congressmen are likely to be eagerly responsive to strong opinion in their own constituencies, they have no sure way of knowing what the majority wants them to do. And usually the majority has no opinion on a particular legislative matter. The representative's responsiveness, therefore, is likely to reflect a minority opinion, especially that of a minority which by its electoral or financial support can affect his chances for reelection. (He also responds to other pressures, internal and external, as we have seen.)

Responsiveness to ephemeral public opinion, however, is not the central test of representative government. The real touchstone is responsibility—the power of the people to hold the legislators responsible for everything they do in Congress. Tools exist for making individual representatives answerable for their actions: for example, the existence of organized criticism by the opposition party and the publication of congressional voting records on selected issues. But once again, congressional procedure tends to make the lines of responsibility indistinct. A bill which you, a citizen, want to see enacted is introduced in the Senate and referred to a committee. It dies quietly behind the closed doors of the committee room. Was your senator responsible for its demise? You have no way of knowing. When the House is considering a measure, an issue of great importance to you arises in the form of a proposed amendment. If the amendment is killed in the committee of the whole, you don't know whether your representative voted for it or against it, for there are no roll call votes taken in the committee of the whole. Likewise, all too often, when the House passes a bill, newspapers report only the roll call vote on its final passage. You are pleased to read that your representative voted as you hoped he would, in favor of the bill. What you don't realize, unless you peruse the *Congressional Record,* is that on the semifinal roll call he may have voted in favor of a motion to recommit the bill, to doom it to oblivion. A fourth procedural obstacle to holding your congressman responsible is the conference committee, with its meetings held in strict privacy and its often important decisions buried in obscure reports.

It would still be possible to hold Congress and congressmen continuously and effectively responsible if the majority party in Congress could base its campaign on a specific program and, when in office, put that program into effect. For instance, if a party's platform consisted of one simple promise to reduce the income tax, and the party gained a clear majority in the House and Senate but for two years failed to cut the tax, at the next congressional elections the people could register their disapproval of such a breach of promise by voting for the other party's candidates. This, however, does not happen. Our constitutional and political system keeps it from happening. There are two constitutional impediments to the creation of responsible national parties: the separation of powers and federalism. The separation of powers make it possible for one party to win the presidency while the other gains control of Congress, as happened in 1956. Which party, then, is to be held responsible for the adoption of a legislative program or the failure to adopt one? As we shall see in more detail in the next chapter, the President has come to be looked upon as a legislative leader; and at the very least he has the power to recommend legislation and veto bills. He shares the burden, then, with Congress; and if he is of a party different from that of the congressional majority, neither party can be held fully responsible for what happens.[6] The federal system leaves each state in control of its share of the national electoral machinery: it determines who may vote and what the nominating process shall be. This means that no national authority can deny a particular party label to a candidate who repudiates the party's program. A national party platform may pledge the party to promote racial desegregation, but under the laws of Alabama, say, the party's nominee for the Senate can still be an ardent segregationist.

This leads us naturally to the other reason why it is so hard to enforce legislative responsibility on a party basis: namely, the nature of the parties themselves. Each of them, as we saw in Chapter 10, is organizationally a loose federation. Neither is a disciplined national unit. Both attract the allegiance of people whose views on public issues differ widely. Their programs are necessarily vague. And if there were a clear-cut, recognized Democratic program in Congress, many Democratic congressmen would feel free to vote against it: likewise with a Republican program. Therefore, it would be unrealistic automatically to hold an entire

---

6 Politicians have been successful, nevertheless, in persuading the voters to blame one party when different parties control different branches. The Democrats, though controlling the House for most of the last two years of a Republican President's term, fixed the blame for the depression on President Hoover. Conversely a Democratic President, Harry Truman, won re-election by his criticisms of a Republican Congress, which he dubbed "the second worst Congress in history."

party responsible for what Congress does or fails to do. It would be both unrealistic and unfair to punish a single representative for the shortcomings of his party's legislative performance. Party leadership, as we have seen, has considerable effect on how congressmen vote, but it is only one of a number of competitors for influence.

Legislative decision-making has sometimes been pictured as the product (usually in the form of a compromise) of a struggle between organized groups, inside and outside Congress. The contestants are different from one controversy to the next. They form alliances to fight on one issue, different alliances to fight on others. The groups speak for powerful interests and accommodate their strategy to the politicians demands for partisan advantage. This is too simple and rough a picture to be completely accurate, for it gives too little weight to historic party attitudes, the influence of congressional leaders, and the purely individual factors of personal conscience and personal likes and dislikes. There is enough truth in it, however, to remind us of the great difficulty of realizing the democratic goal of having representatives answerable to and held responsible by the people. The harder it is justly to fix responsibility on the majority party or on a single representative, the more distant seems that goal.

## Proposals for Change

Three avenues of reform have been suggested as roads to enhancing congressional responsibility and thereby approaching the ideal of what a democratic republic should be.

*Streamlining.* The first and least significant is internal reorganization within Congress itself. If the reformers meant business, of course, they would try drastically to change the apportionment system and abolish the devices which obstruct majority action. Instead, they have concentrated on such alterations as were embodied in the Legislative Reorganization Act of 1946—the enactment of which, incidentally, was a remarkable achievement in view of the reluctance of congressmen to change any of the established institutional peculiarities of Congress. That 1946 statute sought to make Congress and its activities more responsible (or at least more understandable, and without public understanding

Fitzpatrick in the *St. Louis. Post-Dispatch*

### Our three-party system in Congress

As we know, voting in Congress cannot be adequately explained in terms of party affiliation. Nevertheless, it was true before this cartoon was drawn in 1949, and is true still, that important roll-calls reflect a fairly consistent alliance between many southern Democrats and many Republicans—an alliance portrayed as the weird animal at the right of the picture.

there cannot well be responsibility) in two ways. It reduced the number of standing committees by 60 per cent and clarified the jurisdiction of each committee. This was a step toward more clearly fixing committee responsibility and reducing public confusion; but it was not particularly effective, for reducing the number of committees did not reduce the volume of proposed legislation, and to handle the latter scores of new subcommittees had to be established. Second, the statute sought to bring pressure group activity into the full view of the public by requiring the registration of lobbyists and the disclosure of their remuneration. This was helpful, perhaps, in furthering our understanding of congressional behavior. It gave some clues as to just what opinions or interests Congress is responsive to. It did not, however, increase Congress's responsibility to the people as a whole; instead, it reminded us of the hopelessness, under present conditions, of making party responsibility a standard for judging our legislators' conduct.

*Party Discipline.* To create party responsibility has been the goal of a second group of reformers. As they see it, neither Congress as a whole nor individual congressmen can be held responsible for the enactment of a particular program, and so if we are to have responsible government it must be party government. In essence, they would like to have parties which are really committed to legislative programs and which can discipline their own members. Thus party conventions or conferences, held more frequently than every four years, would adopt platforms more explicit than the customary party platforms today. A congressman who then voted against important parts of his party's program would be "read out of the party" and presumably denied renomination. This idea of having a cohesive legislative majority, upon whom responsibility can be fixed, is adapted from the British system. It runs up against our ingrained political habit of having loosely disciplined parties in which legislators may respond to local pressures at least as readily as they respond to national party leadership. It also faces the constitutional obstacle inherent in federalism—the control of the nominating machinery by fifty separate states. A party majority in Congress can deny its party label to anyone it wants, *in Congress,* and can thus deprive him of his place on the seniority ladder; but it cannot prevent him from using the party label in his home state or district, winning the party's nomination, and getting himself re-elected under the party's banner.

The argument for cohesive, disciplined parties is nevertheless a persistent one. Not only does such a party system provide the possibility of truly responsible government; it also gives voters a meaningful choice at the polls, for it assumes that each party will develop a clear-cut program which it will carry out if it gains power. This need for a program which is coherent and can be put into effect is probably the strongest argument that can be made in favor of a revision of our party system. When our great competitors, the Soviet Union and China, can announce "five-year plans" of far-reaching effect on life in those countries, and can carry out those plans, we may be at a disadvantage if our government cannot even develop a coherent legislative program. Americans don't want to trade their democracy for five-year plans. The proponents of party reform suggest, instead, that our government could act more swiftly, consistently, and farsightedly without our giving up democracy. They say that a system of disciplined, "programmatic" parties would make it possible for Congress to make long-range plans with reasonable assurance that these plans will be carried out. They say, furthermore, that when people know what they are voting for—one or the other party's program—and know that if their party wins, the bills which they want to see passed will indeed be enacted, there is more true democracy than when the voters are unsure of the issues and cannot count on any action even though their party wins a majority in Congress.

*Presidential Leadership.* The scope of proposals for "programmatic" parties, however, cannot be confined to party unity in Congress. It must include the presidency. For the presidency is a position of leadership. And if presidential campaigns are not mere popularity contests but involve policy issues, and if party programs mean anything at all, the President is committed to a program. The fulfillment of his and his party's campaign promises depends largely on Congress. Perhaps, then, the road to more responsible government lies in the direction of strengthening the President's legislative leadership—of making his position more like that of a parliamentary prime minister. Suggestions along these lines have, again, been influenced by the British model. Some are very modest. A proposal made many years ago by Woodrow Wilson, for instance, and revived by Senator Kefauver, is that members of the President's cabinet regularly appear before the Congress to answer questions—inquiries about not only executive action but about the

President's legislative program. (Cabinet members, of course, do frequently do this, not before Congress as a whole, but before House and Senate committees.) Some are extreme, requiring amendment of the Constitution. Typical of these radical suggestions was one which would authorize the President, if Congress failed to enact his program, to dissolve the Congress and call for an immediate new congressional election.

Quite conceivably, our future history may show that some or all of these various proposals for strengthening majority control and clearly focusing responsibility were timely and that failure to adopt them dangerously impaired our government's ability both to act swiftly and to plan for the years ahead. Our past history, however, militates against their adoption. From the very beginning of our national existence we have shied away from the idea of complete control by the majority. Likewise, we have been reluctant to allow one man, the President, to dominate the government. Not all Americans are convinced that "programmatic" parties, sharply opposing each other, would be good for the country: a century ago, when the major parties did offer a clear-cut policy choice, the losers would not abide by the decision at the polls and the result was civil war. Finally, there is the familiar argument against all change: for nearly a hundred years we have got along pretty well under our present system, haven't we? It has its imperfections, but any alternative might be worse. The shortcomings of Congress in terms of responsiveness to public opinion and majority responsibility have not aroused widespread dissatisfaction with the institution of Congress itself or with the incoherence of our present political parties. Most people, apparently, are either unaware of them or are ready to put up with them in the belief that they neither imperil the nation nor seriously deviate from the fundamental principles of democracy and representative government.

Some thoughtful observers go further than this. They rejoice in the very things which seem to fall short of the democratic ideal. For, they say, free government demands first of all consensus— a willingness on the part of virtually all the people to obey the rules. The notion of fiercely contending programmatic parties and unified legislative majorities makes them shudder. To them, it seems to portend oppression, disunity, and finally that paralysis of government which leads to dictatorship. Too zealous an insistence on conforming to a "pure" democratic model can lead only to the destruction of whatever democracy we do have. So, they say, it is a fortunate thing that our parties embrace all shades of opinion and cannot with assurance promise to put a program into effect; it is well that the party battle is only one factor in congressional law-making, and perhaps a minor one at that. (In 1962 on nearly half of all roll calls in House and Senate most Democrats and most Republicans combined *with each other* to form a large over-all majority.) It is good, they say, that policies are formed in a struggle between many different interests, a struggle which ends in compromise. Under such a system, government can govern because people will allow it to govern. The nation can stay united and internally at peace. The democratic model, so the argument runs, can remain as a kind of sun, brightening our understanding and warming our efforts to build a free and *somewhat* democratic society; but we had better circle it in wide orbit, for if we get too close to it we shall be consumed.

CHAPTER **15**

# *The Presidency*

The President of the United States is the nation's chief diplomat and the commander-in-chief of its armed forces. Because foreign policy is today a matter of life or death for whole peoples if not of all mankind, and because the United States is the most powerful nation of the free world, the President's primacy in foreign policy makes the presidency the most important office in the country and one of the two or three most important in the world.

It was not always thus. Most of the time for a century (1814-1914) our international relations were of secondary interest to ourselves and of very little significance to anyone else. During that period we had numerous Presidents who did not try to be national leaders. And when, near its end, Woodrow Wilson prophetically described the presidency as the "vital place of action in (our) system," he was not thinking particularly of foreign policy. Rather he was advocating presidential leadership of Congress in matters of domestic legislation. In 1913 he put his precepts into practice, presenting a legislative program to Congress and actively pushing it to enactment; twenty years later, Franklin D. Roosevelt did the same. There emerged a popular image of a "strong" President, meaning one who went beyond the mere words of the Constitution and used all the power and influence at his command to get

447

Congress to pass the bills he proposed. By 1952, if not before, it seemed that, at least in peacetime, legislative leadership was the central task of the presidency and that Presidents would be judged by their performance of that task.

The emphasis, however, was to some extent misplaced, for by 1952 it was partially out of date. We can grant the great significance of the presidency in terms of the making of domestic policy through the persuasion of Congress or by executive action and still realize that, in the age of the hydrogen bomb and the intercontinental ballistic missile, responsibility for foreign policy overshadows everything else in the White House. That modern Americans instinctively grasp this seems apparent from the voters' behavior in 1956. When he came to office in 1953, President Eisenhower, unlike Wilson, Truman, and the two Roosevelts, had no liking for the notion of a "strong" Presidency. Theoretically he preferred the old idea of Congress originating the laws and the President carrying them out; as a practical matter, he could not turn the clock back that far, but in his first term (as in much of his second) his legislative leadership had been desultory and comparatively ineffective. Dissatisfaction was evident when in 1956 the voters elected Democratic majorities to both the House and the Senate: yet simultaneously they reelected Mr. Eisenhower by a very large margin. Why? Because we were at peace, and people believed that our best bet for staying at peace lay in Mr. Eisenhower's continued presence in the White House. (And if war threatened, as it did most ominously the weekend before Election Day, then as a great general he was the best bet for wartime, too.) Admittedly other reasons played a part in both Eisenhower victories, but in 1952 the most effective sentence in his campaign was his foreign-policy pledge: "I will go to Korea," and the 1956 result seemed clearly to show that while Republicans in Congress were blamed for domestic ills, the question of choosing a President turned on considerations of international relations and national security.

We will begin our study of the presidency, then, with a look at these roles of chief diplomat and commander-in-chief. But we must realize that even these roles would be less significant were it not for the importance of all the other parts which a President must play. To some extent, at the very least, he must be a legislative leader, for foreign policy often requires congressional cooperation. To be most effective with Congress, he must operate, too, as the leader of his political party. Congress has delegated to him considerable authority to manage segments of the national economy. The Constitution makes him the head of the executive branch. And in addition to all of these responsibilities, he has the ceremonial duties of "chief of state," and stands before his countrymen and the world as the living symbol of a free people. These are not all completely separate parts, each to be played in a different costume on a different stage. They are all presidential functions. Each adds to the effectiveness of the others. Power in matters of foreign policy enhances a President's influence with Congress, and, vice versa, his skill in leading Congress adds to his effectiveness in foreign affairs. Conversely, a President who fails as a chief executive (by, for example, appointing crooks to high office) finds his influence diminished all across the board. But in the dangerous world we live in, it would take abysmal failure in the White House to deprive him of his predominance as the chief of foreign policy. The Constitution, the nation's history, and the inexorable demands of the present and the future all force that great responsibility onto his shoulders.

## NEGOTIATOR IN PEACE, COMMANDER IN WAR

Foreign policy is aimed at the satisfaction of "national interests" through dealings or other contacts with foreign countries, with full protection to the nation's physical security. In the past, it has been formed out of an amalgam of private economic interests, patriotism, idealistic adherence to general principles, and calculations of how best to prevent or avoid disastrous war; the last of these is probably the most important factor now. It has been carried out mainly through diplomacy (the negotiating of agreements between governments) and war when negotiations fail. War has often been thought of as the result of a failure of diplomacy. This, certainly, would be true of a major atomic war now. In the past, however, war has often been an extension of diplomacy, a calculated part of foreign policy itself. Foreign policy has aimed at preventing war which would be disastrous, but not war which might be won at comparatively little cost. In our own history, the wars with both Mexico and Spain were entered by deliberate choice of the policy-makers on the correct assumption that they would not bring ruin to the United States. The same is true of the War of 1812, except that the optimism of the "war-hawks" on that occasion was not wholly justified. In recent years the stakes have risen. For us, now, they are nothing less than physical and national survival and the maintenance of individual freedom and self-government. The arena has widened, including all the world all the time (where we used to worry occasionally about Great Britain or Venezuela) and the tools have come to include financial aid to other countries, the institutional mechanisms of the United Nations, and the techniques of persuasion beamed at the "uncommitted" people of the world.

In making and carrying out American foreign policy, the President is the prime mover. The Constitution is not explicit about his peacetime role, except for those brief provisions which authorize him to appoint and receive ambassadors and to make treaties with the advice and consent of the Senate. Yet the Supreme Court has referred to the "power of the President as the sole organ of the federal government in the field of international relations" [1]—an overstatement, perhaps, in view of Congress's necessary functions, but a reminder that among nations, our government must speak with one legitimate, official voice, and that voice is the President's.

Presidential utterances purporting to speak for the nation began early. In 1793, as war broke out between Great Britain and revolutionary France, President Washington issued a Declaration of Neutrality. Thirty years later came another historic presidential statement of policy—the Monroe Doctrine. Our own century has seen the promulgation of the "Open Door" policy in China, Wilson's neutrality proclamation in 1914, the Truman Doctrine of containment of communism in the eastern Mediterranean, Eisenhower's commitment of the nation to the defense of Formosa and (less unequivocally) the islands of Quemoy and Matsu, and Kennedy's readiness to use force if the Russians tried to break

---

[1] *U.S. v. Curtiss-Wright Export Corp.*, 299 U.S. 304 (1936).

the American naval blockade of Cuba in October, 1962. The Constitution, of course, gives to Congress the sole power to declare war. Yet the examples just given are in effect presidential pledges, not congressional decisions, to go to war under certain conditions; and neutrality proclamations are virtual pledges not to go to war, at least unless the circumstances change. Thus the President can, and does, take steps which in effect tie Congress's hands, for his commitments are those of the United States and to meet them is a matter of national honor. On the other hand, under the Constitution Congress can, and does, have a considerable negative impact: not so much in its authority to declare war as in the Senate's right to reject treaties and in the congressional power of the purse.

## Treaties and Executive Agreements

Congress has no formal authority to make commitments to other nations, but, though seldom exercised, the Senate's negative power —or, rather, the power of one-third plus one of the senators present and voting—to disapprove of a treaty is a severe limitation on the executive. The classic example of senatorial rejection of a major treaty is, of course, the defeat of the Versailles Treaty at the end of World War I. President Wilson brought that document back from France in the summer of 1919 to find bitter opposition arising. The treaty included the Covenant of the League of Nations and would have made us a member of the League; it also contained provisions which were displeasing to various nations and their equivalent "national origin" interest groups in the United States. Wilson's own actions—his public request for the election of a Democratic Congress in 1918 and his failure to include any prominent Republican on the delegation which accompanied him to the "peace conference" in Paris—made it easy for the Republicans to claim that the President had made the treaty a party issue. They seized on it, in partisan fashion, as an issue which could be turned to their advantage; and eventually the treaty was rejected by the Senate.

The lessons of that debacle have not been forgotten by later Presidents. They realize that any major treaty may well be doomed if it is presented in partisan guise, for Senate approval requires a two-thirds favorable vote, and the minority party is almost sure to hold at least one-third of the Senate seats. They understand, too, the importance of bringing influential senators into consultation and, if possible, into the very negotiations themselves, before any treaty is agreed upon. The political groundwork must be laid very carefully, as it was by President Roosevelt in planning the steps that took us into the United Nations and by President Truman before submitting the North Atlantic treaty to the Senate. Clearly the President is responsible for originating treaties, whether he conducts the negotiations himself or, as is more usual, that task is entrusted to his secretary of state; but equally clearly the omnipresent possibility of Senate rejection dictates the President's preliminary tactics and influences the nature of the treaty itself.

When an international agreement, to be really effective, depends on later legislative action by Congress—as, for example, the passage of an appropriation act—common sense makes it desirable to formulate such an agreement as a treaty. A President would be in a poor position to ask for congressional legislation to carry out an obligation which had not first been approved by the Senate. When such legislation is not immediately necessary, however, or where Congress has already indicated its acquiescence, formal treaty-making can be dispensed with. The President can, instead, make an *executive agreement* with another country or countries. This is just as binding as a treaty and does not require senatorial approval. The "Open Door" policy, referred to above, was embodied in an executive agreement with China; the establishment of formal relations with the Soviet Union in 1933 was accomplished by an executive agreement; and the "destroyer deal" of 1940, when President Roosevelt "traded" over-age destroyers to Great Britain in return for the right to establish bases on certain British islands, was an executive agreement. In the last quarter-century the great majority of our binding arrangements with other governments have taken the form of executive agreements rather than treaties. Many of these have been authorized by Congress, especially those concerning "reciprocal" tariff policies, but others have been purely executive acts, based not on any power delegated by Congress but on the inherent powers of the presidency itself.

The Constitution makes treaties the "law of the land," and the

Supreme Court has held that executive agreements have the same high status. Furthermore, the Supreme Court has held that treaties and executive agreements can deal with matters which the Constitution does not expressly delegate to Congress—undefined subjects of national concern. (Some critics say that such subjects, being undefined, are reserved for state action by the Tenth Amendment.) The range of presidential power is, therefore, very great. So great is it, indeed, that in the 1950's a serious move was made to limit it by amending the Constitution, and a version of such an amendment, originally proposed by Senator John W. Bricker of Ohio, fell only one vote short of Senate acceptance. The Bricker amendment was aimed in part at making executive agreements effective within the United States only with congressional approval.[2] The objections to it were based on principle and on realism. The principle was that the President should and must have a free hand in foreign policy: in a world where every relationship with other countries may be a matter of national survival, and when instantaneous action may be vital, the country must have a single leader with full power to speak in its name and to direct its action. To this principle of presidential supremacy in foreign affairs can be opposed, of course, the principle of government through representatives: after all, the Constitution itself reserves to the Congress, not the President, the power to declare war. But there is a less adequate answer, if any answer at all, to the realistic argument that Bricker amendment or no Bricker amendment, the President's actual power is such as to commit the nation irrevocably when he wishes to do so. He holds this ultimate power chiefly because he is commander-in-chief of the armed forces.

## Commander-in-Chief

Assuming correctly that George Washington would be elected President of the United States, the framers of the Constitution

---

2 Another objective of the Bricker Amendment was to prohibit treaties which were inconsistent with the reservation of state discretion in the Tenth Amendment. The Supreme Court has held that despite the Tenth Amendment, a treaty can authorize the federal government to do things not delegated to it by Article I, section 8. *Missouri v. Holland,* 252 U.S. 416 (1920). That case upheld a treaty for the protection of migratory birds, a matter which the Court had held to be beyond the scope of Congress's power.

may have imagined him leading the army in the field when they agreed to assign the duties of commander-in-chief to the presidency. However that may be, that clause has become a landmark in the history of free government. It placed a civilian official at the head of the armed forces of the nation. No President, in office, has ever worn a military uniform. Experience in many countries has shown that a chief of state who is also a military officer may easily become a tyrant, whereas a government headed by a civilian who does not command the military is ripe for a coup d'etat. In contrast, we have made the presidency a civil office, yet endowed it with ultimate authority over the military. Generals have occupied the White House—Washington, Jackson, Harrison, Taylor, Grant, Eisenhower—but every one of them saw the presidency as a civil office. They did not seize additional power for themselves through their control of the armed might of the nation.

Nevertheless, the power granted by the Constitution is sufficient to strengthen the predominance of the President in foreign affairs. It is of first importance in war; it can also shape international relations in time of peace. The wartime responsibilities of a commander-in-chief are, of course, almost unimaginable, putting a crushing weight on the back of even the strongest President. Consider the Presidents in the three great wars which the United States has fought—Lincoln, Wilson, F. D. Roosevelt. Take a look at their pictures "before and after." The longest foreign war in which we have been engaged was World War II, and in that struggle, above all others, foreign policy considerations vied for attention with purely military plans. Our commander-in-chief had to win the war, but he also felt responsible for developing stable conditions of peace after the victory. The strategy of the Western Allies against Nazi Germany was aimed not only at the military defeat of Hitler, but also at the perpetuation of a workable accord with the Soviet Union and the prevention of Soviet domination of Europe. These two political aims were, of course, hardly compatible. The hope of creating conditions which would avert eventual strife between the West and Russia led President Roosevelt to emphasize the first of them, whereas the British prime minister, Winston Churchill, urged an Anglo-American reconquest of southeastern Europe in the hope of achieving the second.

Military strategy, in other words, was inextricably involved with foreign policy.

The far-reaching impact of the President's military decisions is most dramatically illustrated by two made by President Truman. The first was to drop the atom bomb on two Japanese cities. The second was to "keep the secret" of the bomb from potentially hostile powers and also, unless careful controls were imposed, from the United Nations. The bombing of Hiroshima and Nagasaki was urged upon the President on military grounds, and the subsequent policy of secrecy on the basis of its making the United States unassailably powerful. Hindsight raises questions about these decisions, in terms of the first one's effect on the moral position of America in the present struggle to win men's minds to the cause of freedom, and the second one's futility. Wise or unwise, they made history—and they were the commander-in-chief's decisions.

Mr. Truman made other historic decisions as commander-in-chief. When West Berlin was blockaded in 1948, he refrained from sending ground forces to its aid but directed the air force to fly supplies to the beleaguered people. Within a few hours of hearing the news of the invasion of South Korea in 1950, he ordered American fighting men into action. He did this without consulting Congress and despite the cautious reaction of his secretary of state. Right or wrong, it was the action of a strong President, committing the nation to a course of action which he believed to be required by the circumstances and by our obligations as a member of the United Nations. In each of these instances, foreign policy and military considerations were interwoven: the President had to interpret the nature and extent of our national commitments to our allies, the UN, and the people of West Berlin and South Korea, and weigh the risk of all-out war and the chances of military victory.

Without sending troops directly into action, other Presidents in their capacity as commander-in-chief have brought about situations where war was inevitable or frankly risked. President Polk in 1846 ordered American soldiers into territory claimed by Mexico, after relations between the two countries had been severely strained by their differences concerning Texas and the admission of Texas to the Union. Polk expected that the Mexicans would fight. They did; by the time Congress was asked by the President to declare war, the shooting had begun. In 1955 President Eisenhower felt it prudent to ask Congress to pass a resolution confirming American intentions to defend Formosa and, if necessary, Quemoy and Matsu; but as our forces had long since been committed for that purpose, and the prime value of the American stand was as a deterrent against attack on those islands from the Chinese mainland, Congress felt that it had no freedom of choice in the matter. Mr. Eisenhower's swift decision to land American marines in Lebanon in 1958 was a commander-in-chief's action taken without the specific approval of Congress. It was a military order; yet it was also a foreign-policy decision, designed to check Soviet or Egyptian operations (or both) in the Middle East. Mr. Kennedy's blockade of Cuba, designed to force the Soviet Union to remove its missiles from that island, was ordered with full awareness that war might swiftly result.

Foreign policy, then, is more than treaty-making; it can be made, too, by the movements of planes and ships and men. In the dim past, the President as commander-in-chief seldom made significant policy decisions because, for one thing, he did not have much armed force to command. Now we are in an altogether different age. Whatever the commander-in-chief does or refrains from doing has repercussions all over the world. Inevitably our foreign policy is as readily shaped by the deployment of our might as our military decisions are determined by our foreign policy.

### The "War Power"

The President's constitutional duty to "take care that the laws be faithfully executed" occasionally entails the use of military force on our own soil and in peacetime: thus Cleveland ordered soldiers to Chicago in 1893, Eisenhower sent paratroopers to Little Rock in 1957, and Kennedy dispatched substantial forces to Oxford, Mississippi, in 1962, in each case to support the "law of the land" as decided by the courts. But within our national boundaries it has been in time of war that presidential power has reached its zenith. Technically, its basis is uncertain. It stems partly from the commander-in-chief's authority, but it goes far beyond the commanding of the armed forces. The presidential order removing

Japanese-Americans from their homes in World War II, discussed in Chapter 8, was an exercise of a broad "war power," and so were many of Lincoln's Civil War decrees, including those which increased the army and navy and subjected civilians who discouraged enlistment to the justice of military tribunals without the privilege of the writ of habeas corpus. These executive actions, to be sure, all involved military force to some degree and so were related to the power of the commander-in-chief, but in the main they coerced civilians, not soldiers. In World War II Franklin Roosevelt assumed that his "war powers" included authority to run the economic life of the country. He told Congress quite flatly, in September, 1942, that if it did not enact adequate price-control legislation by October 1, he would impose price controls by executive decree. This threat (which did not have to be carried out, for Congress acted in a hurry) reflected a realization that modern war involves not just armies and navies but the whole citizenry, its achievements in production and its adequacy in distribution.

If Mr. Roosevelt had had to act—and there is no serious doubt that he would have done so if Congress had failed to—would his action have been constitutional, or would it have been checked by the courts? There can be no definite answer to that question. Significant, however, is the fact that during a war, the Supreme Court has inclined to uphold the widest possible use of presidential power. As we have seen, in the first cases involving Japanese-Americans the Court sustained executive. decrees which seemed to many Americans not only to lack any constitutional foundation but actually to violate specific constitutional prohibitions. The Supreme Court did set aside Lincoln's order that civilian objectors to enlistment should be court-martialed and denied the privilege of habeas corpus, in areas where the civil courts were functioning, in *Ex Parte Milligan,* 4 Wallace 2 (1866); but, significantly, this decision was not made until after the war was over.

When there is no *declared* war going on, the question of the extent of the President's "war power" is less clear. During the fighting in Korea, which was a "police action" by the United Nations in which many Americans were dying, a steel strike impeded the production of *matériel* for our armed forces. In April, 1952, while Congress was in session, President Truman ordered his secretary of commerce to seize the steel mills and resume production, the strikers having indicated their willingness to work for the government. The Supreme Court promptly held that the order exceeded the President's authority and was invalid, in *Youngstown Sheet and Tube Company v. Sawyer*,[3] but three justices published their vigorous disagreement with this decision. The *Youngstown* case indicated that even with fighting going on, there were limitations to the "war power" in its extension to economic activities, despite the close relationship between industrial production and military victory. Yet it is reasonable to wonder whether the Court would have decided against the President if the war had been of the magnitude of World War II or if Congress had not been in session when the President acted. The fact that Congress was sitting and could have been asked to pass a bill authorizing the seizure made the President's order appear to be a usurpation of the legislative function; it might have seemed, instead, to be a justifiable action to save the country (like Lincoln's orders increasing the army and navy in 1861) if Congress had not been in session.

### The Role of Congress

Despite rare judicial setbacks, the President's leadership in time of war has been fairly consistently confirmed by Congress. Although he was later harassed by a critical Congress, Lincoln's swift moves in 1861 were later "ratified" by congressional action; so, in effect, was Truman's undeclared war in Korea. Roosevelt's threat to rule by executive decree produced legislative results. There have been occasions when congressmen could safely challenge the President in wartime—witness the vigorous criticism of Polk during the Mexican War, a congressional attack in which young Representative Abraham Lincoln joined. And still today, if the fighting does not seem to jeopardize the national security, the President's conduct of it may be seriously questioned. When President Truman removed General MacArthur from his com-

---

[3] 343 U.S. 579 (1952).

mand in Korea, there was plenty of congressional criticism: in fact, MacArthur was invited to address a joint session of the two houses of Congress and was welcomed as a hero. Yet the significant thing about the MacArthur incident is that, despite the General's glamor and eloquence and the contrasting unpopularity of the Korean War, Congress in effect confirmed Truman's decision. In the atomic age there is little room for political argument over the conduct of a war. The responsibility must be centered in one place, in one commander. That place is the White House and that commander is the President.

But what about the conduct of international relations when there is no "shooting war," but, instead, a ceaseless economic and ideological conflict with unfriendly nations, a conflict which might at any moment develop into armed strife? Such a situation was unknown to us before 1946, but it is here now and seems sure to continue for many years to come. In this kind of a world, can the President prudently be checked by the people's representatives in Congress? In time of crisis, many a congressman feels that it is his patriotic duty to support the President—and we live in an era of perpetual crisis. Even so, however, there are degrees of crisis. Congress may feel that it must vote for whatever the President demands, for the sake of national unity, in moments when war seems immediately in prospect, but is less bound to follow the President when war is less imminent or when the presidential recommendations do not clearly point to military action or national survival.

In foreign policy matters, then, the President must still reckon with Congress. His primacy is recognized and his influence is great; yet the success of his leadership remains in considerable degree dependent on congressional approval. To be the leader of the nation in international affairs, he must also be a leader of Congress. In matters of domestic policy—and the relationship between domestic and foreign policy gets closer every day [4]—the need for him to play the role of legislative leader is equally clear

---

[4] The economic power of the United States in the world may depend in good part on its economic stability and prosperity at home; its ideological influence, especially among the majority of human beings who are dark-skinned, is affected by its own policies concerning human rights.

and decidedly more difficult. His part as "chief legislator," therefore, requires our careful examination.

## THE CHIEF LEGISLATOR

The President is a legislator in two ways. First, he participates
in the legislative process—not as a member of Congress, to be sure,
but as a political leader whose position carries more prestige and
potential influence than that of any congressman. Second, he
"makes laws." In the field of foreign policy, as we have seen, he
makes treaties and executive agreements with other nations, and
these become the law of the land. In an endless variety of domestic
matters, from price supports for farm products to the rules for
allocating graduate fellowships, he issues executive orders or his
subordinates promulgate regulations: these too are the law of the
land. True, a treaty (though not an executive agreement) goes
into effect only with the Senate's approval. True, too, that the
rule-making power is granted by Congress and is limited by conditions with which the executive branch must comply. The President, in other words, is by no means a dictator. All his legislative
influence is but one factor in what Congress does; all his rule-
making power (at least concerning domestic policies in peacetime)
is given him by Congress, and what Congress gives it can take
away. Nevertheless, no other individual has as much legislative
influence and power—if he wants to use it.

### As a Leader of Congress

The authority given to the President by the Constitution in
dealing with Congress is often spoken of as if it were very limited—
he can "merely" make "recommendations from time to time" and,
when he sees fit, disapprove measures passed by Congress. There
has always been great latent force, however, in this authority.
When the President speaks to other countries, he speaks "for the
nation"; it is understandable, then, that many people think that
when he addresses the Congress he is again speaking "for the
nation." The more sophisticated observer may believe that the
President's recommendations are essentially those of a party leader:
but if so, then once again they have extra weight, for they commit

**The President as chief architect of foreign policy.** Above, President Truman in an informal moment with Churchill and Stalin at Potsdam, Germany, where he conferred with the Allies' leaders concerning plans for post-war settlement and for the defeat of Japan, which occurred a month later. Below, the Vienna meeting between President Kennedy and Premier Khrushchev at the United States Embassy Residence in 1961. At right is an interpreter.

The seal of the President, with fifty stars, effective July 4, 1960.

**The White House** was deemed a "bully pulpit" by Theodore Roosevelt, shown in a characteristic pose, middle left, at Evanston, Illinois. For his distant cousin Franklin D. Roosevelt, right, it provided a "fireside" for comparatively informal persuasive radio talks to the people in their own living rooms. President Johnson (top) first chose the surprise news conference in preference to the formal one as he took over the presidential reins. Here he indicates a willingness "to meet with any of the world leaders anytime there is an indication this would be fruitful and productive."

his party to a program and summon his fellow partisans in Congress to fight for that program.

*"Tribune of the People."* The President is the one official (aside from the Vice-President whose office is virtually powerless) who is elected by all the people. His constituency is nation-wide. The local pressures that beat so fiercely on congressional doors are less direct, or at least more diffused, when they reach the White House. Their impact is reduced by their very number and by their tendency to cancel each other out. Many people assume, therefore, that when the President speaks, he speaks for all the people. Presidents themselves incline to assume this. After all, in international affairs the President's word is the word of the nation; why not in all domestic concerns as well? So there is nothing startling in even the somewhat mystical description of the presidency offered long ago by Woodrow Wilson: "A nation is led by . . . a man [to whom] the voices of the nation . . . unite in a single meaning and reveal to him in a single vision, so that he can speak what no man else knows, the common meaning of the common voice."

Now this may not be realistic. In statistical terms, if no other, there may be no such thing as a "common voice." The President of "all the people" was actually the choice of only slightly more than half of those who bothered to vote. Nevertheless, the nature of the office, especially its prestige, its primacy in foreign policy, and its national constituency make the President's words potentially more influential than any other. Theodore Roosevelt, the first of the modern "strong" Presidents, described the White House as "a bully pulpit." Some of his successors have used it not to preach to the people merely for their own good, but for the purpose of influencing Congress. "I will go to the country," warned Woodrow Wilson when he feared that Congress would not pass a bill he wanted—meaning that he would "take his case to the people" and count on them to persuade the Congress to support him. Later he did so, and other Presidents have done the same. They put their case to the people in various ways. The most direct method, nowadays, is the nation-wide television speech, a successor to the broadcast "fireside chat" initiated by Franklin Roosevelt. But the President does not have to go on radio or television in order to be heard. As no other man, he has access to the media of communication. Everything he says or issues is news: every casual remark, every carefully drafted mimeographed statement. One of his most effective means of getting his ideas across to the people is the press conference, a question-and-answer session in the White House attended by Washington correspondents of newspapers, news services, and the radio and television chains.[5]

The very fact that the White House is such a "bully pulpit" enhances its occupant's influence with Congress. When the President takes a stand, his side of the issue, if no other, can be set forth in full before the public gaze. Added to the weight of his arguments is the greatness of his office—and, in some instances, his personal popularity as well. No one else has such a chance to mold public opinion, and it is to public opinion that congressmen ultimately respond.

Nevertheless, the President cannot command; he can only try to persuade. Ingrained partisanship and the deeply felt interests of pressure groups are sure to provide resistance to his efforts. Speeches, press conferences, and prestige are seldom if ever enough to result in favorable congressional action, especially when the controversy is over domestic rather than international issues. A President who relies on them alone is not likely to be a successful legislative leader, however admirable and popular he may be. If he wants to lead Congress, he cannot stay forever "above the battle." More particularly, he must go into the arena of party politics and use his role as party leader to drive his measures to enactment. Even effective party leadership may not be enough: parties are not armies to be led, for competing interests split them into factions, and the opposition party may control Congress as it did throughout President Eisenhower's second term. Still it is the strongest potential weapon in the President's arsenal.

*Party Leader.* The rise of the party system vastly increased the President's legislative responsibility and influence. Responsibility,

---

5 Not surprisingly, it was President Wilson who initiated the press conference system. He and his successors found it useful not only as a way of explaining their stands on issues, but as a "feeling of the public pulse" in terms of the kinds of questions asked by the journalists. Franklin Roosevelt habitually talked "off the record" for a part of the time, giving the reporters unquotable background information—a persuasive technique (for it improved the newsmen's understanding of public problems) which subsequent Presidents have used little or not at all.

because in a presidential campaign he is the party's one real spokesman; few people read the party platform, but millions hear him speak. To persuade people to vote for him, he takes positions on matters of policy and promises results which can be achieved only through the legislative process. The pledges may be vague. They may concern mainly the executive branch and foreign policy as did President Eisenhower's campaign speeches of 1952. But even in 1952 the victorious candidate, speaking for himself and his party, directly or indirectly promised "sounder" financial policies, a less punitive attitude toward business, perhaps even a balanced budget—and all of these involved legislative action. Often the pledges are more specific, and specific or not, the people expect the President to take the lead. Not only the people but the partisan politicians expect him to do so. For ordinarily his record will be the party's record, and their personal fortunes as party candidates for office will be affected by that record. If the President and the President's program are both popular, the candidates of the President's party for all manner of offices will be more popular too: witness the Democratic sweeps in both 1934 and 1936, when the New Deal was at its highest point in public esteem. It didn't matter much, at election time in those years, whether a Democratic candidate for Congress favored all of Franklin D. Roosevelt's program or not: the party label was enough. In revealing contrast is the election of 1956, when President Eisenhower won easily yet the Democrats captured both houses of Congress. There was no question of the President's great personal popularity, but his legislative program was something else again— partly because he had failed to play the role of party leader effectively. Party leadership, unexercised, is no help to a President in getting Congress to adopt his program. Put to full use, however, party leadership can be the greatest single asset a President has in making legislative policy.

A newly inaugurated President has a wonderful chance to lead his party, even granting the loose, undisciplined nature of American political parties. Because he stands before the country as the victorious party's spokesman, a congressman of his party will not lightly oppose him. He is being hailed as a great leader (every President has a "honeymoon" during which he basks in the glow of public acclaim), and, who knows, he may become more popular still. Moreover, even the congressman who is skeptical about the duration of the new President's hold on the affections of the public knows that his own career may be damaged if he defies the White House, for a new President carries the very practical weapon of patronage. Although most federal positions today are under Civil Service, many important ones are not. Over the filling of most of these, the President has ultimate control. The President can use his appointing power to whip his congressional fellow partisans into line. As we have seen, many if not most congressmen are anxious to place some of their constituents in government posts; in times of depression, they are simply besieged by job seekers. Their continuing political success may depend on their getting jobs for these people. They are most reluctant, therefore, to risk losing their chance of placing their constituents by incurring the disapproval of the President.

It is in the first months of a new administration, especially when there has been a shift of control from one party to the other, that this presidential power of conferring or refusing patronage is most effective in keeping congressmen in line. Ordinarily, there are more jobs to be filled then than at any other time. Realizing this, Franklin D. Roosevelt, on coming into office in 1933, deliberately delayed making many appointments until after Congress had put through his far-reaching "recovery" program. The job-hungry Democrats stuck together, following the President's lead. Twenty years later, when the Republicans took over after a long absence from power, the same device might have been used by President Eisenhower to assure him of firm, if temporary, party control. The Eisenhower administration, however, was not ready with a legislative program to present to Congress. When it did present one, a year later, many positions had already been filled and the effectiveness of the patronage weapon was diminished accordingly.

Not rewards and punishments but personal persuasion is also a tool of party leadership which a President can use productively if he inclines to do so. He starts with every advantage: popular approval, constant publicity, and the great prestige of his office. The last is important. If you are invited to the White House, you don't decline; the invitation is a summons. If you have known the

President ever since college, when he was your classmate Bill, he is no longer Bill. He is "Mr. President." The greatness of the office engenders an aura of respect around the man who fills it. We may sneer at the President and tell caustic jokes about him, but we don't do that when we meet him face to face. If he has something to say to us directly and personally, we don't walk out on him; we listen, and we are quite probably impressed.

Presidential persuasion takes various forms, depending largely on the incumbent. Thomas Jefferson, who preferred conversation and letter-writing to making speeches, broke the early custom of appearing in person before Congress to deliver his "messages" reporting on the state of the union and recommending matters for Congress's consideration. A whole century passed during which the potential of presidential speeches to Congress went unrealized. Presidential messages were sent to the Capitol and there read aloud by the clerks of the House and Senate. Then Wilson, a former college professor who loved the lecture platform, changed the pattern. A born orator with a persuasive tongue, he went in person before joint sessions of Congress (the Senate and House sitting together in the large House chamber) to deliver all his major messages. This has been the custom ever since, at least for the annual "state of the union" message and others that may be called for in times of crisis.

Wilson went much further. True to his image of himself as a prime minister, in the early days of his presidency he departed not only from tradition but from his office in the White House to go to the Capitol and occupy an office close to the Senate floor while his legislative program was before Congress. This made quick and easy contact between the Democratic President and individual Democratic senators convenient and normal. What Wilson did in 1913 and 1914, however, did not become a custom. He "got away with it," thus early in his first term; but he was flying in the face of the deep-seated congressional desire for "separateness" which we noted in Chapter 4. No other President has followed his lead. His successors have, however, increasingly regularized their personal contacts with their party's congressional leaders at the White House—at breakfast in Coolidge's day, at early morning weekly conferences in Eisenhower's. Some, espe-

## PARTY LINE-UPS, CONGRESS AND PRESIDENCY, 1854-1962

| Election Year | Congress Elected | House | | | | | Senate | | | | | Presidency |
|---|---|---|---|---|---|---|---|---|---|---|---|---|
| | | Members Elected | | | Gains/Losses | | Members Elected | | | Gains/Losses | | |
| | | D | R | Misc. | D | R | D | R | Misc. | D | R | |
| 1854 | 34th | 83 | 108 | 43 | +48 | −16 | 42 | 15 | 5 | −3 | +5 | Pierce (D) |
| 1856 | 35th | 131 | 92 | 14 | −30 | +23 | 39 | 20 | 5 | −1 | +6 | Buchanan (D) |
| 1858 | 36th | 101 | 113 | 23 | −59 | −7 | 38 | 26 | 2 | −27 | +5 | |
| 1860 | 37th | 42 | 106 | 28 | +38 | −3 | 11 | 31 | 7 | +1 | +8 | Lincoln (R) |
| 1862 | 38th | 80 | 103 | | −34 | +42 | 12 | 39 | | +2 | +3 | |
| 1864 | 39th | 46 | 145 | | +3 | −2 | 10 | 42 | | +1 | 0 | Lincoln (R) |
| 1866 | 40th | 49 | 143 | | +24 | +27 | 11 | 42 | | 0 | +19 | Johnson (R) |
| 1868 | 41st | 73 | 170 | | +31 | −31 | 11 | 61 | | +6 | −4 | Grant (R) |
| 1870 | 42nd | 104 | 139 | | −16 | +64 | 17 | 57 | | +2 | −3 | |
| 1872 | 43rd | 88 | 203 | | +93 | −96 | 19 | 54 | | +10 | −8 | Grant (R) |
| 1874 | 44th | 181 | 107 | 3 | −25 | +30 | 29 | 46 | | +7 | −7 | |
| 1876 | 45th | 156 | 137 | | −6 | −9 | 36 | 39 | 1 | +7 | −6 | Hayes (R) |
| 1878 | 46th | 150 | 128 | 14 | −20 | +24 | 43 | 33 | | +6 | −4 | |
| 1880 | 47th | 130 | 152 | 11 | +70 | −33 | 37 | 37 | 2 | −1 | +3 | Garfield (R) |
| 1882 | 48th | 200 | 119 | 6 | −18 | +21 | 36 | 40 | | −2 | +1 | Arthur (R) |
| 1884 | 49th | 182 | 140 | 2 | −12 | +11 | 34 | 41 | | −2 | +2 | Cleveland (D) |
| 1886 | 50th | 170 | 151 | 4 | −14 | +22 | 37 | 39 | | +3 | −2 | |
| 1888 | 51st | 156 | 173 | 1 | +75 | −85 | 37 | 47 | | 0 | +8 | Harrison (R) |
| 1890 | 52nd | 231 | 88 | 14 | −11 | +38 | 39 | 47 | | +2 | 0 | |
| 1892 | 53rd | 220 | 126 | 8 | −116 | +120 | 44 | 38 | 3 | +5 | −9 | Cleveland (D) |
| 1894 | 54th | 104 | 246 | 7 | +30 | −40 | 39 | 44 | 5 | −5 | +6 | |
| 1896 | 55th | 134 | 206 | 16 | +29 | −21 | 34 | 46 | 10 | −5 | +2 | McKinley (R) |
| 1898 | 56th | 163 | 185 | 9 | −10 | +13 | 26 | 53 | 11 | −8 | +7 | |
| 1900 | 57th | 153 | 198 | 5 | | | 29 | 56 | 3 | +3 | +3 | McKinley (R) |

| Year | Congress | House D | House R | Oth. | D +/- | R +/- | Sen. D | Sen. R | Oth. | D +/- | R +/- | President |
|---|---|---|---|---|---|---|---|---|---|---|---|---|
| 1902 | 58th | 178 | 207 | 1 | +25 | +9 | 32 | 58 |  | +3 | +2 | Roosevelt (R) |
| 1904 | 59th | 136 | 250 |  | −42 | +43 | 32 | 58 |  | 0 | 0 | Roosevelt (R) |
| 1906 | 60th | 164 | 222 |  | +28 | −28 | 29 | 61 |  | −3 | +3 |  |
| 1908 | 61st | 172 | 219 |  | +8 | +3 | 32 | 59 | 1 | +3 | −2 | Taft (R) |
| 1910 | 62nd | 228 | 162 | 1 | +56 | −57 | 42 | 49 | 1 | +10 | −10 |  |
| 1912 | 63rd | 290 | 127 | 18 | +62 | −35 | 51 | 44 | 1 | +9 | −5 | Wilson (D) |
| 1914 | 64th | 231 | 193 | 8 | −59 | +66 | 56 | 39 | 1 | +5 | −5 |  |
| 1916 | 65th | 210 | 216 | 9 | −21 | +23 | 53 | 42 | 1 | −3 | +3 | Wilson (D) |
| 1918 | 66th | 191 | 237 | 7 | −19 | +21 | 47 | 48 | 1 | −6 | +6 |  |
| 1920 | 67th | 132 | 300 | 3 | −59 | +63 | 37 | 59 |  | −10 | +11 | Harding (R) |
| 1922 | 68th | 207 | 225 | 3 | +75 | −75 | 43 | 51 | 2 | +6 | −8 | Coolidge (R) |
| 1924 | 69th | 183 | 247 | 5 | −24 | +22 | 40 | 54 | 2 | −3 | +3 | Coolidge (R) |
| 1926 | 70th | 195 | 237 | 3 | +12 | −10 | 47 | 48 | 1 | +7 | −6 |  |
| 1928 | 71st | 163 | 267 | 5 | −32 | +30 | 39 | 56 | 1 | −8 | +8 | Hoover (R) |
| 1930 | 72nd | 216 | 218 | 1 | +53 | −49 | 47 | 48 | 1 | +8 | −8 |  |
| 1932 | 73rd | 313 | 117 | 5 | +97 | −101 | 59 | 36 | 1 | +12 | −12 | Roosevelt (D) |
| 1934 | 74th | 322 | 103 | 10 | +9 | −14 | 69 | 25 | 2 | +10 | −11 |  |
| 1936 | 75th | 333 | 89 | 13 | +11 | −14 | 75 | 17 | 4 | +6 | −8 | Roosevelt (D) |
| 1938 | 76th | 262 | 169 | 4 | −71 | +80 | 69 | 23 | 4 | −6 | +6 |  |
| 1940 | 77th | 267 | 162 | 6 | +5 | −7 | 66 | 28 | 2 | −3 | +5 | Roosevelt (D) |
| 1942 | 78th | 222 | 209 | 4 | −45 | +47 | 57 | 38 | 1 | −9 | +10 |  |
| 1944 | 79th | 243 | 190 | 2 | +21 | −19 | 57 | 38 | 1 | 0 | 0 | Roosevelt (D) |
| 1946 | 80th | 188 | 246 | 1 | −55 | +56 | 45 | 51 |  | −12 | +13 | Truman (D) |
| 1948 | 81st | 263 | 171 | 1 | +75 | −75 | 54 | 42 |  | +9 | −9 | Truman (D) |
| 1950 | 82nd | 234 | 199 | 2 | −29 | +28 | 48 | 47 | 1 | −6 | +5 |  |
| 1952 | 83rd | 213 | 221 | 1 | −21 | +22 | 47 | 48 | 1 | −1 | +1 | Eisenhower (R) |
| 1954 | 84th | 232 | 203 |  | +19 | −18 | 48 | 47 | 1 | +1 | −1 |  |
| 1956 | 85th | 234 | 201 |  | +2 | −2 | 49 | 47 |  | +1 | 0 | Eisenhower (R) |
| 1958 | 86th | 283 | 154 |  | +49 | −47 | 66 | 34 |  | +17 | −13 |  |
| 1960 | 87th | 263 | 174 |  | −20 | +20 | 64 | 36 |  | −2 | +2 | Kennedy (D) |
| 1962 | 88th | 258 | 176 | 1 | −4 | +2 | 68 | 32 |  | +4 | −4 |  |

SOURCE: *Congressional Quarterly*, Vol. 20, November 9, 1962, p. 2143.

cially Wilson and Roosevelt, have used the telephone, too, to charm, cajole, and if necessary insist.

Not all of this personal persuasion, to be sure, is undertaken as a task merely of party leadership; it is a part of legislative leadership in the larger sense. Sometimes a President confers with an opposition congressman: he must, occasionally, when the opposition controls the Congress. When an international crisis threatens, a private White House conference is likely to be bipartisan. In the main, however, his direct contacts are with his potential followers in his own party. Normally his best chance of getting Congress to do what he wants lies in obtaining their united support.

Whether all of these various means can achieve their goal of leadership of Congress at least when the President's party controls Congress depends first on how skillfully they are used, second on whether the President's program is generally acceptable, and third on whether the President is in his first or second term of office. The effectiveness of his various methods of persuasion depends not only on him but on his subordinates. The men he appoints to posts in the cabinet and in the White House can help him; they can also hurt him, either by tactlessness in personal relations or by failure to give real backing to his program. That program, of course, must have some merit if the President is to obtain any substantial support, and it will not gain united party backing if it is offensive to major factional interests within the party.[6] Finally, though all the tools are in the White House tool chest so long as a President is in office, they get duller and duller as time goes on. There is usually less and less patronage to give out or withhold. Though the respect remains, the early glamor fades. The interests offended by the President's program marshal their forces. Most damaging of all to a President in his second term is the old two-

---

6 F. D. Roosevelt's cautious silence on civil rights issues was undoubtedly dictated by his wish to remain effective as a party leader in Congress. Had he made "civil rights" legislation a part of his program, he would have incurred the wrath of the southern faction of his own party to an extent that would have jeopardized the whole program. President Truman, in contrast, spoke out for "civil rights" and promptly lost effectiveness in Congress, at least with respect to his domestic program. President Kennedy knew well that he was risking implacable southern opposition to the rest of his program when he called for a strong "civil rights" bill in June, 1963.

term tradition now enshrined in the Twenty-second Amendment. This puts everyone on notice that he cannot run again. His party starts looking for a new leader, perhaps one who will have different ideas. The President may still be personally popular and persuasive and he still has the veto power, but with his party and with Congress his affirmative influence is likely to be on the wane.

### As a Lawmaker

We have been considering the President's role as a political and legislative leader, one who must try to command a majority of the legislators. But he is more than a leader of other men. In recent decades he has become responsible for the origin of much of the legislation which he wants Congress to pass, and a lawmaker in his own right by the exercise of broad powers delegated to his office by Congress.

*Administration Bills.* The objective of the President's legislative leadership is the enactment of "his" program—which means that the program must be put together, approved by the President, and introduced as a bill or series of bills in Congress. In earlier times the White House concerned itself little, if at all, with bill-drafting. Even Woodrow Wilson, though acutely aware of his responsibility for pushing a program through Congress, originally stated it in very general terms and then endorsed measures offered by various congressmen—albeit in some instances he conferred with the bills' sponsors and insisted on the inclusion of particular provisions. The emergency of 1933 and the temperament of Franklin Roosevelt, however, brought about a lasting change. The ideas for new legislation in a time of crisis (every bank in the country was closed when Roosevelt took the oath of office) were generated, white-hot, within the executive branch itself. They were discussed with the President, formally drafted by one or more of his subordinates,[7] and taken up to Capitol Hill and given to a willing

---

[7] Most noted of F.D.R.'s draftsmen were Thomas G. Corcoran and Benjamin V. Cohen, lawyers in different executive agencies. Together they drafted the Truth-in-Securities Act (with James M. Landis), the Securities and Exchange Act, and the Public Utilities Holding Company Act. Another major bill, the Wagner Act, was the outgrowth of two years of conferences among a dozen or so lawyers and labor experts, almost all in government positions—although in that case, to be sure, one participant in many of the conferences was Senator Wagner's secretary.

congressman to introduce. Eventually so many agencies and even individual officials were submitting ready-made bills to the legislators that the President, unable to keep up with them, sought to bring order out of chaos by focusing responsibility for their approval in one man. He directed that no bill should be thus submitted until submitted to the director of the budget and found by him to be "consistent with the program of the President." Only when thus endorsed could a bill properly be called an "administration bill." Again there were more of these than Congress, slow-moving as it is, could stomach. Among them the President selected those he deemed worth fighting for. These became known as the *"must* list"—they were the measures which, the President said, Congress must pass. And for some years, Congress passed them.

The pattern set in those depression days, with some modifications, remains in effect today, although its usefulness is limited when the opposition party controls Congress. Many bills originate in the executive agencies. They "clear" the Bureau of the Budget or the White House, and when introduced in Congress are known to be measures approved by the administration. Those that are most important in the President's eyes become his "program." Also a vital part of his program is his annual budget, which embraces many policy decisions, as we saw in Chapter 13. His budgetary proposals, though subject to drastic change in Congress, at least are sure to get some results; Congress must pass appropriation bills if the government is to function. But what about his other policy recommendations embodied in "administration bills"? Since 1936, except during wartime, these have had hard sledding. Congress has resisted presidential pressure for the passage of bills dealing with controversial domestic issues, and often presidential leadership has failed to overcome this resistance even when the President's party controlled the Congress. President Roosevelt was not only hampered, in 1937-1941, by the difficulties inherent in a second term,[8] but had to lead a party which was sharply divided, north and south. President Truman was the victim of not

---

[8] This was before the adoption of the Twenty-Second Amendment, but the two-term tradition seemed unbreakable—Roosevelt himself broke it after war had begun in Europe.

only the same factional strife, but of his own choice of subordinates, some of whom were at best feeble advocates of his policies. President Eisenhower, at first by preference and later for other reasons probably including health, did not noticeably exert himself in an effort to lead either his party or Congress. President Kennedy showed considerable deference to Congress, partly because the coalition of Republicans and southern Democrats left him with only a tenuous majority. When the "civil rights" bill was introduced in 1963, he brought indirect pressure on Congress by inviting sizeable groups of leaders in business, labor, education, and religion to the White House and persuading them of his program's importance. In all these cases, however, a major exception must be made for measures concerning foreign policy. On foreign policy issues all four Presidents marshaled all the legislative support they could find, regardless of party, and achieved considerable success.

*Executive Action.* The other and more direct way in which the President "makes laws" is through the promulgation of executive orders and decrees. Usually these are based on statutes granting him the requisite authority. As we saw in Chapter 4, his actions based on such delegation of law-making authority are usually upheld by the courts, so long as Congress's general purpose is set forth and the statute provides some safeguards against purely whimsical, arbitrary conduct. Whatever legal fictions the Supreme Court may invoke, the fact is that the President and his subordinates are often given broad discretion to determine what is essentially legislative policy. Congress may provide that federal aid should be given to the people of drought-ridden or flooded areas, but the President and his subordinates decide when such aid should be granted, to whom, and (within the limits of appropriated funds) how much. The economic stabilization law enacted during the Korean crisis left it up to President Truman and, later, President Eisenhower to fix, within broad limits, the penalties for violation of executive regulations designed to keep wages from rising rapidly: Congress was in effect saying: "You, Mr. President, can enforce this law when, where, and as strictly as you see fit." Under such circumstances, the President's constitutional duty to take care that the laws are faithfully executed becomes far more than a mere administrative task. Instead of doing what Congress directs, he has to decide whether to do anything at all, and if so, what. In the same way, as Clinton Rossiter has pointed out, laws passed during the financial crisis of the early 1930's empowered the President, in effect, to control, curtail, or even terminate the banking operations of the Federal Reserve System and to suspend trading on the stock exchanges. These laws are still on the statute books. As Mr. Rossiter says, "The President has been statutorily empowered in the event of any future panic like that of March 1933 to declare what amounts to financial martial law." [9]

This presidential role of lawmaker is, of course, intimately connected with his role of chief executive. Indeed, the two may seem to be inextricably interwoven. For an executive is not just a policeman, nor is he a mere automaton carrying out orders. True, the President must administer and enforce the laws made by Congress; but with congressional approval he also makes vital policy decisions and clothes those decisions with the binding force of law. Sometimes he has issued orders without any congressional authorization, and the Supreme Court has held that he was justified in doing so because unspecified powers to maintain the security of the government and the peace of the community are inherent in the presidency itself.[10] In legal theory these are "executive" powers; but their exercise, and the exercise of the legislative authority delegated to him by Congress, would probably have greatly surprised the framers of the Constitution.

---

[9] Clinton Rossiter, *The American Presidency* (New York: Harcourt, Brace & Co., 1956. Paper-backed edition published by the New American Library as a Signet Key Book).

[10] The leading case is *In Re Neagle*, 135 U.S. 1 (1890). Justice Stephen J. Field of the Supreme Court had a mortal enemy in California, David Terry, who threatened to kill him. When Justice Field was going to California on judicial business, President Benjamin Harrison assigned Neagle, a deputy U. S. marshal, to act as his bodyguard. Field and Terry met; thinking that Terry was going to harm the justice, Neagle shot and killed Terry. Neagle was arrested for murder. He petitioned for a writ of habeas corpus. The prosecution argued that Congress had not authorized the President to assign a deputy marshal to guard a Supreme Court justice and that, therefore, Neagle had no official authority and so was acting as a private citizen when he shot Terry. The Court, however, freed Neagle, holding that the President did have the power so to assign Neagle, even though Congress had not said so.

## THE CHIEF EXECUTIVE

The familiar way of looking at the executive function is from the *administrative* standpoint. The successful executive, so the story goes, is he who follows the rules of sound administrative practice and whose organization complies with tested administrative principles. There should be a demarcation between "staff" and "line" agencies; plainly formulated delegation of authority; the "staff" functions should include planning; and throughout the organization lines of authority—the "chain of command"—should be clearly drawn. Moreover, no executive, including the man at the top, should be assigned a "span of control" broader than the limits of human capacity: in other words, a small number of officials should report directly to the President. These principles make a good deal of sense. They do guide the organization of many large corporations and the conduct of their officers. They do apply, too, to the huge business which is the government of the United States—but only to a limited degree.

They are not fully applicable because the presidency of the United States is different from the presidency of a corporation. The head of General Motors is not elected by the people, nor is he a party leader or a national symbol, nor can he issue decrees which bind anyone beyond his own subordinates. In contrast, the President of the United States is answerable to the people. Whether he likes it or not, he is a party politician. He is the ceremonial chief of state. And, as we have just seen, he is a mainspring of national policy.

He is also a chief executive, and as such he does need the proper administrative tools with which to work. At least since 1910, each President has asked that the executive branch be reorganized to bring order out of chaos and make effective, responsible administration possible. Several have established planning agencies, and some have sought to regularize the system of reporting upwards to the chief. All have delegated executive authority. Yet the perfect administrative structure must forever remain an illusion. They can delegate—but, as the sign on President Truman's desk read: "The buck stops here." They can complain, as President Roosevelt did, of the great number of officials who report, personally, to the White House; but they cannot slam the door any more than they can pass the buck, for the presidency is a political as well as an executive office. A corporation president can fire a department head with impunity; seldom will there be anything in the newspapers about it, rarely any protest from the board of directors, never a murmur from the stockholders. In contrast, let the President try to dismiss a member of the cabinet and the repercussions will be felt across the land. He can do it, of course, but he is risking the enmity of that official's friends, of whom there may be many in the country, the party, the administration itself, and most especially the Congress.

Indeed the President, who cannot dictate to Court or Congress, lacks control over a part of the rest of the government—the "quasi-judicial" regulatory agencies established by Congress. Ultimately, administrative control is made effective by "sanctions," especially the right to fire a person. In the case of the regulatory agencies, the President's power of dismissal was curtailed or abrogated by a decision of the Supreme Court, which held that a Federal Trade commissioner who had been appointed with the consent of the Senate could not be discharged by the President for a reason unspecified by statute in the absence of senatorial consent. The decision was in contrast with an earlier one upholding the President's sole power to discharge a postmaster. Together, the two decisions imply that although the President is the head of the executive branch, he is not the head of the regulatory agencies: the latter, despite the analysis of Baron de Montesquieu, seemingly constitute a "fourth branch" of government. We will deal with this distinction in more detail in the next chapter.

Limited particularly by political realities (which are just as "inherent" in his office as is the war power itself), the President who seeks to be a copybook administrator is likely to be distressed and frustrated. In contrast, one who frequently departs from accepted practice may find satisfaction in his executive tasks. Franklin Roosevelt (despite his occasional wish for a narrower "span of control") exuberantly disregarded the maxims of efficient organization again and again. He seemed to view administration as an art, fit for the intuitive innovator, rather than as the practical application of a science of management. During his twelve years in the White House there was a vast amount of administrative confusion, but there was also an unparalleled amount of governmental achievement. Perhaps, as the historian of his era suggests, more important to a President than proper management practices—significant though those may be—is "his ability to concert and release the energies of men for the attainment of public objectives. It might be argued that the essence of successful administration is: first, to acquire the ideas and information necessary for wise decisions; second, to maintain control over the actual making of those decisions; and, third, to mobilize men and women who can make the first two things possible—that is, who can provide effective ideas and information, and who can reliably put decisions into effect." [11]

Executive needs, whether we view them in terms of policy-making or efficient administration, can be met only if the chief is assisted by able people whom he trusts. To them he must turn over much responsibility for action. On them he counts for information and advice. The calibre of his administration depends in good part on the kind of men he appoints to high office and the use that he makes of them. In the past, and to a considerable extent today, the President has counted heavily on the people whom he names to head the departments of the executive branch: from the beginning, these department heads have formed his "cabinet." From time to time, a President has leaned, too, on unofficial advisers. For the last twenty years or so, Presidents have been greatly aided by the establishment of an "executive office" comprised of a group of staff agencies whose duties are to advise and inform the President and assist him directly in the performance of his executive functions.

*The Cabinet.* Nowhere does the Constitution mention the cabinet, nor has any act of Congress created it. Yet it is an established institution of the government and has been so at least since the days of Thomas Jefferson. It was created simply by the choice of early Presidents to call their department heads together for

---

[11] Arthur M. Schlesinger, Jr., *The Coming of the New Deal* (Boston: Houghton Mifflin Co., 1959), p. 522.

consultation and advice. Today it is composed of ten people—the Secretaries of State; the Treasury; Defense; the Interior; Agriculture; Commerce; Labor; and Health, Education, and Welfare; and the Attorney General and the Postmaster General. Nothing prevents the President from inviting other officials to join the cabinet, and some have indeed welcomed the heads of other agencies: yet when this has happened, the newcomers are not generally considered to be "regular" members, so firm is the acceptance of the idea that the real cabinet is composed of department heads and no one else. For instance, in Mr. Truman's day, the federal security administrator had most of the responsibility of the present Secretary of Health, Education, and Welfare, yet lacked "cabinet rank" or status. When by statute the "agency" was renamed a "department," the head of it automatically achieved that status.

The cabinet is an advisory body which meets at the President's pleasure. Its existence does not mean that we have "cabinet government" in the United States—far from it. In Great Britain and other parliamentary democracies, the cabinet is a policy-making unit which makes decisions and stands or falls together. Not so in the United States: the President's cabinet is no more than a group of counselors whose advice the President may accept or disregard, and its members may publicly disagree with one another.

Many observers have, indeed, wondered whether the cabinet is a particularly useful institution. They suggest that its meetings are largely a waste of the time of a burdened President. Two factors decrease the cabinet's potentialities as a consultative body. The first is that its members are themselves busy executives. Each runs a big department and must inevitably specialize on that department's problems. A Secretary of Agriculture has little time to prepare himself to give wise advice on defense policy; a Secretary of the Treasury is not necessarily a competent adviser on labor questions. The second is that the selection of cabinet members is seldom based on their capacity as general policy advisers. The President usually picks them for one of two reasons: either they are specialists in the affairs of the department which they are to head or they bring political strength to the administration. Thus Roosevelt chose the publisher of a farmer's weekly to be his Secretary of Agriculture, and Eisenhower's two Secretaries of Labor were, first, a union official and, second, a personnel and labor relations director. These Presidents and most of the others have also distributed some cabinet posts as if they were political "plums"—rewards for party service—or in the hope of fostering party unity: Lincoln, for instance, appointed his chief rivals for the nomination to his cabinet. By tradition the top cabinet post is that of Secretary of State (tradition long bulwarked by a statute, now repealed, which made that official the successor to the presidency if both President and Vice President should die),[12] and several times that position has gone to a party leader who had just missed the presidency: Henry Clay, William Jennings Bryan, and Charles Evans Hughes were all defeated presidential candidates who became Secretary of State. Today the urgency of foreign affairs points toward naming to that post not party leaders but specialists such as Dean Acheson, the late John Foster Dulles, and Dean Rusk. But neither politicians chosen to placate a disappointed party faction nor experts in particular fields, when brought together, necessarily are well suited as a group to advise a President.

Nevertheless, the cabinet can be useful to a President, if he wishes it to be, as a consultative body, as a means of instilling enthusiasm and unity of direction within the administration, and as a public relations device. President Eisenhower sought to increase its effectiveness in all three respects, establishing for the first time a formal "cabinet secretariat" with the duty of preparing agenda and maintaining records, and allowing some cabinet meetings to be televised. Whether such formal arrangements and such public meetings are conducive to the frank give-and-take usually needed in consultative sessions is open to serious question; but the "institutionalization" of the cabinet was undoubtedly effective in maintaining some cohesion in the Eisenhower administration during long periods when the President himself was incapacitated by illness. In his absence the cabinet continued to meet regularly, with the Vice-President presiding. More important, however, in providing cohesion and continuity, was the "institutionalization"

---

[12] The present law provides that on the removal, resignation, or death or disability of both President and Vice-President, the Speaker of the House shall become President.

of the presidency itself, a process which had hardly begun before the Executive Office was established in 1939, but which gained great significance in the Eisenhower years.

## The Executive Office

For over a century, Presidents got along with at most a handful of personal assistants—a secretary, a stenographer or two (but there were no typewriters in the White House until the eighteen-nineties, and President Wilson typed many of his messages himself), a mail clerk, and a messenger. Until the present century, moreover, they were private employees paid by the President himself. Gradually the staff increased, along with the President's duties. As late as the 1930's however, it was composed of only a few people, whose combined salaries came to $113,188. In contrast, in 1963 President Kennedy requested an appropriation of $4,380,000 for his official needs and his immediate staff.

What had happened was that President Roosevelt, in 1937, had appointed a Committee on Administrative Management to recommend ways of making it possible to perform the executive duties of the presidential office intelligently and efficiently. The committee was headed by Louis Brownlow, a man wise in the ways of politics and seasoned in public administration. The Brownlow committee, like the later commissions headed by Herbert Hoover, studied the organization of the whole executive branch, which is the subject of the next chapter. But it also analyzed the executive functions of the presidency itself, and its recommendations had a profound and lasting impact on that office.

The Brownlow report led to the formal establishment of the Executive Office of the President in 1939. That office, today, consists of the Council of Economic Advisers, the National Security Council, Office of Civil and Defense Mobilization, and the Bureau of the Budget. The first of these, composed of three men, aids the President in meeting his great though unofficial responsibility for guiding the country's economy toward stability and prosperity. The second and third play central roles in the formulation of foreign and military policy. The fourth—the Bureau of the Budget—is the vital one in promoting competent administration. In any large enterprise, budget-making is at the heart of the executive function. Nevertheless, for most of our history, the President had no direct control over it. Even when in 1920 the need for a single *executive* budget for the whole establishment was finally recognized and the President was authorized and directed to prepare and submit such a budget annually to Congress, the agency established to prepare the budget was one long step removed from presidential authority: it was attached to the Treasury Department. In 1939, however, the Bureau of the Budget was transferred to the new Executive Office, where it serves as a focal point and clearing house for the departments' financial requests and proposed legislation and seeks to improve the quality of administrative management throughout the executive branch.

The Brownlow report led also to the creation of a new personal staff for the President, comprised of six assistants who, according to the committee, were to be selfless public servants with a "passion for anonymity." True to form, Mr. Roosevelt, though deserving of credit for the reorganization of the executive, paid less than full attention to the formal administrative opportunities which the reorganization offered: at no time did he fill all six of the authorized positions. Those positions, however, did form a nucleus from which grew President Eisenhower's sizeable personal staff in the White House offices—an assistant to the President or civilian "chief of staff" plus three deputy assistants, the six not-so-anonymous administrative assistants, as well as a special counsel, an assistant counsel, and three secretaries, one of whom handled all relations with the press. Again the great importance of this staff was illustrated by the events following President Eisenhower's heart attack, when the "chief of staff," Sherman Adams, simply took over the executive management functions.

The presidency, now, seems well equipped with the tools of effective administration—so well equipped, indeed, that if a President does not watch out, he may find himself the captive of the presidency as an institution rather than a real chief executive. He can avoid this if he wishes. He can be the master of his administration if he cares to be. He may, on the other hand, prefer to allow his chief executive's role to be shaped largely by the institution which was created to aid him in performing it. No President has placed as much reliance on "staff operations" as President

Eisenhower. Conversely, Mr. Eisenhower voluntarily gave up executive command in a vital area, that of the budget. In 1957, he submitted his budget to Congress with suggestions that Congress might like to change it—a course which disturbed the believers in the executive budget system. Two years later, though he insisted that Congress should not increase his budget, he permitted his inferior officers, the four Joint Chiefs of Staff, publicly to demand increases for their branches of the armed services—and a few days later indicated that he would reappoint three of them when their terms expired. Whether as chief executive the Presidents stand forth as powerful individuals, masters in their own house, or become "organization men" controlled by the institution originally created to help them, depends in good part on their vigor, capacity, and taste for the executive job.

### The Unofficial Advisers

The institutionalization of the presidency may also be bringing to an end the role of the unofficial presidential adviser, the hand-picked confidante who has the President's ear. Probably, however, there will still be room for him. Presidents cannot always find the voice they want to hear in their own official entourage, nor can they always persuade the men they trust most to accept high public positions. Unimpressed by his cabinet, Andrew Jackson consulted with a so-called "Kitchen Cabinet" composed of his friends, men who in the main held minor government posts. Woodrow Wilson counted most on the advice of Colonel E. M. House, who held no official position at all. In Calvin Coolidge's private office sat, much of the time, a Boston merchant named Frank Stearns. Franklin Roosevelt had a "brain trust," men for whom he found minor posts in various departments; later his friend Harry Hopkins came to live in the White House, shared his thoughts, and spoke with, virtually, his voice in delicate foreign negotiations.

Recent Presidents, too, have enlisted "unofficial" help in the preparation of many messages and speeches. Lincoln presumably wrote the Gettysburg Address himself (whether or not on the back of an envelope), and Wilson composed directly on the typewriter. But many drafts of Franklin Roosevelt's speeches were prepared by men he chose, in and out of government, though he changed those drafts sufficiently to make them his own. Presidents Truman and Eisenhower, in contrast, tended to regularize this haphazard kind of procedure, relying largely on their official "anonymous" administrative assistants. Yet even Mr. Eisenhower, for help and advice, did not look exclusively to either his cabinet or his personal staff. When in 1959 he took a strong position in favor of a balanced budget, it was no secret that he had been influenced by two men especially—the president of the board of governors of the Federal Reserve System, William McC. Martin, and George M. Humphrey, a former cabinet officer but in 1959 an unofficial adviser. A man heavily relied on by President Kennedy was, indeed, a cabinet member, but his advice and help was given in fields beyond his own department: the President's brother, Attorney General Robert F. Kennedy.

The "Colonel Houses" of the future may become rarer than in the past, but Presidents, after all, are human. Occasionally, at least, they will turn to the people whom they most like and believe in, regardless of organization charts.

## The Succession

As we saw in Chapter 12, eight Presidents have died in office. Only one of them was succeeded by a Vice-President whom many people had seriously pictured as the right man for the presidency. The tragedy of the President's death stuns the people; even more overwhelmingly, it may stun his successor. "I felt," said Harry Truman, "as though the sun and moon and stars had all fallen on me." Yet the government has survived, and "successor-Presidents" have later won re-election in their own right.

One difficulty faced by Mr. Truman when he took the oath on the evening of April 12, 1945, was that he knew very little of what was going on "on the inside." He was unaware, for instance, that the first atom bomb was nearing completion. Like others before him, he had been leading a quiet life, presiding over the Senate to be sure, but excluded from the center of governmental power. At an earlier stage of our history, the country was not endangered by having an uninformed man—uninformed, at least, with respect to up-to-the-minute details of current controversies—suddenly thrust by fate into the White House. In World War II, the risk was certainly greater; but, fortunately, the struggle in Europe was virtually over when Truman took office, and the whole machinery of government, in the high gear required by war, was rolling ahead strongly. In the years since 1945, however, the development of intercontinental missiles and nuclear power has heightened the urgency of having a President who is "well-briefed" even *before* he takes office.

Doubtless in recognition of this newly urgent need, President Eisenhower entrusted his Vice-President, Richard M. Nixon, with various foreign missions and kept him reasonably well informed. Even more, President Kennedy treated his Vice-President, Lyndon B. Johnson, as a trusted colleague and potential successor. It was well that he did so. A nation shocked by the assassination of President Kennedy on November 22, 1963, took heart at the obvious "smoothness of the transition" to the Presidency of Mr. Johnson. The usual explanation—that Lyndon Johnson, more than any Vice-President since the early days of the republic, was by training and experience qualified for the presidency—was not the whole story. The fact that for nearly three years he had been kept in readiness by being a participant in crucial policy discussions in the White House was important, too.

The death of President Kennedy did arouse new doubts about the succession, however. A Vice-President, carefully selected as a potential President and kept fully informed, can take over without the people suffering a shattering loss of confidence in their government, however deep their sense of personal loss may be. But what if the new incumbent should die, too? Next in line for the presidency is the Speaker of the House of Representatives. He has a full-time job on Capitol Hill—far more demanding than presiding over the Senate, as we have seen. He was not picked or approved by the President as his running-mate and possible successor. He was not elected (even as the tail of the campaign kite) by the people of the country, but by voters in a single Congressional district. And—thanks largely to the Congressional custom of giving great weight to seniority—the Speaker is likely to be an old man. In November, 1963, when John W. McCormack suddenly became next-in-line for the presidency, he was seventy-one years old.

The succession, should the Vice-President become President and then die in office, is determined by statute. From 1886 to 1947, the statute made the Secretary of State next in line. The

Secretary of State is not an elected official, but he is the President's choice and presumably is close to the President at least in matters concerning foreign policy. The 1947 statute, naming the Speaker instead of the Secretary, was more "democratic" in that the Speaker has been elected by some voters, at least, and has been chosen as Speaker by representatives from all over the country. But the Dallas tragedy caused many to suggest, with more urgency than hope, that the old order be restored; they felt that for the sake of the nation's security it was safer to count on a presidentially chosen Secretary of State than a locally elected Representative whom the House has chosen as Speaker.

Another, related, question nagged those who recalled President Eisenhower's heart attack in 1955 and remembered that Lyndon Johnson had suffered an equally serious heart attack that same year. The Constitution provides that if the President shall suffer "inability to discharge the powers and duties of his office" the Vice-President shall perform them "until the disability be removed." But who determines whether the President is unable to do his job? Congress has never agreed upon a method of deciding about a President's "inability." Thrice, for protracted periods, Presidents have been physically incapacitated, and the country has had to get along without any active President.

So central is the office, so contingent are the strength and security of the country on the vigorous discharge of its "powers and duties," that we run a great risk in not closing this constitutional loophole, just as we run a risk when we nominate vice-presidential candidates without giving much thought to their presidential qualifications. Presidents can be "strong" or "weak." They can try to run things themselves or delegate most of their work to others. But when the chips are down, the responsibility is theirs—greater responsibility than rests on any other person in America. On how they meet that responsibility depends their ultimate place in history, and, very likely, the immediate fortunes of the nation. Tradition and custom exalt the office; its power extends beyond the dreams of Constitution-makers; administrative devices make its duties easier to perform; but only great men can keep it great.

CHAPTER 16

# The Executive and Regulatory Agencies

E ach April, hundreds of busloads of high school students descend upon Washington. Long lines of people stand outside the White House, waiting for a brief conducted tour of the President's handsome and historic residence and hoping in vain for a glimpse of the President himself. Then up to Capitol Hill go the sightseers for a brief glimpse of Congress at work. (Too few, however, attend committee sessions, where, as we know, so much of the real work is done; and too often the school vacation coincides with Congress's own Easter holiday, and the corridors and chambers under the great dome are largely deserted.) Some cross the plaza for a probably uncomprehending glance at the Supreme Court. Some, on the way to the Potomac, visit the Bureau of the Mint to see money "manufactured." Then the monuments, museums, and cherry blossoms beckon. Of all the federal government, much the biggest part goes virtually unnoticed. Aside from the Mint, the only operating agency which plays host to a horde of visitors, most of them youthful, is the Federal Bureau of Investigation.

Yet you really don't have to go to Washington to realize the extent and pervasiveness of the executive branch of the government. Take a day in the life of one citizen, a doctor—let's call him Francis Irving. The day is Monday, April 13. It is the day for Dr. Irving's monthly visit to the Veterans' Hospital in a nearby state, for he is a consultant for the Veterans Administration. He taxies to the airport, driving past a row of large, new apartment buildings upon which he casts an approving glance. He flies to a city a hundred miles away and from there is driven over a fine road twenty more miles to the hospital. His call there is short, and and he is back in his own office in the late afternoon in time to open his mail and dictate a few replies. One letter comes from a distressed patient, who complains that the local drugstore has refused to refill the prescription which the doctor gave him without special permission from the doctor. Home again for supper, he hears from his son the details of the opening game of the baseball season, which the boy has watched on television. Then he goes to his study to wrestle with his income tax blanks, which he must fill in and mail first thing in the morning if they are to reach the District Director of Internal Revenue before the April 15 deadline. Dr. Irving splutters over the complications of the forms and grunts crossly over the size of his tax: obviously, he says to himself, the federal government is spending too much money. What was Jefferson's idea? Ah, yes—that government is best which governs least.

It does not occur to him that on this ordinary day, federal agencies have been in the background of much that he has seen and done. The VA, yes, of course: he is on that agency's staff, and they pay him a small fee. But what else? Those apartment houses in the morning—private housing, wasn't it? Yes, but built on land which the city purchased and cleared with financial aid furnished by the Housing and Home Finance Agency. His airplane trip—on the plane of an airline licensed by the Civil Aeronautics Board, on a route designated by it, and at an altitude prescribed in accordance with its regulations. The drive to the hospital—over a highway built with federal aid and the engineering advice of the Bureau of Public Roads in the U. S. Department of Commerce. Back in the office—the mail awaiting him had been brought by the postman, an employee of the U. S. postal service, and the druggist who refused to refill a prescription was obeying a rule of the Food and Drug Administration in the U. S. Department of Health, Education, and Welfare. Home to hear his son describe the Senators' unlikely victory over the Yankees—which the youngster had watched over an unimpeded television channel allotted by the Federal Communications Commission. And finally, the grumbling hours in his study—to meet the demands not only of the tax laws made by Congress, but of the officials of the Internal Revenue Service in the U. S. Treasury Department, who have the job of collecting taxes. He is unhappy about the taxes, but if he stopped to review the day, he might find himself thinking with admiration of the new housing, with gratitude of the speed and safety of his travels, and with approval of the requirement of caution imposed on druggists. He might even stop taking for granted the ability of airplanes and television programs to avoid constant collisions and remember that the day's mail is not wafted to him on the wind. And in the end, he might conclude that Jefferson should be venerated not so much for his remark about "the least government" (however appropriate that was in the eighteenth century) as for his defense of individual freedom: quite specifically, Dr. Francis Irving's complete freedom to gripe about his tax forms and the extravagance of the federal government!

## THE EXECUTION OF THE LAWS

### Enforcement

The task of "faithfully executing" the laws has indeed become a vast one since Jefferson's day. What, in practice, does "executing" mean? We sometimes say that Congress makes the laws and the executive and judicial branches "enforce" them. Such phraseology reminds us of the early ideas about government's proper function: if government's job is to maintain order and protect people from violence, then its laws will be criminal or prohibitory statutes, making certain conduct illegal. The "execution" of such laws is the same thing as their "enforcement." You shall not, says Congress, kidnap someone and take your victim from one state to another; you are under arrest, says the F.B.I. when it catches you doing it. It is a crime, says Congress, to report your income falsely for the purpose of evading taxes; try it, and a treasury agent will be on your trail. Law enforcement is, therefore, included in the executive function.

## Performance

It is not, however, the whole of the executive function. Many federal laws carry no criminal penalties. They are not prohibitions; instead, they direct that something shall be done. The *carrying out* of these directions comprises the major part of the executive duties of the government. Congress establishes a program of old-age insurance; thousands of federal employees, not to mention a great quantity of electronic tabulating machinery, are needed to see to it that each claimant of benefits under that program receives what is due him. A statute says that the workers in a factory can, if they choose, be represented by a union; a federal board arranges for the holding of an election at which that choice is registered. Great sums are appropriated for aid to underdeveloped countries; men and women—not congressmen, but government officials—must do the paper work necessary to transfer the funds, and the field work needed to see how they are spent. These are but a few examples of what could be an almost endless list of tasks which must be performed to "carry out" the laws.

## Policy-Making

The last example, especially, is a reminder that in the process of carrying out the laws, a wide area of discretion is often left to the administrators. The latter become policy-makers in their own right. As we noted briefly in Chapter 4, the complexities of modern society have made law-making an exceedingly intricate business. Increasingly, Congress has acquired the habit of laying down general policies in its statutes and leaving to the executive the task of establishing more detailed policies within that broad framework. The basic reason for this, and the factors which make such "delegation of legislative authority" permissible under the Constitution, were stated by Chief Justice Stone in deciding a case wherein the validity of wartime regulations fixing maximum prices was challenged. These price regulations were issued by an executive official, the price administrator. Congress had enacted a law giving him general authority to prescribe maximum prices, but the act of Congress did not specify the particular price to be fixed for every commodity. Said Chief Justice Stone:

"Congress enacted the Emergency Price Control Act in pursuance of a defined policy and required that the prices fixed by the administrator should further that policy and conform to standards prescribed by the Act. The boundaries of the field of the administrator's permissible action are marked by the statute. It directs that the prices fixed shall effectuate the declared policy of the Act to stabilize commodity prices so as to prevent wartime inflation. . . . In addition the prices established must be fair and equitable, and in fixing them the administrator is directed to give due consideration, so far as practicable, to prevailing prices during the designated base period. . . . Congress has stated the legislative objective, has prescribed the method of achieving that objective—maximum price fixing—and has laid down standards to guide the administrative determination of both the occasions for the exercise of the price-fixing power and the particular price to be established. . . . The Constitution as a continuously operative charter of government does not demand the impossible or the impracticable. It does not require that Congress find for itself every fact upon which it desires to base legislative action. . . . The essentials of the legislative function are the determination of the legislative policy and its formulation and promulgation as a defined and binding rule of conduct—here the rule, with penal sanctions, that prices shall not be greater than those fixed by maximum price regulations which conform to standards and will tend to further the policy which Congress has established. . . . It is no objection that the determination of facts and the inferences to be drawn from them in the light of the statutory standards and declarations of policy call for the exercise of judgment [by the administrator] and for the formulation of subsidiary administrative policy within the prescribed statutory framework."[1]

*Quasi-Legislative Functions.* Chief Justice Stone's language indicates the reason for this particular delegation of "subsidiary" law-making authority—namely, the impracticality of expecting

---

[1] *Yakus v. United States*, 321 U.S. 414 (1944).

Congress to fix a particular price for each of thousands of commodities. It emphasizes the need for a clear statement of Congress's general policy and a set of "standards" to control or guide the administrator.[2] At the same time, the Court's opinion leaves the door open to a great deal of such delegation, for it virtually tells Congress that so long as it includes a policy statement and some standards (and those in the Emergency Price Control Act were hardly precise)—so long, in other words, as it does not wholly abdicate—it can turn over the day-to-day job of law-making to executive officials.

The executive agencies, accordingly, make "subsidiary" laws, which are just as effective as if they had been made by Congress. Often they are significant policy decisions. The secretary of agriculture, for example, has broad latitude in deciding whether, and when, to acquire certain commodities, and at what price; his decision may profoundly affect the whole agricultural economy. A treasury regulation, not an act of Congress, determines whether under certain circumstances graduate fellowships or the compensation of graduate research assistants are taxable or not. Not a statute, but the wage and hour administrator's rule, requires employers to retain their payroll records for a specified number of years. To be sure, the orders and rules and regulations, to be valid, must not contradict an act of Congress and must be within the scope of the general authority granted, and what Congress has granted it can take away. To that extent, the power wielded by the executive agencies is not precisely the ultimate legislative power; but, at the very least, it can be called "quasi-legislative" power.

In another sense, too, administrators perform quasi-legislative functions. As we have seen, some laws contain ambiguous language, and others provide no certain directives for dealing with unexpected circumstances. If a statute established a fellowship program for "graduate students," for instance, would it include in its benefits all those admitted by an accredited university for post-

---

[2] The absence of a precise statement of purpose, and especially of any prescribed standards to which the executive branch had to conform, had led the Court to hold the National Industrial Recovery Act invalid in 1935. *Schechter v. United States,* 295 U.S. 495 (1935).

graduate study, including first-year law school students who had been admitted after their junior year in college? When the Fair Labor Standards Act exempted "administrative" employees from its forty-hour-week provisions, was a stockroom clerk exempted, or a packing room foreman? In these kinds of situations, which are numerous, somebody has to decide what the statute means. Eventually this decision may be made by the courts. In the first instance, however, it is made by the administrator. In effect, he adds to the law passed by Congress new language spelling out what he thinks it means: he does this by issuing "agency letters," or "interpretive bulletins," or, especially when he feels sure of his ground, rules or regulations. Congress or the courts can correct him, but in practice such corrections are rare. For most of us, the "law" embodied in the administrator's interpretive additions to the statute is for all practical purposes the law of the land.

During the first third of this century, the rapid growth of law embodied in rules and regulations gave rise to considerable confusion. How such law was made varied from agency to agency, and although some rulings were publicized, others were not. Citizens trying to obey the law found it ever harder to know what the law was. Eventually, in 1935, Congress passed the Federal Register Act, establishing a daily publication, the *Federal Register,* and in essence providing that substantive administrative orders, rules, and regulations would become effective only upon their being printed in that weighty journal.

*Quasi-Judicial Functions.* In much of the executive establishment, therefore, the policy-making, quasi-legislative function is of prime concern to agency heads and their immediate assistants. In some of it, there is also a task which essentially is neither administrative nor quasi-legislative but resembles more the task of courts and judges—the job of deciding disputes and settling conflicting claims. Are four corporations eager to operate a television station using one particular channel? Obviously only one can use that channel; a federal agency decides which. Does a labor union complain that an employer is violating the Taft-Hartley Act by firing employees who join the union? The employer denies the charge, and a federal board determines whether an "unfair labor practice" has been committed or not. In each case a hearing is held at which the contesting parties present their evidence and argue their side of the case. In deciding such a case, an executive agency is acting in a "quasi-judicial" capacity. It can be reversed by the courts if it has misapplied the act of Congress under which it operates or if it reaches its conclusions arbitrarily, but in the normal course of events its decisions stand and are obeyed.

Such "quasi-judicial" functions are performed from time to time by many agencies throughout the government, but they are usually most notable in the case of the so-called "regulatory commissions," such as the Interstate Commerce Commission and the Federal Communications Commission, which apply to various industries the general policies laid down by Congress. Technically, as we saw in Chapter 4, these regulatory agencies may not be classifiable as parts of the executive branch of the government. Unlike the "old-line" departments, they occupy a peculiar position in the governmental structure, possibly constituting a "fourth branch" of government. This anomalous situation arose out of Supreme Court decisions holding that the President cannot, without senatorial consent, remove from office any commissioner who exercises quasi-judicial functions, except for a reason specified by statute.[3] In his opinion in the first of these cases, Justice Sutherland remarked that the Federal Trade Commission "occupies no place in the executive department" (branch), but left unanswered the question of what "place" the commission does occupy.

The fact is that even quasi-judicial agencies are engaged in political business, in a down-to-earth sense of that phrase. Especially when the statute vaguely directs a commission to decide disputes on some such basis as the "public convenience and necessity" is the door wide open for political maneuvering. Television channels and certain commercial airplane routes, for instance, are incalculably profitable privileges dispensed by government agencies. For the competing claimants to a particular channel, which can be allotted to only one, the financial stakes are very high. And as the agency which has to choose among them is not a court, and so is not protected by the traditions and ethics of the

---

3 *Humphrey's Executor v. United States,* 295 U.S. 602 (1935); *Wiener v. United States,* 357 U.S. 349 (1958).

judicial system, the temptation to exert pressure on its members often seems irresistible. Both congressmen and litigants have ready access to the commissioners, and when—as is not infrequently the situation—no one claimant has a sounder case than any other, personal or political advantage may play a part in the commission's decision.

There was a time when not only quasi-judicial functions, but all executive and administrative duties—the whole field of "public administration"—were assumed by influential scholars and analysts to be "nonpolitical." Indeed, public administration was thought to be not only nonpolitical but to be, in effect, antipolitical; its supposed guiding principle, in contrast to that of politics, was that of scientific rationality. The prophets of public administration put their faith in charts and axioms: they tended to see the problem of running a government as essentially an engineering problem. And of course, to a degree, they were right—but only to a degree. As more people, in days of depression and war, served a hitch in administrative posts, the wider spread an awareness that public administration, while it may profit by the tools of scientific management, is essentially and inevitably and unendingly a part of politics. For administrators make policy, and policy decisions are the ultimate prizes of the political struggle.

## ORGANIZATION

At the center of the "executive establishment" are the President and the agencies which comprise the Office of the President; of these, in organizational terms, the Bureau of the Budget is of special importance. Reporting to the President are the heads of the ten departments and a miscellany of nondepartmental executive agencies and government corporations and "authorities." In the curious no-man's land which we have mentioned, halfway, as it were, between the White House and Capitol Hill, are the regulatory boards and commissions.

### The Departments

Each department is directed by a secretary, appointed by the President (with the consent of the Senate) and automatically included in the cabinet. Each now has at least one undersecretary, second in command, and a number of assistant secretaries, varying roughly in accordance with the size of the department and diversity of its duties. Each includes divisions, offices, bureaus, and sections, the heads of which report through their superiors to a designated assistant secretary or through him to the undersecretary or secretary.

In Part V of this book, when we consider the formulation and execution of important policies, we will have occasion to become sharply aware of the roles played by some of these departments and their subordinate units. Here, therefore, we will take merely a quick, passing look at their major functions.

*State* is the successor of the old Department of Foreign Affairs in the days of the Articles of Confederation. It is responsible for informing and advising the President with respect to international affairs, and, to a large degree, for carrying out his foreign policy. Its Foreign Service provides careers; at home and abroad, for Americans attracted to the life of the diplomat. The American delegation to the United Nations reports to the State Department. Much of the "foreign aid" given to other countries is administered under its supervision. The ordinary citizen's most likely contact with the State Department will occur when he wants to journey abroad, for it has the responsibility of issuing (and sometimes withholding) passports for foreign travel. The department has grown prodigiously in the last quarter-century: this growth is reflected by the size of its "top echelon," where, under the secretary, there serve two undersecretaries, two deputy undersecretaries, and some eleven assistant secretaries.

*Treasury* was originally responsible for the management of the government's finances: the Budget Bureau, for instance, was attached to that department until 1937. Today it shares the tasks of suggesting and making financial policy with other agencies, especially the President's Council of Economic Advisers and the Board of Governors of the Federal Reserve System. It has the tax-collecting function, performed through the Internal Revenue Service; the tariff-administering function, performed through the Bureau of Customs; and it also enforces the laws against illegal trade in narcotics. The Secret Service, a dramatic detective and protective unit which long antedates the FBI, having been formed in 1860 to combat counterfeiters, is a branch of the department and so is the Coast Guard.

*Defense* came into existence, as a department, in 1949, after years of criticism of the division of the armed services into two departments, War and Navy. Not only were the army and navy subject to departmental separation, but between them there was traditional rivalry—and neither looked with favor upon the creation of a third coordinate armed branch, a separate air force. Eventually Congress adopted a plan which retained the old posts of secretary of war (changed, in name, to "secretary of the army") and secretary of the navy and added a secretary of the air force, but put all three under a Secretary of Defense. Only the latter is recognized as a cabinet member, despite the title of "secretary" borne by the other three. Perhaps the most significant thing about any or all of these departments is that they exist as part of the structure of a civilian government. We have never had independent troops, led by a general who recognized only the President as his superior and then only in the President's military capacity as commander-in-chief. Always the ultimate administrative responsibility—and the executive power—has remained in civilian hands. History suggests that this tradition, or institutional arrangement, is indispensable to the preservation of a democracy. A 1947 statute, however, did give (or recognize) new importance to military officials, by formally establishing the Joint Chiefs of Staff, comprised of the heads of the three armed services and a chairman (from one of the services) appointed by the President. The Secretary of Defense thus not only has to wrestle with the problems arising from continued interservice rivalry, but must seek to maintain his primacy, as executive and as policy adviser, in the face of the possible opposition of seven high-ranking officials, every one of whom has direct access to the President.

*Justice* is headed by the Attorney General of the United States, whose post as legal director and adviser was created in 1789, almost a century before a Department of Justice was formally established. The first main task of the department is the direction of most litigation wherein the federal government is a party; the government is, in effect, the Attorney General's client. In trial courts the United States attorneys, appointed to serve in each judicial district, customarily appear, sometimes aided by lawyers from the Washington office; in appeals, including arguments before the Supreme Court, the government is normally represented by the solicitor-general, the "number two" man of the Justice Department, or by one of his assistants. The department's second major duty is that of law enforcement. Except in the areas of enforcement of anti-trust and civil rights laws, which is carried out by litigation under the charge of the Anti-Trust and Civil Rights Divisions of the Department, this is the primary responsibility of one of the department's subordinate agencies, the Federal Bureau of Investigation. It also includes the management of federal prisons. The Attorney General retains his job of "legal adviser" to the President and the latter's subordinates, but as most departments and agencies have their own sizeable legal staffs and some have authority to try their own court cases, and as the President has his own "special counsel" on the White House staff, this function is not as significant as it once was. Justice is also in charge of the administration of the laws pertaining to immigration and naturalization, and, by statute of 1957, includes a Civil Rights Division which is supposed to work toward the prevention of racial discrimination that results in the impairment of federally guaranteed rights.

*The Post Office* is a department primarily administrative in character; it has less discretion and fewer significant policy-making functions than any other department. Its job is to deliver the mail. Almost the only major policy decisions confronting its chief, the Postmaster General, pertain to the enforcement of laws which prohibit the use of the mails for the transmittal of obscene literature or the promotion of gambling or fraudulent schemes. The very absence of burning issues provides one reason why often in history the Postmaster General has been a party politician, even a party manager, frequently serving as chairman of the party's national committee while heading the Post Office Department.[4]

---

4 Another reason, significant in the past, was that postmasterships, long exempt from civil service requirements, provided a broad field for party patronage.

*Interior,* established in 1849, "grew like Topsy," coming to be a kind of holding company for a highly varied conglomeration of special agencies. Its primary concerns, always centered on the western half of the United States, include the irrigation of arid farmland, the regulation of grazing, the management of Indian reservations, and the maintenance of national parks. (The latter, of course, have spread as far east as the coast of Maine, but the movement began with Yellowstone and other western wildernesses.) Since the 1920's, the Bureau of Reclamation, which operates irrigation projects, has built huge multi-purpose dams which not only store water for irrigation, but produce vast amounts of electric energy: the biggest in the country, Grand Coulee on the Columbia River, is such a Reclamation dam. Possessing also a Geological Survey, a Bureau of Mines, a Bureau of Land Management, and a Fish and Wildlife Service, the department seems a logical foundation for a full-scale "Department of Conservation" or "Department of Natural Resources." Its development in that direction was long urged by Harold L. Ickes, who was Secretary of the Interior from 1933 to 1946, and was recommended in 1949 by some members of the first Hoover Commission. Their logical proposals have run up against the hard facts that another department, Agriculture, also deals with natural resources and insists on controlling the national forests, while an "independent" executive agency, the Tennessee Valley Authority, builds dams and has wide responsibilities pertaining to the use of resources in an area including all or parts of eight states, and a regulatory body, the Federal Power Commission, has authority over private dam-building on navigable rivers. Mr. Ickes learned a vital truth about public administration: namely, that it may be easier to move mountains and river beds and build great dams and reservoirs than it is to move a government bureau from one department to another.[5]

---

[5] Throughout the depression of the 1930's and even throughout World War II, Secretary Ickes relentlessly insisted to President Roosevelt that the Forest Service should be transferred from Agriculture to Interior. That the White House door was not slammed in his face is a tribute to both the President's patience and the high value he placed on Ickes's services despite this particular obsession. See *The Secret Diary of Harold L. Ickes* (New York: Simon and Schuster, 1954).

*Agriculture* is a department which, as we have just seen, deals with the conservation of certain natural resources, primarily soil and the products of the soil. Its scientific research and advisory services to farmers are extensive: in the course of the latter, it has developed an unusually close relationship with both local farmers and agricultural schools. The department has some enforcement duties, especially those of securing compliance with the laws requiring the inspection of all meat shipped in interstate commerce. In the last thirty years, however, it has become first and foremost an operating and policy-making agency. It carries out the various farm laws for "price supports" for farm products and acreage control of one crop or another. In doing this, as we have seen, the Secretary of Agriculture can often wield a considerable amount of discretionary policy-making power. Furthermore, the department has often been either a seed bed of ideas for the reshaping of agricultural policies or a conduit for the transmission of such ideas from a pressure group to the Congress.

*Commerce,* like the Departments of Agriculture and Labor, is in some aspects a "special interest" agency. Consider for a moment the difference between these departments and the others. The State Department obviously is not supposed either to represent or to work primarily for the benefit of any one economic interest: it serves the national interest, however that may be conceived. The same is true of the Departments of the Treasury, Defense, and the rest—except for Agriculture, Commerce, and Labor. These are in part promotional units, designed quite frankly to foster the prosperity of farmers, businessmen, and industrial workers. The Department of Commerce, when Herbert Hoover was Secretary, vigorously promoted American export trade, sending its agents abroad to act, virtually, as salesmen for American business. Thirty years later, Mr. Eisenhower's Secretary of Commerce, Sinclair Weeks, clearly assumed that it was his job to express "business opinion" within the administration and to the country at large. In the interim, a variety of new responsibilities had been imposed on the department, chiefly concerning transportation. The Bureau of Public Roads was attached to it; this bureau administers the federal aid program for state highway construction. The Federal Aviation Agency, responsible for enforcing flight safety regulations, reports to the Civil Aeronautics Board but is lodged for administrative purposes in the Department of Commerce, and the same is true of the Federal Maritime Board. Under the Secretary of Commerce are, among other agencies, the Weather Bureau and the Bureau of the Census.

*Labor* was originally part of a "Department of Commerce and Labor"; the Department of Labor was organized separately in 1913. Originally its largest bureau was that of immigration and naturalization, which should remind us of the stake which organized labor had in curtailing the inflow of impoverished immigrants who would work for exceedingly low wages. That bureau was transferred in 1947 to the Department of Justice, leaving the Department of Labor the smallest of the departments. Labor was diminished further when another of its original functions, the conciliation of labor disputes, was transferred to a new and separate Federal Mediation and Conciliation Service. The department administers the Fair Labor Standards Act and the unemployment compensation portion of the Social Security Act. Its Women's Bureau promotes the welfare of working women, a kind of specialized program which, although useful, seems increasingly out of date. The Bureau of Labor Statistics provides economic data of great importance in measuring the cost of living and the rate of unemployment. The department is also responsible for some technical programs arising out of the United States' membership in the International Labor Organization, an agency of the United Nations. All in all, the Secretary of Labor has very limited discretionary power, and when the post was held, as it was for the first twenty years of the department's existence, by a representative of organized labor, it was seldom the source of significant policy proposals. In contrast, Secretary Frances Perkins (the first woman cabinet member) was a vigorous promoter of new programs in the 1930's, especially social security and minimum wages, and twenty-five years later Secretary James Mitchell took an active part in formulating legislative proposals. Neither of these Secretaries could ignore the command of Congress that the department should promote the welfare of wage earners, but neither felt forced to assume that only the strongest labor unions really knew how that welfare could best be promoted.

*Health, Education, and Welfare* is the youngest of the departments, established in 1953. Its forerunner was a nondepartmental
agency, the Federal Security Administration, which handled a
number of expanding programs, especially most of the Social Security program inaugurated in the 1930's. President Truman tried
to give the agency departmental status, but Congress refused because of criticism of the administrator's views in favor of health
insurance. After Truman was succeeded by Eisenhower, the
transition was accomplished. "HEW" deals with the subjects
which its name implies. Much of its work is done in aid of state
and local programs and universities and medical schools, which
receive federal financial assistance, including grants and contracts
for scientific research. Even when such financial support is minimal, as in the case of local public schools, the department conducts
an active program of research and information. Its largest executive tasks are those of administering Old-Age and Survivors Insurance and running the national public health hospitals; its chief
enforcement activity is the policing of foods, drugs, and cosmetics
to require compliance with standards of purity fixed under the
authority of the Pure Food, Drug and Cosmetic Act.

## Other Executive Agencies

The list of governmental bodies which are under the President,
or whose heads report to him, is a long one. Furthermore, except
for the ten departments, it changes frequently. Congress creates
new agencies, or merges old ones, to deal with emergent problems;
the President, with the consent of Congress, shuffles functions and
establishes new administrative units; and in times of crisis, numerous temporary or *ad hoc* agencies appear on the scene. The
nondepartmental executive agencies differ among themselves in
terms of organizational structure. Some resemble departments,
with single chiefs who are not accorded cabinet rank; some are
headed by multi-member boards or commissions. A few take the
form of corporations, yet the seeming independence conferred by
the corporate device does not remove them from ultimate executive control by the President. Of all of these agencies, most of
whose functions are implied by their titles, a few stand out because of the significance of the subjects with which they deal and

the comparatively permanent place which they seem to have achieved in the governmental structure. We will have occasion, in Part V, to learn more of the impact of some of these on policy formation.

In potential long-range importance, the Atomic Energy Commission takes first place. Despite the dominant concern with using nuclear energy for the production of bombs and missiles, control over atomic development has been entrusted to this civilian body. Another organization which deals with military needs, yet is not in the Department of Defense, is the Selective Service System, which administers the "draft." Among the agencies dealing with domestic, civilian problems are the Federal Mediation and Conciliation Service,[6] the Railroad Retirement Board and the National Mediation Board,[7] the Federal Deposit Insurance Corporation, the Veterans Administration, and the Housing and Home Finance Agency. A major regional body under ultimate presidential control is the Tennessee Valley Authority. In Washington are several "staff" or service agencies, whose task is primarily that of assisting the "line" or operating organizations of the government. Significant among these are the Civil Service Commission (personnel), and the General Services Administration (property management).

### Regulatory Boards and Commissions

The device of creating an "independent" commission to regulate a particular kind of economic activity began with the conferring of that status on the Interstate Commerce Commission (railroad rates and routes) in 1889.[8] It flowered in the 1920's and 1930's;

---

6 As we have seen, this took over functions formerly performed by the Department of Labor. The rationale for this change was that the department was assumed to be necessarily "pro-labor," whereas the mediation of strikes required complete impartiality between management and unions. But Secretaries Goldberg and Wirtz nevertheless acted as mediators in major disputes in the 1960's.

7 The political power of the Railway Brotherhoods is reflected by the separate existence of these two agencies. The first handles a special old-age retirement system for railway employees, different from the general Old-Age Insurance program; the second deals with strikes and threatened strikes in the transportation industry, with rules and procedures unlike those applying to other labor disputes.

8 When first created in 1887, tne ICC was attached to the Department of the Interior.

but no such body has been established since New Deal days, unless one includes the Atomic Energy Commission, whose duties have been hardly "regulatory" in the ordinary sense, for there has been no atomic energy industry to regulate. The trend, instead, has been toward increasing the regulatory responsibilities of the departments: thus the Labor Department "regulates" wages and hours, and the Health, Education, and Welfare Department polices the drug industry. The change may reflect, in part, dissatisfaction with the anomalous position of the "independent" agencies in the governmental structure. As the Brownlow report declared way back in 1937, these agencies seem to constitute a "headless 'fourth branch' of the government . . . the Congress has found no effective way of supervising them, they cannot be controlled by the President, and they are answerable to the Courts only in respect to the legality of their action." [9] Nevertheless, the "headless" boards and commissions persist. One reason for their longevity is that they have specialized expert knowledge: a corollary of this is that they have an interested "clientele," familiar with the way they operate and suspicious of any change. Another reason, more theoretical but perhaps as weighty, is that most of them perform quasi-judicial functions and so should be kept as free as possible from "political" (i.e., presidential) control.[10]

One of the "independent" bodies differs from the rest in the breadth of its responsibilities and the absence of quasi-judicial duties. This is the Board of Governors of the Federal Reserve System, which acts as the directorate of a central banking system and profoundly affects the national economy through its monetary and credit-controlling powers. It has a high degree of real freedom from presidential (or any other) control, its seven members being appointed for fourteen-year terms.

The other seven regulatory agencies have more in common

---

[9] *Report of the President's Committee on Administrative Management* (1937), 36.

[10] Louis Brownlow's story of why Congress made the ICC "independent" shortly after the presidential election of 1888 is illustrative: "Mr. Reagan of Texas . . . said that since a railroad lawyer named Ben Harrison had been elected President, he did not trust the President any more in this matter." U. S. Congress, Senate Committee on Labor and Public Welfare, *Hearings on the Establishment of a Commission on Ethics and Government*, 82nd Congress, 1st session, 213 (1951).

with each other. They are the Interstate Commerce Commission, the Civil Aeronautics Board, the Federal Power Commission (hydroelectric installations, natural gas), the Federal Communications Commission (radio, television, telephone), the Federal Trade Commission (truth in advertising, fair competition), the National Labor Relations Board, and the Securities Exchange Commission. All are multi-membered, the members' terms varying from five to seven years. In all but the ICC, the chairman is designated by the President, and in most the chairman is the agency's chief executive. All but the National Labor Relations Board must, by law, be bipartisan. And all reach major decisions through a process of administrative adjudication—a formal adversary proceeding in which, as in a law suit, the parties (including the government) present their competing claims.

## Reorganization

"If the Archangel Michael," said Louis Brownlow in 1937, "could come down and arrange it [the organization of the executive branch] perfectly by the 1st day of March 1937, by the first day of March 1938 you would need another Archangel to come down and adjust it." [11] The demands on government change, and require a readiness and ability to respond by continuous governmental reorganization. This is hard to achieve. Bureaucrats, interest groups, and congressmen have a stake in the maintenance of the status quo. All of them are likely to agree, at any given time, that government by a hodgepodge of overlapping or conflicting agencies which duplicate or stalemate each other's efforts is inefficient and wasteful, but they end up by saying: "Reorganize—but don't touch my agency!" Nevertheless, as the duties of the government have increased and the number of agencies has multiplied, a few major steps have been taken to bring order out of chaos.

The first significant movement in this direction, in the present century, culminated in the passage of the Budget and Accounting Act of 1921. This statute, in "establishing a consolidated budget initiated by the executive, . . . envisioned for the first time the

---

[11] Joint Congressional Committee on Government Organization, *Hearings*, 75th Congress, 1st session, 8.

modern concept of the managerial function of the presidency. It provided the President with the opportunity to present to the Congress and the country a whole fiscal program rather than a series of unrelated parts. It introduced, moreover, a pattern for the development of institutionalized presidential management through staff agencies of fiscal and administrative control." [12] When, in 1939, the Bureau of the Budget was transferred from the Treasury Department to the Executive Office of the President, it began effectively to perform this "control" function, contributing significantly to the efficiency of the operating agencies.

Perhaps still more important was the establishment of the Executive Office itself, in 1939—the lasting monument of Brownlow's Committee on Administrative Management. As we saw in the previous chapter, this development provided the President with the staff which he needed if he was to succeed as a "chief executive."

The idea that the orderliness and efficiency of the executive branch depends, perforce, on presidential authority and discretion was exemplified further by a series of statutes, beginning in the days of Herbert Hoover, which empowered the President to reorganize, subject to a possible veto by Congress. At present, this means that the President can submit a "reorganization plan" to Congress which will become effective in sixty days unless, in the interim, either house disapproves it. As we saw in Chapter 13, this seems like a topsy-turvy method of law-making, but doubts as to its constitutionality have been allayed by giving one house the veto power instead of providing (as earlier statutes did) that the plan would go into effect unless both House and Senate disapproved.[13] However, the extent of presidential authority is limited, for even in granting discretion to the President, Congress

---

[12] Herbert Emmerich, *Essays on Federal Reorganization* (University, Ala.: University of Alabama Press, 1950), p. 24.

[13] A similar statute in New Hampshire, making the governor's plan effective unless both houses of the legislature disapproved it, was held invalid by the New Hampshire Supreme Court. *Opinion of the Justices* 96 N. H. 517 (1950). The reason was that a law requires favorable action by both houses. Although the court was willing to allow such "favorable action" to be indicated by silent acquiescence, it would not permit the reorganization plan to become "law" unless *both* houses acquiesced.

has consistently said, as it were: "This agency or that is untouchable: hands off!" The outstanding "reorganization plan" to go into effect was President Eisenhower's combining of numerous agencies into the new Department of Health, Education, and Welfare.

Aiding Congress and two Presidents, Truman and Eisenhower, in planning reorganization were two commissions headed by a former President, Herbert Hoover. The first Hoover Commission, which issued its series of reports in 1949, concentrated on the proper structure of the executive branch. It appealed for clear lines of authority and responsibility, the rational organization of agencies according to major functions, and considerable decentralization of operations. Its specific recommendations led to the establishment, by Congress, of the General Services Administration and a statute reorganizing the State Department, and there is obviously a close relationship between its proposed "Department of Social Security and Education" and Mr. Eisenhower's plan, four years later, for a Department of Health, Welfare, and Education. Throughout the period of the first commission's existence, Mr. Hoover laid great stress on public relations: never before had "reorganization" been so thoroughly "sold" to the American people. A large and distinguished group, the National Citizens' Committee for the Hoover Report, kept up a constant barrage of educational publicity and propaganda. In twenty states the idea took hold; to examine the structure of state governments, legislatures created "Little Hoover" or "Baby Hoover" commissions.

One strength of the first Hoover Commission was that it refrained, for the most part, from indicating policy preferences. Another was that it did not promise that its proposals would save the taxpayers a specific amount of money. The second Hoover Commission, which reported to President Eisenhower in 1955, failed to observe such caution. Especially it hammered at the alleged unwisdom of various federal programs and activities, urging that they be abandoned. This made it far less effective than its forerunner. Everyone might agree, for instance, that to have a single agency build whatever federal dams and transmission lines Congress might authorize would be better than having a variety of agencies do this job; but there would be violent disagreement with a proposal that Congress should stop authorizing the construction of transmission lines altogether. The second kind of proposal was typical of the second Hoover Commission. Regardless of the latter's wisdom or lack of wisdom, the fact remains that the gloss surrounding the term "Hoover Commission," as a symbol of impartial and useful planning for governmental reorganization, was furnished only by the first of the two bodies which bore that name. It seems safe to predict that its efforts will be repeated—for, as we have seen, the need for reorganization and hence for study of the existing structure is a continuing one, becoming acute from time to time. Doubtless after Mr. Hoover has passed from the scene, "another Archangel" will be summoned to do the kind of job he did so well in 1949.

## THE AGENCIES' RELATIONSHIPS

The reorganization efforts which we have just been considering concerned the institutional relationships of executive agencies with each other and with the Office of the President. In the maintaining of responsible, efficient government these are important factors. By themselves, however, they do not provide the key to sound administration in the public interest. The President's authority to direct might be expanded, the functions of the government allocated with perfect logic, and still the nation be imperfectly served by its officials in Washington. For one thing, the most excellent governmental machinery depends on excellent people to run it; we will discuss the recruitment of personnel later in this chapter. For another, interagency relationships are not the only ones which affect the end product of the administrative process. Departments, bureaus, authorities, boards, and commissions interact with each other and with the White House, but their performance is also affected by their connections with Congress, the courts, and substantial segments of the general public. A brief analysis of all of these relationships should help us to understand the nature of the executive branch's business, in terms of warm and often confused human effort and conflict instead of the cold impersonality of orderly charts of the governmental structure.

## Within the Executive Branch

The towering prestige of the presidential office makes the President the potentially dominant figure, as the framers assumed he would be, in "faithfully executing" the laws. The department heads and their immediate deputies and assistants serve at his pleasure. If he does not formally control, he at least profoundly influences the regulatory commissions: not only does he designate the chairman of most of them, but his very power of appointment of new commissioners often enables him to replace old members with men who agree with him on policy questions. And in two cases—the CAB's certification of airlines to fly foreign routes, and the SEC's suspension of trading on a stock exchange—the "independent" commission's orders are, by statute, subject to presidential modification or veto. Even as chief executive, however, the President works within a political framework. He does not have a free hand. The power to appoint is qualified by the need for senatorial confirmation; the power to discharge is limited by the dangers of adverse public reaction. After the mid-1930's, for instance, no President with an ounce of prudence would have fired J. Edgar Hoover of the FBI, even if he had wanted to.

Departments and regulatory commissions alike are subject to considerable continuing control from two staff agencies. All must deal constantly with the Bureau of the Budget; though the ultimate decision as to appropriations is made by Congress, much depends on what the President recommends, and the President's budget message is mainly prepared by the bureau. All, to a greater or lesser degree, must count on the Civil Service Commission for the selection or approval of much of their personnel.

Finally, every agency, every official, every "bureaucrat" is affected by what some other agency, official, or "bureaucrat" does. On a larger scale we see interdepartmental conflict—witness the long struggle between the Departments of Interior and Agriculture for control of the Forest Service. A vivid example of a similar clash, at the bureau level, is furnished by the rivalry between two dam-building agencies, the Bureau of Reclamation in the Department of the Interior and the Army Engineers under the Department of Defense. Where there is not direct conflict there is necessary dependence which can easily lead to friction. Thus the

SEC's policies can be rendered ineffectual if the Federal Reserve Board pursues a different course, and an FTC attempt to curtail false advertising could be temporarily thwarted by the Postmaster General's failure to bar such matter from the mails.

Within any particular agency, furthermore, tension is likely to arise between subordinate units or their chiefs. It can be abated by friendly personal contacts among responsible officials, but even these may not be enough to overcome it. For interagency jealousy, at any level, is based on a mixture of personal ambitions, policy preferences, and interest group commitments, and of these the first is probably the most pervasive. The lowliest section head or bureau chief is likely to seek more and more authority. If he does not want added responsibility for its own sake, he desires the increased prestige and, perhaps, rank that attaches to the headship of a sizeable agency. And he may want more responsibility, too, either because he enjoys power or because he is filled with zeal for "his" program and convinces himself that only he can carry it out properly. He tends to see his rivals as enemies of the program, determined to sabotage it. When the conflict involves departments or major units it becomes more than personal, of course; one agency's outlook and method of approach toward a particular policy may differ sharply from those of another, and the affected interest groups will inject themselves into the struggle. Much of this interagency conflict goes on out of sight, being waged in terms of seemingly minor personnel changes, obscure alterations of departmental rules, or private conferences with assistant secretaries, cabinet members, or, occasionally, even the President. Often the only publicity it gets is in the form of stories harmful to one contestant, "leaked" by his opponent to a friendly newspaperman.[14] Publicized or not, personal or otherwise, interagency conflict is an ever-present reality in the Washington bureaucracy.

## With the Congress

Normally, an executive or regulatory agency's most frequent congressional contacts are with members of the House and Senate

---

14 Thus a Washington paper once reported that an assistant secretary of a major department had spoken insultingly to a Negro elevator operator. The story was easily traced back to another assistant secretary, his rival for dominance within the department.

committees especially concerned with the agency's work. These committees include both the "subject-matter" committees (the two committees on agriculture, for example, which naturally see much of the officials of the Department of Agriculture) and the appropriations committees, particularly the relevant subcommittee of the House Appropriations Committee. The publicized part of this relationship usually takes the form of formal appearances by high officials at open committee hearings. Much departmental time and effort goes into preparation for these hearings. This is inevitable, for when a department head testifies on matters of policy, he is speaking for the administration to the country as well as to the Congress, and especially in Congress his influence may depend considerably on the skill with which he presents his case. Still, appearances on Capitol Hill do seem to take an inordinate amount of time, making it hard for top executive officials to perform their other duties. Thus between January 15 and February 8, 1959, the Secretary of Defense testified fourteen times (averaging nearly three hours on each occasion) before six congressional committees.

So important, however, is congressional support for any agency or program that these committee demands take top priority. Even more time-consuming—and also, temporarily, destructive of morale—is preparation to meet occasional congressional attacks in the shape of a congressional investigation. The latter is ordinarily commenced by hostile congressmen who make vague charges and then seek to prove them: lurid examples, from yesteryear, are the investigation of the NLRB in the late 1930's (pressed by those hostile to the board's policies, to the CIO, and, indeed, to the purposes of the law which the board administered) and of the FCC in the early 1940's (the project of one representative who resented rumors that he himself had violated the law by accepting a fee to represent a radio station before the commission). The "probe" of the regulatory agencies in the late 1950's was of a more routine partisan nature, a Democratic Congress "checking up" on a Republican administration. It struck pay dirt almost accidentally, exposing the indiscretions of presidential assistant Adams and the highly dubious conduct of a Federal Communications commissioner who promptly resigned; but when the investigating committee's counsel, Bernard Schwartz, dramatically insisted on ferreting out more alleged corruption, the committee dispensed with his services. For the congressmen and the agencies are often linked together by a common orientation toward particular interest groups, especially those which speak for the businesses which the regulatory agencies are supposed to regulate. An investigation which discredits the opposition party is one thing; one which damages the reputation of powerful interest groups is, in the eyes of congressmen supported by such groups, much less desirable.

Interest groups, indeed, often form a kind of bridge between members of Congress and agency officials. Their lobbyists deal with both and may be friendly with both. A senator who takes his cue, on certain issues, from the XYZ Federation is likely to be well disposed toward the bureaucrat of whom the XYZ Federation's lobbyist speaks favorably. Over the years some agencies have formed close alliances with interest groups. The latter have occasionally gained great influence, also, in particular congressional committees—so that, in such cases, the agency-congressional relationship is really a three-way affair, with the interest group fostering mutual confidence between the two.

This kind of connection is, of course, seldom publicized. Even less publicity is given to the procedures, common to most executive and regulatory agencies, by which congressional hostility is allayed and friendly contacts with Congress are maintained. In many offices it is a rule, for instance, that in preparing replies to incoming mail, inquiries from congressmen have top priority. The prudent bureau chief, even the wise Secretary, will break other engagements to suit the convenience of an influential senator. And where appointments to office can be made outside of Civil Service requirements, the bureaucrat who realizes the usefulness of congressional support for his program will ask congressmen to recommend people to fill the vacancies, especially those congressmen who are dominant on the appropriate committees.

## With the Courts

Judicial intrusion in the affairs of the executive and regulatory agencies has taken four major forms. Two we have already men-

Fitzpatrick in the *St. Louis Post-Dispatch*

**Will the real romance get into the show?**

tioned. First are the decisions usually upholding the delegation of legislative authority to the executive branch (see p. 488). Second are the decisions as to the President's formal authority over executive and regulatory bodies. The Supreme Court upheld the exclusive power of the President to dismiss a postmaster [15] and a member of the Tennessee Valley Authority; [16] it denied the ex-

---

15 *Myers v. United States*, 277 U.S. 52 (1926).
16 *Morgan v. United States*, 312 U.S. 701 (1941).

istence of such power in the attempted firing of a Federal Trade commissioner, because the latter served on a quasi-judicial commission.[17] A third line of cases, relating to the discharge of employees on "loyalty" or "security" grounds, we will discuss briefly when we consider personnel administration. The fourth concerns judicial review of the procedures and decisions of quasi-judicial bodies. For many years the courts were unwilling to accept the findings made by such bodies in the course of fixing rates for railroads and other public utilities; the judges seemed to view the regulators with the same suspicion as they viewed legislatures, and inclined to substitute their own judgment for that of the supposedly expert agency. The era of judicial self-restraint, beginning in the 1930's, saved the regulatory decisions from being struck down for lack of "due process of law" whenever the justices disagreed with them. The problem of *"procedural* due process," however, remained. The boards and commissions were vehemently criticized for unfairness in their procedural arrangements. The American Bar Association led the attack, which at long last resulted in the passage of the Administrative Procedure Act of 1946. By 1946, however, improvements in procedure had already taken place, and the statute did little more than codify the best existing agency practices. Decisions by quasi-judicial agencies must be preceded by a fair hearing, with adequate prior notice to interested parties, and must be based on "substantial evidence." An aggrieved party can obtain judicial review, but if the established procedure has been complied with he has little chance of victory in court, save where the statute is unconstitutional or the regulatory agency has incorrectly interpreted it. "Ordinarily this [judicial] review is conducted with general respect for the administrative process and deference to the administrators. . . . The judges have accepted the administrative state." [18]

---

[17] *Humphrey's Executor v. United States, supra.* The doctrine of the *Humphrey* case was reaffirmed in *Wiener v. United States, supra,* wherein President Eisenhower had removed a member of the War Claims Commission for the purpose of replacing him with "a person of my selection."

[18] Merle Fainsod, Lincoln Gordon, and Joseph C. Palamountain, *Government and the American Economy* (New York: W. W. Norton & Co., 1959), p. 88.

## With the Public

By the behavior of administrative officials many people judge their government. For most of us, perhaps, personal attitude counts most of all. Is the Internal Revenue inspector, making a routine "spot-check" of every twentieth tax return showing a substantial income, courteous and reassuring? Or does he seem to be licking his chops at the thought of putting the taxpayer in jail? Does the clerk at the Old-Age Insurance office ostentatiously keep a line of elderly inquirers waiting while he telephones a friend? Is the bureau chief in Washington inaccessible most of the time, supercilious the rest? These small, unimportant personal contacts, when all added together, have an impact on the public's conception of government. Very simply, government seems democratic when officials are patient and courteous, tyrannical when they are not. John G. Winant, thrice governor of New Hampshire, was aware of this when he said that the quality most needed by a government employee was "kindliness."

For many a government agency, however, there is a specialized "public" with a more sophisticated approach. This "public" consists of the interests with which the agency's work is most concerned. In some instances, interest groups feel, with some reason, that the agency exists largely for their benefit: so unions long viewed the Department of Labor, farm organizations the Department of Agriculture, the American Legion the Veterans Administration. Others believe that the agency *should* be administered for their benefit, and seek, in effect, to capture it. This is particularly true of regulatory bodies—and the latter, remember, are by no means exclusively "independent" commissions, but include numerous bureaus in the old-line departments. So cattlemen wished to see the Grazing Service, in the Department of the Interior, headed and staffed by men sympathetic to their desires; the Real Estate Conference Board might be glad to have the Housing and Home Finance Agency headed by a man who preferred delay to public housing. The most obvious pattern of interest group-agency interaction, however, has been woven by the regulatory boards and commissions and the businesses subject to their regulation.

Typically a commission has been created to put an end to an abuse—the charging of destructively high rates, for instance, or the encouragement of irresponsible speculation. It starts off with a zeal for reform, and with public support exemplified by the enactment of the law establishing it. Then, gradually, its vigor seems to abate. Its original purpose of regulating in the public interest, particularly by preventing or punishing abuses, is transmuted into regulation to the satisfaction of the dominant members of the industry regulated, and even into the promotion of the industry. The original object of control becomes instead a client of the controller. There are four main reasons for this change. First, once the initial reforms have been completed, the affected industry emerges from the "doghouse" and fights back against commissions and commissioners who insist on strict regulation. This counterattack is often directed at specific individuals, some of whom have been subjected to campaigns of personal vilification and abuse which have caused them to decline reappointment or to be denied confirmation by the Senate. Second, as commissioners and their staff members become familiar with the industry and interested in its problems, they are often increasingly tempted to leave the government and work for a corporation in the industry, at a greatly increased salary. This possibility sometimes affects their viewpoint while they are still in government service. Third, closely related to the second, is their growing knowledge of the industry's problems and their heightened understanding of the legitimate aspirations of the industrialists. The fourth reason for the typical change really embraces the other three: it is, simply, that the regulators are in constant, daily contact with the regulated and that the great majority of the latter are personable and honest men. The commissioners, then, are not like policemen in frequent touch with criminals. Policemen don't identify themselves with the people they arrest; but the regulators find it hard not to do so with the people they regulate. Senator George D. Aiken summed it up neatly: "Is not most of our trouble in the regulatory commissions due to the fact that the members are thrown in a constant association with the people they are supposed to regulate, rather than the public which they are supposed to represent and protect? It takes almost superhuman powers on the part of a regulatory commissioner, after he has been in office for a certain length of time, not to promote the business he is supposed to regulate instead of regulating it." [19]

This discussion leads us back inexorably to the "personal element"—the concern, ambitions, and reactions of men and women who hold public office. The kind of government we have depends at least as much on those as on the administrative structure. How well the public is served is determined by the character and ability of the public servants. The wise selection and management of personnel is, therefore, the most important single element of the executive process.

## PERSONNEL ADMINISTRATION

At any given time, nowadays, about two and a half million people occupy appointive positions in the United States government. Of these, more than two million are "Civil Service employees" or their equivalent—government work is their career. The remainder are outside of Civil Service for a variety of reasons, the chief of which is that the jobs which they are performing are temporary in nature. That is the main reason, at least, in terms of numbers of people exempted; the most significant exemptions, however, are those of major policy-making and executive positions. These posts, perhaps 1,100 in all, are filled by what have come to be called "political executives," appointed by the President or his subordinates without recourse to any Civil Service examinations.

### The "Political Executives"

Broadly speaking, the noncareer federal executives (department heads, undersecretaries and most assistant secretaries, numerous aides and advisers, and a considerable number of bureau chiefs) have several assets and handicaps in common. On the plus side is their willingness to interrupt their careers in business or a profession, to render public service for at least a brief period.

---

19 U.S. Congress, Senate Committee on Labor and Public Welfare, *Hearings on the Establishment of a Commission on Ethics in Government*, 82nd Congress, 1st session, 213 (1951): quoted in Marver H. Bernstein, *Regulating Business by Independent Commission* (Princeton, N.J.: Princeton University Press, 1955), p. 158.

Perhaps an asset, too, may be their distinction and experience in private life. Generally disadvantageous, however, are the brevity of their tours of duty and their frequent ignorance of the details of the program they are supposed to administer. Nor is the "political executive" likely to be comfortable in Washington unless he has had political experience; the businessman recruited for a high post often finds disconcerting the great difference between running a corporation and running a government agency.

One of the burdens of the latter job, of course, is that of dealing with Congress. Hell hath few furies like a senator scorned. More than one executive has been glad to retreat to private life to escape the vitriolic attacks from congressmen whom he has offended. Sometimes more devastating have been the personal vendettas waged by columnists or commentators against particular agency heads. In recent years exposure to personal abuse, always a hazard of public life, has become potentially more unpleasant than ever because of the ease with which unsubstantiated but terribly damaging charges of "doubtful loyalty" can gain the public ear. As a final obstacle to satisfaction in noncareer public service is the matter of "conflicts of interest," which in this context refers to a conflict between a person's official duties and his private affairs. Must a businessman who has put his savings into the securities of automobile and steel corporations divest himself of his stock before accepting a position as Assistant Secretary of Defense? If he fails to do so, is he fairly subject to criticism on the ground that his financial interest in certain corporations may influence the placing of contracts by the department which he serves? To such questions there are no clear answers, and Congress's early attempts to deal with the problem were unrealistic in their exclusionary results.

Yet "political executives" can still be recruited and render useful service. Why? Obviously one answer, with respect to the highest positions, is prestige. A post in the cabinet confers great distinction on its incumbent. It also gives him an opportunity to handle matters of great moment—to feel the satisfaction of playing a significant part in the affairs of the nation. This kind of satisfaction and self-esteem may be felt, in less degree, in comparatively minor posts. A genuine desire to serve is a conscious motive of many of these temporary officials, though their skeptical colleagues in the permanent "career service" put little stock in it. (The career men apparently feel that most "businessmen in government" are seeking broader experience and contacts to promote their own business prospects.) [20] And whatever the motives for undertaking the job, the job itself may well hold real fascination for an imaginative and industrious person.

The "political executives" come into public service through various routes. Some are political: they gain office through their own political strength or through the use of party patronage. Others are selected by those who get to the top positions early. The attitudes of those top executives largely determine the choice of sources from which to recruit the lesser ones. Thus in New Deal days the preference of a few key officials (and the President) was soon reflected by the appointment, to lesser noncareer posts, of a horde of eager, able, and very young lawyers, with little professional or political experience. Under Harry Truman, most departments were headed by old-time politicians like Truman himself; for most appointments outside of Civil Service, accordingly, party service and political connections were prerequisites. President Eisenhower and his cabinet favored "putting less government in business but more business in government," and hence looked chiefly to the private corporations to provide the "political executives" they needed.

## The Career Service

The great majority of federal employees, in Washington and in still greater numbers scattered all across the country, are "permanent" government servants. About one-quarter of them are women. Generally speaking, they entered the federal service by passing an examination; their salaries (like those of most noncareer employees) are governed by a statute setting up many grades and classifications (from GS 1, $3,305 a year, to GS 18, $20,000); they are protected from arbitrary dismissal; and they have retirement benefits.

Selection on the basis of merit was a goal long sought by re-

---

20 *Businessmen in Government,* Harvard Business School Club of Washington, D.C., 1958.

formers in the last century. The "spoils system" of party patronage brought many unqualified people into the service, and some
corrupt ones. In 1883 Congress passed the Pendleton Act, setting
up a limited Civil Service system which has expanded mightily
over the years. For several decades the approach of the Civil Service Commission reflected the origin of the system: it sought primarily to "keep the rascals out." Its competitive examinations
were less useful in bringing first-rate people into the government
than in keeping ward heelers out of it. As personnel requirements became heavier, however, the need for actively recruiting
people of superior quality made itself felt. In the 1930's the
Civil Service Commission began to take a more affirmative attitude; it sought not merely to bar bad people, but to obtain good
ones. New examinations designed to qualify young men and
women of education and intelligence were devised. Of these,
since 1955, the chief one has been the Federal Service Entrance
Examination, opened frequently to college graduates or persons
of equivalent standing.

Most career employees enter the federal service by taking examinations, though some have been "covered into Civil Service"
by executive orders giving Civil Service status to employees originally outside the system. Most examinations are those of the Civil
Service Commission, but a few highly specialized agencies still do
their own recruiting even of "career" personnel: thus the Foreign Service in the State Department and the FBI in the Department of Justice hold their own qualifying examinations. Most
Civil Service tests are competitive; to fill a vacancy, a department's
appointing officer is offered the names of the three candidates with
the highest marks. In one respect, however, the mark itself is not
based solely on the answers to the examination's questions. If the
applicant is a veteran, he has preferred status: to his original mark
five points are added, or, if he is a "disabled veteran," ten points.[21]

Between four and five thousand career men and women are
responsible policy-makers roughly equal in influence to the lower
echelons of the "political executives." The question immediately

---

[21] Veterans' preference extends beyond the examination process; the statutes
give special advantage or protection to veterans in respect of waiving physical
requirements, administering layoffs, appealing from disciplinary action, etc.

arises: can a person exercise discretionary authority wisely, regardless of whether or not he approves of the program he is supposed to administer? In the case of "political executives," one normally assumes that the head of an agency should believe in what the agency is doing. Should not the same be true of "career executives"? Not necessarily. The temporary official comes into government to do a particular job; if his heart isn't in it, he had better stay home. The career man, in contrast, spends his working life administering policies about which he may feel little or no personal concern. It is his job to put them into effect, and he does that job with all the skill at his command. He knows, too, that his advancement depends in part on how his superiors assess his work, and so he has a very practical reason for serving his chief loyally and well, regardless of whether that chief is a Republican or a Democrat, a radical or a stand-patter. The service he can render is often especially useful to the business or professional man who occupies high appointive office without prior political experience. Frequently the "career executive," over the years, builds a network of personal contacts of political value, especially with congressmen interested in his agency; he acquires "political know-how" which makes him invaluable to his department head. As we saw in Chapter 4, there is a natural hostility or at least suspicion between the legislative and executive branches, but the skillful "career executive," with plenty of time to develop friendly understandings and with awareness of the importance of congressional approval for his agency, can do much to overcome this.

Civil Service employees, whether or not they are politically astute, are supposed to stay out of party politics. The Hatch Act of 1939 forbids them to take any active part in the management of party affairs or in political campaigns. They can vote and privately express their preferences, but, strictly speaking, those are just about the limits of their lawful political activity. Such a strict prohibition, however, has proved difficult to enforce, and there has been little demand for its enforcement. Much more basic to the "civil service" idea—the existence of a career service whose selection and promotion is based on merit—are the protections afforded employees against political reprisal. Thus the tenure system, under which dismissals must be based on "just cause," keeps an arbitrary "political executive" from firing the clerk who refuses to make a campaign contribution.

The separation of civil servants from organizational party pressure, in itself necessary for the preservation of a "career" system, is symptomatic of something more debatable. It reflects the old theory that public administration and politics are, or should be, different kinds of human activity. To the extent that career men act on that belief and become at best professional technicians, at worst spinners of red tape, Civil Service requirements hamper the enthusiastic administration of new and adventurous programs. Fortunately, as we have just seen, numerous career officials are conscious of the mingling of administration and politics and are adept at both.

## Loyalty and Security

Good character has been a prerequisite to qualifying for the federal service since the merit system began, and from the President down, federal officials have taken an oath to uphold the Constitution of the United States. Only since World War II, however, has there been a formal public program for insuring that federal employees are not "disloyal" to the United States or "security risks" whose employment endangers the maintenance of secrecy concerning defense and foreign policies.

President Truman took the first big step in 1947, perhaps to ward off more drastic action by Congress. By that year, hostile feelings between the USA and the USSR were coming into the open. The "cold war" had begun. Truman promulgated a "loyalty order" establishing agency loyalty boards and a top Loyalty Review Board, and making the Attorney General's "list of subversive organizations" influential in determining who was "loyal" and who was not. Federal agents went to work checking up on thousands of their fellow employees; truthful statements, unintentional half-truths, specific but false charges, rumors and gossip all found their way into the files of the FBI and the Civil Service Commission. The Attorney General's list, compiled without benefit of any judicial or even quasi-judicial procedure, was not supposed to be conclusive, nor were the decisions of the various boards: final action could be taken only by the head of the agency where the accused employee worked. But anyone who had belonged to a proscribed organization or failed of loyalty board clearance had little or no chance of remaining in federal employment.

Fitzpatrick in the *St. Louis Post-Dispatch*

**Wrong way to find a needle in a haystack**

Truman's "loyalty order" of 1947 was designed to counteract the threat of subversion within the government; cartoonist Fitzpatrick was one of those who immediately saw it as threatening individual freedom.

The change in administration in 1953 was followed by the abolition of the Loyalty Review Board and the adoption of new nomenclature. "Security" became the key word rather than "loyalty." But in essence the program remained the same, extending not only to people directly employed by the government but also to employees of private firms holding defense contracts. Spurred on by Senator McCarthy of Wisconsin and by its own campaign promises, the Eisenhower administration made a vigorous effort to rid the government of subversives. The result was surprising to those who imagined Reds at every other desk in Washington: at the end of eighteen months of intensive investigation, only 342 employees had been dismissed as "security risks" (mostly because of personal habits leading to indiscretion, rather than subversive activities) and of these some were later reinstated.

The program nevertheless had a damaging effect on morale in the public service. It was widely criticized on various grounds. The concept of "loyalty" as something which could be proved by nonmembership in some organizations was assailed as curiously negative and unsatisfactory. (On a man's record, membership in a left-wing group outweighed such a positive act of loyalty as volunteering for duty in the war.) The fear of "subversion" seemed exaggerated: how could the nation be harmed if a file clerk in a local Old-Age Insurance office turned out to be an ex-Communist? But the chief criticism was directed at the procedure of punishing people without informing them of the charges against them or confronting them with their accusers. The various boards and security officers—as it were, the judges and the prosecutors—had in their hands files showing that anonymous informants, known only as T-1, say, and T-2, had made certain charges against a government employee. But they did not have to tell the employee what the charges were, nor could they tell him who had brought them, for they did not know that themselves. "T-1" and "T-2" might have been patriots, or irresponsible busy-bodies, or malicious enemies of the employee: nobody knew which.

Since 1948 the Supreme Court has, with some difficulty, avoided the necessity of ruling squarely on the constitutionality of such procedure. Challenged again and again to do so, it has found other grounds upon which to base its decisions in favor of federal employees. In one such case it decided that the old Loyalty Review Board had acted outside of the specific authority granted to it by executive order; [22] in another, that the relevant executive orders

---

22 *Peters v. Hobbv.* 349 U.S. 331 (1955).

and rules did not clearly embrace "nonsensitive" positions and so presumably applied only to "sensitive" ones wherein "security risks" could be really dangerous; [23] and in a third, that the executive orders were not to be construed to direct dismissal without confrontation.[24] In the last case, however, the opinion of the Court suggested a strong disapproval of discharge by anonymous accusation. In this it was echoing an off-the-cuff statement by President Eisenhower: "In this country if someone dislikes you or accuses you, he must come up in front. He cannot assassinate you or your character from behind without suffering the penalties an outraged citizenry will inflict. . . . If we are going to continue to be proud that we are Americans, there must be no weakening of the code by which we have lived—including the right to meet your accuser face to face." On the other hand, Mr. Eisenhower's Attorney General insisted that the demand for confrontation of witnesses would "hamstring" the whole security program, saying that "undercover agents, paid informers and casual informers" must be "guaranteed anonymity." The issue remains in doubt. A 1961 decision [25] followed the logic of Greene v. McElroy in upholding a dismissal, without confrontation of the accusers, where the procedure had been explicitly authorized by the President or Congress; but there were four dissenting justices, and the appointment of Justice Goldberg in 1962 soon appeared to be transforming this four-man minority in civil liberties cases into a five-man majority.

Beyond serious doubt is the fact that most federal employees are trustworthy and reasonably industrious Americans, many of whom find that public service gives them a chance to do what they like best to do, or a sense of being useful, or, best of all, both. Its essential rewards were once summed up by one who, though not technically a "career" man, worked for many years in both state and federal government: "The first is the deep inner satisfaction that comes from working, with others equally dedicated, for the public weal. Special exhilaration is the lot of the man who throws

---

23 Cole v. Young, 350 U.S. 900 (1955).

24 Greene v. McElroy, 360 U.S. 474 (1959).

25 Cafeteria and Restaurant Workers Union, Local 473, AFL-CIO v. McElroy, 367 U.S. 886 (1961).

his efforts, not into securing an advantage for client or business or self, but into building a stronger city or state or nation. . . . No less essential to the fullness of life is the sheer day-to-day fun that comes from working on a government job in a field that arouses one's interest. . . . Joy in the job, the excitement of being in the main stream of something important and worthwhile, are perhaps the most attractive features of a public career." [26]

---

26 Paul M. Herzog, "Government Service as a Career," *The Archbishop* (North Andover, Mass.: Brooks School, May, 1954).

# CHAPTER 17

# *The Law and the Judges*

Throughout this study of our government, we have been reminded again and again of the underlying rules and their interpreters—the Constitution and the justices of the Supreme Court of the United States. Yet it would be a mistake to assume that the Constitution, "supreme law" though it is, is the only law that holds our society together, just as it would be an error to think that the Supreme Court by itself constitutes the whole judicial branch of the national government. There are many other federal courts, as well as a far greater number of state and local courts, and these courts by no means confine themselves to the business of construing the Constitution. (Neither does the Supreme Court, though constitutional interpretation has come to be regarded as its biggest and most significant task.) In a civilized society, judges and judicial tribunals provide peaceable means of definitely and finally deciding certain types of disputes. Sometimes in frontier communities in our own old West, suspected thieves were hunted down by posses and hanged from the nearest tree; in olden times across the sea, two citizens who claimed ownership to the same plot of ground settled their argument with broadswords. Now, instead, the guilt of the suspect, the ownership of property, and all manner of other questions affecting the liberties and rights of individuals and the peace and good order of the community are decided through a judicial process and in accordance with something called "law." Because courts deal with "law" and judges are trained and are presumed to be knowledgeable in the "law," we had better think for a moment about what "law" does and what it is.

Law has four basic functions or objectives. First, it protects the individual against the arbitrary action of government: this is the fundamental principle of "constitutionalism." Second, it protects individuals and the society itself against wrongdoing by other individuals; it prohibits and punishes actions which the society deems criminal and gives redress to the injured person. Third, it provides the means for the orderly settlement of disputes through established procedures generally accepted as just and fair. Fourth, it gives stability and certainty to private arrangements made by or among individuals: if you make a proper will, for instance, you can reasonably expect that after you die your property will be divided as your will provides, and when you sign a two-year lease for a house, you assume that you can stay in that house for those two years if you comply with the lease and pay the rent on time. This fourth purpose, unlike the others, is not wholly or perhaps even primarily protective: it not only maintains accepted forms of the social and economic order, but aids in the development of new forms. The modern corporation, for example, was a lawyers' invention, made possible by the legal decisions and rules affecting the private rights and liabilities of the owners of productive enterprise.

We have seen something of how legislators and administrators go about making those decisions and rules which, for convenience, we can call "statute law." But what about the courts and the judges who preside over them? In the course of our country's history it is law as applied or made through the judicial process which has had the greatest impact on the way we comport ourselves and on the organization of our society. DeTocqueville observed long ago that we in the United States were the most legally minded people on earth; we were in 1835, and are now, ever conscious of the impact of law or the need of it ("There ought to be a law!") even though we are not quite sure what it really is or where it came from. Ignorance of the law, we often hear, is "no excuse" for wrongdoing. Likewise, a self-governing people cannot be safely ignorant of the existence of law and the ways in which it is applied or made. Uncertainty about what "law," in the larger sense, really is, is more excusable; even the greatest scholars of legal history and jurisprudence have differed among themselves as to the true nature of law.

## THE NATURE OF LAW

### Different Conceptions of Law

Obviously a subject which, all through the ages, has engaged the intellects of some of the world's greatest philosophers cannot be encompassed in a few short pages. Yet we should at least gain some awareness, here, of the ideas about law which have most influenced the people directly concerned with it—the lawyers and especially the judges. The "bench and bar"—the judges and the attorneys—of present-day America are affected, both consciously and unconsciously, by the beliefs and customs of earlier times. Indeed, modern differences of opinion about what "law" is and what the judicial duties are with respect to it are really nothing new. Similar differences have persisted for centuries. Way back in 1345, in *Langridge's Case,* tried in a royal court of England, the following colloquy took place, illustrating three contrasting conceptions of law:

> R. Thorpe (who was the lawyer for the plaintiff, addressing the judges): I think you will do what others have done in the same [kind of] case, or else we do not know what the law is.
> Hillary, J. (a Justice of the court): It is the will of the Justices.
> Stonore, C. J. (Chief Justice): No; law is that which is right.[1]

Here the last speaker, the chief justice, takes the position that has been dominant most of the time in the development of Anglo-American law—the law of England transplanted to the United

---

[1] Common Bench, 1345. *Year Book,* 19 Edw. III 375, quoted in Harold J. Berman, *The Nature and Functions of Law* (Brooklyn: The Foundation Press, Inc., 1958), pp. 21-22. Professor Berman is a leader in the movement to include courses in law (not for professional training but as part of a general education) in the undergraduate social science curriculum.

States. "Law is that which is right." But who or what is the ultimate arbiter of right and wrong? The imperfections of humanity
put that ultimate decision beyond man's certain reach. If, then,
law is that which is right, it must be something more than a mere
human invention. If not admittedly divine in origin, it still must
be closely related to universal principles, lacking divine authority
only because it must be transmitted through the frail reasoning
powers of human beings. At the least, then, it is a consistent body
of principles reached by the process of "right reason"; a judicial
decision arrived at by faulty reasoning would not really be "law"
at all.

The idea that there is a close relationship between law and
divine authority can be illustrated by a famous remark uttered
by the great chief justice of England, Edward, Lord Coke, in
1607. When, angered by Coke's decision in a case, King James I
insisted that it be decided as he wished and reminded the chief
justice that, after all, he was the King and so "not under any
man," Coke defiantly replied: "Under no *man*, but *under God
and the Law*." Nearly three centuries later a clergyman could
conclude a hymn entitled "The Word of God" with the lines:

> Man's laws but catch the music
> of the eternal chime.

About fifty years ago an influential American teacher of law,
Joseph H. Beale, omitted any reference to the deity in his description of the subject, yet pictured something certainly superhuman:
law, he said, must be uniform, general, continuous, equal, certain,
and pure.[2]

This conception of a higher law, transmitted through the
power of human reasoning into the rules and decisions governing
everyday life, was prevalent in the United States—at least among
judges and lawyers—for the major part of our national existence.
In one form or another, it has many devotees today. Its appeals
are many and they run deep. Perfection, certainty, continuity:
are these not worth striving for here below in the knowledge that
they must exist above? The rhythmic reassurance sounds in Mere-

---

[2] Summarized in Jerome Frank, *Law and the Modern Mind* (New York: Brentano's, Inc., 1930), 48.

dith's sonnet "Lucifer in Starlight"—as the vainglorious, defiant archangel fell from heaven, "around the ancient track marched, rank on rank, the army of unalterable law." There is, surely, a close connection between Meredith's astronomy and Beale's philosophy.

The trouble, today, is that we know that not all the stars are constant in their courses, and likewise many articulate Americans have come to doubt the existence of an immutable and perfect body of law. Some who never went so far as to acknowledge the existence of either a divine law applicable in secular courts or an only slightly less-than-divine "natural law," but who nevertheless venerated the "common law of England" as a foundation of our society, began to point out even the common law's lack of universal consistency. Their starting point was similar to that of Hillary, J.: "It is the will of the Justices." Law, in this view, is what courts actually rule in deciding the disputes before them. Furthermore, it is "law" only to the extent that the decision can be authoritatively enforced: in other words, it is effective only within the jurisdiction of the particular court making the decision. If, therefore, the highest state court of state A holds that a contract is binding only when it is set forth in writing, that is the "law" *in that state;* but in state B, the court may decide that an oral contract is binding, and this will be the law in state B. This conception of law, as something made by government officials and enforceable by government officials within the area where they have authority, was summed up in Mr. Justice Holmes' famous statement that "the common law is not a brooding omnipresence in the sky." [3] Some critics of the older notions went further still. "The will of the Justices," they suggested, was itself often the product of psychological forces rather than logical reasoning: Jerome Frank's *Law and the Modern Mind,* published in 1930,

---

[3] In the nineteenth century, the Supreme Court assumed that there was a general common law. Thus it declared that a federal court in a given state was not bound to follow the decisions of the courts of that state applying the common law; the state decisions could have misstated the law. *Swift v. Tyson,* 16 Peters (1842). This assumption of the existence of a common law which transcended jurisdictional boundaries came under increasing criticism in the present century, and eventually it was repudiated by the Supreme Court itself in *Erie Railroad Co. v. Tompkins* 304 U.S. 64 (1938).

tended to describe law as a combination of Hillary, J.'s artless statement and the doctrines of Dr. Sigmund Freud.

When Hillary, J. said that the law is what the judges decide, the attorney, Thorpe, suggested that really it is what the judges *can be expected* to decide. He saw law in terms of *predictable* rules which the court, the organ of the state, will make and enforce, whether the rules be "right" or "wrong"; to find the law, Thorpe implied, you simply find out what courts have decided in cases similar to your own. This view of the law, then, is that it is a predictable body of decisions made by courts guided by *precedent* or reached after arguments showing how the case before the court is *analogous* to cases decided earlier or *distinguishable* (logically different) from them. The emphasis is on law as a fairly continuous and logical set of rules made by officials of the government and sanctioned by the power of the government.

The old courtroom colloquy of 1345, then, illustrates three ways of "looking at law." A fourth gained status in the world of jurisprudence at about the same time, half a century ago, that sociology was achieving recognition. This fourth school of theorists saw law primarily as an instrument of social control, with courts' chief functions being to balance competing interests and shape the ever changing social system while maintaining its order and unity. Some recent writers, indeed, have pictured Supreme Court decisions as resolutions of interest conflicts, seeming to suggest that the Supreme Court, like Congress, is a political cockpit wherein contending interest groups struggle and the stronger wins.[4] To be sure, as we have seen, the Supreme Court is in one sense a political institution. Yet even when the Supreme Court is dealing with constitutional issues, it is not counting heads and voting in the hope of popular approval; and in the everyday business of other courts, the political struggle is generally irrelevant. Judges do decide cases, and their decisions are influenced by their predispositions and personalities. Often they consider the impact of a possible decision on not just the parties before them, but on society as a whole. Customarily they study precedents and reason by analogy: they are trained to do so, and the lawyers appearing

---

[4] See, e.g., Jack W. Peltason, *Federal Courts in the Political Process* (Garden City, N. Y.: Doubleday & Co., 1955.)

before them frame their arguments accordingly. Yet what the judge does is not the whole of law. For he does it within a framework that stretches back over the centuries. Whether the framework was divinely inspired, or imperfectly man-made, or constructed by a nearly superhuman effort to ascertain the "right," it subtly controls the judge's conduct and guides the judicial pen. That framework is the common law.

## The Common Law

From their predominantly English heritage the original thirteen states took and applied in their courts the "common law of England." Furthermore, they extended its sway to great areas out of which new states were soon to be carved: for this "northwest territory," the Northwest Ordinance of 1787 prescribed "judicial proceedings according to the course of the common law." Eventually, it was predominant in all states except Louisiana,[5] though all of them enacted statutes occasionally modifying its rules. Today in more than half the states the common law of crimes remains in force; for instance, if the legislature has made no law defining the crime of burglary, a court would assume that to be guilty of burglary one must have "broken and entered in the night-time"—the old common-law definition of that felony.[6]

Again, in the absence of a statute, a lawsuit for damages suffered in an automobile collision would be governed by the common-law doctrines of "negligence" and "contributory negligence." The trials themselves would conform to common-law concepts of fairness and propriety: hearsay testimony, for example, would be excluded not because any legislature had ordered its exclusion, but because under the common law it was inadmissible.

The common law thus covers crimes and torts (civil wrongs

---

[5] Before its acquisition from Napoleon in 1803, Louisiana under French rule had become accustomed to the "continental" or "civil" legal system, one based on the codification of rules which, to a large degree, adapted the maxims of ancient Roman law.

[6] Although a court would thus deal with a familiar and long-defined crime, it would be most reluctant to *develop* any new common law of crimes, to meet changing circumstances. There is a natural objection to prosecutions for conduct which has not been specifically defined and determined, in advance, to be criminal; the definitions are made either by the legislature or by a very long line of ancient judicial decisions.

for which damages can be sought), contracts, procedure, and property rights. Originally its most important concern was real property: the ownership of land. In an agricultural community, land is the paramount interest; in a country only slowly emerging from feudalism, the relationship between the owners, the tenants, and the laborers on the land was the most significant economic relationship. And the common law of England began when that "green and pleasant land" was a country of farms and forests, in the age of nobles and serfs. Henry II, in the twelfth century, established a rudimentary judicial system for the nation which he ruled, and soon the cases heard by these English courts began to be "reported" or summarized in writing, the summaries being preserved in the "Year Books" like the one which reported the conversation in Langridge's Case. Gradually the decisions of the judges began to form discernible patterns. One court held that under certain conditions, a man's will could prevent the sale of his land by his heirs only for a given period; later, to settle the same kind of dispute, another court would find in this decision a good reason for making a similar decision. In the beginning there were no judicial precedents: judges had to be guided by their own "right reason" or, perhaps, by their estimate of what the community would consider reasonable and just.[7] By 1600, however, there were precedents a-plenty to cover the most usual types of cases, and the use of such precedents was facilitated by the monumental labors of the aforementioned Edward Coke. Here was a truly astonishing man. Attorney-general, leader of Parliament, chief justice, Coke still had time to compile and analyze the common-law precedents in a lengthy treatise; and, by precept and example, he stimulated the practice of reporting cases fully, in contrast to the often laconic summaries of "Year Book" days. Emphasizing the perfection, completeness, and certainty of law, Coke distilled from the precedents a body of rules and maxims. A century later, these were enlarged and clarified by a legal scholar, Sir William Blackstone, and thereafter for about a hundred and fifty years in England and, too, in young America,

---

[7] Bracton, writing in the thirteenth century, mentioned about 2500 decisions, but did not imply that they created binding precedents.

Blackstone's *Commentaries on the Law of England* provided the foundation of most legal training.

*Courts of Equity.* The belief in perfection or the need for certainty, or both, thus "hardened" the common law into a body of immutable principles. Soon it appeared, however, that the common law was not "complete": it did not always provide what people believed was just redress for civil wrongs. For instance, it permitted a person to collect damages from another man who had broken a contract with him, but it made no provision for requiring the fulfillment or "specific performance" of the contract. For many a purchaser of land, however, money as damages for a broken contract was not what he desired. He wanted to occupy the property and have the former owner get out. So as the common law became more rigid, it was necessary to create a complementary legal system which would do "equity," especially in the form of granting relief of a type not furnished under the common law, "specific performance" of contracts or "injunctions" forbidding the commission of wrongful acts. The English courts of equity, like the early common-law courts, thus began making new precedents. Both in England and the United States, courts of law and courts of equity existed side by side, their jurisdiction depending on the kind of relief sought by the litigant. Yet such was the strength of the belief in perfection or the desire for certainty that equity's precedents, too, hardened into fairly rigid rules. As any budding lawyer needed to know these rules just as thoroughly as he needed to master the common-law doctrines, the formal separation of judicial administration into courts of law and courts of equity became a useless complication; but the merger of the two, permitting a single court to rule on both types of cases, was long in coming. Only in 1947, for example, was the old distinction obliterated in New Jersey.

The principles of the common law and the maxims of equity fostered certainty and helped judges decide many difficult cases by referring to something other than their own whims or consciences. The rules and maxims of one age, however, could not take into account the altered community structure and social viewpoints of another. A legal system fit for a rural community was not likely to settle all the disputes arising from the Industrial

Revolution. Nor was the notion of "justice" held by an English yeoman of the seventeenth century necessarily the same as the notion of "justice" held by New Yorkers today. And so as old ways of living and thinking gave place to new, the law changed too—or, if one agreed with Professor Beale, the judges' rational processes found in the law rules applicable to the new conditions. Changes or new discoveries in the common law came gradually. Seldom if ever were they abrupt reversals of ancient maxims; rather they grew out of the familiar process of analyzing the precedents and finding *distinctions* between the facts of the cases which had given rise to those precedents and the facts now before the court. The common law, Holmes said, was a "seamless web." The judges kept weaving it in fresh patterns, yet they did not break the threads with the past.

It was this slowly changing, gradually growing body of the common law which underlay the American legal system in our country's earliest days and profoundly influences it today. To be sure, the influence of modern skepticism has wrought a great change in even the judicial conception of it. As we have seen, Holmes' view that the law consisted of particular, enforceable judicial decisions (which might differ from state to state) rather than being a uniform "omnipresence in the sky" gained wide acceptance.

*The Expansion of Statute Law.* The old idea of the completeness and uniformity of "law" suffered a further great change in the present century. Sixty years ago it was possible for a scholar to write that of the various forms which law takes, *statutes* were the least important. Compared to judge-made (or "judge-found") law, legislation was indeed altogether insignificant. That cannot be said today. Over and over, legislatures have invaded the precincts of the ancient law. No longer, in many states, is burglary "breaking and entering in the night-time"; a statute defines it otherwise. No longer in the devolution of realty confined by a rule made by an English judge in 1574; state statutes make different rules. No longer are the very procedures in the courtroom wholly governed by the common law; they must comply with "codes of procedure" adopted by state legislatures. Rights and remedies are fixed, today, more by statutes than by judicial precedents. Yet the influence of the common law persists. Although some statutes in effect reverse the common law, many simply codify it. In recent decades, the legal profession has taken the lead in an effort to "restate" the law pertaining to various branches of human activity—contracts, torts, agency, for example—and to foster the enactment of uniform legislation in the various states. Who thus "restates" the law and drafts the bills? Lawyers: men learned in the common law, men trained in the time-tested ways of reasoning by analogy from judicial precedents. Present-day Americans put more reliance on statute law than their fathers did, but in legislatures as well as in courtrooms the spirit of the common law is still pervasive.

## ELEMENTS OF THE JUDICIAL PROCESS

This chapter is not the place for an extended analysis of the judicial process, any more than it was for a detailed study of jurisprudence, but any understanding of the work done by the judicial branch of government (whether national or state) requires a grasp of a few fundamentals of judicial procedure.

### Adversary Proceedings

The first of these is that in the main, court decisions result from the workings of what is called an *adversary process*. There are exceptions to this: judges usually issue orders making wills effective, for instance, without any disputants or "adversaries" appearing before them. The chief business of trial courts, however, is to try cases in which one "party" is opposing another "party." In a criminal case, the "parties" are the government on the one hand and the accused "defendant" on the other. In the typical civil case or "lawsuit," the complaining party is the "plaintiff" and the party he is suing is, again, the "defendant." It is disputes between parties which are settled in court by the verdicts of juries or the rulings of judges, as the case may be.[8]

---

[8] Not all disputes are settled in court; a great majority of civil cases, though they begin with formal legal proceedings, end by an agreement or "settlement" between the parties, voluntarily reached by the parties rather than imposed by the judge.

## Actual Controversies

Second, *the dispute must be a real one:* the parties must really be adversaries, with conflicting interests at stake. Courts cannot properly entertain cases wherein the contending parties are actually on the same side, both wanting the same result. Years ago a statute went into effect requiring a reduction in railroad fares. Promptly a railroad company official arranged with a friend to test the constitutionality of this statute through a trumped-up lawsuit. The friend asked to buy a ticket, saying that he would not pay more than the new statutory price. The railroad refused to sell the ticket to him at that price. He bought a ticket at the price charged by the railroad, higher than the maximum allowed by the statute, and then brought suit against the railroad for the difference. When the case was tried, and later when it was appealed, the plaintiff's lawyer made no effort to win it for his client; on the contrary, he joined with the railroad's lawyer in arguing that the statute was unconstitutional. Eventually the Supreme Court held that this case should never have been tried at all, for the parties were not really adversaries: they both wanted the same result.

This does not mean that all "trumped-up" cases are thrown out by the courts. A test of constitutionality can be desired and a lawsuit properly instituted for that purpose—so long as the parties are genuinely opposed to each other and so give the court the benefit of hearing both sides fully presented. It must be admitted, too, that sometimes if the case takes the form of an adversary proceeding, judges will shut their eyes to the lack of any real conflict: the obvious example of this can be found frequently in the divorce courts, where the unhappy "parties" often formally oppose each other, yet are both anxious that the divorce be granted.

A few states give their highest courts one task which departs from the general rule that only actual controversies between opposing parties should be decided. They permit "advisory opinions" as to the validity of pending state legislation. In such a state, a legislature which is considering a bill may request and obtain from the state's supreme tribunal a statement of whether the measure, if enacted, would be constitutional or not. The Supreme

Court of the United States, however, has no such function. The validity of an act of Congress cannot be tested until the act is in effect and some person asserts that it deprives him of his constitutional rights.

## Justiciable Questions

The next prerequisite is that the controversy must be *justiciable,* raising a question that can properly be settled by judicial proceedings. A professional baseball player might sue his club's owners for payment of his salary, and the case would be heard; but no court would consider his protest against an umpire for calling him out at third, even though his disagreement with the umpire is angry and vocal. Normally, in a civil suit, the plaintiff in his "pleadings"—the formal, written complaint which begins the suit —must show that he has somehow been injured or imminently threatened with injury by the defendant. The injury must be substantial; when damages are sought, it must be measurable in terms of money. If your agreed-upon salary is $600 a month, failure to pay it for a month obviously results in your suffering measurable injury—a financial loss of $600. For this you can sue. But what's the price tag on an umpire's upraised thumb?

Now it is easy enough to say that a dispute between a baserunner and an umpire does not constitute a justiciable controversy. Some far more significant cases, however, have been rejected by the Supreme Court on similar grounds. The first and most famous of these was the case of *Luther v. Borden,* 7 Howard 1 (1849). That case arose out of "Dorr's Rebellion" in Rhode Island in 1842, wherein a group of Rhode Islanders, claiming that the old colonial charter under which the state was governed disfranchised the masses, wrote a new constitution and elected Thomas W. Dorr as governor. The established state government declared "martial law" and put down the uprising. In the course of doing so, Borden, a member of the state militia, entered the home of Luther, one of Dorr's adherents, and arrested him. Luther sued for damages, claiming that Borden was merely a private citizen—the old charter government having allegedly been superseded by Dorr's government—and so, having no authority to enter his house, had unlawfully trespassed on his property. Damages can be assessed for

trespass: so far, then, the case appeared fit for judicial consideration. The central issue, however, was which government was the
legitimate government of Rhode Island at the time of Luther's arrest. And this, in turn, depended on the validity of Luther's claim
that the old government was unconstitutional because it was not a
"republican form of government" guaranteed to the states by Article IV of the Constitution.

The Supreme Court denied Luther the right to make this claim
(upon which his whole case largely rested) in a judicial proceeding.
Chief Justice Taney declared that it raised not a judicial but a
*political question.* That question could be answered by Congress,
when it decided to seat senators and representatives elected under
either the old charter or Dorr's constitution; but it was not a
matter for any court to pass upon. On several occasions since, the
Supreme Court has avoided some heated questions by calling them
"political." In *Colegrove v. Green,* 328 U.S. 549 (1946) an Illinois
voter sought to have a "gerrymander" of Illinois' congressional
districts declared invalid. The Supreme Court (with three dissents) agreed on the dismissal of the complaint, Justice Frankfurter saying: "Courts ought not to enter this political thicket.
The remedy for unfairness in districting is to secure state legislatures that will apportion properly, or to invoke the ample powers
of Congress. . . ." The "political thicket" was entered in 1962 in
the case of *Baker v. Carr,*[9] when the Court, with six separate
opinions being written and Frankfurter vigorously dissenting,
held that a district court had jurisdiction to hear a case in which
voters challenged the apportionment of seats in the Tennessee
legislature. This significant decision was promptly followed by a
spate of suits to compel reapportionment, in various states. It also
cast new doubt not only on the meaning of the phrase "political
question" but on the likelihood of the Court's invoking it in important cases in the future.

### Ripeness for Adjudication

Courts have little patience with litigants who come before them
without first availing themselves of other proper means of getting

[9] 369 U.S. 186 (1962).

what they want. A plaintiff who sues for damages without having already demanded payment from the defendant would get short shrift in court. And when a plaintiff is claiming that some government agency has deprived him of his rights, normally he must seek all the administrative remedies open to him before a court will hear his suit. If, for instance, he is an old man who believes that the amount of his monthly federal old-age benefit is less than what he is entitled to, it would be futile for him to go to court until he has filed a claim with an administrative body, the Social Security Administration in the Department of Health, Education, and Welfare and has insisted on a hearing before that agency's appeals board. Most courts are so overwhelmed by pending litigation that they are glad to get rid of cases not yet "ripe" for their decision.

To sum up: ordinarily, to be decided in judicial proceedings, a case must be a genuine controversy between adversaries who stand to gain or lose by the outcome; the controversy must be of a nature appropriate for judicial determination, raising questions that can be effectively answered by a court; and the issue must be ready for judicial determination, all other possible means of deciding it having been exhausted. Yet all these conditions could be satisfied and a plaintiff be left at the starting post if he failed to bring his suit in the right court, one having "jurisdiction" or authority to decide his particular case. We cannot, once more, examine fully the complications of all jurisdictional questions, but it is time to observe the structure of the judicial systems in the United States and the broad outlines of the authority of the various courts which comprise them.

## THE JUDICIAL STRUCTURE

### The State Courts

The great preponderance of the people's legal business takes place in one or another of the state and local courts. Here most criminal cases are tried; here most civil disputes are decided. In these courts the disposition of a deceased person's property is determined, the transfer of deeds to real estate is registered, divorces are granted or denied, and the adoption of children is approved.

Generally speaking, litigants in these state courts can appeal the lower tribunal's decision to a higher court, often to the highest court of the state. Only occasionally, as we shall see, can they go still further and obtain a hearing before the United States Supreme Court. Yet the small percentage of state decisions which are ultimately reviewed in Washington include some of the most significant constitutional cases in our history. We cannot well study the federal government's judicial branch, therefore, without being aware of the existence and general shape of the judicial systems of the states.

Every state constitution provides for a "judicial branch," a system of local courts with varying jurisdictions. In each state these head up, ultimately, into a final appellate court. This is usually called the "Supreme Court" of the state, although in New York, confusingly, the title of "Supreme Court" is given to the system of major trial courts, with the court at the apex of the appellate structure being named the Court of Appeals.

Not only in nomenclature, but also in functions and methods, the state judicial systems vary somewhat. Usually, for instance, the county is the primary *geographic* unit of jurisdiction: if you were charged with burglary you would be tried in the court of the county where the crime took place, and if you wanted to probate a will, you would go to a court in the county where the deceased resided. In some states, however, there are also city courts of more local jurisdiction; and at the base of the structure in many states are the part-time local "justices of the peace." States vary also in the extent to which they divide up the *functional* jurisdiction of their courts. Many of them have assigned matters pertaining to wills, real property, and sometimes domestic relations to courts which do not handle criminal cases or other kinds of civil actions: witness such titles as "surrogate," "probate judge," and "land court." In a few, separate "juvenile courts" have been established to deal only with cases involving youthful offenders.

## The Federal Courts

Article III of the Constitution says that there shall be one United States Supreme Court, and authorizes Congress to establish "inferior" courts. This Congress has done. It has created a system of trial and appellate courts, wherein in practice most litigation brought in the federal courts is completed. Only a very small proportion of such litigation reaches the Supreme Court of the United States.

*Trial Courts.* At the base of the federal government's judicial pyramid are the courts which try cases—the United States district courts. Each state (and the District of Columbia) comprises at least one judicial "district"; some large states are divided, geographically, into more than one, so that there are now 87 district courts. In each district sit from one to eighteen judges (not together, for each trial is presided over by a single judge) bringing the total number of such judges, active now, to 307. In addition, Congress has established some "legislative courts" including the Court of Claims, which passes initially upon claims against the federal government, for back pay, for example, or for reimbursement for money allegedly spent on authorized government business.

Federal trials take place in the district court's courtroom. Here a single judge presides. Here juries sit. Here decisions are made, verdicts handed down, sentences imposed. And here most cases end, although the loser who believes that an error of law has been committed by the judge can appeal to a higher tribunal.

The Constitution, as we saw when we considered *Marbury v. Madison,* makes the Supreme Court itself a "trial court" for certain kinds of cases, over which it is given "original jurisdiction" by Article III. Rare indeed, however, is the case which begins as well as ends in the Supreme Court. Once in a great while an interstate dispute, over rights to divert the water of a great river, for instance, or to tax the estate of a rich man who died in one state but left property in another, has been brought directly to the Supreme Court by the complaining state; but the highest tribunal of the nation is primarily an appellate court, reviewing the claims that error has tainted the proceedings in the courts below.

*Appellate Courts.* Except for the few instances where statutes (or, in the case of the Supreme Court, the Constitution) provide otherwise, the task of the federal appellate courts is solely to pass on the legal questions raised by those aggrieved litigants who claim that error was committed in the trial of the case. The error might be a mistaken ruling of the judge excluding certain offered evidence; it might be his refusal to dismiss the case because the statute under which it was brought was unconstitutional; it might be in his one-sided instructions to the jury, or in his failure to explain the law correctly to the jury; it might consist of his failure to declare a mistrial when a jury is exposed to misleading newspaper headlines prejudicial to the defendant; it might be found in any one of a host of other procedural decisions which any trial judge must make. The thing to remember is that the hearing of an appeal is not a new *trial:* in an appellate court there is no jury and

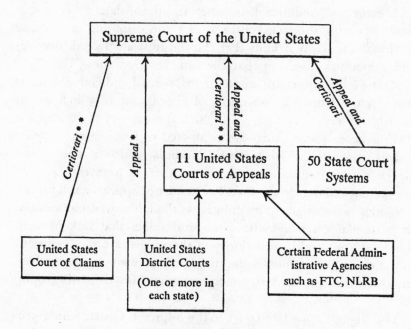

### Diagram Showing the Appellate Authority of the Supreme Court

\* Direct appeals from district courts are allowed only in very special circumstances to save time when time is crucial, as when a federal statute has been invalidated, or a federal injunction has blocked a vital process of state government.

\*\* A Court of Appeals, like the Court of Claims, may certify to the Supreme Court "any question of law . . . as to which instructions are desired." This device is now seldom used because certified questions tend to raise hypothetical, rather than real, issues. These the Supreme Court shuns for the same reasons which have impelled it to avoid giving advisory opinions.

From Wallace Mendelson, *The Constitution and the Supreme Court* (New York: Dodd, Mead & Company, Inc., 1959).

no witnesses are called to testify. Instead, the lawyers for the contending parties submit written briefs and make oral arguments on the disputed points of law. The appellate court does not sav whether the *result* of the trial—verdict for the plaintiff or for the defendant, guilty or not guilty—was right or wrong. That is not the appellate court's function. It reviews the *conduct* of the trial. If it finds that during the trial no error of law was made, damaging to the losing party, then the judgment or verdict of the trial court is *affirmed*. If, on the other hand, the appellate court decides that such error was committed, it issues an appropriate order, sometimes *reversing* the trial court's ruling and disposing of the case forthwith (as when it finds that the statute was, indeed, invalid) and sometimes directing that the case be tried anew.

Most of this appellate work, in the federal judicial system, is done by the United States courts of appeal, one of which sits in each of the eleven *circuits* into which the country is divided for this purpose. These courts are composed of from three to seven judges (nine in the District of Columbia, which is one of the eleven circuits); usually three sit together to hear the lawyers' arguments and decide the case. Each court of appeals has a presiding judge, who assigns to his colleagues the job of writing opinions in particular cases and also often undertakes that task himself. These, if approved by a majority of the judges, are the "opinions of the court." Occasionally the judges disagree among themselves, in which case the minority members may file "dissenting opinions."

The highest appellate court is the Supreme Court, which proceeds in a similar manner. The nine justices study the record of the case and the lawyers' briefs, hear the arguments, and vote on the decision. Usually, too, because most cases come to them only after being heard and decided by a lower appellate tribunal, they analyze that appellate court's published opinion. The chief justice decides who shall write the Supreme Court's opinion, and other justices are free to write dissents. Sometimes when they agree with the result but feel that the Court's opinion is incorrectly reasoned or omits an especially significant point, justices also file "concurring opinions," stating their own reasons for siding with the majority.

In reading the opinions of appellate courts, it is wise, though not always easy, to try to distinguish between the reasons expressed by the court which are necessary for the decision of the particular case, and the additional material which often creeps into those opinions. In legal Latin, this distinction is between the *ratio decidendi* and the *obiter dictum*. The former provides the legal rule which must be followed by lower courts in similar cases; the latter is an expression of opinion which may indicate what the judges believe, but which establishes no legal rule or binding precedent.

The significance of this distinction should not blind us, however, to the frequent importance of *obiter dicta* in Supreme Court opinions. Often the statements of the Court, though not essential to the particular case, give a strong hint as to what its attitude would be in other cases. Sometimes, too, the Court has deliberately gone beyond the immediate needs of the occasion to expound general doctrines of constitutional law. This was the particular forte of Chief Justice Marshall, whose *obiter dicta* were great educational media, shaping the people's ideas about the Constitution. In more recent times Chief Justice Warren's long opinion in *Watkins v. United States*,[10] touching on matters far afield from Watkins' claim that he had been within his rights in refusing to answer a congressional investigating committee's questions, seemed plainly intended to remind Congress and the voters of the general constitutional limitations on such investigating committees' powers.

Appellate courts are not required to write long opinions, or even short ones. They do so, ordinarily, because in a free society they feel obliged to explain to the people the reasons for their holdings. But they will not express their views on the "merits" of a case—the questions of substance raised by the litigants—unless they find, first, that the case is properly before them for adjudication. It must have been brought, in the first place, in the right court, a tribunal authorized to handle this particular kind of dis-

---

10 354 U.S. 178 (1957).

pute; it must then have been brought to the appellate court in the manner prescribed by law. The first thing that the lawyers must show the judge is that the court has *jurisdiction* to decide the case before it.

## THE JURISDICTION OF THE FEDERAL COURTS

As we have seen, most litigation is conducted in state courts. Both contending parties may be, for instance, residents of Michigan; one therefore sues the other in the courts of Michigan. (Which Michigan court he should begin with depends on what the Michigan constitution and statutes say about the trial of cases of the kind he is bringing.) However, although the preponderance of legal business is still in the state courts, the workload of the federal judiciary has constantly increased. That workload is based on the jurisdiction conferred on the federal courts by Article III of the Constitution. The framers of that article could hardly have foreseen the amount of litigation which eventually would be brought before those inferior courts which they were authorizing Congress to create: they could not envisage those great changes in the economic life and transportation facilities of the country which led to a vast increase in the business of the federal government's judicial branch.

### The Constitutional Basis

The jurisdiction of the federal courts, in terms of parties and subject matter, covers, first, cases arising under the Constitution, laws, and treaties of the United States; for example, when an act of Congress gives employees a right to sue their employers for wages legally due them, they can bring this suit in the United States district court. It covers, second, those cases involving "Ambassadors, other public Ministers and Consuls" which were discussed in *Marbury v. Madison;* such cases, if any, may be brought directly to the Supreme Court. Third, it embraces disputes concerning shipping on the high seas, including crimes committed thereon; a sailor who kills another on a fishing trawler off the Grand Banks would be tried for murder in a federal court. Fourth, it covers cases in which the United States government is either the plaintiff (or prosecutor) or defendant; such cases mostly arise under the "laws of the United States," but may also include demands by injured individuals which are brought to the Court of Claims. Fifth, it includes disputes between states; these, again, can be brought directly to the Supreme Court. And finally, and in terms of sheer volume most important, the federal judicial power extends to controversies between citizens of different states.

If you drop in, some morning, at the courtroom of a United States district judge while a trial is in progress, you might find a luckless seaman on trial for his life. More likely, the defendant will be someone accused of cheating on his federal income tax, or possibly a corporation charged with monopolistic practices in violation of the anti-trust laws. (If it should be an anti-trust case which you happen upon, don't stick around for the verdict: such cases are vastly complicated and sometimes the trial alone takes several months.) Most probably, however, you will find a civil suit being tried, in which the plaintiff is a person who has been hurt in an automobile accident and the defendant is the owner of the "other car" or an insurance company. Why are such cases tried in the federal court? They are tried there, in great numbers, because the parties are citizens of different states: you, say, are a Rhode Islander, but it was a car from Massachusetts that knocked you down or the car's owner is a Connecticut trucking corporation.

The present number and scope of federal statutes, the growth of interstate business, and the ease of interstate transportation—these are the factors that the framers could hardly have imagined which have crowded the dockets of the federal courts. To be sure, the Constitution does not say to each of us: "If you sue a citizen of another state, you can bring your suit in a federal court." It authorizes the federal courts to handle cases where there is such "diversity of citizenship" between the parties, but it leaves to Congress the authority to establish the "inferior courts" and, within the limits of Article III, to prescribe their jurisdiction. An act of Congress now provides that the federal courts' "diversity of citizenship" jurisdiction shall apply only to cases where $10,000 or more is at stake. Even so, in 1962 the federal district courts were laboring with a backlog of some 81,000 untried cases.

Because those dockets are so crowded, year by year a smaller percentage of the total volume of cases is ultimately reviewed by the Supreme Court. Some appealed cases the Supreme Court is required to consider, but in the great majority of instances the lawyer who says that he will "fight this all the way to the Supreme Court" is whistling in the wind. There would have to be a dozen Supreme Courts to decide all the federal cases wherein such ultimate review is sought.

## The Supreme Court's Jurisdiction

The scope of the Supreme Court's authority to review the decisions of other courts is determined by Congress, while to a large degree the extent of the exercise of that authority is decided by the Court itself. By statute, the Court is required to consider cases appealed to it from state courts in certain circumstances, but it has wide discretion in deciding whether or not to consider most of the cases wherein review is sought.

*The Right of Appeal.* A litigant who loses in the highest state tribunal authorized to decide his case (usually the state's supreme court) can appeal to the Supreme Court of the United States if he has claimed some right under the federal Constitution or statutes and that claim has been rejected. For example, he may have been convicted of breaking a state law prohibiting the publication of Socialist newspapers. Appealing to the supreme court of the state, he claims that the state law violates the Fourteenth Amendment of the Constitution—in other words, he says that he has a constitutional right to publish his paper. If the state court rejects his argument and affirms his conviction, he can then appeal to the United States Supreme Court, which, if the "federal question" which he raised is a substantial one, *must* then accept the parties' briefs, hear the arguments of counsel, and either affirm or reverse the state court's decision.

The catch, here, lies in that word "substantial." Even when a litigant assumes that he has an absolute right of appeal, the Supreme Court might not hear his case, for it does not have to do so if the justices deem that the "federal question" in his case is "insubstantial." As the pressure of business on the Court has grown, so has the need of winnowing out the less significant cases, and there has been a growing tendency to reject even the appealed cases on the ground that the issues which they present are not sufficiently important for the court's attention. As Chief Justice Vinson explained a few years ago, "To remain effective the Supreme Court must continue to decide only those cases which present questions whose resolution will have immediate importance far beyond the particular facts and parties involved." [11]

*The Writ of Certiorari.* Most of the Supreme Court's business "comes up on *certiorari*"; that is, the losing party in the state supreme court or the U.S. court of appeals petitions the Supreme Court to order the court below to "certify" to it the entire record of the case. (*Writ of certiorari,* then, is an "order to certify," so that the Supreme Court may decide the case.) Whether or not to grant the petition, issue the writ, and hear the case is a matter to be determined by the Supreme Court. Again, it could not grant all the petitions which come to it and still keep abreast of the disputes which it must settle. There would simply not be enough time to hear all these cases; years would elapse before the arguments could be delivered and the opinions written. Most petitions for certiorari, therefore, are rejected. Such rejection leaves the lower court's ruling intact. It makes that lower court's decision final. But it does *not* necessarily imply that the Supreme Court agrees with the lower court. In a case wherein it refuses to grant certiorari, the Supreme Court takes no position at all on the merits of the legal issues involved.

When, however, at least four justices out of the nine on the Supreme Court believe that a case should be heard, the court issues the writ as requested and proceeds to give full consideration to the merits of the dispute. This discretion is not lightly or whimsically exercised. The court has its own customary and understandable reasons for granting certiorari. One—about which justices often differ among themselves—is the relative importance of the issue raised, as described in the petition for the writ. Another is the need for uniformity in the law: if similar cases have been decided differently by courts of appeals in two or more

---

[11] Address before the American Bar Association, September 7, 1949, 69 Sup. Ct. VI (1949).

circuits, obviously there is need for the one final decision which only the Supreme Court can render.

In Chapter 5, when we considered the Supreme Court's great function of judicial review, we saw how the frequent ambiguity of constitutional clauses gives to the Supreme Court a considerable area of choice when it interprets the Constitution. Now we see, also, that the justices have wide discretion not only in deciding cases but in choosing which cases to decide. Yet, as we also saw in Chapter 5, the choice is not exclusively their own. The Constitution gives Congress the final say as to the scope of the Supreme Court's appellate jurisdiction. Angered by a decision on a particular question—such as the alleged denial of "due process" to witnesses before congressional committees or to people detained in police custody without prompt arraignment—Congress might enact a law forbidding the Supreme Court to decide such questions in the future. Yet the right to "due process" is a constitutional right which can be invoked by a person who claims that he has been arbitrarily deprived of his life, liberty, or property. Some court must pass upon his claim. If Congress should prevent the Supreme Court from doing so, the final decision of such "due process" questions would be made by the eleven courts of appeal and the fifty supreme courts of the states. Governmental conduct deemed fair and reasonable in one circuit or state might, in a different circuit or state, be held to violate the fundamental law of the country. The Constitution, the "supreme law of the land," could mean several different things, in different parts of the United States. The obvious disadvantages of such fragmentation of the Constitution have kept Congress from making sweeping inroads on the Supreme Court's appellate jurisdiction. Despite occasionally vigorous efforts to curtail the Court's power, it remains supreme.

And so the justices constitute the dominant tribunal in one of the three great branches of the government, the one furthest removed from the people, and they have the power profoundly to influence the shape and form of American government, the national economy, and the social customs of the country. Because they hold this power in their hands, to understand our political system we must know more about them, especially how they reach the seats of the mighty and how they meet their great responsibilities.

## THE JUSTICES OF THE SUPREME COURT

### The Process of Selection

If you want to be a congressman, you "throw your hat into the ring." If you seek a presidential nomination, you may stump the country or, while coyly disclaiming any interest in the office, arrange to have your name constantly in the headlines, your picture on a magazine cover, your face and voice on television. But no one in his right mind would campaign for a position on the Supreme Court of the United States. The most he could do would be to have friends bring his suitability to the attention of the President; and even this might be a dubious course to take, for overt eagerness for the job is normally a disqualification for it. The idea that "the office should seek the man" has little practical validity in the matter of filling most elective posts, but it is dominant in appointments to judicial positions, especially those on the Supreme Court.[12]

The responsibility for the selection rests with the President. For advice and suggestions he can turn whenever he wishes—to his Attorney General, to trusted friends, to political advisers, to distinguished lawyers or former judges, and perhaps, even, to the sitting justices, though few of the latter are likely to be willing to advise him. In making up his mind he may prudently seek to ascertain whether the Senate would confirm the nomination of the man he is considering for the post. But the ultimate choice is his.

What leads him to the selection that he makes? What are the qualifications that fit a person to be a Supreme Court justice? The

---

12 On rare occasions, men frankly aspiring to the Supreme Court have been able, through their close personal acquaintance with the President, to mention their hopes to him directly without incurring his resentment: Robert H. Jackson seems to have done so and was appointed by President F. D. Roosevelt. But this is the exception, not the rule.

Constitution fixes none; there is not even a legal requirement that every justice must be a lawyer or have had legal training. No age limits are set, no rule requires that different parts of the country be represented on the Court, there is no constitutional or statutory provision for bipartisanship. To find out what, in fact, are or have been the important qualifications for membership on the Court, we have to look at the justices themselves, past and present. Doing that, we find only two prerequisites that seem generally and consistently applicable. First, all justices have in fact been lawyers. Second, they have all been men. And although the first prerequisite will doubtless endure, the increasing number of women in the legal profession seems likely, eventually, to be reflected by the appointment of a woman to the Court.[13]

So, then, when a vacancy occurs, all we can safely predict is that a lawyer will be named to fill it. Which lawyer? In answering that question, Presidents and their advisers appear to have given varying amounts of weight to a number of considerations and factors which they deem relevant.

*Age.* Although the Court's august dignity might be diminished by the appointment of a platoon of boyish justices, a white-bearded bench is also open to criticism: thus a "debunking" book about the Court, published shortly before Roosevelt's attack on it in 1937, was entitled *The Nine Old Men.* One by-product of the controversy in the 1930's was the passage of legislation permitting justices who have served for at least ten years to retire at seventy, on full pay. This implied, at least, a preference for men under that age. When a vacancy occurs, therefore, a President naturally seeks to fill it with someone "not too young and not too old." Of the last twelve appointees, eight were in their fifties when named to the court. One was forty-eight, one was sixty-two, and two, Justices Stewart and White, were unusually young—forty-one and forty-four, respectively.

*Experience.* Four appointments by President Eisenhower seemed to evidence his assumption that judicial experience is an

---

13 Florence Allen of Ohio, appointed by President Coolidge in 1927, is the only woman yet to serve as a U.S. court of appeals judge.

important qualification for appointment to the Supreme Court. Justices Harlan, Whittaker, and Stewart were all "promoted" from the court of appeals, and Justice Brennan from the highest court of New Jersey. Perhaps, however, the actual experience of the first two of these gentlemen was less significant than their apparent experience. Although they each bore the *title* of "Judge," thus making their nominations seem appropriate, not one of them had really had much experience on the bench. Whittaker had served on the court of appeals only three years, Harlan for only a few months. The Supreme Court's history does not indicate that previous work as a judge is a prerequisite either for appointment or for greatness as a Supreme Court justice. Some of the historic figures had, indeed, served long on state courts before their elevation: one thinks of Holmes and Cardozo. But others, such as Hughes, Stone, Jackson, and Warren (Eisenhower's first appointee) came to the Court after distinguished careers in politics and government service. The eminence of such men reminds us that greatness on the Court requires not so much the technical knowledge gained on an appellate bench, as statesmanship in the largest sense. It also demands a high degree of legal craftsmanship which is not an exclusively judicial attribute: thus Brandeis came to the Supreme Court directly from a successful private practice, and F. D. Roosevelt appointed two distinguished law professors.

*Reputation.* Usually a President intends—not always with complete success—to appoint men whose general reputation makes them acceptable to the public, the legal profession, and the Senate. Most voters know little about the quality of particular judges and lawyers, but on rare occasions one becomes so preeminent that his appointment is almost inevitable. President Hoover could hardly have seen eye to eye with Benjamin N. Cardozo, chief judge of the New York Court of Appeals in 1930; yet to fill a Supreme Court vacancy he named Cardozo, whose towering fame made any other selection almost unthinkable. In such instances, the reputation of the President himself is at stake. Ten years later, the one judge in the country whose name was universally revered was Learned Hand of the U. S. court of appeals; F. D. Roosevelt escaped the necessity of appointing him only because of his advanced age.

The nominee's eminence is not always a source of strength in winning senatorial confirmation. Big men make enemies. Brandeis was a famous lawyer, but his confirmation was achieved only after a bitter fight involving not only the legal profession but leading laymen: the president of Harvard University, for instance, demanded that the Senate reject the nomination, while Harvard's aged ex-president led the pro-Brandeis forces. The one nominee actually rejected in this century, John J. Parker, had been an able appellate judge, but his decisions had made enemies who brought about his defeat. A President who wants to "play it safe" in terms of winning senatorial approval can, however, play one trump card. He can nominate a member of the Senate itself. The Senate's "club spirit" is so strong that such a nomination is virtually certain to be confirmed. Thus in 1937, Roosevelt's "Court-packing" plan aroused such animosity that when a vacancy occurred that summer, doubts were expressed that any Roosevelt nominee would be accepted. The President settled those doubts by unexpectedly naming a senator, Hugo L. Black.

*Residence.* As in the selection of his cabinet, the President in making nominations for the Supreme Court may give some thought to "geographical balance." Other things being equal, he would prefer to have the justices come from a variety of states. This is seldom a consideration of major significance. Throughout the 1930's three of the justices were New Yorkers, and few if any voices were raised in criticism. Some regional representation, however, does seem important. The Court must frequently reflect the general viewpoint as to what is fair or what "shocks the conscience"; and if social viewpoints differ from one major part of the country to another, then there is good reason to heed sectional origin or background in appointing justices. The fact that three southerners graced the Court at the time of its unanimous decision outlawing school segregation undoubtedly was a moderating factor in the aftermath. Southern criticism of the Court for that decision was violent enough, as it was—but it would have been still fiercer if all the justices had been northerners.

*Religion.* Ideally, perhaps, a man's particular religious faith

Fitzpatrick in the *St. Louis Post-Dispatch*

### Above and beyond the call of politics

This was drawn in 1953 after Chief Justice Vinson's death. President Eisenhower filled the vacant chair by appointing a politician, Earl H. Warren—but the latter quickly showed, by his conduct on the bench, that he agreed that the Court is indeed "above and beyond the call of politics."

should have no bearing on his qualifications for the Court. The President who makes the appointments, however, is a political leader and, as we saw in Chapter 9, religious interests have a political impact. There is no direct evidence that religious preference has dictated any selection. The circumstantial evidence suggests that it has. Since 1916 there has been at least one Jewish member of the court, and for some years two: when Justice Frankfurter retired in 1962, he was succeeded by Arthur Goldberg. And since 1894, except for one seven-year period, at least one seat on the court has been occupied by a Roman Catholic.

*Partisanship.* Most appointments have gone to men of the same political party as the President who chooses them. This, however, is by no means an unbreakable rule. Of President Truman's four appointees, one, Senator Burton, was a Republican; of President Eisenhower's five, one, Judge Brennan, was a Democrat. In the main, though, a President is under pressure to give this pre-eminent recognition to a member of his own party, though such partisan pressure is not as heavy as it is in the case of lesser judicial appointments. Although the honor is seldom or never bestowed simply as a reward for political services, the rumored promise of F. D. Roosevelt to appoint Senator Robinson, a move forestalled by Robinson's death, would have fallen into that category. Byron K. White, President Kennedy's first appointee, had been prominent as an organizer of the 1960 campaign. Possibly the naming of the Attorney General to the Court, which frequently happens (e.g., McReynolds, Stone, Jackson, Murphy, Clark) can be classified as a "political" choice in terms of either gratitude for services performed or of "kicking upstairs" a man whose cabinet post the President wished to give to someone else. The selection of Justice Brennan by President Eisenhower had obvious political overtones. It occurred during the presidential campaign of 1956, when the Republican managers had high (and justified) hopes of making large gains among eastern urban Catholic voters, most of whom were registered Democrats. For a Republican President, running for reelection, to choose an eastern urban Catholic and Democrat for the Supreme Court was a skillful political move, wholly aside from the excellent qualifications of its chief beneficiary.

If party politics, however, plays an inevitable role in the selection process, it is of no visible significance in the conduct of the justices once they are appointed. As members of the Court, they are acutely aware that their position is completely apart from the party battle. Political ambitions, as we have seen, have on rare occasions affected individual justices, such as McLean in *Dred Scott* days. Charles Evans Hughes, when a sitting justice, was nominated for President in 1916. Although nothing in his judicial record gave any evidence of his judgment's being affected by ambition, it was a poor precedent. It has never been repeated, though in 1948 Justice Douglas did not discourage some efforts to promote his nomination, and in early 1956, when President Eisenhower was ill, there were rumors that he would step aside for Chief Justice Warren. The Chief Justice fittingly scotched the rumors. The Court would be in sorry plight if it appeared to be a stepping stone to the presidency. The party politician who takes his seat on the Supreme Court, therefore, ceases to be an active partisan or politician.

*Viewpoint.* Judges are human. Although they must abjure partisanship and ambition, they still have their opinions about right and wrong, their convictions about the role of government under the Constitution. Accordingly, in selecting men for the Supreme Court, Presidents are likely to prefer people whose general outlook seems to be like their own. Franklin Roosevelt chose justices reputed to be "liberal"; without knowing how they would decide particular cases, he could guess that they would interpret the Constitution as permitting a broad exercise of federal power over the economy, yet vigorously protecting First Amendment liberties. At best, however, he could only guess; and such guesses sometimes turn out wrong. One of F. D. Roosevelt's appointees eventually gained a reputation as a leader of the "conservative wing" of the court. Much earlier, Theodore Roosevelt made a bad guess; he chose Oliver Wendell Holmes, Jr., with confidence that Holmes on the Court would "vote right" on an important antitrust case. Holmes promptly voted the other way, and the President was bitterly angry. In 1959 rumors persisted, despite official denials, that President Eisenhower was surprised and upset by the judicial views of his first appointee, Chief Justice Warren. Usually, though, it is not too hard to guess right. President Harding correctly assumed that all the justices he named were "sound" (i.e., conservative) men, and other Presidents, in selecting old and trusted friends (as Coolidge chose Stone, and Truman both Vinson and Minton) presumably knew how these men reacted to problems of statecraft. Even so, times change and so do men. In former days it was said of the justices, "few die and none resign," and although today retirement is made financially easier, many justices stay on the bench to a ripe old age. Some grow in intellectual power as the years advance; in others, early attitudes harden into inflexible prejudices. The very independence of the Court fosters the intellectual development, or at least change, of its members.

## The Justices' Tenure

All federal judges are appointed "for life or good behaviour," which means that so long as they are not removed for wrongdoing —and no Supreme Court justice and only four lower court judges have been impeached and removed—they can stay on the bench as long as they like. The reason, as we know, is that life tenure is one safeguard of the independence of the judiciary. In Chapter 5 we saw that most state judges are assumed to be impartial even though they are popularly elected; we noticed, too, that the appointed Supreme Court justices are not so "independent" that they lightly and needlessly flout Congress. Secure in their own personal positions, they are nevertheless concerned for the status and influence of the Court as an institution. Furthermore, they do not live in a world apart, but, like other men, hear the wind rising and feel which way it is blowing. All this is true: yet the fact remains that life tenure means that no justice is personally answerable to the President, to the Congress, or to the voters for his decisions. His freedom of action is greater than that of the other leading officials of our government.

When a vacancy occurs through a justice's death or retirement, it is not filled, ordinarily, until after the successor has been nominated by the President and confirmed by the Senate. So confirmed, the successor immediately begins his term, with life tenure. So when a justice has died when Congress was not in session, the President has almost always left his post unfilled until Congress reassembles. Then, and not until then, a nomination is sent to the Senate for its approval. In the interim, the Court gets along well enough with eight justices instead of nine.[14] Justices, of course,

---

[14] Occasionally, when, because a vacancy exists or a justice is ill or absent, only eight justices consider a pending case, they have divided four to four. In such a situation, the Court issues no opinion. The decision is to leave undisturbed the ruling of the appellate court from which the case came, but it does not establish any constitutional doctrines or create a precedent which lower courts are bound to follow in later cases.

are not the only officials subject to Senate confirmation. Many positions, such as cabinet posts and ambassadorships, are filled in the same way. Vacancies may occur when Congress is not in session; if this happens, a statute provides that the President, alone, may make an *interim* appointment, the appointee to serve during Congress's recess and through the next session of Congress. If by that time the Senate has not confirmed his nomination, he must relinquish his post. This is all very well for cabinet members and ambassadors, but it is not consistent with the idea of judicial independence. It means that an *interim* Supreme Court justice must decide cases and write opinions while anxiously awaiting senatorial approval. He may be tempted to weigh each decision in terms of the senatorial opposition which it will arouse. Accordingly, with only three exceptions before 1953, Presidents avoided making such *interim* appointments to the Supreme Court, and the new justice took his seat only when it was definitely his for life. President Eisenhower broke this tradition; Chief Justice Warren and Justices Brennan and Stewart all were appointed by him while Congress was in recess. The first two were confirmed quickly enough when Congress reconvened, but Justice Stewart waited for many tense months in 1959 while senatorial critics of his opinions delayed his confirmation. All that time he was a member of the Court, voting on the hotly disputed cases that came before it. This unhappy experience made doubly welcome an early return to the old and sound custom by which no justice, once on the bench, is beholden to any senator.

## The Work of the Justices

The Supreme Court "sits" for a term roughly equivalent to the old academic year, beginning in October and usually winding up in early June. The visible working hours seem short. Four days a week, the Court convenes at noon and, with a luncheon break, remains in session only until about four-thirty. During most of that period, the justices sit behind a long raised bench and listen to lawyers' arguments. They may, and often do, interrupt to ask questions. But the questions are important. They not only clarify the facts, but often test the validity of counsel's argument by pushing it to its logical extremes.

Friday is given over to the Court's weekly "conference," at which the justices vote on the cases which have been argued, and the responsibility for preparing the opinions is assigned. These are decidedly secret affairs; in fact, the decisions are held in strict confidence until they are formally announced in court. Only a justice could say whether a given case produced a long discussion at the Friday session or was settled by a quick vote—and he won't tell. The Court's written opinion on the case is circulated to all of the justices well before its announcement, so that they may prepare dissents or, occasionally, their own concurring opinions.

When the Court is ready to announce its decision it does so on Monday, before hearing new cases argued. The justice whom the chief justice has selected to write the opinion in a particular case reads it aloud in the courtroom. When he finishes, any dissenting justice may, if he wishes, read his dissenting opinion, although dissents are often left unread. Sometimes, in accordance with the old English practice, the judges do not read opinions but express them orally without benefit of manuscript. This, however, is a somewhat risky practice. Purely oral opinions can lead to ill-considered exaggeration, as when Justice McReynolds, passionately dissenting from a majority ruling, declared that "The Constitution is *gone.*" (That phrase does not appear in McReynolds' written dissent, printed in the official report of the case.[15])

The working hours of the members of the Court are not as light as their formal schedule implies. The volume of business the Court transacts makes this clear. In the 1960–61 term, for example, the Court disposed of 1,911 cases. Of these, 1,643 were petitions for *certiorari;* all were studied, and about 10 per cent were granted. The Court concluded 118 cases, with the issuance of full "opinions" announcing the decision, not to mention numerous concurring and dissenting opinions filed by individual justices. The largest number of decided cases, 42, were civil suits in which the federal government was a party and the interpretation of a federal statute or order was necessary for a just disposition of the case.

---

15 *Norman v. Baltimore & Ohio Railroad Co.*, 294 U.S. 240 (1935).

There were 34 criminal cases, 25 of these coming up from the federal courts and 9 from the state courts. Civil cases in which states were involved as parties numbered 25. In 16 cases both litigants were private persons, and in 1 case the original jurisdiction of the Court was invoked. In order to meet this caseload, the justices must do a substantial amount of homework, reading records and briefs and writing opinions. Their responsibility is great, and their efforts to reach the right decision and state their reasons carefully and persuasively are correspondingly intense.

Even the summer months are not wholly a vacation season for them. Ordinarily, at the end of the term in June, a justice faces a big summer job of reading and analyzing scores of petitions for *certiorari* and recommending to his colleagues whether or not, in each instance, the writ should issue and the case be heard. In all of their duties, justices are not unaided; each of them employs one or more "law clerks" to assist them in checking precedents and sometimes in writing first drafts of opinions. Justices Holmes and Brandeis, years ago, instituted a practice of having a new clerk each year, annually selecting an outstanding member of the graduating class at Harvard Law School. Several justices now follow this system, drawing on other law schools as well as Harvard.

*Perception of the Judge's Role.* As they go about their work, what particular factors influence the justices' performance of their duties and personal conduct? Without psychoanalyzing individuals, we can observe a number of institutional foundations of the official and unofficial behavior of virtually every justice.

First, they are men who have had legal training and, even at the outset, possess some awareness of the nature of the judicial function. More than that, they have a deep respect for their high office. If they come to the Supreme Court from lower courts or from law schools, they have not only a broad knowledge of constitutional history but the habit of thinking like lawyers—analyzing precedents, noting distinctions, reasoning by analogy. If they come directly from active political life, bringing to the Court a useful knowledge of social and political realities, they often seek to supplement these by a self-imposed renewal of their more strictly legal education: former Governor Warren and especially ex-Senator Black thus turned themselves into legal scholars. The "collegial" nature of the Court, a group of men whose only direct, personal responsibility is to each other, itself impels the justices to strive for technical excellence and so win the respect of their colleagues.

Their very independence increases their sense of the importance of impartiality. They feel the obligation both to be and to appear impartial. This leads the conscientious justice to refrain from discussing constitutional questions either in public speeches or private conversation. A series of public lectures, for example, by Justice Frankfurter dealt with the Court in our system of government only in the most general and familiar terms, the speaker neatly avoiding any mention of issues which might come before the Court. Justice Brandeis, who regularly invited friends to weekly tea parties, armed himself beforehand with topics of conversation far removed from the judicial realm—the dairy cooperatives of Denmark, or the savings banks' life insurance system in Massachusetts. Even when they touch more directly on the questions of the day, the justices usually take care to deal in generalities. The tradition of personal self-restraint is a compelling one.

Both effort and self-restraint stem largely from their conception of the role of the Supreme Court, which they see as a necessary and beneficent instrument in the governing of a free people. When the Court is under attack, individual differences are subordinated.[16] Thus in 1937 Brandeis, long a leading "dissenter," joined in exposing the fallacies of President Roosevelt's alleged reasons for wishing to add to the numerical size of the Court. And though dissenting opinions often contain sharp and, rarely, almost unseemly language, in at least one famous instance all the justices agreed on the need for unanimity. That was in the "desegregation" case of 1954. When a majority of the justices voted to hold state school segregation laws unconstitutional, it was apparent to all nine that the decision would cause widespread criticism and bring the court under vehement attack. In such a situation, the effective-

---

[16] Of course, even when the Court is not under attack, justices often suppress their doubts about a particular decision or opinion. Many significant cases have been decided by a unanimous Court. In recent years, however, the habit of filing individual opinions, both concurring and dissenting, has markedly increased.

ness and reputation of the Court might be weakened by any appearance of judicial disagreement. For the sake of the Court's immediate and future authority, differences of opinion had to be surrendered. And so when, after long delay, the decision in *Brown v. Board of Education* was finally announced, it was the unanimous decision of the Supreme Court.

What we have said here about the justices applies, in large degree, to other judges as well, even to those who win their state judicial posts through partisan elections. Not without reason have men who served briefly on a local court preferred thereafter always to be addressed as "Judge," even when, like Cordell Hull, they later rise to national eminence as representative, senator, and secretary of state. There is a stately dignity about judicial office, recognized or felt by the judge and by the rest of us as well. So long as we remember that judges are human and courts are fit subjects for reasonable criticism, this aura of authority is an asset to a society which desires both liberty and stability, both freedom and order. For whatever the essence of law may be, the existence and acceptance of legal rules distinguishes a free society from the nations governed by despots' whims. "Equal Justice Under Law," the phrase carved above the entrance to the Supreme Court building in Washington, is the expression of a central ideal in American life. That ideal can be realized only through the instrumentality of the judicial system.

PART *Five*

# THE GOVERNMENT IN ACTION

CHAPTER **18**

# Government and the National
# Economy

The nature and role of government in the United States have been determined not so much by a preconceived ideology as by experience, self-interest, and institutional machinery facilitating compromise among contending forces. We seem to be an essentially practical people. In the long run, we have followed a down-to-earth, practical course, even when that course caused us to stray from the path of presumably immutable political principles. Our parties, for instance, are highly useful conglomerations of groups with different ideas, in sharp contrast to the ideological parties in western Europe. Our policies are seldom planned long in advance as parts of a complete, coherent program; they are, instead, responses to immediate practical needs or demands. Even our one supposedly fixed constellation, the Constitution, is like the stars themselves in constant motion and looks different from different angles and at different times.

Nevertheless ideas about what government should be and do have had a pervasive influence all through our history. These ideas have not been mere intellectual playthings. They have been put to work by individual people, official bodies, and interest groups for the purpose of influencing policy formation by the national government. They have never become so dominant (save, perhaps, in the Supreme Court, over a thirty-year span) as to over-shadow practical requirements for an extended period, but they have helped create attitudes toward government. They have been part of the American political atmosphere.

We have already glimpsed some of the earliest ideas in action: the theories of the framers of the Constitution and the contrast-ing approaches of Hamilton and Jefferson. About the latter pair, it would be misleadingly easy to say that Hamilton was simply an activist, a centralizer, a "big government" man, and Jefferson the opposite. Underlying their conflict were contrasting visions of what they wanted America to become—a country wherein com-merce and industry would dominate or an essentially agrarian society. The imperatives of the Industrial Revolution and the Union armies' triumph at Gettysburg settled that issue in the nineteenth century. And then, with the northern victors riding high and great business fortunes piling up, a large part of the country came under the sway of an idea about government—an idea foreshadowed plainly enough by the agrarian Jefferson, yet well suited to the purposes of the new industrialists. This was a belief in laissez faire, the French phrase commanding government to "let [things] be" which we considered briefly in our study of Supreme Court decisions on "substantive due process" issues. Because laissez-faire ideas have had lasting influence (though not enduring dominance) and because they were intimately related to an economic theory still embraced by many Americans, we should take a further look at them.

## THE DOCTRINE OF LAISSEZ FAIRE

To the reasonably well-educated American of the late nine-teenth and early twentieth centuries—not the professional econo-mist or philosopher, but the ordinary college graduate or successful businessman—the doctrine of laissez faire, with some practical, nonideological modifications, seemed to be the proper political philosophy for a country of thriving economic enterprise. The opening of the "boundless west" created innumerable opportunities for private profit; the floods of immigration insured industrialists and investors of a cheap labor supply and so of higher profits still. Clearly America was the daring businessman's oyster—if the government would just let him alone. And, so the theory ran, by letting him alone the government would be making its contribution to the maintenance of a satisfactory, self-regulating economic system, a system beneficial, or at least just, to all the people.

The economic side of laissez faire was projected through the influence of a Scottish writer, Adam Smith, whose book *The Wealth of Nations* had appeared way back in 1776. On Smith's theories later economists built elaborate superstructures. To their students—and we are concerned here with what busy, informed, and influential Americans understood and thought, not with the refinements of economic theory—these added up to one axiom: namely, that a free market, wherein anyone can compete and where prices are fixed by the "law of supply and demand," produces a proper economic system. By "free market" they meant conditions of buying and selling in which (1) government played no part, save possibly to prevent outright thefts or other crimes; (2) any producer could offer his goods for sale, and any consumer could buy them; and (3) if more goods were offered than buyers wanted, prices would be reduced to the point where they would be purchased, whereas if there were more buyers than goods, more demand than supply, then prices would be raised. When the price of a commodity fell, some producers would get discouraged and go out of business, thus reducing supply and so increasing the price. When heavy demand drove prices up, new producers would sniff a profit and enter the competition, increasing supply and so bringing prices down again. Always prices would be fluctuating close to the point of equilibrium, the point where they were high enough to insure a profit and low enough to be within the people's reach. This self-adjusting price mechanism, however, would work only if the door of the market was left wide open to competing producers. It depended on freedom of the market not only from governmental price-fixing, but also from any impediments to the unlimited access of competitors.

The emphasis on competition dovetailed neatly with the chief scientific theory of the nineteenth century—Darwin's theory of evolution and "the survival of the fittest." Professors expounded laissez-faire economics as a great social philosophy. A British philosopher, Herbert Spencer, was the prophet of the movement, and his books were widely read in this country (far more than in Britain). Preachers who were reluctant to accept Darwin could still praise Adam Smith and teach that it was each man's Christian duty to get rich. In the post-Civil War decades, laissez faire became closer to being a national ideology than any other idea in our history except democracy itself.

Yet the very businessmen who did much to sponsor the spread of this ideology were far too practical to swallow it whole. Although the Spencerian philosophy excluded government from economic life, American industry had from the beginning counted on government intervention in economic life. Specifically it had sought and gained the advantages of a governmentally imposed tariff on foreign imports. This was not merely intervention; it was the government imposing an obstacle to free competition in the market place by barring a competitor's goods or forcing him to raise the price for them. It was "wrong," then, from the standpoint of both philosophy and economic theory. Yet no one seriously expected the tariff laws to be repealed—and they weren't.

## Government Intervention

By the turn of the century the influence of Spencer and Smith, though still strong, was on the wane. Its final chance of permanent domination of American thought faded in the 1930's. Obvious reasons for its decline included (1) the monopolization of the markets for many commodities, impeding free competition and "automatic" price adjustment, and requiring government intervention to break up the monopolies and restore competition; (2) its treatment of labor as a commodity with a typically fluctuating price: an oversupply of labor often drove that "price," or wage, down to a pittance, creating misery and poverty which aroused humanitarian demands for governmental action; and (3) the failure of the self-adjusting mechanism to work perfectly, or at least to adjust quickly enough. Instead of moderate fluctuations in prices, the system produced drastic price changes and seemed to make inevitable a recurrent "economic cycle" of booming prosperity followed by hard times. The great depression which began in 1929 unleashed a growing skepticism toward the eternal rightness of the old doctrines. President Herbert Hoover, to be sure, never lost his faith in them: he insisted on limiting government intervention almost wholly to comparatively modest loans to corporations and rejected suggestions that the federal government should either come directly to the relief of unemployed people or put them to work on new public projects. Hoover believed, then and ever after, that if he had been reelected in 1932 the essential rightness of the economic system would have reasserted itself and that, without significant governmental aid, prosperity would have returned. But three years of hardship exhausted the patience and confidence of millions of Americans. Hoover's defeat, or more realistically the New Deal programs of 1933-1937,[1] marked a revolution in American thought concerning the role of government. In essence, wisely or unwisely we turned back from the semi-ideological path to the pragmatic, experimental one. The government "took arms against a sea of troubles," and the voters approved. Since that period the national government has been immersed in the economic problems of the nation and has readily acted in an effort to solve them. In 1946 Congress confirmed what every politician long had realized, the ultimate responsibility of the government for the country's prosperity, measured by the "full employment" of its available men and women.[2]

Yet laissez-faire doctrine remains a part of the intellectual equipment of many Americans. Though once despised by Alexander Hamilton, it still attracts especially the industrialists upon whom Hamilton built his hopes for America. In practice they

---

[1] Hoover's defeat by Franklin D. Roosevelt hardly seemed epoch-making when it occurred on November 2, 1932, for Roosevelt in his campaign had not vigorously assailed the old laissez-faire doctrines. On the contrary, he had criticized Hoover for creating new federal commissions and had called for balancing the budget.

[2] The Employment Act of 1946, though more an expression of belief than a concrete program, was enacted only after a long and complicated political struggle, expertly recounted by Stephen K. Bailey, *Congress Makes a Law* (New York: Henry Holt and Co., 1950).

may count on government tariffs, subsidies, and contracts, yet some of them invoke the old ideas as reasons why it is wrong for government to conduct business operations of its own, especially those that compete with private enterprise.[3] Just as New Dealers criticized laissez faire as a doctrinaire myth leading to widespread misery, so modern conservatives view government intervention as "creeping socialism," momentarily practical but in the long run a threat to freedom. Both groups can agree, however, that the issue is basically one of degree: how far, and in what respects, should government intervene in the economy? How far, and in what respect, does it do so?

It is to that last question that we address ourselves in this chapter and, to a considerable degree, in the two that follow it. Here we will deal with some of those public policies designed to maintain or modify the economic system and its chief segments. In the next chapter, we will examine programs primarily concerned with the protection of individuals, and in Chapter 20 the government's management of our natural resources; in considering both of these topics, we will readily observe their close relationship with the subject of the present chapter. Thus a social security program, though directly benefiting this unemployed man or that old lady, has a broad economic effect, and so does the harnessing of a river to produce great quantities of electric power. Social insurance and the sale of energy are both "interventions" in the country's economic life, just as are the policies to be considered in the present chapter—the management of the market, the encouragement of prosperous production, and the restraint of private economic power.

## STABILIZATION AND THE PROMOTION OF PROSPERITY

Three economic ills, historically, have led to demands for government intervention into the free market for the purposes of regulating the price structure and maintaining a high level of

---

3 A good example of the assumption that such activities (whether useful or not) are just plain *wrong* is furnished by the report of the second Hoover Commission in 1955, discussed briefly in Chapter 16 of this book.

private employment. The first is cyclical depression—the down-swing of the classical economic cycle. In the past this has usually been marked by a rapid decline in prices ("deflation"), wide-spread unemployment, and an increase in business failures. The second is inflation—a sharp rise in the general price level, causing a "high cost of living" and bringing distress to those, such as elderly pensioners, who live on fixed monetary incomes. The third is stagnation—a cessation or slowing down of the growth of business enterprise, causing hardship for small business especially and creating a seemingly permanent reservoir of several million unemployed.

Prices are at the heart of all these problems. The price level is affected by many factors, among which are the monetary and fiscal policies of government. As we have just seen, in classical economic theory prices were assumed to adjust themselves; but even this self-adjustment presupposed the existence of an ade-quate amount of money, the issuance of which was a proper gov-ernmental responsibility. And whenever the self-adjustment system failed to work smoothly, demands for an active, self-con-scious governmental monetary policy increased.

## Monetary Policy

If you think of money as a commodity like a loaf of bread, you will see at once that an increase in the price of bread means a decrease in the value of money. When the bread is worth more money, the dollar is worth less bread. What causes a decrease in the value (or price) of money? One cause, certainly, is the rela-tionship of supply to demand. If money is abundant but there is not much bread, the oversupply of money causes a drop in its worth. The "price" of money falls, the price of bread rises. Conversely, if money is in short supply, it becomes more valuable; people will offer more to obtain it. For a dollar the grocer will pay ten loaves of bread instead of only five. In other words, he lowers the price of bread from twenty cents a loaf to ten cents a loaf. Inflation, then—a rise in the price of goods and services—may result from an increase in the supply of money, deflation from the contraction of the supply of money.

The most acute and general suffering in our history arising

out of the swings of the economic cycle has come in times of depression—deflationary periods, marked by falling prices, wage cuts, losses instead of profits, and widespread layoffs and unemployment.[4] In such times the pressure on government to employ monetary policy to counteract the deflation has often been heavy. Increase the supply of money, the argument has run, and the tide will turn. In former times this kind of argument concentrated on the simplest device for increasing the supply; namely, the issuance of more money by minting more coins or "starting the presses rolling." Economic analysis has shown, however, that what affects the value of money is not merely the amount of it in physical existence, but the amount of it in *circulation;* dollar bills kept under a mattress for twenty years do not add to the national economy's effective supply of money, however much they may reassure the old lady who hides them there. Furthermore, money is not all coins and greenbacks. A very substantial amount of it consists of bank deposits, created when a bank agrees to permit a business firm to draw money from the bank, up to a certain amount, whenever it wants to do so. The establishment of such a deposit in effect creates new money where none was before, for the business firm, though it may give the bank a mortgage on its property, puts no dollar bills into the bank.

Monetary policy, therefore, deals not only with the amount of currency to be issued but with its circulation and with the amount of credit (bank loans or deposits, long-term corporate borrowing, and installment purchase contracts) which may be extended. Its goal is price stability—if not the permanent maintenance of a particular price level, at least a degree of stability sufficient reasonably to safeguard the value of the dollar on the one hand and to prevent sudden disastrous deflation on the other. Partly because of its theoretical ineffectiveness, more because of the fear that the printing presses, once started, could never be stopped, the issuance of more dollar bills has not been a signifi-

---

4 Although Americans have often felt the impact of deflation, they have largely escaped the disasters that can accompany a rapid inflation like that which occurred in Germany in the 1920's, when the price of goods rose so swiftly that money became worthless, and the people whose property was chiefly in the form of money were in desperate straits.

cant method in American monetary policy. The less direct instruments, of manipulation of the amount of money in circulation and credit controls, are the chief tools used by the government.

*The Federal Reserve System.* The main responsibility for the formulation and execution of monetary policy is vested in the Federal Reserve System and its Board of Governors. The system consists of twelve regional Federal Reserve Banks and privately owned "member banks." All national banks must be members of the system and some state banks are permitted to be; the total membership includes banks holding about 85 per cent of all the commercial banking assets of the country.

The Federal Reserve Board can affect the supply of circulating money (and hence the general price level) in three ways. First, as we have just seen, much "new money" is created by bank loans and deposits; but the Federal Reserve Act permits member banks to maintain deposits only to the extent that they hold, in cash or its equivalent, reserves amounting to a certain percentage of their total deposits. This "reserve requirement" is flexible. In most large city banks it ranges from 10 per cent to 20 per cent. Between those limits, the Federal Reserve Board determines what it shall be. When the board raises the reserve requirement, it thereby reduces the permissible amount of bank loans. When it lowers it, it stimulates new loans and deposits. So if the board fears inflation, it increases the reserve requirement, and if it feels that the economy needs "a shot in the arm," it reduces it.

Second, through a committee on which it holds a majority, the board can direct the Federal Reserve Banks to buy and sell government securities on the open market. The sale of bonds brings in money which increases reserves and so, like the lowering of the reserve requirement, enables the banks to lend more money, thus having an inflationary effect. The purchase of bonds, reducing the cash reserves, has the opposite effect.

Both the changing of reserve requirements and open market operations thus may have an impact on the amount of bank loans and business investment. The availability of funds, in turn, has an effect on the interest rate. Interest is the price paid for borrowed capital. If there is plenty of money to lend, the price charged by the lender drops. Thus lowered reserve requirements and open-market sales of government securities, by increasing the amount of lendable funds, tend to decrease the interest rates charged by the banks to borrowers. The board also affects the interest rate more directly by fixing the "rediscount rate" charged by Federal Reserve Banks when they make loans to member banks.[5] Announcement of a rise in the rediscount rate is a signal that the board is seeking to slow down an inflationary boom by discouraging the expansion of credit.

The Federal Reserve Board has so much independence, discretion, and prestige that it is the prime maker of day-to-day monetary policy. To some extent, however, the field is shared by the Treasury Department. The latter's role has had special significance since the national debt has risen to huge figures (from about $40,000,000,000 in 1939 to more than $308,000,000,000 in 1964). The management of the debt is the Treasury Department's business. Frequent financing and refinancing are accomplished through the issuance of government securities. The marketability of such securities depends considerably on the interest the government is ready to pay and the time fixed for repayment. These, determined by the Treasury Department, may influence the cost and nature of private credit transactions and thus have some inflationary or deflationary effect. Obviously a truly coherent, consistent monetary policy depends on cooperation between the Treasury Department and the Federal Reserve Board.

### Fiscal Policy

To many who endured hardship in the great depression, monetary policy seemed to be a feeble defense against economic disaster. Some blamed the Federal Reserve Board for not using it vigorously and quickly to halt the frenzied boom of the 1920's before the crash occurred in 1929. Others, however, believed that by themselves the board's weapons were inadequate to cope with

---

[5] Technically, these are purchases of the "commercial paper" which the original borrower has given to the member bank as evidence of his debt and security for its payment. They resemble, however, loans backed by the same security, and the "rediscount rate" is in effect the equivalent of interest—the price paid by the borrowing bank.

the powerful forces of the economic cycle. In the ensuing decade, the government sought to relieve suffering and restore prosperity—not by drastic monetary inflation but by a series of programs whose cost far exceeded revenues. These programs had to be financed by borrowing. Although at first this "deficit spending" seemed to violate all sound notions about government finance, eventually it gained status as an application of "fiscal policy." Fiscal policy has been defined as "the use of government expenditure and revenue as balancing factors to secure economic stabilization." [6] In brief, this means that in times of economic recession, government should reduce taxes and increase its expenditures, thus encouraging both capital investment and consumer purchases. In days of full employment, on the other hand, it should increase taxes and cut expenditures, thus reducing the amount of money in circulation and so checking a possibly harmful inflation. The formulation of fiscal policy has not been entrusted to any one administrative agency; it remains primarily the responsibility of Congress. Its effectiveness as a stabilizer remains uncertain, for although deficit spending is in itself inflationary, the amount of it needed to turn a depression into a boom is unknown. Traditionally the swings of the economic cycle have reflected psychological changes in the business atmosphere, specifically, intangible things called "confidence" or "lack of confidence." And, traditionally, the very presence of a badly unbalanced budget has impaired "confidence" and discouraged new investment, thus to some extent counteracting its inflationary effect. Nevertheless, in the last twenty years the idea that there can and should be such a thing as fiscal policy has become respectable. Indeed it has been accepted, as an idea, by dominant factions in both parties, though the Eisenhower administration declined to put it to full use during two "recessions" in the 1950's. In 1963, something new was added by President Kennedy's demand that Congress cut taxes at a time when there was no general economic recession. The Kennedy proposal appeared to be based on the belief that a recession would soon occur (following the pattern of the 1950's) and on the fact that, despite the country's

---

[6] James A. Maxwell, *Fiscal Policy* (New York: Henry Holt and Company, 1955).

prosperity, there was a persistent "hard core" of unemployment and the national rate of economic growth was much slower in the United States than in some other countries.

## Other Influences on Stabilization

Confident forecasters often tell us that there can be no repetition of the great depression. They point to the possibilities of fiscal policy—a vast public works program, for instance—in taking up the temporary slack in private enterprise, and they speak of the safeguards against disaster embodied in statutes enacted in the 1930's. Of these the most significant is the nation-wide system of state unemployment compensation laws, which provide that people who lose their jobs will for some months receive weekly payments from the state's unemployment compensation fund. This, for a time, keeps money—purchasing power—in their pockets. It cushions the shock of a recession, delaying, for example, the impact of a shutdown in a big factory on all the retail stores and service stations in the town where the factory is located. Unemployment compensation is therefore a handy shield against depression, and so is old-age insurance, which similarly provides people with some "spending money" which many would not otherwise have. Together, however, these could not check for long any major deflationary onslaught. What they could do is give the government time to get a public works program under way.

Because fiscal policy was born of depression, and changes in monetary policy have usually been sought by those hurt in hard times, most of the emphasis on economic stabilization has been directed toward curing a deflation. In wartime, however, the shoe is on the other foot. Then the demand for goods and services far outruns the supply, there is a manpower shortage, and so both prices and wages start to rise precipitously. War quickly creates the spectre of a runaway inflation. This danger leads to direct government control of the price structure. Thus in World War II the Office of Price Administration was established, empowered to fix maximum prices for most of the goods sold in the nation; simultaneously, other agencies put a "freeze" on wages. The effectiveness of these efforts is shown by their results: in five war years

(1941-1945) the general consumer price level went up 22 per cent whereas in the first three years after controls were relaxed or eliminated, it increased 33 per cent. The experience also indicated, however, that direct price-and-wage controls are enormously complicated and difficult to administer and probably impossible to enforce save in the atmosphere of high patriotism engendered by war.

How to deal with an unhealthy peacetime inflation, then, remains a prime question of stabilization policy. Monetary policy alone won't check a runaway boom. The application of an anti-inflationary fiscal policy runs up against the demands for more government spending (for defense, among other things) and the popular resistance to any new taxes. The issue is clouded, furthermore, by the fact that all stabilization policy must be based to a large degree on guesswork. Responsible experts may conclude, even during a business recession, that the real danger is inflation, and so refuse to take strong anti-recession measures (this was the attitude of the Federal Reserve Board during much of the "slump" of 1957-1958); but neither they nor anyone else can be certain that they are right. Finally, as we shall see later in this chapter, a new inflationary force has made itself felt since World War II: the inflationary "wage-price spiral" arising out of collective bargaining agreements between big unions and big corporations. When these agreements have raised wages, they have been consistently followed by price increases, seemingly regardless of general economic conditions. They were a factor, certainly, in causing the curious phenomenon of 1957-1958, when recession and unemployment were accompanied not by deflation but by higher prices. They pose a new and tough problem for the stabilizers.

### The Politics of Stabilization

Some of the political battles of yesteryear over monetary policy we have mentioned earlier in this book. Go back almost to the beginning: what was one reason for the Philadelphia Convention being held? It was the monetary policy of a few states, which inflated their currency in response to the demands of debtors. Skip more than a century, and we find Bryan leading a crusade for "free silver," preaching the inflationary doctrine of the debt-ridden farmers.[7] In each case, substantial property interests were threatened chiefly by the conflicting interests of those who had borrowed money to finance their farms. In each case, the latter lost. Bryan's second defeat, in 1900, virtually finished monetary policy as an election issue. One group, however, retained its special concern for questions of coinage and currency: this was the silver-mining industry in the West. A solid "silver bloc," of fourteen senators from seven states, kept up the pressure for the remonetization of silver or at least the governmental purchase of it at a price profitable to the industry. In the mid-1930's they gained an eloquent non-senatorial spokesman in the person of Rev. Charles R. Coughlin, the "radio priest" of Royal Oak, Michigan; and by 1939 their senatorial leader, Pittman of Nevada, who had reached the chairmanship of the Senate Foreign Relations Committee, used that post to exact concessions for silver from President Roosevelt in return for his support of the President's foreign policy.

In the meantime, however, the usable instruments of monetary policy had been turned over to the Federal Reserve Board (established in 1913) and thus substantially removed from the party battle. The board is certainly engaged in politics, in the large sense, and is not immune to pressures; but it has an unusual degree of freedom from both presidential and congressional influence. President and Congress were and are, however, confronted with the issues inherent in the formation of fiscal policy. When the New Deal began in 1933, its leader, F. D. Roosevelt, was inclined to dally with monetary notions (in his first inaugural address he called for "an adequate but sound currency," whatever that may mean) but apparently gave little thought to fiscal policy as such. He did insist, however, on "putting first things first," which to him meant spending the government's money to succor the millions of unemployed and to give them work on public projects. This resulted in expenditures which far exceeded revenues. The budget was unbalanced, and the government had to

7 Silver had been discontinued, as a basis of currency, by Congress in 1873. Bryan sought to repeal "the Crime of '73" and remonetize silver as a step toward increasing the amount of currency, raising prices, and making it easier for debtors to pay their debts.

borrow. The Republican opposition fiercely denounced such "unsoundness"; when the national debt rose to $29,000,000,000, serious citizens foresaw national bankruptcy and ruin. (Today the debt is more than ten times that sum, yet the country seems to survive.) It appears that as late as 1937, Roosevelt himself assumed that a balanced budget was a desirable end in itself and hoped to restore it. By that time, however, his supporters had begun to justify the spending program in terms of fiscal policy. In hard times it was right and wise, they said, for the government to borrow and spend, for an unbalanced budget would create purchasing power, raise prices, and "prime the pump" of private enterprise. Their prophet was a distinguished British economist, John Maynard Keynes. The economic theories of Keynes have been analyzed, acclaimed, and denounced for thirty years, but whatever their shortcomings, they produced an erudite and, to many, a convincing justification of deficit financing during a depression. Fiscal policy, as a consciously wielded instrument of government, is largely a Keynesian creation. Bipartisan recognition of its existence was formally accorded to it by the passage of the Employment Act of 1946.[8]

How fiscal policy should be applied was the source of political conflict in President Eisenhower's regime. In the face of a minor recession in 1953-1954 and a more serious one in 1957-1958, the President, the Treasury, and the Federal Reserve Board insisted that the real danger was inflation. Their critics, pointing to 5,000,000 unemployed, urged spending programs (for example, expenditures for new schoolhouses, new public housing, and more weapons) which, they said, would be useful in their own right and would also restore prosperity. To this the President could answer that fiscal policy to raise prices was no sure cure for a recession in which prices were rising anyway. Temporary hard

---

[8] This statute begins with a "declaration of policy" as follows: "It is the continuing policy and responsibility of the Federal Government to use all practicable means consistent with its needs and obligations and other essential considerations of national policy, with the assistance and cooperation of industry, agriculture, labor and State and local governments, to coordinate and utilize all its plans, functions, and resources for the purpose of creating and maintaining, in a manner calculated to foster and promote new competitive enterprise and the general welfare, conditions under which there will be afforded useful employment opportunities, including self-employment, for those able, willing, and seeking to work, and to promote maximum employment, production, and purchasing power."

times brought out a heavy anti-administration vote in the congressional elections of 1954 and 1958, but the President did not yield. Instead, as conditions improved, he took a firmer stand in favor of an anti-inflationary policy of budget-balancing by cutting expenditures. This position accorded with his instinctive preferences, born of early laissez-faire assumptions. He maintained it with some success through the use of the veto power. But when a steel strike occurred in 1959, neither the President nor Congress was prepared to deal effectively with the "wage-price spiral." This new inflationary force gave rise to a basic and unanswered question far deeper than any immediate impact on prices. That question was whether practicable monetary, fiscal, or other public policies could counteract this force, or whether, instead, the price level was passing outside of the government's sphere of influence and would hereafter be chiefly determined by neither supply and demand nor public policy, but by the decisions of a few leaders of huge aggregates of private economic power.

Eisenhower's successor, John F. Kennedy, sought to answer that question in 1962 when he intervened personally, first to extract a promise from union leaders that they would not make immediate wage demands on the steel industry, and then to prevent "Big Steel" from nevertheless raising steel prices. Kennedy's vehement criticism of an announced price increase made him, in turn, the object of vehement criticism from those who professed to speak for free enterprise and laissez faire. The withdrawal of the price rise was accomplished without resort to legal action. Nevertheless, the fact that the steel companies withdrew it is a reminder of the great extent of the government's potential influence on industrial policies—influence based on both its historic power to break up monopolies and its newer role as a major customer of heavy industry.

## THE PROMOTION AND RESTRAINT OF INDUSTRY AND LABOR

### The Promotion of Business

The Founding Fathers, unimpressed by Adam Smith if, indeed, they were aware of his existence, took for granted that govern-

ment should concern itself with productive enterprise. To some
of them this meant that it should positively promote the development and prosperity of manufacturing. Hamilton's "Report on
Manufactures," in 1793, outlined a full program for the encouragement of private industrial enterprise through government
credit, subsidies, and a protective tariff.[9] Of these the one which
promptly became a permanent part of the country's economic
policy was the tariff. The tariff, in the early days, produced a significant share of federal revenues. Later it came to be justified as a
defensive instrument, protecting American industry—both profits
and wage scales—from the inroads of destructive foreign competition. Thus it was and still is often said to be a shield for the
American way of life. If Americans buy inexpensive foreign goods
instead of the goods made in American factories where the workers get decent wages, how can American manufacturers stay in
business and American labor make a respectable living? For most
of our history, however, the tariff has been more than a weapon of
defense. One of the main purposes of its early sponsors was to promote new enterprise by promising future protection to entrepre-
neurs and investors. As the decades passed, the duties charged on
many imported articles came to exceed by far the amount needed
to equalize the cost of foreign and domestic production. Tariffs
went up so high as virtually to exclude many foreign goods from
the American market, leaving American producers free to compete
only with each other instead of with the rest of the world.

After the Civil War, laissez faire became a philosophical justification for vigorous, profitable, and often ruthless private
exploitation of the country's resources. It also permitted the concentration of economic power in comparatively few hands. In
competition where the rule was "the devil take the hindmost,"
the strongest grew stronger still. The corporation which had the
most capital, for instance, could take a loss and undersell its rivals,
temporarily but often long enough to drive them out of business.
As we shall see in a moment, the government sought to slow
down this process of concentration by the passage of anti-monop-

---

9 Hamilton's concern for industry, as opposed to agriculture, was indicated by
his proposal to impose no tariff on imports of raw materials. Uninterested in
"protecting" American agriculture from foreign competition, he wanted manufacturers to be able to obtain their raw materials at the lowest possible price.

oly laws, but the process continued nonetheless. Partly this was
due to the expansion of accessible markets through improvements
in transportation. Partly it was the result of the savings made
possible by mass production and mass selling. To a noteworthy
degree, however, it has in recent decades been encouraged by the
federal government itself.

Without necessarily intending to do so, the government promotes not merely business, but bigness, through policies which
result in large corporations becoming ever more dominant. One
of these policies, with respect to a particular industry—oil and
gas—is expressed in the corporate income tax law. It allows oil
and gas producers a so-called "depletion allowance," a tax deduction of $27\frac{1}{2}$ per cent of their gross sales, not to exceed 50 per
cent of their net income. The justifications for this allowance are
that in taking oil out of the ground, the producers are using up
capital which they can never replace and that the deduction will
encourage them to search for new sources of oil. Thus it promotes
a vitally important industry. However, it also appears to increase
the advantage of the large companies in the industry over the
small ones; big business, paying big taxes, saves a great amount
of money when big tax deductions are permitted. This money the
large corporations can use to expand their operations and
strengthen their position in the industry.[10]

Other policies fostering big business's domination of the economy have stemmed from the demands of military preparedness.
Corporations were induced to operate new defense plants during
World War II and the Korean War, for instance, by another kind
of tax favor—a provision that they could amortize the cost of the
plant in five years. This meant that in those five years, they would
be paying far less in taxes than they would have under the normal
amortization provisions of the law. Most companies profiting by
this arrangement were in industries where concentration and bigness were already the rule; "accelerated amortization" made them
bigger and stronger still. More significant, however, is the matter

---

[10] See Supplementary Treasury Department Statement on Special Depletion
Allowances, House of Representatives Ways and Means Committee, 81st Congress,
2nd Session, *Hearings*, February 6, 1950.

of defense contracts themselves. Annually these run into astronomical figures, amounting to close to 10 per cent of the total national income. They profoundly affect the economic system. And once again, the way they are awarded promotes not just industry as a whole, but primarily the largest and most powerful corporations. The latter frequently seem most obviously suited to do the job that is needed, quickly and efficiently: they have the plant capacity, the manpower, the know-how. More often than not, they get the contracts. The Department of Defense unquestionably seeks to award contracts to those best fitted for the task required, but in terms of the economic system the result is the increase of the power of a few concerns and the consequent decline of the old competitive system, especially in the basic heavy industries.

### Restraints on Industry's Power

The old competitive system assumed, of course, free access to the market by all who wished to produce and sell goods and services. Its price mechanism depended on this; high prices would be brought down, you recall, only by the appearance of new producers attracted by the chance to make a profit. The whole machinery was thrown out of kilter by *monopoly,* for if one producer got control of the marketing of a product, he could keep his prices high, regardless of shrinking demand, as long as his capital reserves lasted. Moreover, if he was selling a really necessary commodity, he could make his customers "pay through the nose," safe in the knowledge that no one would offer them the same commodity for less money.

*Rate Regulation.* It was this this last aspect of monopoly power—the matter of "charging all the traffic will bear"—which in 1887 brought about the first significant federal legislation for the regulation of business. Some railroads, especially in the rugged West, were very nearly "natural monopolies"; the one that first preempted the shortest, swiftest route through the mountains had a great advantage over any possible competitor. And when two or three did compete, they found it mutually advantageous to divide the traffic and agree on the rates which each would charge. Often unworried about competition, therefore, the railroads could demand almost any price they liked for shipping wheat and other crops from the farms to the urban centers of distribution. To live, the farmers had to ship and sell their wheat; to ship it, they had to pay such high freight rates that they lost money and sank deeper into debt. They therefore pleaded for governmental control over railroad rates. State legislation was not enough to help them. In 1887, accordingly, Congress passed the Interstate Commerce Act. The looseness of the statute and judicial hostility toward it made it a futile instrument of regulation for nearly twenty years, but in 1906 a new law, the Hepburn Act, gave the Interstate Commerce Commission the needed rate-fixing authority. This it still continues to exercise, though it may give less emphasis today to the protection of shippers than to the economic health of the railroad industry, for in the modern age the railroads are hard-pressed competitors with other forms of transportation.

Railroads are "public utilities," licensed by government and permitted to use public facilities on the condition that they serve the public generally. So are streetcar and bus and trucking companies, telephone companies, electric light corporations, oil and gas pipelines. Partly because these were often "natural monopolies," partly just because they were "public utilities," all of them have been subjected to rate regulation. Most of such regulation takes place at the state and local level; but the interstate operations of buses and trucks, telephone communications, and pipelines are subject to federal control exercised, respectively, by the ICC, the Federal Communications Commission, and the Federal Power Commission.

*The Prevention of Monopoly.* In great areas of enterprise not embraced by the term "public utilities," monopoly power reared its head in the 1870's. Erstwhile competitors pooled their resources in mergers, trusts, and holding companies. Growing companies, backed by ample capital from the investment bankers,[11] drove their less well-financed rivals to the wall and then bought their assets at low prices. By the 1890's a single corporation

---

11 The prototype of the great financiers of this era was John Pierpont Morgan, head of J. P. Morgan & Co., whose offices were on Wall Street in New York City. To many Americans, the term "Wall Street" thus came to symbolize monopoly power.

virtually controlled the oil industry, another the steel industry, another the rubber industry, another the sugar refining industry, and so on—the list was a long one. And in 1890 the government struck back by passing the Sherman Act, the first of several statutes which together constitute what we call the anti-trust laws.

In the beginning the Sherman Act was a feeble gesture. Though it outlawed all "combinations in restraint of trade" in interstate commerce—in other words, one would think, all sizeable monopolies that interfered with a fully competitive market—it depended for its effectiveness on the determination of the attorney-general, to whom enforcement was entrusted, and on sympathetic interpretation by the Supreme Court. In the years that followed its enactment, many an attorney-general lacked the requisite enthusiasm, and the Court virtually rewrote the law, giving itself the power to decide what was an illegal monopoly and what was not. It did this by declaring that the Sherman Act really meant to prohibit not "every combination" but "every *unreasonable* combination." [12] As to what was "unreasonable," the Court itself had the final say in every case.

For many years the Court tended to find most tight monopolies —consolidations or mergers putting almost an entire industry under the control of a single corporation—"reasonable" and therefore lawful. It struck down, however, looser monopolistic arrangements, such as price-fixing agreements among competitors, regardless of whether they were "reasonable" or not.[13] Eventually, in 1945, the "rule of reason" was narrowed, the Sherman Act, in one case, being given the meaning which, to the layman, its language had always seemed to have. Monopolies, regardless of their "reasonableness," were unlawful.[14] In the last fifteen years this doctrine, in turn, has been modified: the Court inclines to read the law as prohibiting a concentration of economic power sufficient "to control prices or exclude competitors." [15]

---

12 *U.S. v. Standard Oil Co. of New Jersey,* 221 U.S. 1 (1911). Chief Justice White's opinion illustrated the Court's acceptance of doctrinaire laissez faire economics when it expressed a belief in "the inevitable operation of economic forces and the equipoise of balance in favor of the rights of individuals which resulted."

13 *U.S. v. Trenton Potteries Co.,* 273 U.S. 392 (1927); *U.S. v. Socony-Vacuum Oil Co.,* 310 U.S. 150 (1940).

14 *U.S. v. Aluminum Company of America,* 148 F. 2d 416 (1945).

15 *U.S. v. E. I. duPont deNemours & Co.,* 351 U.S. 377 (1956).

The early judicial interpretations of the Sherman Act showed that the justices assumed not that monopoly was an evil, but that it was sometimes achieved by evil or "unreasonable" and hence unlawful means. The same attitude was reflected by Congress's enactment, in 1914, of two laws, the Clayton Act and the Federal Trade Commission Act, which were based on the similar assumption that unfair trade practices—price-cutting conspiracies, misleading advertisement, etc.—were destroying competition. The outlawing of such practices, however, failed to halt the trend toward industrial concentration. Almost immediately World War I occurred, giving big business the advantages which it inevitably gains in wartime. Later the belief in price competition waned. In the depression year of 1933, the anti-trust laws were, in effect, suspended while the country tried the experiment of the National Industrial Recovery Act, under which industrial groups were supposed to agree on "codes of fair competition" for their industries. A primary objective of such codes was to prevent the competitive lowering of prices by desperate producers faced with falling demand for their goods. The act was a failure; enforcement of it had collapsed long before the Supreme Court gave it its death blow in 1935.[16] A year later, however, Congress moved again to put limits on price competition when it passed the Robinson-Patman Act, a complex statute aimed at protecting independent retailers from the low-price competition of the big "chain store" distributors. The effort to help the small businessman in his struggle with his bigger rivals who could operate with lower unit costs then shifted to the states, many of which enacted "fair trade" laws requiring uniformity in the pricing of particular commodities sold at retail. Congress tried to help this attempt to protect the retailer from the competition of mail-order or "discount" houses, but the "fair trade" movement ran up against numerous judicial obstacles. It did indicate, however, a concern for "competitors" instead of a belief in price competition. Price uniformity may help to keep small businessmen in business, but it contradicts a fundamental assumption of the old competitive free enterprise system.

---

16 *Schechter v. U.S.*, 295 U.S. 495 (1935).

Meanwhile the anti-trust laws remain on the statute books. A division of the Justice Department, under an assistant attorney-general has the job of enforcing them by investigating complaints, analyzing reports of Federal Trade Commission investigations, and bringing court action against those accused of violations—sometimes criminal prosecutions, more often civil suits aimed at obtaining a court's order to dissolve the monopoly or cease from illegal monopolistic practices.[17] Actually much of American business, especially the basic heavy industries such as steel, is now organized so that without unlawful monopoly, either one giant corporation overshadows all the rest, or a handful of large companies (as in the case of automobiles) do almost all of the producing. Price wars are the last things these corporations want, and they are equally averse to unceasing price fluctuations reflecting changes in the ratio of supply to demand. Much of the time there is a noticeable similarity in the prices asked by competitors, without any wrongdoing being charged; therefore, the conviction of several officials of large electric companies, in 1961, for conspiring to fix prices came as a distinct stop to much of the business community. A year or so later, a Supreme Court decision,[18] applying the more stringent clauses of the Clayton Act rather than the more tolerant standards of the Sherman Act, forced dissolution of a merger between a large manufacturer and a sizable retailer of its products. Statutes designed to insure competition, especially price competition, in a market open to all comers may seem increasingly out of date, but they still serve as safeguards against total monopoly, and, as we shall see, they may be significant in imposing checks on any alliance between corporations and labor unions to control prices and markets.

## The Politics of Competition

Our governmental approach to the organization of the industrial system is replete with paradox. The initial paradox lay in the nineteenth century theory of economics which assumed both

---

17 Private suits, for heavy damages, may also be brought by those claiming to be injured by illegal monopolistic practices.

18 *Brown Shoe Co. v. U.S.*, 370 U.S. 294 (1962).

competition and governmental abstention. Actually it was impossible to have both. Monopolies destroyed competition, and only government could break up monopolies or protect the public against monopolistic, noncompetitive prices. Yet while it opposed monopolies with one hand, with the other the federal government accepted big business, made use of it, and adopted tax policies that fostered it, even though the inevitable result was a diminution of price competition.

The early anti-monopoly fervor, as we have seen, was strongest in the agricultural West. Because of the influence of the Nebraskan, Bryan, it might have been the basis of an enduring Democratic issue; but in 1902 the Republican Theodore Roosevelt, seeing a chance for his party to regain its historic foothold in the West, seized the "trust-busters" banner. In his regime, the anti-trust division of the Department of Justice was given for the first time appropriations adequate for its needs. Not all Republicans, however, followed Roosevelt's lead. Indeed, in the 1912 campaign the unwillingness of Roosevelt's successor, Taft, to assail monopoly vociferously was a factor in the split in the Republican ranks. In that contest, trust-busting was a leading subject of the speeches of the Progressives under Roosevelt and of the victorious Democratic candidate, Wilson; the regular Taft Republicans were on the other side.

That was the last campaign in which monopoly was a major issue. After World War I the shape of the industrial system was becoming fixed; in much of it, not monopoly but "oligopoly"—domination of an industry by a few huge corporations—had become the rule. Vigorous anti-trust enforcement campaigns, like those launched by Assistant Attorneys General Thurman Arnold under Franklin Roosevelt and Stanley N. Barnes under Eisenhower, made no perceptible change in the pattern. The Public Utility Holding Company Act, passed in 1935 after a bitter battle in which the holding companies, backed by other business interests, succumbed to the implacable persistence of Roosevelt and his New Dealers, seemed at the time to be a significant setback for big business and gave the President a chance to claim victory over the "economic royalists." This act imposed a so-called "death sentence" on certain huge corporations, each of which controlled a number of electric companies operating in several states. Yet, in the long run, even this drastic statute came to seem like King Canute bidding the tide to stop rising. By the late 1930's the old trust-busting fervor was dormant. When in 1938 a presidential hopeful, Robert H. Jackson, tried to arouse it, his series of able speeches on the subject fell on deaf ears. A searching investigation of monopoly practices conducted by Congress's Temporary National Economic Committee (TNEC) produced a wealth of information but no fruitful demand for corrective action. And if the fervor was dormant in the 1930's, it seemed to have died away forever after World War II.

For this there were several reasons. One was the general acceptance of big business as an instrument of efficient production, leading to a constantly higher standard of living. Another was the consolidation of the countervailing power of big labor unions, and a third was the fact that the government had embarked on a broad program to prevent economic disaster on the nation's farms. Neither the labor nor the agricultural interests, therefore, were as hostile to the bigness of business as they had been in days of yore. The small business interest, seemingly a natural opponent of oligopoly, could seldom match the political influence of the great corporations; furthermore, as we have seen, in politics small business was accustomed to letting the big business pressure groups speak for the whole business community. The final and perhaps most important reason for the lack of concern with the diminution of competition was the long period of general prosperity beginning in 1939.

Prosperity leads to satisfaction with things as they are. If people are well off, why worry about the fact that in basic industries prices are no longer fixed simply by supply and demand, but are, rather, determined by dominant producers, perhaps in tacit agreement with each other? The era of "administered prices" has been, generally, a thriving period of economic growth. Only theorists and those who are actually hurt are likely to complain. Should hard times come and many millions be laid off, the old complaints could, conceivably, be voiced again by labor. Even in days of prosperity for most of the people, agriculture has not shared equally in the boom; although in recent decades the farmers have been stirred only to demand more federal protection for themselves, a disastrous farm depression might reawaken the ancient antagonism toward big business. Because of the status achieved by unions and the governmental commitments to agriculture, however, any revival of the "trust-busting" spirit seems unlikely.

## The Protection and Restraint of Labor Unions

The right of most of the wage earners in most of American industry to organize for the purpose of bargaining collectively with their employers has been guaranteed by federal law since 1933. The first statute extending this protection to all nonexecutive workers engaged in work affecting interstate commerce (which, as we saw in Chapter 5, now means almost all productive enterprise) was the National Industrial Recovery Act. Section 7a of that statute forbade employers to penalize their employees for joining a union. The law was held unconstitutional, in a case which did not involve its labor provisions, on May 27, 1935; but within two months section 7a was in effect revived by the passage of the National Labor Relations Act, commonly known as the Wagner Act. Twelve years later that law, in turn, was reenacted in significantly altered form as the Labor Management Relations Act of 1947—the Taft-Hartley Act.

This basic labor law makes it an "unfair labor practice" for an employer to discourage the unionization of his employees by refusing to hire a person unless he promises to refrain from joining a union,[19] or by firing or otherwise discriminating against a person who does join. It also forbids an employer to sponsor a union himself. The law provides machinery by which employees can determine, through an election, what union, if any, they wish to represent them. This machinery is administered by the National Labor Relations Board, which also has the duty of enforcing the law. When the Board is shown, usually by signed membership cards, that there is a substantial demand for union representation, it holds an election in which the choice is between "no union" and one or more designated unions. When complaints of "unfair labor practices" are brought to the Board, its general counsel may institute quasi-judicial proceedings, and the latter

---

[19] The exaction of such a promise has long been known as a "yellow-dog contract."

may conclude with a formal Board order to cease and desist from such practices. If the order is disobeyed, the Board then seeks an order of a U.S. court of appeals directing obedience to the Board's decree; failure to comply with the court's command constitutes punishable contempt of court.

The existence of these legal protections for union organization has brought about a great change in the American economy since 1933. Before that date, only the Railway Brotherhoods had been given equivalent protection by the federal government. Most of American industry was "unorganized." Most labor unions were small and weak. Most decisions· as to wages and working conditions were dictated by the employer; the lone employee, normally with little or no savings and often in real need of a job, had to take what he could get. Unions not only lacked statutory protection but faced seemingly implacable judicial hostility. Again and again, both federal and state courts forbade their efforts to bring economic pressure on an employer to force him to deal with them and on many occasions declared that their attempts to organize stamped them as conspiracies illegal under the common law.

The NIRA's section 7a and the Wagner Act changed the situation, and the new picture, confused at first, came into focus when the Supreme Court upheld the Wagner Act in 1937.[20] Quickly total union membership, numbering hardly 3,000,000 in 1932, doubled, trebled, quadrupled: today it numbers close to 18,000,-000. A major reason for its growth was the statutory prohibition of private efforts to prevent it. There was, however, another reason, based on a profound change in the nature of the American labor movement. This was the rise of industrial unions. Most earlier labor organizations had been craft unions: that is, a worker joined a union composed of people pursuing the same trade or craft as he did. It did not matter whom he worked for. A plumber gravitated toward the plumber's union, a carpenter to the carpenter's union. Most of these "building trades" unions, along with some others, were leagued together in the American Federation of Labor. In 1936. however, under the leadership of John L. Lewis, the Committee for Industrial Organization was formed for the purpose of promoting unionism based not on the individual's

---

20 *National Labor Relations Board v. Jones & Laughlin Steel Corporation,* 301 U.S. 1 (1937).

trade but on the industry in which he worked. The CIO [21] split away from the AFL and, with crusading zeal, went about the task of bringing all the workers in automobile factories into a single new union, the United Automobile Workers, all workers in steel mills into the United Steelworkers, and so on, industry by industry. Thus "big unions" arose, each one tied to a particular industry. In basic industries where one or only a few corporations were dominant, an agreement between the largest companies and the union came to fix a pattern for wages and working conditions throughout the industry; conversely, a strike against the leading companies could bring production in the whole industry to a critical standstill. Industry-wide unions led, in practical effect, toward industry-wide bargaining and occasional industry-wide strikes.

Though benefiting by governmental protection, however, unions are by no means free from all governmental restraints. Restrictions on their conduct are often imposed by state and local law, as, for instance, the prohibition of mass picketing. At the national level, the Taft-Hartley Act has defined "unfair labor practice" to include certain union tactics, such as secondary boycotts, strikes to force an employer to deal with a union other than the one already recognized as the employees' bargaining agent, and insistence on the payment of wages for "services which are not performed"—the practice of "feather bedding," as it is called. The 1947 statute also authorizes the President, in the case of a major strike, to appoint a fact-finding board; if he does so, the strike must be suspended for eighty days. President Eisenhower made use of this provision in the autumn of 1959, to suspend a nation-wide steel strike. In the summer of 1963, a new prospect of federal intervention was created by a threatened railroad strike. The strong possibility that all the railroads in the country would stop running renewed demands for outlawing strikes and compelling arbitration of labor disputes where a strike would close down a public utility.

The Taft-Hartley Act modified some of the protection given Unions by the Wagner Act. It strengthened the right of the em-

---

21 The name was later changed to Congress of Industrial Organizations, retaining the original initials.

ployer to try, by oral argument, to persuade his employees not to join a union; conversely it forbade unions, just as it forbade employers, to "coerce" anyone into joining a union. An exception to this noncoercion rule, however, was made with respect to a "union shop" agreement. A union shop is one wherein all employees in the bargaining unit covered by the agreement must, as a condition of continued employment, belong to the union, joining it either promptly or after a probationary period. Under federal law today, a union shop is legal. However, the Taft-Hartley Act permits each state to prohibit the union shop in that state. Between 1947 and 1961, nineteen states did so through the passage of so-called "Right to Work Laws," but available evidence indicates that for the most part these laws have been widely ignored.[22]

A further restraint on union power is contained in the antitrust laws. Although for a long time the Sherman Act was applied rigorously against unions, since 1940 the Supreme Court has so construed that statute, as amended and amplified by later laws, as virtually to free unions from anti-trust controls—with one significant exception. Anti-trust prosecutions may still be successful where unions and employers, acting in concert, seek to control prices and impede competition: thirty-two of such cases have been brought since 1945, and a plan to bring many more was publicized in 1959. The precedent for this campaign is a Supreme. Court decision holding that the law was violated by agreement between a union and manufacturers and installers of electrical equipment, providing that manufacturers would sell only to installers who had contracts with the union and installers would buy only from manufacturers who had contracts with the union. By making such an agreement the union, according to the Court, unlawfully "participated with a combination of business men who had complete power to eliminate all competition among themselves and to prevent all competition from others." [23]

Allegations of connivance between some unions and some employers were one reason why the Senate, in 1957, instituted a

---

22 See, e.g., Frederic Meyers, *"Right to Work" in Practice,* A Report to the Fund for the Republic (New York: Fund for the Republic, 1959).

23 *Allen-Bradley Co. v. International Brotherhood of Electrical Workers,* 325 U.S. 797 (1945).

special investigation of labor "racketeering" and other practices. The investigators, headed by Senator John L. McClellan of Arkansas, disclosed several instances of such connivance. They also heard evidence (which was widely publicized) of corruption among union officials and tyrannical control of certain unions by their officers. In 1959 Congress enacted a law aimed primarily at protecting union members against these abuses of power by highhanded or dishonest labor leaders. The enactment of such legislation injected the federal government into the internal affairs of unions, not so much to impose significant new restraints on their bargaining power as to police their dealings with their own members.

## The Politics of Labor

The dangers of oversimplified assumptions in political analysis are neatly illustrated by the history of federal labor legislation. We might assume, for instance, that congressional decisions can be predicted in terms of the amount of pressure applied by interest groups. A cause vigorously supported by large, effective pressure groups will win; without such support, it will lose. But take a look at the statutes we have just been considering—the NIRA of 1933, the Wagner Act of 1935, and the Taft-Hartley Act of 1947. The first two were "pro-labor" laws, yet they were enacted when unions were numerically weak and politically confused. The third imposed restraints on unions at a time when they were great in size and well organized for political action. Clearly we must look beyond the weight of organized pressures for the explanation of such congressional behavior.

For many years the leaders of the labor movement assumed that Congress could have little concern with unions, for prior to 1937 its power to regulate commerce was limited by the Supreme Court's interpretation of the Constitution.[24] Labor saw as its

---

[24] The Court recognized, of course, Congress's power to regulate interstate transportation, as distinguished from the production of goods for interstate commerce. Accordingly, transportation employees could and did seek congressional action to assure them of the right to organize. This they obtained in the passage of the Railway Labor Act of 1926. The Railway Brotherhoods possessed political influence out of all proportion to their size, partly because their internal discipline gave them economic power, partly because they had active members in all parts of the country, and partly because of their social status—railroad employees were long viewed as "the aristocracy of the labor movement."

"enemy," therefore, not the Congress, or the President, or any political party, but the courts—especially the federal courts, which broke strikes by issuing *ex parte* injunctions (temporary restraining orders issued on an employer's complaint, without hearing both sides) and which applied the anti-trust laws severely against unions. Before the great depression, therefore, most unions desired from Congress only legislation to restrain the courts. The AFL's president, Samuel Gompers, urged the passage of the Clayton Act in 1914 because he thought, incorrectly, that it would exempt unions from the Sherman Act. In the late 1920's, labor's chief legislative objective was the elimination of the *ex parte* injunction. This was accomplished in 1932 by the passage of the Norris-LaGuardia Act—but it is interesting to note that in the Senate, that pro-labor measure was introduced by a senator who hailed not from a great industrial state but from rural Nebraska. He was hardly a tool of organized labor. Indeed, by 1932 the labor movement was in a bad way. The AFL's membership, shrinking slightly through the 1920's, had dropped precipitously to less than 3,000,000. Many local unions had given up the ghost. The Norris-LaGuardia Act seemed, therefore, to stem more from the reforming zeal of the old, traditionally anti-court Progressivism of Theodore Roosevelt and the elder La Follette than from any fear of political reprisal by the labor interest.

Gompers' successor, William Green, did urge the inclusion of section 7a in the NIRA in 1933, and the AFL supported the Wagner bill two years later; but, again, in both cases the pressure which organized labor could exert was limited by its numerical weakness. Although section 7a was a "shot in the arm," stimulating union organization for a brief period, the National Recovery Administration's failure to enforce it soon resulted in another drop in union membership. So it would be misleading to describe the New Deal's labor legislation as simply a response to interest group pressure. Nor can we find the reason for it in the individual leadership of the chief New Dealers. Franklin Roosevelt had no personal enthusiasm for unions as such and gave no support to the Wagner bill until after it had passed the Senate. What, then, caused its enactment? Its personal sponsorship by one man, Senator Robert F. Wagner, may have been one contributing factor; the skill and zeal of its draftsmen, mainly young government lawyers unconnected with the labor movement, another. Perhaps more important, though, was a kind of *reverse* interest group influence. From 1933 through 1935, the prestige of business, particularly big business, was low. Many people in office and out of it put the blame for the depression on the whole big business world—financiers, holding company presidents, corporation executives. In such an atmosphere, the opposition of organized business, especially the National Association of Manufacturers speaking mainly for large corporations, might well have helped the Wagner bill rather than hurt it. And the very fact that industry was big and powerful, while labor was comparatively small and weak, made a bill to equalize their strength seem fair and desirable to many impartial voters.

We are suggesting, here, a theory that in a recognized conflict between two competing interests, the weaker of the two may emerge victorious—if, being small, it is not generally unpopular, and if its larger opponent has incurred temporary public disfavor. That seems to be what happened in 1935. Such a theory may explain, too, what happened in 1947. By that time organized labor's political assets seemed to equal or exceed those of business. But its very size and power cost it public sympathy, and a series of nation-wide strikes after the end of World War II made it unpopular. Accordingly, the unions could not prevent Congress's passing the Taft-Hartley Act by large majorities in both House and Senate, so large that President Truman's veto of the measure was easily overridden.

There are other reasons why labor's accretion of economic power has not been fully translated into political success, even since the AFL and CIO were reunited in 1955. One is that there is no such thing as a completely controlled "labor vote." Union leaders may endorse candidates, but many union members will vote against them.[25] Another lies in the structure and customs of Congress, particularly the filling of committee chairmanships on

---

25 This was obviously the case in 1952, when substantial numbers of union men and women voted for Eisenhower instead of the candidate officially supported by most of organized labor, Stevenson. It was illustrated, too, by the heavy vote for F. D. Roosevelt in 1940 in the mining section of West Virginia, despite the endorsement of Willkie, Roosevelt's opponent, by President Lewis of the United Mine Workers.

the basis of seniority. This brings to the top, as we have seen, men who have served long in Congress. In the main, such men come from districts or states where one party is far stronger than the other. So when the Democrats control Congress, many chairmanships are held by southerners; when the Republicans have a majority, the chairmen are likely to come from rural or small-town areas in the Middle West. These are precisely the two areas where dislike for the whole idea of unionism remains most vehement. In August, 1959, for example, ninety-five House Democrats joined Republicans in adopting a measure, called the Landrum-Griffin amendment, which was bitterly opposed by union spokesmen; of the ninety-five, all but three were from the South.

Often thwarted, therefore, in Congress, responsible labor leaders have occasionally encouraged union intervention in party machinery, especially that of the Democratic party. Since the days of Bryan, labor endorsements have usually gone to Democratic candidates; in New Deal days, the Democratic party itself seemed to be largely a coalition of the labor and agricultural interests. (The strength of this coalition persisted through the election of 1948, when the Democratic candidate won despite the loss of several traditionally Democratic southern states.) In the 1958 election, some Republicans, such as Goldwater of Arizona and Knowland of California, took a vigorous anti-labor stand. They seemed at times to be campaigning against Walter Reuther, vice-president of the AFL-CIO, rather than against their Democratic opponents. Such tactics, it seemed, could only push the union leaders more firmly into the Democratic column. But southern influence in the Democratic party, combined with southern reluctance to welcome the labor movement, hinders the unions' effectiveness within the party in the same way as it is impeded in the Congress.

Despite lingering opposition to unionism, one great political issue of the next decade involving labor may arise out of the comparatively recent attitude of cooperation between unions and management. This attitude is of most significance in the great basic industries where a few dominant firms can impose "administered prices" on their customers. So long as the cost of a wage increase can be offset, or more than offset, by a rise in prices, what is there to stop unions and corporations from obtaining an ever larger share of the national wealth? In the course of bargaining, unions customarily produce figures tending to prove that their wage demands can be met without a price increase; management counters with figures of its own, tending to prove the opposite. Whichever is right, wage increases in such industries as steel have regularly been followed by sharp price increases. The fear of just such a wage-price spiral underlay President Eisenhower's plea for "holding the line" in the steel strike of 1959 and President Kennedy's public criticism of the short-lived steel price increase in 1962. Presumably they were thinking of the unequal impact of inflation. If everyone's income went up along with prices, nobody would be hurt; but if only corporate profits and union workers' wages went up, then many groups of people might be hurt.

The second, greater, issue of the immediate future arises out of "automation"—the replacement of men by machines. The bitter railroad dispute of 1963 was caused, basically, by a mechanical change, from steam to diesel-powered engines back around 1940. This and other improvements made many jobs appear to be unnecessary; the men who filled them or the unions which insisted that they be filled were accused of "feather bedding." After various fact-finding bodies had agreed that many of these employees were unnecessary for the safety of the railroad, management decided to dismiss some 65,000 workers. This kind of action could not well be negotiated as part of ordinary labor-management relations: as was pointed out at the time, collective bargaining could not "resolve the national collision of the railroads with the railroad unions, for in that confrontation an industry with declining revenues desperately seeks relief far beyond the scope of collective bargaining: it proposes that the unions . . . bargain their members out of jobs and their organizations out of existence." [26] To keep the railroads running, not collective bargaining but political action was required.

While the railroad industry was unusual in that 65,000 men were deemed by management to be dispensable all at once, newly-perfected machines and processes are steadily increasing produc-

---

26 Paul Jacobs, *Now What Could This Be?* (Santa Barbara, Calif.: Center for the Study of Democratic Institutions, 1963).

Fitzpatrick in the *St. Louis Post-Dispatch*

## What of our big country?

Big strikes (such as those in 1946, when this cartoon was drawn)
make it easy to see that union-management strife threatens the
public welfare. But the opposite side of the shield—union-management cooperation—presents new problems which, though not so
visible, may come to have even more impact on the national
economy.

tion in other industries and displacing men who belong to other
unions. This gives rise to a twofold political problem. It increases
temporary unemployment, and it creates a situation—or a series of
bitter disputes—with which the existing collective bargaining machinery cannot effectively deal.

Automation, then, may well be the biggest "labor issue" of the
next decade. Its impact on industry, however, was preceded to a

large degree by its impact on another segment of the economy—agriculture. Mechanical advance was changing the aspect of the American farm before the diesels came in large numbers to the railroads, and long before the modern computer was invented. It made farms of vast acreage economically feasible. Nevertheless, "big farming" does not yet dominate the agricultural scene, and in agriculture old-fashioned price competition persists. The old Adam Smith economic model—millions of small competitors, selling at fluctuating prices which they cannot control—continued long after oligopoly and comparatively rigid prices had become the rule in much of industry. The resulting disparity in economic power and well-being brought government to the aid of agriculture many years ago. Agricultural policies of the future will inevitably be influenced by what government does, or fails to do, with respect to the wage-price spiral in the concentrated basic industries.

## THE PROMOTION AND RESTRAINT OF AGRICULTURE

In 1800 approximately 85 per cent of the American people lived on farms. Today nearly 90 per cent live in cities. Nevertheless, agriculture is a necessity if the country is to be fed; some 20,000,000 people, living on about 3,700,000 farms, depend directly on it for their livelihood; and, thanks to the system of equal senatorial representation of all states large and small, the farmers speak with a loud political voice. Depression on the farms contributes, slowly but surely, to depression in the rest of the economy, for farmers annually buy some $26,000,000,000 worth of production goods and a great amount of consumer goods as well. The prosperity of agriculture is of importance to the whole community. This interdependence has been a justification for the government's programs to aid the farmer.

### Land and Credit

Successful farming depends on arable, usable land. For ages such land has existed on this continent, but only a little more than a hundred years ago did much of it become available for the kind of agricultural production that we know today in the states of the Middle West and the great plains—production, on predominantly one-crop farms, of produce not to be consumed on the farm but to be shipped to central markets. The coming of the railroads made this kind of farming possible. It also increased the demand that the federal government, which held title to the western lands, should make those lands freely available to settlers. The cry of "free soil" was finally heeded when Congress passed the Homestead Act of 1862, opening the public domain for settlement in 160-acre tracts. Settlers would gain ownership, free of charge, after five years of residence. The Homestead Act thus promoted not only agricultural growth, but the development of the comparatively small "family-style" farm.

In the same year, Congress also enacted the first Morrill Act, which gave land to the states for the establishment of agricultural (later agricultural and mining—"A & M") colleges. This was a major step in a program that had begun some years before and has greatly expanded since—a program of federal assistance in the development of agricultural arts and the most productive use of the soil. In 1914 Congress established the "county agent" system, through which the Department of Agriculture cooperates with the land-grant colleges in a broad project of "extension" service for farmers. This was the earliest sizeable and successful joint federal-state-local system put into operation. It depended in part on local financial support and even more on the receptivity of the farmers—you can try to teach a person, but you can't make him listen if he doesn't want to. Local cooperation was largely achieved by having the responsible "teacher," the county agent, selected by state and local bodies, though he also became a federal official.

The knowledgeable use of the land, plus the advance of mechanical invention, in recent years has made much American soil far more productive than it ever was before. Even so, a substantial proportion of farmers are constantly in debt. The vagaries of both the weather and the competitive market result in bad years following good ones. The mortgage may be nearly paid off one autumn, but new borrowing may be required the next. The need for credit on easy or reasonable terms has long been felt on the farms, so acutely that the federal government, to maintain if not promote agriculture, has stepped in to provide it. Federal credit agencies were first established in 1916. These have come to include federally chartered land banks in which the borrowing farmers, organized in farm loan associations, hold stock; production credit corporations, which make short-term loans; and a special banking system for agricultural cooperatives. In each case the government made an original large subscription to the stock of the corporation, a loan which in the case of the land banks has been fully repaid. The federal lending agencies thus eased the credit needs of many reasonably prosperous farmers who held title to their farms, but did not help those who were worst off—small farmers on unproductive land, especially tenant farmers and sharecroppers who did not own the land they ploughed. During the great depression the government came to the aid of these people through special loans made by the Resettlement Administration and through the Farm Security Administration's encouragement of cooperative ventures for leasing land, providing housing, and buying feed and farm equipment. In 1946 these agencies were, in effect, succeeded in limited form by the Farmers' Home Administration, which lends money to tenants seeking to buy the farms where they live and to very small farmers who want to enlarge their holdings.

## Prices and Production

If farmers saw debt and the need for credit as their great problems in earlier days, for the last forty years the central issues of agricultural economics and politics have turned on the amounts of crops produced and the prices paid for them. As we have seen, farm prices are acutely responsive to changes in supply and demand. An example of this was the experience of World War I. At the beginning of that war, net annual income realized by the country's farmers was about $3,500,000,000. By 1919, in response to an overwhelming world-wide demand for agricultural products, it had shot up to over nine billion. In this period, farmers increased supply, too, by farming millions of acres hitherto lying fallow or never ploughed before. While the war lasted, the increase of supply could not keep up with the growing demand. As Europe recovered from the war's devastation, however, demand dropped off rapidly, creating a situation where the new wartime acreage produced an oversupply. Prices fell as sharply as they had risen, total net income dropping all the way to $3,600,000,000 by 1921.

This example reminds us of the competitive nature of agriculture. When demand diminishes, the average farmer, unlike a great corporation, cannot simply reduce his production (by closing a couple of plants and laying off employees, for instance) and maintain the former price for his products. To keep going, he has to sell what he grows promptly and for whatever price he can get. An era of low farm prices may drive him off the land altogether, but as long as he stays a farmer he must keep on producing, adding to the total supply and so keeping prices down. Conversely, high prices stimulate him to produce more than ever, if he can.

In the late 1920's when agricultural prices were falling while others rose, and especially in the early 1930's when total net farm income shrank to less than two billion dollars, the solution of the agricultural problem seemed to lie in the assurance of a reasonable minimum price for farm products. Governmental policies were devised to achieve this objective. Those policies, modified in some particulars, have continued to this day. They are based on three concepts: the propriety of the government's paying farmers for their crops, in loans or outright purchases; the restriction of production; and the need for "parity" for agriculture.

*Parity.* The concept of parity is that when he sells his produce, the farmer should be paid enough money to enable him to buy as much as he could buy with the price paid him for the same amount of produce in some earlier, reasonably prosperous year. In other words, if 1954 is assumed to be the "base year" and in 1954 two thousand bushels of wheat were sold for enough money to pay for a brand new four-door sedan, then in 1964 two thousand bushels of wheat should again bring a price equal to that of a similar new car. If, in the meantime, automobile prices have risen, the "parity" price of wheat in 1964 would be higher tnan the actual price of wheat was in 1954; if automobile prices have fallen, it would be lower.

This simple illustration of the general idea of parity, of course, conceals a quantity of difficult problems. For example, which comparative "base years" does one pick? The prices of which non-agricultural goods and services should be compared? Such questions are almost innumerable. They have led to revisions of the parity formula, which at best is an exceedingly complex calculation of price relationships, to the extent that the parity principle itself has been called a "statistician's nightmare." [27]

*Price Supports.* However calculated, the parity price has for nearly two decades been the measuring stick for the amounts paid out of the federal treasury to farmers who raise certain designated crops. Since the passage in 1938 of the second Agricultural Adjustment Act, the core of the farm program has been the government's readiness to lend money, taking surplus crops as full security for the loan, or in the case of perishable dairy products, to purchase the surplus. The amount paid for a given kind of product is determined by the parity formula; the government offers not the exact parity price per bushel or hundred weight or bale, but a fraction of it as Congress or, within limits, the Department of Agriculture may determine. Thus the farmer is assured of receiving at least a minimum price for his crop, even that part of the crop which he cannot sell in the market at that price.

Not all agricultural products are thus "supported." Actually, measured in terms of total market sales, a little less than half of agriculture is effectively guaranteed a minimum price. Price supports go primarily to the producers of six so-called "basic" crops —wheat, corn, cotton, rice, tobacco, and peanuts. The other chief beneficiary is the dairyman. When loans are made, the government, through the Commodity Credit Corporation in the Department of Agriculture, receives and stores the crop. Theoretically it may get its money back eventually by selling the crop so stored. Actually, however, what was a surplus for the farmer is usually a

27 Fainsod, Gordon, and Palamountain, *Government and the American Economy* (New York: W. W. Norton & Co., Inc., 1959), p. 156.

surplus for the government too. Therefore the amounts stored have filled government warehouses to bursting, growing larger year by year. In 1962 the government held in storage nearly 1,200,-000,000 bushels of wheat and over 67,000,000 tons of feed grain. By 1959 the Secretary of Agriculture was predicting that in 1960, the wheat surplus in the government's hands would amount to a billion and a half bushels. The existence of these huge surpluses has caused federal expenditures, in loans and storage costs, running to well over a million dollars a day; President Eisenhower reported in 1959 that "for wheat, cotton, and rice producers who have allotments of one hundred acres or more, the net [federal] budgetary expenditures per farm for the present fiscal year are approximately as follows: wheat, $7,000 per farm; cotton, $10,000 per farm; rice, $10,000 per farm."

The increasing surpluses reflect, in part, heightened agricultural productivity. Modern techniques and machinery have markedly increased the yield per acre for many crops; the following table [28] shows this for the six "basics" of the price support program. In every case, much more was grown on an acre in the 1960's than was grown ten or twelve years before:

| | Corn (bu.) | Wheat (bu.) | Rice (lbs.) | Cotton (lbs.) | Tobacco (lbs.) | Peanuts (lbs.) |
|---|---|---|---|---|---|---|
| Average 1939-43 | 31.2 | 16.4 | 2101 | 249.7 | 985 | 703.8 |
| Average 1952-56 | 41.1 | 18.7 | 2693 | 404.9 | 1333 | 952.3 |
| Average 1959-61 | 56.4 | 23.9 | 3393 | 446 | 1695 | 1195 |

Increased productivity per acre is one great handicap to governmental efforts to maintain farm prices by the restriction of supply —that is, by the limitation of production.

*Little Pigs and Soil Banks.* The federal government's first

---

28 *"Toward a Realistic Farm Program"* (New York: Committee for Economic Development, 1957), p. 11, and *Statistical Abstract of the United States, 1962* (Washington, D.C.: U.S. Bureau of the Census, 83rd edition, 1962), pp. 651-652.

effective moves to raise and maintain agricultural prices were concentrated not on price supports, but on the reduction of supply, to bring the latter into balance with the reduced demand of the depression era. Under the first Agricultural Adjustment Act, passed in 1933, payments were made to farmers who agreed to produce less than they had been producing. They were thus induced to leave acres uncultivated and little pigs unborn. So total supply was reduced and prices rose. In 1936 this act was held unconstitutional by the Supreme Court,[29] and two years later, as we have seen, the system of supporting prices by loans against surplus crops replaced the method of increasing them by paying for nonexistent commodities.

How to deal with the agricultural surplus became a pressing problem once again after World War II. Loans at a fixed high percentage, such as 90 per cent, of parity assured farmers of a good price. A product thus supported was, accordingly, produced in ever greater quantities. A flexible price support system, in effect for some crops, permitted the Department of Agriculture to make loans at a lower percentage of parity when a surplus was in the offing; this lowered prices somewhat, but hardly slowed the rate of production. High fixed price supports, as in the case of wheat and corn, were made conditional on the growers agreeing to a system of production limitation by acreage allotments or market quotas. The wheat limitations, however, contained loopholes in the form of minimum production allowances per farm and a minimum of total acreage to be permitted—acreage sufficient to produce more wheat than could be sold on the open market at the support price. The corn limitations were rejected by the corn growers themselves in 1958.

In 1956 the Eisenhower administration sought to solve the surplus problem through the device of the "Soil Bank." Twenty-three years before, Secretary Henry A. Wallace had been bitterly assailed for "killing little pigs," but actually the aim of his New Deal program was akin to that of Eisenhower. In each case, the purpose was to reduce supply by paying farmers not to produce. The "Soil Bank" plan, under which farmers took acreage out of

---

[29] *U.S. v. Butler*, 297 U.S. 1 (1936).

production and were compensated for so doing, had little effect on total production. Surpluses continued to mount. Government costs rose; the prices of unsupported or flexibly supported agricultural commodities fell. And as they fell, the breeze of political unrest once again stirred the long grasses on the farms.

## The Politics of Agriculture

In simpler days when government did little for the farmer, many farmers could agree on what it should do to cure their real or fancied ills. Oppressive railroad rates led to a widespread demand, sparked by the National Grange, for rate regulation. Debt, made disastrous by deflation, brought strong agricultural support to the cause of "free silver," led by William Jennings Bryan. And falling farm income during the booming 1920's and desperate early 1930's found the agricultural states presenting a well-nigh united front in Congress, regardless of party. This "farm bloc," in the Senate composed equally of Republicans and Democrats, demanded action. First it fought for a plan to support prices by export subsidies, which was blocked by presidential veto; then it got behind the New Deal's farm program. In the latter case, the legislation was the product of close cooperation between department officials, state college experts and a pressure group, the American Farm Bureau Federation. This triumvirate had worked together for many years; the county agent system, mentioned above, had cemented their alliance, for where the AFBF was strongly organized, the county agent was likely to be the Federation's nominee.

Vigorous governmental action, however, gave rise to new issues which tended to divide the agricultural interest. In the New Deal period, the Farm Security Administration's often unorthodox and experimental attempts to improve the lot of tenant farmers and sharecroppers, many of whom were Negroes, aroused strong opposition, especially in the South; the AFBF, speaking for the more prosperous cotton growers, fought the agency tooth and nail and finally brought about its dissolution. In this controversy the AFBF came into conflict with another pressure group, the National Farmers Union. The split has continued. More and more the AFBF has come to represent the big commercial producers, especially of cotton and corn; the smaller NFU, whose strength is chiefly in wheat-growing areas, argues the case for the "family farm." This division is symptomatic of developing political alignments: corporate farming versus individual farming, wholly owned farms against heavily mortgaged farms, crop against crop, prosperous against poor. Thus in recent years the NFU agreed with the Kennedy administration's emphasis on high supports with strict controls, while the leadership of the AFBF supported the view previously taken by the Eisenhower administration that lower supports and few controls are the appropriate methods of dealing with farm surpluses. Accordingly, the NFU supported the Kennedy administration in the 1963 referendum of wheat farmers on a proposed wheat program which called for unprecedented tight controls on the production of wheat. The AFBF fought the program and was widely credited with bringing about its defeat.

In the late 1950's a new group, the National Farmers' Organization, was formed largely among hog farmers of the Middle West. The NFO emphasizes direct action by the farmer rather than legislative solutions to the problems of agriculture. Pointing to the success of labor unions, it advocates withholding produce from the market until buyers enter into negotiated collective bargaining agreements for higher prices. Although the NFO does not yet have enough members to carry out this program successfully, its appearance indicates a disillusionment with legislative means of improving the lot of farmers. And this disillusionment may well be reflected in an impasse in Congress on agricultural legislation, which has made it very difficult to enact any constructive farm bill.

This legislative impasse is the result of the proliferation of interests within agriculture. Conflicts exist between producers of different crops; for example, livestock raisers do not want high price supports for the grain which they feed to their livestock. Important conflicts also exist between different producers of the same crops, arising out of the competition between new and old producing areas or competing varieties of the same crop. The old bipartisan farm bloc has disintegrated. Since the early 1950's, congressional voting on agricultural issues has tended to follow party lines. In part this may be due to calculations of political advantage; the Democrats, especially, have sought to capitalize on farm discontent.[30] But probably, in the main, it reflects the complexity of a problem to which no one has a certain answer. When a question is so huge and complicated that interest alignments are splintered and every proposed solution seems inadequate, the legislator's most defensible course may well be that of voting with his party.

The problem of agriculture, of course, is but one part of the much larger issue which has been central to this whole chapter—the extent and nature of governmental intervention in the economic life of the country. The economy, as we can hardly emphasize enough, is interdependent. A failure in one substantial segment of it sooner or later brings harm to the rest. Monetary and fiscal policies have an impact on the whole of it. Whether government permits or restrains the concentration of economic power in a few groups affects the prosperity of every other group. Yet we should not think of government's intervention solely in terms of economic groups; the individual counts too, and much of what the national government does is directed toward the satisfaction of individual needs. Programs designed to meet those needs are the subject of the next chapter.

---

30 Clearly there is no solid "farm vote." Many agricultural districts, for instance, have voted Republican year after year, regardless of economic conditions. But the votes of many farmers, like those of other people, are affected by circumstances and tend to be cast against the party in power when times are hard. Thus in 1956, when in most of the country Eisenhower rolled up much greater majorities than he had four years before, in agricultural Kansas and Nebraska his former majorities were sharply reduced.

CHAPTER 19

# Government and the Protection of the Individual

You will recall that in the very first chapter of this book, we took note of a guess that human governments came into existence to provide individuals with protection against harm—security which no man could achieve all by himself. That security, in the early days of our own national existence, was assumed to mean security of person and property. It was taken for granted that government should protect a person from the physical harm that might be done him by men of violence and from the loss of his property by theft or willful destruction. These protective functions, of course, were in part directed against potential foreign foes. In this aspect they constitute the task of "national defense," which we will discuss in Chapter 21. But most of the time, fortunately, we are not at war with enemy nations. To a great extent, therefore, the protection afforded us by government is "internal and domestic"—a shield against the depredations of some of our fellow countrymen, even our neighbors, a safeguard against assault and murder, arson and robbery.

In the laissez-faire days of rugged individualism, many Americans believed that such protective functions should be limited to

610

the prevention or punishment of just such familiar crimes. Even in that era, however, it was realized that the physical security of person and property could be threatened and destroyed by other things than crime. Accidental fire, for example, was a frequent and fearful destroyer; and so by the 1840's, a few cities were pioneering in establishing public fire-fighting units. Infectious disease killed many more people than did murderers, and so in the 1850's and the following decades, several state governments made somewhat tentative efforts to promote "public health" (that is, to protect the individual's health) by requiring the observance of minimum standards of sanitation. In the so-called Progressive Era of the early 1900's, government's duty to protect property was extended by broadening the concept of crimes against property; a person's property was seen to be threatened not only by burglars in the nighttime, but by the fraudulent schemer who robbed the gullible by misrepresentation and deceitful advertising. Eventually, in the 1930's, the idea of property as consisting only of tangible possessions was discarded. For most men, in those depression days, the most precious possessions of all were a steady job or a dependable income. At the same time, the old laissez-faire shackles on governmental action were cast aside, and so government assumed the task of protecting the individual against the disaster of unemployment.

Governmental authority to protect or promote health, welfare, safety, and morals, often spoken of as the "police power," has through most of our history been concentrated in the state governments. Indeed, it is the right to exercise such authority that is implicitly "reserved" to the states by the Tenth Amendment. Therefore, to a very large degree, such functions are performed not by the federal government but at the local level. The uniformed policeman on the corner is a city policeman, the health inspector in the restaurant's kitchen is a state inspector, the social worker checking up on the needs of an old-age pensioner is a state or county or city welfare official. More and more, however, the national government has intervened in this whole "police power" area. It has often done so indirectly: using its constitutional power to tax and spend, it has offered financial assistance to the states, encouraging the development of health and welfare programs which conform to prescribed federal standards. It has intervened directly, too. Its authority to regulate interstate commerce has enabled it, for instance, to arrest criminals who cross state lines and to provide that workers in most of industry shall receive at least a minimum wage; its power to tax and spend has been used to create a national system of retirement insurance. The whole pattern of increasing federal intervention reflects the change in physical and economic realities which has brought Los Angeles within five hours' distance from New York and has made individual prosperity dependent not alone on one's own efforts but also on the condition of the whole national economy.

## FOR SAFETY AND HEALTH

### Federal Police Activities

Most crime is local. From the earliest days of the Republic, however, some activities were deemed criminal under federal law—for example, the counterfeiting of United States currency. With the coming of the railroads, Congress from time to time declared certain uses of interstate transportation to be criminal, such as the shipment of lottery tickets, the transportation of women for immoral purposes, and, later, the transmission of motion pictures of prize fights. Here Congress was using its power to regulate interstate commerce as a basis for protecting the "public morals"—though just why movies of boxing matches should have been deemed immoral may baffle us today. In the modern age, however, the federal government's intrusion into the traditionally local field of law enforcement has been caused chiefly by the difficulty of catching criminals who have committed "local" crimes. The automobile made it easy for many such miscreants to escape from the jurisdiction where they performed their lawless acts. So Congress, again using its interstate commerce power, came to the aid of local law-enforcement officials by enacting a series of statutes, most of those with continuing significance becoming law in the early 1930's. Among these are laws which make it a federal crime to abduct a person across a state line (the so-called Lindbergh anti-kidnapping law), to transport stolen property worth more than $500 across a state line (a law especially useful in catching criminals trying to escape in stolen automobiles), and to flee out of a state in order to escape prosecution. Using its implied power to establish banks, Congress also made the robbing of a national bank a federal crime.

Furthermore, the list of federal crimes has always included treason to the country and in World War I came to embrace a number of activities which, though not treasonable, were deemed to be "subversive." In this area, the most significant statute in recent years has been the Smith Act of 1940, which we discussed in Chapter 6.

The laws of Congress, we must remember, are part of the "supreme law of the land." Therefore when Congress makes a particular act a crime, every police officer in the country is bound to enforce that law by arresting the criminal and holding him for trial. The local policeman, for instance, does not stand idly by while a national bank is being robbed, saying "That's a federal crime, so it's none of my business." However, the converse is not true: the criminal statutes of a state are not national laws. A burglary of a person's home is ordinarily no concern of the federal government—unless and until the burglar flees with his loot across the state line or escapes from the police and drives out of the state.

**The FBI.** The need for a substantial federal police force, therefore, has been felt only in comparatively recent times. To combat counterfeiting, to be sure, the Treasury Department early established its Secret Service. For many years, other federal agencies with a need for criminal detectives simply borrowed Secret Service agents from the Treasury Department; but in 1908, Congress severely limited such borrowing (though presidential bodyguards, to this day, are Secret Service men), whereupon President Theodore Roosevelt directed the Attorney General to organize an "investigative service" in the Department of Justice. This was the beginning of the Federal Bureau of Investigation. In World War I the FBI expanded, but its effectiveness was impaired by haphazard recruiting (for a while it was a patronage dumping ground) and its reputation was damaged by its disregard for constitutional rights (as in the "Palmer raids" of 1919 and 1920) and by the embroilment of its chief, William J. Burns, in the unsavory corruption of the Harding administration. The change came after

Harding's death, when President Coolidge appointed Harlan F. Stone as Attorney General. Stone, in turn, named a young FBI man, J. Edgar Hoover, as director of the FBI with the understanding that the FBI would be a specially recruited career service, trained not only in investigative methods but also in the observance of constitutional guarantees.

The FBI's chief, an effective organizer, had an instinctive knack for public relations. His agency became perhaps the first police unit in history to win great and general popularity. Youngsters in the 1930's delighted in imagining themselves, not as space cadets, but as "G-men"—a phrase apparently first publicized in 1933 when one Kelly, a cornered kidnapper, shouted "Don't shoot, G-men, don't shoot!" As various gangsters left over from the Prohibition days were hunted down, critics claimed that the FBI often arrived on the scene just in time to claim the credit: be that as it may, Hoover and his agency unquestionably won a warm degree of public confidence.[1]

The "national security" responsibilities of the FBI have taken first place among its duties since the Smith Act became law and World War II created a new crisis. In the post-war period, some FBI agents infiltrated the small Communist party of the United States, and a host of others gathered data concerning the past histories, affiliations, and opinions of thousands of federal employees. All such data are placed in what the FBI calls its "raw files." A good part of them are indeed "raw"—unverified and often untrue gossip. Director Hoover stated that the FBI's function is not to evalute this raw data but simply to present the facts to employing officials and security boards for them to assess. As we saw in Chapter 16 the FBI depends considerably on informants whom its agents believe trustworthy but who remain anonymous. Emphasizing the fact-gathering function, FBI men frequently say that their agency is in no sense a policy-making organization; some skeptics, however, have claimed that it has influenced policy through its ready cooperation with congressional investigating committees and

---

[1] The close connection between Director Hoover and a helpful journalist is illustrated by the following sentence in an account of a gangster's capture: "As the FBI closed in on Buchalter, Walter Winchell broadcast a radio appeal for the gang leader to surrender, with a promise that his civil rights would be respected by the FBI." Don Whitehead, *The FBI Story* (New York: Random House, 1956).

the widely publicized statements of its director concerning the Communist threat inside this country. Meanwhile the FBI continues to serve as an efficient enemy of crime which has interstate aspects, and, increasingly, as an educational center for local police forces eager to improve their techniques for detecting and combatting crime.

## Federal Health Activities

For nearly a century the protection of people's health has been a major function of state governments. The early "sanitary codes" were followed, in state after state, by hospitalization programs: indeed, one of the most inspiring stories in the history of local government is that of how, sparked by the evidence gathered by an indomitable woman, Dorothea Dix, the states gradually stopped chaining insane people like dangerous animals and instead built hospitals for the treatment of their illness. In the main, responsibilities for health remain in the states today. The federal government, however, also plays a significant part.

Directly, it provides (through the Veterans Administration) hospital and outpatient care for veterans, and (through the Public Health Service in the Department of Health, Education, and Welfare) medical and hospital facilities for Coast Guard personnel, merchant mariners, Indians, federal prisoners, and drug addicts. Its armed services, of course, also have their own medical and surgical units. Through the National Institutes of Health, it conducts and sponsors medical research. It began the inspection of meat in 1890. And since 1906, it has sought through the Food and Drug Administration to protect consumers from the effects of poisonous food and drugs—and since 1938, cosmetics also—sold in interstate commerce. Granted inadequate appropriations, the Food and Drug Administration has never been able to test and control more than a small fraction of the commodities it is supposed to regulate.

Indirectly, the national government assists in health protection through a variety of financial grants-in-aid, bringing needed support to state public health agencies. An important new grant-in-aid program began in 1948 with the passage of the Hill-Burton Act, under which the federal government contributes one-third of the construction cost of new hospitals. In the decade following the enactment of that law, aid for building over 3,500 hospitals and related facilities was authorized, involving federal expenditures of approximately a billion dollars.

Since 1956, grants-in-aid have also been made available to states to assist them in paying the costs of medical care for certain indigent people. As we shall see, the federal government gives financial support to various state "public assistance" programs, chief among them the provision of old-age pensions to elderly, needy people. When a pensioner is ill, some states increase the amount granted, to meet the cost of treatment. Federal aid encourages all to do so.

## AGAINST FRAUD AND FOLLY

The old legal maxim *caveat emptor,* which means "let the buyer beware," was well suited to the purposes of those engaged in the ruthless pursuit of profits. It fitted neatly, also, into the philosophy of rugged individualism which deemed financial success a virtue and financial failure a mark of the unfit. The great impresario of the nineteenth century, Phineas T. Barnum, is supposed to have said that "one is born every minute"—meaning, in the inelegant phrase, one sucker, one naïve human being who can easily be fooled by clever men. As American enterprise burgeoned, much of it, presumably most, was conducted "on the level"; but all manner of pursuits were also interlarded with charlatans, impostors, and frauds.

Among the most glaring fraudulent practices were those of some manufacturers and salesmen of so-called patent medicines. Perhaps this was because people were (and are) often most gullible when they are in trouble and hope to find a cure for their real or fancied ills. Patent medicine frauds became widespread, and early in the present century they were given lurid publicity by "muck-raking" national magazines. Public indignation was aroused not only by tragic stories of illness and death caused by poisonous food, drugs, and medicines, but also by the willful lies told by those who made and sold products which, though physically harmless, were actually worthless. That the deceivers took the money of poor and suffering people might not, by itself, have caused governmental intervention. That they aroused false hopes of cures for fatal diseases, however, was a factor which swayed the balance in favor of protecting the weak and guillible. Accordingly, the Pure Food and Drug Law of 1906 included prohibitions against false labeling and fraudulent misrepresentation.

The drive to protect consumers against fraud was a part of the progressive movement, reaching a climax with the passage of the Federal Trade Commission Act in 1914. That statute gave the FTC the duty of restraining "unfair competition," and one unfair method of competition may be false advertising. The commission spends much of its energies, today, in efforts to prevent deception of consumers.[2] Long restricted by narrow judicial interpretations of the original statute, since the passage of an amending law in 1938 it has had broad authority. Nevertheless, like the Food and Drug Administration, it does not have resources nearly adequate to police the whole vast business of branding, labeling, and advertising. To a large degree consumers must look to private organizations, such as Consumers Union, Consumers' Research and Better Business Bureaus for protection against those who would prey on the naïve and the susceptible.

The indignation against fraudulent purveyors in the muckraking days was mild compared to the fury with which many Americans blasted bankers, "Wall Street," and the stock exchanges after the stock market crash of 1929. Psychologists might have found that their anger was really directed at themselves for being taken down the garden path to indulge in gambling with their life's savings—for gambling the securities investment craze of 1927-1929 certainly was. Instead they turned on those whom they

---

[2] The old-time "medicine men" are not extinct. The FTC's report for the fiscal year 1953, for instance, included a long list of orders which it had issued in that year, to "cease and desist" from deceptive practices. Among the latter were claims that "Static Master instantly destroys static-surface attraction with polonium, a harmless by-product of the Uranium-Radium series, when in fact polonium can be highly dangerous; that Parfum de Soir, Danse Apache, or Bois de Rose are imported from France or that they contain gold; that Dolcin is 'economical' or 'low cost' or that it is effective treatment for rheumatic fever, fibrositis, myositis, neuritis, sciatica, lumbago, bursitis, etc.; or that Thorkon will convert 'a nagging, quarrelsome, irritable woman into a good wife and mother . . . unless such . . . conditions are caused by Vitamin B1, B2, niacinade, or iron deficiencies,' which instances, the FTC assures us, are quite rare." Fainsod, Gordon, and Palamountain, *Government and the American Economy* (New York: W. W. Norton & Co., Inc., 1959) p. 228.

618 **The Government in Action**

blamed for leading them astray. These included some investment bankers who had, indeed, misled investors into buying certain foreign bonds. Mainly, however, they were executives, bankers, brokers, and speculators who had not engaged in unlawful fraudulent practices. They had simply played the ruthless, competitive game of the securities exchanges, rigging markets, letting useful friends buy stock at low prices, urging small investors to buy shares of stock "on margin" (which meant, in effect, with money they didn't have but hoped to get when the price of the shares went up)—all for the purpose of reaping a legitimate financial harvest.

It has been said that in Wall Street there are bulls, bears, and lambs; the bulls and bears, the big traders and manipulators, are supposed largely to control the market, whereas the lambs, the little investors, get shorn. The great crash brought all three down together.

The New Deal laws regulating the securities business were, therefore, only partially aimed at the prevention of fraud; they were designed, as well, to protect people from the consequences of their own folly. The Securities Act of 1933 required full disclosure of pertinent information whenever a corporation issued new securities for sale, so that every potential investor could know what he was buying before he bought it. The Securities Exchange Act of 1934 broadened this requirement to embrace all securities, new and old. It also authorized the governmental imposition of restrictions on trading "on margin," and provided for regulation of the operations of stock exchanges and over-the-counter markets to prevent manipulative and unfair practices. Margin requirements are set by the Federal Reserve Board; otherwise the administration of these laws is the responsibility of the Securities and Exchange Commission. The SEC's task was made somewhat easier when the New York Stock Exchange voluntarily put numerous reforms into effect in the late 1930's, after its former president had gone to Sing Sing for grand larceny. Although the exchange markets still offer temptations to those who hope for large, quick gains and may instead suffer serious losses, unwise gambling is now, at least, discouraged, and even the gambler is protected against sharp dealings.

## TOWARD A MINIMUM LEVEL OF DECENT SUBSISTENCE

By far the greatest governmental programs for the protection of the individual are those designed to make certain that he will have money in his pocket—enough, at least, to live on, not luxuriously but decently. As we have seen, the idea that an individual's decent subsistence is a matter of public concern flowered only recently. For most of our history, the poor were seen as fit objects of private charity, not of public assistance. Most cities had their hopeless paupers, whom they herded into "poor houses" and treated as something less than citizens; but self-respecting people could not bear to take the "pauper's oath," and struggled on as best they could. When in 1937 Franklin Roosevelt said that he saw "one-third of a nation ill-housed, ill-clad, and ill-nourished," he was describing a condition which had always existed: in prosperous times the fraction might have been somewhat smaller, but poverty and privation were nothing new in America.

Any direct governmental attack on poverty long faced two great obstacles. One was the widespread belief in laissez faire. The other was the narrow interpretation of the Constitution, in terms both of restricted federal power and the limitations on state power imposed by the due process clause. When humanitarian reformers breached the laissez faire walls, the Supreme Court shored them up again. A few states, prior to 1929, did manage to institute very modest systems of aiding needy old people, leaving them in their own homes and refraining from classifying them as paupers. But when states tried to provide that active workers should be paid a living wage, their attempts were thwarted by the Court,[3] and judicial disfavor likewise prevented most effective federal action. The Court did, however, leave the door open to possible federal aid for state programs to assist the needy.[4]

The first obstacle trembled at the crash of 1929, and both fell

---

[3] *Adkins v. Children's Hospital,* 261 U.S. 525 (1923); *Morehead v. Tipaldo,* 298 U.S. 587 (1936). These decisions were overruled in *West Coast Hotel Co. v. Parrish,* 300 U.S. 379 (1937).

[4] *Massachusetts v. Mellon,* 262 U.S. 447 (1923), in which the Supreme Court upheld a federal grant-in-aid made to assist a state in carrying on a child-welfare program.

to pieces in the 1930's. From 1933 through 1938, Congress and state legislatures enacted measures designed, in one way or another, to assure people of having enough to live on, and from 1937 onward the Supreme Court gave its general approval to such measures.

These laws were not solely humanitarian in purpose. The federal work relief program, for instance, in which the Works Progress Administration employed millions of otherwise unemployed people at "subsistence wages," was a Godsend to most of those millions, but it also was supposed to rejuvenate the national economy by increasing the total spending power of consumers. A similar double motive underlay social security laws, minimum wage laws, and farm price-support laws. To the social worker, these statutes meant the relief or prevention of destitution in the case of old Mrs. X, unemployed Mr. Y., and impoverished Farmer Z. To the Keynesian economist they meant additional purchasing power with which to stimulate the wheels of private industry. The social worker's viewpoint was least noticeable, of course, in the formulation of agricultural legislation, which we discussed in the previous chapter. Except for the Farm Security Administration's attempts to help sharecroppers and tenant farmers, that legislation was and is plainly based more on economic than on humanitarian concepts. Still, insofar as the government puts a floor under farm prices, it affords considerable protection to the individual farmer, just as when it puts a floor under wages it helps those who work in industry to escape from abject poverty.

## The Fair Labor Standards Act

Most industrial and commercial employment in the United States today is subject to the provision of the Fair Labor Standards Act, which is administered by the Wage and Hour Division of the Department of Labor. As originally passed in 1938, the statute prescribed a minimum hourly wage of thirty cents for workers engaged in interstate commerce or the production of goods for interstate commerce. The minimum was supposed to rise, in steps, to forty cents; subsequent amendments had brought it to a dollar by 1958, with pressure building up for a further increase to a dollar and a quarter. Actually, considering the general rise in

Fitzpatrick in the *St. Louis Post-Dispatch*

### "Now me!"

When the essential features of the Social Security Act were held constitutional by the Supreme Court in May 1937 (when this cartoon was drawn) a bill for national minimum wages was pending in Congress, stalled in part by doubts about its constitutionality. The bill was eventually enacted, almost a year later, and passed successfully through the judicial gates in 1941. Fitzpatrick apparently thought that the Court's emphasis on "welfare," in the 1937 decisions, indicated that a minimum wage law would be held valid; actually the Fair Labor Standards Act was sustained as an exercise of Congress's power to regulate interstate commerce.

the cost of living, the present minimum is only a little more, in terms of what a person can buy with it, than the original one.[5]

---

[5] In many states, persons employed in work not covered by the federal statute are given some (usually less) protection by state minimum wage laws.

From the humanitarian standpoint the need for such legislation, long asserted by a knowledgeable few, became generally apparent as soon as it began to be enforced. Some New Englanders, for instance, had rather smugly assumed that although the law might be needed in "backward" states (presumably in the South) it would have no effect in progressive New England, where working conditions were good and wages were high. They were shocked, therefore, by what the wage and hour inspectors found in 1939—for example, factories within twenty miles of Boston where piece workers earned on the average as little as fifteen, twelve, or in one plant seven cents an hour. Violations were not confined to New England, of course, any more than they were confined to the South. Vigorous enforcement of the law brought substandard wages up; returning prosperity soon brought them up still more.

The Fair Labor Standards Act not only prescribes a minimum wage, but also requires that a person who works overtime—that is, in excess of forty hours in a week—shall be paid "time and a half" for his overtime hours. This means that for each hour in excess of forty, he gets one and a half times the amount of his regular hourly pay. The statute also finally accomplished what Congress had tried unsuccessfully to do many years before; it effectively prohibited child labor by forbidding the shipment in interstate commerce of goods upon which children had worked. You will remember that just such a law had been held unconstitutional in *Hammer v. Dagenhart;* in 1941, that decision was at long last overruled, the Supreme Court upholding the child labor provisions of the Fair Labor Standards Act.[6] A goal long sought by humanitarian reformers was thus achieved.

## The Social Security Act

The most far-reaching single "humanitarian" piece of legislation in our history, however, was the Social Security Act, signed by President Franklin D. Roosevelt on August 14, 1935. As originally proposed, this law described its own purpose as being to "alleviate the hazards of old age, unemployment, illness, and de-

---

[6] *United States v. Darby Lumber Co.,* 312 U.S. 100 (1941).

pendency." This was a modest and reasonably accurate description. No act of Congress could bring complete economic security to every American. Probably no act should. But in a time when the industrious were idle and the thrifty man suffered equally with the ne'er-do-well, it seemed indeed appropriate for government to "alleviate the hazards" of an economic system that could bring such hardship to millions of worthy citizens.

*Public Assistance.* In the first quarter of the twentieth century, a number of states inaugurated very modest welfare programs under which payments were made regularly out of the public purse to help certain people in dire need. This was "categorical" assistance, given to needy people in designated categories. The chief forms of assistance were old-age pensions for indigent individuals over sixty-five or, more often, over seventy years of age; "mothers' aid" for families in which, typically because of the death, absence, or incapacity of the father, young children did not have enough to live on; and aid to blind people unable to support themselves. In every case, however, the amount of assistance granted was niggardly, and even in the most generous states the grants were hedged around by obstacles such as the requirement that the recipient must have lived continuously within the state for at least five or even seven years. Monthly old-age pensions, in 1934, averaged as low as $1.22 in Nebraska and, believe it or not, 69 cents in North Dakota; more than half of the twenty-eight states with old-age pension laws paid less than $10 a month, and in three there were no available funds and no pensions were paid at all. Yet at this very time the need for help was increasing, for depression and unemployment had impoverished millions. The problem of the needy aged, furthermore, was becoming more acute regardless of the depression. In a stable agricultural society, old people normally work on the farm as long as they can and then are cared for, still in the old farmhouse, by their children; but the steady trend away from the land and into the cities disrupted this familiar pattern. More and more, the old folks were left to shift for themselves. Frequently they ended up with less than enough money to maintain even a "minimum standard of decency and health."

The federal government came to the help of these needy "categories" of individuals when Congress passed the Social Security Act. The first "title" or chapter of that statute authorized federal grants-in-aid to the states, to help the states to pay the cost of assisting the needy aged. Subsequent titles authorized similar support for state programs of "mothers' aid" (re-named "aid to dependent children"), aid to the needy blind, aid to crippled children, and maternal and child care. All of these grant-in-aid programs, plus an additional one added in 1950 for people over fifty who are "permanently and totally disabled," are now supervised by the Department of Health, Education, and Welfare. In terms of cost and the number of people helped, by far the largest are old-age assistance and aid to dependent children. Spurred on by the availability of federal funds, every state passed legislation which met the standards imposed by Congress, including more generous residence requirements, local administration by personnel selected on a merit basis,[7] and, in the case of old-age assistance, eligibility at age sixty-five. By 1961, 2,267,000 elderly people were receiving old-age assistance, in monthly payments which averaged, for the whole country, approximately $68 per person. Of this $68, slightly more than half was contributed by the federal government. Administration, however, including the important decisions as to what constitutes "need" and how much each individual should receive, is the responsibility of the states. Also in 1961, 2,764,000 children were being supported by state programs for aid to dependent children; the national average payment per family was just over $120 a month, with the federal treasury again shouldering a little more than half of the total cost.

All of these federally aided public assistance programs are based on individual need. They are, in effect, public charity replacing or supplementing private charity. They put a little cash into people's otherwise empty pockets. They are not uniform national programs; they are based on state laws whose provisions vary widely, and are carried out by state and local officials. The offer of federal money did, however, make these programs not national, to be sure, but nation-wide; every state rose to the bait. And the

---

7 Congress struck this requirement from the original bill in 1935, but reinserted it in the law by an act passed in 1939.

conditioning of federal aid on compliance with a few federal standards gives the national government supervisory responsibility and hence considerable influence on the shaping and administration of the various state programs.

*Old-Age and Survivors Insurance.* Sharply contrasting with the public assistance programs fostered by the Social Security Act is the national system of retirement insurance established by the same statute. This is a contributory system and for the most part a compulsory one, although for some groups, especially the self-employed, participation is voluntary. About nine-tenths of all persons in paid employment in the United States are covered by it. From them, and equally from their employers, contributions are exacted equal to a small percentage of their wages.[8] To them, after they reach the age of sixty-five and at least partially retire from paid employment, it regularly pays old-age benefits. The latter are measured, to a large degree, by the amount contributed by the individual concerned; under the formula established in 1962, they could vary between $40 and $127 per month. Additional monthly benefits are paid when the insured's wife reaches sixty-five, and also with respect to dependent children under eighteen, subject to a family maximum of $254.10. A widow of an insured worker, when she reaches the age of sixty-two, is entitled to three-quarters of the benefit which would have been paid to him, and special provisions give added protection to widows with dependent children.

Formally called Old-Age and Survivors Insurance and often shortened to OASI, this is the program most generally referred to simply as "social security." Constitutionally, it is founded on Congress's power to tax and spend for the general welfare; the so-called contributions are actually taxes. It is a single national program, administered by the Treasury Department and the Department of Health, Education, and Welfare. The individual states have nothing to do with its administration. It is not based

---

8 In 1961, the tax amounted to 6¼ per cent on the first $4,800 of earnings or wages paid during the year, 3⅛ per cent being paid by the employer and 3⅛ per cent by the employee. The rate is scheduled to rise by steps until it reaches 4⅝ per cent each by 1969, for a total of 9¼ per cent. Self-employed persons covered by the program pay 1.5 times the employee rate.

on individual need; it covers men with high salaries as well as those with low wages and pays benefits to the wealthy and impecunious alike.

Indirectly, of course, the spectre of increasing urgent need was a factor in the establishment of the system. As the average life span grows longer, the proportion of aged people in the total population rises. In a largely urban, industrial country many old folks are likely to have too little to live on. The framers of the Social Security Act, therefore, saw the insurance program as one which, in the long run, would check the rising costs of public

# 18.6 MILLION BENEFICIARIES

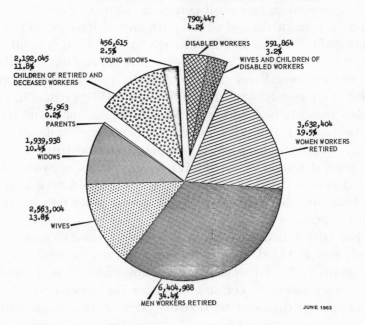

790,447
4.2%
DISABLED WORKERS

591,864
3.2%
WIVES AND CHILDREN OF
DISABLED WORKERS

456,615
2.5%
YOUNG WIDOWS

2,192,045
11.8%
CHILDREN OF RETIRED AND
DECEASED WORKERS

36,963
0.2%
PARENTS

1,939,938
10.4%
WIDOWS

2,563,004
13.8%
WIVES

3,632,404
19.5%
WOMEN WORKERS
RETIRED

6,404,988
34.4%
MEN WORKERS RETIRED

JUNE 1963

*Department of Health, Education, and Welfare—Social Security Administration*

### How beneficiaries of Old-Age, Survivors, and Disability Insurance are divided

The original Social Security Act of 1935 provided Federal Old-Age Benefits. Amendments in 1939 extended benefits to dependents and survivors; and disability benefits were added in 1956. The impact of the extension is shown here in two substantial slices representing monthly benefits paid to younger people—widowed mothers and their children, and disabled workers and their dependents.

assistance. State old-age pensions, paid on the basis of need, would become less important and less widespread, as more and more elderly people received a monthly check from the national government not because of their poverty but as a matter of right. In addition, as we have seen, economists of the New Deal period welcomed the assurance of sustained purchasing power in elderly consumers' hands. The purchasing power theorists, however, were even more hopeful about the stabilizing effects of the third major aspect of the Social Security Act—the promotion of state programs for paying regular unemployment compensation benefits to people who lose their jobs.

*Unemployment Compensation.* The principle underlying the nation-wide system of state unemployment compensation laws is that employers should bear some responsibility for supporting those of their employees who lose their jobs through no fault of their own and try unsuccessfully to find other suitable work. Note the phrase *"some* responsibility"; no employer is bound to pay a man whom he lays off, for the remaining years of that man's life. But each employer is called upon to make some provision for paying something to that man for at least a few weeks or months while he seeks other employment. Employers meet this responsibility by making contributions to unemployment compensation funds. Out of these funds unemployment benefits are paid.

The contributions, like those for old-age insurance, are equal to a percentage of wages paid. However, unlike old-age insurance, unemployment compensation laws do not require employee contributions, except in Rhode Island. In two other states, employees contribute toward disability insurance. In every state, some provision is made for scaling the rate of employers' contributions up or down, depending on the condition of the fund or the individual employer's success in avoiding unemployment among his own workers. Prosperous times mean fewer payments of unemployment benefits; hence the amount of unspent funds increases, and in many states when it reaches a certain point further contributions from employers are diminished or suspended. This system of "merit rating," or gearing contribution rates to the amount paid out in benefits, theoretically stimulates businessmen to try to eliminate the recurrent seasonal unemployment long typical in many industries. Probably its main effect on businessmen, however, is to make them anxious to keep individual benefit rates as small as possible. Unemployment compensation benefits are, in fact, limited in both amount and duration. The amount varies considerably from state to state, and the maximum benefit period (after an uncompensated working period, usually of one week) is likewise far from uniform. The national averages for 1961 were $33.80 per week for a potential period of twenty-seven weeks.[9]

The coverage of unemployment compensation is less than that of old-age insurance, as most states exempt farm laborers, domestic servants, and persons working in very small businesses which have less than four employees. Nevertheless, over two-thirds of the country's labor force is protected. The amount of their protection is insufficient for a comfortable living. However, although it is so small that it hardly encourages the unemployed man to sit idly at home, it is often large enough to supplement whatever savings or credit he has and so tide him over a bleak period. And, once again, it prevents the sudden disappearance of purchasing power, thus dulling the impact of large layoffs on the economy of the communities affected.

Unemployment compensation, like public assistance, is a subject of state laws and state administration. These state laws came into effect because of Congress's passage of the Social Security Act.[10] In the case of unemployment compensation, however, federal grants-in-aid played an insignificant part in persuading the states to act. The federal government does grant each state enough money to meet its purely administrative costs, including the expenses of a state-wide system of public employment exchanges. It does not, however, pay any share of actual benefits to the un-

---

[9] The recession of 1958 caused many workers to remain idle so long that they exhausted their rights to benefits, and also caused a heavy drain on the unemployment compensation reserves of the hardest-hit industrial states. Accordingly, Congress enacted a temporary law, authorizing federal advances to states for the payment of benefits for twenty additional weeks.

[10] Wisconsin passed an unemployment compensation act in 1932, but promptly suspended its operation, so that it did not actually become effective until after the Social Security Act was passed.

employed. Instead, the federal government imposes a 3 per cent payroll tax on employers and then permits each employer to offset against nine-tenths of that tax the amount he has contributed to a state unemployment compensation fund.[11] In other words, if his payroll tax for a given period is $300 and his state contribution is $270, he pays only $30 of the federal tax.[12] When this tax first came into effect, its impact everywhere was the same: every state legislature decided that rather than have the payroll tax be paid into the federal treasury to be spent for any purposes that Congress might determine, the money, or at least the 90 per cent of it permitted by the law, should be collected by the state for the benefit of its own unemployed.

Federal leadership thus brought state laws into being, but federal responsibility for the operation of those laws is limited. The Treasury Department acts, as it were, as banker for all state unemployment funds. The Department of Labor approves the administrative grants-in-aid, enforcing a few standards, some of which, such as a merit system for personnel and a fair hearing for aggrieved claimants, are similar to those imposed in connection with grants-in-aid for public assistance. Primarily, however, unemployment compensation, like public assistance, is the task of the various states. Under the Social Security Act, only Old Age and Survivors Insurance is a strictly national program.

### HOUSING

The individual's need for a decent place to live has grown more pressing as we have become an increasingly urban society. The poor man who cannot meet the mortgage payments on his modest home moves out, hunting for some abode within his means. The hopeful but penniless young couple hunts unsuccessfully for a place to live that is both decent and dirt cheap. In crowded cities and suburbs fast filling up, where can they go?

---

11 The Wisconsin law provided, not for a state-wide fund, but for separate "reserve accounts" maintained by the contributions of each employer.

12 When an employer's contribution rate is reduced from the state maximum because of his good employment record or the sufficiency of the state's unemployment reserves, he can offset against the federal tax both the amount of contributions he actually paid and the amount he was thus properly excused from paying.

The likelihood is that the best they can pay for is substandard housing. Whether they admit it or not, they become slum dwellers—and slums have long since been proved to be a social menace, breeding illness, infant mortality, juvenile delinquency, and crime. The provision of decent housing for those who lack it and cannot pay the prices charged by private owners is primarily a local function, but the federal government assists cities and towns to perform it.

As a matter of fact, the federal government's first program in the housing field had nothing to do with local governments, but was a relief measure directly helping people who were in danger of losing their homes because of their inability to pay their mortgagees. Established in 1933, the Home Owners Loan Corporation loaned them money so that, in most cases, they could keep their homes. This was a highly successful venture in terms of both the beneficiaries and the federal government. When, after eighteen years, the HOLC wound up its operations in 1951, it had a surplus of about $14,000,000.

The HOLC was, initially, a depression agency. The federal aid program for local public housing was likewise inaugurated in the depression, getting its start with the passage of the Federal Housing Act in 1937; it has continued, with many ups and downs, under a further statute enacted in 1949, providing for governmental assistance to individuals, for home financing, as well as to local public housing bodies for construction of low-rental housing. The various agencies concerned with these matters are combined in the Housing and Home Finance Agency. The HHFA has two main concerns. One is with the extension of credit to finance the building and owning of homes (and also, by a recent addition to the statute, college dormitories). A nation-wide home loan banking system, the purchasing of GI (veterans') mortgages, and mortgage insurance are the chief parts of this program. The other major objective is the creation of more low-cost rental housing in cooperation with local housing authorities. Some of this is public housing. Some of it is built and operated by private developers with governmental encouragement. Under a statute of 1949, which succeeded the original act, the Public Housing Administration, a constituent agency of the HHFA, has charge of

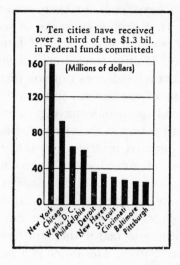

1. Ten cities have received over a third of the $1.3 bil. in Federal funds committed:

(Millions of dollars)

New York, Chicago, Wash. D.C., Philadelphia, Detroit, New Haven, St. Louis, Cincinnati, Baltimore, Pittsburgh

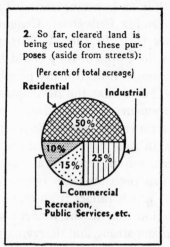

2. So far, cleared land is being used for these purposes (aside from streets):

(Per cent of total acreage)

Residential — Industrial — 50% — 10% — 15% — 25% — Commercial — Recreation, Public Services, etc.

*The New York Times*

## Urban Renewal

the federal end of a cooperative federal-local program of slum clearance and new construction. The slum clearance law (Title I of the Housing Act of 1949) is designed to bring private capital into the work of urban redevelopment. Working with a local redevelopment authority which is ready to acquire substandard or slum properties, the PHA arranges for a federal grant to repay the city for two-thirds of the loss which it takes in buying such properties and reselling them at a markdown to private developers. Nearly three hundred cities had joined in such programs within the first ten years of the PHA's existence.

## THE POLITICS OF WELFARE

Decidedly until World War II, and to some extent today, the issues concerning public welfare upon which men have divided have been deeply grounded in philosophical outlooks and beliefs. First is the question of the individual's responsibility for his own condition. The extreme of old-fashioned doctrine was illustrated in 1937 by the remark of a kindly, experienced congressman. Speaking when millions of Americans were out of work, he said that the unemployed should not be viewed with scorn and hatred, for their plight was not really due to their evil ways: "God made them lazy and incompetent." Ten years later the then president of Columbia University, Dwight D. Eisenhower, spoke of social security with distaste: if security was the prime goal of human beings, he implied, they could find it most conveniently behind prison walls. Indeed many people of adventurous outlook incline to the belief that the development of the human spirit and the advancement of civilization depend on people having to stand on their own feet and make their own way in the world. Artificial props, in this view, weaken our spiritual muscles; governmental support softens the moral sinews of Americans. Disagreement with this position takes two forms. One is the humanitarian attitude, which ranges from mere pity for the poor and weak to a conviction that in the modern age only the government can enable many strong and deserving people to realize their full potentialities and have decent, productive lives. The other is a belief in interdependence—privation for part of the population is assumed to be damaging or dangerous for all the rest of it. As F. D. Roosevelt put it, paraphrasing Lincoln, the nation could not long endure "half boom and half broke."

The second philosophical issue concerned the role of the national government. Under the Constitution, health and welfare were traditional state responsibilities. Would not federal intrusion into these fields violate basic constitutional principles? Would it not, in fact, lead to a centralization of power, threatening individual freedom? Proponents of federal action answered that the problems of privation were nation-wide and needed nation-wide solutions. They were willing to leave to the states broad responsibilities, provided that the states met those responsibilities; but they also read the Constitution as permitting a considerable degree of direct federal action, and on this the Supreme Court eventually agreed with them. They believed that freedom was endangered less by federal programs to aid those in want than by the failure of government to meet the economic needs of the people.

## The Institutional Framework

The nature of the federal system, indeed, had a profound effect on the shaping of programs to succor the poor and protect individuals from disaster. Within that system, as we have seen, the national government has often promoted state action by offering money or property to the states for particular programs. The grants of land for state colleges was an early example; more significant, as a precedent for later laws, was the Federal Highway Act of 1916, which inaugurated a large financial grant-in-aid program for state road-building. Other grants-in-aid were provided during World War I. By 1935, then, when the social security bill was considered, there was ample experience with grants-in-aid, and this form of federal sponsorship seemed beyond attack on constitutional grounds. The pattern of the public assistance provisions of the Social Security Act was, therefore, generally acceptable. The issue was not whether grants-in-aid were proper. Instead, it involved the formula by which the amount to be granted was determined and the nature and extent of federal standards to be observed as a prerequisite of any state's eligibility for aid.

A very different problem was created by proposals to help industrial employees by imposing new costs on industry. A minimum wage law meant increased expense for many employers, and unemployment compensation meant more taxes. Assuming the need for such protective measures all across the country, could the states do the job? Theoretically, yes; but the practical answer was no. Any state that took the lead by passing such a law was raising the cost of doing business in that state, thus making it harder for industry in the state to compete successfully with industry in other states. Therefore few states were willing to begin. (As we have just seen, even Wisconsin, though pioneering with an unemployment compensation statute, decided not to put it into effect.) The question, then, was how to reach the goal in every state in the Union. In the case of minimum wages, there seemed to be no feasible way of promoting nation-wide state action; accordingly, the federal government acted directly through the national Fair Labor Standards Act. In the case of unemployment compensation, the tax-offset device was used to push each state into establishing a state program. This complicated method, rather than the more familiar grant-in-aid, was selected mainly for constitutional reasons. Framers of the social security bill feared that although usual grants-in-aid, out of the general funds in the United States Treasury, were valid, a grant specifically financed by a particular earmarked payroll tax would be frowned upon by the Supreme Court. They knew, on the other hand, that the court had upheld a tax-offset scheme designed to persuade every state to pass an inheritance tax [13] and so felt hopeful that a similar device to promote state unemployment compensation laws would likewise be approved.

Constitutional doubts (well founded in 1935, though later proved unnecessary) thus provided one reason for promoting state systems of unemployment compensation instead of instituting a single uniform national program. Another reason, however, was that there was no general agreement as to what a single uniform program should be. The suspended Wisconsin law provided for individual "reserve accounts" for each employer, to which his employees could look for their unemployment benefits; but influential experts and some groups, especially labor unions, preferred a system wherein contributions from all employers would be placed in a single "pooled fund." Furthermore, there were differences as to whether employees should be required to contribute. Opponents of a single national program pointed out that the states constituted "experimental laboratories," especially suited for testing the wisdom of different kinds of legislation in an untried field.

None of these doubts and arguments prevented the enactment of a single national old-age insurance law. This part of the Social Security Act, however, had much the hardest sledding in Congress. It broke away from the familiar federal pattern, and for a time it seemed to have the weakest constitutional basis.[14] It was such a vast scheme that to many critics it seemed unworkable; they did not foresee the feats of recording that could be performed by modern business machines. In the face of such objections, its sponsors argued that in a mobile age, social insurance

---

[13] *Florida v. Mellon*, 273 U.S. 12 (1927).

[14] In 1936 the Supreme Court invalidated the first Agricultural Adjustment Act, which levied processing taxes and earmarked the receipts for the payment of benefits to farmers. *United States v. Butler*, 297 U.S. 1 (1936). This decision seemed to doom the old-age insurance program, for in effect the latter consisted of collecting payroll taxes to cover the cost of paying old-age benefits. However, in the course of the Supreme Court's famous "switch" of 1937, the old-age insurance program was sustained as a valid exercise of Congress's power to tax and spend for the general welfare. *Helvering v. Davis*, 301 U.S. 619 (1937).

designed to cover a person throughout his mature life had to be national in scope if it was to work at all.

## The Impact of Interests

Most of this chapter has dealt with the protection of consumers and people who are or might come to be in need. All of us are consumers, but our "consumer's interest" is for that very reason so widespread, and so taken for granted, that it has never been the basis of sustained, organized, and effective pressure on the national scale.[15] Organizations purporting to speak for it have usually been very small, often really representing only the views of two or three dedicated individuals. Similarly, the poor and potentially poor constitute a highly uncertain basis for a pressure group; most people are reluctant to wave the banner of their own poverty and unwilling to assume that they will need help in hard times ahead. Most protective welfare legislation, therefore, seems to have been produced less by pressure groups than by circumstances. When the circumstances of, say, a major economic depression are combined with the fact that the millions of impoverished people have the vote, the pressure for action exists without large organizations furnishing it. The interests of those who welcome governmental help are therefore politically potent, even though unorganized. Franklin Roosevelt and his assistants realized this in the 1930's; when one of them began to worry because the Republicans were pinning the tag of "welfare state" on the New Deal, another replied: "Well, what's so bad about that? People like to know that the administration is concerned about their welfare, so they'll vote for us." They did.

Two organizations, it is true, have played a part in the drive for adequate care for aged people. One of these was primarily a social group, the Fraternal Order of Eagles. Early in the century the Eagles made old-age pensions their special "cause" and pushed effectively for legislation in several states. The other, a product

---

[15] The Consumers League, sparked by the late Lucy Randolph Mason, has been an informative organization for half a century, but not a politically influential one. It did wage the judicial battle in behalf of early state laws protective of working women. Attorney Louis D. Brandeis was brought into the case of *Muller v. Oregon* (wherein he originated the "Brandeis brief" mentioned in Chapter 5) through his sister-in-law's connection with the Consumers League.

of the depression, was a nation-wide organization of clubs formed to sponsor the Townsend Plan, a vague scheme for levying a "transactions tax" and paying every elderly person $200 a month. Dr. Francis E. Townsend and the promotors of his plan avoided the difficulty of organizing people on the basis of their poverty by appealing, instead, to their pride as deserving senior citizens, to whom a grateful nation should pay its debt of gratitude in monetary form. The movement gained many followers in 1934 and 1935, so many that some historians have assumed that the old-age provisions of the Social Security Act were passed in response to Townsend pressure, or at least in order to head off the enactment of the Townsend Plan. The assumption is incorrect. The New Deal administration was committed to an old-age pension program before the Townsend movement gained any noticeable strength, and in 1935 the plan's backers carried very little weight in Congress. The movement perisisted, however, gaining more skillful political leadership as time went by, and it could claim at least some credit for the 1939 amendments to the Social Security Act, which made somewhat more generous provisions for the aged.

Preponderantly but not unanimously, business interests have lined up against most national protective or welfare legislation. In the contests over the Pure Food and Drug Act of 1906 and its successor, the Pure Food, Drug, and Cosmetic Act of 1938, and in the process of their administration, heavy opposition pressure was brought on legislators and rule-makers alike by substantial portions of the proprietary drug industry and advertisers.

Substantial appropriations for aid to local housing authorities for public construction have been fiercely and often successfully resisted by private developers, the Real Estate Conference Board being especially effective.[16] These private interests were aided,

---

16 In contrast to public housing grants, the redevelopment program's hottest political sparks are often struck at the local level. Slum clearance requires people to leave their homes, which have to be torn down preliminary to building new apartments. Whether their homes are slums or not, they tend to object. They also worry about where they are going to move to: this is an increasingly acute problem, for the substandard sections of the old central cities of metropolitan areas are becoming heavily populated by Negroes, who all too often find it hard to relocate. Ironically, therefore, redevelopment frequently arouses the most passionate resentment among the very low-income groups which, in the long run, it is supposed to benefit.

in 1959, by the Eisenhower administration's opposition to any increase in federal spending; the President first indicated that he would veto a large authorization bill being considered by the House, and then did veto a much more modest bill.

When the issue was social insurance through payroll taxes, the National Association of Manufacturers fought grimly against old-age insurance and unemployment compensation alike. The impact of business pressure was reflected in the crucial House vote on the Social Security Act—a vote on a motion to strike out the old-age insurance provisions.[17] On that question, business-oriented Democrats yielded to party and presidential pressure for the bill, Republicans, of course, did not: the motion was defeated by a vote that very largely followed party lines. In contrast, businessmen were more noticeably divided as to unemployment compensation, a number of prominent manufacturers and retailers supporting it; and the unemployment compensation provisions received congressional approval without any struggle on the floor of either house. In the following year, 1936, the Republicans made old-age insurance (but not unemployment compensation) a major campaign issue, picturing it as a program of human enslavement and suggesting that the payroll tax would be squandered and benefits never be paid. This attack backfired and was never repeated. On the contrary, under the Republican administration of the 1950's, old-age insurance coverage was expanded and both taxes and benefits increased.

Labor union pressure, as we saw in the last chapter, had less than an overwhelming impact in the 1930's, and was especially slight on the legislation we are considering here. The American Federation of Labor, after long opposing unemployment compensation, endorsed it in 1932, but its support was a decidedly minor factor in congressional consideration of the social security bill. In recent years, the unions have pressed for a uniform national system, and, in lieu of that, for supplemental federal support for state systems. Labor had a more direct interest in the passage of the Fair Labor Standards Act, though in the long struggle preceding the enactment of that statute the AFL at times

---

[17] Technically, this was a motion to recommit the bill to the Ways and Means Committee, with instructions to delete the old-age insurance sections.

seemed more concerned with blocking proposals it dislikes~~
with obtaining a minimum wage law. Recently the combined
AFL-CIO has exerted steady pressure for increasing the minimum
wage.

The unions for over twenty years have shown special concern for
another form of social insurance: namely, a national health insurance law. But here, as we saw in Chapter 9, they have run up
against a pressure group which, with respect to matters concerning
medicine, is more influential than they are. This is the American
Medical Association. Before World War I, it seemed reasonable
to guess that the first broad scheme of social insurance in the
United States would be a plan for meeting the costs of medical
care. Earlier, in both Germany and Great Britain, health insurance had headed the social insurance parade, and influential
American doctors looked favorably on the idea, and in 1917 the
state senate in New York passed a state health insurance bill that
had strong professional support. At the end of the war, however,
the leadership of the AMA changed, and, guided by Dr. Morris
Fishbein, the organization began its long, unceasing campaign
against whatever it decided to call "socialized medicine." [18] When
the social security program was being devised, health insurance
was deliberately omitted for fear that AMA opposition would kill
the whole bill. That this was a prudent decision was shown fifteen
years later by the fate of President Truman's health insurance
proposals, and again in the 1960's when Congress rejected President Kennedy's more modest "Medicare" proposal for national
health insurance for aged people.

Broadly speaking, the present statutory programs for individual
protection present few, if any, purely partisan issues. The two
main pure food laws were sponsored by the two Roosevelts, the
first a Republican, the second a Democrat. Public assistance
grants-in-aid evoke bipartisan support, though business influence
in the Republican ranks tend to make Republicans more cautious
about increasing the grants. Old-age insurance has not been a

---

[18] In the 1920's and 1930's, the AMA denounced private plans, like that of the
present Blue Shield, for the voluntary prepayment of medical costs.

matter of serious party contention since 1936. For good or ill, the "welfare state" is here to stay.

### The Influence of Individuals

Pressure politics is likely to be practiced most effectively by a vigorous organization which has at stake something quite specific, usually something to its immediate practical advantage. When, however, the issue is the protection of great numbers of people, especially people who through poverty, ignorance, or pride are largely inarticulate and unable or unwilling to organize even in their own self-interest, political action is nearly always sparked by a few zealous and persistent individuals.[19] Often sneered at as impractical idealists, these reformers occasionally seem to prove that a few people's single-minded devotion to a cause can produce momentous political results. At least we can wonder whether governmental action would have been taken if such inspired zealots had not fought for it. So it was in the last century, when a lone woman, Dorothea Dix, campaigned for humane treatment for the insane, and a village storekeeper, Lemuel Shattuck, for public sanitation; so it has been in more recent decades, in the case of several of the programs considered in this chapter.

The list of individuals who by their own efforts influenced public opinion could be a long one; we could begin with the famous social worker, Jane Addams, and the crusaders for child welfare, Julia Lathrop and Grace Abbott, but a full-length honor roll would be too long for inclusion here.

In the years of the progressive era, the fight for pure food laws was led by one man, Dr. Harvey W. Wiley, chief chemist of the Department of Agriculture. He had no great pressure group to support him, but did enlist the interest of widely read journalists who dramatically publicized the tragedies resulting from the sale of toxic and falsely advertised food and drugs. From about the same time on through the New Deal period, the effort for better labor standards was kept continuously alive largely by two people,

---

[19] The power of the Anti-Saloon League, crusading to protect people from the bottle, is a noteworthy exception to this general proposition.

Dr. and Mrs. John B. Andrews. True, they operated through an organization known as the American Association for Labor Legislation, but this was not much of a pressure group; it consisted chiefly of the handful of subscribers to the labor legislation journal which the Andrewses published. In the same period, the tiny American Association for Social Security was not an organization which made politicians quiver; but its leaders, Abraham Epstein and I. M. Rubinow, assembled the facts, wrote the books, and perfected the arguments which statesmen later used to obtain affirmative action.

Famous statesmen, too, have their place along with the forgotten reformers. We saw in Chapter 5 how Louis D. Brandeis, a Boston lawyer, devised the factual brief which led to the upholding of a state labor law for women. Brandeis was a many-sided man; in part he was a reformer, though certainly not a single-minded zealot. He has left two legislative monuments. One, which does not particularly concern us here, is the system of inexpensive savings bank life insurance in Massachusetts. The other, surprisingly, is the particular device used to promote unemployment compensation. In 1932, when Brandeis was a Supreme Court justice, his son-in-law was appointed to administer the original Wisconsin unemployment compensation law. However, as we have seen, that law was held in abeyance. It seemed likely to be discarded altogether unless the competitive handicaps with which it confronted Wisconsin industry could be removed by the passage of similar statutes in the other states. How could the states be persuaded to act? Justice Brandeis provided the answer. He mentioned to his son-in-law the Supreme Court's decision in *Florida v. Mellon,* wherein a tax-offset plan to induce the passage of state inheritance tax laws had been upheld. That was all he had to do. His Wisconsin relative and officials of the U. S. Department of Labor set to work drafting a bill which later became the basis of the unemployment compensation provisions of the Social Security Act.

The passage of that act itself owed much to two individuals in high office, President Franklin D. Roosevelt and Secretary of Labor Frances Perkins. The President (sometimes described as "a social worker at heart") devised the successful strategy for its enactment. The loyal Secretary Perkins, a trained social worker, captained the team that actually hammered out the broad program and put its many variegated parts together. In an area where pressure groups were weak and the voices of the aging reformers were growing thin and feeble, such personal political leadership was indispensable.

CHAPTER **20**

# Government and the Country's
# Resources

The growth of the United States from a small, largely agrarian
seaboard federation to a great, powerful nation was caused not
alone by human heroism or human invention. Both, certainly,
played their part. But a large part must also be accorded to what
the pioneers found waiting for them here—half a continent rich
beyond imagination in the physical resources upon which a good
life could be founded. First there was land, plentiful and fertile,
covered with trees and hiding vast wealth beneath its surface.
Second there was water—not just the oceans but innumerable lakes
and rivers, waterways which could serve as arteries of commerce
and waterfalls which could turn the millers' wheels. And today
we must add to land and water a third great resource, air. Oxygen,
of course, has always been necessary for human life; but only in
the present century has there come to be public concern not only
for the purity of the air we breathe, but also for the air as the
resource which we use for the fastest methods of transportation
and communication.

In the air and on the navigable lakes and streams, the public
has a paramount interest. Private rights to such air and water are

642

generally not rights of ownership, but privileges granted by government for the temporary use of these resources. In contrast, most of the land in the United States is privately owned. There are those with a philosophical bent, however, who see even private ownership of land as a very limited right: the "owner," they suggest, is really holding the land as a trustee for future generations. And, of course, they may be right in emphasizing the public's ultimate interest in even privately owned land, for government can at any time take (or reassert) possession of such land. Aside from the private holdings subject to this governmental right of eminent domain, there are still vast tracts owned outright by the national government, and smaller areas by states and local units. Broad and unceasing, therefore, is the concern of government with the physical resources of the territory over which it rules. In the United States the federal government is deeply involved in the preservation of many of those resources and the uses to which all of them are put.

## THE CONSERVATION OF LAND AND WATER

For nearly three centuries, without let or hindrance, white men exploited, wasted, and destroyed the natural resources of America. Sometimes they did this because they were greedy and heedless of the future: if a whole forest could be cut down and the timber sold at a good profit today, why worry about tomorrow? Sometimes they were wasteful through ignorance, like the farmers who, never having heard of contour ploughing, ploughed their furrows straight up and down the hillside and then watched acres of their best topsoil being washed down those man-made channels in the spring rains. Sometimes they were destructive for the fun of it, like the hunters who slaughtered thousands of bison and left their carcasses rotting on the great plains. But mostly they were just people trying to get along, building homes and communities and roads in what seemed to them a never-ending wilderness. They simply could not imagine that there was any limit to the physical richness of America.

But there was. As population expanded and the whole country was settled, America's natural wealth was seen not to be boundless after all. Farms that had been eroded for generations ceased to provide the farmers with a good living. Where forests had once grown, deserts encroached. Not only was there danger in the disappearance of soil and trees, but peril, too, in the failure to control water in the great rivers: floods destroyed cropland, and swiftly growing cities faced eventual extinction if they could not harness and put to consumptive use in their factories and homes the streams which rolled, undammed, to the sea. Awareness of all these dangers led, near the turn of the century, to the conservation movement, which found its chief political voice in President Theodore Roosevelt. The movement might have been foreseen as early as 1891, for in that year the federal government first began significantly to restrict settlement on the public lands.[1] Theretofore, the public domain, in small tracts, was "up for grabs." Now parts of it began to be "reserved" or "withdrawn from settlement." The withdrawal of acreage—its preservation, that is, for public purposes—proceeded slowly until Roosevelt became President in 1901. Then the amount of land withdrawn from settlement increased rapidly, until, today, the "reserved" public domain constitutes more than half the territory of eleven western states. The purpose of reserving it was to conserve the nation's resources. At an epochal conference of state governors in 1908 Theodore Roosevelt stated the issue: "The wise use of all our natural resources is the great material question of today. . . . These resources are the final basis of national power and perpetuity. It is ominously evident that these resources are in the course of rapid exhaustion."

### Forests

If Theodore Roosevelt was, as he has been called, the godfather of the conservation movement, its father was Gifford Pinchot and among its most influential relatives was John Muir. Pinchot, one of the first professional foresters, had been appointed chief of the Department of Agriculture's Division of Forestry in 1898; Muir was a famous naturalist. It is not surprising, therefore, that the early conservationists were primarily concerned

---

[1] Yellowstone Park had been established in 1872, but the other national parks were not established until the twentieth century.

with saving the forests and the surviving wilderness areas of the United States. An expanded Forest Service was established in 1905, with a program of maintaining the nation's supply of wood, protecting watersheds and wild life, promoting recreation in wilderness areas, and regulating forage grazing. Pinchot led a campaign for the federal acquisition of "forest reserves," which are now called national forests and encompass some 181,000,000 acres. These acres contain about one-third of the nation's commercial timber. The government is not in the wood-processing business, but does regulate cutting on federal lands, permitting it on a "sustained yield" basis; [2] from the sale of timber stumpage in eleven western states, it received nearly $90,000,000 in 1957.

Always a threat to forests and wildlife, and today their greatest hazard, is fire. The Forest Service seeks to prevent fire loss on the lands which it controls; it also supervises a grant-in-aid program to assist the states in fighting forest fires. This is an endless battle. Despite the improvements made in inspection and warning systems and in equipment, some 23,500,000 acres, both publicly and privately owned, were burned in the single year of 1950.

Despite the unsuccessful insistent demands of the late Secretary of the Interior Harold Ickes that the Forest Service be transferred to his department, it remains in the Department of Agriculture. Not only does the service deal with a "crop," but forestry's relationships with agriculture are close. Especially it concerns cattlemen and sheepraisers, for in the West much of the land included in the national forests is suitable for upland grazing. It involves, too, protection against wind erosion and "dust storms" in times of drought. After the fearful droughts of the early 1930's, the federal government embarked on an affirmative tree-planting program to develop a protective "shelter belt" of trees running through the great plains from North Dakota to the Texas panhandle. [3]

The federal forest program was not developed and is not run without continuous political conflict. In the early days the great

---

[2] Forests need frequent thinning; the important thing is that the right trees are cut and provision is made for continual replenishment.

[3] This was a favorite project of Franklin D. Roosevelt, a man of many varied interests who, on being asked his occupation by an election official (he was then President) replied cheerfully: "Tree grower."

lumber companies fought it. The Oregon legislature, influenced by them, petitioned against the creation of Pinchot's forest reserves. Today the issues are different; the national forests provide a continuing source of supply for the lumber companies, but the organized grazing interests have frequently urged turning over the national forests' grazing acreage to state control. The stockmen naturally believe that they could be more influential with state legislatures than with the Forest Service. Some corporate influence, too, has been on the side of the preservation of as much state control as possible. (Actually most of the nation's timberland is in private hands and so most forest practices are regulated by the states when they are regulated at all.) Usually on the side of strict regulation of cutting, limitation of grazing, and expansion of the national forests have been several organizations which retain much of the fiery zeal of the early conservationists, such as the Conservation Foundation, Inc., the Save-the-Redwoods League, and the professional Society of American Foresters.

### Soil

As we saw in the case of the shelter belt, tree-planting or "afforestation" is one means of protecting topsoil. Others include contour ploughing, crop rotation, and planting crops which enrich the soil instead of depleting it. The early conservationists, emotionally attached to the grandeur of the wooded mountains and their birds and bears and beavers, paid comparatively little heed to the need for conserving soil, but by 1934 a survey showed that nearly 300,000,000 acres had been made useless or severely damaged by erosion, and in 1947 a soil expert could say quite positively: "We have ruined more good land in less time than any nation in recorded history." [4] With the beginning of the cooperative agricultural extension program in 1916, some concern was paid to this wastage; but soil conservation is a complicated scientific business, and few county agents could be expected to be well versed in it. Furthermore, in the last analysis soil-saving practices

---

[4] Hugh H. Bennett, "The Coming Technological Revolution in the Soil," *Science,* January 3, 1947, quoted in Fainsod, Gordon, and Palamountain, *Government and the American Economy* (New York: W. W. Norton & Co., Inc., 1959) p.717.

must be those of individual farmers, who may incline to be "sot in their ways," reluctant to change their familiar methods. Despite county agents, state agricultural colleges, and the extension service's cooperative research, erosion continued.

The federal government stepped effectively into the picture in 1935. Congress passed the Soil Conservation Act, which established the Soil Conservation Service in the Department of Agriculture. The SCS promoted the establishment, under state laws, of local soil conservation districts, of which there are now close to three thousand. Though local and run by farmers within the district, these districts are not designed to operate in isolation. They work with the SCS, which brings to them the needed expertise in soil conservation practices and which, on request, may prepare a plan for the most productive and soil-saving use of the land within a district. The program, in effect, is based on the interest of some local farmers in soil conservation, their willingness to learn and to educate and persuade their neighbors, and the knowledge and tact of the SCS experts.

The other federal agency most directly concerned with soil conservation is the Bureau of Land Management in the Department of the Interior, which administers the Taylor Grazing Act of 1934. The latter pertains to grazing on the "public domain"—the western land still owned by the national government and not included in national forests or national parks. The statute was strictly a conservation measure, designed to protect some 80,000,-000 acres (soon increased to 142,000,000) from erosion resulting from the destruction of forage cover by overgrazing. On these acres, grazing is lawful only if it complies with rules limiting the amount of grazing and fixing fees to be paid by the stockmen. The latter have brought heavy pressure to weaken federal control and put the real power in the hands of local advisory committees of stockmen, who may or may not be concerned with soil conservation. Like the silver miners whom we considered in Chapter 18, the stockmen are comparatively few in numbers but, because they live in thinly populated western states, are overrepresented and hence influential in the Senate. However, since the death in 1953 of their leading spokesman, Senator Pat McCarran of Nevada, they have been less successful than heretofore in their effort to substitute self-regulation for federal control.

## Minerals and Oil

The valuable resources *under* the public lands are treated by the federal government in three different ways. First, all uranium is reserved for the sole use of the government under the Atomic Energy Act of 1946. Second, oil and gas, sodium, phosphates, potassium and sulfur may be exploited by private operators under leases. These leases are intended to limit the amount of exploitation in accordance with national needs; their clauses are enforced by the Geological Survey in the Department of the Interior, which also inspects the lessees' drilling operations. Other mining on the public domain is governed by an old statute, the Mining Law of 1872, under which a private developer can, at very little cost, claim sole rights to mine a twenty-acre tract where he has "located" minerals. He can also use the surface of the tract; actually, there is very little mining on the public lands, the "locaters" often claiming mining rights as a means of acquiring some inexpensive acreage for lumbering or grazing purposes.

Readiness to permit such use of the public domain by lumbermen masquerading as miners caused sharp partisan criticism of the Eisenhower administration early in its regime. Far more significant as a political issue, however, has been the conservation of oil.[5] Of all the scandals of the Harding administration (1921-1923) the best remembered concerned oil—the leasing, on terms highly favorable to the lessee, of rights to exploit oil deposits under public lands in Wyoming known as the Teapot Dome naval oil reserve. Charges of bribery and corruption forced the Secretaries of the Navy and Interior out of office. The latter was prosecuted, and the lease itself was terminated by court order. Ironically, this scandal, which the Democrats expected to use as a winning issue in the next election, gave them no partisan advantage and instead weakened their strongest presidential aspirant. Harding died in 1923 and Calvin Coolidge, succeeding to the presidency, could run as the Republican nominee in 1924 saying truthfully that

---

[5] About 95 per cent of all oil produced in the United States is under privately owned land. Its production is regulated by state laws. The federal government supports state laws conserving oil by prohibiting the shipment, in interstate commerce, of oil produced in violation of the state's requirements.

no oil had dirtied his hands. On the Democratic side, however, the leading contender for the nomination, William G. McAdoo, had in his law practice represented some business interests of the very oil man who was accused of bribing a cabinet officer. Although McAdoo was not involved in the corruption, the mere smell of oil was enough to weaken his "availability" and prevent his nomination.

Oil more recently discovered under submerged coastal lands, chiefly under the so-called "tidelands" of Texas and Louisiana, caused hot political controversy after World War II. President Truman claimed these deposits in the name of the national government. The Supreme Court upheld his claim. The states affected, however, wanted to own these deposits in order to receive revenue, in the form of royalties, from the companies exploiting them. The oil companies preferred state control despite the existence of state oil conservation laws, because they assumed that federal oil conservation policies would be much stricter than those of Texas and Louisiana. Three times Congress passed bills giving these national resources to the states. Twice the bills were killed by President Truman's veto. The third was signed by President Eisenhower in 1953, after he had carried usually Democratic Texas in the 1952 election largely because he had supported the oil interests' demands and his rival, Stevenson, had opposed them.

## Water

Unlike forests and soil and minerals, water is normally a self-replenishing resource. It does not have to be "conserved" in the sense applied to other natural resources. Of course you may hear plenty about "conserving water" if you live in Tucson, Arizona, or spend a very dry summer in St. Louis County, Missouri. Don't water your lawn for more than an hour; don't water it at all! But if you keep the faucets shut you will not thereby keep any water imprisoned at the edge of the desert, nor will you refill the Missouri River. Rivers run to the sea. When temporarily they fail to provide all the water that people want (either because drought has lowered their levels or because too many people line their banks) the immediate need is to control the *use* of the water, sharing it so that everyone can use a little though not as much as he desires. This is a problem of allocation of resources, not conservation.

A permanent water shortage, however, may give rise to practices akin to conservation. Replenishment is a goal of the sustained-yield program in the forests and the planting of soil-building crops, and under the same heading we can properly place the still experimental efforts to replenish water supplies by artificial rainmaking. Although skeptics may feel that the Hopi Indians' annual snake dance is as productive of rain as the scientific efforts of meteorologists, still the aerial "seeding" of clouds might be developed into a significant method of filling rivers and reservoirs. More important and more certain of results is the *holding back* of surplus water so that instead of rolling, wasted, to the ocean, it can be put to human use when it is needed. This kind of conservation is accomplished by building dams and regulating the flow of water over those dams. Such dams create storage basins and make possible a steadier flow below the dam, keeping the depth of ship channels more nearly uniform throughout the year. They may also conserve much arable land by preventing destructive floods. Since Congress passed the Flood Control Act of 1936, the federal government, through the Army Corps of Engineers, has been engaged in a large-scale program of building floodwalls, levees, and dams designed to prevent flood damage. A small share of the cost of this program is borne locally, but in the main it is federally run and federally financed. Furthermore in some river basins, as we shall see, flood control is one of several purposes underlying federal developmental programs run by agencies other than the engineers.

The ultimate authority to regulate the flow of most sizeable rivers in the United States rests with the national government, for the Constitution empowers Congress to legislate with respect to "navigable streams." Although the federal interest in water may have been expressed by the Theodore Roosevelt progressives in terms of conservation ("saving this priceless resource for the benefit of all the people"), the issues it creates pertain not so much to the conserving of water as to the ways rivers are used, who uses them, and for whose advantage. These have been fighting political issues for more than half a century.

## THE USES OF RIVERS

Fresh water can be wasted and it can destroy good land, but it is a vital resource for any great nation. Many are the uses of rivers. In our homes we drink their water and wash in it. Factories use billions of gallons of it every day. Ships sail on it. Fish breed in it. Some of it is diverted into canals which, running into arid areas, make the desert bloom. And as it tumbles over waterfalls and dams it turns the turbines which produce electricity. All these uses are interrelated. To be sure, through most of our history, governments acted as if they were not interrelated; only in the last few decades have the possibilities of "multi-purpose" river basin development been realized. Yet the connection has always been there, and we cannot well comprehend the politics of water unless we are keenly aware of its existence.

### Consumption

Domestic and industrial use of water is primarily a matter of local concern. Where great cities have arisen in areas with little rainfall, however, the local government by itself cannot meet the needs of the people. The plight of the rapidly growing city of Los Angeles, California, early in this century is an example of this. Its needs could be satisfied only by diverting some of the water of the Colorado River, three hundred miles east of the city. But the other states of the Colorado Basin also wanted to use its water. After years of negotiation, an interstate compact or "treaty" was agreed upon, dividing up the available water. Congress approved the Colorado River Compact in 1927, six states promptly joined in it, and so for a time at least Los Angeles was assured of a sufficient water supply.

The consumers' interest in water includes not only the quantity of the water but its quality. Here, of course, the water drinker and the industrialist are joined by those who enjoy swimming and boating and fishing and by the specialists in public health. All of them are hurt by pollution—pollution caused partly by sewage, partly by the extraneous elements that are mixed with the water as it is used by industry before returning to the river. (About 100 billion gallons of water are used in industry every day.) Everybody would like the water to be clean, but few are ready to assume the great expense of making it so. Congress made a rather modest gesture against pollution in 1956, its Water Pollution Control Act authorizing federal legal action to abate pollution on an interstate river if a downstream state so requests and expanding a grant-in-aid program (supervised by the Public Health Service) which had begun on a very minor scale in 1948, to stimulate state and local pollution control programs.

## Navigation

Navigation on the inland waterways of the United States is largely made possible by federal expenditures. This has been noticeably true since the coming of the railroads and especially in the modern age of trucking. Most river transport is feasible only because of continuing efforts of the army engineers and other federal agencies to maintain channels and embankments. Its importance in the national economy is slight. In terms of local economic interests, however, it is significant; for this reason, and because of the favorable publicity which usually comes to a congressman for "doing something for the district," internal navigation measures have strong political backing. The rivers and harbors measures proposed in Congress have long been called "pork-barrel" bills, the idea being that each representative is eager to obtain "pork," in the form of a levee, a deepened channel, and the like for his constituency. Politically, then, Congress's power over navigation serves often as the source of a form of local patronage. Legally, it has at times furnished a constitutional justification for great federal river development projects in which other purposes are in fact far more important.

## Irrigation

If you fly across the western states in clear weather (after all, this is the region "where the skies are not cloudy all day"), look down at the ground far below you. For many minutes you may see only what looks like miles and miles of brown, barren earth, some of it flat, some of it wrinkled, all of it apparently empty. Then, in striking contrast, comes a patch of vivid green. From your plane's height this patch looks small, but you may estimate correctly that it is one or two hundred miles square. Then comes more brown land, and another patch of green. What you are seeing is a vast, arid, waterless desert, in parts of which men have made crops and fruit trees grow in abundance by bringing water from faraway rivers to give life to the dry soil. Irrigation has made portions of the desert productive places fit for human living.

The country's first sizeable irrigation system was constructed by the Mormon settlers in Utah more than a century ago. There and in other western states, without federal assistance, more and more of such projects were begun, and from the time when the first irrigation canals were dug in 1848 until 1900, about 10,000,-000 acres were made productive by bringing water to them. These private cooperative ventures, however, were costly, and after land close to the rivers was irrigated, the digging of long canals to more distant areas became impossibly expensive. Then, as we have seen, at the turn of the century came a growing concern for the prevention of waste of natural resources. Soil which would be luxuriantly productive if it only had water was being wasted for lack of water. To stop this waste, it should be irrigated. So in 1902 Congress passed the Reclamation Act, putting the federal government into the business of bringing and selling water to farmers in the arid portions of seventeen western states. In twenty years the total amount of land irrigated by both public and private efforts more than doubled; today some seven million acres get their water from federal reclamation projects.

The 1902 statute established a reclamation fund, consisting of receipts from the sale of public lands. Into this fund go, also, the payments made by the water users, who are charged a sufficient amount to meet the construction costs of the project. (These charges are spread out over a long period, so the annual payment by the water user is small.) Out of the fund, supplemented in recent years by sizeable appropriations from general funds, comes the money to build and operate the irrigation projects. The system is run by the Bureau of Reclamation in the Department of the Interior. The latter must not only dig ditches and long canals, but build dams. River flow varies greatly from season to season, but the need for irrigation water does not vary accordingly; therefore, dams must be built so that when the river is full, water can be stored in reservoirs, available for irrigation in the periods the river resembles a dry creek.

The framers of the Reclamation Act realized that provision of "federal water" was bound greatly to enhance the value of the land irrigated. There was a danger, therefore, that "land sharks" would buy up such land while it was still arid and then sell it at a huge profit after it came under irrigation. Partly to prevent this, and partly to perpetuate the familiar American "family farm," Congress in the Reclamation Act provided that water would be furnished only to holdings which did not exceed 160 acres, or 320 acres where the owner and his wife both lived on the farm. Private and state reclamation projects do not necessarily contain any such acreage limitation, but the latter remains as a central part of the federal statute.

### Power and Multi-Purpose Development

Although the primary purpose of a Bureau of Reclamation dam might be irrigation, the very existence of the dam constitutes a potential source of electric power. Early in its career, therefore, the bureau began to produce power as a kind of by-product of its main work. While the amounts so produced were still small, Congress directed that in marketing such power the bureau should give preference to certain designated customers—municipalities and other public bodies, and, later, rural cooperatives. Beginning in the late 1920's, however, the bureau's power operations assumed a new significance as Congress authorized the construction of the first of a series of high dams, each one capable of producing great quantities of electric energy.

The first huge reclamation dam, the Hoover Dam on the Colorado River, was built in connection with the needs of Los Angeles and the Colorado River Compact states, discussed above. In the next decade came enormous projects on other rivers, especially the Columbia River in Washington and Oregon and the Tennessee River in the South. The great Grand Coulee Dam on the Columbia not only was the world's largest power plant, but made possible the reclaiming of 1,200,000 acres of upland desert land in southeast Washington. The development of the Columbia illustrated more, however, than the possibilities of combining power production with irrigation. The purposes of flood control and navigation could be served, too, especially if dams were located not only on the main river but on its tributaries as well. And in the construction of Bonneville Dam near Portland, Oregon, and in the location of dams further upstream, special consideration had to be given to the preservation of the Columbia River salmon, which is born upriver, goes to sea, and then must return upriver to breed. If the salmon's return were blocked by impassable dams, there would soon be no more salmon. The Bonneville Dam, accordingly, contains gently stepped "fish ladders" up which the salmon can easily climb.

The Columbia, then, is the scene of multi-purpose development, embracing not just the main river but much of the river basin. However, it is not a unified program, the product of a single area-wide plan. Responsibility is divided among various federal agencies on the basis of function, with no one agency responsible for the whole development. In this lack of unity the Columbia and other rivers where reclamation dams are the center of multi-purpose activity differ sharply from the one great unified program of river basin development, that of the Tennessee Valley Authority.

The TVA, established in 1933, is a unique federal agency. It has been described as a "semi-independent, quasi-autonomous government corporation," [6] operating a huge electric power business the receipts from which largely pay the costs of developing and running an area-wide multi-purpose program. The area is the watershed of the Tennessee River, covering some 40,000 square miles in parts of eight states. The purposes are the production and marketing of electric power, flood control, the improvement of navigation, recreation, and the promotion of conservation practices. (Irrigation is unnecessary, as the region gets adequate rainfall.) TVA agricultural experts teach and demonstrate efficient farming and soil conservation practices and conduct research beneficial to both farmers and the fertilizer industry. For the rest, the TVA's activities are centered around its twenty dams and eight

---

[6] C. Herman Pritchett, *The Tennessee Valley Authority* (Chapel Hill, N.C.: University of North Carolina Press, 1943).

large steam plants. The dams and the transmission lines fanning out from them have made possible the electrification of 90 per cent of the farms of the Tennessee Valley and have also stimulated industrial growth and prosperity. The steam plants are not merely supplemental to the dams, "standing by" to take up the slack when the water in the river is low; they are vital factors in meeting the demands of the area's largest utilizer of electric power, the atomic energy installations at Oak Ridge.

Headed by a presidentially appointed three-man board of directors, under which serves a single general manager, the TVA has its own "capital" city, Knoxville, Tennessee; its own personnel and merit system, separate from Civil Service and traditionally hostile to political patronage; its own financial resources including authority to borrow money by issuing its own bonds (though the subjection of its financial operations to congressional appropriations and General Accounting Office procedures has been a source of constant argument); and its own regional constituency. Its apparent achievement in bringing prosperity to a region which had seemed economically doomed gave the TVA world-wide fame by the late 1930's, and prompted suggestions that similar "authorities" should be created to develop other river valleys, especially those of the Missouri and the Columbia. But doubts persisted in some quarters about the validity of TVA as a matter of principle, regardless of its practical achievements; and to these doubts were added complex political conflicts, inside government [7] as well as among private organizations.

### River Basin Politics

By itself, a flood control program is hardly a likely subject of national political controversy. Nobody likes floods. River navigation, as we have seen, is sometimes a political bonanza, but seldom has been the source of a major political issue. (An exception is the St. Lawrence River Seaway, long advocated by midwestern agricultural and industrial interests and bitterly opposed in New

[7] Harold L. Ickes, Secretary of the Interior from 1933 to 1946, developed an almost pathologically jealous hatred of the TVA and seized every opportunity to undercut plans for the expansion of the "authority" idea.

York and New England.) In contrast, the building of dams which may serve these purposes but which provide irrigation water and produce electric power have sparked some of the hottest political conflicts in our history.

The issues have been centered on multi-purpose projects for irrigation and power. As far as irrigation is concerned, for more than half a century the crucial political question has been the 160-acre limitation. Its defenders have held fast to the position taken by its originators and have gained the support of those organizations which, like the National Farmers Union, believe in the "family-sized farm" as an article of faith. They have described the opponents of the limitation as speculative land grabbers eager to turn a public investment to their private enrichment. The rise of large-scale, mechanized, corporate farming, however, tends to put the defenders at a logical disadvantage. Often, in the argument, the issue of acreage gets lost in a larger issue—the role of government in developing and selling electric power. Reclamation policy since 1902 has included both acreage limitation and public power development, and the friends or enemies of one tend to be the friends or enemies of both.

The public power issue concerns the building of dams and power plants and the transmission of energy for resale. For a long time most of the people's rivers were assumed to be fair game for any utility corporation that wished to dam them. Not until 1920 did the federal government, under the Federal Water Power Act, treat the building of power dams on navigable streams as a privilege for which the would-be builder had to obtain a federal license. This, of course, did not halt private development—development which might or might not constitute the most efficient and generally beneficial use of public property but was highly profitable to the licensed corporation. Utility companies grew in wealth and influence. Often they were grouped under a single holding company, the latter having a controlling interest in all the major operating electric companies in a region embracing several states. Thus utility "empires" grew up. Their rates were subject to state regulation, but often they sought to control state regulatory commissions and legislatures with considerable success.

By the time that the depression shattered the holding company pyramids, the "power trust" had long been a prime target of anti-monopolists. A quarter-century earlier, Theodore Roosevelt had spoken of it as the "most threatening growing monopoly." During the 1920's, that old conservationist Gifford Pinchot, by now governor of Pennsylvania, led the public power forces, proposing a state-run grid of transmission lines to cover several eastern states. In the Senate, George W. Norris of Nebraska fought successfully to keep the federal government's Wilson Dam at Muscle Shoals on the Tennessee from being sold to private operators. High electric rates caused protests, and many conservative home owners and businessmen decided that public power might be preferable to monopolistic private power.[8] By 1930, forty-three cities and towns in Massachusetts alone had their own municipal power plants. The rising storm engulfed the private companies when, almost simultaneously in the period from 1929 to 1933, congressional investigation disclosed the length to which the electric light industry had gone to influence not only politicians but students and newspaper readers,[9] and the great holding company pyramids, such as that of Samuel Insull, came crashing down into financial ruin.

By 1933, therefore, the stage was set for public development. The laws authorizing the TVA and the many new reclamation dams were enacted without much effective opposition. A precedent for the erection of a very high dam by the federal government had already been created, in the spectacular shape of Hoover Dam on the Colorado; but this was a structure needed to solve the water problems of the southwest and financially beyond the scope of private capital. Moreover, and most important, from Hoover Dam the federal government had built no transmission lines. The energy generated there was available only to those who could come and get it—it was for sale at the dam ("at the busbar" is the usual phrase) to whatever private company built transmission lines

---

8 Thus a former president of the United States Chamber of Commerce, John H. Fahey, said: "As a businessman I would prefer private ownership, but when the public cannot obtain the best possible service at the lowest possible cost, the advantages of private ownership disappear."

9 It was found, for instance, that the industry kept on its payroll numerous college and business school professors. And a controlling interest in a leading Boston newspaper was held, in practical effect, by the International Paper and Power Company.

to the dam. In contrast, the later projects included not only dams but transmission lines, carrying electricity directly to the preferred customers of the government. And those preferred customers did not include private power companies.

Today the two central issues remain: who shall build the dams and who shall build the transmission lines? Since its dark days, the industry has recovered much of its prestige and political influence. The election of President Eisenhower, who once referred to the TVA as "creeping socialism," marked a change in public policy: plans for federal dam-building were slowed, and a choice dam site at Hells Canyon on the Snake River was awarded to the Idaho Power Company for the construction of a lower dam than the one previously planned by the Department of the Interior. Furthermore the Eisenhower administration, reverting to the position taken by President Hoover many years before, favored selling federal power at the busbar and so frowned on the erection of governmental transmission lines. The policy of the 1950's was based on three ideas. First, public power projects were deemed dangerous to free enterprise, for, not having to pay taxes or dividends, the public projects had a competitive advantage over private companies and could slowly drive them out of business. Second, where a dam was so large as to be beyond the resources of private capital, the government having built the dam should stay out of business and foster private enterprise by selling the power at wholesale to private corporations for resale. Third, in any power development the federal government should not be dominant; there should be "partnership" between it, the states, and private business. These three policy objectives were welcomed and reiterated by the utility industry.

Opponents attacked all three. As to the first, they pointed out that despite the huge federal developments since 1933, more than four-fifths of the electricity used in the country was still generated and sold by private corporations. Second, they repeated the historic slogan that a public resource should not be used for monopolistic private gain: selling power at the busbar, they said, would deprive domestic and industrial consumers of the benefit of low-cost electricity, and would, instead, present to the corporation which acquired the power an opportunity to make a handsome profit. Third, they protested against the "meaningless vagueness" of the "partnership" idea—which, indeed, was never clarified in practical terms.

President Kennedy, in the 1960's, did not continue to advocate "partnership," but his own policy did not promptly and clearly emerge. Years before, as a young congressman, he had sided with the private companies. As a candidate for President, he had expressed a change of viewpoint and won a good deal of support from public-power advocates. In his early years in the White from public-power advocates. His successor, President Johnson, had been a strong supporter of the New Deal's public-power program, when he served in the House in the late 1930's and early 1940's.

In the long and continuing political struggle over river basin development the lineup of interests was and is easily discernible and predictable—essentially, the private producers, strongly organized, against small consumers who want plenty of electricity at low rates. The latter, to a degree uncommon among consumers generally, have some organizational influence. The rural cooperatives, receiving low-cost public power through the Rural Electrification Administration, form an effective pressure group; in a contest, the advocates of public power can also summon to their side the National Farmers Union and some labor unions. More than most defenders of the so-called "liberal" position, they can count, too, on substantial support from southern spokesmen in Congress: indeed, the self-styled "public power bloc" in the House was once headed by a representative often described as a reactionary, John E. Rankin of Mississippi. This southern support for public power is partly an echo of the old rural anti-monopoly, anti-Wall Street sentiment, and partly a reflection of region-wide popular approval of the TVA. It makes the issue very nearly a partisan one, though some eastern Democrats in Congress oppose public power and some Republicans (especially in the northwest where, as in the Tennessee Valley, great government projects have long been in operation) have tended to support it.

## THE USES OF THE LAND

The chief products of the land used by men are visible vegetation and minerals and oil extracted from underground. Aside

**The uses of the soil.** Grand Coulee Dam, Washington State, top, the largest concrete dam in the world, is one of several government dams in the valley of the Columbia River. Like other government dams, such as those in the Tennessee Valley and California, it produces great quantities of electric power, and so is the center of continuing political conflict. But in the arid West such dams also make possible the irrigation of otherwise unproductive land. Farmers on much of our irrigated land can produce only because the Department of the Interior constructs reclamation projects. The potato farm at left, irrigated by surface pipe, had previously been fallow for forty years. This Idaho farmer also profited from the advice of the Department of Agriculture as to planting "on the contour." At right is shown scientific strip planting in Wisconsin, guided by the advice of Department of Agriculture experts. The Wisconsin farmer had been a "cooperator" with the Department for ten years before this picture was taken.

**The government as manager of prosperity.** The Harbor Freeway, Los Angeles, at top, is not only an example of federal-state cooperation in building highways but also a reminder of the uses of governmental expenditures for public works to stabilize the economy (see page 575). Today, indeed, the fortunes of much of American industry, such as the McDonnell airplane manufacturing plant, Saint Louis, Missouri, below, are to a considerable degree dependent on a continuing high rate of governmental expenditures.

from the way products are used, however, there is the matter of
the use of the land surface. That land surface makes the existence
of farms possible. Over it run the roads by which most of us, even
in this space age, still travel. It provides the building sites upon
which homes and stores and factories are constructed and great
cities grow. We take for granted, and so tend to overlook, the fact
that the land surface is a first essential for any organized society,
whether agricultural or urban.

With the use of land for farming and with the disposal of its
agricultural products we dealt in Chapter 18. We saw, earlier in
the present chapter, that minerals and oil were to some extent objects of governmentally directed conservation. With respect to the
use of most mineral products, the federal government has little
to say, save in wartime when they have been allocated for defense
purposes. The interstate marketing of oil and its sister product,
natural gas, are, however, subject to a degree of federal control.

## Transportation

*Pipelines.* The pipelines through which oil and natural gas are
carried are as much a part of the nation's transportation system
as are railroads with tank cars or the highways on which travel
the big trucks with their tailboard signs of "Danger—Flammable."
In the case of oil, Congress aids state conservation programs, as
we have seen, by barring the interstate transportation of oil illegally produced. Oil markets and prices are affected, too, by presidential actions excluding or admitting foreign oil. Natural gas,
a relative newcomer in interstate commerce (pipes for long-dis-
tance transmission were not perfected until the late 1920's) is
regulated by the Federal Power Commission. Congress in 1938
directed the latter to control prices charged for natural gas not
only by interstate transporters but also by oil companies selling
natural gas to the interstate transporters. Pressure from both oil
and gas interests, centered in the southwest, twice led to the passage of bills excluding "independent producers" of natural gas—
that is, oil companies selling gas to pipeline companies—from
federal regulation, but both were vetoed. Truman's veto in 1950
was in part a response to strong counterpressure from mayors of
large northern and eastern cities, who purported to speak for con-

sumers objecting to possible higher prices. The mayors' efforts failed to prevent the passage of the second bill, in 1956, and apparently had no effect on President Eisenhower, but the latter reluctantly vetoed the bill because of the aura of attempted bribery that surrounded its passage.[10]

*Railroads and Highways.* From the time of the first railroads in the 1830's until after the Civil War, most Americans viewed railroads as an unmixed blessing. Especially the farmers of the new west longed for them. The federal government played a vigorous part in their promotion, through making its western public lands available for roadbeds; where the roadbeds should be located was often a burning political issue, one which, indeed, may well have influenced the nation's history.[11] But beginning in the 1870's, as we have seen, the farmers' welcome turned to hatred. From the west, from desperate men struggling to stay alive, came the cry for regulation; the government's response to that demand, the establishment of the Interstate Commerce Commission, we considered briefly in Chapter 18. In recent years not the farmers but the railroads have been hard pressed to keep alive. The gasoline engine dimmed the future of the iron horse. Long before airplane travel became habitual, the use of overland routes by trucks and family cars was cutting into the railroads' business. More and more, today, the ICC is confronted with railroads' requests for permission to curtail unprofitable passenger service and raise passenger rates. (Raising the rates, of course, decreases the number of passengers, which in turn justifies a further reduction in the number of passenger trains.) Suburban lines have been particularly hard hit. The railroad industry long

---

[10] Senator Case of North Dakota, a friend of the bill, declared in the Senate that he had been offered a cash "contribution" by an individual easily traced to one of the oil companies supporting the measure.

[11] There is considerable evidence that in urging repeal of the Compromise of 1850 and thus disturbing the precarious status quo upon which many based their hope of avoiding civil war, Senator Stephen A. Douglas of Illinois was speaking for railroad interests bent on securing a main northern route from the Mississippi to the Rockies, as opposed to one further south. See Gerald M. Capers, *Stephen A. Douglas* (Boston: Little, Brown & Co., 1959). At about the same time, the Gadsden Purchase from Mexico of land which later became part of New Mexico and Arizona was negotiated by interest spokesmen (Ambassador Gadsden himself was a railroad man) bent on securing the most practicable southern railroad route to the Pacific.

ago hoped that effective federal regulation of buses and trucks would limit the threat of competition and supported the movement that led to the passage by Congress of the Motor Carrier Act of 1935, vesting regulatory power over public motor carriers in a separate division of the ICC. Large-scale bus and trucking companies also welcomed this legislation, hoping that it would reduce competition from newcomers. Their hopes have, in practice, come nearer realization than those of the railroads. The latter, with few exceptions, continue to lose ground.

Not regulatory but highly promotional has been one federal activity in behalf of those who drive motor vehicles, whether for pleasure or for profit. This is the program of grants-in-aid for highway construction and maintenance. When the Federal Highway Act inaugurated this program in 1916, few thought that good automobile roads might spell the doom of railroads or at least deprive them of their passenger traffic. To be sure, railroads and farm organizations tried to have the legislation give first place to building short roads from farming communities to railroad stations. The simplicity of the time, however, is illustrated by the fact that one of the first vocal pressure groups for federal aid for road-building was the Wheelmen of America, a national association of bicyclists. Since those quiet days we have seen thousands of miles of federally aided roads stretch across the country, with a new network of cooperatively built interstate highways now under construction. Federal aid takes the form not only of monetary grants but of consultative planning and engineering services provided by the Bureau of Public Roads in the Commerce Department.

The present 41,000-mile interstate highway program is, indeed, virtually a federal project, for the federal government is committed to paying 90 per cent of the cost, with state and local units footing only 10 per cent of the bill. Congress in 1957 decided to finance the program by establishing a highway construction trust fund. It earmarked federal gasoline tax receipts for deposit in the fund, out of which the grants would then be made. Within two years, it became apparent that unless the gasoline tax was raised, or other tax receipts earmarked, there would not be enough money in the fund for construction to proceed as scheduled.

Faced with this problem, and with President Eisenhower's insistence that the program be kept on a "pay-as-you-go" basis (i.e., financed by special earmarked taxes on the highways' users), Congress had to seek a solution under heavy pressure from organized interests, including gasoline producers (oil companies), automobile manufacturers, and transportation companies.

The old idea that the primary use of roads was to bring produce from the farm to either the market or the railroad depot has long since been replaced. Roads are for vacationers to dash thousands of miles to mountains or seashore and for trucks to transport heavy goods across the country. Roads are for people to drive on, to and from work, or to and from the shopping center. Today America's roads serve a predominantly urban society. As railroads, joining distant cities, gave rise to new cities along their routes, so highways, circling great cities, have hastened the growth of the modern suburb. They have influenced the use of the land for the construction of new homes and new industrial plants.

### Urban Survival and Suburban Expansion

With startling speed America is becoming a nation of densely populated metropolitan areas. The trend away from the farms began long ago, but that trend, at first, was toward urban areas both great and small. In the last twenty years both internal migration and the birth rate have centered the growth of the population in the bigger cities and their environs—the 212 "standard metropolitan areas," as the Bureau of the Census calls them. Between 1950 and 1960, those metropolitan areas grew four times as fast as the rest of the country. By 1960 almost two-thirds of all the people in the country lived in metropolitan areas; experts estimate that nearly 70 per cent will by 1975. The population "explosion" has been most marked outside of the formal jurisdictional limits of the great cities. Not the central or core cities of metropolitan areas have swiftly become more crowded, but the citified suburbs and, more and more, new semi-rural suburbs further from the old center. Semi-rural today, perhaps, but likely to be urban tomorrow. As both light industry and department stores have moved to the suburban belt far from downtown, property values in the central city have fallen and decay has spread.

The most prevalent use of the land, then, we may properly call urban or metropolitan use. The immediate responsibility for its direction rests on local governments which, as we have seen, are subordinate units of the states. For guidance and assistance, one might expect a city to turn to the state government. Traditionally, however, there is in many states a political conflict between rural interests and urban interests, particularly big-city interests. Often the metropolitan areas are underrepresented in the state legislature. Therefore as urban and metropolitan problems have become more acute, cities have turned directly to the federal government for aid, as we saw in the preceding chapter when we considered public housing.

The feature which distinguishes a "metropolitan" from an "urban" problem is the existence, in a metropolitan area, of a great number of separate governmental units—dozens or scores of suburban cities, towns, and villages, one or more counties, and all manner of special districts for schools, water, fire protection, etc., each with its own function and, often, its own taxing power. Some metropolitan areas, furthermore, such as New York, Philadelphia, Chicago, and St. Louis, spread out across state lines.[12] In all such places, the coordination of plans for healthy development—for an efficient highway system, mass transit operations, disposal of wastes, allocation of water, and planned utilization of the land for residential or industrial purposes—is difficult to achieve.

These are local questions, but they are also common problems confronting most Americans. Accordingly, an increasing demand may be expected for national assistance in solving them. Federal aid for housing and airport construction and miscellaneous "community facilities" are steps in this direction. In the late 1950's Senator Joseph Clark of Pennsylvania, a former mayor of Philadelphia, urged the establishment of a new Department of Urban Affairs. It was high time, he suggested, for the federal government to recognize the shift in the social complexion of America. If the farmers, now a small numerical minority, have

---

[12] Some experts forecast a situation where "metropolitan area" may itself become an obsolete concept; for example, they foresee, within a couple of decades, a virtually unbroken built-up, urban belt running all the way from Boston to Richmond, Va.

their Department of Agriculture, why should not the city dwellers, the great majority, be able likewise to turn to a federal agency
for leadership, advice, and financial aid? Conceivably a federal aid
program could even bring about some governmental unification
in the metropolitan areas and influence the planning of land use
for urban and suburban purposes. But when President Kennedy
sought to create the new department, Congress first rejected his
proposal and then specifically prohibited its inclusion in any future "reorganization plan" (see page 503) that might be initiated
by the President.

## THE USES OF THE AIR

Men dreamed for centuries of using the air for transportation
before the Wright brothers took off from the sands at Kitty Hawk
in 1903. To use it, without the aid of connecting wires, for the
communication of sights and sounds was something that seemed
still more visionary until Marconi's invention of the wireless in
1896. Today the air, like forests and soil and rivers and oil deposits, is available for human use, not just for breathing but
for the profit of those who exploit it and the convenience or
enjoyment of their customers. In this respect it is, moreover, a
national resource. It is public property, in effect held by the government in trust for the people, and vital to the nation's safety
in times of peril.

### Radio and Television

The radio industry got started after World War I. Soon chaotic
competition created a jumble of noise on the airways and economic confusion among the competitors. Both listeners and broadcasting corporations demanded federal regulation, even in those
days of the prevalence of laissez-faire thinking. To meet an indis-
putable need, Congress passed the Federal Radio Act in 1927,
establishing a Federal Radio Commission. (An indication of Congress's philosophic distaste for such governmental intervention
is the fact that this commission was originally set up as a temporary agency.) The successor statute, basic to regulation of the

use of the airwaves today for both radio and television, was passed in 1934—the Federal Communications Act, which substituted a Federal Communications Commission for the earlier body.

The FCC is authorized to allocate air space through the issuance of renewable three-year licenses to broadcasters. In doing this, it is directed to foster competition within the broadcasting industry and strictly to refrain from curtailing free speech on the air. As the licensee is supposed to serve the public convenience and necessity, the FCC has potential authority (despite its being forbidden to censor programs) to require particular kinds of programming, but it has made little use of this authority. To satisfy its possible demands broadcasters do produce occasional sustaining programs, not subsidized by advertisers; but usually such "public service" programs come at hours when the audience is small. The commission did, however, reserve FM channels for ᴐrofit educational radio broadcasting, and in 1953 reserved t one-tenth of the TV channels for educational stations.

ιe battle to obtain a broadcasting license is often fierce. The ᴛ gets the sole right to use a designated wave length in a ιar area. This permits him to sell time on the air and reap profits—so large that one licensee is reported promptly to sold his license for $8,000,000. Although the license is a ιorary one, creating no vested rights, the licensee knows that l probability it is his for keeps. If, when he seeks to renew it, ces competing applicants, the very fact that he is in business ᴜ him an advantage. Almost always the FCC renews the ιse.

making the original choice among applicants, the com- on is directed to consider a number of factors. One of these ᴇ maintenance of competition. In the 1940's, some commis- ᴛs felt it their duty to foster diversity in the dissemination ᴇws and so frowned on any broadcasting applicant who was ᴇd to a newspaper. Their view did not prevail. Other criteria ᴛhe applicant's engineering standards and financial soundness. ᴗᴛᴛen, however, the decision ultimately turns on the conclusion that one applicant rather than another is best fitted to serve the public convenience and necessity—a criterion so vague that it gives the FCC almost unlimited discretion, and so makes the commissioners constant targets of the kind of pressure on regulatory agencies which we considered in Chapter 16.

The statute confronts the broadcasters with a different kind of political question by providing that a station (or network) allotting time to a political candidate must give equal time to his opponent. Taking this literally, it means that not only major party nominees but inconsequential fly-by-night independent candidates must be allowed to use up the station's highly valuable time. Furthermore, it gives rise to the question, when is a candidate not a candidate? In the summer of 1959, after Senator Hubert Humphrey's friends, but not Humphrey himself, had announced that he was an aspirant for the Democratic presidential nomination in 1960, one network promptly canceled its invitation to him to appear on a Sunday afternoon press-interview program. It feared that if he appeared, all other aspirants would be entitled to equal time. Another major network decided that for the purposes of the "equal time" rule, Humphrey was not a candidate and so could appear on its comparable show without his rivals having to be invited. The confusion caused by the "equal time" rule is obvious; but its defenders can properly ask whether private broadcasters should be permitted to give one candidate free time on the air while denying the same privilege to his opponent. The FCC has been insistent on equal treatment, including the selling of comparable time to candidates who pay for their programs, and has held that when a station's own commentators indulge in political comment, equal time must be given to those whom they criticize. But what comment justifies an answer? Indeed, how can the political slanting of news broadcasts, by "editorial selection" that results in building up one candidate or one issue and omitting mention of the others, possibly be prevented except by willing adherence to some inarticulate concept of fair play? These are difficult questions, important to the future of American politics. For the airwaves, though public property, are potential sources not only of great private profits, but also of great private political power.

## Civil Aviation

The use of the air for transportation by privately owned

carriers was made possible by federal financial aid. This has taken three forms. Federal grants to states and local governments have helped to pay for the construction of airports, without which the airlines could not operate. The Post Office Department has paid airlines for carrying the mail. As this is payment for a service, it perhaps should not be classified as "aid," but until 1953 the "air mail pay" received by many airlines far exceeded the cost of the service. Some airlines could not have existed without that extra pay or federal subsidy. Since 1953, direct subsidies, now administered and accounted for separately from true air mail pay, have been reduced, but they are still available to hard-pressed lines and are required to keep local service or "feeder" lines in operation.

Both the need for public financial support and the obvious need for uniform, enforceable rules for the safety of air transportation made public regulation of the industry inevitable. The allocation of routes and the approval of rates and charges are the responsibilities of the Civilian Aeronautics Board. Though its work in this field is patterned on that of the older transportation agency, the ICC, its problems, particularly that of awarding routes, are akin to those of the FCC. Permission to fly from New York to Miami, for instance, is a prize as eagerly sought as a license to broadcast with a powerful transmitter over a clear channel; and the criteria for deciding who should get the prize are very nearly as vague in one case as in the other, although of course the CAB has more leeway because more than one airline can fly the same route.

The CAB also investigates aviation accidents, but the air safety rules—the traffic regulations of the air—are promulgated and enforced by the Federal Aviation Agency in the Department of Commerce. The latter is entrusted with the task, too, of coordinating the operations of military aircraft with civilian flying, a difficult job and one of growing significance as more and more high-speed jets zoom across the sky.

## Space Exploration

Earth's atmosphere is a highway not only between cities and continents, but between our planet and space. Mechanical invention having conquered the air, men's minds turned toward the possibilities of travel in the realms beyond the atmospheric limits. What had seemed unimaginable or at least fantastic as recently as World War II swiftly became a topic of common and rational conjecture. And it approached reality when on October 4, 1957, the Soviet Union launched the first sputnik—a man-made satellite circling this planet.

The initial shock of sputnik, in this country, was felt largely in terms of international rivalry and national defense. Little serious thought was given to the possibilities of the great blank spaces of the universe, or the cold solid bleakness of the moon, as resources which peaceful men could turn to their advantage. Nevertheless the possibilities of such use exist; it is too early to say whether Americans or others will use space as a launching place from which to destroy mankind or as a means of learning more about the earth and the universe, and even, eventually, as a highway to distant planets.

In the United States, planning for space exploration was at first chiefly a Defense Department function. In 1958, however, Congress established the National Aeronautics and Space Administration, an executive agency responsible to the President, responsible for major operations beyond the earth's atmosphere. NASA is now committed to placing a man on the moon by 1970 and to the development of a network of communications satellites, the latter in cooperation with private industry. On February 20, 1962, John H. Glenn became the first American "spaceman" to circle the earth, going around three times. Within fifteen months three others had followed him, the third, L. Gordon Cooper, completing twenty-two orbits.

Politically, the exploration of space has been viewed by some observers as an intriguing issue which might be exploited to a candidate's advantage. When satellites became an old story (our span of enthusiasm seems strangely short) and the United States had more of them in space than did the Russians, the issue lost much of its glamor. But then when living men went into space, interest revived; and a "race to the moon" against the Russians was an idea that appealed to many Americans. But as not everyone agreed on its importance, and even the Russians by 1963 were saying that they didn't want to race, space exploration was destined to become a national political issue. The issue involved more than just whether or not to have a "track meet" in the cosmos. It included the question of whether Americans still had the pioneers' sense of adventure. It raised highly conjectural arguments about the need to be "first in space" as a matter of national defense. More quietly, though equally conjecturally, leading scientists pondered the scientific opportunities that the conquest of space might offer; as one of the more confident of them wrote: "One hundred years from now the new knowledge attained in space research will surely have paid untold, unforeseen, and unexpected dividends." [13]

## ATOMIC ENERGY

The space age is also the atomic age or, properly speaking, the nuclear age. As air is used as a pathway to the universe, so earth's long-familiar resources have made it possible to utilize the fundamental energy of the universe. Minerals and the old sources of power, water and coal, were brought together by man's imagination and inventiveness to produce fissionable material and to explode it. For human purposes, the potential wonders of atomic or nuclear energy are probably far greater than those of the moon and all the distant planets put together.

In 1946, less than a year after a single atomic bomb destroyed the large Japanese city of Hiroshima, Congress passed the Atomic Energy Control Act. It did so in the realization that this newly found resource was not only so destructive but so incredibly powerful and valuable that for the safety of the nation and of humanity it had to be developed only under public, national control. At that time, the exploitation of nuclear energy involved the construction of huge installations and a process far beyond the financial means of private enterprise. Strong arguments, therefore, were made in favor of letting well enough alone by allowing the army to continue to make bombs, without worrying about the future. But to these arguments there were two answers. Each was in the form of a challenging question. First, should the military

---

[13] Lee A. DuBridge, "Sense and Nonsense About Space," *Harper's Magazine*, August, 1959, pp. 21-28.

have sole possession of a resource of such devastating power, on the one hand, and of so many potential civilian uses on the other? The second question stemmed from the first: should not every effort be made to explore and develop the beneficial peaceful uses of the atom?

Congress thus faced several related issues. It decided to entrust control not to the military, but to a new and wholly civilian agency, the Atomic Energy Commission. This choice was made over vehement opposition, the opponents preferring to vest ostensible control in a commission which would be only a part-time body and on which officers of the army and navy could serve. One reason for the decision, urged by the Atomic Scientists of Chicago (an organization composed of men who had worked on the Manhattan Project in developing the original atom bomb, and the forerunner of the American Association of Atomic Scientists), was that a civilian agency was much more likely than a military one to foster creative research leading to peaceful use. Although the scientists were pleased with Congress's conclusion on this point, they were less happy about the provisions of the statute which imposed a high degree of secrecy on the new commission's operations. As a famous research scientist put it, "When you lock the laboratory door, you lock more out than you lock in." [14] Ever since the act was passed, scientists have objected to its security requirements and the way in which the commission has enforced them. Many of them believe that because the scientific imagination knows no national boundaries, heavy emphasis on security is futile and discourages research.

In the statute of 1946 Congress also took a long step toward deciding whether private enterprise should take first place in the exploitation of the new resource for civilian purposes. To be sure, in the debate on the bill this issue was hardly mentioned; the emphasis was all on bombs. Nevertheless, Congress did make the tremendously significant decision that not only should all fissionable material belong to the government, but also that the huge business of owning and operating the facilities for producing such material should be a government monopoly.

---

[14] C. F. Kettering, quoted in James R. Newman and Byron S. Miller, *The Control of Atomic Energy* (New York: McGraw-Hill Book Company, 1948), p. 15.

This monopolistic position was modified by Congress in 1954 at the urging of the Eisenhower administration. The 1954 statute authorized the commission to foster the development of private reactors and atomic power plants. But the very high construction costs, plus the expense of making the new projects physically safe as the commission required, made the price of atomic power far too high for commercial use. Under the chairmanship of Lewis Strauss, the commission persisted in counting heavily on private development; its congressional critics, chiefly Democrats, insisted that in the absence of significant private development, the AEC should build new reactors and power plants itself. To some extent the argument, basically, is reminiscent of the clash between the public power and private power interests in connection with river basin development.[15] But it is complicated by a sense of urgency, a feeling that the nation which first puts the new resource to its fullest possible use will emerge as the undisputed leader of the world.

Although the commercial use of nuclear energy has not yet been proved feasible, the by-products of the AEC's work, especially radioactive isotopes for research in medicine, industry and agriculture, has brought rapid scientific advance, most dramatically in the field of medical science. Yet the fact remains that the most dramatic use yet made of nuclear energy was a tragic one—the destruction of the populations of Hiroshima and Nagasaki. Whether in the long run it will prove to be the ultimate destroyer or a blessing to mankind remains to be seen. Which it will be may depend in large part on the skill and wisdom with which the government of the United States conducts its relations with the other nations of the world.

15 Had it not been for the government's dams in the Tennessee and Columbia valleys, atomic energy would hardly have been developed in this country by 1945. The vital installations at Oak Ridge, Tennessee, and Hanford, Washington, were made feasible by the power generated at the TVA dams and Grand Coulee Dam, respectively.

CHAPTER 21

# Government, Foreign Policy, and National Security

The most fundamental question confronting the American people is whether we can survive in a world where tens of millions of lives could be wiped out overnight. The next great question is whether we can not only survive physically but can retain our heritage of freedom, our material prosperity, our "way of life." The answers depend on our relationships with the other countries and peoples of the world. If our foreign affairs should deteriorate to the point of nuclear warfare, the civilization that we know and cherish would probably be destroyed; the "United States" might remain, as a name and even as a sovereign governmental power, but the impoverished survivors of the holocaust would be forced by desperation into a strange and authoritarian form of social, economic, and political organization. Apart from the avoidance of nuclear conflict, the maintenance of our standard of living may well be the crucial foreign policy issue. If because of economic pressure from abroad we should fail to maintain it, or if our growing wealth is gained at the expense of hundreds of millions of people on other continents, the resulting conflict of economic ambitions and demands could easily lead to all-out war.

674

Although foreign policy, therefore, is primarily directed to insuring the national security, it must and does have many facets.
It is not just a matter of reaching agreements with other countries,
important as those agreements are. It is also a question of the extent and nature of military power. And it involves, too, vitally
important economic questions, including the maintenance of the
vigor of our domestic economy and the encouragement or dis-
couragement of foreign trade and industrial growth abroad.

## BASIC APPROACHES TO FOREIGN POLICY

### Power

Any nation's position in the world—its influence in world
politics and its relationship with other countries—depends largely,
perhaps chiefly, on its physical might. This is ordinarily interpreted in terms of the size and potential effectiveness of its
armed force. Thus for a century the British navy, which "ruled
the waves" of the world's oceans, made possible the British empire
and British economic control of much of the globe's land surface.
So in the 1930's Adolf Hitler not only rearmed Germany as a
preliminary to his intended domination of the world, but based
his calculations on assumptions of the military weakness of his
rivals and their unwillingness to fight. And since World War II
both the United States and the Soviet Union have sought national
security through development of nuclear bombs and missiles,
possession of the means of dropping them, and repeated asser-
tions of readiness to drop them should the need arise.

Military might today depends on both manpower and industrial
capacity. Wholly aside from nuclear weapons, when one country
has a well-equipped army much bigger than its neighbor it may
dominate that neighbor if it wishes: certainly the imminence of
the Soviet army, not the threat of atomic destruction, was a primary cause of Czechoslovakia's fall to communism in 1948 and
the swift suppression of revolt in Poland and Hungary in 1956.
To be effective, however, an army must be armed. Behind it must
be a vigorous "defense" industry, with sufficient skilled manpower, adequate plant facilities, and ready access to raw materials.
In a tyranny, the comparative size of such an industry can be de-

Fitzpatrick in the *St. Louis Post-Dispatch*

**In the laboratory of human affairs**

termined by the government: almost all of the country's industry
can be devoted to building weapons, without much regard to the
effect on the people's standard of living—as Hitler put it, "guns
instead of butter." In a free country the problem is more difficult.
Where, as in the United States, industry is geared mainly to the
satisfaction of ordinary consumers' desires, a swift shift to "guns
instead of butter" would be very hard to make in peacetime, for
it would drastically lower the standard of living. And it could not
be made effectively and quickly enough, even in wartime, if the
private economy was out of kilter—if depression had disrupted
the industrial system, or demands for reduced federal spending

had led to the dismantling of vital plants, or trade barriers against foreign imports had cost us the raw materials we need.

To underpin its military power, therefore, the United States needs a healthy internal economy. Economic strength does not automatically make a nation powerful, in this age when war may allow so little time for the conversion of industry to military production. But in a free society armed might does require a vigorously functioning economy. (Russian leaders were well aware of this, when, predicting a major depression in the United States following World War II, they assumed that such a depression would clear the road for the Soviet Union's domination of the world.) It requires, too, access to raw materials found only outside of the country. The government's economic policies, with respect both to industrial growth at home and trade abroad, are accordingly vital factors in the achievement of military power.

## Ideals

For most of our history we were in so little danger of physical destruction that we could afford to be very lightly armed. From the end of the War of 1812 until World War I, foreign attack upon our shores was virtually unthinkable. We fought two wars with foreign countries during that century, to be sure, but neither involved any serious danger to the homeland. The first, the war with Mexico, was an example of the use of superior power for an assumed national advantage; it was essentially a war of conquest, far removed from high ideals or principles. The second, the war with Spain in 1898, was very different. Its purpose was to drive out of Cuba a European power that was not seriously threatening American interests. Undoubtedly a hope for economic exploitation of Cuba's raw materials underlay some of the support given to the war by some American business interests, but the American people were stirred far more by the iniquities of Spanish rule in Cuba. They saw the war as one for the liberation of the downtrodden Cubans, not conquest. And its curious imperial by-product, the capture of the Philippines, left many Americans troubled and uneasy. Theodore Roosevelt, who had seized his moment as Acting Secretary of the Navy to order the attack on Manila, later privately repented, and it was with considerable relief that the United States eventually relinquished this outpost of empire.

During the time when the United States neither cared nor needed to be a great military power, its efforts at leadership in international affairs were necessarily confined to the praising of democracy and to sporadic peace-making. Americans saw themselves as setting a good example for the rest of the world to follow and were inclined to give verbal encouragement to democratic movements elsewhere. (This habit began early in our history, taking root in sometimes surprising places: for instance, in every Democratic national platform from 1800 to 1848, the Democrats sent to the French people a message of hearty approval of their alleged efforts to bring the ideals of the French Revolution to reality.) From behind the shield provided by the British navy, the United States government decried the warlike propensities of Europe and urged arbitration processes to replace war. Perhaps the climax of this former kind of foreign policy was Theodore Roosevelt's peace conference at Portsmouth in 1905, called to bring an end to the Russian-Japanese war.

The habit of insistently professing ideals as the basis of foreign policy was not one that always endeared us to other nations, to whom it often seemed unrealistic, smug, or even hypocritical. Nevertheless, it persisted. It has survived the immersion of America in world-wide political struggles, in which, according to the expounders of *realpolitik* (power politics), principles are insignificant and only power counts. Woodrow Wilson's call to arms in 1917, to "make the world safe for democracy," got a deep emotional response. In the 1920's, President Coolidge's Secretary of State, Frank B. Kellogg, negotiated a series of treaties by which nations renounced "war as an instrument of national policy"—a renunciation which seemed sheer hypocrisy to some, but a hopeful statement of principle to others.

In the modern age of the great dictators, the tendency of Americans to speak of foreign affairs in terms of ideals and principles continues, though perhaps with less assurance than in the past. The loss of assurance has not been due to any condoning of the cruelties of police-state tyranny in Nazi Germany or Communist

Russia or Red China. It has been caused by a growing awareness that we are engaged in what may be a mortal struggle with (for the moment) one very powerful totalitarian state. If to gain an advantage in that struggle we believe that we need the assistance of some other dictator, we incline to swallow our distaste for tyranny or to decide that he is not a cruel tyrant, after all. Not all Americans, by any means, easily surrender principles to the demands of power politics; vigorous objections are often voiced, for instance, to dealing on an amicable basis with Tito of Yugoslavia, and a few protests still are made against official American gestures friendly to Franco and Salazar, the dictators of Spain and Portugal. But the responsible makers of foreign policy, acutely aware of very tangible danger, incline to discard ideological consistency as a basis of action. They do continue the custom of presenting their policies to the public in terms largely of principles and ideals. If to some these ideals seem unrealistic, it would be highly unrealistic to assume that they have no effect on the framing of American policy.

## Relationships

Even when the happy combination of the Monroe Doctrine and the British navy kept hostile powers away from American shores, the people of the United States could not be wholly oblivious of the rest of the world. To many Americans, as late as 1941, "splendid isolation" seemed preferable to involvement in international life, but the processes of science and invention worked inexorably against them. Today the possibility of our country's being an impregnable fortress is gone forever. The national security, therefore, cannot depend solely on the kind of turreted walls that used to protect medieval cities, or on forts with gun emplacements at every harbor entrance, or even on a network of radar installations and a stockpile of interceptor weapons, useful though those might be. It is based, instead, on policies which involve various kinds of relationships with other nations. In peacetime these range from alliances, on the one hand, to nonrecognition on the other. With nations wherein the government is controlled by those who deem American interests consistent with their own, we make treaties of friendship and mutual security; upon such agreements, indeed, we may build a whole cooperative structure of defense against armed attack. With one extremely large and powerful nation, Red China, we declined to have any formal relations at all even after it had held full power over the territory and people of China for fifteen years.[1] Between our alliances, on the one hand, and our refusal to recognize the rulers in Peking, on the other, lie three broad categories of relationships— those with the potentially important "neutrals," the so-called Russian satellites, and the Soviet Union itself. Toward the "neutrals" our attitude has been uncertain, partly because we seem to jump to the conclusion (born, presumably, of moral conviction of our rightness) that those who are not for us must be against us. Thus the Indian statesman, Nehru, was often denounced in some portions of the American press as a Communist sympathizer, despite the harsh measures he had taken against Communists in India; and the creation of the United Arab Republic, not having been sponsored by Britain or the United States, was widely reported to be a Communist-inspired movement rather than one based on nationalist Arab sentiment and hostility toward Israel. Toward the subservient nations bordering the Soviet Union, the approach has sometimes seemed far distant from reality. American talk about "liberation" rang hollow indeed when blood flowed in the tragic streets of Budapest in 1956. In direct dealings with the Soviet Union, however, realism has taken first place.[2] The road toward agreement between rivals with such conflicting aims as the USA and the USSR is inevitably a long one and sometimes seems impossibly blocked. A mutual hope to avoid a nuclear war, however, has led both sides occasionally to seek "accommodation"— some minor policy modification designed to ease current tension— and, in 1963, a more far-reaching agreement on a treaty to ban the testing of nuclear weapons in the atmosphere.

The relationship of the United States to all other nations is significantly affected by the existence of the United Nations and

---

[1] Some of our allies have seen in our nonrecognition of China a typical American adherence to a moral judgment in the face of reality.

[2] Even the Yalta agreement of 1945, paving the way for Russian domination of eastern Europe, can be classified as "realistic," as it was based on Stalin's promise to fight Japan.

the country's commitments under the UN Charter. Although most foreign policy is embodied in "unilateral" decisions or, at most, agreement among a few allies, the very existence of the United Nations provides opportunities for preparing the way by public discussion and for subjecting any policy to hostile criticism. The British, French, and Israelis felt the impact of such hostile criticism in the UN when they started war against Egypt in the fall of 1956; and though the Russians, at about the same time, seemed less impressed by UN condemnation of their ruthlessness in Hungary, the very fact that the UN Assembly condemned it encouraged those who put their faith, as Woodrow Wilson did, in the eventual good influence of the "opinions of mankind" on international affairs.

Tied in with diplomatic and military relationships are economic ones. Treaties of friendship may provide far less cement to bind nations together than trade agreements lowering tariff walls. The fostering of new industry and more productive agriculture in underdeveloped countries may win friends among the uncommitted "neutrals"—at least both the Russians and the Americans seem to think so. Economic desires and rivalries underlay the old imperial wars of the nineteenth century, and, it would seem, the Japanese aggression of 1941; conversely, economic ties or arrangements designed to mitigate rivalries and satisfy needs are an important part of any design for peace.

The making of foreign policy, then, today involves both diplomatic and military decisions, both economic programs and appeals to principles and shared ideals. Its chief aspects since World War II may be briefly traced. Beginning in 1947, the government of the United States acted on the assumption that the Soviet Union was an aggressive power bent on the acquisition of control over territories beyond its borders and, eventually, the whole world. It therefore adopted the policy of "containment," declaring its readiness to resist Communist aggression anywhere in the world. So in 1948, when the western entrance to Berlin was subjected to a ground blockade by the Communist rulers of East Germany, the United States air force flew supplies to the beleaguered people of the city, and in 1950 President Truman ordered American forces into Korea within a few hours of receiving the news of a

Communist invasion. After it was proved that the Russians possessed nuclear bombs, the "containment" policy, of meeting every aggression with armed force, became increasingly dangerous. In 1954, Communist invasion of Indo-China evoked no effective American response; but otherwise Secretary Dulles persisted in proclaiming the country's readiness to fight, believing that a firm show of such readiness (as on the islands off the shore of China, and in Lebanon to which troops were sent in 1958) would deter the aggressors. The chief deterrent, however, was deemed to be the power and determination to drop nuclear bombs on the enemy in case of war. When Russian missiles were discovered in Cuba in 1962, and President Kennedy demanded their withdrawal and ordered our navy to halt Soviet ships approaching Cuba, there was nothing empty about the threat of imminent nuclear devastation.

In furtherance of the "containment" policy, the United States entered into a series of treaties with non-Communist countries. The most significant of these was the North Atlantic Treaty of 1949. Today the North Atlantic Treaty Organization (NATO), consisting of fifteen nations,[3] is in effect an international military body, created to provide resistance to any attack upon the territory of any of its members—or, to put it more bluntly, to try to defend western Europe against the Russian armies. Closer relationships with western European countries were also furthered by the Marshall Plan of 1947 and subsequent programs for massive American economic and military aid; later, considerable assistance, mostly economic, was furnished also to the so-called "neutrals," the industrially underdeveloped countries, chief of which is India.

Although the western allies were in general accord on defensive policies toward Russia, they tended to disagree on policies relating to the Far East and Near East. In 1949 the Communist Chinese,

---

[3] Belgium, Canada, Denmark, France, Iceland, Italy, Luxemburg, The Netherlands, Norway, Portugal, the United Kingdom, the United States, Greece, Turkey, and West Germany. Generally similar "mutual security" treaties, under which each country agrees to "act to meet the common danger in accordance with its constitutional processes," are those with Australia and New Zealand (1952) and countries of South East Asia (SEATO, 1954). A promise to "assist in meeting the attack" on a western hemisphere country is included in the Inter-American Treaty of Reciprocal Assistance (1947).

having driven the remnants of Chiang Kai-Shek's army to the island of Taiwan (Formosa), took full command of the mainland of China. Great Britain and others of America's allies gave formal recognition to the new regime. The United States not only refused to do so, but in the next decade earnestly considered the possibility of fighting the Red Chinese in Viet Nam and on Quemoy and Matsu, islands only a few miles from the Chinese coast. Western European statesmen were quietly but urgently opposed to taking these risks of all-out war. Conversely, the United States strongly and publicly opposed the attempted seizure, by force, of the Suez Canal in Egypt by the British and French in 1956.

Crawford in the *Newark News*

**The escape valve**

The Korean War, the Suez crisis, and the status of Red China all involved the United Nations. American leadership brought UN forces to the defense of Korea. An unusual combination of

American and Russian opposition halted the Anglo-French invasion of Egypt. (To be sure, unilateral threats from either or both countries might have stopped it, but the fact was that the UN provided the sounding board for the opposition and the machinery—a small international "police force"—for keeping the peace.) The question of the admission of Red China to the UN was tied up with American nonrecognition, the United States insisting that Chiang's government on Taiwan was still the government of China and so was still entitled to the council seat allotted to "China" by the United Nations Charter. Thus the UN is a forum for the expression of both agreement and disagreement. Lacking power in the ordinary sense, it represents an ideal and carries influence; and its operating affiliates, such as the World Health Organization and the International Labor Organization, make it a living reality in widely dispersed parts of the world. Although American policy is certainly not dictated by the UN, and often seems to be formulated with little regard for that body, the United Nations as an organization provides a part of the institutional framework within which almost every nation's foreign policy, including our own, is made.

## THE MAKING OF FOREIGN POLICY

The main primary participants in foreign policy formulation are, on the diplomatic side, the Department of State, on the military the Department of Defense and the Joint Chiefs of Staff, and on the economic the Treasury Department and, again, the Department of State. Policy coordination is sought through the National Security Council in the Executive Office of the President. The final responsibility rests on the shoulders of the President, who in some instances may or must share it with Congress; as we saw when we considered the presidency in Chapter 15, Congress has influence on foreign policy, but in this field the President, although not supreme, is usually more influential than in any other.

### The President and the National Security Council

Historically Presidents have relied on their Secretaries of State to handle questions of policy in international relations or have stepped in, as Wilson and F. D. Roosevelt did, and done the job themselves. But the change in the nature of foreign policy-making —the significance of trade and economic aid programs, and particularly the impossibility of treating diplomatic and military decisions as if they had no bearing on each other—was reflected in the National Security Act passed by Congress in 1947. Under this statute was established the National Security Council, headed by the President and including the Vice-President, the Secretaries of State and Defense, the director of the Office of Civil and Defense Mobilization, and such agency heads as the President may appoint to it or invite to attend the meetings. Among the latter, in regular attendance have been the chairmen of the Joint Chiefs of Staff and the Atomic Energy Commission, the Secretary of the Treasury, the Director of the Budget, and the Director of the Central Intelligence Agency, a highly secret organization which, administratively, is under the NSC. The council has a full-time executive secretary and a planning board whose function is to clarify issues and present possible alternative courses of action to the council for its consideration. Also under the council is its Operations Coordinating Board, responsible for seeing to it that the policies agreed upon are implemented. Actually the NSC is more of an advisory body than a decision-making or operating one, although the President can, if he wishes, accept its recommendations. When the latter are unanimous, he is of course tempted to do so—though the very fact that the NSC is a representative council whose members speak for different agencies and viewpoints makes it likely that any unanimous recommendation will be an imprecise compromise.[4] When the agencies represented on the NSC persist in their differences, the President must choose between their views (not necessarily on the basis of whose plan gets the most votes at the council's session), or postpone making any decision.

The NSC's chief value lies, probably, in its functioning as a forum for responsible discussion and a clearinghouse of ideas. (Its subordinate agency, the CIA, is likewise a clearinghouse for all the "intelligence" gathered by not only its own operatives but

---

[4] See Hans J. Morgenthau, "Can We Entrust Defense to a Committee?" *New York Times Magazine,* June 7, 1959, p. 9.

those of other agencies.) It brings together spokesmen for the diplomatic and military viewpoints. Under President Eisenhower, furthermore, most council discussions have taken place with the Director of the Budget participating, and with the effect of every proposal on the budget a subject for consideration. Some critics of the NSC profess alarm at the intrusion of the military in a policy-making body. They see this as a dangerous compromise of the principle of civilian control and would prefer to think of the armed services solely as operating units, ready to implement whatever policies the President and his civilian advisers agree upon. Other critics complain that NSC deliberations are conducted with a constant awareness of the budgetary implications of foreign and military policies; such policies, they say, should be made to meet the demands of national security and the budget altered to fit them rather than the other way around. Defenders of the NSC system reply that in a dynamic age when the course of diplomacy is inevitably shaped by swiftly changing factors of military capability, the pooling of diplomatic and military knowledge must be a prerequisite to policy-making. Some of them believe, too, that the nation's economic strength is at least partially dependent on whether the budget is balanced and that budgetary limits should therefore be recognized by the policy-makers. In any event, the ultimate responsibility is the President's. He can decide whether to give first place to military and budgetary viewpoints or not—although, as we shall see, his decisions may occasionally be modified by Congress.

Actually, accepted tradition impels most Presidents to look first and foremost, for advice on foreign policy questions, not to the Defense Department or the Joint Chiefs of Staff [5] or the director of the budget, but to the Secretary of State. This has been true even since the creation of the National Security Council. President Truman put great trust in Secretary Dean Acheson, and President Eisenhower obviously relied heavily on Secretary John Foster Dulles. Even when Secretary Dulles was at the height of his great

---

[5] So closely intertwined are major foreign policy questions and military considerations that the opinions of the Joint Chiefs are sought eagerly by Congress on such matters as the ratification of a nuclear test ban treaty—which means that a prudent President, too, must give considerable weight to their views.

influence, to be sure, the President listened carefully to financial advisers who urged reduced expenditures—but this did not necessarily imply that there was any conflict between them and Dulles, who seemed ready to tailor his policies to their budgetary wishes. Sometimes Presidents in the past have paid comparatively little attention to State Department advice; Wilson and F. D. Roosevelt each acted, so it was often said, as "his own secretary of state," and President Kennedy's special assistant, McGeorge Bundy, was a significant foreign policy adviser. But the complications of the modern age make considerable presidential reliance on the State Department a necessity.

## The State Department

In most countries there is a "Ministry of Foreign Affairs." The American equivalent is the Department of State. To be sure, the statute of 1789 which originated the position of Secretary of State said nothing about his acting as "foreign minister"; it simply charged him to assist the President in any manner that the latter directed. From that vague beginning has grown an agency, under the Secretary's direction, which not only finds facts and formulates policy but conducts operations, too, especially in the running of "overseas missions" in which diplomatic, military, and economic policies are implemented.

*Policy-Making.* Actually, as we have seen, the ultimate responsibility for foreign policy rests with the President and to some extent with Congress, but as an informed adviser the Secretary of State has great influence on its formation. He, in turn, must count on subordinate agencies within his own department for information and advice. Available to him are high officials—for example, the undersecretary, the counselor of the department, the undersecretaries for political and economic affairs—and bureaus headed by assistant secretaries. Four of these bureaus are established along geographical lines, dealing with the problems of four different parts of the world; a fifth concerns itself with the United Nations. In addition, there is an assistant secretary for policy-planning who heads a coordinating research group which at times in the recent past has had considerable impact. The theory of the policy of "containment" of Communist power, a fundamental in all our international dealings throughout the 1950's, was first publicly set forth in 1947 by the then head of the policy-planning staff, George Kennan.

All of these officials, including the "desk men" in the various bureaus, tend to acquire detailed and expert knowledge of the particular subjects or countries in their special charge. As experts they often become effective advocates of particular policy proposals. A major task at the higher levels of the department, therefore, is that of settling interbureau differences. Fortunately this does not require constant compromise to keep peace among the bureaus, for almost all of the responsible officers are career men, unlikely to resign even though their views are rejected. Rather, what the Secretary and his top assistants often have to do is to choose promptly and decisively between different recommendations—and to make sure that their decisions are consistent with each other, so that the United States will not, for instance, simultaneously support the conflicting claims of two rival nations.

Two erstwhile independent operating agencies, which in the 1950's were brought under the Secretary of State's control in matters of policy, play some part in policy formation despite their "operating" status. One of these, the United States Information Agency, broadcasts by radio all over the world. It is required to adhere to the policy "line" laid down by the Secretary, but sometimes unexpected events occur justifying comment by the USIA, where no clear policy has been decided. In such instances the USIA, if unable to obtain a clear directive from the department, may occasionally establish a "line" by itself—though since congressional criticism of the "Voice of America" cost the agency its former complete independence, the USIA inclines to exercise great caution. The second is the Agency for International Development (AID), in charge of foreign economic assistance programs. Though the AID and its predecessor, the International Cooperation Administration, have been administratively a part of the State Department since 1955, the AID is semiautonomous, reporting only to the Secretary and often, with his approval, presenting its own case to Congress. Its director is not only the chief of an operating agency, but a policy adviser to the President.

Policy recommendations, at every level, are based on a variety of factors. First, as we have seen, is knowledge of the facts—knowledge acquired, in considerable part, from the reports of State Department diplomats and other operatives in foreign lands. Second are American commitments to other governments, through formal treaties, informal understandings, and membership in the United Nations; once any policy's success depends on the continuing agreement of some other country or the latter's confidence in the United States, later policies must not lightly cancel that agreement or destroy that confidence. Foreign governments' opinions and probable reactions are therefore important factors in shaping American policy. American public opinion itself is a significant factor, too, though it would be a mistake to suppose that the State Department is swayed by every fluctuation of viewpoint indicated by a sample poll. The department's public affairs bureau does put an ear to the ground occasionally, hoping to hear what the "informed" public is saying, but its more important function is to increase the size of that public by an educational or public relations program. It is public opinion, informed or uninformed, spontaneous or guided by interest groups, *as reflected in Congress* that has a real impact on the State Department, for although the discretion of the President and his advisers is broader in the field of foreign affairs than anywhere else, still the success of many a policy depends on congressional approval. The department's Office of Congressional Relations is therefore an important one, although far less important than the impact which the Secretary of State himself makes on the relevant committees of Congress.

*Operations.* The department's implementation of foreign policy takes place mainly in "overseas missions" in every section of the globe.[6] In about three-quarters of the countries to which these missions are sent, the chief of mission holds the rank of ambassador; in the rest, that of minister. Attached to the mission

---

6 One operating function performed in Washington is the issuance of passports to American citizens wishing to travel abroad. Policies sometimes prescribed by the Secretary, sometimes left largely to the director of the Passport Division, have led to the denial of passports to numerous people, and the frequent refusal to permit Americans to travel in China. Arbitrary denials of passports, without a hearing and a statement of reasons for the denial, have been held unconstitutional by the Supreme Court.

are Foreign Service officers of the State Department, staffing its political, economic and cultural sections. Also under the direction of its chief, though hired and assigned by other departments, are staff personnel representing the Defense Department and, in many places, the Departments of Labor and Agriculture.

Under the Constitution, ambassadors are the personal representatives of the President of the United States.[7] Many of them, through much of our history, were selected for reasons only remotely connected with diplomatic experience or skill. Rich men who contributed heavily to a winning presidential campaign were often rewarded with major ambassadorships; minor ones frequently went to smaller contributors or temporarily unemployed party politicians. Occasionally, still, the desire to reward party service obviously plays some part in their selection, but the crucial nature of international relations has increasingly made some special knowledge or skill a prerequisite for an ambassadorial post. As ambassadors have to entertain on a scale which often far transcends the appropriations for that purpose, independent wealth remains a great asset to anyone who desires an ambassadorship, and party regularity is an asset too. Since World War II, however, more and more embassies have been headed by the State Department's own career diplomats, men who began as lowly Foreign Service officers and worked upwards toward an ambassadorial climax.

The department's career service itself has undergone a transformation within the last decade. Formerly there was a sharp distinction between its Foreign Service and its Washington-based civil servants. The increase in overseas activity after World War II, however, brought many of the civil servants into foreign capitals. They worked alongside of the Foreign Service officers, but were governed by different rules of recruitment and tenure and salary scales. The resulting friction caused Secretary Dulles to appoint a Public Committee on Personnel, headed by former President Henry M. Wriston of Brown University. The Wriston

---

[7] F. D. Roosevelt was roundly criticized for referring, in a campaign speech, to "my ambassador . . . Joe Kennedy." His critics claimed that he should have said "our" ambassador or "the United States ambassador."

report [8] led to the gradual integration of department personnel into a unified Foreign Service and to a drastic change in the methods of recruiting new employees. The requirement of long specialized training, previously necessary for admission to the Foreign Service, was discarded. Now, once or twice each year, able college students are invited to apply and to take general examinations which cover a wide field of knowledge, although they usually emphasize history, politics, and economics somewhat more than other subjects. The examinations are hard, but require no special "cram" courses; and although mastery of a foreign language is essential to a permanent diplomatic career, the applicant who passes the rest of the examination may be qualified for work in the department on a probationary basis, without meeting the language requirement until later.

Even at comparatively humble levels, the job of representing the United States abroad is an exacting one. Day by day, it may run the gamut from property management (buying a new desk for the counselor of embassy's secretary) to freeing American goods from the clutches of a mistaken customs officer, to interceding with the local authorities on behalf of an overstimulated American tourist. It may consist of making arrangements for the distribution of medicine to village clinics or demonstrating new machinery to farmers. Always it includes two things: the assimilation of information (all Foreign Service officers are, quite openly, the "eyes and ears" of their country) and the representation of the United States, for people tend to judge America by the Americans they come to meet and know.

At the higher levels, the groundwork for major diplomatic achievements is often laid by conferences between the ambassador and the foreign minister of the country to which he is accredited. Ordinarily, of course, these exploratory conversations are set in motion by policy decisions at the highest level of all, that of the Secretary of State or the President back in Washington. The ambassador is carrying out their directives. In recent years, in contrast to the past, the Secretary of State and the President them-

---

8 *Toward a Stronger Foreign Service* (Washington, D.C.: Government Printing Office, 1954).

selves have frequently engaged in face-to-face negotiations with their foreign counterparts, traveling thousands of miles to do so. Times have changed indeed. Many Americans professed to be horrified when President Wilson sailed to attend the peace conference at Paris in 1918, but few if any were disturbed by President Eisenhower's airplane journeys to Europe and Asia forty-one years later. The man who largely guided American foreign policy for the first six years of Mr. Eisenhower's presidency, Secretary Dulles, relied heavily on personal contacts with foreign officials and was constantly on the move from one capital to another. In 1963, President Kennedy's European trip included what was virtually a campaign tour of West Germany, at a time when De Gaulle of France was seeking to persuade the West Germans to be less cooperative with the United States.

## The Department of Defense

There was once a time when decisions to strengthen the armed forces of the United States could be made by civilians who were not experts in shipbuilding or the manufacture of explosives. A battleship was a battleship, a cannonball was a cannonball. If the President, acting on the advice of the diplomats, urged Congress to appropriate more money for the navy, there was little need to worry about the possibilities of building new ships or to ask naval experts about their future usefulness. If such ships were useful now, new ones like them could be built readily and would be useful five or ten years hence. Changes in the arts of war came slowly.

Today, in contrast, only experts know—and sometimes they can merely guess—whether new instruments of war or defense can be built at all. Only they can know, or reasonably guess, whether proposed weapons will be obsolete as soon as they are manufactured. And only they can predict with authority the effectiveness or destructive power of weapons in existence or on the drawing boards. These experts are sometimes found in corporate research departments or universities; occasionally they are free-lance writers or even congressmen; but their influence is likely to be greatest if they are connected with official agencies charged with responsibilities for national defense—the Atomic Energy Commission and, especially, the armed services linked together in the

The years of peace. The rustic scene of Washington, above, was copied from a sketch made in 1801 by Nicholas King, the city surveyor of the then new city of Washington. Into the "President's House" (in the center, hardly recognizable as the White House we know) in this same year moved Thomas Jefferson, who once said that "that government is best which governs least." The building at the right was Blodgett's Hotel, built in 1793 and used as a residence for Congressmen and Senators. Later it was used for some sessions of Congress during the building of the Capitol, and even once served as the temporary Capitol. Below, the little city of Washington in Andrew Jackson's time, when the work of government could be carried on in just a few buildings, including the dominant White House, left, the Capitol with its then unimpressive dome, and a few small office buildings in between. Compare this view with the view of the same area today at the top of the next page.

In 1960. Above, the vast Pentagon building, nerve center of defense planning and military administration. Below, the stately Mall running from the Washington Monument, with the Lincoln Memorial beyond, to the Capitol. To both north and south of it are row on row of ponderous but impressive office buildings where much of the vast job of governing is done.

country's military establishment by the Department of Defense. That department's home, the huge building on the Virginia side of the Potomac River known as the Pentagon, is a center of influence on foreign policy because foreign policy is shaped in part by military power, and the Pentagon provides the informed estimates of the extent and quality of American military power in a world of swift technological change.

*Policy-Making.* Defense officials are influential not only because they are assumed to know how effective existing weapons are and future ones may be, but also because they are judges of the military potential of other nations. Knowledge of foreign armaments is acquired by civilian agencies, especially the CIA, as well as by the intelligence units of the armed services, but the armed services and the top Defense Department officials use that knowledge as a basis of military planning. Such military planning seems, today, inextricable from diplomatic planning. For instance, if the Pentagon reported that new hostile installations in "Ruritania," threatening American air bases in Turkey, could be "neutralized" only by acquiring new bases in Albania and equipping them with newly invented missiles, the diplomatic question would be whether to make a deal with Communist-oriented Albania in order to get the bases in that country. Merely by insisting on the importance of protecting the bases in Turkey, air force generals would to some degree influence the decision about dealing with Albania.

Not always, of course, must military estimates of foreign power or, particularly, foreign intentions be accepted; if they were, our international relations might be guided wholly by generals and admirals. A great general, Douglas MacArthur, incorrectly estimated both the reaction and the power of the Chinese Communists when late in 1950 he pushed through North Korea to the border of China, confident that the Chinese would not fight or, if they did, would make an unimpressive showing. Chinese soldiers promptly poured across the Yalu River and forced MacArthur to retreat southward. Generals and admirals have their opinions, naturally, on such questions as the Soviet Union's capacity to destroy European and American cities and the possibility of using nuclear weapons in isolated "limited" wars without starting a global conflagration. Trained to win wars, they may feel strongly, too, that in any conflict every effort must be made to achieve total victory. Thus MacArthur, pushed back by the Chinese in Korea, urged the bombing of Chinese bases in China; and in 1955 the chairman of the Joint Chiefs of Staff, Admiral Radford, was reported to favor an all-out nuclear attack on Communist forces besieging Dien Bien Phu in what was then still French Indo-China. What these military leaders saw as questions of military policy, however, were recognized by others as matters of foreign policy. An attack on bases within China, President Truman and Secretary of State Acheson believed, would not only increase the difficulty of keeping the Korean War from becoming a world war, but might cost us the support of our Atlantic allies, especially Great Britain. Nuclear war in Indo-China was ruled out by President Eisenhower for similar reasons. The fact remains that military leaders in proposing military policies thereby intervene in the making of foreign policy, and although their views do not necessarily prevail, they are given respectful consideration.

Respect for their opinions is often particularly evident in Congress. The Pentagon has established a close working relationship with the congressional standing committees on the armed services, especially the House committee long headed by Representative Carl Vinson of Georgia, and the policy views of generals and admirals are often reflected in congressional debates. When President Truman dismissed General MacArthur from his command in 1951, Congress reacted by inviting the General to address a special joint session of the House and Senate. Congressmen habitually show deep respect for the uniform [9] and a readiness to accept without much question high officers' estimates of the military (and hence, to a considerable degree, the international) situation.

If army, navy, and air force leaders spoke with a single voice, their impact on policy-making both in the executive branch and in Congress might be greater than it is. Rivalry between the services, however, persists, despite their alleged "unification" in the Department of Defense. The essential question upon which

9 It is noteworthy that the Senate's censure of one of its own members, Joseph McCarthy, took place not as a result of his many irresponsible denunciations of civilians, including State Department officials, but only after he had publicly insulted a general of the U.S. army.

they divide is: what kind of war to prepare for? In approaching that issue, each service tends to assume a position like that of a private interest group in similar circumstances—each often appears to be convinced that the national security can best be protected by *its* holding the predominant place in the system of national defense. It may be argued that all great wars in the past have been decided, in the last analysis, by the foot soldiers, and any future wars will likewise be won by them. Or that airplane carriers and nuclear submarines are the vital instruments of successful modern warfare. Or that land-based aircraft, capable of dropping nuclear bombs, will determine the fate of the world. So run the conflicting claims. Notice how closely they are connected with basic foreign policy questions. For example, the army's readiness to fight a small "brushfire" war in some remote area might lead to a decision to promote and protect American or anti-Communist interests in that area, on the assumption that the war could remain limited in scope. On the other hand, the assumption that wars cannot be limited but must be prevented by threats of "massive retaliation" in the form of nuclear bombing of large cities gives first importance to the Strategic Air Command. Each service tends to favor that policy which depends primarily on the strength of that service. And each, foreseeing the eventual predominance of the intercontinental ballistic missile as the ultimate weapon, has sought zealously for control of ICBM development.

*Operations.* The administration of programs providing military aid to foreign countries is the responsibility of the Secretary of Defense and his assistant secretary for international security affairs. In addition to supplying material, the services have conducted "training missions" to acquaint some foreign forces with the uses of new weapons. Aside from the direct assignment of American men, ships, planes, and guns to overseas duty—such as the protective forces in Korea and the air bases in the southwest Pacific area—the chief involvement of United States forces with foreign operations is their participation in the NATO military establishment, under the command of NATO's Supreme Headquarters in Paris. Though a civilian council has ultimate authority over the disposition of NATO's forces, active direction is centered in the Supreme Headquarters. NATO's top command post has been held by a series of American generals, one of whom left that position to run successfully for the presidency of the United States.

To operate, the military establishment must have men. For manpower the armed services have depended largely on the draft or selective service system. The Selective Service Act of 1940 instituted the first peacetime draft in American history; and after World War II, though the size of the forces was drastically reduced for a time, that system was continued. Officers are trained at the service academies at West Point, Annapolis, and Colorado Springs (the traditional Army-Navy football rivalry has often been cited, without convincing proof, as a reason why unification of the services is difficult) or come up from the ranks of enlisted men. A vigorously sponsored college training program has created a reserve officers' corps; about 340,000 college students were enrolled in the ROTC in 1960, of whom, on the basis of past experience, about 90,000 seemed likely to remain in the reserve beyond the required period of service.

To a degree unparalleled in any other part of the executive branch, the Pentagon engages in a massive public relations program. This includes not only its own motion picture studio but extensive cooperation with private motion picture producers; television shows, many of which are donated by stations as "public service" programs; assistance in the preparation of books and magazine articles and promotion in placing them with publishers; and the furnishing of speakers and exhibits to grace all manner of affairs, from patriotic observances to county fairs, all over the country. Furthermore, in recent years colleges and universities have come to count on the Defense Department and the AEC, together, for hundreds of millions of dollars' worth of research contracts. These contracts are for needed research, but they also spread the Pentagon's influence. Obviously the Defense Department considers public understanding and approval of its activities as a matter of great importance.

It is important because, among other things, defense takes a huge bite out of the taxpayer's dollar. The maintenance and strengthening of the armed forces, in the manner in which their commanders deem necessary, requires favorable action by Congress in passing appropriation acts. Not always, to be sure, do the military leaders win the support of the executive officials who frame the original budget for submission to Congress. Thus, shortly before the Korean War, budget requests were cut sharply by President Truman's Secretary of Defense, Louis Johnson. In 1953 President Eisenhower and Secretary Charles E. Wilson, urged on by the Secretary of the Treasury, George Humphrey, sought "more bang for a buck"—they insisted on reduced budgetary requests. In 1959 the service chiefs publicly objected to the President's budget recommendations. Their objections were numerous and detailed; an example is army General Maxwell D. Taylor's comment: "No funds are provided to initiate production of tactical equipment and [anti-missile] missiles. My reservation in this area arises from the unopposed ICBM threat and my conviction that the importance of obtaining this unique anti-missile weapon at the earliest possible date outweighs the possible financial risks inherent in initiating selective production now." The careful cultivation of congressional support and the Pentagon's public relations programs mean that the budget battle does not necessarily end with executive decisions. The services have on occasion gained from Congress what the Secretary of Defense, the budget director, and the President have agreed should not be given them.

Civilian reluctance to go along with every budget request does not imply lack of concern for national defense. It may reflect a judgment that the particular arms requested won't work, or will take too long to produce, or would be inconsistent with over-all foreign policy. But it may and does also result from a weighing of priorities. This is made obvious by General Taylor's comment, when he indicated that the civilian executives' failure to recommend appropriations for an anti-missile missile was based on "possible financial risks." In other words, the President and his advisers had to balance the probabilities of the need for and success of the missile against their conviction that the soundness of the national economy required cutting expenditures and balancing the budget. Thus economic considerations may profoundly affect the strength and operations of the Department of Defense. Questions of economic policy, indeed, are involved not only in armament decisions but in the whole complex structure of our international relations.

## Economic Policy

The impact of economic considerations is felt not only in determining the size and quality of a defense program but also in direct dealings with other countries. The American position in relation to the rest of the world is greatly affected by the status of international trade and the economic assistance offered by the United States.

*The Tariff.* In foreign trade, as we have seen, the United States was for more than a century concerned primarily with the protection of domestic industrial producers. Foreign imports which might otherwise have competed with American products were subjected to customs duties, often heavy enough to make their importation unprofitable. As American enterprise grew, however, American producers sought foreign markets. Trade is a two-way street; if you want people to buy your products, you must be willing to buy theirs. The high tariff walls erected after World War I were, therefore, charged with drying up American markets abroad and took some of the blame for the depression. In 1934 American trade policy changed direction, the Trade Agreements Act (renewed every few years since) leading to executive agreements with other countries to reduce tariffs and promote trade. This was a program of "bilateral" bargaining, with one country at a time. The economic interdependence of much of the world made it hard for such bilateral arrangements to achieve much, though they were a step in the direction of more international exchange of goods. After World War II, the United States joined in an effort to foster multinational trade agreements, among several nations, through participation in the thirty-five nation General Agreement on Tariffs and Trade (GATT) of 1947. GATT was little more than an indication of readiness to reduce tariffs; it did not actually lower them. It did, however, impose on the signatory nations an obligation to refrain from sudden and arbitrary tariff increases.

As a huge "free trade" area itself (remember that the Constitution forbids any state to impose a tariff against goods brought in from another state) the United States has naturally viewed sympathetically the efforts to create something approaching a similar free-trade area embracing the countries of western Europe. However, as British interests have remained dubious about the establishment of a European "common market," or even hostile toward it, American encouragement has been cautiously limited. Meanwhile, however, after twenty years of the Reciprocal Trade Act, the old spirit of protectionism appeared to be rejuvenated in the United States during the 1950's. The President's discretion under that statute was limited by amendments which pointed invariably in the direction of higher tariffs. The trend disturbed those who saw in freer trade among nations a way to satisfy the basic wants of all peoples and thus to relieve economic tensions that may lead to demands for more territory and so to war.

*Economic Assistance.* Upon the establishment of the United Nations, the United States became an active participant in two of its agencies which affect economic stability and growth in much of the world, the International Monetary Fund and the International Bank for Reconstruction and Development. But one of the most dramatic and effective foreign economic programs was set in motion by the United States alone, outside of the United Nations. This was the plan proposed on June 5, 1947, by Secretary of State George C. Marshall and approved by Congress in the following year. It called for massive American loans and grants to nations devastated by war and lacking the capital with which to restore a fully productive economy. Marshall's recommendation reflected a basic foreign policy decision: namely, that the United States would have to bring swift and substantial help if several western European countries were to be saved from Communist domination.[10] In effect, it implemented the "containment" policy. Economic assistance went to Great Britain and western European nations (including, by additions to the program in 1949 and 1950, West Germany and Austria) and to Greece and Turkey,[11] and,

---

[10] Poverty and discontent had made Communist parties in France and especially Italy strong contenders for political power in those countries in 1947 and 1948.

[11] Mr. Truman asked Congress for $400,000,000 for Greece and Turkey in March, 1947, at the same time that he proclaimed the "Truman Doctrine" of containment.

later, Korea, Southeast Asia and the Philippines. The program of economic aid has continued to be a cornerstone of modern American foreign policy.

In "point four" of his inaugural address in January, 1949, President Truman called for a "bold new program . . . for the improvement and growth of underdeveloped countries . . . to stir the peoples of the world into triumphant action, not only against their human oppressors, but against their ancient enemies—hunger, misery, and despair." Although the humanitarian emphasis of this appeal stirred many imaginations, it had less effect on Congress than did the more direct anti-Communist aspect of the Marshall Plan.[12] The "bold" program was whittled down to one of piecemeal aid and substantial support for the technical assistance operations of the United Nations. In 1957, however, Congress established a Development Loan Fund for the making of "soft" loans, repayable in the currency of the borrower, to spur economic growth in underdeveloped countries.

One form of American economic aid antedated the Marshall Plan by many years. This consists of the lending operations of the Export-Import Bank, a federal agency established in 1934. The bank operates on a business basis, extending international credits which have made possible the development of steel mills, industrial plants, irrigation projects, and other public works in foreign countries. Its loans are "hard"—repayable in American dollars— and are made on the condition that the equipment required must be obtained in the United States. This condition may have much to do with the ease with which the bank gets its appropriations from Congress, in contrast to the annual congressional battle over Agency for International Development appropriation bills. In its first twenty-five years of existence, the Export-Import Bank authorized some $10,000,000,000 in credits and, by the end of that period, had earned a profit of nearly a billion dollars.

Export-Import loans, plus sales of farm surpluses for foreign

---

12 As originally proposed by Secretary Marshall, Marshall Plan aid would have been offered to all the wartime allies. By the time Congress made the Marshall Plan effective by passing the Foreign Assistance Act of 1948, however, the Soviet Union had announced that it would reject the offer and caused its satellite nations to do likewise.

currencies which were then granted or loaned back to the pur-
chasers, and gifts of further farm surpluses to charitable organizations for shipment abroad, actually amounted to more dollars of
foreign economic aid in 1958 than were voted by Congress for the
official economic assistance program. The inclusion within that
program of the new Development Loan Fund, however, seemed
certain to shift the balance in subsequent years.

In contrast to Congress's tendency, in critical times, to "go
along" with the President's diplomatic decisions and to listen with
some awe to generals and admirals, the legislators regularly intervene, vigorously and critically, in the economic area of foreign
policy. It is in that field that political controversy is most consistently apparent. Yet as a body representative of the people, Congress cannot and does not ignore any major foreign policy
questions, muted though the official debates may be in days of
danger. For in our time the questions of foreign policy have become the central political questions confronting the country and
the world.

## THE POLITICS OF FOREIGN RELATIONS

"Politics stops at the water's edge" is a statement of a goal, not
a fact. In a democracy, foreign policy decisions, like other policy
determinations, are the product of familiar political forces. To
be sure, knowledgeable men have argued that they should not be.
A respected and keen analyst of foreign affairs, Walter Lippmann,
has seen in democratic (or, as he calls it, "Jacobin") influence on
foreign policy a source of great danger to the West. The great
mass of the people, he suggests, regularly react mistakenly to international issues; they are moved by emotion and a desire for ease
and comfort when the times demand cool thinking and Spartan
qualities. Therefore the hard, unpopular course that leads to
greater eventual national safety is avoided, and instead we stum-
ble along a smoother path leading to disaster. So Lippmann implies, urging that the choices in foreign affairs should be made
by the comparatively few men truly competent to make them,

with the people's representatives in Congress acting only as a check against corrupt or wholly irresponsible conduct.[13]

A former Secretary of State, Dean Acheson, has to some extent echoed the Lippmann view. He has expressed a preference, at least, for the customary acceptance of executive leadership on international questions.[14] And indeed a strong case can be made for the position that in the complex and dangerous business of settling issues of war and peace, the experts should be not merely on tap but on top. Most Americans certainly are ill informed about world affairs. Many have only the vaguest notion even of geography; it is all too easy to find college seniors who think that Oslo is in Spain and the river Rhone in Germany. When it comes to the significance of foreign statesmen, changes in other nations' governments, or the sources of sharp dispute between two far-off countries, the poll-taker with his questionnaire draws many a blank. Not only knowledge but sustained interest seems lacking. Polls have shown that although a large percentage of the people name foreign policy issues as "most important" at a moment when wide publicity is given to threats of war, their interest slackens as soon as the publicity dwindles. The danger may be as great as ever, but if it does not produce sensational front-page news, most Americans prefer to disregard it.

Despite the public ignorance and seeming unconcern, however, the proponents of executive control have some hard questions to answer. First, does the superior knowledge of the experts mean that they also have better judgment than anyone else? Not necessarily. Second, which experts should be dominant? Mr. Lippmann, though joining in what has been called "the denigration of the masses," [15] would hardly wish to put foreign policy into the hands of the generals, admirals, or nuclear physicists. Third, how can

---

13 Walter Lippmann, *Essays in the Public Philosophy* (Boston: Little, Brown & Co., 1954).

14 Dean Acheson, *A Citizen Looks at Congress* (New York: Harper & Brothers, 1956). It might be noted, a bit ironically, that as a leader in the Democratic party's advisory council, ex-Secretary Acheson felt free to be highly critical of his Republican successor's policies and to urge changes in them.

15 Charles O. Lerche, Jr., *Foreign Policy of the American People* (Englewood Cliffs, N.J.: Prentice-Hall, Inc., 1958).

official obliviousness to public opinion be squared with the principle of democratic government, wherein the temporary rulers are answerable to the people? In reply to that last question, a State Department official has suggested that a kind of special public opinion is worth heeding: "Our national policies should reflect the will of the people, a will that is not distorted by false propa-

Drawing by Modell, copr. © 1958 The New Yorker Magazine, Inc.

*"From the cyclotron of Berkeley to the labs of M.I.T.,*
*We're the lads that you can trust to keep our country strong and free."*

ganda or slogans, that is based upon a solid knowledge of all the facts, that has taken into account all factors and considerations, and has resulted from open and active debate so that all points of view have been thoroughly aired and discussed." [16]

Now it may be true, as George Kennan has asserted, that "a

[16] Francis H. Russell, "The Function of Public Opinion Analysis in the Formulation of Foreign Policy," *Department of State Bulletin,* March, 1949. Mr. Russell was then director of the department's Office of Public Affairs; later he became ambassador to New Zealand.

good deal of our trouble [in formulating and implementing a consistent long-range foreign policy] seems to have stemmed from the extent to which the executive has felt itself beholden to short term trends of public opinion in the country and from what we might call the erratic and subjective nature of public reaction to foreign policy questions." [17] But there are obvious reasons why the executive does feel itself so "beholden." First, the President is himself an elected official and a party leader. In getting elected he is highly likely to appeal to the voters' "erratic" or emotional reactions, and in the course of doing this to make a number of commitments. Second, he hopes either to be reelected himself or to have his party's candidate win the next election. Third, to make much of his policy effective—especially programs like those of foreign military assistance and economic aid which cost a lot of money—he must depend on congressional support; and Congress is influenced by the opinions of ordinary voters who are indeed swayed by propaganda and whose "will" is seldom "based upon a solid knowledge of all the facts." Fourth, whenever war threatens, every responsible leader knows that the country's strength depends in good part on the unity of its people. In one sense this is a reason for strong executive leadership—congressmen are responsible leaders, too, and will often subordinate their own opinions to the need for national unity. Thus in 1955, President Eisenhower asked for and received from Congress, by a nearly unanimous vote, a "blank check" authorizing him to go to war, if he thought it necessary, to defend Quemoy and Matsu, despite many congressmen's grave doubts about the wisdom of such a course. Again in 1958, the President's action in dispatching troops to Lebanon seemed to some senators and representatives to be unwise, yet for weeks no serious criticism was voiced in Congress. However, no President can be sure that his judgment of the national danger will always be shared by the public or the Congress. If it is not, the steps that he takes or proposes may divide and weaken the nation. He must, therefore, always keep in mind the probable public reaction to his policies.

That public reaction is likely to be conditioned by several

---

[17] George Kennan, *American Diplomacy, 1900-1950* (Chicago: University of Chicago Press, 1951), p. 93.

factors aside from "solid knowledge." These can be roughly classified into five broad categories: orientation, partisanship, national origin, economic interests, and personal hopes and fears.

## The Factor of Orientation

Not polls but observation and history together imply that any analysis of the politics of United States foreign policy can profit by a very general classification of Americans into two groups. The first is composed of those to whom there have been handed down, through the generations, traditional assumptions about society and government that seem to stem from ancient Greece, but developed most understandably in England beginning in the seventeenth century. These unwritten assumptions include a theoretical belief in equality and, often, a practical limitation of it; a respect for continuity and a distaste for disorder and drastic change; and a realization that denial of freedom for one threatens freedom for all. Underlying all these is faith in an unexpressed, indefinable code, representing the consensus of wise and responsible men of this and former ages on what individual and social conduct ought to be—an invisible standard of excellence in deportment and achievement. Some American leaders have viewed "western civilization" in these terms. In the early years of World War I, for instance, Woodrow Wilson could speak of "peace without victory" among the warring European nations because he assumed that all of them except, perhaps, Russia, abided by the same basic code of honor and conduct. Only when Kaiser Wilhelm's ministers unquestionably broke the code by directing submarine warfare against neutral American ships did Wilson decide that the German government was not "civilized" and so feel ready to go to war against it. And in World War II many Americans saw everything that they most deeply believed in mortally threatened by the Nazi war against Great Britain. Long before Pearl Harbor they were singing "The White Cliffs of Dover" with emotion, and pouring out money for "Bundles for Britain" and "Aid to the Allies"—which, again, primarily meant Britain.[18]

---

18 A poem widely quoted in those days, "The White Cliffs" by American poetess Alice Duer Miller, concluded with the lines: "In a world without an England, I would not wish to live."

This tradition inspires probably a rather small minority of Americans, but though comparatively few in number they have always been great in influence. In the past they have included many of the best-educated people in the United States, men and women of social prominence and financial power. Patriotic Americans, they view the American future as inextricably tied to the future of the "West," especially Great Britain. Their orientation, in international affairs, is toward England and western Europe.

Much more numerous are the Americans who are neither consciously nor subconsciously much concerned about the past. Western traditions, in their view, are all very well, but this is America, a nation formed by revolution against the old ways. Such people have found the true romance not in ancient Athens or Buckingham Palace or the unwritten code, but in the individual struggle for success, the humming of the turbines, and the adventure of building a great and free country. Their more articulate spokesmen have limned the pioneers and preached the glories of egalitarian democracy. Of them Carl Sandburg wrote "The People: Yes!" They are not inclined to share, at least with any enthusiasm, the transatlantic orientation of the traditionalists; in fact, perhaps in reaction to that viewpoint, their concern about foreign affairs has often been directed the other way, across the Pacific. Thus many who opposed every pro-British gesture by the American government toward Hitler were enthusiastic about checking Japan's territorial ambitions; and more recently some favored bombing China, in defense of Korea or Chiang Kai-Shek, at the risk of severing our alliance with Britain. In the main, however, their attention has been devoted to the United States apart from the rest of the world. Not surprisingly, then, the "progressives" of the Midwest and mountain states—the LaFollettes, Wheeler, Borah, and other vigorous reformers on the domestic front—were spokesmen for isolationism in international affairs.[19] Joining them were the conservative midwestern descendants of

---

[19] The most dramatic figure in the "America First" movement to keep out of World War II was the famous transatlantic flyer, Charles A. Lindbergh. Whatever Lindbergh's conscious reason may have been, it may be significant that his father had been an old-time "progressive" representative from Minnesota.

the pioneers and of people who had emigrated from Europe to escape hardship or political persecution.

Of course it would be a mistake to draw sharp, firm lines between these two broad classifications. Many Americans react favorably, at different times, both to the appeals of traditional western civilization and to the pioneer, Europe-be-hanged spirit. And the great transformation of much of the world into two armed camps—the years of "cold war" with the Soviet Union —have made many old differences of orientation obsolete. Nevertheless, the predominance of one viewpoint or the other profoundly affected American political history; and because tradition is an important factor in politics, the effects still persist. When the question, for instance, concerns more foreign aid, support for the United Nations, or close cooperation with Great Britain, opposition to these policies tends to center in the Middle West, the old home of both "progressivism" and "isolationism." Popular support for them, in contrast, is likely to be strongest among the people whose forebears, at least, professed and handed down the ancient values.

## National Origins

The difference in orientation stems in part from the fact that Americans have personal or ancestral roots in many different countries. Indeed one shrewd observer, Samuel Lubell, has seen midwestern isolationism as a product not of a democratic, pioneering concern for practical problems close at hand, but of the bitter reaction of Americans of German stock to the entry of the United States into World War I against Germany.[20] His analysis, based on the returns in heavily German-American counties in elections beginning in 1920, shows sharp fluctuations in voting behavior whenever issues concerning American relations with Germany were involved. This hardly proves that isolationism— or "nationalism," in the more recent verbiage—was born in 1917 out of German-American resentment; but Mr. Lubell's statistics do remind us of the great political importance of national origin

---

20 Samuel Lubell, *The Future of American Politics* (Garden City, N.Y.: Doubleday & Co., 1953).

groups in the electorate. A small but dramatic example of the way many Americans identify themselves with the country of their forebears was provided by Italo-American voters in East Boston, Massachusetts, in 1940. That almost solidly Democratic ward had given Franklin Roosevelt big majorities in 1932 and 1936. On June 10, 1940, however, in a speech at Charlottesville, Virginia, Roosevelt spoke bitterly of Mussolini's last-minute attack upon France, which was already crumbling before Hitler's onslaught. Harshness toward Mussolini would probably have cost the President little Italo-American support, but in his speech one sentence bitterly offended Italo-Americans: "The hand that held the dagger has struck it into the back of its neighbor." When Roosevelt ran again the next fall, East Boston's Republican vote tripled.

National origin interests, as we saw in Chapter 9, strongly affect the conduct of both legislators and executive officials. Strongly Irish-American districts have been traditionally anti-British. Representatives of Polish-American constituencies are almost automatically in the forefront of any denunciation of Russia. (They have plenty of companions, to be sure.) Not only congressmen but presidential aspirants are acutely aware of the impact of ancient national prejudices and hatreds on voting behavior.

The Zionist interest—a compound of religion and nationalism—has had a considerable and lasting effect on American foreign policy. How much the holding of the Jewish vote (which had been preponderantly Democratic since 1932) was a factor in President Truman's decision to encourage and recognize the new state of Israel in 1947 no one can possibly say, but that it played some part can hardly be denied. The intense pro-Israel feelings of many voters continue to influence policy at every level. In the making of decisions affecting the oil-producing areas of the Middle East, where anti-Israel emotions are constantly whipped up by the propaganda agencies of the United Arab Republic, American policy-makers face the difficult task of simultaneously keeping the Arab countries out of the Communist orbit and discouraging their aggressive intentions toward Israel. This task is theirs partly because of possible domestic political repercussions and partly because of the national commitment, made at the very outset, to support Israel.

## Partisan Factors

As the making of an international commitment by a President in the name of the United States binds future administrations, so the making of a foreign policy decision by a President has occasionally determined partisan stands on international affairs. A prime example is Wilson's advocacy of our participation in the League of Nations in 1919 and 1920. Wilson was a Democrat, about to retire from office. The Democratic standard-bearers in the 1920 election felt bound to take up his cause and made it the central issue of their unsuccessful campaign. For sixteen years thereafter, to be sure, the Democrats backed further and further away from "internationalism." The lasting partisan effect of the League fight was felt, instead, by the Republicans. Early in World War I leading Republicans, among them former President Taft, had urged the establishment of an international "League to Enforce Peace." In 1918 the Republican state convention in New York had endorsed the idea of a league of nations. Yet after Wilson, a Democrat, had become the leader of pro-League sentiment, the Republican position swiftly changed. To be sure, Taft and a few others, in the 1920 campaign, urged the election of the Republican candidate, Harding, as "the surest way to get us into the League," but such an argument seemed at the time curious and, in hindsight, fantastic. In effect, Wilson's internationalist course (and his making it appear to be a personal and a partisan issue) turned the Republicans onto the isolationist path, which they followed until World War II. So we see that when a President leads in a particular foreign policy direction, the opposition party may oppose that policy simply because it needs a clear-cut issue to present to the voters. Thus when McKinley, a Republican President, kept the Philippines, the Democrats promptly became "anti-imperialists." And in 1952 the Republican campaign talk about "unleashing Chiang Kai-Shek" was really an attempt to condemn the previous Democratic administration's policy in China—a seizing on something to oppose rather than a realistic promise of future action.

Such semiautomatic partisan reaction, however, has been tempered by the rise of bipartisanship in foreign policy questions.

(Secretary Cordell Hull preferred the term "nonpartisanship.")
In present-day terms, this had its beginning in 1942, when a Republican senator, Arthur Vandenberg of Michigan, long a convinced and influential isolationist, decided that he had been
wrong. At that time the Democratic President, F. D. Roosevelt,
was looking forward to the problems of the postwar period and
was anxious for a bipartisan approach to their solution. He believed that Wilson's political mistakes had doomed our entry into
the League, and he was determined to avoid any repetition of
those mistakes. With enthusiasm, therefore, he learned of Vandenberg's "conversion." Vandenberg believed that Pearl Harbor
disproved the thesis which he himself had long expounded, to the
effect that we could stay at peace while the rest of the world was
at war. He became a militant internationalist. Roosevelt welcomed him and directed Secretary Hull to work with him not
only in planning the structure of a new international organization, but in influencing public opinion. From 1943 on, Vandenberg and other Republican leaders joined in the planning
councils and the international conferences, and bipartisan teams
of speakers went out to carry the message to the country. Fortunately for Roosevelt's aims, the Republican nomination in 1944
went to Thomas E. Dewey of New York, who had never been
closely aligned with the isolationist faction of his party and relied
heavily on the advice of a man rooted in the European tradition,
John Foster Dulles. Dulles and Hull, as the candidates' emissar-
ies, agreed that foreign policy should not be a fighting issue in
the presidential campaign of that wartime year, and Roosevelt
and Dewey adhered to that bargain.

Bipartisanship led us into the United Nations with only six
dissenting votes in the Senate. It saved President Truman when
he acted swiftly in defense of Greece and Turkey. It enabled
that Democratic President to make a formidable record in
foreign policy—the Marshall Plan and the North Atlantic
Treaty—even though for two years the Republicans controlled
Congress. It was not applied to issues arising in the Far East; but
otherwise, it gave the "internationalists" a wide margin in Congress.

Bipartisanship did not mean unanimity or the end of debate

and criticism. It did not cover every subject of foreign policy: our relations with China remained a partisan issue at least into the 1950's. But it did bring a majority of Republicans and Democrats together, for a time, on many international issues, and it also gained status as an approved idea in American politics. Increasingly, political leaders in taking policy positions have disavowed partisanship, as if partisanship were reprehensible. This tendency makes for unity, often an important factor in convincing other nations of American determination. It makes presidential leadership easier, for by definition it means that a goodly number of the opposition party joins with many of the President's party in support of his policy. (Actually, in the Eisenhower regime, the President received more over-all foreign policy support in Congress from Democrats than from Republicans.) It is sharply criticized, however, by those who believe that the parties' basic function is to provide significant alternatives for the voters to choose between. These critics suggest that the absence of a responsible party program in foreign affairs makes it easier for many congressmen to vote in accordance with their personal whims, the prejudices of their constituents, or, especially, the wishes of local economic interests dominant in their constituencies.

## Economic Interests

In three broad segments of foreign policy economic interests play a significant part. These are the areas of international trade, foreign military, economic, and technical assistance, and the construction of the weapons of war.

Long ago people laughed at a presidential candidate, Governor W. S. Hancock, for saying that "the tariff is a local issue." But, to a degree, he was right. As we have seen, it is also most decidedly a national question; but if you were a representative you would know what Governor Hancock meant. To the manufacturers in your district and the people they employ, the tariff is a local issue of great immediate importance. A reduction in duties on foreign imports may introduce new competition that reduces profits, might result in operating losses, and could conceivably cause the plant to close and the workers to be unemployed. Not every tariff

cut has such disastrous results, by any means, but the mere suggestion of a cut is enough to set the alarm bells ringing—and the
congressman hears them. As tariff-making is now so largely an
executive function, he cannot do much about the matter on the
floor of the House; but he knows that the economic interests of
his constituents—or a vocal number of them, at least—are on the
side of protection, and when any issue involving foreign trade
does come before Congress, he may vote accordingly. Conversely,
he may come from an area largely dependent on exports, in which
case he will tend to favor measures stimulating the international
exchange of goods.

These predispositions, based on local economic interests, are
factors also in congressional action authorizing foreign aid. The
strengthening of industry in other countries may eventually lead
to more competition for American producers in markets at home
and abroad. Fear of foreign competition produces votes against
foreign aid, just as the danger of Russian encroachment produces
votes for it. A shift in the pattern of congressional voting on
foreign aid measures since the early 1950's reflects the impact of
the protectionist idea. As the South, traditionally an exporting
agricultural area whose spokesmen favored lower tariffs, has become increasingly industrialized, southern support for foreign
aid bills in Congress has dwindled. The alliance of southern
Democrats and midwestern Republicans, long effective in domestic matters, has begun to appear in this important area of foreign
policy, too, despite the deep-rooted traditions of southern internationalism and midwestern isolationism.

The furnishing of billions of dollars' worth of aid to other
nations directly affects another economic interest, that of the
taxpayer. Supporters of foreign assistance programs have to make
a convincing case for their bills: they must show that the assistance is needed and that the funds advanced are usefully spent.
Congressmen have inclined to respect the opinion of the President and his advisers that aid is required, but have become increasingly insistent on information about just how it is used. In
this they speak for taxpayers who don't want their money thrown
away.

The taxpayer's concern is one of four facets of the impact of economic interests on the rate of expenditure for arming the United States itself. A second, closely related to it, is the matter of fiscal policy; with defense by far the largest item in the budget, there is not much room for substantial budget-cutting elsewhere. If President and Congress believe that a drastic reduction of federal expenditures is needed to assure economic stability, they are going to have to cut the arms budget—or at least they are going to have to weigh the importance of cutting it against the importance of building more planes, submarines, and missiles. In striking this balance they run up against another economic question: while a reduced arms budget may wipe out an unstabilizing, inflationary federal deficit, what immediate effect will it have on a substantial segment of American industry? In some places, for instance, airplane factories provide more employment than any other business. If the airplane company's contracts with the Pentagon are canceled, its manufacturing or assembling activities will be drastically curtailed and thousands of workers will be laid off. Both industry and labor, therefore, have a direct stake in continuing defense production at a high rate—a very substantial stake, in view of the fact that the defense budget annually runs to a total of more than forty billion dollars. So it is no wonder that some aspiring politicians, speaking in cities where, for instance, airplane factories are located, commit themselves enthusiastically to a foreign policy wherein an ever growing air force is the chief element of physical power.

There was a time when arms manufacturers and international financiers together were viewed as the black sheep of American foreign policy. In the years between the two world wars, many Americans came to think that the United States had entered the first one to save the overseas investments of New York bankers and that armament corporations were bent on causing future wars for their own financial benefit. A Senate investigation in the 1930's did disclose that some companies had, indeed, financed pressure campaigns to disrupt international disarmament conferences and even, in one instance, to encourage hostilities between two South American countries. Congress promptly passed "neutrality" legislation designed to prevent shipment of arms from the United States to belligerent nations. After Hitler had begun his assault on Europe in 1939 this legislation was repealed, but the fact that it was ever enacted serves as a reminder of the people's desire for peace.

## The Personal Factor

In previous chapters we have considered the impact of individuals on various aspects of politics, referring especially to a few influential men and women. In speaking of the desire for peace, however, the individual is virtually Everyman. The intensity of that desire, of course, does vary from person to person. But only those afflicted with what psychologists call a "death wish" can actually welcome the thought of all-out war in the atomic age.

In former times the yearning for peace was often assumed to be a special attribute of mothers of sons of the right age for military service. "I didn't raise my boy to be a soldier" was supposedly a woman's cry, not a man's. Just why fathers were thought to be harder-hearted is unclear; political history shows men to have been just as ready as women to vote for candidates who would "keep us out of war" or who, as in the 1952 election, gave hope of bringing armed strife to an early end. Today not just for the young men and their relatives, but for every human being, the basic question is survival—not only survival for themselves and their loved ones, but the perpetuation of the institutions they hold dear and the existence of future generations. It was one thing to fight to protect a way of life and insure its continuation for the benefit of later Americans. It is another to fight a war which, whatever nation "wins" it, would destroy the familiar fabric of American life and might, through the effects of radiation released by nuclear explosions, change the aspect and very nature of generations yet unborn. Many Americans, not fully aware of the destructive power of nuclear missiles or at least unwilling to accept the facts, still think in terms of "victory" in an all-out war. An increasing number, however, with either more knowledge or more imagination, have come to view nuclear warfare as the ultimate, final tragedy for the nation and mankind. Philosophical pacifism is probably hardly more prevalent than it ever was. A logical insistence on peace as the only alternative to annihilation, however, is far more widely asserted than in the preatomic years.

Most of those who thus give a top priority to peace appear to agree that military power—the ability to destroy any enemy—is necessary to prevent war. (Armament races have led to wars in the past, but those armaments were not totally destructive; the nation with the greatest power always hoped to escape unscathed, a hope that cannot be wisely entertained in the age of intercontinental missiles.) But even so, many of them have questioned the need and wisdom not of making nuclear weapons, but of exploding them in peacetime. Each such explosion, they argue, increasingly poisons the atmosphere and the food men eat through the radioactive fall-out it produces. They see the question of this "testing" of nuclear explosives as one which involves the future of the human race, for a high degree of radioactivity leads to sterility, mutations, and abnormal births.

The question became a political issue in 1956. Late in his campaign for the presidency, Adlai Stevenson proposed that the United States should offer to stop testing atom bombs if the Russians would agree to do likewise. The proposal was widely misunderstood: Democratic campaigners were dismayed when people said to them: "I was for Stevenson, but why does he want to give the atom bomb to the Russians?" (This question was frequently asked, despite the fact that the Soviet Union had exploded a hydrogen bomb as early as 1953.) It was scorned by Stevenson's opponents. After the campaign smoke cleared, however, the pressing nature of the question became more generally comprehended. By 1958 the Eisenhower administration had agreed with the Russians to suspend "testing" for a year; by 1959, facing the competing demands of a vocal pressure group, the National Committee for a Sane Nuclear Policy, on the one hand and the insistence of the military establishment and Atomic Energy Commission on the other, the President had appointed a special committee of scientists to ascertain and report on the extent and limits of the fall-out danger. From 1959 on, the United States urged a "test ban" on a reluctant Kremlin. When, in 1963, Russian-Chinese relations worsened, the Soviet leaders at long last agreed to the modest proposals of the Americans and the British; and at once the question of the ratification of the ensuing treaty became a major political question in the United States. Personal, human concern for health and survival, mixed with distrust of Soviet intentions, made what had seemed to many to be just "campaign talk" in 1956 a deeply-felt issue in 1963.

It was part, of course, of the larger questions of foreign policy as a whole, and of who should direct it in a free democracy. Despite the tendency to put great faith in the wisdom of executive leadership, despite the arguments in favor of doing so, in the last analysis the issue of a person's life or death is of primary concern to *him*. So the individual American is entitled to hold opinions about his country's relations with the rest of the world; and so long as democracy has any vital meaning, his expression of those opinions will be a factor in shaping the destiny of the nation.

PART *Six*

PART Six

CHAPTER **22**

# *The Unrelenting Questions*

Prophecy is always difficult and often foolish. As Americans move into the latter part of the twentieth century, however, they might well take note of enduring issues of politics and government which have vexed the country in the past and seem certain to confront it in the future. Certain, that is, if the nation is not engulfed in Armageddon, to emerge, if at all, as a very different country from the one that we and our forebears have known and loved.

For the nation and the world, the exceedingly narrow footbridge across the Valley of the Shadow must be trod with infinite care. It is a long, long bridge. The issues of foreign policy, which in the final analysis are the issues of survival, will not quickly be melted away by the warm sun of peace. Since nuclear fission and fusion were added to the storehouse of men's achievements, the possibility of swift extinction has been present, and it always will be. Americans are forced to be aware of that fact, now and in future decades. They have to face the probability, too, that the temptation to use nuclear weapons will persist because, for a long

719

time to come, there will be hostile rivalry between some of the nations which possess them.

## THE NEW NATIONS

When in the preceding chapter we discussed the foreign policy of the United States, we quite understandably made frequent mention of the tense relations between this country and the Soviet Union. It would be a mistake, however, to assume unquestioningly that that tension, that clash of principle and power, will always be the chief source of the danger of war. In times not long past, other nations have dreamed of world dominion by armed conquest. If encouraged by the possession of lethal weapons, they could follow leaders, as they have before, down the nightmare path of world destruction. Since World War II, moreover, perhaps the greatest historical movement (one which we tend to overlook, in our preoccupation with the Soviet threat) has been the nationalist uprising of erstwhile colonial peoples, yellow and brown and black. This revolution, which has shaken much of Asia and Africa, is by no means completed. No man can foretell with certainty its ultimate effect upon the world's trade, political institutions, and hopes for peace. With assurance, however, we can assume that American foreign policy in the future will have to take the new nations and the needs and aspirations of their citizens into far more serious account than it has in the past.

## RED CHINA

Already it is obvious that one Asian country which, in terms of its internal organization and dealings with the West, might well be called a "new nation," is looming as one of the great powers in world affairs. That country is China. For nearly a century before 1949 China, though an independent nation, was weak and subservient. European nations carved out spheres of economic influence within it, the United States joining the parade with its "open door" policy announced in 1901. The "open door" was a gateway to foreign exploitation of Chinese resources, open equally to all comers: an agreement, in effect, among western nations to maintain equal rights, among themselves, in China, on the safe assumption that the Chinese would meekly accede to their demands for economic concessions. The great change came with the Chinese Communist revolution. That that revolution had close ideological ties with Moscow there can be no doubt, but Red China is no satellite of the Soviet Union. Furthermore, the Chinese revolution was more than an internal uprising. It was, in addition, a war to drive the "foreign devils" out—to wipe out the influence of the white western nations in the affairs of China.

In population, Red China is the largest nation in the world. In industrial and military strength it is comparatively small— now. But the tyrants who rule it have from the first expressed a determination to make it a great power, if possible the most fearsome power on the globe. The government in Peking, the legitimacy of which the United States so long has refused to recognize, commands vast human resources and can direct its people, willing or unwilling, to work with desperate fervor to arm their country. In 1963, perhaps imbued with confidence that they would soon possess nuclear weapons, the Red Chinese leaders defied the Kremlin. They denounced Khrushchev as being, as it were, "soft on capitalism." They scorned the doctrine of "coexistence" and the treaty to limit nuclear testing. It seems hard to imagine, but a powerful Red China bitterly hostile to both the United States and the Soviet Union could force those "cold war" foes to make common cause to restrain the Chinese and prevent a holocaust.

We face, then, an age of continuing crisis. It may be an age of increasing opportunity, too—opportunity to forge new links between peoples by the understanding treatment of their special problems. But there is, and will be always, the danger of war, and with it the demand for national security. That being so, a question that has arisen in the past will remain urgent in the future— whether we can achieve national security without sacrificing the basic liberties of individual Americans. As we saw in Chapter 6, it may be cogently argued that those liberties themselves are a source of national strength, but history proves that times of crisis give rise to forceful demands for the suppression of criticism and dissent. Those demands have been made before and they will be made again, confronting Americans with basic moral, constitutional, and political issues.

## EQUAL RIGHTS

Closely related to individual liberties is the matter of equal rights, regardless of race or color. Here again, as we all know, the issue is unresolved. It is not a regional issue. Negroes in the North have not been subjected to segregation laws, but they have been subjected to plenty of unofficial segregation in such matters as housing and employment. As they have increased in number in many northern cities, the problems and tensions created by discriminatory practices—particularly residential segregation—have increased as well. If the Supreme Court's interpretation of the Fourteenth Amendment made segregation a national issue in one sense, social habits and prejudices make it a national or at least a nation-wide issue in another. Patience with gradual change had worn thin by 1963, a year full of Negro marches, sit-ins, and demonstrations—a year, too, in which Congress considered far-reaching legislation and many cities began local efforts to promote equality of opportunity. The timetable was speeded up, but harmonious solution of the problems was still a long way off.

The issue of equal rights has a potential impact on American foreign policy. This country's future may be profoundly affected by the attitude toward the United States shown by the people of Africa and Asia—and that attitude may depend in good part on the actual status of the American Negro.

## THE COSTS OF GOVERNMENT

The critical political questions of the coming years are not all born of international conflict or the need for influence in the world. Now that "big government"—partly the fruit, of course, of wars and foreign tension—is here to stay, a basic question is how the costs of government are to be met and what the nation's wealth shall be used for. The national budget, relying heavily on personal and corporate income taxes and spending heavily for national defense, is only a part of the whole picture. State and local governments tax and spend, too. The individual's taxes, therefore, may include such levies as local retail or sales taxes, state and federal excise taxes (as on gasoline, for instance) and, bearing most heavily on many, federal income taxes and local

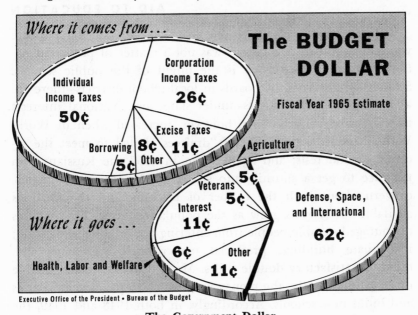

The Government Dollar

> The conflict between defense spending and budget balancing is made sharply apparent by the chart above. Note that more than 70¢ out of every dollar spent by the Federal government goes for meeting fixed obligations or for national security. (This includes a substantial part of the items for interest and for veterans.) The remaining amount—less than 30¢ out of every dollar—leaves little, if any, room for substantial economies; inevitably any really substantial budget cuts would require reducing the military or national security items.

property taxes. Why are these taxes imposed? They pay for things most of us want—armed power, welfare assistance, police protection, hospitals, schools.[1] The question is, how much do we want

---

1 Justice Holmes has been quoted as saying: "I like to pay taxes; with them, I buy civilization." When he died, Holmes left the residue of his estate simply to "The United States of America," with no strings attached.

the things that government provides? We cannot get them without paying for them.

## AID TO EDUCATION

This question leads us to one issue of the immediate future which for most of our history was not a matter of particular national concern. That issue is the plight of the public schools. Schools are governed by boards in local school districts—there are about 36,000 such districts—under state laws. National interests in the quality of schooling, however, increased when in World War II a startling number of "draftees" failed to meet the so-called mental tests, and again when in 1957 the Russians won the race to get a sputnik into space. In the intervening years, concern about both the caliber of teaching and the facilities available for schools grew as the population grew. Low salaries discouraged capable people from entering the teaching profession; inadequate buildings produced overcrowded classrooms and, often, unsatisfactory double shifts. Many districts seemed unable or unwilling to raise the money with which to pay decent salaries and build new schools. Accordingly, in both 1948 and 1949, the United States Senate passed bills for federal aid to education. These measures, however, died in the House, victims of a stalemate between those who wished to aid only public schools and those who wanted to leave each state free to spend some of the federal money to help parochial school students. Since that time, the school problem has grown worse, and seems certain to become still more acute.[2]

The issue of federal aid to education reminds us of some familiar basic questions and stirs thought about others. Involved in it is the conception of federalism—specifically, the question of how far, if at all, national government should go in paying the bills of state and local programs. Fear is expressed that aid for education, unlike aid for highways or hospitals or welfare pay-

---

[2] The National Defense Education Act of 1958, a congressional response to sputnik, provided a modest federal scholarship and loan program, but did not deal with the plight of the elementary and secondary schools.

ments, may open the door to uniform national indoctrination of the whole country's school children. Belittling that fear (and in the effort to refute it they can point to the history of the land-grant colleges) many educators reply that without federal aid, more and more millions of American children will be badly educated—at the very time when the country needs the utmost in capability and informed intelligence. In this instance as in others, however, the question of federalism can easily be transformed into a question concerning the nature of taxation. Schools rely preponderantly on local property taxes. In many localities, owners of real estate, feeling that their homes are already burdensomely taxed, have rejected further increases in the property levy. Federal aid would, in effect, relieve the pressure on the local property taxpayer and distribute some of the burden among the corporations and individuals who pay federal income taxes.

## OUR OWN CHOICES

Consideration of the federal principle and the incidence of taxation, however, should not obscure the more fundamental question, asked above: how much—how intensely—do we want the things that government provides? The householder wants better schools, but does he want them badly enough to give up his television or to get a cheaper car, so as to have the money to pay higher property taxes? In 1958 a widely read and stimulating book, J. K. Galbraith's *The Affluent Society*,[3] suggests that because of advertising pressure, a desire to conform, and an uncertainty about human values, most Americans bought many goods and services that they did not particularly want and certainly did not need. If some of these expenditures were transferred to the "public sector" of the economy—that is, if they were paid out in taxes—they could buy things which people really need, such as more playground space, more housing, and, especially, more schools. Such a suggestion at once raises the question of what kind of taxes should be levied (Professor Galbraith, perhaps a bit uneasily, proposed sales taxes) and the deeper philo-

---

3 J. K. Galbraith, *The Affluent Society* (Boston: Houghton Mifflin Co., 1958).

sophical problem of the extent to which the government should control the spending habits of the people. Indeed, perhaps the basic question is whether we are ready to cast aside completely the old laissez-faire doctrine—whether, that is, we are confident that in a "mixed economy," wherein government engages substantially in enterprise alongside of private corporations and individuals, economic growth and prosperity will flourish and personal liberties and rights will be protected.

When we ask to what extent the government should control the people, however, we should not forget that in the United States the government itself is a government *of* the people. And here we approach the final unrelenting question—the success or failure of the American political adventure. In this country our political institutions seem secure. There will be no attempt to disrupt this Union of, now, fifty states; we are "one nation, under God, indivisible." Modifications in the powers and procedures of the presidency, Congress, and Supreme Court there may be from time to time, but given the absence of a final cataclysm, the constitutional framework will remain much the same. Changes in the nature and use of the nation's less formal political machinery may count the most. Some aspects of its nature, to be sure—the two-party system, the habit of nominating local men for Congress, the balancing of a national ticket—have very nearly attained institutional status; swift and drastic changes in them are difficult and improbable. But institutional modifications there will be, and new policies devised. Their nature will depend largely on the way Americans put their political machinery to use and meet their personal political responsibilities. Conceivably the making of great decisions will be taken out of the people's hands, and effectively removed, even, from the grasp of their elected representatives. It is imaginable that the principle of popular government through majority rule, embraced so enthusiastically in America more than a century ago, will prove unsuited to the age of jets and rockets. Possibly the selfishness of politically powerful groups, oblivious of the national interest, will produce policies that do the country harm—and that this, in turn, will arouse a demand for limiting free organization for political action.

Yet democracy has survived those periods of war when Presidents made command decisions regardless of constitutional restraints. The American political system has adapted itself to great social and economic changes in the past. And the Republic has survived, too, the "pestilence of faction." The democratic principle assumes that all men and groups, selfish or not, will be heard, and that the country is served better by considering their claims than by labeling them as unfit to participate in the making of public decisions. It assumes, too, that a man serves his country well when, with knowledge of its governmental system and a sure grasp of the issues, he strives for what he believes to be the national interest by active participation in the political process.

# *Suggested Reading*

Anyone who has ever been a college undergraduate knows that the "selected bibliographies" included in textbooks are totally ignored at least nine-tenths of the time by at least nine-tenths of the students. In every large class, however, a few are eager to go beyond the assignments and read widely on their own, and many more wish occasionally to dig deeper into some particular field that interests them. But almost every student, under the pressure exerted by other courses and various aspects of college life, finds his time for "outside reading" severely restricted; and where library copies are constantly in use, financial limitations often restrict his capacity to buy books. The suggestions here are offered with these handicaps in mind. Many excellent books are omitted. In the selection of a comparative few, thought has been given to their readability, brevity, and low price. Not all of them, to be sure, are "easy reading" or short; if a subject is worth grasping, it is worth the student's intellectual effort required to grasp it. Nor are all of them inexpensive, but a considerable number can be obtained in paperback editions. (These are marked by asterisks; as time passes, perhaps several not now so marked will be published as paperbacks.) Each of them, however, is suggested in the belief that by reading it, the student will deepen or broaden his understanding of one or more aspects of American government and politics.

PART I

In the course of recorded history, the opinions of an ancient Greek, Aristotle, have probably had more continuous influence on political thought in the western world than those of any other man. Aristotle's ideas are the basis of much of a book full of interesting speculation about the nature of government, Leslie Lipson, *The Great Issues of Politics* (Englewood Cliffs, N.J.: Prentice-Hall, Inc., 2nd ed., 1960). Fundamental in the development of the national government in the United States were the ideas of John Locke, *Of Civil Government* * (Chicago: Henry Regnery Company—a Gateway book). Interesting analyses of government and politics, frequently comparing the American system with those of other countries, are presented in Austin Ranney, *The Governing of Men: An Introduction to Political Science* (New York: Henry Holt and Co., 1958), and Karl Loewenstein, *Political Power and the Governmental Process* (Chicago: University of Chicago Press, 1957). Helpful to the student of the American system may be Jack C. Plano and Milton Greenberg, *The American Political Dictionary* * (New York: Holt, Rinehart & Winston, 1962).

Aristotle's work was based on as "scientific" an observation of political behavior as the world knew for many centuries, but it was more the product of intuition, contemplation, and logical reasoning about what ought to be than of accurate measurement and reporting. In the sixteenth century the first great realistic essay on politics appeared, Niccolo Machiavelli, *The Prince* * (New York: Oxford University Press, 1935). It relates to the city-states of Renaissance Italy but is well worth reading today, for the ruthless portion of the power-hungry man's nature hasn't changed much. Machiavelli reported what he saw. Today, political scientists try to do this with the aid of the mathematical tools developed in our technological age. For introductions to their work, see Herbert J. Storing (ed.), *Essays on the Scientific Study of Politics* (New York: Harcourt, Brace & World, 1962), and Robert A. Dahl, *Modern Political Analysis* * (New York: Spectrum Books, 1963).

Democracy is the subject of a short, eloquent, and stirring appraisal by A. Powell Davies, *Man's Vast Future: A Definition of Democracy* (New York: Farrar, Straus & Young, 1951) and a series of thoughtful lectures by John H. Hallowell, *The Moral Foundation of Democracy* (Chicago: University of Chicago Press, 1954). A significant reinterpretation of the ideal of democratic government, insisting that Americans departed from it in their zest for equality and popular participation, is Walter Lippmann, *Essays in the Public Philosophy* (Boston: Little,

Brown & Co., 1955). A French observer challenges us to re-examine our taken-for-granted assumptions about the strength of our democratic system, in a highly readable book: R. L. Bruckberger, *Image of America* (New York: The Viking Press, 1961).

In considering the development of political ideas in the United States, a good starting point would be Carl Becker, *The Declaration of Independence* * (New York: Alfred A. Knopf, 1924—a Vintage book). The most famous analytical work by a foreign observer, reporting on the practice of American democracy long ago, is Alexis de Tocqueville, *Democracy in America* * (New York: Alfred A. Knopf, 1945—a Vintage book, 2 vols.). Alan P. Grimes, *American Political Thought* (New York: Henry Holt and Co., 1956) summarizes ideas that underlie the country's institutions; a new collection of readings on the same subject is Andrew M. Scott, *Political Thought in America* (New York: Rinehart & Co., 1959). A more controversial book, Louis Hartz, *The Liberal Tradition in America* (New York: Harcourt, Brace & Co., 1955), presents one scholar's vivid interpretation of its political history. The enduring influence of eighteenth-century political thought makes Merrill D. Peterson, *The Jefferson Image in the American Mind* (New York: Oxford University Press, 1960), timely and worth reading. Encompassing both is a distinguished book by a political historian, Richard Hofstadter, *The American Political Tradition* * (New York: Alfred A. Knopf, 1951—a Vintage book).

### Part II

*Making the Constitution.* Appropriate also in Part I because of its analysis of the political ideas of leaders in colonial America, Clinton Rossiter, *Seed-Time of the Republic* (New York: Harcourt, Brace & Co., 1953), is relevant here because of its consideration of colonial government, the shape of which influenced the Constitution-makers. Of more direct impact were the government and the difficulties of the states under the Articles of Confederation, the subject of Allan Nevins, *The American States During and After the Revolution 1775–1789* (New York: The Macmillan Co., 1927). On the nature and significance of the concept of constitutional government, see C. H. McIlwain, *Constitutionalism, Ancient and Modern* * (Ithaca, N.Y.: Cornell University Press, 1940—a Great Seal book). The members and proceedings of the Constitutional Convention of 1787 have been described and discussed in many books; among the best are Max Farrand, *The Fathers of the Constitution* (New Haven, Conn.: Yale University Press, 1921) ; Charles

Warren, *The Making of the Constitution* (Boston: Little, Brown & Co., 1928); and a more colorful account, Carl Van Doren, *The Great Rehearsal* (New York: The Viking Press, 1948). The idea that the Founding Fathers were spokesmen for the special interests of creditors was first popularized in a famous book, Charles A. Beard, *An Economic Interpretation of the Constitution of the United States* (New York: The Macmillan Co., 1913). Beard's analysis has been subjected to sharp, perhaps too sharp, attack by Robert E. Brown, *Charles Beard and the Constitution* (Princeton, N.J.: Princeton University Press, 1956) and a more balanced and fruitful reevaluation by Forrest McDonald, *We the People: The Economic Origins of the Constitution* (Chicago: University of Chicago Press, 1958). The famous series of articles, *The Federalist Papers,* which helped persuade Americans to adopt the Constitution, are printed in whole or in part in various volumes: one edition is edited by Beard, under the title *The Enduring Federalist* (Garden City, N.Y.: Doubleday & Co., 1948); another by R. H. Gabriel, *The Federalist* * (New York: Liberal Arts Press—an American Heritage Series book); another by H. S. Commager, *Selections from the Federalist* * (New York: Appleton-Century-Crofts—a Crofts Classic).

*Federalism.* The concept of federalism is meticulously defined by an Englishman, K. C. Wheare, *Federal Government* (London: Oxford University Press, 3rd ed., 1953) who finds that few countries besides the United States can be called truly federal states. See also a collection of able essays edited by an American scholar, Arthur W. Macmahon (ed.), *Federalism, Mature and Emergent* (Garden City, N.Y.: Doubleday & Co., 1955). The shift of much authority from the states to the national government in the present century, especially in the 1930's, gave rise to a number of books. Jane Perry Clark, *The Rise of a New Federalism* (New York: Columbia University Press, 1938) is a scholarly discussion of the change. Present-day arguments about the extent of federal power remind us of similar controversies a century ago; for the way the South sought to settle the question, see Charles Robert Lee, Jr., *The Confederate Constitution* (Chapel Hill, N.C.: University of North Carolina Press, 1963). The best book on the modern working of the federal system is William Anderson, *The Nation and the States* (Minneapolis, Minn.: University of Minnesota Press, 1955).

*Separation of Powers.* With the swiftness of modern transport and communication has come increasing uneasiness about a system whose built-in "checks" are intended to be restraints on quick, national action, and the result has been a number of recent books criticizing the system. Of these, the most widely read is James M. Burns, *The Deadlock of*

*Democracy* (Englewood Cliffs, N.J.: Prentice-Hall, 1963). See also Rowland Egger and Joseph P. Harris, *The President and Congress* * (New York: McGraw-Hill Book Co., 1963); Robert A. Wallace, *Congressional Control of Federal Spending* (Detroit: Wayne State University Press, 1960); and Stephen Horn, *The Cabinet and Congress* (New York: Columbia University Press, 1960).

*Judicial Review.* The Supreme Court's role of "umpire of federalism" is explored in John R. Schmidhauser, *The Supreme Court as Final Arbiter in Federal-State Relations* (Chapel Hill, N.C.: University of North Carolina Press, 1958). Judicial review as a whole, and its impact on our governmental system, is the subject of a great many good books, though some are "dated" in the sense that they argue about issues that were "hot" when they were written: still, such issues have a way of recurring. Thus Charles Warren, *The Making of the Constitution, supra,* argues interestingly and convincingly that the framers intended that the Supreme Court should have authority to invalidate acts of Congress, and Robert K. Carr, *The Supreme Court and Judicial Review* (New York: Rinehart & Co., 1942) suggests in a vigorous, readable essay that the justices abused this power. Carl B. Swisher, *American Constitutional Development* (Boston: Houghton Mifflin Co., 2nd ed., 1954) is a good historical account of the adaptation of the Constitution to changing conditions through judicial interpretation. A concise little book, E. S. Corwin and Jack W. Peltason, *Understanding the Constitution* (New York: Henry Holt and Co., rev. ed., 1958) helps the student to achieve the goal indicated in its title. Concise and stimulating is Charles L. Black, *Perspectives on Constitutional Law* * (Englewood Cliffs, N.J.: Prentice-Hall, 1963), and worth perusing is a longer work that emphasizes the inescapable political role of the Court, Loren P. Beth, *Politics, the Constitution, and the Supreme Court* (New York: Harper & Row, 1962). (Other books pertaining to the Supreme Court will be suggested under the heading of Part IV.)

*Freedom and Justice.* The literature of liberty is so extensive that it is hard to pick and choose. Perhaps the best starting point would be a nineteenth century classic, John Stuart Mill, *On Liberty* * (Chicago, Ill.: Henry Regnery Co.—a Gateway book) or a compilation of essays edited by Howard Mumford Jones, *Primer of Intellectual Freedom* (Cambridge, Mass.: Harvard University Press, 1949). On the present question of reconciling the principle of individual freedom with the threat of international communism, the basic issue is concisely presented by Harold W. Chase, *Security and Liberty* * (New York: Random House, 1955); see also Thomas I. Cook, *Democratic Rights versus*

*Communist Activity* * (New York: Random House, 1954). Readers of John C. Miller, *Crisis in Freedom* (Boston: Little, Brown & Co., 1951), a lively, dramatic account of the period of the Alien and Sedition laws, may note an implied comparison between those days of fear of "Jacobins" and the more recent alarm about Communists. Well worth reading is a soberly brilliant book on liberty as a source of national greatness, Alan Barth, *The Loyalty of Free Men* * (New York: The Viking Press, 1951—a Vintage book). A contrasting view, that to deserve freedom men must first be virtuous, is presented by Walter Berns, *Freedom, Virtue, and the First Amendment* (Baton Rouge, La.: Louisiana State University Press, 1957).

A long but basic work on the meaning of the First Amendment is Zechariah Chafee, *Free Speech in the United States* (Cambridge, Mass.: Harvard University Press, 1948). Leonard W. Levy, *Legacy of Suppression* (Cambridge, Mass.: Harvard University Press, 1961), however, presents historical evidence indicating that the framers of the First Amendment thought of it as a less sweeping guarantee of individual liberty than some "libertarians" assume it to be. On religious liberty and the separation of church and state, see Philip B. Kurland, *Religion and the Law* (Chicago: The Aldine Press, 1962), and Loren P. Beth, *The American Theory of Church and State* (Gainesville, Fla.: University of Florida Press, 1958). The right "peaceably to assemble and petition for a redress of grievances" is basic to the right of free expression: see David B. Fellman, *The Constitutional Right of Association* (Chicago: University of Chicago Press, 1963).

On procedural safeguards, two very different works are recommended: a brief essay on the privilege against self-incrimination, Erwin Griswold, *The Fifth Amendment Today* * (Cambridge, Mass.: Harvard University Press, 1955) and a thorough analysis of the whole field, David Fellman, *The Defendant's Rights* (New York: Rinehart & Co., 1958). Some of the English beginnings of the concept of due process are stirringly told in the biography of Lord Coke—Catherine Drinker Bowen, *The Lion and the Throne* (Boston: Little, Brown & Co., 1957), the reading of which is an enriching experience.

**Equal Rights.** The question of equality is dealt with trenchantly in Henry A. Myers, *Are Men Equal?* * (Ithaca, N.Y.: Cornell University Press, 1945—a Great Seal book), and American willingness to open the country's gates to all alike—and its more recent unwillingness to do so— is the subject of a series of essays collected in Benjamin M. Ziegler (ed.), *Immigration: An American Dilemma* (Boston: D. C. Heath & Co., 1953). On the specific question of the Negro's rights, well worth reading are C. Vann Woodward, *The Strange Career of Jim Crow* * (New York: Oxford University Press, 1957—a Galaxy book) and Arnold Rose, *The Negro in America* * (Boston: The Beacon Press, 1948), the latter being the authorized condensation of Gunnar Myrdal's great sociological study of the Negro problem, *An American Dilemma* (New York: Harper & Brothers, 1944). Group action aimed at victory through litigation is described by Clement Vose, *Caucasians Only: The Supreme Court, the NAACP, and the Restrictive Covenant Cases* (Berkeley, Cal.: University of California Press, 1959). Since 1954, many authors have analyzed various aspects of the reaction to the Supreme Court's desegregration decision of that year: see, for instance, John Bartlow Martin, *The Deep South Says "Never"* * (New York: Ballantine Books, 1957); Brooks Hays, *A Southern Moderate Speaks* (Chapel Hill, N.C.: University of North Carolina Press, 1959); and Albert P. Blaustein and Clarence C. Ferguson, Jr., *Desegregation and the Law* (New York: Alfred A. Knopf, 1957). An interesting study of the federal judges who were given the responsibility of implementing the decision "with all deliberate speed" is J. W. Peltason, *58 Lonely Men* (New York: Holt, Rinehart & Winston, 1961). Specific instances of tension are the subject of Daisy Bates, *The Long Shadow of Little Rock* (New York: David McKay Co., 1963), who writes from the viewpoint of an NAACP leader, and Benjamin Muse, *Virginia's Massive Resistance* (Bloomington, Ind.: Indiana University Press, 1961). The most disturbing book about the whole problem is James Baldwin, *The Fire Next Time* (New York: The Dial Press, 1963).

## PART III

***Pressure Groups.*** The theory of the "group basis of politics" was given its first modern statement by Arthur F. Bentley, *The Process of Government* (Chicago: University of Chicago Press, 1908) and has been further expounded by David B. Truman, *The Governmental Process* (New York: Alfred A. Knopf, 1951). Neither of these books is easy reading, but both are significant. Donald C. Blaisdell, *American Democracy Under Pressure* (New York: The Ronald Press, 1957) weaves theory and practice together in a vigorous account of interest groups at work. Good studies of particular interests and pressure groups include the following: Oscar Handlin, *Race and Nationality in American Life* * (Boston: Little, Brown & Co., 1957; Garden City, N.Y.: Doubleday & Co., 1955—an Anchor book); Peter Odegard, *Pressure Politics: The Story of the Anti-Saloon League* (New York: Columbia University

Press, 1928); Clifton Brock, *The Americans For Democratic Action* (Washington, D.C.: Public Affairs Press, 1962); and Armin Rappaport, *The Navy League of the United States* (Detroit: Wayne State University Press, 1962).

*Parties.* What American political parties should be has long been a subject of hot scholarly debate. On the side of having them stand for clearly defined opposing programs are E. E. Schattschneider, *Party Government* (New York: Rinehart & Co., 1942), and *Toward a Two-Party System* (New York: Rinehart & Co., 1950), a report of the American Political Science Association's committee on political parties, headed, incidentally, by Professor Schattschneider. On the same side of the issue are Stephen K. Bailey, *The Condition of Our National Parties* * (New York: The Fund for the Republic, 1959), a lively, imaginative, and comparatively practicable proposal for change, and Austin Ranney, *The Doctrine of Responsible Party Government* * (Urbana, Ill.: University of Illinois Press, 1962). Pendleton Herring, *The Politics of Democracy* (New York: W. W. Norton & Co., 1940) states the case for keeping each party "pluralistic" rather than "programmatic," suggesting that a party's central function is that of playing the "broker's" role between interests and government.

Political history in terms of party conflict is readably recounted by W. E. Binkley, *American Political Parties: Their Natural History* (New York: Alfred A. Knopf, 3rd ed., 1958). The beginning of the party system in the United States is skillfully presented by William Nisbet Chambers, *Political Parties in a New Nation* (New York: Oxford University Press, 1963). Amos R. E. Pinchot, *History of the Progressive Party 1912-1916* (New York: New York University Press, 1958) is an "inside story" of the Bull Moose movement, and the turgid history of a small group that, among other things, played the role of a political party is well told by Irving Howe and Lewis Coser, *The American Communist Party: A Critical History* * (Boston: The Beacon Press, 1958). Not third-party, but essentially one-party politics in a whole region is the subject of V. O. Key, *Southern Politics in State and Nation* (New York: Alfred A. Knopf, 1949), a detailed analysis of political structure, attitudes, and operations in the southern states. When that book was written, "southern politics" was almost wholly "white politics"; today, both South and North, the Negro vote is of importance, and so James Q. Wilson, *Negro Politics* (Glencoe, Ill.: Free Press, 1960) is a significant book.

Many years ago, the author of the present book found reading Frank Kent, *The Great Game of Politics* * (Garden City, N.Y.: Doubleday &

Co., 1923—an Economica book published by Smith, Keynes & Marshall, Buffalo, N.Y.) both a fascinating and a chilling experience for a politically unsophisticated undergraduate who had not realized the extent that money and local party organizations count in politics. The corruption of city machines half a century and more ago, still not wholly irrelevant, was colorfully described by Lincoln Steffens, *The Shame of the Cities* * (New York: McClure, Phillips Co., 1904—an American Century Series book published by Sagamore Press, Inc., N.Y.). Modern local party organization is described in James Q. Wilson, *The Amateur Democrats* (Chicago: University of Chicago Press, 1962). For a study of national party organization, see Hugh A. Bone, *Party Committees and National Politics* (Seattle, Wash.: University of Washington Press, 1958). The Eagleton Foundation's Series of Case Studies in Practical Politics (published in New York by Holt, Rinehart & Winston, beginning in 1958) all of them brief and down to earth, include Philip S. Wilder, Jr., *The Republican National Committee Chairman in the 1958 Campaign* * and Francis Carney, *The Rise of the Democratic Clubs in California.* *

*Nominations and Elections.* The Eagleton Foundation's Series also contains studies of the nominating process: Rhoten Smith and Clarence Hein, *Republican Primary Fight: A Study in Factionalism,* * and Joel Sterns, *Selecting a Senatorial Candidate,* * the first concerning Kansas and the second New Jersey during the 1958 congressional campaign. For an account of the real beginning of the primary movement, see A. F. Lovejoy, *La Follette and the Establishment of the Direct Primary in Wisconsin, 1890-1904* (New Haven, Conn.: Yale University Press, 1941). Presidential nominations are the subject of Paul Tillett, *Inside Politics: The National Conventions* * (Dobbs Ferry, N.Y.: Oceana Publications, 1962); and the struggles to win them, as well as the post-convention campaign, are brilliantly recounted in Theodore H. White, *The Making of the President, 1960* (New York: Atheneum Publishers, 1961). The much-debated question of the machinery for electing a President is thoughtfully considered in Lucius Wilmerding, *The Electoral College* (New Brunswick, N.J.: Rutgers University Press, 1958). Campaigns cost money: a good short account of their financing is J. B. Shannon, *Money and Politics* * (New York: Random House, 1959), and a more substantial one is Alexander Heard, *The Costs of Democracy* (Chapel Hill, N.C.: University of North Carolina Press, 1960). An Eagleton study of the effort of the American Heritage Foundation to persuade everyone to contribute a small amount to the party of his choice is John W. Crawford, *Dollars for Democracy.* * Stanley Kelley,

Jr., *Professional Public Relations and Political Power* (Baltimore, Md.: Johns Hopkins University Press, 1956) is a startling, fascinating account of high-pressure "selling" of issues and candidates.

Few politicians, if any, have more interestingly and thoughtfully described what it is like to run for office than Stimson Bullitt, *To Be a Politician* (Garden City, N.Y.: Doubleday & Co., 1959). Robert E. Merriam and Rachel M. Goetz, *Going Into Politics* (New York: Harper & Brothers, 1957) is one of several respectable essays on the same subject. Some writers of fiction have dealt effectively with the general field of politics and individual successful politicians: see Edwin O'Connor, *The Last Hurrah* * (Boston: Little, Brown & Co., 1956—a Bantam book), which is based on characters in Boston, and Robert Penn Warren, *All the King's Men* * (New York: Grosset & Dunlap, Inc., 1946—a Bantam book), laid in Louisiana.

As is obvious from the text, the key book on voting behavior (though others will undoubtedly be soon appearing) is Angus Campbell and others, *The American Voter* (New York: John Wiley & Sons, 1960); but a shorter and very wise evaluation of poll-taking as a tool for understanding voting behavior is V. O. Key, Jr., *Public Opinion and American Democracy* (New York: Alfred A. Knopf, 1962). A surprising historical analysis of the behavior of the voters in 1928 (when, most people assumed, Alfred E. Smith was badly defeated because he was a Catholic) is Ruth C. Silva, *Rum, Religion, and Votes: 1928 Reexamined* (University Park, Pa.: Pennsylvania State University Press, 1962). A leading exponent of the "behavioral" approach to the study of politics presents his case in Heinz Eulau, *The Behavioral Persuasion in Politics* * (New York: Random House, 1963). An interesting study of why some people "switched" to the Republican ticket in 1952 and others didn't is Lawrence P. Fuchs, *The Political Behavior of American Jews* (Glencoe, Ill.: Free Press, 1956).

Covering the whole area discussed in Part III is a book of well-selected, almost invariably interesting essays by various authors, Henry A. Turner (ed.), *Politics in America* * (New York: McGraw-Hill Book Co., 1956). And for more than half a century the mellow wisdom of an English writer has contributed so much to the understanding of politics in a democracy, on both sides of the Atlantic, that it has been reprinted again and again: Graham Wallas, *Human Nature in Politics* * (Lincoln, Neb.: University of Nebraska Press, 1962; originally published in 1908).

## PART IV

**Congress.** Bertram M. Gross, *The Legislative Struggle* (New York: McGraw-Hill Book Co., 1953) is a knowledgeable book developing the idea that Congress is the vortex of whirling intergroup conflict. A pioneering, partly mathematical analysis of the party structure in Congress is David B. Truman, *The Congressional Party* (New York: John Wiley & Sons, 1959). Both intergroup strife and party influence are considered in James A. Robinson, *Congress and Foreign Policy-Making* (Homewood, Ill.: The Dorsey Press, 1962). That group or partisan advantage is often an underlying aim of Congressional investigations is a major theme of the outstanding book on investigating committees, Telford Taylor, *Grand Inquest* (New York: Simon and Schuster, 1955).

A personalized and mostly admiring description of the House of Representatives is furnished by Neil Macneil, *Forge of Democracy* (New York: David McKay Co., 1963); in contrast, one of the best critical books about it—not new, but not outdated—is James M. Burns, *Congress on Trial* (New York: Harper & Brothers, 1949). A balanced, critical appraisal of the Senate is Donald R. Matthews, *United States Senators and Their World* (Chapel Hill, N.C.: University of North Carolina Press, 1960). Recently, some Senators, feeling frozen out of positions of real influence in the Senate and believing that its structure and procedure badly need to be reformed, have taken their case to the public: Joseph S. Clark and others, *The Senate Establishment* * (New York: Hill & Wang, 1963). The standard scholarly work on the Senate's power to approve or reject presidential nominations for important positions is Joseph P. Harris, *The Advice and Consent of the Senate* (Berkeley, Cal.: University of California Press, 1953). One significant contest over such confirmation is described in an Eagleton Foundation case study: James N. Rosenau, *The Nomination of Chip Bohlen.**

Good studies of Congress and congressmen doing their job are Daniel A. Berman, *A Bill Becomes a Law: The Civil Rights Act of 1960* (New York: The Macmillan Co., 1962), and Stephen K. Bailey and Howard D. Samuel, *Congress at Work* (New York: Henry Holt & Co., 1952). For the real flavor of congressional life, the writings of congressmen themselves are best: see especially Jerry Voorhis, *Confessions of a Congressman* (Garden City, N.Y.: Doubleday & Co., 1947); the letters of the late Representative Clem Miller of California in John W. Baker (ed.), *Member of the House* (New York: Charles Scribner's Sons, 1962); and the vivid introduction in John F. Kennedy, *Profiles in Courage* * (New

York: Harper & Brothers—a Pocket book).

*The Presidency.* Outstanding as a clear, short, lively analysis of the President's many functions is Clinton Rossiter, *The American Presidency* * (New York: Harcourt, Brace & Co., 1956). Harold J. Laski, *The American Presidency* * (New York: Harper & Brothers, 1940—a Universal Library book), written near the end of the New Deal period, was a trail-blazing justification of expanded presidential power; its ideas are still provocative. Excellent books which trace the historical development of the office are George Fort Milton, *The Use of Presidential Power* (Boston: Little, Brown & Co., 1944) and Wilfred E. Binkley, *The Man in the White House* (Baltimore, Md.: Johns Hopkins University Press, 1958). On the office of Vice-President, see Irving G. Williams, *The American Vice-Presidency: New Look* * (New York: Random House, 1954).

Richard F. Fenno, Jr., *The President's Cabinet* (Cambridge, Mass.: Harvard University Press, 1959) is one of the very few published studies of the cabinet as an institution, and the only recent one. The establishment of the executive office of the President is one of the subjects covered in the second volume of the autobiography of the remarkable man who headed the committee which proposed it, Louis Brownlow, *A Passion for Anonymity* (Chicago: University of Chicago Press, 1958). See also Barry D. Karl, *Executive Reorganization and Reform in the New Deal* (Cambridge, Mass.: Harvard University Press, 1963).

Much can be learned about the presidency by perusing the biographies and memoirs of the men who have held the office. A list of such books would be too long to include here. Without any desire to exclude others, books about two "strong" Presidents, one from each party, will be mentioned: Henry F. Pringle, *Theodore Roosevelt* * (New York: Harcourt, Brace & Co.—a Harvest book) and James M. Burns, *Roosevelt, the Lion and the Fox* * (New York: Harcourt, Brace & Co., 1956). "Inside" stories of President Eisenhower's administration have been told by two of his associates: Emmett J. Hughes, *The Ordeal of Power* (New York: Atheneum Publishers, 1963), and Sherman Adams, *First Hand Report* (New York: Harper & Brothers, 1961). When President Kennedy succeeded Eisenhower, he read and praised Richard E. Neustadt, *Presidential Power—The Politics of Leadership* (New York: John Wiley & Sons, 1960). Mr. Kennedy's special counsel wrote thoughtfully of his chief's job, in Theodore C. Sorensen, *Decision-Making in the White House* (New York: Columbia University Press, 1963). For a good glimpse of a President feeling the weight of responsibility, read an exciting novel: Fletcher Knebel and Charles W. Bailey,

*Seven Days in May* (New York: Harper & Row, 1962).

**The Executive Branch.** Administrative organization and reorganization are not subjects conducive to light summer reading. Important to any student of public administration, however, are two fairly recent books (older ones are regretfully omitted): Fritz Morstein Marx, *The Administrative State* (Chicago: University of Chicago Press, 1957) and Emmette S. Redford, *Ideal and Practice in Public Administration* (University, Ala.: University of Alabama Press, 1958). Two books present the problems of the first Hoover Commission in a readable and interesting fashion: Bradley D. Nash and Cornelius Lynde, *A Hook in Leviathan* (New York: The Macmillan Co., 1950) and Herbert Emmerich, *Essays on Federal Reorganization* (University, Ala.: University of Alabama Press, 1950). J. Roland Pennock, *Administration and the Rule of Law* (New York: Rinehart & Co., 1941), though not new, is still a highly useful study of critical factors in the development of quasi-legislative and quasi-judicial functions in executive agencies. J. Leiper Freeman, *The Political Process: Executive Bureau-Legislative Committee Relations* * (New York: Random House, 1955) is a short study of the subject indicated in its title. The most authoritative work on regulatory commissions is Henry J. Friendly, *The Federal Administrative Agencies* (Cambridge, Mass.: Harvard University Press, 1962).

Considering federal personnel, Paul P. Van Riper, *History of the United States Civil Service* (Evanston, Ill.: Row, Peterson and Co., 1958) deals with the development of a competitive merit system, while the role of the non-career official, drawn to service in Washington for a brief period, is the central subject of Marver H. Bernstein, *The Job of the Federal Executive* (Washington, D.C.: The Brookings Institution, 1958). A thorough, competent exposition of personnel administration is Felix A. Nigro, *Public Personnel Administration* (New York: Henry Holt and Co., 1959). Since 1947, the imposition of uncertain standards of loyalty and security on government employees has stirred numerous writers, most of them highly critical; among good recent studies of the subject are the Association of the Bar of the City of New York, *Report of the Special Committee on the Federal Loyalty-Security Program* (New York: Dodd, Mead & Co., 1956) and Ralph S. Brown, *Loyalty and Security: Employment Tests in the United States* (New Haven, Conn.: Yale University Press, 1958). For accurate, absorbing and sometimes shocking accounts of actual incidents, see Adam Yarmolinsky (ed.), *Case Studies in Personnel Security* * (Washington, D.C.: Bureau of National Affairs, Inc., 1955).

**Law and the Courts.** Perhaps because law is a profession requiring years of special training, comparatively few really good books about it have been written for the layman. Attempts to write such books have often either disastrously oversimplified or have dealt with concepts beyond the reader's ready comprehension. However, some of these worthy efforts have had better results. Recommended are the following, on the general nature of law and the judicial process (the list could be longer and omits some "classics"): Max Radin, *The Law and You* \* (New York: New American Library—a Mentor book), Charles P. Curtis, *It's Your Law* (Cambridge, Mass.: Harvard University Press,. 1954), and Henry J. Abraham, *The Judicial Process* (New York: Oxford University Press, 1962); also a series of startlingly witty lectures to embryo law students, Karl N. Llewellyn, *The Bramble Bush* (New York: Columbia University Law School, 1930, rev. ed., 1951), and two brilliant, iconoclastic books by a lawyer who became a federal judge, Jerome Frank, *Law and the Modern Mind* (New York: Brentano's, Inc., 1930) and *Courts on Trial* (Princeton, N.J.: Princeton University Press, 1950). Judge Frank raised serious questions about the efficacy of the adversary process and the jury system: these questions (among other things) were implicitly raised again by a bestselling novel, Robert Traver, *Anatomy of a Murder* \* (New York: St. Martin's Press, 1958— a Dell book). One of the few other good American novels about law is James Gould Cozzens, *The Just and the Unjust* (New York: Harcourt, Brace & Co., 1942).

The interrelationships of politics and law—especially constitutional law—have increasingly interested political scientists. See Victor G. Rosenblum, *Law As a Political Instrument* \* (New York: Random House, 1955), Jack W. Peltason, *Federal Courts in the Political Process* \* (New York: Random House, 1955), and Walter F. Murphy and C. Herman Pritchett, *Courts, Judges, and Politics* (New York: Random House, 1961).

The Supreme Court of the United States is the subject of Robert G. McCloskey, *The American Supreme Court* (Chicago: University of Chicago Press, 1960), and a set of short and pithy lectures by a late Justice, Robert H. Jackson, *The Supreme Court in the American System of Government* (Cambridge, Mass.: Harvard University Press, 1955). The continuing division within the Court in the 1950's and early 1960's is expertly explained by Wallace Mendelson, *Justices Black and Frankfurter: Conflict in the Court* (Chicago: University of Chicago Press, 1961). Among many excellent biographies of, or books about, Supreme Court Justices, only a few can be mentioned here: David B. Loth, *Chief Justice: John Marshall and the Growth of the Republic*

(New York: W. W. Norton & Co., 1949); Max Lerner, *The Mind and Faith of Mr. Justice Holmes* (Boston: Little, Brown & Co., 1943); Alpheus T. Mason, *Brandeis: A Free Man's Life* (New York: The Viking Press, 1946); Harlan Phillips (ed.), *Felix Frankfurter Reminisces* (New York: Reynal & Co., 1960); H. M. Christman (ed.), *The Public Papers of Chief Justice Earl Warren* (New York: Simon & Schuster, 1959).

PART V

Like a helicopter dusting crops, this part sweeps over so many fields (though hovering here and there) that the pruning of a list of good relevant reading must be done ruthlessly and with a high degree of subjectivity on the part of the pruner. To keep the list to manageable size he must leave out many enlightening and readable works; and (perhaps fortunately) he does not even have room to explain just why he selects the particular books suggested here rather than others.

*Government and the Economy.* Sidney B. Fine, *Laissez Faire and the General Welfare State* (Ann Arbor, Mich.: University of Michigan Press, 1956) provides a fine summary of nineteenth century American attitudes, beliefs which were prevalent until the Great Depression. The revolutionary change in the early 1930's is described in a superb history, Arthur M. Schlesinger, Jr., *The Coming of the New Deal* (Boston: Houghton Mifflin Co., 1959), which tells the story of the beginnings of many of the programs discussed in this part of your text. The lives and thoughts of some leading spokesmen of the earlier period are well sketched by Robert G. McCloskey, *American Conservatism in the Age of Enterprise* (Cambridge, Mass.: Harvard University Press, 1951). The concentration of economic power under a largely laissez-faire system was brought out in 1932 in a very influential book, Adolph A. Berle, Jr., and Gardiner C. Means, *The Modern Corporation and Private Property* (New York: The Macmillan Co., 1932, 2nd ed., 1940). When this book appeared the country was already in the throes of disillusion, which had begun when the bottom fell out of the stock market in October 1929—an event vivaciously described by J. K. Galbraith, *The Great Crash* (Boston: Houghton Mifflin Co., 1955). With respect to the present nature of the economy, Adolph A. Berle, Jr., *Power Without Property* (New York: Harcourt, Brace, and Co., 1959) is a brief and penetrating study of the role of the vast corporation in American life.

For deeper analyses of various aspects of monetary and fiscal policy see Charles C. Abbott, *The Federal Debt* (New York: The Twentieth Century Fund, 1953) and Paul J. Strayer, *Fiscal Policy and Politics* (New York: Harper & Brothers, 1958). Walter Adams and Horace M. Gray, *Monopoly in America* (New York: The Macmillan Co., 1955), while hardly objective in tone, is a short, challenging book filled with examples of the stimulation of monopoly by government. An excellent history of labor unions in America, up through World War II, is Foster Rhea Dulles, *Labor in America* (New York: Thomas Y. Crowell Co., 1949); a more detailed account of part of that period is contained in Marc Karson, *American Labor Unions and Politics, 1900-1918* (Carbondale, Ill.: Southern Illinois University Press, 1958). The present condition of the labor movement is analyzed and its problems succinctly stated in a refreshingly dispassionate book by a British economist, B. C. Roberts, *Unions in America* * (Princeton, N.J.: Industrial Relations Section, Princeton University, 1959). The shift from ideological struggle to equal bargaining by big and powerful bargainers, and the effect that this change has had on the leadership of unions, is described by Richard A. Lester, *As Unions Mature* (Princeton, N.J.: Princeton University Press, 1958). Though none of the foregoing books about labor is complex or dull, anyone in search of lighter reading on the subject might enjoy Richard A. Bissell, *Seven and a Half Cents* (Boston: Little, Brown & Co., 1953), a novel from which was adapted the successful musical comedy, *Pajama Game.*

A very different kind of novel, Frank Norris, *The Octopus* * (Garden City, N.Y.: Doubleday & Co., 1901—a Bantam book) might serve as an interesting introduction to the farm problem, especially if followed by that indignant author's second volume in his planned but never-finished "trilogy of the wheat," *The Pit* * (Garden City, N.Y.: Doubleday & Co., 1903—a Bantam book). The first of these stories, especially, gives the reader an idea of why farmers demanded regulation of railroad rates. As to more recent agricultural policies, one aspect is discussed by a leading agricultural economist in a book with an irritable title, John D. Black, *Parity, Parity, Parity* (Cambridge, Mass.: Harvard Committee on Research in the Social Sciences, 1942); two more recent works, both of them short, clear, and to the point, are Troy J. Cauley, *Agriculture in an Industrial Economy* (New York: Bookman Associates, 1956) and Willard W. Cochrane, *Farm Prices* (Minneapolis, Minn.: University of Minnesota Press, 1958).

This chapter on economic policies owes much to a thorough and informative volume, Merle Fainsod, Lincoln Gordon, and Joseph C. Palamountain, Jr., *Government and the American Economy* (New

York: W. W. Norton & Co., Inc., 1959). A shorter work, covering several subjects dealt with in this part of your text, is Jack W. Peltason and James M. Burns, eds., *Functions and Policies of American Government* (Englewood Cliffs, N.J.: Prentice-Hall, Inc., 1958).

*Government and the Protection of the Individual.* When we think of law enforcement we think of the FBI. Donald F. Whitehead, *The FBI Story* (New York: Random House, 1956) is a highly laudatory account of that organization; Max Lowenthal, *The Federal Bureau of Investigation* (New York: Sloane Associates, 1952) a sharply critical one. But there are other "federal policemen" on the job: in the Post Office Department's Inspection Service, for instance—see John N. Makris, *The Silent Investigators* (New York: E. P. Dutton & Co., 1957) and in the Treasury—see Andrew Tully, *Treasury Agent: The Inside Story* (New York: Simon & Schuster, 1958). The drive to free the food and drug industries, and their products, from poisonous elements is the subject of Oscar E. Anderson, Jr., *The Health of a Nation: Harvey W. Wiley and the Fight for Pure Food* (Chicago: University of Chicago Press, published for the University of Cincinnati, 1958), and James H. Young, *The Toadstool Millionaires* (Princeton, N.J.: Princeton University Press, 1961). The legislative struggle for a federal minimum wage law is described in Burns' *Congress on Trial*, mentioned above; an Eagleton Foundation Series study, Gus Tyler, *Raising the Minimum Wage,*\* deals with the recent efforts to amend it. For background on welfare programs generally, see Arthur M. Schlesinger, Jr., *The Crisis of the Old Order* (Boston: Houghton Mifflin Co., 1957) which includes a description of the economic plight of millions of people in 1930-1933. Frances Perkins, *The Roosevelt I Knew* (New York: The Viking Press, 1946) contains a first-hand account of the inauguration of federal relief and social security policies.

A short yet detailed story of the enactment of one major law is told by a man who helped to shape it: Edwin E. Witte, *The Development of the Social Security Act* (Madison, Wis.: University of Wisconsin Press, 1962). Eveline Burns, *Social Security and Public Policy* (New York: McGraw-Hill Book Co., 1956), deals with policy problems in the field of welfare and social insurance. One of those problems seems sure to reflect the increase in longevity: as you wonder about the long future, look at John J. Corson and J. W. McConnell, *Economic Needs of Older People* (New York: The Twentieth Century Fund, 1956). Another may concern medical care and the cost of paying for it, questions considered in Herman M. Somers and Anne R. Somers, *Doctors, Patients, and Health Insurance* (Washington, D.C.: The Brookings Institution, 1961). As population increases, the need for adequate housing intensifies. The continuing housing problem is the subject of Edward C. Banfield and Morton Grodzins, *Government and Housing in Metropolitan Areas* (New York: McGraw-Hill Book Co., 1958), and one extremely troublesome aspect of it is emphasized in a report of the Commission on Race and Housing, *Where Shall We Live?* * (Berkeley, Cal.: University of California Press, 1958).

**Government and the Country's Resources.** For a good over-all introduction, see Norman C. Wengert, *Natural Resources and the Political Struggle* (New York: Random House, 1961). Various aspects of federal conservation policies are well described in Arthur H. Carhart, *The National Forests* (New York: Alfred A. Knopf, 1959); Freeman Tilden, *The National Parks* (New York: Alfred A. Knopf, 1958); Marion Clawson and Burnell Held, *The Federal Lands: Their Use and Management* (Baltimore, Md.: Johns Hopkins University Press, 1957); Howard W. Ottoson (ed.), *Land Use Policy and Problems in the United States* (Lincoln, Neb.: University of Nebraska Press, 1963); and Philip O. Foss, *Politics and Grass: The Administration of Grazing in the Public Domain* (Seattle, Wash.: University of Washington Press, 1960). If trees and flowers and birds are included as "natural resources," as indeed they should be, then it is appropriate to mention here an alarming and controversial book, about the impact of insecticides, including the government's spraying programs: Rachel Carson, *Silent Spring* (Boston: Houghton Mifflin Co., 1962). The affirmative side of the development of an important resource, oil, is pictured in Ruth Sheldon Knowles, *The Greatest Gamblers: The Epic of American Oil Exploration* (New York: McGraw-Hill Book Co., 1959); the seamy side, oil as a focus of political corruption, in M. R. Werner and John Starr, *Teapot Dome* (New York: The Viking Press, 1959). The politics of water has been the subject of case studies of a government agency (the Army Engineers) acting as a highly effective pressure group: Arthur A. Maass, *Muddy Waters: The Army Engineers and the Nation's Rivers* (Cambridge, Mass.: Harvard University Press, 1951) and of governmental efforts to develop the potential resources of the Connecticut River: William Leuchtenberg, *Flood Control Politics* (Cambridge, Mass.: Harvard University Press, 1953). Vincent Ostrom, *Water and Politics* (Los Angeles: The Haynes Foundation, 1953), deals chiefly with a city's problems, but those were inevitably related to the Colorado River Compact. The TVA has been the subject of numerous books; among the best (though, of course, enthusiastically favorable) is one by an early chairman of the Authority, David E. Lilienthal, *TVA: Democracy* *on the March* \* (New York: Pocket Books, Inc., 1944). More dispassionate is C. H. Pritchett, *The Tennessee Valley Authority* (Chapel Hill, N.C.: University of North Carolina Press, 1943). The impact of pressure groups on the TVA's policy decisions is well described by Philip Selznick, *TVA at the Grassroots* (Berkeley, Cal.: University of California Press, 1949); and one bitter controversy which was widely viewed as "private power versus TVA" is the subject of Aaron Wildafsky, *Dixon-Yates: A Study in Power Politics* (New Haven, Conn.: Yale University Press, 1962).

The Editors of *Fortune, Exploding Metropolis* \* (Garden City, N.Y.: Doubleday & Co.—an Anchor book) graphically warns of the imminence of insoluble land-use problems in an urbanized society. Robert life, and Morton Grodzins, *The Metropolitan Area as a Racial Problem* \* (Pittsburgh, Pa.: University of Pittsburgh Press, 1958) deals with one critical question which may acquire increasing significance.

William L. Lawrence, *Men and Atoms* (New York: Simon and Schuster, 1959) is a lucid account of atomic development, tinctured with optimism. The possible nonmilitary uses of nuclear energy are interestingly explored in a report of the American Assembly, *Atoms for Power* (New York: American Assembly, Columbia University Press, 1957). Harold Green and Alan Rosenthal, *Government of the Atom* (New York: Atherton Press, 1963) is an able study of an important subject.

***Government, National Security, and Foreign Policy.*** Can a free and democratically governed country formulate and carry out the kind of consistent foreign policy required in a world of perpetual crisis? The moods, attitudes, and hopes that underlie the handling of our international relations are ably discussed by a behavorial scientist, Gabriel A. Almond, *The American People and Foreign Policy* \* (New York: Harcourt, Brace & Co., 1950; New York: Frederick A. Praeger, rev. ed., 1960); and, somewhat more intuitively, by a historian, Dexter Perkins, *Foreign Policy and the American Spirit* (Ithaca, N.Y.: Cornell C. Wood, *Suburbia: Its People and Their Politics* (Boston: Houghton Mifflin Co., 1958) deals with various facets of present-day metropolitan University Press, 1957). The present-day prophet of *realpolitik,* Hans J. Morgenthau, in his *Politics Among Nations: The Struggle for Power and Peace* (New York: Alfred A. Knopf, 2nd ed., 1954) and *Dilemmas of Politics* (Chicago: University of Chicago Press, 1958) is concerned less with the "spirit" than with the country's striking power, for such power, as he sees it, is the central factor in all international relations.

Human survival is certainly in the national interest: how to achieve it, and at the same time safeguard other national interests, is the central problem of our foreign policy. On the making of that policy, see Cecil V. Crabb, *American Foreign Policy in the Nuclear Age* (Evanston, Ill.: Row, Peterson & Co., 1960) and James N. Rosenau, *National Leader-ship and Foreign Policy* (Princeton, N.J.: Princeton University Press, 1963). The test-ban treaty of 1963 aroused a flicker of optimism that a road to peace—and survival—could be found through gradual dis-armament, but some of the great difficulties in that course are shown by John W. Spanier and Joseph L. Noges, *The Politics of Disarmament* (New York: Frederick A. Praeger, 1962), and by Thomas C. Schelling and Morton H. Halperin, *Strategy and Arms Control* (New York: The Twentieth Century Fund, 1961). On this whole question, see also Robert A. Levine, *The Arms Debate* (Cambridge, Mass.: Harvard University Press, 1963), and Emile Benoit and Kenneth E. Boulding, *Disarmament and the Economy* (New York: Harper & Row, 1963).

The search for peace through armed strength includes the forging of alliances, most important of which is NATO: see Massimo Salvadori, *NATO: A Twentieth Century Community of Nations* * (Princeton, N.J.: Van Nostrand Co., 1957—an Anchor book). But cooperation among *all* nations is another road: to point the way to such a road is the function of the United Nations. An engineer who is also an unusu-ally clear and refreshing writer has described that body: David Cush-man Coyle, *The United Nations and How It Works* * (New York: New American Library, 1958—a Mentor book). Of interest, also, are a much longer book, Inis L. Claude, *Swords Into Ploughshares* (New York: Random House, 2nd ed., 1959) and Robert E. Riggs, *Politics in the United Nations* * (Urbana: University of Illinois Press, 1958). Also recommended are Francis O. Wilcox and H. Field Haviland, *The United States and the United Nations* (Baltimore, Md.: The Johns Hopkins Press, 1961), and Lincoln P. Bloomfield, *The United Nations and United States Foreign Policy* (Boston: Little, Brown & Co., 1960).

B. M. Sapin and R. C. Snyder, *The Role of the Military in American Foreign Policy* * (Garden City, N.Y.: Doubleday & Co., 1954) is a much-cited short study of the topic described on its title. A good history of the subject, emphasizing the long anti-militaristic tradition and the recent departure from it, is Arthur A. Ekrich, *The Civilian and the Military* (New York: Oxford University Press, 1956). Another helpful book is Edgar S. Furniss, Jr., *American Military Policy* (New York: Rinehart & Co., Inc., 1957).

The substance of American foreign policy is dealt with in many books; one of the best short historical accounts is George Kennan,

*American Diplomacy, 1900-1950* (Chicago: University of Chicago Press, 1951). A more recent and critical analysis is that of Norman Graebner, *The New Isolationism* (New York: The Ronald Press, 1956). Excellent also is William G. Carleton, *The Revolution in American Foreign Policy* * (New York: Random House, 1957). Who should make foreign policy? As we saw, Walter Lippmann, *Essays in the Public Philosophy* (Boston: Little, Brown & Co., 1954) argues that it is the executive's responsibility. Without sharing Lippmann's gloomy view that popular control is to blame for all the disasters of the last century, a brilliantly written little book by a former secretary of state, Dean Acheson, *A Citizen Looks at Congress* (New York: Harper & Brothers, 1957) seems to agree that there should be public recognition of the necessity of executive leadership. Robert A. Dahl, *Congress and Foreign Policy* (New York: Harcourt, Brace & Co., 1950) is a distinguished, fairly short study of congressional participation before, during, and immediately after World War II. An occasion when Congress took the initiative is the subject of an Eagleton Foundation study, James A. Robinson, *The Monroney Resolution.** The pro's and con's of taking foreign policy issues out of party politics, and the question of whether they have been so removed, is discussed by Cecil V. Crabb, *Bipartisan Foreign Policy: Myth or Reality?* (Evanston, Ill.: Row, Peterson and Co., 1957). An old partisan issue, in days when it had more effect on internal affairs than international ones and also after World War I, is the tariff; certainly today tariff policy is an integral part of foreign policy. President Eisenhower's special commission on international trade emphasized this; its chairman, a steel corporation executive, wrote a short and influential personal statement—Clarence B. Randall, *A Foreign Economic Policy for the United States* (Chicago: University of Chicago Press, 1954). For a short discussion of the issue of reconciling a sound foreign policy with the demands of domestic producers, see Howard S. Piquet, *The Trade Agreements Act and the National Interest* (Washington, D.C.: Brookings Institution, 1958). An important recent study of the subject is Raymond A. Bauer, Ithiel de Sola Pool, and Lewis A. Dexter, *American Business and Public Policy: The Politics of Foreign Trade* (New York: Atheneum Publishers, 1963). See also, Charles P. Kindleberger, *Foreign Trade and the National Economy* * (New Haven, Conn.: Yale University Press, 1962).

Diplomacy, or at least the diplomatic jobs and personnel to do them, have changed over the years—but how much? Richard Harding Davis, *The Consul* (New York: Charles Scribner's Sons, 1911) is a stirring short story (which had some political impacts) about simpler times, told by one of America's greatest storytellers. Yet the preposterous intrusion of political patronage into the workings of the Foreign Service is still observed, in these more difficult days, in William Lederer and Eugene Burdick, *The Ugly American* (New York: W. W. Norton & Co., 1958), a bestseller which deals roughly, perhaps too harshly, with American overseas missions in Southeast Asian countries. (For an amusing take-off of *The Ugly American*, to be read after finishing the book, see H. L. Downs, "Ambassador in the Boondocks," *The New Republic,* April 27, 1959.) A more serious treatment of the purposes of such overseas missions is Edward S. Mason, *Economic Planning in Underdeveloped Areas* (New York: Fordham University Press, 1958). Young people interested in service abroad might find profit in Harlan Cleveland and Gerard J. Mangone, Jr. (eds.), *The Art of Overseasmanship* (Syracuse, N.Y.: Syracuse University Press, 1957), which concerns preparing Americans for civilian foreign duty, and Charles E. Wingenbach, *The Peace Corps* * (New York: The John Day Co., rev. ed. 1963). A girl contemplating matrimony with a fledgling Foreign Service officer might learn something from Beatrice Russell, *Living in State: The Trials and Travels of a Foreign Service Wife* (New York: David McKay Co., 1959). A more serious study is Michael H. Cardozo, *Diplomats in International Cooperation* (Ithaca, N.Y.: Cornell University Press, 1962). The head of the diplomatic branch is the subject of Don K. Price (ed.), *The Secretary of State* * (Englewood Cliffs, N.J.: Prentice-Hall, 1960), and Norman A. Graebner (ed.), *An Uncertain Tradition* (New York: McGraw-Hill Book Co., 1961).

Many college students may take a personal interest in Gene M. Lyons and John W. Masland, *Education and Military Leadership: A Study of the ROTC* (Princeton, N.J.: Princeton University Press, 1958) and in William H. Riker, *Soldiers of the States: The National Guard in American Democracy* (New York: Public Affairs Press, 1957). Having similarly direct impact on some, and general interest for many more, will be H. H. Ransom, *Central Intelligence and National Security* (Cambridge, Mass.: Harvard University Press, 1958). Significant books concerning the place of the military in our whole political system are Samuel P. Huntington, *The Common Defense* (New York: Columbia University Press, 1962); Paul Y. Hammond, *Organizing for Defense* (Princeton, N.J.: Princeton University Press, 1961); and Morris Janowitz, *The Professional Soldier, A Social and Political Portrait* (Glencoe, Ill.: Free Press, 1960). The great crisis over Cuba in October, 1962, when any internal military and diplomatic differences were resolved by the President's taking the "calculated risk" of blockading arms-carrying Russian ships, is the subject of Henry M. Pachter, *Collision Course* * (New York: Frederick A. Praeger, 1963).

## PART VI

The question of survival, and what we might make of it, is trenchantly discussed by an articulate nuclear scientist, Harrison Brown, *The Challenge of Man's Future* * (New York: The Viking Press, 1954—a Compass book). The perils and dangers of a changing world make demands on us for greater knowledge of nations and continents asserting new-found power and influence; profitable reading, therefore, are John K. Fairbank, *The United States and China* (Cambridge, Mass.: Harvard University Press, rev. ed., 1958), a book which is much more about China than about the United States; Herbert Feis, *The China Tangle* (Princeton, N.J.: Princeton University Press, 1963), the ablest account of our foreign policy at the time of the Communist take-over; Chester Bowles, *Ambassador's Report* (New York: Harper & Brothers, 1954), by a man who has served twice as our envoy to India; a pioneering study of South Africa, Gwendolen M. Carter, *The Politics of Inequality* (New York: Frederick A. Praeger, 1958); and two books about the erstwhile "Dark Continent," Thomas R. Adam, *Government and Politics in Africa South of the Sahara* * (New York: Random House, 1959), and Walter Goldschmidt, *The United States and Africa* * (New York: The American Assembly, Columbia University, 1958). What might follow atomic war, or might even occur without it if people generally became fearful not only of war but of freedom itself, is vividly described in a famous novel of life in a totalitarian society, George Orwell, *1984* * (New York: Harcourt, Brace & Co., 1949—a Signet book). May we be in danger of losing our freedom not because of war or fear of war, but because of a mistaken belief that government should provide individual security, engage in economic endeavor, and plan and direct private enterprise for the public good? Yes, says F. A. Hayek, *The Road to Serfdom* * (Chicago: University of Chicago Press, 1944—a Phoenix book), an essay that was widely read and much praised. Yet another widely read book, J. K. Galbraith, *The Affluent Society* * (Boston: Houghton Mifflin Co., 1958) assumes that government should continue to play a large role in economic affairs and suggests that we would be better off, in things that count in a good life, if it played a still larger one. The issues raised by these two books may be clarified by reading Robert Heilbroner and Peter L. Bernstein, *A Primer on Government Spending* * (New York: Random House, 1963). The temptation to relax and assume that everyone is well off, implicit in Galbraith's title, is spurned in a bitter reminder of poverty in the United States, Michael Harrington, *The Other America* (New York: The Macmillan Co., 1962).

What we, as a people, do value is one of a host of topics covered in an extraordinarily full, challenging picture of present-day American society, Max Lerner, *America as a Civilization* (New York: Simon & Schuster, 1957) which, though not a textbook, is a course in itself, a good follow-up to one in the basic elements of American government and politics. As we think about where we are heading, it would be appropriate to read Saul K. Padover, *The Meaning of Democracy* * (New York: Frederick A. Praeger, 1963). Finally, it is a pleasure to recommend a brief volume of lectures delivered by a wise historian, who, knowing the past and keenly aware of the present, could look forward without foolish optimism but with calm hope: Carl Becker, *Freedom and Responsibility in the American Way of Life* (New York: Alfred A. Knopf, 1945).

# The Constitution of the United States

W e the People of the United States, in Order to form a more perfect Union, establish Justice, insure domestic Tranquility, provide for the common defence, promote the general Welfare, and secure the Blessings of Liberty to ourselves and our Posterity, do ordain and establish this Constitution for the United States of America.

## ARTICLE I

*Section* 1. All legislative Powers herein granted shall be vested in a Congress of the United States, which shall consist of a Senate and House of Representatives.

*Section* 2. 1. The House of Representatives shall be composed of Members chosen every second Year by the People of the several States, and the Electors in each State shall have the Qualifications requisite for Electors of the most numerous Branch of the State Legislature.

2. No Person shall be a Representative who shall not have attained to the Age of twenty five Years, and been seven Years a Citizen of the United States, and who shall not, when elected, be an Inhabitant of that State in which he shall be chosen.

3. Representatives and direct Taxes shall be apportioned [1] among

---

[1] Changed by Sixteenth Amendment.

the several States which may be included within this Union, according to their respective Numbers, which shall be determined by adding to the whole Number of free Persons, including those bound to Service for a Term of Years, and excluding Indians not taxed, three fifths of all other Persons.[2] The actual Enumeration shall be made within three Years after the first Meeting of the Congress of the United States, and within every subsequent Term in ten Years, in such Manner as they shall by Law direct. The Number of Representatives shall not exceed one for every thirty Thousand, but each State shall have at Least one Representative; and until such enumeration shall be made, the State of New Hampshire shall be entitled to chuse three, Massachusetts eight, Rhode-Island and Providence Plantations one, Connecticut five, New-York six, New Jersey four, Pennsylvania eight, Delaware one, Maryland six, Virginia ten, North Carolina five, South Carolina five, and Georgia three.

4. When vacancies happen in the Representation from any State, the Executive Authority thereof shall issue Writs of Election to fill such Vacancies.

5. The House of Representatives shall chuse their Speaker and other Officers; and shall have the sole Power of Impeachment.

*Section* 3. 1. The Senate of the United States shall be composed of two Senators from each State, chosen by the Legislature thereof,[3] for six Years; and each Senator shall have one Vote.

2. Immediately after they shall be assembled in Consequence of the first Election, they shall be divided as equally as may be into three Classes. The Seats of the Senators of the first Class shall be vacated at the Expiration of the second Year, of the second Class at the Expiration of the fourth Year, and of the third Class at the Expiration of the sixth Year, so that one third may be chosen every second Year; and if Vacancies happen by Resignation, or otherwise, during the Recess of the Legislature of any State, the Executive thereof may make temporary Appointments until the next Meeting of the Legislature,[3] which shall then fill such Vacancies.

3. No Person shall be a Senator who shall not have attained to the Age of thirty Years, and been nine Years a Citizen of the United States, and who shall not, when elected, be an Inhabitant of that State for which he shall be chosen.

---

[2] Provision for counting a slave as "three-fifths of a person" eliminated by Fourteenth Amendment.

[3] Changed by Seventeenth Amendment.

4. The Vice President of the United States shall be President of the Senate, but shall have no Vote, unless they be equally divided.

5. The Senate shall chuse their other Officers, and also a President pro tempore, in the Absence of the Vice President, or when he shall exercise the Office of President of the United States.

6. The Senate shall have the sole Power to try all Impeachments. When sitting for that Purpose, they shall be on Oath or Affirmation. When the President of the United States is tried, the Chief Justice shall preside: And no Person shall be convicted without the Concurrence of two thirds of the Members present.

7. Judgment in Cases of Impeachment shall not extend further than to removal from Office, and disqualification to hold and enjoy any Office of honor, Trust or Profit under the United States: but the Party convicted shall nevertheless be liable and subject to Indictment, Trial, Judgment and Punishment, according to Law.

*Section* 4. 1. The Times, Places and Manner of holding Elections for Senators and Representatives, shall be prescribed in each State by the Legislature thereof; but the Congress may at any time by Law make or alter such Regulations, except as to the Places of chusing Senators.

2. The Congress shall assemble at least once in every Year, and such Meeting shall be on the first Monday in December, unless they shall by Law appoint a different day.[4]

*Section* 5. 1. Each House shall be the Judge of the Elections, Returns and Qualifications of its own Members, and a Majority of each shall constitute a Quorum to do Business; but a smaller Number may adjourn from day to day, and may be authorized to compel the attendance of absent Members, in such Manner, and under such Penalties as each House may provide.

2. Each House may determine the Rules of its Proceedings, punish its Members for Disorderly Behaviour, and, with the Concurrence of two thirds, expel a Member.

3. Each House shall keep a Journal of its Proceedings, and from time to time publish the same, excepting such Parts as may in their Judgment require Secrecy; and the Yeas and Nays of the Members of either House on any question shall, at the Desire of one fifth of those Present, be entered on the Journal.

4. Neither House, during the Session of Congress, shall, without the

---

4 Changed by Twentieth Amendment.

Consent of the other, adjourn for more than three days, nor to any other Place than that in which the two Houses shall be sitting.

*Section* 6. 1. The Senators and Representatives shall receive a Compensation for their Services, to be ascertained by Law, and paid out of the Treasury of the United States. They shall in all Cases, except Treason, Felony and Breach of the Peace, be privileged from Arrest during their Attendance at the Session of their respective Houses, and in going to and returning from the same; and for any Speech or Debate in either House, they shall not be questioned in any other Place.

2. No Senator or Representative shall, during the Time for which he was elected, be appointed to any civil Office under the Authority of the United States, which shall have been created, or the Emoluments whereof shall have been encreased during such time; and no Person holding any Office under the United States, shall be a member of either House during his Continuance in Office.

*Section* 7. 1. All Bills for raising Revenue shall originate in the House of Representatives; but the Senate may propose or concur with Amendments as on other Bills.

2. Every Bill which shall have passed the House of Representatives and the Senate, shall, before it becomes a Law, be presented to the President of the United States; If he approve he shall sign it, but if not he shall return it, with his Objections to that House in which it shall have originated, who shall enter the Objections at large on their Journal, and proceed to reconsider it. If after such Reconsideration two thirds of that House shall agree to pass the Bill, it shall be sent, together with the Objections, to the other House, by which it shall likewise be reconsidered, and if approved by two thirds of that House, it shall become a Law. But in all such Cases the Votes of both Houses shall be determined by Yeas and Nays, and the Names of the Persons voting for and against the Bill shall be entered on the Journal of each House respectively. If any Bill shall not be returned by the President within ten Days (Sundays excepted) after it shall have been presented to him, the same shall be a Law, in like Manner as if he had signed it, unless the Congress by their Adjournment prevent its Return, in which Case it shall not be a Law.

3. Every Order, Resolution, or Vote to which the Concurrence of the Senate and House of Representatives may be necessary (except on a question of Adjournment) shall be presented to the President of the United States; and before the same shall take Effect, shall be approved by him, or being disapproved by him, shall be repassed by two thirds of

the Senate and House of Representatives, according to the Rules and Limitations prescribed in the Case of a Bill.

*Section* 8. The Congress shall have Power 1. To lay and collect Taxes, Duties, Imposts and Excises, to pay the Debts and provide for the common Defence and general Welfare of the United States; but all Duties, Imposts and Excises shall be uniform throughout the United States;

2. To borrow Money on the credit of the United States;

3. To regulate Commerce with foreign Nations, and among the several States, and with the Indian Tribes;

4. To establish an uniform Rule of Naturalization, and uniform Laws on the subject of Bankruptcies throughout the United States;

5. To coin Money, regulate the Value thereof, and of foreign Coin, and fix the Standard of Weights and Measures;

6. To provide for the Punishment of counterfeiting the Securities and current Coin of the United States;

7. To establish Post Offices and post Roads;

8. To promote the Progress of Science and useful Arts, by securing for limited Times to Authors and Inventors the exclusive Right to their respective Writings and Discoveries;

9. To constitute Tribunals inferior to the supreme Court;

10. To define and punish Piracies and Felonies committed on the high Seas, and Offences against the Law of Nations;

11. To declare War, grant Letters of Marque and Reprisal, and make Rules concerning Captures on Land and Water;

12. To raise and support Armies, but no Appropriation of Money to that Use shall be for a longer Term than two Years;

13. To provide and maintain a Navy;

14. To make Rules for the Government and Regulation of the land and naval Forces;

15. To provide for calling forth the Militia to execute the Laws of the Union, suppress Insurrections and repel Invasions;

16. To provide for organizing, arming, and disciplining, the Militia, and for governing such Part of them as may be employed in the Service of the United States, reserving to the States respectively, the Appointment of the Officers, and the Authority of training the Militia according to the discipline prescribed by Congress;

17. To exercise exclusive Legislation in all Cases whatsoever, over such District (not exceeding ten Miles square) as may, by Cession of particular States, and the Acceptance of Congress, become the Seat of

the Government of the United States, and to exercise like Authority over all Places purchased by the Consent of the Legislature of the State in which the same shall be, for the Erection of Forts, Magazines, Arsenals, dock-Yards, and other needful Buildings;—And

18. To make all Laws which shall be necessary and proper for carrying into Execution the foregoing Powers, and all other Powers vested by this Constitution in the Government of the United States, or in any Department or Officer thereof.

*Section* 9. 1. The Migration or Importation of such Persons as any of the States now existing shall think proper to admit, shall not be prohibited by the Congress prior to the Year one thousand eight hundred and eight, but a Tax or duty may be imposed on such Importation, not exceeding ten dollars for each Person.

2. The Privilege of the Writ of Habeas Corpus shall not be suspended, unless when in Cases of Rebellion or Invasion the public Safety may require it.

3. No Bill of Attainder or ex post facto Law shall be passed.

4. No Capitation, or other direct, Tax shall be laid, unless in Proportion to the Census or Enumeration herein before directed to be taken.[5]

5. No Tax or Duty shall be laid on Articles exported from any State.

6. No Preference shall be given by any Regulation of Commerce or Revenue to the Ports of one State over those of another: nor shall Vessels bound to, or from, one State, be obliged to enter, clear, or pay Duties in another.

7. No Money shall be drawn from the Treasury, but in Consequence of Appropriations made by Law; and a regular Statement and Account of the Receipts and Expenditures of all public Money shall be published from time to time.

8. No Title of Nobility shall be granted by the United States: And no Person holding any Office of Profit or Trust under them, shall, without the Consent of the Congress, accept of any present, Emolument, Office, or Title, of any kind whatever, from any King, Prince, or foreign State.

*Section* 10. 1. No State shall enter into any Treaty, Alliance, or Confederation; grant Letters of Marque and Reprisal; coin Money; emit Bills of Credit; make any Thing but gold and silver Coin a Tender in Payment of Debts; pass any Bill of Attainder, ex post facto Law, or

---

[5] Changed, with respect to income taxes, by the Sixteenth Amendment.

Law impairing the Obligation of Contracts, or grant any Title of Nobility.

2. No State shall, without the Consent of the Congress, lay any Imposts or Duties on Imports or Exports, except what may be absolutely necessary for executing its inspection Laws: and the net Produce of all Duties and Imposts, laid by any State on Imports or Exports, shall be for the Use of the Treasury of the United States; and all such Laws shall be subject to the Revision and Controul of the Congress.

3. No State shall, without the Consent of Congress, lay any Duty of Tonnage, keep Troops, or Ships of War in time of Peace, enter into any Agreement or Compact with another State, or with a foreign Power, or engage in War, unless actually invaded, or in such imminent Danger as will not admit of delay.

### ARTICLE II

*Section* 1. 1. The executive Power shall be vested in a President of the United States of America. He shall hold his Office during the Term of four Years, and, together with the Vice President, chosen for the same Term, be elected, as follows

2. Each State shall appoint, in such Manner as the Legislature thereof may direct, a Number of Electors, equal to the whole Number of Senators and Representatives to which the State may be entitled in the Congress: but no Senator or Representative, or Person holding an Office of Trust or Profit under the United States, shall be appointed an Elector.

3. The Electors shall meet in their respective States, and vote by Ballot for two Persons, of whom one at least shall not be an Inhabitant of the same State with themselves. And they shall make a List of all the Persons voted for, and of the Number of Votes for each; which List they shall sign and certify, and transmit sealed to the Seat of the Government of the United States, directed to the President of the Senate. The President of the Senate shall, in the Presence of the Senate and House of Representatives, open all the Certificates, and the Votes shall then be counted. The Person having the greatest Number of Votes shall be the President, if such Number be a Majority of the whole Number of Electors appointed; and if there be more than one who have such Majority, and have an equal Number of Votes, then the House of Representatives shall immediately chuse by Ballot one of them for President; and if no Person have a Majority, then from the five highest on the List the said House shall in like Manner chuse the

President. But in chusing the President, the Votes shall be taken by States, the Representation from each State having one Vote; A quorum for this Purpose shall consist of a Member or Members from two thirds of the States, and a Majority of all the States shall be necessary to a Choice. In every Case, after the Choice of the President, the Person having the greatest Number of Votes of the Electors shall be the Vice President. But if there should remain two or more who have equal Votes, the Senate shall chuse from them by Ballot the Vice President.[6]

4. The Congress may determine the Time of chusing the Electors, and the Day on which they shall give their Votes; which Day shall be the same throughout the United States.

5. No Person except a natural born Citizen, or a Citizen of the United States, at the time of the Adoption of this Constitution, shall be eligible to the Office of President; neither shall any Person be eligible to that Office who shall not have attained to the Age of thirty five Years, and been fourteen Years a Resident within the United States.

6. In Case of the Removal of the President from Office, or of his Death, Resignation, or Inability to discharge the Powers and Duties of the said Office, the Same shall devolve on the Vice President, and the Congress may by Law provide for the Case of Removal, Death, Resignation, or Inability, both of the President and Vice President, declaring what Officer shall then act as President, and such Officer shall act accordingly, until the Disability be removed, or a President shall be elected.

7. The President shall, at stated Times, receive for his Services, a Compensation, which shall neither be encreased nor diminished during the Period for which he shall have been elected, and he shall not receive within that Period any other Emolument from the United States, or any of them.

8. Before he enter on the Execution of his Office, he shall take the following Oath or Affirmation:—"I do solemnly swear (or affirm) that I will faithfully execute the Office of President of the United States, and will to the best of my Ability, preserve, protect and defend the Constitution of the United States."

*Section 2.* 1. The President shall be Commander in Chief of the Army and Navy of the United States, and of the Militia of the several States, when called into the actual Service of the United States; he may require the Opinion, in writing, of the principal Officer in each

---

[6] Modified by the Twelfth Amendment and, to some extent, by the Twentieth Amendment.

of the executive Departments, upon any Subject relating to the Duties of their respective Offices, and he shall have Power to grant Reprieves and Pardons for Offences against the United States, except in Cases of Impeachment.

2. He shall have Power, by and with the Advice and Consent of the Senate, to make Treaties, provided two thirds of the Senators present concur; and he shall nominate, and by and with the Advice and Consent of the Senate, shall appoint Ambassadors, other public Ministers and Consuls, Judges of the supreme Court, and all other Officers of the United States, whose Appointments are not herein otherwise provided for, and which shall be established by Law: but the Congress may by Law vest the Appointment of such inferior Officers, as they think proper, in the President alone, in the Courts of Law, or in the Heads of Departments.

3. The President shall have Power to fill up all Vacancies that may happen during the Recess of the Senate, by granting Commissions which shall expire at the End of their next Session.

*Section 3.* He shall from time to time give to the Congress Information of the State of the Union, and recommend to their Consideration such Measures as he shall judge necessary and expedient; he may, on extraordinary Occasions, convene both Houses, or either of them, and in Case of Disagreement between them, with Respect to the Time of Adjournment, he may adjourn them to such Time as he shall think proper; he shall receive Ambassadors and other public Ministers; he shall take Care that the Laws be faithfully executed, and shall Commission all the Officers of the United States.

*Section 4.* The President, Vice President and all civil Officers of the United States, shall be removed from Office on Impeachment for, and Conviction of, Treason, Bribery, or other high Crimes and Misdemeanors.

## ARTICLE III

*Section 1.* The judicial Power of the United States, shall be vested in one supreme Court, and in such inferior Courts as the Congress may from time to time ordain and establish. The Judges, both of the supreme and inferior Courts, shall hold their Offices during good Behaviour, and shall, at stated Times, receive for their Services, a Compensation, which shall not be diminished during their Continuance in Office.

*Section* 2. 1. The judicial Power shall extend to all Cases, in Law and Equity, arising under this Constitution, the Laws of the United States, and Treaties made, or which shall be made, under their Authority;—to all Cases affecting Ambassadors, other public Ministers and Consuls;—to all Cases of admiralty and maritime Jurisdiction;—to Controversies to which the United States shall be a Party;—to Controversies between two or more States;—between a State and Citizens of another State;—between Citizens of different States,—between Citizens of the same State claiming Lands under Grants of different States, and between a State, or the Citizens thereof, and foreign States, Citizens or Subjects.[7]

2. In all Cases affecting Ambassadors, other public Ministers and Consuls, and those in which a State shall be Party, the supreme Court shall have original Jurisdiction. In all the other Cases before mentioned, the supreme Court shall have appellate Jurisdiction, both as to Law and Fact, with such Exceptions, and under such Regulations as the Congress shall make.

3. The Trial of all Crimes, except in Cases of Impeachment, shall be by Jury; and such Trial shall be held in the State where the said Crimes shall have been committed; but when not committed within any State, the Trial shall be at such Place or Places as the Congress may by Law have directed.

*Section* 3. 1. Treason against the United States, shall consist only in levying War against them, or in adhering to their Enemies, giving them Aid and Comfort. No Person shall be convicted of Treason unless on the Testimony of two Witnesses to the same overt Act, or on Confession in open Court.

2. The Congress shall have Power to declare the Punishment of Treason, but no Attainder of Treason shall work Corruption of Blood, or Forfeiture except during the Life of the Person attainted.

## ARTICLE IV

*Section* 1. Full Faith and Credit shall be given in each State to the public Acts, Records, and judicial Proceedings of every other State. And the Congress may by general Laws prescribe the Manner in which such Acts, Records and Proceedings shall be proved, and the Effect thereof.

---

[7] Changed by the Eleventh Amendment, with respect to certain cases wherein a state is a party.

*Section* 2. 1. The Citizens of each State shall be entitled to all Privileges and Immunities of Citizens in the several States.

2. A Person charged in any State with Treason, Felony, or other Crime, who shall flee from Justice, and be found in another State, shall on Demand of the executive Authority of the State from which he fled, be delivered up, to be removed to the State having Jurisdiction of the Crime.

3. No Person held to Service or Labour in one State, under the Laws thereof, escaping into another, shall, in Consequence of any Law or Regulation therein, be discharged from such Service or Labour, but shall be delivered up on Claim of the Party to whom such Service or Labour may be due.[8]

*Section* 3. 1. New States may be admitted by the Congress into this Union; but no new State shall be formed or erected within the Jurisdiction of any other State; nor any State be formed by the Junction of two or more States, or Parts of States, without the Consent of the Legislatures of the States concerned as well as of the Congress.

2. The Congress shall have Power to dispose of and make all needful Rules and Regulations respecting the Territory or other Property belonging to the United States; and nothing in this Constitution shall be so construed as to Prejudice any Claims of the United States, or of any particular State.

*Section* 4. The United States shall guarantee to every State in this Union a Republican Form of Government, and shall protect each of them against Invasion; and on Application of the Legislature, or of the Executive (when the Legislature cannot be convened) against domestic Violence.

### ARTICLE V

The Congress, whenever two thirds of both Houses shall deem it necessary, shall propose Amendments to this Constitution, or, on the Application of the Legislatures of two thirds of the several States, shall call a Convention for proposing Amendments, which, in either Case, shall be valid to all Intents and Purposes, as Part of this Constitution, when ratified by the Legislatures of three fourths of the several States, or by Conventions in three fourths thereof, as the one or the other Mode of Ratification may be proposed by the Congress; Provided that

---

8 Made obsolete by the Thirteenth Amendment.

no Amendment which may be made prior to the Year One thousand eight hundred and eight shall in any Manner affect the first and fourth Clauses in the Ninth Section of the first Article; and that no State, without its Consent, shall be deprived of its equal Suffrage in the Senate.

## ARTICLE VI

1. All Debts contracted and Engagements entered into, before the Adoption of this Constitution, shall be as valid against the United States under this Constitution, as under the Confederation.

2. This Constitution, and the Laws of the United States which shall be made in Pursuance thereof; and all Treaties made, or which shall be made, under the Authority of the United States, shall be the supreme Law of the Land; and the Judges in every State shall be bound thereby, any Thing in the Constitution or Laws of any State to the Contrary notwithstanding.

3. The Senators and Representatives before mentioned, and the Members of the several State Legislatures, and all executive and judicial Officers, both of the United States and of the several States, shall be bound by Oath or Affirmation, to support this Constitution; but no religious Test shall ever be required as a Qualification to any Office or public Trust under the United States.

## ARTICLE VII

The Ratification of the Conventions of nine States, shall be sufficient for the Establishment of this Constitution between the States so ratifying the Same.

Done in Convention by the Unanimous Consent of the States present, the Seventeenth Day of September, in the Year of our Lord one thousand seven hundred and Eighty-seven, and of the Independence of the United States of America the Twelfth. In witness thereof We have hereunto subscribed our Names.

## AMENDMENTS

### ARTICLE I

Congress shall make no law respecting an establishment of religion, or prohibiting the free exercise thereof; or abridging the freedom of speech, or of the press; or the right of the people peaceably to assemble, and to petition the Government for a redress of grievances.

## ARTICLE II

A well regulated Militia, being necessary to the security of a free State, the right of the people to keep and bear Arms, shall not be infringed.

## ARTICLE III

No Soldier shall, in time of peace be quartered in any house, without the consent of the Owner, nor in time of war, but in a manner to be prescribed by law.

## ARTICLE IV

The right of the people to be secure in their persons, houses, papers, and effects, against unreasonable searches and seizures, shall not be violated, and no Warrants shall issue, but upon probable cause, supported by Oath or affirmation, and particularly describing the place to be searched, and the persons or things to be seized.

## ARTICLE V

No person shall be held to answer for a capital, or otherwise infamous crime, unless on a presentment or indictment of a Grand Jury, except in cases arising in the land or naval forces, or in the Militia, when in actual service in time of War or public danger; nor shall any person be subject for the same offence to be twice put in jeopardy of life or limb; nor shall be compelled in any criminal case to be a witness against himself, nor be deprived of life, liberty, or property, without due process of law; nor shall private property be taken for public use, without just compensation.

## ARTICLE VI

In all criminal prosecutions the accused shall enjoy the right to a speedy and public trial, by an impartial jury of the State and district wherein the crime shall have been committed, which district shall have been previously ascertained by law, and to be informed of the nature and cause of the accusation; to be confronted with the witnesses against him; to have compulsory process for obtaining witnesses in his favor, and to have the Assistance of Counsel for his defence.

## ARTICLE VII

In suits at common law, where the value in controversy shall exceed twenty dollars, the right of trial by jury shall be preserved, and no fact tried by a jury shall be otherwise re-examined in any Court of the United States, than according to the rules of the common law.

## ARTICLE VIII

Excessive bail shall not be required, nor excessive fines imposed, nor cruel and unusual punishments inflicted.

## ARTICLE IX

The enumeration in the Constitution, of certain rights, shall not be construed to deny or disparage others retained by the people.

## ARTICLE X

The powers not delegated to the United States by the Constitution, nor prohibited by it to the States, are reserved to the States respectively, or to the people.

[The first ten Amendments were adopted in 1791.]

## ARTICLE XI

The Judicial power of the United States shall not be construed to extend to any suit in law or equity, commenced or prosecuted against one of the United States by Citizens of another State, or by Citizens or Subjects of any Foreign State. [Adopted 1798.]

## ARTICLE XII

The Electors shall meet in their respective states, and vote by ballot for President and Vice-President, one of whom, at least, shall not be an inhabitant of the same state with themselves; they shall name in their ballots the person voted for as President, and in distinct ballots the person voted for as Vice-President, and they shall make distinct lists of all persons voted for as President, and of all persons voted for as Vice-President, and of the number of votes for each, which lists they shall sign and certify, and transmit sealed to the seat of the government of the United States, directed to the President of the Senate;—The President of the Senate shall, in the presence of the Senate and House of Representatives, open all the certificates and the votes shall then be counted;—The person having the greatest number of votes for President, shall be the President, if such number be a majority of the whole number of Electors appointed; and if no person have such majority, then from the persons having the highest numbers not exceeding three on the list of those voted for as President, the House of Representatives shall choose immediately, by ballot, the President. But in choosing the President, the votes shall be taken by states, the representation from each state having one vote; a quorum for this purpose shall consist of a member or members from two-thirds of the states, and a majority of all the states shall be necessary to a choice. And if the House of Representatives shall not choose a President whenever the right of choice shall devolve upon them, before the fourth day of March next following, then the Vice-President shall act as President, as in the case of the death or other constitutional disability of the President.[9]—The person having the greatest number of votes as Vice-President, shall be the Vice-President, if such number be a majority of the whole number of Electors appointed, and if no person have a majority, then from the two highest numbers on the list, the Senate shall choose the Vice-President; a quorum for the purpose shall consist of two-thirds of the whole number of Senators, and a majority of the whole number shall be necessary to a choice. But no person constitutionally ineligible to the office of President shall be eligible to that of Vice-President of the United States. [Adopted 1804.]

## ARTICLE XIII

*Section* 1. Neither slavery nor involuntary servitude, except as a punishment for crime whereof the party shall have been duly convicted, shall exist within the United States, or any place subject to their jurisdiction.

*Section* 2. Congress shall have power to enforce this article by appropriate legislation. [Adopted 1865.]

---

[9] Modified by the Twentieth Amendment.

## ARTICLE XIV

*Section* 1. All persons born or naturalized in the United States, and subject to the jurisdiction thereof, are citizens of the United States and of the State wherein they reside. No State shall make or enforce any law which shall abridge the privileges or immunities of citizens of the United States; nor shall any State deprive any person of life, liberty, or property, without due process of law; nor deny to any person within its jurisdiction the equal protection of the laws.

*Section* 2. Representatives shall be apportioned among the several States according to their respective numbers, counting the whole number of persons in each State, excluding Indians not taxed. But when the right to vote at any election for the choice of electors for President and Vice President of the United States, Representatives in Congress, the Executive and Judicial officers of a State, or the members of the Legislature thereof, is denied to any of the male inhabitants of such State, being twenty-one years of age, and citizens of the United States, or in any way abridged, except for participation in rebellion, or other crime, the basis of representation therein shall be reduced in the proportion which the number of such male citizens shall bear to the whole number of male citizens twenty-one years of age in such State.

*Section* 3. No person shall be a Senator or Representative in Congress, or elector of President and Vice President, or hold any office, civil or military, under the United States, or under any State, who, having previously taken an oath, as a member of Congress, or as an officer of the United States, or as a member of any State legislature, or as an executive or judicial officer of any State, to support the Constitution of the United States, shall have engaged in insurrection or rebellion against the same, or given aid or comfort to the enemies thereof. But Congress may by a vote of two-thirds of each House, remove such disability.

*Section* 4. The validity of the public debt of the United States, authorized by law, including debts incurred for payment of pensions and bounties for services in suppressing insurrection or rebellion, shall not be questioned. But neither the United States nor any State shall assume or pay any debt or obligation incurred in aid of insurrection or rebellion against the United States, or any claim for the loss or emancipation of any slave; but all such debts, obligations and claims shall be held illegal and void.

*Section* 5. The Congress shall have power to enforce, by appropriate legislation, the provisions of this article. [Adopted 1868.]

## ARTICLE XV

*Section* 1. The right of citizens of the United States to vote shall not be denied or abridged by the United States or by any State on account of race, color, or previous condition of servitude.

*Section* 2. The Congress shall have power to enforce this article by appropriate legislation. [Adopted 1870.]

## ARTICLE XVI

The Congress shall have power to lay and collect taxes on incomes, from whatever source derived, without apportionment among the several States, and without regard to any census or enumeration. [Adopted 1913.]

## ARTICLE XVII

The Senate of the United States shall be composed of two Senators from each State, elected by the people thereof, for six years; and each Senator shall have one vote. The electors in each State shall have the qualifications requisite for electors of the most numerous branch of the State legislatures.

When vacancies happen in the representation of any State in the Senate, the executive authority of such State shall issue writs of election to fill such vacancies: *Provided,* That the legislature of any State may empower the executive thereof to make temporary appointments until the people fill the vacancies by election as the legislature may direct.

This amendment shall not be so construed as to affect the election or term of any Senator chosen before it becomes valid as part of the Constitution. [Adopted 1913.]

## ARTICLE XVIII

*Section* 1. After one year from the ratification of this article the manufacture, sale, or transportation of intoxicating liquors within, the importation thereof into, or the exportation thereof from the United States and all territory subject to the jurisdiction thereof for beverage purposes is hereby prohibited.

*Section 2.* The Congress and the several States shall have concurrent power to enforce this article by appropriate legislation.

*Section 3.* This article shall be inoperative unless it shall have been ratified as an amendment to the Constitution by the legislatures of the several States, as provided in the Constitution, within seven years from the date of the submission hereof to the States by the Congress. [Adopted 1919.] [10]

## ARTICLE XIX

The right of citizens of the United States to vote shall not be denied or abridged by the United States or by any State on account of sex.

Congress shall have power to enforce this article by appropriate legislation. [Adopted 1920.]

## ARTICLE XX

*Section 1.* The terms of the President and Vice President shall end at noon on the 20th day of January, and the terms of Senators and Representatives at noon on the 3d day of January, of the years in which such terms would have ended if this article had not been ratified; and the terms of their successors shall then begin.

*Section 2.* The Congress shall assemble at least once in every year, and such meeting shall begin at noon on the 3d day of January, unless they shall by law appoint a different day.

*Section 3.* If, at the time fixed for the beginning of the term of the President, the President elect shall have died, the Vice President elect shall become President. If a President shall not have been chosen before the time fixed for the beginning of his term, or if the President elect shall have failed to qualify, then the Vice President elect shall act as President until a President shall have qualified; and the Congress may by law provide for the case wherein neither a President elect nor a Vice President elect shall have qualified, declaring who shall then act as President, or the manner in which one who is to act shall be selected, and such person shall act accordingly until a President or Vice President shall have qualified.

*Section 4.* The Congress may by law provide for the case of the death of any of the persons from whom the House of Representatives may choose a President whenever the right of choice shall have de-

---

[10] Repealed by the Twenty-first Amendment.

volved upon them, and for the case of the death of any of the persons from whom the Senate may choose a Vice President whenever the right of choice shall have devolved upon them.

*Section* 5. Sections 1 and 2 shall take effect on the 15th day of October following the ratification of this article.

*Section* 6. This article shall be inoperative unless it shall have been ratified as an amendment to the Constitution by the legislatures of three-fourths of the several States within seven years from the date of its submission. [Adopted 1933.]

## ARTICLE XXI

*Section* 1. The eighteenth article of amendment to the Constitution of the United States is hereby repealed.

*Section* 2. The transportation or importation into any State, Territory, or possession of the United States for delivery or use therein of intoxicating liquors, in violation of the laws thereof, is hereby prohibited.

*Section* 3. This article shall be inoperative unless it shall have been ratified as an amendment to the Constitution by conventions in the several States, as provided in the Constitution, within seven years from the date of the submission hereof to the States by the Congress. [Adopted 1933.]

## ARTICLE XXII

*Section* 1. No person shall be elected to the office of the President more than twice, and no person who has held the office of President, or acted as President, for more than two years of a term to which some other person was elected President shall be elected to the office of the President more than once. But this Article shall not apply to any person holding the office of President when this Article was proposed by the Congress, and shall not prevent any person who may be holding the office of President, or acting as President, during the term within which this Article becomes operative from holding the office of President, or acting as President during the remainder of such term.

*Section* 2. This Article shall be inoperative unless it shall have been ratified as an amendment to the Constitution by the legislatures of three-fourths of the several States within seven years from the date of its submission to the States by the Congress. [Adopted 1951.]

## ARTICLE XXIII

1. The District constituting the seat of Government of the United States shall appoint in such manner as the Congress may direct:

A number of electors of President and Vice President equal to the whole number of Senators and Representatives in Congress to which the District would be entitled if it were a State, but in no event more than the least populous state; they shall be in addition to those appointed by the states, but they shall be considered, for the purposes of the election of President and Vice President, to be electors appointed by a state; and they shall meet in the District and perform such duties as provided by the twelfth article of amendment.

2. The Congress shall have power to enforce this article by appropriate legislation. [Adopted 1961.]

## ARTICLE XXIV

*Section* 1. The right of citizens of the United States to vote in any primary or other election for President or Vice President, for electors for President or Vice President, or for Senator or Representative in Congress, shall not be denied or abridged by the United States or any State by reason of failure to pay any poll tax or other tax.

*Section* 2. The Congress shall have power to enforce this article by appropriate legislation.

# Index

East Front of the Capitol

Treasury

Smithsonian Institute

City Hall

Greenoughs Statue of Washington

Pension Office

Jackson Hall

Washington fro

Navy Yard

Georgetown College

Aqueduct

# *Washington City and Georgetown, 1849*